The Bells of Russia

THE
BELLS OF
RUSSIA

History and Technology

Edward V. Williams

PRINCETON UNIVERSITY PRESS : PRINCETON, NEW JERSEY

Published by Princeton University Press, 41 William Street, Princeton, New Jersey 08540
In the United Kingdom: Princeton University Press, Guildford, Surrey

Library of Congress Cataloging in Publication Data will be found
on the last printed page of this book

ISBN 0-691-09131-5

This book has been composed in Linotron Caledonia

Clothbound editions of Princeton University Press books are printed on acid-free paper,
and binding materials are chosen for strength and durability

Printed in the United States of America by Princeton University Press
Princeton, New Jersey

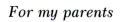

For my parents

Contents

Contents

Contents

Illustrations

Permission has been obtained for all material where possible.

Tables

Preface

In that same year [1530] and on that night, in the hour when Ivan Vasil'evich, Grand Duke of all Russia, was born, at that time in [the city of] Great Novgorod, a bell of good size was cast for the Cathedral of St. Sophia, by order of the God-loving Metropolitan Makarij, Archbishop of Great Novgorod and Pskov; and in Novgorod and in the entire Novgorod region, there is not [a bell] of such magnitude; it blasts like an awesome trumpet.

—PSRL III (Novg. II), p. 148, my translation

CENTURIES before church bells first rang in Kievan Russia, trumpets had resounded in ancient Egypt and Israel. Their stentorian voices pierced the din of battle with signals for tactical maneuvers, called great encampments to assembly, and rang out at appointed times during temple rites. In late antiquity rhythms struck on wooden and metal semantra eventually displaced these trumpet fanfares as a summons to services in the Byzantine East. And in time, untuned bells assumed in Russia the favored position that semantra had held in Byzantium. Russian bells, named and blessed, are associated with some of the most colorful episodes in the history of the old regime.

In Moscow especially the surging accompaniment of the Russian church bells seemed a canopy beneath which unfolded the city's rich and turbulent history. Ridolfo Fioravanti introduced Muscovites to Italian technology in the founding of bells and cannon in the late fifteenth century; and soon after, the capital, with its hundreds of gilded and copper-covered cupolas rising from churches and monasteries, was filled with the sound of ringing bronze. The bells rang in the births of sovereigns, announced their coronations, marriages, and battle triumphs, and tolled their deaths. They served rites of the church as well as ceremonies of state, investing the reigning monarch with powerful aural regalia and affirming Moscow's spiritual destiny as the Third Rome.

Russian bells resemble Western bells in their form, but unlike the bells that most Westerners know, they are stationary in their mounting and are untuned. They are rung by manually swinging an internal clapper to produce rhythmic patterns derived from signals struck on Byzantine semantra. This practice is in sharp contrast to the ringing of most tuned bells in the Western world, whether in performing polyphonic music on the keyboard and pedals of a carillon with its stationary bells or ringing changes by setting bells themselves in motion to meet their internal, free-swinging clappers. Russian bells also reached extraordinary sizes and weights in the sixteenth to the nineteenth centuries at the hands of master founders and pious, ambitious rulers. Andrej Chokhov cast a bell of over 2,000 puds (72,226 pounds) for Boris Godunov in 1599; Aleksandr Grigor'ev cast a bell of at least 10,000 puds (361,130 pounds) for Aleksei Mikhailovich in 1655; and in 1735 Mikhail Motorin cast Tsar-Kolokol for Empress Anna Ivanovna at 12,000 puds (433,356 pounds), a bell whose magnitude remains unchallenged to this day in the annals of bell founding.

By the late nineteenth century the constant ringing of the smaller bells in Moscow vied with the clatter of droshkies tearing through the city, sparks streaming in their wake as the horses' iron-clad hooves beat nerve-jangling rhythms on the stone thoroughfares. But the deep, resonant strokes on the larger Russian bells, like the nocturnal wail of a distant train, filled the soul with ineffable spaciousness. For the Russian people, from the imperial family in St. Petersburg to the peasants in remote provincial villages, the *zvon* (collective sound) of church bells added an aural dimension to the visual splendors of Russian Orthodoxy.

After 1917 the zvon over Russia gradually faded. Many of the bronze inhabitants of Russia's bell towers were either destroyed in the two world wars or sacrificed to economic progress during the interval between. Only a few fine ensembles of bells survive that descendants of the Orthodox can hear today, but in the hands of skilled ringers they still stir the imagination and call back the past. In the following chapters the history of Russia's bells and even some of the legends surrounding bells and bell ringing in tsarist Russia are presented for the first time in a Western language.

Cultural historians have generally recognized Ivan III's Kremlin architecture as a visible expression of Moscow's ascendancy over Russia, but with few exceptions they have largely overlooked the city's equally imposing sonic analogue. One reason the "soundscape" of Moscow has not been pursued in Western scholarship is that to musicologists without command of the Russian language the historical development of Russian bells and their liturgical function have remained inaccessible; even with knowledge of the language, the sources, widely scattered throughout an extensive literature, are not easily obtained. Most of the sources I consulted in my research are from collections at the University of Kansas, the University of Illinois at Urbana-Champaign, the University of North Carolina at Chapel Hill, Duke University, the Library of Congress, and the Lenin State Library of the USSR in Moscow.

My study of Russian bells and bell founding began in the fall of 1970 when I was invited to participate in a session devoted to "Spiritual Motifs in [Russian] Art" at the Bi-State (now Central) Slavic Conference at the University of Kansas. In a twenty-minute paper entitled "An Aspect of Russian Nationalism: The Voice of Orthodoxy in the Art Music of Nineteenth-Century Russia," I hastily introduced a few examples of Russian composers' use of chants, polyphonic liturgical music, and bell sounds in their music. Six minutes of general remarks on bell motifs in Russian music soon expanded into study of the history of bells and the technology of bell founding in Muscovy. James Scanlan, now at The Ohio State University, planned the original panel and in that capacity helped launch the research that has resulted in this book.

In this volume I have viewed bells, bell ringing, and the technology of founding as salient manifestations of certain religio-political attitudes in pre-revolutionary Russia. I have focused on defining the historical and technological aspects of the subject, presenting the individual dramas of the great bells, and interpreting the collective cultural significance of the zvon. A subsequent volume will examine the role of bells in the offices and liturgies of the Russian Rite, the impact of bell ringing on Russian architecture, literature, and music, and evidence for regarding Russian bells and bell ringing as aural icons.

The historian will, I hope, experience no difficulty in the present volume with the musical and acoustical aspects of the subject, and the musicologist without extensive prior knowledge of Russian history should be able to follow developments in Russian bell founding through references to contemporary events in political and military history. The glossary at the back of the book is designed to facilitate the reader's acquaintance with the basic terminology of founding and campanology as well as certain titles and institutions from Russian and Byzantine culture.

Acknowledgments

THE INTEREST, encouragement, and generous assistance of several institutions and numerous friends and colleagues have gone into the preparation of this volume. I am indebted to the University of Kansas for a sabbatical leave in 1980-1981, three Summer Research Grants from the Faculty Research Fund, and an allocation from the Small Grants' Fund to assist with the production of illustrative material. The summer awards allowed me to spend time as an Associate at the Summer Research Laboratory on Russia and Eastern Europe at the University of Illinois in Urbana-Champaign. The support services at the National Humanities Center during my year as a fellow and the award of a fellowship from the American Council of Learned Societies contributed substantially to the completion of this study.

At the University of Kansas the dedicated work of Mary Kay, director of Interlibrary Services, and her staff at Watson Library has put a remarkable number of sources at my disposal from collections in this country and abroad. Marianne Griffin, Maria Alexander, Marilyn S. Clark, Galina Kuzmanović, and Tina Spray have all cheerfully expedited innumerable loan requests and responded to my questions on bibliographical materials. At the Kenneth Spencer Research Library James Helyar and Alexandra Mason have been particularly helpful. A special word of thanks is due Albert Gerken, carillonneur at the University of Kansas, who took time from his busy schedule to read the manuscript and offer suggestions. Kenneth E. Rose, professor of mechanical engineering, read and critiqued technical material in Parts IV and V. Other colleagues at the University of Kansas who have willingly assisted with various aspects of this volume include Stephen Addiss, John T. Alexander, James Barnes, Gary Bjorge, Herbert Galton, Gerald Mikkelson, Philip Montgomery, Oliver Phillips, Michael Shaw, and Elden Tefft.

A significant portion of my research was carried out during the summers of 1976, 1977, 1979, and 1982 at the Summer Research Laboratory on Russia and Eastern Europe in Urbana-Champaign. Established by Ralph T. Fisher, Jr., and directed by Benjamin Uroff and Marianna Tax Choldin, this summer institute and the resources and collections at the University of Illinois continue to enrich the work of hundreds of scholars each year. In the Slavic and East European Library, Laurence H. Miller, Marianna Tax Choldin, June E. Pachuta, Mary P. Stuart, and Rebecca Atack have all given generous assistance and guidance and have procured from foreign libraries a great number of sources essential to the completion of my work. Frederick V. Lawrence, professor of civil engineering and metallurgy at the University of Illinois, advised me on the historical development of arc welding. For their help with translations from Russian and Polish, I am happy to acknowledge the skilled assistance of Gene Barabtarlo and Piotr Gorecki.

At the National Humanities Center, that haven for scholars in the Piedmont forest of North Carolina, the initial draft of this volume was written between July 1980 and August 1981. I am grateful to William Bennett, then director of the center, and to the gifted members of his staff for their dedication. The center's librarians, Alan Tuttle and Rebecca Sutton, and their assistants obtained many items from libraries at Duke University and the University of North Carolina at Chapel Hill as well as loans from other institutions. My sincere thanks also go to the center's patient and skilled typists, Karen Carroll, Madeline Moyer, Jan Paxton, and

Cynthia Edwards, who produced the first draft of this manuscript.

Diane O. Ota of the music department at the Boston Public Library granted permission to use materials in the Allen A. Brown Collection, and Harvard University extended me the privilege of using the resources of Widener Library. In the European Division of the Library of Congress Robert V. Allen and David H. Kraus were both extremely helpful in advising me of holdings in the Russian collection appropriate to my work. The Embassy of the People's Republic of China in Washington gave me information on bells in Peking. For their numerous and varied contributions to this book, I wish also to thank W. Averell Harriman, George F. Kennan, Percival Price, Tillman Merritt, Kenneth Levy, John Meyendorff, Miloš Velimirović, William F. Newman, Franz Peter Schilling, Warren Cowgill, Zhenia Yashemsky, Milford Myhre, John Erickson, Ann Kleimola, David Miller, Diane Touliatos-Banker, Gordon Holland, K. Anikovich, M. P. Tsukanov, V. I. Erokhin, V. I. Lebedev, Vance Thurston, Brian Davies, Eugenia Felton, Carol Worley, Vera Sehon, Charles Andrew, and Timothy Barker.

At Princeton University Press the late Christine K. Ivusic expressed early interest in this study and offered generous guidance as I prepared the manuscript for submission. Tam Curry's exemplary skills as copyeditor have strengthened my work immeasurably and removed its stylistic infelicities. I am grateful for her revisions and suggestions in shaping this book for publication. Thanks are also due Sue Bishop, who has designed the book.

Finally, I wish to thank my parents, Blenus and Kathryn V. Williams, for their encouragement during a decade of research. I also remain in their debt for many helpful comments as drafts of chapters were completed. This book is dedicated to them.

Though I am indebted to all who have played a part in the completion of this project, I hasten to claim as my own whatever imperfections or misunderstandings may be present.

Edward V. Williams
Lawrence, Kansas

Author's Explanatory Notes

IN TRANSLITERATING titles and names of publishers for Russian works published before October 1918, I have made no distinction between "и" and "i," or between "e" as "ie" and "e" as "io" or "yo"; both of the latter have been transliterated as a Roman "e" (capitalized at the beginning of sentences or proper names). I have used the following Roman transliterations for the accompanying Cyrillic letters: й = j, ъ = ", ы = y, ь = ', ѣ = ě, э = ė, ю = iu, я = ia, ѳ = th, and ѵ = ẏ. Transliteration of other letters is more standardized.

Translated rather than transliterated forms are used for names or place names whose translations are familiar and easily recognized: Alexander I instead of Aleksandr I, and Peter the Great instead of Petr Velikij; Moscow instead of Moskva, Yaroslavl instead of Iaroslavl, and the Trinity-Sergius Lavra instead of Sviato-Troitskaia-Sergieva lavra. The soft sign (') at the end of such city names as Tver and Yaroslavl is dropped in the text though preserved in titles. Certain frequently used foreign terms (semantron, bilo, klepalo, zvonnitsa) are not italicized in the text after their initial appearance.

Since the subject of this study largely falls before the October Revolution of 1917, and before the subsequent change from the Julian to the Gregorian calendar in 1918, no attempt has been made to render Old Style dates before that year as New Style. However, Russian years expressed on bell inscriptions and in chronicles as *anno mundi* (A.M., "from the creation of the world") have been converted to *anno Domini* (A.D., "from the year of the Lord") to facilitate identification. Unless otherwise indicated, dates following the names of rulers are their regnal years.

Special pitches for the fundamental, hum tone, and other partials on bells, as well as for the tuned pitches of chimes and carillons, are indicated according to the following system.[1]

The units of Russian measurement used in this study and their American equivalents are:

1 *versta*	=	3,500 feet or 0.663 miles (500 *sazheni*)
1 *sazhen'*	=	7 feet (3 *arshiny*)
1 *arshin*	=	28 inches (16 *vershki*)
1 *vershok*	=	1.75 inches
1 *pud*	=	36.113 pounds (40 *funty*)
1 *funt*	=	0.903 pounds[2]

Anglicized plurals are used in the text for most of these units (puds, not *pudy*; funts, not *funty*). To simplify conversion, puds and funts are rounded off to the nearest whole number in pounds (e.g., 150 puds = 5,417 rather than 5,416.95 pounds).

Whenever possible, note has been made of such Russian monuments as bells, bell towers, churches, and monasteries that have been severely damaged or destroyed. In some cases, however, the present condition or even the very existence of monuments cited in Russian publications before World War I and the Revolution has not been possible to verify.

Part I
Early Instruments of Convocation

1

Voices of Ancient Trumpets

IN LENINGRAD on the granite embankment of Vasilevsky Island opposite the Academy of Arts, two Egyptian sphinxes flank a landing stage whose steps descend into the Neva (figure 1). Brought to St. Petersburg from Thebes in the spring of 1832, this pair of sphinxes had guarded the entrance to a temple that Amenhotep III had built near the Nile at the beginning of the fourteenth century B.C.[1] Beneath the desert sun, these syenite creatures had once heard the bellowing of royal trumpets. Then, after more than three millennia in Egypt, they reached St. Petersburg during the final century of the old regime, and in their new home in the snows of northern Russia they met the rhythmic music from St. Isaac's untuned bells across the river. The prehistory of Russian bell ringing begins in Egypt with the crafting and blowing of metal trumpets, essentially in the presence of the Leningrad sphinxes.

Ancient Egypt, Israel, Greece, and Rome

Among the "wonderful things" brought to light in 1922 with the opening of the tomb of Tutankhamen (d. mid-fourteenth-century B.C.) were two trumpets, a silver one and a slightly shorter copper or bronze instrument, both with some gold overlay (figure 2).[2] A third trumpet of bronze from Roman Egypt is preserved in the Louvre.[3] These three trumpets, together with certain idiophones, are the only ancient Egyptian instruments still capable of reproducing their original sound.[4]

Hickmann has described the timbre of the two trumpets from the tomb of Tutankhamen as "raucous and powerful, particularly in their low sounds."[5] Plutarch remarked *circa* A.D. 120 that residents in the Egyptian towns of Busiris and Lycopolis had already ceased to use the trumpet (*salpinx*, or σάλπιγξ) in their rites because it made "a noise like an ass," an animal regarded as a demonic beast because of its resemblance to the god Typhon.[6] The apparent braying noises emitted from these relatively short ancient trumpets may have resulted from the fairly high pitch of their ground tone and from the restricted number of notes available above this pitch.[7]

In the ancient world end-blown metal trumpets served as military instruments but were also sounded in certain ceremonies and rituals of a sacred or semisacred nature. The straight Egyptian trumpet or *šnb* occurs so frequently in a military context in Egyptian art beginning with the New Kingdom (1567-1085 B.C.) that there can be no doubt that it was used for signaling during battle.[8] An early representation of the šnb appears *circa* 1480 B.C. on a relief from the Temple of Hatshepsut at Thebes (figure 3), showing a trumpeter leading a procession of soldiers at a festival during her reign.[9] In another example, also from Thebes, a trumpeter, possibly sounding cadence on the šnb, faces a file of six armed soldiers and an officer.[10]

1. Landing stage with two Egyptian sphinxes on the Neva embankment before the Academy of Arts in Leningrad. From V. A. Kamenskij, ed., *Pamiatniki arkhitektury Leningrada*, 2d ed., rev. and enl. (Leningrad, 1960), 424, fig. 1. Permission of Strojizdat, Moscow.

Evidence for the use of trumpets in Egyptian rites of worship is less abundant. Despite engraved figures of the gods Rê-ʿHorakhti, Amon-Rêʿ, and Ptah on the lotus-shaped bells of the two trumpets from Tutankhamen's tomb, Howard Carter believed that these instruments had functioned in a military capacity. Each of the three Egyptian deities, Carter maintained, probably served as tutelary patron of a legion in the imperial Egyptian army.[11] Several scenes from Dynasties IV, V, and VI, however, show trumpeters standing in boats and may represent a ceremonial use of the trumpet in barques for the dead as early as the third millennium B.C.[12] Stronger evidence for the trumpet's role in the cult of the dead during the Roman period in Egypt is found in a painting on an Egyptian coffin from A.D. 212, which shows a trumpeter sounding his instrument before Osiris (figure 4).[13] Furthermore, Eustathius, Archbishop of Thessaloniki (fl. A.D. 1175), ascribes the invention of the trumpet to Osiris and reports its use in rites associated with worship of this god.[14]

To what extent the silver trumpets of the ancient Hebrews were modeled on Egyptian instruments is still not certain, but their length and form as well as their manufacture from leaves of silver are features common to the trumpets of both peoples.[15] The earliest mention of trumpets as instruments of convocation appears in Numbers 10:1 and 2, where God commanded Moses on Sinai to make two trumpets (*ḥazozeroth*), each from a whole sheet of silver. A detailed description of the silver Hebrew trumpet appears in Josephus, who reports that it was "little less than a cubit" (17 to 21 inches) in length and that it had a straight, narrow tube terminating in a bell flare.[16] The well-known relief on the Arch of Titus in Rome (after A.D. 81) shows a late rendering of a pair of ḥazozeroth, which, together with other sacred objects, was removed from the Temple when Jerusalem fell to the Romans in A.D. 70 (figure 5). But the two straight trumpets carved on the Arch of Titus are closer in appearance to the long Roman *tuba* than to ancient Egyptian prototypes.[17] It is possible that the sculptor of this relief never had seen ḥazozeroth himself and carved into this panel on the Arch of Titus the form and shape of the *tubae* he had known in Rome.

If details on trumpets as cultic instruments in ancient Egypt are meager, account of their ritual use in the encampments on Sinai is clearly set forth in the tenth chapter of Numbers. In fact, four different functions are cited for the ḥazozeroth Moses fashioned in the wilderness, among them their use as ritual or cultic instruments.[18] Because the musical resources of ancient trumpets were extremely limited, the ḥazozerah, for calls to assembly, was used both singly and in pairs. This practice established at an early date a precedent for distinguishing signals through contrasts in volume and perhaps in pitch. When two trumpets were sounded

2. The copper or bronze (A) and silver (B) trumpets from the first half of the fourteenth century B.C., found in the tomb of Tutankhamen. From Hans Hickmann, *Catalogue général des antiquités égyptiennes du Musée du Caire, nos. 69201-69852* (Cairo, 1949), pl. 87B. Permission of the Library of the Egyptian Museum, Cairo.

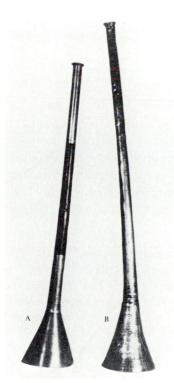

together, "all the assembly shall assemble themselves . . . at the door of the tabernacle [tent of meeting] of the congregation." If one trumpet was blown, then only the princes or heads of the tribes were summoned.[19]

An alarm signal, sufficiently distinct from the call for assembly, sounded four times for breaking camp and dismantling the Tabernacle. At the first alarm, the eastern quarter of the encampment prepared to move out. When the second, third, and fourth alarms were sounded, the southern, western, and northern quarters followed. These four alarms relied upon a series of commands issued through the temporal spacing of four blasts.[20]

The military role of trumpets in ancient Israel, first stated in Numbers 10:9, is articulated in great detail in the Dead Sea scroll that contains *The War of the Sons of Light against the Sons of Darkness*, written perhaps in the second half of the first century B.C.[21] But even in their military capacity, trumpets were used principally to remind Hebrew soldiers of the religious nature of warfare.[22] The priestly privilege of blowing trumpets, unequivocally established on Sinai, was maintained over the centuries even on the field of battle, and priests' trumpets bore inscriptions dedicating them to their sacred purpose. Though signals both on silver ḥazozeroth and on *shofaroth* (rams' horns) were blown during battle, directions in *Sons of Light against the Sons of Darkness* explicitly state that the former are to be blown by six priests and the latter are to be sounded by the Levites.[23]

In the Tabernacle on Sinai and later in the Temple silver trumpets were sounded on certain days and at prescribed moments during sacrificial rites.[24] In Jerusalem ḥazozeroth were also blown at the beginning of every month, on solemn days, and on festive occasions, including the coronations of Hebrew kings. Trumpets are specifically mentioned in the Bible at the anointing and crowning of Joash in the ninth century B.C.[25] The Bible further reports 120 priests blowing trumpets during the national rejoicing that accompanied the dedication of Solomon's Temple *circa* 950 B.C.[26]

In the Temple the silver trumpets were blown

3. Detail from a relief on the south side (lower colonnade) of the Temple of Deir el Bahari, Thebes, ca. 1480 B.C., showing an Egyptian trumpeter leading a procession at a festival during the reign of Hatshepsut. From Edouard Naville, *The Temple of Deir el Bahari*, pt. 6 (London, 1908), pl. 155.

4. Painting on an Egyptian coffin from the Roman period (A.D. 212) showing a trumpet being blown before Osiris. From Hans Hickmann, *La Trompette dans l'Egypte ancienne*, Supplément aux Annales du service des antiquités de l'Egypte, notebook no. 1 (Cairo, 1946; reprint ed., Nashville, TN, 1976), p. 16, fig. 22. Permission of The Brass Press.

during the three breaks in the daily singing of Psalms.[27] At each of these pauses in the psalmody, the priestly trumpeters blew three blasts, and each time the people prostrated themselves.[28] The Talmud preserves a description of the use of trumpets during the sacrificial rites of the Second Temple, which Zorobabel built after the Babylonian Captivity:

The deputy high priest stood on the horn of the altar with the flags in his hand, and two priests on the table of the fat [pieces] with two trumpets in their hands. They blew a teki'ah [prolonged], a teru'ah [staccato] and a teki'ah, and then went and stood by Ben Arza, one on his right hand and one on his left. When he bent down to make the libation the deputy high priest waved the flags and Ben Arza struck the cymbals and the Levites chanted the Psalm. When they came to a pause a teki'ah was blown, and the public prostrated themselves; at every pause there was a teki'ah and at every teki'ah a prostration. This was the order of the regular daily sacrifice for the service of the House of our God.[29]

Though both the Greek salpinx and the Roman *tuba* were primarily used as military instruments, they also participated in religious rites and state ceremonies. When the salpinx was blown in rituals, as it was on occasion, it was called "the sacred trumpet" (σάλπιγξ ἡ ἱερά).[30] It was a long, straight trumpet, generally of metal, which terminated in a bell (κώδων), the wide mouth of the instrument.[31] A vase painting from the first half of the fifth century B.C. shows a hoplite sounding a salpinx (figure 6). Together with the *cornu*, *lituus*, and *bucina*, the *tuba* was a Roman instrument of Etruscan origin. *Tubae* were also blown in Roman cult music, and their players, the *tubicines*, even enjoyed a privileged position. Twice each spring, the *tubae* blown in religious, military, and state functions were blessed in a ceremony called *tubilustrium*.[32] A straight, cylindrical instrument terminating in a bell, the Roman *tuba* was usually made of bronze sections and measured about 4.33 feet.[33] Because of the unusual length of both the salpinx and *tuba*, the players of both often wore a mouth band (φορβειά or *capistrum*). Classical writers have used the Latin words *terribilis* and *rauca* to describe the sound of *tubae*.[34]

Signals blown on ancient trumpets were limited to rhythmic calls on one or two pitches and could be distinguished through pitch and tone—low and full or high and thin. These instruments were therefore generally capable of producing three kinds of signals: (1) a blast at a high dynamic level, (2) a sustained tone of moderate intensity, and (3) a quavering sound produced through rapid alternations of the fundamental and an overblown note.[35] In all probability, early Christian communities in Upper Egypt adopted these three kinds of articulation on the trumpet for their first calls to services.

Early Christian Egypt

During the early fourth century, when Christians were permitted to assemble freely without fear of persecution,[36] St. Pachomius (ca. 290-346) aban-

doned his eremitical life to embrace and propagate a coenobitical, or communal, monastic ideal. About 320 he committed himself to the new movement at Tabennesis.[37] Numbers of other Egyptian anchorites also renounced their solitary existence in the desert to follow Pachomius and chose a regulated monastic ideal, which called for a structured life of daily worship, work, and communal meals. In the Thebaid along the Nile Pachomius established and supervised no fewer than eleven foundations for his spiritual protégés.[38]

St. Jerome's Latin translation of the fourth-century monastic rule that bears the name of Pachomius contains two passages in which the blowing of a trumpet (*tuba*) is cited as a summons to the assembly hall.[39]

III. Whenever he hears the voice of the trumpet as a call to assembly, he leaves his cell immediately, meditating on a passage of scripture all the way to the door of the assembly hall.[40]

IX. When the sound of the trumpet announces an assembly during the day, he who arrives late for prayer at that place will in turn be chastised with the previously stated [manner of] rebuke and will remain in the refectory.[41]

In the Greek texts of the second passage published by Boon and Lefort the noun "salpinx" appears.[42] St. Jerome's use of the noun *tuba* in his translation of the first passage, however, may indicate that the signaling instrument was also designated a salpinx in the Greek source from which he worked, or that he has introduced *tuba* as the instrument that issued the call to assembly. (The word "salpinx" does not occur in the Greek versions of Boon and Lefort.) In the Latin version of the second passage the noun *clangor* and the verb *increpuerit* both suggest the unmusical timbre of the ancient trumpet. The Greek verb βοήσῃ (shouts; cries) carries a similar connotation. And the choice of words in both the Greek and Latin versions of the rule presents reasonable evidence that the ancient trumpet served the early Christian communities as their first instrument of convocation.

Jerome's use of the noun *signum* (signal) in more than a half-dozen instances in his translation of

5. Relief panel on the Arch of Titus in Rome (after A.D. 81) depicting the triumphal Roman procession following the capture and sack of Jerusalem in A.D. 70. Objects from the Temple carried in the procession include the seven-branch candlestick (left) and a pair of trumpets (right). Permission of Alinari/Art Resource.

Pachomius' rule[43] and his use of *tuba* only twice should not be taken as evidence that *tuba* is a mistranslation or an error. Nor should the reference to "beating" or "striking" as a call to prayer in the Greek and Coptic fragments of the rule be understood to rule out trumpets as another means of announcing services.[44] As late as the beginning of the ninth century, Theodore, abbot of the Studion Monastery from 798 to 826, instructed the *kanonarch*, the cleric who struck the semantron, to "sound forth the wood like a trumpet" (σάλπιζε . . . τὸ ξύλον).[45] He suggests in his choice of metaphor the historical precedence of the trumpet and the lingering memory of its calls to services.

A passage from chapter 8 in the *Protoevangelium Jacobi* says that a trumpet called together the widowers in Palestine (including Joseph) among whom a husband was to be chosen for the twelve-year-old Mary: "And the heralds went forth over all the country round about Judaea, and the trumpet of the Lord (ἡ σάλπιγξ κυρίου) sounded and all men ran thereto."[46] On the basis of Harnach's belief that

6. Painting on an Attic vase (ca. 475 B.C.) of a hoplite blowing a *salpinx*. From *Die Musik in Geschichte und Gegenwart* 12, plate 38, fig. 3 (opposite col. 801). By permission of the Museo Teatrale alla Scala, Milan.

the *Protoevangelium Jacobi* originated in Egypt, Georg Stuhlfauth finds evidence in this passage for the sounding of trumpets in Christian Egypt as early as the mid-second century. The anonymous author of this apocryphal gospel, he maintains, has probably transferred an early Christian custom of trumpet blowing as a call to assembly in second-century Egypt to an event that allegedly took place in Palestine at the end of the first century B.C.[47]

Though prototypes for trumpets blown in early Christian communities were probably the silver Hebrew ḥazozeroth, no iconographical sources have survived. Representations of trumpets on a Jewish coin of the Bar Kokhba period and of the *tuba* and salpinx may be the closest visual information available.

During the fourth century at intervals throughout the day and night, the strident cries of trumpets shattered the quiet within the walled monasteries of Upper Egypt. Trumpet calls woke the inhabitants of these foundations from their sleep and called them from their cells and from their work. The trumpet assembled them several times a week for group instruction—often by Pachomius himself—and for daily prayers in the morning and evening.[48] The trumpet also summoned the devout to the assembly hall for the Eucharist on Saturdays and Sundays and to the two common meals taken each day.[49]

From the bells of these metal instruments came signals that ordered the lives of monks in the Thebaid. But their voices were soon to be replaced in the Christian East by rhythmic calls of another kind—the striking of a mallet on wood.

2

Holy Wood and Holy Iron

AT THE END of the sixth or beginning of the seventh century John Climacus in *Scala paradisi* (Κλῖμαξ τοῦ παραδείσου) speaks of signals for convocation from "the spiritual trumpet" (ἡ πνευματικὴ σάλπιγξ).[1] By this expression he implies that some other instrument of convocation had already displaced the trumpet on Sinai, and further suggests that the newer instrument had also absorbed something of the trumpet's sonic and symbolic essence. Rainer Stichel may be correct in assuming that a wooden beam or board was in use in Egypt as early as the fourth century.[2] Two passages in the fourth-century *vita* of Pachomius mention "striking" or "hitting" something to summon monks to the morning office and to communal meals,[3] though they do not specify an instrument or surface on which the signals were struck. A.-J. Festugière assumes that a wooden plank or semantron (*la simandre*) must have been the object that received the blows.[4] But later accounts from Palestine and Egypt suggest that the semantron itself had not emerged by that time.

About 420 both Palladius and John Cassian cite in specific terms the custom in Palestine and Egypt, respectively, of knocking with a hammer or mallet on each monk's cell (presumably on cell doors) to assemble monastic communities for worship and work.[5] This hammer Palladius calls "the awakening hammer" (τὸ ἐξυπνιαστικὸν σφυρίον). The earlier striking action mentioned in the *vita* of Pachomius therefore seems far more likely to refer to striking on cell doors than to sounding a semantron as Festugière has surmised. Had Pachomius

known the semantron, which, sounded from a central location within the monastery compound, could be heard simultaneously by all monks, surely the author of his *vita* would have mentioned "wood" in connection with striking and later monastic communities would have adopted the more efficient, more trumpetlike instrument of convocation.

In his study of the origins of the semantron Stichel draws attention to a Jewish practice of knocking on the doors of houses with a wooden hammer, a custom attested to by the year A.D. 200 in the Palestinian Talmud.[6] Whether any connection exists between this Jewish practice and striking cell doors in early Christian monasteries has yet to be established. But Stichel speculates that the hammer may have replaced the *shofar* for signaling in Jewish circles during the early Christian era, which may possibly be relevant to the close association of the semantron and trumpet in the Christian East.[7] Whatever earlier relationship may eventually be revealed between hammer and ram's horn, the evidence transmitted through the Greek verb κρούειν (to hit or strike) in the *vita* of Pachomius and in the works of Palladius and John Cassian is sufficient to establish a percussive precedent for the semantron by the early fifth century.

The Emergence and Dissemination of the Semantron

By the end of the fourth century, then, trumpets as signaling instruments seem already to have seen their best years of service and were probably in the process of being replaced in monasteries by hammer blows on cell doors.[8] By the fifth and sixth centuries, however, the *vitae* of certain saints, in addition to their references to simply "striking," were beginning to cite "striking on the wood" (κρούων εἰς τὸ ξύλον and τῷ ξύλῳ ἔκρουον), which seems to indicate more persuasively the presence of the semantron or similar instrument.[9] Use of the semantron would obviate the need to summon each individually from his own cell. Thus by the beginning of the sixth century wooden semantra must have taken the place, physically if not symbolically, of both trumpets and hammer blows on cell doors as signals for convocation in the monasteries of Egypt, Palestine, Sinai, and possibly even in Christian communities of the Far East.[10]

Several notices in the *Pratum spirituali* of John Moschus (d. 619/620) that describe monastic conditions in Palestine at the end of the sixth century reveal that "striking the wood" (πρὸ τοῦ κροῦσαι τὸ ξύλον) had become the normal method of signaling for services and that the duty of sounding such calls had been assigned to the *kanonarchos*.[11] By the early years of the seventh century larger urban churches in the Levant had also begun to adopt the semantron. And the semantron was sounded when the relics of the martyr Anastasius (d. 628) were transferred from Persia to Caesarea in Palestine; as the procession approached the city, the faithful were summoned to the new church of the Theotokos (Virgin) by the sounds of "the holy wood."[12] But the freedom of using this instrument was suddenly restricted when Islamic conquerors descended upon the Christian East.

In 638, after a four-month siege, the Arabs occupied Jerusalem. Upon entering the city, they drew up the so-called Covenant of ʿUmar, which detailed a number of regulations to be imposed on Christian liturgical practices, among them a restriction on signals used for calls to worship.[13] An early eighteenth-century mistranslation of this clause by Simon Ockley suggested that Christians in Jerusalem had been ringing bells to announce their services,[14] an error not challenged until Edward Gibbon (1737-1794) intuitively questioned the report, doubting "whether this expression can be justified by the text of Al Wakidi, or the practice of the times."[15] Gibbon's suspicions were well founded, for the word in the Covenant of ʿUmar translated as "bells" is not *jaras* but *nākūs* or *nāqūs*, an instrument that is not a bell at all but two suspended logs "made to swing toward each other and touch, producing a booming sound not unlike that of a great bell."[16] What the clause in the covenant sought to limit was the volume of the sound from the nākūs. The Christians in Jerusalem were actually admonished "to beat the nākūs only gently in [their] churches," that is, not to make too much noise.[17] In other cities under Arab domination similar restrictions were placed on the time and manner of issuing calls to worship. In some areas striking the nākūs was proscribed before and after Muslim prayers.[18]

For more than four and a half centuries of Arab domination (638-1099) the nākūs served Christians in Jerusalem as their sole instrument of convocation. When Godfrey of Bouillon and his crusaders gained custody of the city in 1099, a member of his retinue reported that Jerusalem contained no bells and that bell ringing was not to be heard in the city.[19]

Though the bell was the convocational instrument favored in the West and striking the wood was favored in the Christian East, the semantron was not altogether unknown in Western Europe. It even appeared there along with bells, although to a more limited extent. Before the mid-sixth century Western sources do not specify the instrument used to summon monks or nuns to offices, instead using the ambiguous term *signum* (sign or signal). Caesarius of Arles may have had in mind the semantron when he used the term *signum* in his *Regularis ad virgines* (ca. 513);[20] the first reference to a church bell sent to Europe—from North Africa to the Italian peninsula—only appeared about two decades later. Likewise, the Rule of St. Benedict of Nursia, probably formulated between 530 and 540, may intend the Late Latin word *signus* to mean semantron, although by this time a church bell was presumably more of a possibility.[21] The instrument in these two early references, however, is uncertain.

A later reference gives clear evidence of the presence of the semantron in the West. Amalarius of Metz, in chapter 21 of *De ecclesiasticis officiis* (823), specifically compares the different characters of the wood and the bronze in calling the faithful to services:

Furthermore, the pomp of signals, which was produced by bronze vessels, is abandoned, and the sound of wood, somewhat more humble than the sound of bronze, is produced as required to call people to church. It is possible even that this, a more humble custom of the Roman Church than that in use today, is copied from ancient times and especially from that time when [the church] was in hiding in catacombs because of its persecutors: for until the present day, the younger Rome [Constantinople], which in ancient times was governed under one lord [the emperor] with old Rome, maintains the use of wood, not because of a lack of bronze, but because of a venerable tradition.[22]

No evidence has yet appeared to support Amalarius' theory that semantra were used in catacombs during the period of persecutions. Probably no signaling instrument of any kind was sounded before the fourth century that would betray Christians in their subterranean meetings.[23]

Though a few instances of striking the wood as calls to services can be cited from Europe,[24] the bell was indisputably preferred in the Latin West. In fact, beyond Byzantium and those regions that fell under Constantinople's liturgical influence, use of the semantron was quite limited. The true home of the semantron remained the Christian East.

By the middle of the eleventh century striking the semantron is clearly specified and established in the Typikon or Rule of the Studion Monastery in Constantinople.[25] A century and a half later Archbishop Antonij of Novgorod, who visited the imperial city in 1200, noted that even at Hagia Sophia, the great church of the Byzantine Empire, the clergy did not ring bells but struck a small hand semantron as a call to the morning office: "[The Greeks] do not have bells at Hagia Sophia, but holding in the hand a small semantron, they strike for Orthros [Matins]. And they do not strike for the Liturgy and Vespers, but at other churches they strike for both."[26]

A description of the Church of the Holy Apostles in Constantinople by Nikolaos Mesarites (ca. 1200) further illustrates the significance of the semantron in the imperial city a few years before the Fourth Crusade and Latin occupation (1204-1261). This church was one of the central houses of worship in the city, and the faithful assembled here for worship in the evening, in the morning, and at noon when they heard the semantron; Mesarites here draws a forceful comparison between the rhythms of the mallet on the wood and the beating of the human heart.[27]

Thus although the first bells may have been sent to Constantinople in the second half of the ninth century,[28] more than three hundred years later a foundation as important and as richly endowed as the Church of the Holy Apostles was still using the traditional semantron as its instrument of convocation. At the beginning of the fifteenth century, shortly before the Empire fell to the Ottoman Turks, Symeon, Archbishop of Thessaloniki (d. 1429), re-

7. Wooden hand semantra from Mt. Athos: 1. Karakalou Monastery, Agioi Apostoloi; 2. Protato, Karyes; 3. and 4. Grigoriou Monastery; 5. Chilandari Monastery; and 6. Unidentified. The length of these instruments ranges between 4.33 and 6.56 feet. From Fivos Anoyanakis, *Greek Popular Musical Instruments* (Athens, 1979), 96, fig. 60. Permission of the Holy Monastery of the Virtuous Forerunner (St. John the Baptist), Serrai.

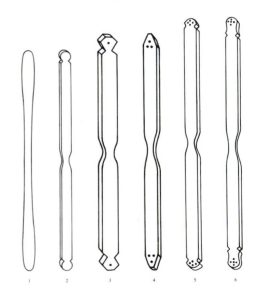

8. One method of striking a portable wooden semantron. From *Acta Sanctorum, Iunii 2* (Antwerp: 1698; reprint ed., Brussels, 1969), xxv. By permission of Editions Culture et Civilisation.

9. Another method of striking a hand semantron, at the Great Laura on Mt. Athos. From Anoyanakis, *Greek Popular Musical Instruments*, 36, pl. 11. Permission of the author.

affirmed the preeminence of the semantron at Greek churches and monasteries.[29]

The Semantron and the Sideron

The semantra that have served Greek monasteries and churches for calls to worship are of several sizes and types. N. V. Pokrovskij divides them into three general categories: the large wooden semantron, the small wooden semantron, and the iron or copper semantron.[30] All are mentioned in medieval sources and can still be heard today.[31] The smaller wooden semantron, which a player can carry in a procession, is called a "small semantron" (σήμαν-τρον μικρὸν), "hand semantron" (χειροσήμαν-τρον), or "little wood" (μικρὸν ξύλο).[32] Allatius describes it as an unblemished, resonant, and care-fully planed plank up to 20 feet long (he probably meant 10), about 4.5 inches wide, and about 1.5 inches thick.[33] It is most resonant when made of maple, linden, ash, or chestnut.[34] The board is hewn with an axe and must not be split or cracked. Its shape is not perfectly straight but slightly curved. Each end is either rounded or terminates in a simple ornamental shape in which one to five small holes are bored (figure 7). Three holes symbolize the Holy Trinity; four or five holes are arranged in the configuration of a Greek cross.[35]

The hand semantron can be held in two ways. The center of the board can be balanced on the player's left shoulder and the instrument held in place by a cord that passes through a hole in the plank's midpoint and is firmly clenched between the player's teeth (figure 8). This frees both of the

10. Detail of an angel striking a hand semantron on a wooden panel "The Dormition of St. Ephraem" by Emmanuel Tzanfournari (Christian Museum of the Vatican Library). From Jean Baptiste Seroux d'Agincourt, *Histoire de l'art par les monuments*, 5 (Paris, 1823), pl. 82. Courtesy of the Duke University Libraries.

11. Large wooden and iron semantra at the Chilandar Monastery, Mt. Athos. From Alexandar Deroko, *Athos: The Holy Mountain* (Belgrade, [1966]), pl. 47. Permission of Turistička štampa, Belgrade.

player's hands to strike the board with wooden mallets, simultaneously or alternately.[36] For the other method of carrying a hand semantron, the board must be tapered slightly toward the point of balance at its middle. The left hand of the player can then grasp the instrument at its narrower midpoint, while the right hand holds the mallet to strike the board, first in one place and then in another (see figures 9 and 16). A detail in the background of a wooden panel representing the Dormition of St. Ephraem by Emmanuel Tzanfournari shows an angel ascending a slope and sounding a hand semantron in this manner (figure 10).[37] In addition to the longer portable semantron, Kazanskij mentions having seen on Mt. Athos a somewhat shorter wooden hand semantron, less than 56 inches long, about 3.5 inches in width, and less than an inch in thickness.[38]

The larger wooden semantron, known as a "great semantron" (μεγασήμαντρον or σήμαντρον μέγα), is stationary and is usually suspended on one or two chains at shoulder height in the narthexes of churches or in monastery towers or arcades (figure 11).[39] It can be more than 10 feet long, as much as 2 feet wide, and 4 inches thick.[40] It is fashioned from the same kinds of dry and unblemished wood as the hand semantron and often assumes the same general form (without the narrower midpoint). It may also have shaped ends in which holes have been bored. Both these holes and the attenuated thickness of the wood at either end enhance the vibrations of the beam when it is struck (figure 12).[41]

The considerable size and weight of the great semantron require that special mounts be devised that are secure at the same time they do not dampen the vibrations of the wood. One solution has been to chisel out at least one rectangular section in the wood on the narrow top surface of the instrument, to form a slot through which a bolt can be passed to anchor the chain that suspends the semantron. Another has been to bolt a clamp to the upper face of the beam; and another has been to bore holes into the top side of the beam and insert hooks by which to hang the instrument.[42] The great semantron, thus suspended, is then struck by a monk, or sometimes two, with wooden mallets in each hand.

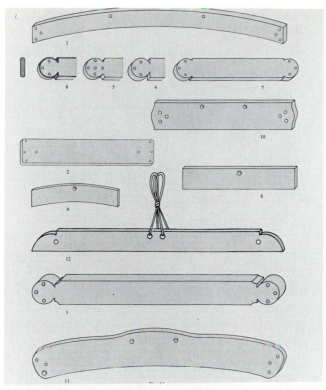

12. Large wooden semantra. Mt. Athos: 1. and 2. Chilandari Monastery; 3. and 4. Great Laura; 5. Stauroniketa Monastery; 6. Protato, Karyes; 7. Koutloumousi Monastery. The Meteora: 8. and 9. Agiou Stefanou Monastery; 10. Varlaam Monastery; 11. Metamorfoseos Monastery. Kastoria: 12. Church of the Taxiarchos. These instruments range in length between 3.93 and 12.33 feet, their width varies from 9 inches to 1.96 feet, and their thickness runs between 1.18 and 5.11 inches. From Anoyanakis, *Greek Popular Musical Instruments*, 97, fig. 61. Permission of the Stauroniketa Monastery, Mt. Athos.

Strictly speaking, the Greek word "semantron" should be reserved for wooden instruments, large or small, struck with wooden mallets. The metal instrument of iron or copper is more properly designated a *sideron* (σίδηρον), meaning "iron," or "holy iron" (ἅγιον σίδηρον or ἁγιοσίδερο) (cf. σάλπιγξ ἡ ἱερά, "the sacred trumpet").[43] But "semantron" has become the generic term used for all instruments of this family, regardless of their substance. Semantra were being made from iron as early as the fifth or sixth century;[44] today metal semantra are still being struck at foundations on Mt. Athos.

Like their wooden counterparts, metal semantra can be either small or large. A small one—a short bar of iron about 10 to 12 inches long and 3 to 4 inches wide—is usually suspended from a rope, which the player holds in his right hand while he strikes the iron bar with a metal hammer in his left (figure 13). Larger metal semantra are stationary, suspended on chains, and struck with an iron hammer or sometimes by two. The sound produced on such an instrument resembles the clear tone of a bell, a timbre some Greeks and Bulgarians consider more agreeable than that of Russian bells.[45]

The larger metal semantra are much more varied in form than the wooden ones. Some are only slightly falcate; others are bent more deeply into shapes suggesting boomerangs, horseshoes, or even circles. Still others appear as rectangular iron plates with holes for hooks. Additional small holes (most often three) at each end are characteristic features of metal as well as wooden instruments (figures 7 and 12, 14 and 15).[46]

Unlike bells, which have been traditionally cast with inscriptions, semantra are rarely inscribed. Two exceptions have been published. On a wooden se-

13. Striking a small iron semantron. From *Acta Sanctorum, Iunii* 2: xxviii. By permission of Editions Culture et Civilisation.

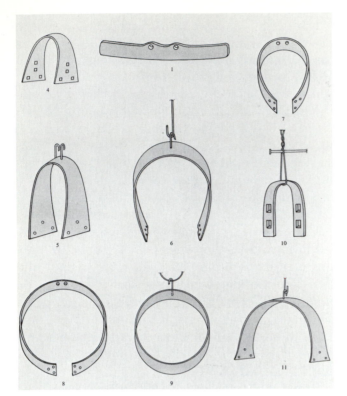
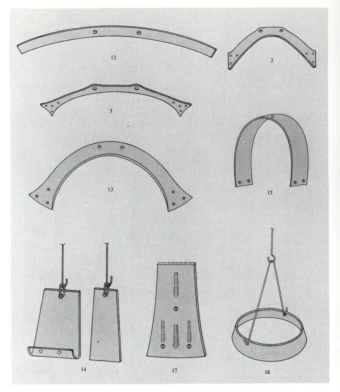

14. Iron semantra. Mt. Athos: 1. Great Laura; 2. Dionysiou Monastery; 3. Docheiariou Monastery; 4. Philotheou Monastery; 5. Xeropotamou Monastery; 6. Chilandari Monastery; 7. Karakalou Monastery; 8. Iviron Monastery; 9. Panteleimon Monastery; 10. Chapel of the Dormition of the Theotokos (Molybokklesia), Karyes; 11. Protato, Karyes. The Meteora: 12. Roussanou Monastery; 13. Agiou Stefanou Monastery. 14. Monastery of St. Athanasios Koubara, Attica; 15. Byzantine Church of the Saviour, Amfissa; 16. Monastery of the Cross, Samos. Mt. Athos: 17. Dionysiou Monastery. From Anoyanakis, *Greek Popular Musical Instruments*, 98-99, fig. 62. Permission of the author.

mantron used at the Dionysiou Monastery on Mt. Athos an unsophisticated Greek poem was carved in which the semantron, speaking in the first person, reflects upon its sylvan origins and its present function in the monastery:

Where are you from, o wood?
You have known me as a tree in the middle of the
    forest.
I was then felled and cut out by an axe;
I now hang in the house of the Lord,
The hands of devout deacons govern me,
And when they strike me with a hammer, I send forth
    sounds,
That all might come to the house of the Lord,
That they might find remission for [their] sins.[47]

Lenoir has published a four-line Latin inscription

on a French semantron which hung at the entrance to the chapter house of the Abbey of Clairmarest near Saint-Omer:

Mine is an awesome lot, because I am an announcer of
    death,
And at my sound hearts are suddenly troubled.
When anyone dies, [someone] comes running to me,
And at appointed hours I send forth signals for work.[48]

The large wooden semantron at the Karakalou Monastery on Mt. Athos had a somewhat less awesome lot; at feeding time each day monks would strike a simple rhythm to summon the monastery's cats.[49]

The mallets used for striking both wooden and metal semantra are found in several shapes, the main a distinction being between mallets that have a single head and those with two.[50] A mallet with two heads is capable of producing more rapid rhythmic patterns than one with a single head.[51]

The cleric charged with sounding the semantron varies from source to source and apparently from one location to another. In the last years of the nineteenth century three stone fragments were uncovered in Palestine with the words τῶν ξύλων φύλαξ (the guardian of the woods, i.e., semantra), an office Leclercq believes was similar to that of a sacristan.[52] John Moschus (d. 619/620) and Theodore of the Studion Monastery (759-826) both cite the kanonarch as the cleric who in addition to chanting kanons also struck the semantron.[53] Elsewhere Theodore names the *aphypnistes* (ἀφυπνιστής) as the person who woke monks from their sleep with the sound of the wood.[54]

The Bilo and the Klepalo in Russia

The Russians, spiritual and cultural protégés of Byzantium, had received their faith from Constantinople by the end of the tenth century, with the Byzantine semantron in accompaniment. In Russia this instrument was known as a *bilo* (pl. *bila*), and its metal counterpart as a *klepalo* (pl. *klepala*).[55] According to one source, because there were no trees in Kievan Russia whose wood produced a resonant sound, the Russians generally struck iron or copper klepala.[56]

The earliest notice of the bilo on Russian soil is contained in two passages from the Lavrentian Chronicle under the year 1074, which indicate that the bilo was already in use near Kiev at the Monastery of the Caves (later Kievo-Pecherskaia Lavra) by this time.[57] The first reference describes events surrounding the death of St. Theodosij, igumen (abbot) of the monastery (1062-1074), who fell mortally ill shortly after celebrating the liturgy on Easter Sunday of that year. "After he had fallen ill and had been sick for about five days, he directed [the brothers] to carry him out to the courtyard at seven in the evening; the brothers took [him] on a sled and placed him before the church. He then ordered all the brothers called. So the brothers struck the bilo and all were assembled."[58] A second notice

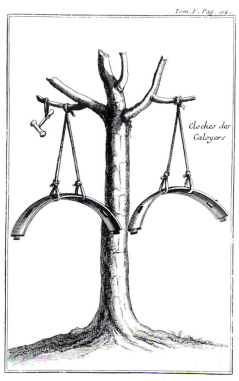

Tom.1. Pag. 114.

Cloches des Caloyers

15. Two arc-shaped metal semantra suspended from the branches of a small tree. From Pitton de Tournefort, *Relation d'un voyage du Levant* (Paris, 1717), betw. pp. 114 and 115. Courtesy of the Kenneth Spencer Research Library, University of Kansas.

from the same year mentions the bilo incidentally, reporting that a wise monk of the monastery named Matthej, on leaving the church, sat down to rest beneath the bilo.[59]

Sources confirm that bronze bells and the bila or klepala coexisted in Kievan Russia at least from the second half of the eleventh century. If any distinction can be drawn between the use of these two instruments from the meager information available before the Mongol invasion, the bell seems to have been favored in the larger and wealthier urban churches, and the bilo or klepalo used in monasteries and smaller parish churches. At the Monastery of the Caves, however, the most important monastic foundation in Russia at this time, only the bilo is reported. It seems that a large number of parish churches and monastic foundations could not afford bells and so struck the bilo or klepalo for their calls to services.[60]

16. Miniature from a Life of St. Sergej: Greeting the saint, who calls for a hand bilo to be struck to assemble the monks of the Holy Trinity Monastery (later the Trinity-Sergius Lavra). From a MS. in the Trinity-Sergius Lavra, f. 173ᵛ, published in G. A. Uvarov, "Bilo" (Materialy dlia arkheologicheskago slovaria), *Drevnosti: Trudy Moskovskago arkheologicheskago obshchestva* 2 (1870), 5.

asteries in the Novgorod region depended upon klepala or bila.[64] A miniature from a late sixteenth-century Russian manuscript with the Life of St. Nicholas the Miracle Worker shows a monk striking a large suspended bilo as a call to the morning office (figure 17).[65]

Olovianishnikov describes a fourteenth-century iron klepalo, formerly in the Church Archeological Museum of the Petersburg Ecclesiastical Academy, that may be the oldest extant Russian instrument of its kind.[66] This klepalo may in fact be the same instrument that Findejzen identifies as coming from Novgorod and dates not later than the fifteenth century.[67] In 1925 this klepalo was in the collections of the Archeological Institute of Leningrad. Two other old klepala are preserved in the Novgorod Museum: one is iron, bow-shaped, and dates from the sixteenth century; the other is cast-iron and quadrangular. Peter I donated the latter to a Novgorod monastery at the beginning of the eighteenth century as recompense for some old cannon he had requisitioned.[68]

In the mid-nineteenth century and even at the beginning of the twentieth century the rhythms of bila and klepala could still be heard in some of the more remote areas of Russia.[69] Some village

The use of bila or klepala was still reported, sometimes with bells, at the end of the fourteenth century. A chronicle entry of 1382 laments the destruction that Khan Tokhtamysh wreaked on Moscow during a Mongol attack in that year, noting that "there is no ringing of bells nor [striking] of bila."[61] Slightly later Epiphanius the Wise writes in his *vita* of St. Sergej of Radonezh (1314-1392) that St. Sergej ordered a hand bilo struck before entering the church of the Holy Trinity Monastery with his brothers (figure 16).[62] And as late as the sixteenth century, when Russian church bells began to increase significantly in size and number, the bilo or klepalo had still not entirely been replaced, especially in rural areas. Before receiving its first bell in 1558, the Novgorod Church of St. Philip had been served by only an iron klepalo.[63] Even in the early 1580s some churches and mon-

17. Detail from a sixteenth-century manuscript containing the "Life of Nicholas the Miracle Worker," formerly in the Rumiantsev Museum, Moscow, shows figure striking a large bilo as a call to the morning office. From N. Sultanov, *Obraztsy drevnerusskago zodchestva v" miniatiurnykh" izobrazheniiakh" izslědovanie po rukopisi XVI věka: "Zhitie Nikolaia Chudotvortsa,"* Pamiatniki drevnej pis′mennosti i iskusstva 8 (St. Petersburg, 1881), Tablitsa 10, fig. 79 (p. 147 in MS).

churches and less affluent monasteries, in fact, continued to strike bila until the end of the old regime. The Old Believers, too, used bila at their sketes in the Altai region and in Siberia right up until the time of the Revolution.[70]

From the first ingenuous rappings on the cells of Egyptian and Palestinian monks to the rhythmic fantasias heard today in Greek monasteries, "striking the wood" has remained the preferred manner of calling the faithful to services at Orthodox foundations in the eastern Mediterranean. The semantron survived the fall of Constantinople; and the Ottoman Turks, who proscribed bell ringing in the territories they conquered, encouraged the striking of wood. Now before dawn each day on Mt. Athos mordant rhythms of awakening hammers still ruffle the darkness, their wooden fanfares calling monks to the morning office.

3

Bells in the Medieval World

Bells in the Latin West

THE EARLIEST known reference to the use of a bell as a signal for Christian convocation appears about 535 in a letter that Fulgentius Ferrandus, a deacon in Carthage, wrote to his friend Eugippius, abbot of a monastery near Naples.[1] A bell (*campana*), Ferrandus advises, would considerably facilitate Eugippius' task of calling his monks to daily services:

During all the hours that are set aside for appropriate prayers, you are not only permitted but also have time to be presented to the divine countenances [i.e., to pray]. Only you yourself do not practice this alone but call many others to take part in this good work, to serve which ministry the most holy custom of the most blessed monks has established [the ringing of] a resonant bell. Because you ordered [it], we have sent this [bell] to Your Holiness. I have not permitted my name to be inscribed on it because the Holy Spirit has already written it on your heart.[2]

From the information that Ferrandus transmits, both directly and indirectly, Georg Stuhlfauth has drawn several conclusions. By 535, but probably even earlier, bell ringing seems to have already been established among North African churches in the vicinity of Carthage.[3] Passing mention of bell ringing in Lower Egypt not quite two decades later lends credence to this suggestion. At least by around 551 when Apollinaris arrived in Alexandria as the Byzantine emperor Justinian's appointment to the

patriarchal throne of that city, bells were rung to call people to the church where the new patriarch read imperial letters from Constantinople.[4] But Ferrandus' shipment of a bell from North Africa to Eugippius near Naples and the tone of Ferrandus' instructions tacitly indicate that bells were not yet being used on the Italian peninsula.[5]

That Ferrandus apparently did not allow his name to be inscribed on the bell Eugippius ordered also suggests that despite the absence of engraved inscriptions on extant church bells from before the seventh century, the custom of inscribing bells may have been practiced earlier than previously thought.[6] The bell was presumably made in Carthage, but we cannot be sure of this. Neither can we conclusively determine the bell's size or its method of manufacture, though we can postulate that it was uncast, like the small hand bells that Irish missionaries, monks, and priests were using by this time.

Besides the word *campana* that Ferrandus uses to designate "bell" in his letter to Eugippius, there are other Latin nouns that occur in early Western sources: among them *cloca* or *clocca*, *nola*, and *signum*.[7] The last is the most problematical and equivocal of the four. In ancient Rome *signum* meant "sign" or "signal" and carried no connotation of the instrument used to produce the signal. *Signum* might therefore be sounded on a trumpet, semantron, or bell. For both Caesarius of Arles and St. Benedict of Nursia in the first half of the sixth century the word still carried a meaning more general than specific.[8] But *signum* eventually came to be synonymous with "bell."[9] And there can be little doubt that Gregory of Tours, writing in the second half of the sixth century, meant "bell" when he used *signum.* Not only does he clarify his meaning through such verbs as *movere* (to move) and *commovere* (to set in motion) but in one passage he even cites the use of a rope (*funis*) to move the instrument.[10] Gregory of Tours is the first writer to record the presence of church bells (*signa*) and bell ringing in the West with any frequency.[11]

Notices of the ringing of church bells proliferate rapidly from the beginning of the seventh century, perhaps due in part to official sanction for their liturgical use, which Pope Sabinianus (604-606) is alleged to have given.[12] Monastery bells began to be sounded at appointed times during the day and night to awaken monks, to call them to offices and masses and to the refectory, and to "ring them to bed."[13] Bells also appeared at a few parish churches, though they were rung less frequently. And with bell casting (instead of forging and riveting) in French-speaking territory, which began toward the beginning of the seventh century and flourished from the eighth, a greater number of bells were produced. The more important role that church bells were beginning to assume during the Carolingian period is substantiated by the first evidence of structures built especially for bells. In Rome Pope Stephen II (752-757) raised a tower above the basilica of Old St. Peter's in which to hang three bells for calling clergy and people to daily offices.[14]

Only during the ninth century did bells begin to come into general use for small village churches. Sources indicate that each parish church was expected to have at least one bell to ring for services.[15] Moreover, the *Excerptiones* required priests in England at this time to ring bells at certain hours. And around 970, rules for bell ringing were promulgated in England through *Regularis concordia,* a code of monastic law.[16] Thus almost 450 years after the first Western record of the ringing of a church bell (in Ferrandus' letter to Eugippius) bell ringing was finally established in the services of the Western church.

Bells in Byzantium

The early history of bells in Europe is as sharply focused as sources will permit. Less clear is the appearance and role of church bells in the Byzantine East. During the seventh, eighth, and ninth centuries, when bell ringing was spreading among churches in the West, the Greeks were still announcing their services by striking the semantron. No document has yet appeared to indicate that church bells were present or rung in Constantinople prior to the last third of the ninth century.[17] In fact, the first notices of church bells intended for use in the imperial city appear solely in Western sources that record a shipment of bells from Venice to Constantinople.

The three Western sources that report this event agree only on a few very general points: the request for bells that Orso (Ursus) II Partecipazio, Doge of Venice, received from a Byzantine emperor; the origin and destination of the bells and the fact of their shipment; and the general time of the transaction.[18] John the Deacon says that it was a set of twelve bells; and Andreas Dandolo, without specifying their number, indicates that the bells were bronze. The three sources contain no information on the size, weight, or shape of these bells,[19] though they were probably of cast bronze, among the earliest examples of the "primitive" bell (see next section of the chapter).

Discrepancies in details and conflicting information among the sources only obscure the year the bells were shipped from Venice, the name of the Byzantine emperor who ordered them, and his purpose for requesting them. Both Dandolo and Goar concur that Orso II (*reg.* 864-881) sent the bells to Emperor Michael in 865, a year that would have been the first or second in Orso's administration and would have fallen at the end of the reign of Emperor Michael III, called "the Drunkard" (842-867). But John the Deacon identifies the emperor as Basil I (867-886), whose reign overlapped Orso's years as doge.

Just as John the Deacon and Goar disagree on the date of the shipment of the bells and the identity of the emperor, so they also disagree on the place where the bells were hung on reaching Constantinople. Goar reports that Michael installed the bells in the belfry beside the Church of Hagia Sophia. Because substantial evidence confirms that no bell tower was attached to Hagia Sophia before the thirteenth century, however, Goar's statement can only be dismissed as erroneous.[20] John the Deacon's account contains the most logical explanation for the shipment of the Venetian bells. He reports that Basil installed the bells in his "newly built church," obviously referring to the Nea Ekklesia, completed in 881. But if the bells had indeed been hung at Basil's new church, why do the two Greek writers Symeon Magister and George the Monk not refer to them or to any bells in their descriptions of this church?[21] In view of the novelty that Western bells would have represented at the Nea Ekklesia in the ninth century, their not being mentioned is difficult to explain.

Perhaps the Venetian bells were never actually sent to Constantinople. There is sufficient reason to question the information in the three Western sources. Not only has no Greek document appeared to confirm, correct, or amplify these notices, but subsequent writers, both Byzantine and Western, have been silent regarding any such bells. If Venetian bells were still being rung in Constantinople in the late tenth century, or were known to have rung, why does Liudprand of Cremona make no mention of them in his account of his embassy to the court of Nicephorus Phocas in 968-969, especially in light of his rabid anti-Greek posture and Western chauvinism?[22] Perhaps the bells were indeed shipped from Venice, but for one reason or another never reached Constantinople. This would explain both the strange silence in Greek sources and the conflicting information that Dandolo, John the Deacon, and Goar transmit.

Even if Orso's Venetian bells did not reach Constantinople at the end of the ninth century, the Greeks could scarcely have escaped the sound of bells from several Latin churches that served European residents of their city in the tenth and eleventh centuries.[23] But they remained largely indifferent to bells and before the thirteenth century did not generally employ them at their own churches,[24] preferring instead the traditional semantra. Indeed, the very fact that bells were rung at churches that observed the Roman Rite may have increased the distance that Greeks maintained at that time between bell ringing and their own services. It is only the rare Greek source before 1204 that makes any reference to bell ringing in a Byzantine foundation.[25] The strong preference for the bell in the Roman Catholic West and the semantron in the Orthodox East became, in fact, one of the most symbolic manifestations of the separation between the two halves of the Christian world.[26] Both Archbishop Antonij of Novgorod (ca. 1200) and Theodore Balsamon (ca. 1140-ca. 1195) make pointed references to this divergence.

[The Greeks] adhere to [the use of] the semantron according to the Angel's instruction, but the Latins ring bells.[27]

Through the Latins—unfortunately separated from us and whose hearts have been hardened by Satan even if they are softened in their words beyond oil—is transmitted another custom of calling people to churches. They make use of one kind of signaler—the bell.[28]

Eustathius, Archbishop of Thessaloniki during the last quarter of the twelfth century and witness to the Norman capture and sack of his city in 1185, expresses the Greeks' surprise over the Normans' aversion to the semantron: "At that time we came to wonder: Why do [the Normans] not shrink from striking the large signal bells overhead near the Church of the Myrobletos, but, on the other hand, they are offended by the wood at the Metropolis, which announces the holy service?"[29] The widening gulf between Rome and Constantinople was to be confirmed in its true extent by the tragic events of the Fourth Crusade.

During the fifty-seven years of Latin occupation in Constantinople (1204-1261) the conquerors built a number of new churches and monasteries within the city walls and rang bells to announce the Mass and offices. Olovianishnikov believes that bells had been used so seldom in Byzantium between the tenth and thirteenth centuries that the occupation actually served to introduce bell ringing to the city.[30] In any case, as a result of this Western presence in

Constantinople, the Greeks' use of bells for their own services began to increase rapidly. Nicephorus Gregoras' history of the reign of Andronicus II Palaeologus (1282-1328) makes frequent reference to Byzantine church bells and bell ringing.[31]

Among the most visible records of the Western impact on late Byzantine architecture are the bell towers that began to appear on Greek churches and in Greek monasteries from the beginning of the thirteenth century. Bell towers had already appeared in the Levant during the Crusades, but only during and following the Latin occupation of Constantinople did they become part of Byzantine church architecture.[32] The French architect Guillaume Joseph Grelot conveys valuable information on the now-vanished bell tower that once stood on the western side of Hagia Sophia.[33] This structure, dating from the first half of the thirteenth century, is believed to have been the work of Western masons, who presumably installed in it bells they had brought with them from Europe.[34] Pachymeres (1242-ca.1310), in his history of the reign of Andronicus II Palaeologus, speaks of the use of bells for calls to services at the great church as though bell ringing were already an established practice.[35]

Bell towers on churches at Mistra and elsewhere are evidence of the use of bells at Byzantine foundations during the final decades of the Empire.[36] And the growing importance of bells in the Eastern church is expressed in an inscription of 1427 on the campanile bell tower at the Vatopedi Monastery on Mt. Athos: "[This] splendid [tower] contains ringing bells above, calling the faithful to sing a hymn to God."[37]

Sources from the Palaeologan era transmit almost no data that could give even the most general idea of the inroads that bells had made on the traditional use of the semantron in the East. One later witness, however random, is an anonymous Greek poem on the Turkish siege of Constantinople in 1453. The poet writes that the city then contained three hundred semantra and sixty-two bells, or almost five semantra for every bell.[38] Even if these figures cannot be verified, the poet makes clear that bells had by no means displaced semantra at this time. Toward the beginning of the fifteenth century, moreover, Symeon, Archbishop of Thessaloniki, mentions only wooden semantra on which calls to worship were sounded in his city. Of bells he says nothing.[39]

Even so, the first Turkish attack on Constantinople in early April of 1453 was accompanied by a mêlée of sounds, and prominent among them was the ringing of church bells:

The emperor [Constantine XI Palaeologus] made his rounds of the entire city, exhorting his people, inspiring them with hope in God, and he ordered [bells] to ring throughout the city to call the people together. The Turks, however, when they heard the great sound of bells, let loose with the voices of fifes and trumpets and a countless number of large drums, and there was great and utterly terrible carnage: . . . for the howling and crying and weeping and sobbing of the people and the noise of siege guns and the ringing of bells were fused into a single sound, and it was like great thunder.[40]

On the eve of the final Turkish assault Constantine XI, the last Byzantine emperor, ordered icons and relics carried through the streets of the doomed city as church bells rang.[41] Mutual desperation erased differences as Greeks and Latins worshiped together in Hagia Sophia for the last time. Before dawn the following morning, May 29, 1453, bells were heard again. This time they sounded an alarm as the enemy launched its attack.[42] But their wild pleas were drowned by the trumpets, fifes, and cymbals of the Turks.[43] And soon the cacophony of Christian bells and Moslem trumpets was engulfed by the pandemonium of battle. Salvos from one enormous Turkish cannon shook all of Constantinople. Between 5:00 and 6:00 A.M. the Turks breached the land walls and several hours later they were in possession of the city. From that moment, church bells in Istanbul were silenced for four hundred years. Mehmet the Conqueror permitted Christians to maintain their "churches and burying-places," but he signed a treaty with the Genoese that contained a clause reminiscent of a restriction in Covenant of 'Umar after the Arabs' capture of Jerusalem more than eight centuries earlier: "let [the Greeks] not ring bells."[44]

The bells of Greek churches, even if spared in-

18 (*left*). The Bell of St. Patrick's Will, perhaps from the fifth century, a riveted hand bell in the National Museum of Ireland, Dublin. From André Lehr, *Van paardebel tot speelklok: de geschiedenis van de klokgietkunst in de Lage Landen*, 2d rev. ed. (Zaltbommel, The Netherlands, 1981), fig. 12. Permission of the author.

19 (*right*). The riveted bell called "Saufang" (early seventh century), Church of St. Cecilia, Cologne. From Albert Lenoir, *Architecture monastique*, Collection de documents inédits sur l'histoire de France, 3d ser.: Archéologie (Paris, 1852), 160.

itial destruction, soon became Turkish prisoners of war. In the final years of the fifteenth century a German knight reported seeing bell mortuaries in Adrianople with piles of bronze fragments that Turkish soldiers had collected.

We went further into another house close by, which was full of whole and broken Christian bells which had been captured in Christian countries and carried there, from which cannon are cast. It was told me that each Turk, when he crosses a mountain or the sea to conquer a country, must bring back a piece of a bell. Such a collection made by three or four times a hundred thousand men makes a mighty heap, from which innumerable mighty cannon are cast.[45]

The bells in the Latin bell tower of Hagia Sophia were among those eventually confiscated in Istanbul to provide gun metal for Turkish artillery. When Grelot saw the bell tower around 1670, it was already empty; sometime after his visit the tower itself was demolished.[46]

The Forms of Medieval European Bells

Though Ferrandus' letter suggests that a church bell was first heard in Latin Europe in the lower Italian peninsula, the oldest extant Christian bells in the West are those associated with missionary activity in northwestern Europe. Irish bells and their descendents in England, Scotland, and Wales were fashioned from sheets of iron or copper, forged and riveted into the roughly rectangular form of a cowbell. Of the numerous examples of riveted bells preserved today in Ireland, the most famous and one of the oldest (possibly from the fifth century) is the hand bell known as the Bell of St. Patrick's Will (*Clog-an-eadhacta Phatraic*) (figure 18). This small bell was made from two sheets of iron and given an iron handle on top. It is thought to be the Bell of the Testament that was mentioned in 552 in the Annals of Ulster and was found that year in the tomb of St. Patrick (d. 461).[47]

The Irish prototypes underwent significant changes on the Continent toward the end of the sixth and beginning of the seventh centuries, assuming larger and heavier rounded forms, which were sometimes dipped in molten bronze to afford protection against rusting and to improve somewhat the quality of their clanking tone.[48] From small hand instruments, riveted bells grew to over a foot in height and were eventually hung in raised structures to facilitate the dissemination of their sound. The early seventh-century bell "Saufang," which formerly belonged to the Church of St. Cecilia in Cologne, is made from three iron plates that have been rounded at the crown and riveted together (figure 19).[49] Although still a riveted bell, "Saufang" represents a transitional stage. It was once hung in a tower or belfry from the iron strips attached to its crown.[50]

The forging of riveted bells from sheet metal remained a European practice from the fifth to the middle of the eleventh centuries, but experiments in bell casting eventually led to the modern bell, a form that was preceded by three successive but overlapping stages. The first phase, which resulted in the cup-shaped "primitive" bell, began toward the end of the eighth century and lasted approximately four centuries, into the early years of the thirteenth century. The second phase, which produced the Theophilus bells, appeared in the eleventh century and continued until about the middle of the thirteenth. Primitive and Theophilus bells, therefore, were roughly contemporaneous with the Romanesque style in architecture. Their successor, the "archaic" bell, paralleled the Gothic period, extending from the late twelfth to the fourteenth century. The modern bell appeared around the mid-fifteenth century in the Low Countries, but founders' experiments in proportions and tuning continued for two more centuries and culminated in the ideal form, profile, and tone quality that the Hemony brothers began to produce in Holland around the mid-seventeenth century.

Primitive bells were convex in shape and had a rounded head; their profiles show a uniform wall thickness. But their relatively thin wall at the strike point of the clapper remained an inherent structural weakness. To prevent these frail bells from fracturing under repeated blows from their clappers, a circular metal band or collar was added sometime during the tenth century to reinforce the outside surface of the lip, a structural innovation

22. An eleventh-century Theophilus bell of beehive shape from Aschara near Gotha, now in the Bell Museum in Apolda, E. Ger. Margarete Schilling, *Glocken und Glockenspiele* (Gütersloh, W. Ger.: Prisma Verlag, 1982), 17. Permission of Klaus G. Beyer, Weimar, and Franz Peter Schilling, Apolda.

20 (*left*). The "primitive" bell of Canino (eighth or ninth century), Lateran Museum, Rome. From Lehr, *Van paardebel tot speelklok*, fig. 14. Permission of the author.

21 (*right*). The "primitive" Siena bell of 1159. From Lenoir, *Architecture monastique*, 160.

that also improved the resonance.[51] Of extant examples of primitive bells the oldest is thought to be the Tuscan bell of Canino (figure 20). Its inscription is partially obliterated, so the year of founding is illegible, but according to paleographical evidence from that portion of the inscription still preserved, it probably dates from the eighth or ninth century.[52] About a half-dozen primitive Italian bells have survived from the late eleventh and twelfth centuries, including the bell of Siena (figure 21).[53]

The primitive bell was still popular when the first so-called Theophilus bell appeared, with stocky proportions that made it resemble a beehive. A fine eleventh-century example from Aschara near

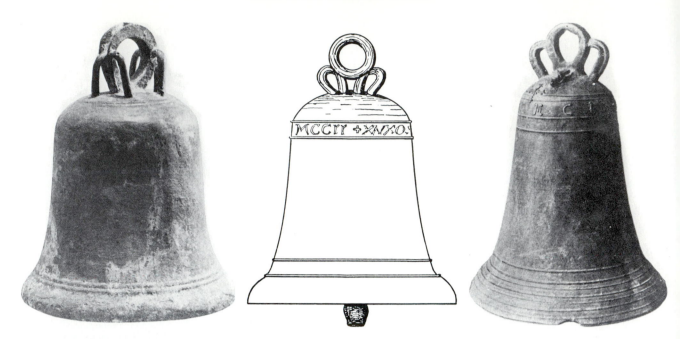

23 (*left*). The undated church bell found in Söderby-Karl in Uppland, assigned to the beginning of the twelfth century, now in the State Historical Museum, Stockholm. From Nils-Arvid Bringéus, *Klockringningsseden i Sverige*, Nordiska Museets Handlingar 50 (Stockholm, 1958), 21. fig. 1. Permission of the Antikvarisk-topografiska arkivet, Stockholm.

24 (*center*). Drawing of the "archaic" bell of Fontenailles, Normandy (1202), now in the Bayeux Museum. From Arthur Lynds Bigelow, *Carillon* (Princeton, 1948), 37.

25 (*right*). The "archaic" bell of 1184 in the Bargello Museum, Florence. From Satis N. Coleman. *Bells: Their History, Legends, Making, and Uses* (Chicago, 1928), 59.

Gotha now belongs to the Bell Museum in Apolda, East Germany (figure 22).[54] Its waist is almost cylindrical, and a recessed Latin inscription states that a certain "Wolfger" was the founder. Its ring is described as *dumpfe* (dull, hollow). The oldest Swedish bell, an instrument of similar form, was discovered in 1916 and has been assigned to the beginning of the twelfth century (figure 23).[55]

In the latter twelfth and early thirteenth centuries the archaic bell developed, whose waist was attenuated into a "sugarloaf" form that was more conical than cylindrical. One of the principal features that distinguished the longer-waisted archaic bell from the older primitive bell was the change,

for acoustical reasons, from a convex to a slightly concave waist. The head of the bell was still rounded like that on the cup-shaped and beehive bells, but the collar that had reinforced the lip of the primitive bell was now cast as part of the bell itself to provide a greater mass of metal at the clapper's strike point. This thickening of the lower bell wall resulted in a stronger form that resisted cracking and in greater resonance—though the bell was still untuned, and its ring far from satisfactory by modern standards (Curt Sachs has described the tone produced by both primitive and archaic bells as "disappointing, flat, and whining").[56] Two of the oldest extant examples of the archaic bell are an instrument of 1202, formerly of Fontenailles in Normandy, now preserved in the Bayeux Museum (figure 24), and a Florentine bell from 1184 (figure 25).[57] Among the earliest bells in Eastern Europe is a Polish instrument, the bell of Gruszowo, which was probably cast in the late thirteenth century.[58]

Though European bells continued to be cast in the "archaic" sugarloaf shape into the fourteenth century, a new form began to emerge toward the end of the thirteenth, whose waist was somewhat shorter and whose tone was considerably richer and more resonant.[59] By the mid-fifteenth century founders in the Low Countries had developed the form and proportions that would generate the most euphonious combination of partials when struck. The sound-bow was gradually tapered upward into a thinner waist, and founders began initial attempts to tune bells by chipping away metal from the inside of the lip. Other major changes were the gradual flattening of the earlier hemispherical head into a top plate and shoulders and the reduction of the bell's height in proportion to its lower diameter.[60]

Changes in the form and acoustical properties of bells in the Low Countries during the first half of the fifteenth century were soon followed by a shift of leadership in bell founding from Italy to the Netherlands. Work here culminated in the bells that the Hemony brothers cast in Holland between about 1642 and about 1680. These Dutch bells were founded with shapes, profiles, and proportions that permitted them to be accurately tuned, both individually and in concert with other bells.[61] And with this development, the modern European bell had emerged.

The appearance of the modern bell had come too late for the Greeks. Although they had culti-vated bell ringing to some extent during the last two centuries of their Empire, church bells were only beginning to secure a place in Byzantium when their tenuous hold was suddenly broken by the Turkish conquest in May of 1453.[62] The proscription of bell ringing in Istanbul, lamented in many accounts by Western travelers, who seemed to sense a certain aural vacuum in the Turkish capital,[63] was finally rescinded in 1856. But by that time bells and bell ringing in the Orthodox East had found their true home in Russia. From Thebes, Sinai, Jerusalem, and Constantinople, the voices of trumpets and the rhythmic speech of semantra were to be amplified a thousandfold in the bell ringing that swept Russia on the great church feasts before 1917. As raucous blasts from silver ḥaẓoẓeroth had signaled prostrations of worshippers in the Temple at Jerusalem, so centuries later would choruses of untuned bells accompany prostrations of the faithful in the churches of Moscow and St. Petersburg. The Leningrad sphinxes in their youth had heard the trumpet calls that launched a protracted sonic migration that pushed northward for several thousand miles from the Nile to the Neva, which they now overlook, and extended across three millennia from the ancient to the modern world.

Part II
Bells in Russian History

4

The Rise of Bells in Russia

THE THOUSAND-YEAR reign of bells in Russia has unfolded in six stages of historical, cultural, and industrial development. The presence of bells and bell ringing in Kievan Russia is first recorded in the mid-eleventh century. Then between 1237 and 1241 the Mongol invasion marked the beginning of the second epoch. After two and a half centuries of Oriental suzerainty, and contemporaneous with Ivan III's declaration of independence from Mongol authority in 1480, Ridolfo Fioravanti introduced Western technology to bell founding in Muscovy and launched the third period in the history of Russian bells. In the sixteenth century the rate of production at the Moscow Cannon Yard increased dramatically while the quality of castings improved as well. Like other sectors of the Russian economy, however, the cannon yard suffered serious setbacks in productivity at the beginning of the seventeenth century during the Time of Troubles (1598-1613), a time of dynastic crisis, social upheaval, civil war, and foreign domination in Muscovy. These fifteen years of turbulence precede the beginning of a fourth period in Russian bell manufacture, which accompanied the reigns of the first Romanov tsars from 1613 until the end of the seventeenth century.

Though continuity in industrial development links the seventeenth-century tsardom of Muscovy with Imperial Russia, the Great Northern War of Peter the Great became a watershed not only in Russia's political and military history but also in Russian founding. Peter's struggles with Sweden during the first decade of the eighteenth century demanded new standards of production from the state foundry and inaugurated a fifth stage in the development of Russian bells. This period extended throughout the century and saw the decline in the importance of the Moscow Cannon Yard. Privately owned plants, which emerged during the late seventeenth and eighteenth centuries, produced the church bells cast in Russia from the closing of the Moscow Cannon Yard in 1802 until the end of the old regime. This period of more than a century defines the sixth and final stage in Russian bell manufacture. Between 1917 and the end of World War II, Russian bell founding ceased, some of Russia's finest bells were destroyed, and the remarkable "soundscape" of prerevolutionary Russia disappeared.

Kievan Russia

Though the beginning of Russian history is traditionally dated from 862—the year that Riurik is reported to have established his authority at Ladoga north of Novgorod—the presence of bells on Russian soil is not confirmed until 1066,[1] some years after the conversion of Kievan Russia to Byzantine Christianity. Details surrounding the introduction of the new faith into pagan Russia are not abundant, but there is general agreement among scholars that Prince Vladimir's baptism of his subjects at Kiev in 988/989, officially known as "the conver-

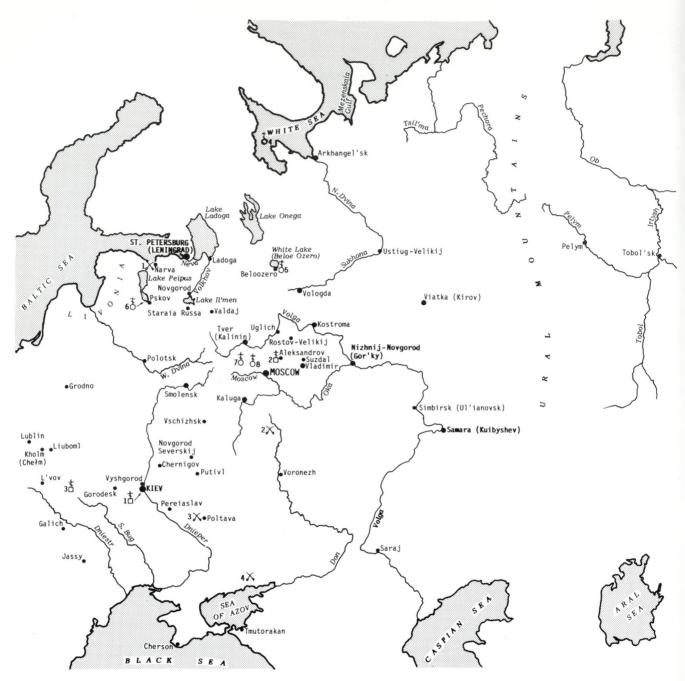

Some important cities, religous foundations, and battle sites associated with the history of bells and bell founding in Russia.

Battles ✕ (1) Narva (1700); (2) Kulikovo Pole (1380); Poltava (1709); (4) Kalka River (1223).

Lavras ☩ (1) Kievo-Pecherskaia Lavra; (2) Trinity-Sergius Lavra; (3) Pochaevskaia-Uspenskaia Lavra; (The Alexander-Nevsky Trinity Lavra was located in the city of St. Petersburg.)

Monasteries ☩ (4) Solovetskij Monastery; (5) Kirillo-Belozerskij Monastery; (6) Pskovo-Pecherskij Monastery; (7) Monastery of Joseph of Volokolamsk; (8) New Jerusalem Monastery.

sion of Russia," was only the culmination of a protracted process of conversion that took place in a series of waves, each of which was temporarily checked by pagan opposition. This process seems to have begun as early as the second half of the ninth century.

Sometime around 864 Photius, Patriarch of Constantinople, sent a bishop north into the land of the "Rhos." Sources do not disclose this prelate's place of residence, and apparently his labors among the pagan populace were ephemeral. But at the time his work appeared of sufficient scope for Photius to declare in an encyclical of 867 to the other eastern patriarchs that the Rhos had abandoned their godless pagan religion to embrace the pure and unadulterated Christian faith.[2] About 874 Patriarch Ignatius may have sent a second prelate to the Russians, but this did not prevent a reversion to paganism after 882 with the capture of Kiev by Oleg, Riurik's successor and the first ruler of all Kievan Russia.

Seventy-five years later the Russian princess Olga was baptized in Constantinople and requested that the German emperor Otto I appoint a bishop to serve Kiev. A monk named Adalbert from the Benedictine Monastery of St. Maximin at Trier was ordained bishop and set out for Kiev. But he did not remain there long. After no more than two years (961-962) another strong surge of pagan reaction drove him from the city. Though Olga's baptism apparently had no appreciable effect on the general population, it may have been influential among members of the ruling class, for her grandson, Vladimir I, "the Great," prince of Kiev from 980 until 1015, effected the official conversion of the Russian state.[3]

The presence of churches in Kiev and other pagan Slavic regions is indicated at least four decades before Vladimir's baptism of his subjects. By the end of the reign of Igor (912-945) a church dedicated to St. Elias was functioning in Kiev.[4] Abūl Ḥasan ʿAlī ul-Masʿūdī, an educated Arab traveler, not only confirms an established Christian presence on pagan Slavic territory by 956 but he also transmits what may be the first evidence for the use of church bells among Slavic tribes.[5] "The Slaviane are divided into many groups of people, some of whom are Christians; among them are pagans as well as sun worshipers. . . . Their tribes are largely pagan, which cremate their dead and worship them. They have many cities, as well as churches, where they hang bells on which they strike with a hammer, just as our Christians [those living among the Arabs] strike a board with a wooden mallet."[6]

Masʿūdī is careful to distinguish between the *Slaviane* (Slavs) and the *Rusy* (Russians), and the customs he describes above he clearly associates with the former. Because he does not unequivocally identify the region where these church bells were rung, it is not possible to determine whether he is referring to eastern Slaviano-Russian tribes on the Volga or to western and southern groups along the Danube.[7] The impression Masʿūdī conveys is of a region that is still predominantly pagan but not without some churches in a number of urban centers, which own and ring bells. He also implies, since he makes no statement to the contrary, that these churches with bells were built for and primarily attended by native Christians, not by foreign merchants trading in these cities. Masʿūdī's comparison of bell ringing at these churches with the striking of wood by Christians elsewhere is significant in itself and indicates that bells, not semantra or bila, were the instruments of convocation in these new foundations.

The baptism of Vladimir, probably in 987 or a year or so earlier, preceding his marriage to Anna, sister of Byzantine Emperor Basil II, was an event that soon led to the conversion and transformation of Kievan Russia.[8] Pagan customs did not disappear overnight; they even persisted in rural Russia until the end of the nineteenth century. By the eleventh century, however, Christianity had become firmly rooted in the major towns of Kievan Russia, and the Russian nobility, if not the population at large, had resolutely embraced Greek Christianity and was prepared to defend its faith.

Several important stone churches appeared in Russia at the end of the tenth and in the first half of the eleventh centuries. About 990 Vladimir constructed the first masonry church in Kiev, dedicated to the Dormition (Assumption) of the Holy

Virgin but better known as the Desiatinnaia or Church of the Tithe.[9] The Church of St. Irene soon followed, and a little later, Yaroslav's splendid new Cathedral of St. Sophia (begun 1037).[10] To the north another stone Cathedral of St. Sophia rose inside the kremlin at Novgorod by 1052.[11]

Not until almost eighty years after the conversion of Russia are bells (*kolokoly*) first cited in a Russian chronicle. An entry from 1066 in the First Novgorod Chronicle records the seizure of Novgorod by Prince Vseslav Briachislavich of Polotsk and his removal of bells and chandeliers from the St. Sophia Cathedral.[12] This notice, the first unequivocal confirmation of bells on Russian soil, suggests that they were being rung in Novgorod by the time the new stone church was finished, if not earlier. The removal of the bells from the cathedral was an action typical of invading princes. Throughout the military history of medieval Russia, even into the sixteenth century, church bells were treated much like prisoners of war when cities were captured. Carried off with other booty as trophies of conquest, they were displayed and rung in the towns of the victors.[13]

The sixteenth-century *vita* of Antonij Rimlianin (b. Rome, 1067; d. Novgorod, 1147) relates the saint's miraculous nocturnal arrival in Novgorod in 1106, when "[bells] began to sound for the morning office as is customary, and the saint heard a great sound of bells (*zvon" velik"*) in the city."[14] Even if the volume of the zvon over Novgorod in the early twelfth century is exaggerated, this passage nevertheless suggests that many Novgorod churches at that time were ringing bells.

The Hypatian Chronicle provides the first reference to bells in Kiev, reporting the seizure of bells at Kiev in 1146 by Prince Iziaslav Mstislavich, eldest son of Prince Mstislav of Novgorod.[15] A subsequent removal of all bells from Kiev occurred in 1171 following another attack on the city.[16] A third twelfth-century reference to bell ringing, or, in this case, to its absence in Vladimir northeast of Moscow, is transmitted in an entry of 1169. After all the churches of Vladimir had been closed, there was heard "neither ringing [of bells] (*zvonen'ia*), nor singing throughout the entire city and in the cathedral."[17]

One, possibly two, references to bells from the end of the twelfth century appear in the epic poem *Slovo o polku Igoreve* (The Tale of Igor's Campaign), presumably written between 1185 and 1187.

"Horses whinny beyond the Sula;
glory rings (*zvenit' slava*) in Kiev;
trumpets blast in Novgorod [-Severskij];
banners stand fast in Putivl."[18]

For [Vseslav] in Polotsk they began to ring the bells
    (*pozvonisha . . . v" kolokoly*) early
for the morning office at St. Sophia:
but he heard the sound (*zvon"*) in Kiev.[19]

Bell ringing is only suggested in the first passage, but the second indicates clearly that bells were being rung at a Russian church by the mid-eleventh century.[20]

Information on bells in Russia before the Mongol invasion is meager and provides no unequivocal answer to the question of the source or sources of bells in Kievan Russia—did they come from Byzantium, whose faith the Russian princes had embraced, or from cities in Western Europe, with which the Russians carried on extensive trade? That bells may have reached Russia from both the Byzantine East and the Latin West is also a possibility.[21]

There can be little doubt that the semantron was brought to Russia from Byzantium; and the bilo is first cited in a Russian chronicle in 1074, a few years after but still contemporaneous with the earliest citation of bells. But the argument for acknowledging Byzantium, specifically Constantinople, as the source of bells in Kievan Russia seems to be based principally on reports that a set of bells shipped from Venice was present in Constantinople toward the end of the ninth century (see Chapter 3). And as we have seen, the actual receipt of the Venetian bells in Constantinople cannot be established beyond all doubt, nor is there evidence of bell founding in the Byzantine capital before Mas'ūdī's report of church bells in Slavic territory by the mid-tenth century.

Mas'ūdī's account may thus be the earliest record of the actual possession and use of church bells in the entire Christian East north of Alexandria. It would antedate by at least a few years both Liudprand of Cremona's oblique reference to a striking bell in the clock mechanism at the Nea Ekklesia in the *Antapodosis* (955-962) and Athanasius' directive (after 958) that a bell be sounded to assemble monks at the Great Laura on Mt. Athos. Almost a century separates Mas'ūdī's account from the Byzantine notice of a bell circa 1040 that awoke Emperor Constantine IX Monomachus at Constantinople. It may even be that church bells were in use in southern Russia before their alleged appearance in Byzantium.

In contrast, by the mid-tenth century, church bells had been known in the Latin West for four hundred years, and their general use well established there for at least a century. Moreover, from the beginning of the tenth century, if not earlier, Russian merchants had traversed an overland trade route to cities in Western Europe, their presence first being recorded in south German territory between 903 and 906.[22] In all probability, then, the bells that Mas'ūdī reported among the Slavs around 950 were carried overland from the West. That Kiev had been served, if only briefly, by a bishop from Trier in 860 and 861 lends further credence to arguments favoring a Western source for the first bells in Russia.

Dynastic ties increased Kiev's contacts with the West at the end of the tenth and throughout the eleventh centuries. One or possibly two of Vladimir the Great's wives were from Czechia.[23] And even after the formal schism of 1054 between the Byzantine East and the Latin West, marriages continued to be contracted between Western princes and Russian princesses. Sviatoslav, son of Yaroslav the Wise (1019-1054), married the sister of the bishop of Trier; and two other Russian princes took as their wives the daughters of Otto, a Saxon margrave, and of Leopold, count of Stadt. Two daughters of Yaroslav married Western kings: in 1051 Anna became the queen of Henry I of France; and a few years earlier Anastasia had married her cousin An-

26. Bell with a recessed Latin inscription unearthed in 1957 at the site "Maloe gorodishche" near the village of Gorodsk in the Zhitomirskaia oblast'. From R. I. Vyezzhev, "Kolokola drevnego Gorodeska," *Kratkie soobshcheniia Instituta arkheologii*, issue 9 (Kiev, 1960), p. 104, fig. 1. Permission of Vsesoiuznoe agentstvo po avtorskim pravam (hereafter VAAP), Moscow.

drew of Hungary, though she lived at the court of Henry IV of Germany from 1061.[24]

In addition, economic ties with the West were substantially strengthened in both Kiev and Novgorod by the mid-eleventh century. Conversion of the Hungarians to Christianity during the reign of Stephen I (997-1038) opened up commerce between Kiev and Regensburg (Ratisbon) along the Danube in addition to trade that flowed through Prague and Cracow.[25] Russian embassies were sent to Alstadt in Thuringia in 1040 and to Goslar in 1043.[26] And about this time direct trade began to flourish between Novgorod and German-speaking centers, commerce that had formerly passed through Visby on the island of Gotland.[27] Two churches for Western merchants were established in Novgorod—St. Peter's for Germans and St. Olaf's for Gotlanders—and at Ladoga another church for Gotlanders was dedicated to St. Nicholas. In Smolensk a Latin church also served European resi-

27. Bells and bell fragments from archeological excavations at Kiev. Nos. 1 and 2: two bells discovered in 1824 in the foundations of the Desiatinnaia Church; no. 3: a bell unearthed in 1937, not far from the site of the Desiatinnaia Church; no. 4: a bell found in 1907 on Khorevaia Street. From M. K. Karger, *Drevnij Kiev*, 1 (Leningrad, 1958), 570, pl. 43. Permission of VAAP, Moscow.

dents.[28] And in Kiev, a commercial center of international importance and the point where two major trade routes converged, a number of churches of the Latin Rite were established for the colony of foreign, mostly German, merchants. Several were already present in the tenth century, and Western sources mention a Roman Catholic church in Kiev dedicated to the Virgin and active between 1222 and 1240.[29]

The strongest evidence of a Western source for Russian church bells appeared in 1957 with the recovery of a whole bronze bell of the beehive type with a complete Latin inscription around its shoulder (figure 26). It was found on the site called "Maloe gorodishche" of the former medieval city of Gorodesk, and from its recessed inscription, which translates "Gottfried (Godefridus) engraved the inscription on this vessel," and a comparison of its form with medieval Western instruments, Vyezzhev concludes that this bell was an eleventh-century bell cast on German-speaking territory and imported to Gorodesk.[30] Indeed, in both these details the Russian bell closely resembles the eleventh-century German bell from Apolda (see figure 22), and its cannons are quite similar to those on the Swedish bell in Stockholm, assigned to the beginning of the twelfth century (see figure 23). By analogy, a northern European provenience is also quite possible for the whole bell unearthed in the foundations of the Desiatinnaia Church at Kiev and the bell discovered in 1907 on Kiev's Khorevaia Street (figure 27, nos. 1 and 4). It is not impossible, of course, that Western founders cast these bells on location at both Gorodesk and Kiev. All that can be stated with certainty is that at least one bell rung in Kievan Russia bore a Latin inscription and closely resembles northern European Theophilus bells from the eleventh and twelfth centuries.[31]

Archeological digs undertaken in Kiev during the 1820s and 1830s on the site of the Desiatinnaia Church uncovered two other bronze bells. Only the lower portion and the loop-shaped cannons from the top remained of one bell, but the other, except for the inside crown staple from which its clapper had been suspended, was still in a fairly good state of preservation (figure 27).[32] Since they contain no inscription, these two bells cannot be assigned with certainty to the reign of either Vladimir I (980-1015) or Yaroslav the Wise (1019-1054), but they were very likely commissioned by one of these two Kievan princes.[33] In 1833, at the same time the foundations of the Desiatinnaia Church were being excavated, other foundations were discovered in Kiev thought to be those of the Church of St. Irene. Among the objects to emerge from this site were fragments from a church chandelier and another bronze bell.[34] Three other bells have subsequently been unearthed at archeological sites in Kiev and its vicinity, and bell fragments have surfaced in various other locations during the late nineteenth and mid-twentieth centuries (figure 27).[35] The five whole or nearly whole bells recovered from these excavations can be regarded as the oldest surviving bells in Russia, in all probability antedating the Mongol assault on the city in 1240. But they contain no inscriptions, so not even an approximate date of founding can be assigned, nor is it possible to establish whether they were of local manufacture or imported from abroad. Skilled metal workers were active in Kievan Russia by 1194, when the Lavrentian Chronicle reports that the roof of the Suzdal Cathedral was recovered with tin and that Russian draftsmen, not foreign masters, were employed for the project.[36] So it is plausible that Russian founders and metal workers may also have cast bells without foreign assistance by the beginning of the thirteenth century.[37]

In 1946 a bell fragment was found during excavations on Kiev's B[ol'shaia] Zhitomirskaia Street that contained two letters—ТЬ . . .—of what had once been a Cyrillic relief inscription.[38] Two years later the workshop of a medieval foundryman active before the Mongol invasion was uncovered on the grounds of the historical preserve known as "Ancient Kiev" (*Drevnij Kiev*). On the floor of this structure were found pieces of various bronze objects, including a bell fragment and a piece from some other large bronze vessel, which had evidently been brought into the workshop to be melted down and recast.[39] These discoveries considerably strengthen the possibility that the bells unearthed at Kiev were cast in Russia, probably in Kiev.

Archeological projects undertaken during the 1930s and 1940s in the lower church at Old Grodno have also brought to light the remains of two bells.[40] One of these had obviously fallen before the fire of 1183, which destroyed the town, since its pieces bore no traces of concentrated heat. On a fragment from this bell were four Cyrillic letters, part of a rather crude relief inscription: РАБУ (*rabu*, possibly the word "servant" in the expression "servant of God," referring to the founder).[41] This fragment is not only one of the oldest bell pieces in Russia but is also among the earliest examples of an Occidental bell with a relief inscription.[42] The second

28. The bell of 1341 for the Church of St. George (Iurij), now preserved in L'vov. From Karol Badecki, *Dzwony starodawne z przed r. 1600 na obszarze B. Galicji* (Cracow, 1922), 9, fig. 4.

bell certainly fell during the fire of 1183, for fragments of it were reduced to shapeless chunks of metal under the intense heat. Because one of its fragments weighed 27.14 kg. (almost 60 pounds), this bell had evidently been an instrument of considerable size.

In 1223 Mongol horsemen rode suddenly out of Asia and threatened settlements on the steppes. Despite Russian princes' vigorous reaction, the Asian cavalry defeated the princes' combined armies that year on the banks of the Kalka River north of the Sea of Azov. The Mongols vanished as mysteriously as they had appeared and were not seen again in Russian territory for fourteen years. But when they returned in 1237, cutting a swath of destruction through much of the Kievan lands, they altered the course of Russian history for the next two and a half centuries.

The Mongol Period

Between 1237 and 1241 Mongol invaders either killed or enslaved a significant proportion of the Russian population, sacked and burned their towns, and drew industrial production to an abrupt halt. The full impact of the Mongol conquest fell on commercial centers in the south—Kiev, Chernigov, Pereiaslav—where long-established trade routes were suddenly cut off.[43] From the mid-thirteenth to the mid-fourteenth centuries bell founding in Russia, together with other kinds of manufacturing, was in chaos. Not only had the conquerors destroyed most of the important towns and their metal-working shops but, even more deleterious, they were forcing skilled artisans, including foundrymen, from workshops in Russia to serve Khan Batu at Saraj or even the Great Khan in his capital in Asia.[44] It took Russian towns and their inhabitants the better part of a century to regain economic and industrial stability.

A few Russian towns in the west and northwest escaped both the carnage and subjection to Mongol rule, though even their commercial life was not unaffected.[45] But these towns stood to gain much from the new alignment in Russia. With the south so devastated, commercial and political power quickly shifted from Kiev to towns in the north and west, a process begun almost a century earlier, in the 1150s, but accelerated by the effects of the Mongol invasion. And as the severity of Mongol domination began to subside after the mid-fourteenth century, towns such as Novgorod, Pskov, Ustiug-Velikij, Tver, and Moscow had begun to emerge as important centers of industry and bell founding. At the same time, the way was being prepared for Moscow's eventual assumption of military, political, and ecclesiastical leadership during the second half of the fourteenth century and its

domination of Russian industry from the second half of the sixteenth century.[46]

For two decades following the Mongol invasion Russian chronicles are silent about bell ringing. And when notices begin to reappear, their number is small; no more than a half-dozen such references exist for the second half of the century. But they establish the presence of bells in such widely scattered towns as Kholm, Nizhnij-Novgorod, Smolensk, Liuboml, and Ustiug-Velikij. The most important of these notices, dating from 1259, tells of a fire in Kholm at the Church of St. John (Ivan): "[Prince Daniil Romanovich of Galicia] brought bells from Kiev, he cast others there [in Kholm]; all were caught in the fire."[47] Even if this passage does not prove conclusively that the bells Prince Daniil had ordered cast in Kholm were the work of Russian rather than foreign foundrymen, it nevertheless stands as the earliest dated reference to bell founding on Russian soil.

Around 1288 a Galician prince, Vladimir Vasil'kovich heard "wonderful bells" at the Church of St. George in Liuboml, where "there were not such [bells] in all the land."[48] Thus the volume of bell sound must have begun to reach a significant level, at least in Liuboml, by the end of the thirteenth century. Moreover, the adjective *divny* (wonderful) that the chronicler uses to describe the sound of the bells implies that these bells were superior in tone to anything the prince or chronicler had heard elsewhere. Two years later there appears the earliest citation of a Russian bell that had been named. In 1290 two princes of Rostov-Velikij, Dmitrij and Konstantin, sent Bishop Tarasij in Ustiug-Velikij a bell named "Tiurik'" upon the consecration of his church.[49]

The first chronicle notice of large bells in Russia dates from 1305, when "two large bells" (*dva kolokola velikaia* [sic]) were reported damaged in Rostov.[50] Notices of "a large bell" and "three large bells and two small," the first indication of relative sizes, appear in chronicles under 1342 and 1346 respectively.[51] Although chronicles do not give approximate weights, these bells probably weighed no more than 100 puds (3,611 pounds).[52] Indications of increased sizes and weights of bells in the early fourteenth century are followed, not surprisingly, in 1394 by the first mention of a bell structure in Russia on the kremlin walls of Pskov;[53] larger and heavier bells would of course need more substantial structural support.

Two fourteenth-century bells are among the oldest with Russian inscriptions. A bell of 915 pounds founded in 1341 was cast "during the reign of Prince Dmitrij by order of Igumen Ev″fimij for [the Church of] St. George (Iurij). And Skora Iakov wrote [this inscription]" (figure 28).[54] Skora Iakov, it is clear, did not found the bell but only prepared its inscription. Identification of Prince Dmitrij is not entirely certain.[55] A copy of the inscription from another fourteenth-century bell is preserved in a manuscript from the Cistercian Monastery at Trok in Lithuania: "Hereby I, Iakov Ondreevich, a servant of God (*rab″ Bozhij*), with my mother Ul′iana Aleksandrovna . . . [have] cast this bell at the Church of St. . . , Parask[eva] in Vilna, in the year 6887 [1379]."[56] This is the only citation in medieval sources of the participation of a Russian woman in bell founding.

Throughout most of the first three-quarters of the fifteenth century, chronicles offer little additional information on bell founding. Even in the highly productive period of founding in Moscow between 1475 and 1500 no details are forthcoming on the size and weight of bells or on casting procedures or the technology used in the manufacture of bells. Chronicles only routinely record that bells were cast, damaged as a result of fires and raids, and recast.[57] But at least three fifteenth-century Russian bells survive to the present day. The earliest of these is a 20-pud (722-pound) bell cast in 1420, the oldest in a quartet of bells known as the "Four Brothers" at the Trinity-Sergius Lavra in Zagorsk.[58] Another bell, cast by a Novgorod foreman named Mikula, is preserved in the Great Gostinopol′skij Monastery on the Volkhov River in the vicinity of Novgorod and bears the inscription, "in 6983 [1475] foreman Mikula cast [this] bell for [the Church of] St. Nicholas by order of Archbishop Feofil of Novgorod during the reign of Grand Duke

29. Mikula's bell of 1475 for the Great Gostinopol′skij Monastery near Novgorod. From N. N. Rubtsov, *Istoriia litejnogo proizvodstva v SSSR*, pt. 1, 2d ed., rev. and enl. (Moscow, 1962), p. 234, fig. 28. With permission of Izdatel′stvo "Mashinostroenia," Moscow.

Ivan Vasil′evich [Ivan III]" (figure 29).[59] A third, now in the Organnaia Palace Museum at Kolomenskoe, was cast on October 10, 1488, by a certain "Fed′ko" (Fedor) at the Borovskij Pafnut′ev Monastery in the Kaluga province.[60]

Of particular importance for the political future of Russia, as well as for the development of Russian bell founding, was the transfer in 1326 of the see of the Russian metropolitan from Vladimir to Moscow, a move that was to make Moscow the matrix of Russian Orthodoxy, and also the center of

30. Miniature from the second Ostermanovsky volume showing the founding of a bell at Tver in 1403. Two furnaces can be seen from which the molten metal flows into the bell mold. From A. V. Artsikhovskij, *Drevnerusskie miniatiury kak istoricheskij istochnik* (Moscow, 1944), 79, fig. 25. Permission of Moscow University Press.

political power.[61] The next year the Mongols bestowed on Ivan I Kalita (1325-1341), ruler of Moscow, the title of Grand Duke (*Velikij kniaz'*).[62] Moscow's eventual supremacy over its longstanding political rival Tver was foreshadowed in 1339 when Ivan removed a bell from Tver's Cathedral of the Saviour and ordered it transported to Moscow.[63]

With the Russian victory over the Mongols at Kulikovo Pole in 1380, the ascendancy of Moscow was assured.[64] Though Mongol raids continued to plague Russian cities throughout the fifteenth century, Moscow had struck a vital blow that would be followed in time by the final liberation of Russia from foreign domination. The very year of the Battle of Kulikovo Pole the icon of St. Dmitrij of Thessaloniki was transferred from Vladimir to Moscow, and in 1395 the most venerated icon in all Russia, the Virgin of Vladimir, was placed in the Uspensky Cathedral within the Moscow Kremlin.[65]

Favored with a location advantageous for transportation and trade, natural protection on three flanks, the support of the Russian Church and its metropolitan, and the shrewdness of its princes, Moscow was also emerging as one of the leading centers of bell founding in Russia. The first indication of Moscow's burgeoning position in bell manufacture is the selection in 1342 by Archbishop Vasilij of Novgorod of "a genial man named Boris," a Muscovite foreman, to cast a large bell (of unspecified weight) for the Novgorod Cathedral of St. Sophia.[66] This Boris is the first bell founder in Russia whose name has been recorded. The commission is noteworthy if only to show the older city's recognition of the technical competence of at least one Muscovite founder. In 1346 a foreman named Borisko (thought to be the same Boris), called "Rimlianin" (the Roman), by order of Moscow's Grand Duke Simeon "the Proud" (1341-1353) and his brothers, Ivan and Andrej, cast five bells—three large and two small.[67] By 1420 founders in Pskov sought Moscow's expertise in casting lead plates for a new roof on the Cathedral of the Holy Trinity and were sent a Muscovite foreman who taught a Pskovian named "Fedor" to cast the plates.[68]

Statements that indicate continuous growth in the number of bells rung and the volume of the zvon in Russian towns begin to appear by the end of the fourteenth century.[69] In Moscow both bells and bila were temporarily silenced following the Mongol attack of 1382, only two years after the Battle of Kulikovo Pole.[70] But with the resurgence of founding, bells lost during the siege were soon replaced and the city's zvon restored.

During the last quarter of the fourteenth century Moscow significantly strengthened its military hegemony over other Russian towns through the power of its artillery. Bell founders already established in Moscow also became manufacturers of cannon, and by the beginning of the fifteenth century a considerable number of heavy weapons were being cast.[71] With the first recorded use of artillery in Russia in 1382 and the earliest dated founding of Russian cannon a little more than a decade later began that precarious relationship between the instrument of the church and the instrument of battle that has posed a threat to bells in virtually every region of Europe.[72]

Moscow's principal rival in bell founding by the early fifteenth century was Tver, an important city northwest of Moscow with political aspirations of its own.[73] Even more than Moscow, Tver had established and maintained close ties with the West and with European industrial developments; thus it was probably here that Western innovations in founding were first received. In 1403 a chronicler described as "beautiful" the voice of a bell cast at Tver as "Blagovestnik" for the Cathedral of the Saviour (*byst' glas" ego krasen"*).[74] By 1447 a Tver cannon foreman, Mikula Krechetnikov, was reported to have no peer in his field, even among foreign founders.[75] But Moscow's longstanding rivalry with Tver, in both politics and bell founding, suddenly ended when Ivan III, Grand Duke of Moscow (1462-1505), annexed Tver in 1485.

Fourteen years earlier Ivan III had subdued Novgorod and by 1478 had forced this prosperous mercantile center to recognize the authority of Moscow. The bell that had rung to summon Novgorod's town assembly (*veche*), and to proclaim the town's independence (figure 31), was seized and transported to Moscow (figure 32).[76] Ivan III thus made the veche bell his prisoner and extinguished one of the few manifestations of oligarchical rule in Russia.[77] Despite its political bondage, Novgorod continued to provide cultural nourishment for Moscow an entire century after its conquest and was artistically eclipsed by Moscow only toward the end of the sixteenth century.[78]

Opinion differs on the fate of Novgorod's veche bell. Wherever it was hung in Moscow—presumably on the Kremlin wall near the Spasskij Gate—it would have been prominently displayed.[79] It is

31. Summoning the veche in Novgorod by ringing the veche bell. From O. I. Podobedova, *Miniatiury russkikh istoricheskikh rukopisej k istorii russkogo litsevogo letopisaniia* (Moscow, 1965), 297, fig. 122. Permission of VAAP, Moscow.

believed to have been recast at 150 puds (5,417 pounds) in 1673 as the Moscow *nabatnyj* (alarm) bell. Then by edict of Tsar Fedor Alekseevich, it was sent in 1681 to the Nikolaevskij-Korel'skij Monastery in the Arkhangel'sk province because its midnight ringing disturbed the tsar's sleep.

Though Ivan III had drawn Novgorod into Moscow's thrall, Ivan IV, "the Terrible," ruthlessly crushed the last vestiges of Novgorod's independent spirit and in 1570 ordered two to three thousand of its citizens slain.[80] A legend arose that when Ivan IV rode onto the bridge to cross from the

32. The Novgorod veche bell being transported on a sled to Moscow. From Podobedova, *Miniatiury*, 301, fig. 124. Permission of VAAP, Moscow.

commercial (east) side of the Volkhov River to the St. Sophia (west) side, a bell being rung in the cathedral belfry spooked his horse, which suddenly fell to its knees. The enraged tsar punished the offending bell by having its "ears" (cannons) cropped. A similar legend is attached to another crop-eared bell at the Church of St. Nicholas Usokha in Pskov, Novgorod's "younger brother," whose voice was also reputed to have startled the tsar's horse.[81] Neither the Novgorod nor the Pskov legend reveals the fate of the horse.

After his marriage in 1472 to Sophia (Zoë) Palaeologus, niece of Constantine XI, the last Byzantine emperor, Ivan III took a strong personal interest both in the development of founding and in the raising of a splendid new architecture within

the Kremlin. In 1474 he sent his ambassador, Semen Tolbuzin, to Italy to recruit skilled architects, engineers, and technicians for this work.[82] Most illustrious of the numerous Italians who accepted Tolbuzin's invitation was the Bolognese architect, engineer, and founder, Ridolfo Fioravanti (1415/20–ca. 1486), whose influence culminated in a new group of monumental buildings within the Kremlin.[83] Between 1475 and 1509 three new churches—whose Byzantine form and Italian Renaissance detail were crowned with cupolas and crosses of gold—became compelling statements of the aspirations of Ivan III and his successor, Vasilij III.[84]

In addition to his work as an architect, Fioravanti is also reported to have minted coins and cast bells and cannon, though none of these works have survived. And as his commissions increased during the 1480s, he invited other skilled workers from Italy to join him in Moscow. A Venetian foreman, Paolo (Pavel) Debosis, arrived in 1483, and following him, a steady influx of foreign masters, including two brothers, Giacomo (Yakov) and Pietro (Petr) Friazin, who served as Fioravanti's assistants. Under the tutelage of the Italians, a number of Russians were introduced to, and soon became proficient in, Western techniques of casting.

Fioravanti's most significant contribution to Russian founding was his introduction of new European technology to Moscow's Cannon Shop (*Pushechnaia izba*), established *circa* 1479 near the Kremlin's Spasskij Gate. The Cannon Shop burned down in a fire of 1488 but was rebuilt the following year. It burned down again in 1500 and was reestablished as a much larger operation. Sources from the first years of the sixteenth century indicate that its new location was near the left bank of the Neglinnaia River. In descriptions of damage from a fire of 1547, the plant is called the Cannon Yard (*Pushechnyj dvor*).[85] The Moscow Cannon Yard was to be the principal producer of fine bells and field weapons in Russia for three hundred years.[86]

In 1490, if not earlier, Ivan III took the first steps to reduce Moscow's dependence on England, Denmark, Sweden, and Holland for their copper and tin by recruiting foreign metallurgists, prospectors, and mining engineers to help Russians locate and exploit native metal resources. Two Germans in the tsar's service explored the Pechora region in the north and in 1491 discovered deposits of copper and silver along the Tsil'ma River in this area.[87] Russia did come to rely less and less on the importation of metal from abroad, but throughout the sixteenth century and most of the seventeenth the country continued to be dependent to a great extent on Western European expertise in discovering, extracting, and processing the ores.

Through the initiative of Ivan III, then, the last quarter of the fifteenth century saw an unprecedented burst of founding in Moscow; and during the sixteenth century Russian bell casting there entered a new era of expansion and technological development. A full century after the Russian victory at Kulikovo Pole, Ivan III succeeded in liberating Muscovy from Mongol domination[88] and thus prepared Russia to assume both spiritual and industrial leadership in the Christian East.

5

Bells in Muscovite Russia

ON JULY 11, 1613, Mikhail Fedorovich Romanov, newly crowned Tsar of All the Russias, was escorted in momentous procession from the Uspensky Cathedral across the Kremlin's central square beneath a baldaquin of wildly ringing bells. For three days other bells throughout the capital joined the joyous zvon from the Kremlin to proclaim the coronation of a new sovereign and the advent of a new dynasty.[1] Unwittingly this zvon also rang in a new age in Russian bell founding. European and Russian founders at the Moscow Cannon Yard had cast magnificent bells and cannon throughout the sixteenth century. They had learned well the founding techniques of their Italian teachers, brought to Moscow at the end of the fifteenth century; and now they continued to develop their skills and increase their production. Founders in Pskov and Novgorod had also produced many fine bells by the end of the sixteenth century and were worthy rivals of the Muscovites.[2] But Russian founders at the state cannon yard soon eclipsed them and eventually even surpassed their Western mentors in the art of bell founding and in the magnitude of their castings.

Pskov and Novgorod

The founding yards in sixteenth-century Pskov, located in its Zapskov'e and Zavelich'e districts, were largely managed by families of artisans.[3] These foundries cast bells for Pskovian churches and monasteries, for the St. Sophia Cathedral in Nov-

gorod, and for other towns in northern and northwestern Russia.[4] As early as 1520 and 1521 the Andreevs—Mikhail, Onufrij (also Anufrij), and Maksim—founded two large bells, one of 100 and the other of 200 puds (3,611 to 7,223 pounds), for the Spaso-Mirozhskij Monastery; and for at least thirty years between 1520 and 1550 they were among Pskov's leading founders.[5]

Mikhail Andreev was the most gifted of the Pskovian founders and was apparently an accomplished founder by the time he came to Pskov in about 1520. His biography is limited to information that is transmitted on his bells, but from this and from the Italianate decorative devices he used on his bells, V. A. Bogusevich has identified him as a grandson of Ridolfo Fioravanti. Bogusevich further speculates that Mikhail received his early training in Moscow under Italian masters.[6] We know from chronicles that Fioravanti's son Andrea accompanied him to Russia. And Andrea, according to Bogusevich, was the father of Mikhail Andreev.

Mikhail was probably the founder who produced the large bell cast in 1530 by order of Archbishop Makarij for the Novgorod Cathedral of St. Sophia. This bell of 250 puds (9,028 pounds) was said to have been cast on the same night and during the very hour in which Ivan Vasil'evich (the future Ivan IV) was born.[7] Since Mikhail was the most experienced bell founder in northwestern Russia at the time, he and his brothers would have been likely candidates for carrying out such an important commission.[8]

Mikhail begat an illustrious dynasty of bell founders. Though productivity during the second half of the century—to judge from Pskov bells extant before World War II—did not equal Andreev's earlier level, a brief resurgence in activity seems to have occurred in the late 1580s and 1590s just before bell founding at Pskov shows a sharp decline (Appendix A).

Bell casting in Novgorod, according to Tikhomirov, had emerged as early as the mid-fourteenth century and owed much to the founding art of its "younger brother," Pskov, though Novgorod foremen did not begin to challenge the work of Pskovian founders until after 1550.[9] Among the first bell founders active during this period in Novgorod was a foreman named Ivan, who produced a bell in 1554 in thanksgiving for the city's deliverance from an epidemic of plague.[10] There is also reported in the second half of the sixteenth century a large bell of 500 puds (18,057 pounds) commissioned by Metropolitan Pimen of Novgorod (d. 1571) to serve the St. Sophia Cathedral as its "Blagovestnik."[11]

Unlike the concentration of the founding industry within the town of Pskov, Novgorod founders were spread over a much more extensive territory. Within Novgorod itself, however, founding was also organized in the family *artel'*, or association for common work, but there were a number of independent artisans as well. Thus established, bell production in Novgorod continued throughout the seventeenth and the first quarter of the eighteenth centuries. The work of two families, the Matveevs and the Leont'evs, became particularly distinguished, and some of the Leont'evs eventually moved to Moscow at the end of the seventeenth century to work at the Moscow Cannon Yard.[12]

The Moscow Cannon Yard

Despite the significant achievements in bell founding in both Pskov and Novgorod, bell production at the Moscow Cannon Yard had surpassed that in the two older cities by the end of the sixteenth century. In 1510, the year political freedom in Pskov was abrogated, Vasilij III forced a considerable number of Pskov's citizens, including bell founders,

to relocate in Moscow. With other founders from such towns as Voronezh and Kostroma, the Pskovians continued their work in Moscow, where they attained a high degree of perfection in their art. Novgorod, after Ivan IV's massacre at the beginning of 1570, lost to Moscow a number of bells from its churches and monasteries, symbols of Moscow's newly established authority there.[13] Among these bells was Pimen's "Blagovestnik" bell, which was removed from the zvonnitsa of the St. Sophia Cathedral and carried to the tsar's residence at Aleksandrov.[14] The political subjugation of these two great founding centers and relocation of their workers gave Moscow an undeniable advantage in Russian bell founding.

In its industrial diversity, Moscow in the sixteenth century had even begun to rival such great Western European founding centers as Paris and London.[15] And a diversity of professional skills distinguished the work of individual foremen at the Moscow Cannon Yard, where a founder was required to master each step of the founding process, and thus intimately acquainted with his craft, produced castings of the highest quality. The Russian foreman was permitted to choose the size, dimensions, and weight of smaller bells and of light artillery, including the wall thickness of the former and the caliber of the latter. This gave him the opportunity to develop individual designs for the smaller castings, but it also significantly limited their rate of production. In the second half of the sixteenth century, when new regulations began to specify both the weight and dimensions for light artillery and smaller signal bells—which probably promoted the founding of more items in this size—founders began to focus their creative skills on designing a more limited number of siege cannon, heavy artillery, and large bells.[16] To avoid difficulties in transporting castings of such size and weight to purchasers in distant towns, foremen from the Moscow Cannon Yard and their assistants often had to travel to any place within the territories of Muscovy to undertake on-site production or repair of heavy cannon and bells.[17]

The first Russian bells of significant size were cast in the early sixteenth century, and chronicles began to specify the weight of individual bells (earlier chronicle notices suggested only relative size and weight, with the adjectives *velikij* or *men'shij*). In 1501 Ivan Afanas'ev (or Athanas'ev) is said to have founded in Novgorod a bell of 450 puds (16,251 pounds) called "Medved'" (Bear), which, although recast in 1775, still hangs in the Ivan Velikij Bell Tower within the Moscow Kremlin.[18] In 1503 Petr Friazin, a European founder at the Moscow Cannon Yard, cast another large bell, containing 350 puds (12,640 pounds) of copper alone.[19]

Three other bells of unusual weight appeared in Moscow and Novgorod during the early 1530s, two of which seem to have been the work of a foreign founder. In 1532 Nikolai Friazin cast what was the largest bell yet founded in Russia, at a weight of 500 puds (18,057 pounds).[20] A year later Nikolai Nemchin cast another bell, twice as heavy, at 1,000 puds (36,113 pounds).[21] These two bells in all probability were the work of a single European master whose given name was Nicholas, Nikolaus, or possibly Nicola or Niccolò.[22] The inscription on a bell called "Lebed'" (Swan) that hangs today in the Kremlin's Ivan Velikij Bell Tower identifies it as the bell cast by Nikolai in 1532 at 445 puds. The difference of 55 puds is probably the result of recasting the original in 1775.[23] The 1,000-pud bell of 1533 reportedly hung in its own wooden structure in the courtyard of the Kremlin. The third monumental bell cast in Russia at this time was the 250-pud (9,028-pound) bell of 1530 allegedly founded in Novgorod to commemorate the birth of the future Ivan IV, a bell that may have been the work of Mikhail Andreev.[24]

No bells are recorded cast in Muscovy in the second half of the sixteenth century that rival those cast in the first half. The reason for this is simple. After a fire in 1547 destroyed a considerable portion of the Kremlin's defensive wall and the cannon positioned on it, Ivan IV took immediate steps to replace the lost weapons.[25] The tsar's struggles with the Khanates of Kazan and Astrakhan in the 1550s and the protracted war in Livonia (1558-1583) further meant that for much of the second half of the century founders at the Moscow Cannon Yard concentrated their efforts on the production of weapons rather than the founding of large bells.[26]

Observations made by two foreign visitors in Moscow in the 1560s and 1570s concerning Russian bells add a few personal impressions to the meager accounts in Russian chronicles. Raffaello Barberini in 1565 commented on the extraordinary number of wooden and masonry churches in Moscow, observing that there was scarcely a street on which there were not several churches. Barberini further noted that on the Feast of St. Nicholas the incessant bell ringing in the city was as wearisome as it was unbearable.[27] Heinrich von Staden from Westphalia records how the zvon over Moscow was suddenly silenced following the Crimean khan's attack on the city in May of 1571, when a great number of Moscow's bells were either broken or melted in fires.

The next day [the Crimean Khan] had the palisades or suburbs, which were very large, set afire. Many monasteries and churches were there. The city, the palace [Kremlin], the oprichnina court, and the suburbs burned down completely in six hours. It was a great disaster, because no one could escape. Not three hundred persons capable of bearing arms remained alive. The bells in the temple and the walls they hung on [collapsed], and the stones killed those who sought refuge there. The temple and church tower, together with all the ornaments and icons, were completely burned out. Only the walls remained standing. The bells that hung in the tower in the middle of the palace melted, cracked, and fell to the ground, some in pieces. The largest fell and broke apart. The bells in the oprichnina [court] fell to the ground; likewise all the bells that hung in wooden churches and monasteries inside and outside the city.[28]

The Moscow Cannon Yard was no doubt the scene of unusual activity by the end of the Livonian War as its workers recast the bells lost during the Crimean khan's devastation of the city. By the late 1580s Moscow's zvon had apparently been restored. Jerome Horsey and Giles Fletcher, two Elizabethan visitors to Russia at that time, both mention the almost incessant ringing of bells that could be heard day and night throughout the city.[29]

The achievements of more than thirty outstanding Muscovite bell and cannon foundrymen reported during the reign of Ivan IV are all overshadowed by the work of Andrej Chokhov, generally considered the father of the Moscow school of founding.[30] No biographical information on Chokhov exists beyond random data gleaned from inscriptions on his work. But we know he was active for at least sixty years between 1568, when his casting was first mentioned, and 1629, the date of his last known work. His career spans the two periods of relative stability that flank the Time of Troubles (1598-1613), and his art links the Rurikid and Romanov dynasties. Records, if not extant examples, of Chokhov's art survive from the reigns of four of the tsars he served: Ivan IV, Fedor I, Boris Godunov, and Mikhail Romanov.[31] We also know that Chokhov was a student of Kashpir Ganusov, active in Moscow during the 1550s and 1560s, and he appears to have been engaged during the first half of his career chiefly in the casting of cannon and harquebuses.[32] His art matured at the end of the sixteenth century during the reign of Fedor Ivanovich, culminating in his masterpiece of 1586, "Drobovik," the great cannon of 2,400 puds (86,671 pounds), known today as Tsar-Pushka (Tsar Cannon).[33] The refinement of his decorative plan and his remarkable sense of design and proportion are fully evident in this weapon. It stands today in the Kremlin not far from its equally famous eighteenth-century companion, Ivan and Mikhail Motorin's Tsar-Kolokol (Tsar Bell). Of the more than twenty pieces of artillery that bore Chokhov's name, twelve are still preserved.[34]

During the second half of his career Chokhov founded several bells of exceptional size and weight. At the beginning of the short reign of Boris Godunov (1598-1605) he produced one great bell for the Moscow Patriarchate, known as the Kremlin Godunov Bell of 1599, and another in 1600 for the Holy Trinity Monastery.[35] The Godunov Bell was one of Chokhov's finest achievements in founding, and at an estimated weight of about 2,173 puds (78,474 pounds), it was also one of the most ambitious casting projects undertaken in Russia until that time. Its metal has since been thrice recast,

finally in 1735 as Tsar-Kolokol, which makes Chokhov's bell the "great-grandfather" of this supreme Russian bell. In 1621 Chokhov cast four bells for the Kremlin's Ivan Velikij Tower, but his "Reut" bell, founded the following year at 2,000 puds (72,226 pounds), rivalled his earlier work.[36] For this bell the tsar conferred on him a state award.[37] In addition to his own achievements in casting, Chokhov was also active in training a large number of apprentices at the Moscow Cannon Yard and thereby left the stamp of his genius on a whole generation of Muscovite foremen (see Appendix B).

One unfortunate bell in sixteenth-century Russia was closely associated with an event in 1591 that was to precipitate a dynastic crisis and pave the way for Boris Godunov to ascend the Russian throne. This bell, weighing a modest 19 puds, 20 funts (704 pounds), originally hung in the tower of the Cathedral of the Transfiguration (Spaso-Preobrazhenskij sobor) in the town of Uglich on the Volga 125 miles northeast of Moscow.[38] Not long after the death of Ivan IV in 1584 his young son, the tsarevich Dmitrij, the boy's mother, Mariia Nagaia, and her family, the Nagois, were sent from Moscow to live in Uglich. As potential threats to the throne of Tsar Fedor, Dmitrij's half brother, they were watched closely by a representative of the tsar, Mikhail Bitiagovskij, who had been assigned to Uglich in 1590.[39]

On Saturday, May 15, 1591, shortly after lunch, a commotion rose in the courtyard of the palace where Dmitrij was playing *tychka* with four of his friends, a game in which a knife is thrown at a target. Suddenly an alarm was sounded from the cathedral's bell tower (figure 33), and Mariia Nagaia rushed outside to find her young son dead from a throat wound.

The repeated strokes of the bell quickly drew the citizens of Uglich to the square, where they were soon seething with outrage. Bitiagovskij, plunging into the crowd, made his way to the bell tower to try to silence the alarm, but the bell ringer had locked himself in and the alarm continued to sound. The townspeople, assuming that Dmitrij had been murdered by agents of the tsar and Boris Go-

33. Seventeenth-century panel showing the death of the Tsarevich Dmitrij at Uglich on May 15, 1591. A ringer in the bell tower of the Cathedral of the Transfiguration (upper left) is sounding the alarm. From Ronald Hingley, *A Concise History of Russia* (New York, 1972), 55. Permission of Bibliothèque Slave, Paris.

dunov, took matters into their own hands and proceeded to lynch Mikhail Bitiagovskij and his son Daniil. Twelve people were killed and considerable property destroyed in this spontaneous administration of mob justice.[40]

The people of Uglich, especially the Nagois, paid dearly for their precipitous actions. Boris Godunov, a brother-in-law of the then childless Fedor Ivanovich and the power behind his throne, dealt decisively with all offenders—animate and inani-

34. The bell at Uglich on which the alarm was rung at the death of the Tsarevich Dmitrij and which was exiled to Tobol'sk in western Siberia. The engraved inscription recounts the bell's unusual history. Courtesy of the Uglich Museum of History and Art.

mate—and virtually decimated the population of the town. Some citizens were executed, others were incarcerated, and about a hundred people were exiled to Pelym, a newly established town in western Siberia.[41] Authorities in Moscow also treated the bell that had sounded the alarm as if it had been a willful participant in the alleged crime. As a symbolic gesture, they had it lowered from the cathedral tower and flogged a hundred twenty times; then they had its clapper removed and one of its "ears" (cannons) lopped off. As a final sentence, the crop-eared bell (*kornoukhij kolokol*) was banished to Siberia with the exiled citizens. For an entire year the exiles pushed eastward, dragging the bell on a sledge through swamps and forests and across the Urals. When they reached Tobol'sk, Prince Lobanov-Rostovskij, the *voevoda* (military governor), registered the bell as "the first inanimate exile from Uglich," and from that day this bell has borne the sobriquet *ssyl'nyj*—"exiled."[42]

For three centuries the Uglich bell remained in Tobol'sk. It was initially hung in the bell tower of the Church of the All Merciful Saviour, where it struck the hours and served as the *nabatnyj* (alarm) bell.[43] Later it was moved to the bell tower of the St. Sophia Cathedral to function as the bell on which the canonical hours were announced and also as one of the smaller (*zazvonnye*) bells in the tower. In 1836 or 1837 it was relocated again and, by order of Archbishop Antonij, suspended under a wooden cover near the Church of the Holy Spirit adjacent to the archbishop's residence in Tobol'sk.[44] There it served as "Blagovestnik."

In December 1849 forty citizens of Uglich initiated requests to return the bell to its original home,[45] arguing that it had already been sufficiently punished for its "crime." The mayor of Tobol'sk countered that since the bell had been banished for life, its sentence had not yet been fully served. The question of the bell's rightful home would have to be decided by the Russian courts.[46] Uglich's attempts to recover its exiled bell were frustrated for almost forty years because of insufficient documents in the archives of the Yaroslavl eparchy that would establish beyond all doubt that the Tobol'sk bell was the same bell that had rung in Uglich on May 15, 1591.[47]

But finally in 1888 Uglich's petition was granted, and four years later the hapless bell was drummed out of Tobol'sk and ceremoniously accompanied to Uglich by its own commission. Its missing "ear" and clapper were restored on the way, as it floated up the Volga on a steamboat specially designated for this journey. Late in the evening of May 20, 1892, a throng in Uglich greeted the bell's arrival, installed it in a temporary belfry, and posted an honor guard around it throughout the night. The next morning at 9 A.M., following the Liturgy, a prayer service of thanksgiving (*moleben*), and a procession of the cross, the bell's dense and solemn tone resounded once more through the town and over the Volga. The citizens of Uglich then passed beneath the bell, and each took his turn to swing the clapper. For years after its homecoming, townspeople would ring the bell on May 15, recalling the dark and menacing voice that had foretold Russia's Time of Troubles.[48] Today the bell hangs in the Uglich Museum of History and Art where its Gogolesque biography is recounted for visitors (figure 34).

The addition of more and more bells to Moscow's churches and the gradual deepening of pitch through the casting of bells of greater size and weight led to an overpowering zvon in the capital by the end of the sixteenth century. Foreign visitors were astounded by the massive sound generated on great feasts and special state occasions. A Danish account notes "the powerful rumble" of Kremlin bells that greeted the arrival of Prince John in Moscow in September of 1602 instead of the trumpet flourishes and drum rolls customary in Denmark.[49] Petrus Petrejus (Per Persson), who was in Moscow between 1608 and 1611, observed that each church or monastery owned and rang a minimum of four or five bells, and some even had between nine and twelve bells.[50] If Stephan Kakasch's report of 1,500 churches and monasteries in Moscow in the first years of the seventeenth century is accurate, then a conservative estimate of the bells in the city based on the figures of Petrus Petrejus would put their number at approximately 6,000.[51] Whatever their total number, when they were all rung simultaneously, the zvon was so great that conversations were not possible on the city streets.[52]

The First Romanovs and the Great Age of Russian Bell Founding

Production at the Moscow Cannon Yard fell off sharply during the Time of Troubles (1598-1613) and did not recover fully until the mid-1630s.[53] But with the accession of Mikhail Fedorovich Romanov (1613-1645) began a vigorous quest to stand Russian industry back on its feet by freeing it from dependence on foreign sources of metal ores. As his predecessor Ivan III had done at the end of the fifteenth century, Mikhail Fedorovich summoned foreign geologists to Russia and financed large-scale exploration. This prospecting continued throughout the seventeenth century. Veins of copper were discovered west of the Urals near Solikamsk in the 1630s and additional deposits appeared in the Yenisej region in 1658. In 1653 a copper smelting plant had opened in Kazan, but by 1666 the ore from this deposit was exhausted. In the 1670s copper was being mined near Novgorod, near Olonets Kolonets not far from Lake Onega, and about one hundred fifty miles from the Mazenskaia Gulf in the White Sea.[54] All this copper production, along with the extraction and processing of substantial amounts of iron as well as deposits of tin and lead, encouraged the expansion of founding in Russia during the reigns of Mikhail Fedorovich and his successor, Aleksei Mikhailovich (1645-1676). And yet Muscovy was still unable to meet its own industrial needs for these metals and continued to import copper ore, principally from Sweden, and tin, from England and Denmark.[55]

Russian names began to appear more frequently among founders active during the early seventeenth century as skilled native workers replaced the large number of foreign foremen employed in Russian plants.[56] Novgorod appears to have been home to a significant number of these Russian foundrymen; apparently this city had not only maintained but had even increased its productivity in bell founding. That names of bell founders from Pskov appear less often indicates that Pskov, once Moscow's principal rival in founding, was no longer a power to be reckoned with.

Though a great number of extant Russian bells from the seventeenth century were cast in Moscow and Novgorod, decentralization of the industry is also evident. Largely because the Moscow Cannon Yard could not keep pace with the increasing number of orders for larger bells, smaller workshops began to spring up in such places as Kazan, Ustiug-

Velikij, Sol'vychegodsk, Vologda, Beloozero, Belaia, and Kiev.[57] Even cloistered monks were sometimes engaged in casting.[58] This meant that foundrymen from the Moscow Cannon Yard had to do less traveling to carry out on-site casting of very heavy objects.[59]

Another new feature of bell founding in seventeenth-century Russia was the rise of private workshops in Moscow.[60] These family-owned foundries shared the hereditary nature that the profession had earlier assumed in Pskov—and indeed in the course of the century such family names as Danilov, Dubinin, Ivanov, Kuz'min, Leont'ev, and Motorin became synonymous with founding—but they were also operated partially in conjunction with the Moscow Cannon Yard. The domestic workshops in Moscow appear to have been first established on a small scale. Founders continued their association with the state cannon yard, but they began to cast bronze articles on their own on the side, mainly church bells; and they would even work out certain details of a new state casting project in their private workshops.[61] Since the production schedule at the Moscow Cannon Yard was never fixed but depended on orders whenever they were received, these founders, through projects undertaken in their own workshops, were assured of a more or less constant flow of work and were able to supplement their incomes as well.

Gradually these domestic workshops developed into flourishing private plants. One of the most important of these was the plant of the Motorin family. The first of the Motorin founders was Fedor Dmitrievich, active in Moscow from about 1650 to about 1685, during which time he cast a number of large bells weighing from 200 to 1,275 puds (7,223 to 46,044 pounds).[62] By 1686 Fedor Dmitrievich owned and managed a private bell foundry in Moscow's Pushkarskaia settlement, a plant that his two sons, Dmitrij and Ivan, and later his grandson Mikhail (son of Ivan) inherited and expanded. Castings from the foundries of Iakov Dubinin and Mart'ian Osipov were also noted for their high quality. Dubinin, moreover, was a frequent recipient of the "tsar's stipends" or bonuses for his skills in bell founding. During the eighteenth century these private foundries accounted for a large number of the bells produced in Russia, and they replaced the Moscow Cannon Yard when it ceased operation in 1802.

If most Russian bells founded in the sixteenth century weighed in the hundreds of puds, the great bells from the seventeenth century weighed in the thousands. Through their casting technology, founders at the Moscow Cannon Yard achieved magnitudes in weight and size that astonished West European visitors.[63] In 1654 when Emel'ian Danilov (fl. 1640-1654) recast the Kremlin's ruined Godunov Bell, he increased its weight to 8,000 puds (288,904 pounds). The bell shattered upon testing, but Tsar Aleksei Mikhailovich had it immediately recast by Aleksandr Grigor'ev, a precocious founder not yet twenty years old. Grigor'ev's great bell of 1655, weighing perhaps 10,000 puds (361,130 pounds), was the largest and heaviest ever rung in Russia and served the Kremlin for more than twenty-seven years until it was destroyed in a fire of 1701.[64] Two other monumental Russian bells cast in the seventeenth century, especially noted for their rich tone, were Khariton Ivanov's bell of 1,000 puds (36,113 pounds) founded in 1678 for the Simonovskij Monastery in Moscow and Aleksandr Grigor'ev's bell of 1667 cast at 2,125 puds 30 funts (76,767 pounds) for the Savvino-Storozhevskij Monastery near Zvenigorod.[65]

With the dramatic growth in size and weight of certain bells in Moscow came a proportionate increase in the volume of the zvon. Travelers to Moscow in the mid-seventeenth century compared what they heard to thunder. They said that vibrations generated through the concerted ringing of the city's bells were so powerful that the ground itself trembled.[66]

Throughout most of the seventeenth century the Moscow Cannon Yard was administered by the Cannon Bureau (*Pushkarskij prikaz*),[67] which, despite the presence of foreign foremen at the foundry, managed to keep detailed plans of the plant out of the hands of foreign visitors and Western publications. The location of the cannon yard was indicated on virtually all maps of the city published in Europe during the seventeenth century. But even today its exact plan and appearance remain conjectural.[68] The plan of Moscow from 1610 dedicated to Sigismund III of Poland seems to have been drawn from memory; it shows a single foundry warehouse inside the cannon yard compound (figure 35). A. M. Vasnetsov depicted the Moscow Cannon Yard in 1918 as he imagined it would have looked in the seventeenth century and also shows only one foundry warehouse (figure 36), though there are believed to have been two. A seventeenth-century plan of the entire foundry complex published by Vladimir Lamanskij, on the other hand, shows two foundry warehouses and visually confirms information in printed sources (figure 37). Inside the warehouses were permanent casting pits, with machinery constructed over each pit so that items cast could be hoisted to ground level after founding. The cannon yard also included a number of workshops. Facing the courtyard around the two warehouses were forging shops for blacksmiths, and in the central compound were a well and scales for weighing metal. Adjacent to the cannon yard stood the Church of Ioakim and Anna, with the courtyards of individual workers situated nearby. The state foundry had access to the Cannon Bureau's reference library of technical material on metals, founding, and related subjects.[69]

Personnel at the Moscow Cannon Yard largely belonged to the three general ranks of foreman (*master*), foundryman (*litets*), and apprentice (*uchenik*), but there were also numerous workers with lesser skills to assist.[70] Foremen were expected to be equally proficient in such highly diverse skills as the selection of molding materials, the construction of molds and furnaces, the melting of metals, and casting itself. Ridolfo Fioravanti had exemplified such diversification at the end of the fifteenth century. With the appearance of larger plants and greater production capacity in the seventeenth century, founders by necessity became more highly specialized in their work, but their knowledge of the profession continued to be quite broad. Since most bells called for decorative programs to be applied to the false bell before the cope or upper mold was made, foundries sometimes called upon engravers or icon painters to design this ornamentation.[71]

Normally there were several senior foremen at the Moscow Cannon Yard, one of whom was recognized as chief because of his seniority. At the end of the sixteenth and beginning of the seventeenth centuries Andrej Chokhov was the first in command and as such received the highest annual salary.[72]

Although most foremen at this time were Russian, foreign masters continued to work in Russian foundries during the reigns of the first Romanov tsars. Both Russian and European foremen carried out their projects individually with the help of assistants and apprentices.[73] But occasionally, more so later during the reign of Peter I, tension surfaced between them. The Europeans, invited to Moscow to teach their casting skills and techniques to Russian workers, drew salaries much higher than those paid their Russian peers, and they generated ill will when they purposely withheld professional secrets.[74]

Foremen and foundrymen received three kinds of allowance in addition to their annual salary: a bread allowance for food, various grains, and salt; a clothing allowance; and an "apprentice" allowance given to foremen who were responsible for the training and care of apprentices.[75] The amount of these allowances was determined by the seniority and responsibilities of the individual worker. Rewards in the form of money or provisions (especially cloth) were normally bestowed by the tsar as special bonuses to recognize the successful completion of a very large project or a significant number of smaller items. By the end of the seventeenth century the tsar's bonuses were being dispensed so regularly that founders came to regard them as obligatory after completing a special project and complained if they were not forthcoming.

Apprenticeship, as a system for training younger workers, probably existed to some extent in Kievan Russia, and by the fourteenth and fifteenth centuries legal documents governed most relations

35. Detail of the Moscow Cannon Yard (no. 19) on the Neglinnaia River, from the so-called Sigismund Plan of Moscow, 1610. From S. P. Barten'ev, *Moskovskij Kreml': v" starinu i teper'*, 1 (Moscow: 1912), fig. 44.

between foremen and their apprentices. At the beginning of the fifteenth century the institution of apprenticeship was discussed in the code known as the Pskov Sudebnik as though it were already a tradition of long standing.[76] And from the end of the century Italian masters at the Moscow Cannon Yard were beginning to instruct Russian apprentices.

The majority of apprentices were youths in their midteens, often the sons, nephews, or other relatives of foundrymen. This tendency to pass on founding skills to younger relatives would have perpetuated the profession within certain families. But the extraordinary number of apprentices whom Andrej Chokhov and Aleksej Ekimov (Iakimov) (fl. 1618-1641) trained during the reign of Mikhail Romanov served to broaden the base of the profession and to insure the continuity and success of casting in Moscow throughout the seventeenth and even into the early eighteenth centuries.

Apprentices in private workshops were bonded to their foremen through a contract (this registration was not required at the Moscow Cannon Yard) and thus, for a normal training period of five years,

36. View of the Moscow Cannon Yard in the seventeenth century, as A. M. Vasnetsov has represented it in a drawing of 1918, "The Cannon-Casting Yard on the Neglinnaia River." The large round building with a conical roof contains the furnaces. On the street outside the compound under a small pavilion some smaller bells are on display. From L. Bespalova, *Apollinarij Mikhajlovich Vasnetsov 1856-1933* (Moscow, 1956), 132. Permission of VAAP, Moscow.

became in effect indentured servants of their master.[77] The foreman was responsible for the housing, feeding, clothing (including shoes), and complete instruction and training of his apprentices and would use their allowances to provide these material necessities. In addition, an annual salary of four to seven rubles was normally given to each apprentice.[78] The following agreement between Dmitrij

Fedorov and Ivan Motorin was contracted on December 13, 1694:

Hereby I, Dmitrej Fedorov, of the town of Skopin, in the present two hundred third year [A.D. 1694], on the thirteenth day of December, I have given this document to foreman Ivan, son of Fedor, Motorin to wit: for me, Dmitrej, to live with him, Ivan, in his yard from the above written date until that same date five years hence; and the entire time that I am living with him to obey and respect him, Ivan, and his wife, and his children in all matters and to perform any kind of work that he, Ivan, orders; not to drink and not to carouse, and not to steal by any kind of pilfering; not to steal his goods and not to run away; and not to leave before having completed my term [of training]; not to incur any

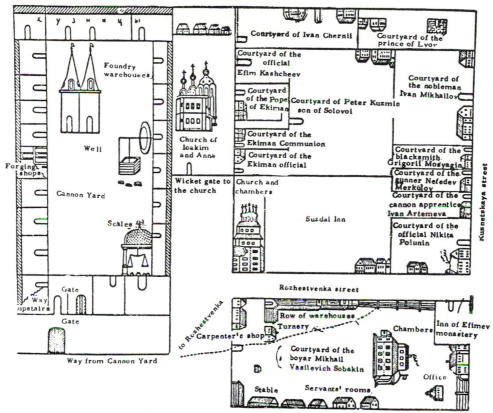

37. Seventeenth-century plan of the Moscow Cannon Yard (left). From Vladimir Lamanskij, ed., *Sbornik" chertezhej Moskvy eia okrestnostej i goroda Pskova XVII stolětiia* (St. Petersburg: 1861), plan no. XVII. Redrawn and relabeled in English in N. N. Rubtsov, *History of Foundry Practice in USSR*, trans. from the Russian [2d ed.] (New Delhi, 1975), 55, fig. 23. Used by permission of the National Science Foundation, translated and printed for the Smithsonian Institution by the Indian National Scientific and Documentation Centre, New Delhi, under the National Science Foundation's Special Foreign Currency Science Information Program.

kind of losses; drink and food and clothes and shoes his household [is] to provide for me; and I have contracted for service at four rubles a year, and will receive this money when my apprenticeship has been served. And they have signed this document for me as a guarantee for all [of the above]. (The signatures of the guarantors follow.)[79]

The contract served to protect a foreman from any disorderly conduct on the part of his apprentices. Since apprentices were bonded, their guarantors had to forfeit from 10 to 50 rubles if they did not follow their foreman's orders.

To protect apprentices from the whims of foremen contracts sometimes specified that foremen must not abuse their students. One of the most common abuses, notwithstanding, was a foreman's illegal extension of his apprentices' training period as defined in the contract. At the Moscow Cannon Yard it could sometimes last more than two decades.[80] This unethical practice was sometimes motivated by the lack of new positions at the yard for those youths who had already successfully completed their stated period of apprenticeship. But it most frequently resulted from a foreman's attempt to use well-trained and low-salaried workers for his own profit. After serving as apprentices for fifteen years, Mikhail Pavlov and Iakov Ivanov in 1677 finally petitioned the tsar for permission to work as bell founders in their own right and to escape from an overextended period of service to Khariton Ivanov.

To the Tsar, . . . your slaves (*kh[o]lopi*) at the Cannon Bureau (*Pushkarskij prikaz*), Mishka Pavlov and Iakushka Ivanov, bell[-founding] apprentices, petition [literally: beat our foreheads]. By your great Majesty's order, we, your slaves, have been serving and working for you, great Majesty, for more than fifteen years as bell [-founding] apprentices in Moscow and on assignments in various cities; and, for us, your slaves, Majesty, that bell[-founding] activity and the work of [making] bell molds is routine; we know how to make bell molds for casting on our own, but without your great Majesty's order, we dare not establish ourselves [independently]; we fear the enmity of our own foreman, Khariton Ivanov; but we your slaves, Majesty, have perished and been brought to utter ruin by Khariton's oppressive assignments. Merciful Soverign . . . take pity on us, your slaves; order us, Majesty, as our bell[-founding] work to undertake a bell mold for casting on our own, as you, great Majesty, prescribe. Tsar-Sovereign, have mercy.[81]

Though a number of foundry workers endured illegally extended apprenticeships, others became foremen at an unusually young age. Emel'ian Danilov at age twenty-four and Aleksandr Grigor'ev when not quite twenty had each successfully cast a monumental bell.

For an apprentice to rise to the rank of foundryman or foreman, he had to produce, after many years of practice, a major work in which he demonstrated his skills in founding.[82] This casting project was then evaluated by his own foreman and by other invited specialists. An apprentice who successfully passed this inspection was eligible to be advanced. Occasionally, less gifted trainees found themselves transferred from one foreman to another. One hopeless apprentice, who had been judged incapable of becoming a successful founder and who had been the student of numerous foremen, was finally assigned to the manufacture of horseshoes.[83]

At the beginning of January 1700 Peter the Great celebrated his reform of the Russian calendar with an order to fire cannons and ring church bells for an entire week.[84] But his great war with Sweden would soon force him to sacrifice the bells to the cannons. In order to feed foundries the metal necessary for the immediate casting of heavy weapons, Peter, like others before and since, raised his sights to the bronze inhabitants of his country's bell towers. Not since the Mongol invasion in the thirteenth century was there carried out such wholesale destruction of church bells in Russia.

6

Bells in Imperial Russia

HOSTILITIES with Sweden in the Great Northern War at the very beginning of the eighteenth century had drastically curtailed Russia's supply of iron and copper ore from that country, its principal source. To tap new deposits of these ores in the Urals and Siberia, Peter the Great (1682-1725) put renewed energy into promoting the eastward settlement of workers, a policy introduced during the reigns of his predecessors.[1] This vigorous development of the country's resources took on new urgency when as a result of their disastrous rout at Narva on November 19, 1700, the Russians retreated and abandoned their artillery to the Swedes; this left them virtually without ordnance.[2] The young tsar took extraordinary measures to reequip his army. He requisitioned all older pieces of Russian artillery, demanded increased production at the Moscow Cannon Yard, and ordered the private bell foundry of Ivan and Dmitrij Motorin to begin casting weapons.[3] Bells were also collected—a quota from each Russian church and monastery according to its size and wealth—and brought to foundries where they were melted down and recast as cannon.[4] As a result of Peter's fiat many of Russia's oldest bells were lost, but the tempo of Russian founding was accelerated almost overnight, and new bases of manufacturing were established.

In his efforts to increase productivity at the Moscow Cannon Yard, Peter introduced new standards of discipline to control the quality of personnel and to govern their professional behavior. A directive dated April 17, 1702, focuses on drunkenness as one of the leading impediments to production at the cannon yard and exhorts foremen to dismiss incapable apprentices and to retain only good, sober workers.[5] Peter also shortened the period of apprenticeship and established special schools to provide professional training for a greater number of workers. He established state rewards to recognize special achievements and create additional incentives for increased production. As a result, the production of ordnance at the Moscow Cannon Yard rose more than 150 percent between 1700 and 1701. Whereas only a hundred mortars were produced in 1700, the following year workers cast more than two hundred and forty-five cannon, twelve howitzers, and twelve mortars.[6]

Despite a setback in bell casting at the beginning of the eighteenth century and the loss of a large number of bells, the new foundries that began to appear in the hinterlands by the second half of the century were producing new bells.[7] Deposits of tin in Russia never proved adequate for domestic requirements, but mining operations developed in the Urals and Siberia provided enough copper by the mid-eighteenth century to meet the needs of Russian foundries. While Peter the Great's development of mining and reforms in Russian industry were largely salutary, however, the impact of the latter on Russia has been compared to the shock of the Mongol invasion. Each turned the country in new directions.[8]

The Decline of the Moscow Cannon Yard and Rise of Private Bell Foundries

Peter the Great's drastic measures to revitalize the Moscow Cannon Yard could not prevent this two-hundred-year-old institution from slipping into a century-long period of decline.[9] The establishment of other munitions factories in various regions of Russia was one factor in the cannon yard's diminishing importance. Another was the establishment of St. Petersburg at the beginning of the eighteenth century as a second capital more accessible to the West; it replaced Arkhangel'sk as Russia's principal northern port and soon began to challenge Moscow as a leading center of manufacture and founding.[10] The rise of privately owned bell foundries in the second half of the century further weakened the Moscow Cannon Yard's precarious position.

St. Petersburg's proximity to the scene of conflict during the Great Northern War only increased its importance as a center for the production of war matériel. In 1713, the year following the official transfer of the government to the new capital, the Cannon Yard (*Pushechnyj dvor*) there began production.[11] In January of 1714 the foundry had thirty-six workers under the supervision of foreman Semen Leont'ev. To increase production in March and April of that year Peter ordered one-third to one-half of all available workers at the Moscow Cannon Yard reassigned to the St. Petersburg foundry, followed by workers sent from Tula. By the 1720s, when the name of the foundry was changed to the St. Petersburg Arsenal, there were up to two hundred foremen and workers engaged in various aspects of founding. Though the principal mission of the St. Petersburg foundry was to manufacture cannon, it also cast bells, among other bronze objects.[12]

Although fine examples of bronze casting appeared in St. Petersburg during the first four decades of the eighteenth century, the art of Muscovite master Ivan Fedorovich Motorin (ca. 1660-1735), son of Fedor Dmitrievich and brother of Dmitrij Fedorovich, eclipsed the work of all other founders active in Russia at this time.[13] He is principally remembered today, with his son Mikhail, as the creator of the Kremlin's Tsar-Kolokol during the early 1730s.[14] But in 1687 Ivan Motorin and his brother Dmitrij had just jointly inherited their father's bell foundry.[15] They continued to work as foremen at the Moscow Cannon Yard while they supervised casting at their own plant.[16] The earliest notices of Ivan's work as a bell founder appeared in 1692 when he successfully completed a bell of 120 puds 8 funts (4,341 pounds), for the Staro-Preobrazhenskij Monastery at Staraia Russa in the Novgorod region, and a bell for the Church of St. John (the Evangelist) in Bronniki, beyond Moscow's Tver Gate in the Bronnaia suburb. Four years later he cast a bell of 200 puds (7,223 pounds) for the Church of the Trinity in Upper Sadovniki on the Bersenevka Embankment.

Although Ivan Motorin was occupied throughout most of the first decade of the eighteenth century in producing cannon for the tsar's army, records show that he also founded several large bells around this time.[17] Indeed the need for new Kremlin bells arose in the first year of the new century when many bells, including Grigor'ev's great bell of 1655, were lost in the fire of June 19, 1701.[18] One of Motorin's bells, his alarm bell (*nabatnyj kolokol*) of 1714, is of considerable historical interest, for it is thought to be a recasting of Novgorod's veche bell that Ivan III brought to Moscow in 1478.[19] Motorin's bell, placed in the Kremlin's Nabatnyj Tower on the wall flanking Red Square (see figure 43), bears an inscription below its shoulders stating that it was "cast in the year 1714 on the 30th day of July from an old broken alarm bell for the Spasskij Gate of the city of the Kremlin. Its weight is 150 puds [5,417 pounds]."[20] On the lower portion of the sound-bow near the lip a brief second inscription identifies Motorin as its founder (figure 38).

Motorin's alarm bell was one of the bells on which the tocsin (alarm) was sounded during the Muscovite insurrection in September of 1771 known as the Plague Riot.[21] When the riot had been put down, Catherine II sought the persons who had sounded the alarm, but unable to identify the guilty parties, the frustrated empress instead punished Motorin's Kremlin bell by having its clapper re-

38. Ivan Motorin's alarm bell (*nabatnyj kolokol*) of 1714, now
in the Kremlin's Oruzhejnaia palata (Armory). From A. M.
Andreev, *Moskovskij Kreml'* (Moscow, 1958), pl. 188. Permission of VAAP, Moscow.

moved. Catherine no doubt visited her wrath on Motorin's bell particularly—of all the bells in Moscow that sounded the alarm—because, mounted in the Nabatnyj Tower in the Kremlin wall, it had overlooked scenes of violence on both sides of the Spasskij Gate on September 16. For thirty-two years, then, Motorin's bell hung mute in the Nabatnyj Tower. In 1803, when the tower was undergoing repairs, the bell was removed and placed in the Kremlin Arsenal. Later it was transferred to the Oruzhejnaia palata (Armory), where it is preserved today, a superlative example of Ivan Motorin's art.[22]

In 1726 and 1727 Motorin undertook two projects for St. Petersburg: a bell of 200 puds (7,223 pounds) for the cathedral in the Peter and Paul Fortress, and the next year, a zvon or ensemble of ten bells for the (old) Cathedral of St. Isaac.[23] Three years later Motorin recast a Novgorod bell dating from 1556, which had hung in the zvonnitsa near the St. Sophia Cathedral inside the Novgorod kremlin. The weight of this recast bell was 420 puds (15,167 pounds). Finally, in 1732, while working on Tsar-Kolokol, Motorin founded a 1,000-pud bell (36,113 pounds) called "Uspensky" (Assumption) for the Kievo-Pecherskaia Lavra.

What promised to be the crowning achievement of Motorin's distinguished career came in 1730 with his acceptance of the commission from Empress Anna Ivanovna to recast the pieces of the great bell that Grigor'ev had founded in 1655 for Aleksei Mikhailovich. But Motorin did not live to see a successful casting of his own great bell. He died on August 19, 1735, less than a year after his unsuccessful attempt. But his son Mikhail carried on his work and cast the bell, Tsar-Kolokol, in the early morning hours of November 25, 1735. The weight of this bell, counting loss of metal during the melting and casting process, has been calculated at 12,000 puds (433,356 pounds). It remains the world's largest bell as well as the high-water mark in Russian bell founding. Tsar-Kolokol stands today in the Kremlin on a stone pedestal at the foot of the Ivan Velikij Bell Tower.

Several other monumental bells would be founded in Russia after Tsar-Kolokol, but never again on such a scale. On orders from Empress Elisabeth Petrovna, a bell of 1716 was recast in 1748 at the Trinity-Sergius Lavra. The weight of the former bell, 3,319 puds (119,859 pounds) according to the inscription on the other, was increased by 681 puds (24,593 pounds), but the new bell, also known as Tsar-Kolokol, was not raised into the first bell tier of the lavra's tower until 1759. Another enormous bell for the Moscow Kremlin was the work of Konstantin Slizov, who in 1760 recast a sixteenth-century bell for Elisabeth Petrovna. Slizov's new Uspensky Bell, weighing 3,551 puds 4 funts (128,241 pounds), was rung in the Kremlin on great feasts until it fell and shattered when Napoleon ordered the Kremlin's Ivan Velikij Bell Tower blown up in October of 1812.

At least three privately owned bell foundries were active in Moscow by the end of the eighteenth century. One of these was the Motorin foundry, which on the death of Mikhail Motorin in 1750, passed into the hands of Konstantin Slizov, then to a founder named Kalinin, and in 1813 to Mikhail Bogdanov. Another was the Finliandskij plant, which had been established in 1774. And a third, belonging to the Samgin brothers, had begun production in 1793.[24]

Private bell foundries also appeared in other regions of Russia during the second half of the eighteenth century. A foundry in the Perm district, which a German traveler described in 1774, was equipped with two furnaces, each of which had its own casting pit.[25] Inscriptions on three mid-eighteenth-century bells—two from 1754 and one of 1755—record that Slizov had cast them at Yaroslavl, at the factory of Dmitrij Maksimovich Zatrapeznov.[26] Another Yaroslavl plant that appeared soon after Zatrapeznov's was the foundry of the Company of P. I. Olovianishnikov and Sons. The earliest bell bearing the Olovianishnikov name (Grigorij Thedorov[ich] Olovianishnikov) is dated June 15, 1766, and was cast at 163 puds, 8 funts (5,894 pounds) for the town of Rostov-Velikij. The Olovianishnikov plant dated its first year of operation by this bell.[27]

The Last Century of Bell Founding
in Russia

At the close of the eighteenth century the casting of cannon and other ordnance was transferred from the Moscow Cannon Yard to the arsenal at Briansk and the cannon yard became a magazine for the storage of munitions. In 1802 these stores were moved to the Kremlin Arsenal, and the buildings and facilities of the former cannon yard were demolished. Two years after the Moscow Cannon Yard closed down, there were thirteen bell factories operating in Russia producing bells of various sizes.

Sources that list Russian factories in 1811 and 1812 do not distinguish between bell foundries and foundries manufacturing other bronze items. But we know that 4,220 bells were produced in Russia during 1811 and that the number dropped by more than half, to only 1,726, as a result of the French invasion in 1812.[28]

It was on the afternoon of September 2, 1812, as the clock in the Kremlin's Spasskij Tower struck four, that ringers in the Ivan Velikij Bell Tower beginning to sound *blagovest* for the evening office suddenly stopped. Those within the Kremlin were surprised. But at that moment a crowd came running through the Troitskij Gate crying, "Save yourselves, Orthodox believers! The French are at our heels!"[29] The thirty-nine days that the *Grande Armée* spent in Moscow culminated in Napoleon's orders to blow up certain structures in the Kremlin and elsewhere in the city. The French began mining the Kremlin on October 19, and the first explosions were detonated two days later.

By the two first explosions part of the walls, and one of the towers towards the river, were destroyed; by the third, the church of St. Nicholas, and the four great bells of Moscow were blown up with tremendous violence; at the same moment, the lofty tower of Ivan Veliki . . . was rent from the top to the base. The fourth shock was by far the most dreadful, . . . a concussion succeeding, that shook the whole city to its foundations.[30]

Another witness compared the raw red brick ex-

posed in the bell tower's fracture to a gaping wound and observed that three large bells lay upside down on top of the rubble hurled down from the explosions.[31] Debris from the tower also rained down into the pit that still held Motorin's Tsar-Kolokol, almost burying the giant bell. Among the bells lost during the third detonation, was Slizov's Uspensky Bell, and with Mikhail Bogdanov's recasting of it in 1817, the age of founding Russia's bronze giants came to an end.

The Napoleonic invasion dealt Russian bell founding a crippling blow. The economy as a whole recovered and went on to experience rapid growth between the mid-1830s and 1861 (the year the serfs were emancipated).[32] But bell founding was never the same. Foundries were mainly small, semi-professional, private factories staffed by workers whose skills were primitive and outdated.[33] Compared with other areas of manufacturing, the production of bells in most cases remained quite low.[34] The decline in the overall quality of bells in the late nineteenth century is epitomized in the exclamation of an anonymous Russian founder: "Sound! What do we care about sound? We sell by the pound. Sound doesn't weigh anything."[35] Only a few private foundries achieved distinction through fine finish and a superior tone quality.

In the mid-nineteenth century the Samgin and Bogdanov plants mentioned at the end of the preceding section cast the majority of large bells in Moscow.[36] Estimates at this time place the number of bells being rung at Moscow's monasteries and parish churches at 2,145 to 2,500.[37] A further conjecture places the total weight of Moscow's bells at around 100,000 puds (3,611,300 pounds). This great mass of metal, suspended in towers throughout the city, was sufficient, as one observer has remarked, to have exhausted an entire mine.

Newly founded Russian bells, along with other Russian manufactured items, could be seen in open markets at many of the fairs that sprang up across the country during the nineteenth century. Of the fairs where bells were regularly exhibited and sold, the largest and most famous was the annual fair in July and August at Nizhnij-Novgorod, "almost on

39. The bell market at the Nizhnij-Novgorod Fair. From Chloe Obolensky, *The Russian Empire: A Portrait in Photographs* (New York, 1979), 227, pl. 308.

the border of Europe and Asia" at the confluence of the Volga and the Oka. The products and goods at this fair were organized in "rows" (*riady*), each of which identified the merchandise displayed— e.g., Fur Trade Row, Striped Linen Row, Soft Goods Row, and Soap Row.[38] A section of the fair near the Alexander Nevsky Cathedral was designated the *kolokol'nyj riad*, and here, in graduated ranks, Russian bells, some weighing hundreds of puds, were suspended from a stout log framework. Potential buyers as well as the curious strolled back and forth beneath the bells and occasionally paused to grasp a clapper. Throwing it against the sound-bow they bent their heads and shut their eyes to judge the thunderous voice of the bell "with an air as pleased as if they were listening to birdsong" (figure 39).[39]

During the last quarter of the nineteenth century bell manufacture in Russia showed very little fluctuation in its rate of production.[40] Data for 1894 reveal that some twenty-five foundries had a gross annual product of 923,000 rubles.[41] But among these plants, less than half were producing bells of high quality. And by the turn of the century bell founding had became concentrated in the four provinces of Moscow, Novgorod, Penza, and Poltava.[42] Moscow produced most of the larger bells as well as those noted for the power of their sound and the purity of their tone.[43]

Moscow, like Nizhnij-Novgorod, maintained its own bell market, and at the All-Russian Exhibition of 1882 in Moscow the Samgin, Finliandskij, Olovianishnikov, and Ryzhov foundries displayed their bells.[44] The first two foundries, located in Moscow, and the third, in Yaroslavl, had been producing bells since the last third of the eighteenth century. But the Ryzhov foundry in Khar'kov, established in 1858, was not yet a quarter of a century old, and the quality of its workmanship was judged to be slightly inferior when compared with that of the three older factories. A specialty of the Ryzhov foundry, however, was the production of "carved" bells, or bells cast with apertures in their walls, an ornamental feature that their founders believed also increased the purity of their tone.[45]

At the All-Russian Exhibition in Nizhnij-Novgorod in 1896 bells from ten Russian foundries were on display. In his review of these exhibits Nikolaj Findejzen singled out three of the ten foundries for special comment. The Samgin bells he found to be excellent both for their tone as well as their finish. He thought the Finliandskij foundry produced some of the most beautiful bells on display from the standpoint of their external finish and decoration, though he did not find their sound completely satisfactory. In his estimation, the Olovianishnikov bells from Yaroslavl were equal in quality to those of Samgin and Finliandskij. Bells on display from the other seven foundries, he observed, revealed nothing that was particularly outstanding.[46]

The Olovianishnikov bells were widely known for their excellence. Scarcely a province in Russia was without at least one of them, and they rang abroad in Greece and Bulgaria, and at Jerusalem, Istanbul, and Karlsbad.[47] Before the October Revolution bells from the Olovianishnikov foundry had been exhibited in a number of Russian and international shows, where they received numerous awards for their superior quality.[48] The plant had also been honored by visits from three Russian emperors and a number of grand dukes.[49] In consultation with Aristarkh Izrailev, the Olovianishnikov foundry began to produce tuned bells in 1882, possibly motivated by a desire to increase its sales to churches in the West where tuned bells were preferred.

The year 1913, the last full year of peace and the tricentennial of the Romanov dynasty, was also one of the last years of bell production in Russia. In that year at least nineteen foundries were still casting bells.[50] But thereafter, bell founding once more bowed to the more pressing demand for weapons and other war matériel.

Over a hundred bells were sent to Nizhnij-Novgorod (now Gorki) in 1915 from churches in the Baltic provinces and Poland in order to save them from the advancing Germans. These "Latin" bells ranged in weight from 250 pounds to three or four tons and were estimated to be worth over half a million dollars. One of them bore a casting date of 1650; the inscription on another indicated that it had originally been a gift to its church from Charles XII of Sweden (1697-1718). Whether these displaced bells were ever returned to their church towers in Baltic towns and cities after the armistice cannot be verified. In the summer of 1922 they were still to be seen at Nizhnij-Novgorod where church bells had formerly been sold at the great summer fair.[51]

The Soviet Epilogue

Following the October Revolution in 1917 bell founding in Russia came to an end. There was no reason to continue production of church bells in a state that had officially disassociated itself from the Orthodox Church and its rites. There were sharp conflicts between church and state, however, concerning existing bells. After church and monastery lands had been nationalized in a decree of December 4, 1917, the Orthodox Church protested and made clear that if attempts were made to confiscate church property, including bells, the faithful would be called to "the defense of the church by the ringing of bells, or [by] sending out of messengers, or by other such means."[52] But another decree at the beginning of 1918, which established the separation of church and state, guaranteed the church's right to perform religious ceremonies as long as they did not interfere with public order and the rights of citizens.[53] And a year later the Commissariat of Justice even went on record as approving funeral processions accompanied by church banners and the tolling of bells.[54]

Under the new regime church bells have at best been preserved as national treasures, at worst either

40. The bell foundry of the Company of P. I. Olovianishnikov and Sons formerly at Yaroslavl. Some of the company's bells are on display under the pavilion on the left. From N. Olovianishnikov, *Istoriia kolokolov" i kolokololitejnoe iskusstvo*, 2d ed. enl. (Moscow, 1912), betw. pp. 410 and 411.

sold to countries whose supplies of copper and tin had been depleted during World War I or converted into farm and industrial equipment in the Soviet Union.[55] In June of 1923 reports came that numerous villages were selling their church bells to raise funds for improving agriculture and supporting education.[56] After vigorous encouragement from the press of Komsomol (Young Communist League), peasants in some villages began pulling down bells even before local authorities could organize such efforts.[57] And Stalin—not unlike Peter the Great, who had harvested Russia's bells more than two centuries earlier to provide new cannon for his war with Sweden—ordered many bells removed from their towers to be recast as tractors. One of the first cities to empty its bell towers was Stalingrad (now Volgograd),[58] and by the early 1930s bell tiers in hundreds of Russian towers were vacant.

In his short story "Mahogany" Boris Pilnyak describes how "pulleys, beams, and jute ropes" were used to pull the bells down from "their high perches in belfries" at Uglich in 1928: "They fell with a roar and a thud, digging holes some five feet into the ground. . . . The whole town was full of the moaning of these ancient bells."[59] Vasilij Peskov also recalls the end of bells in his village of Orlov: "A huge crowd gathered. The women crossed themselves and said that the bells would be made into tractors. Indeed, that same year a new tractor, its spurs glittering in the sun, drove down the length of the village street, making real to us boys the strange transformation from bell to machine."[60]

The bells that were not destroyed were often simply silenced by fiat, as on June 30, 1930, when the Moscow Soviet issued a ban on bell ringing in the capital and in towns and cities surrounding.[61]

The aural metamorphosis that took place in the Soviet Union during the late 1920s and early 1930s as a result of all this activity began with the rhythmic pulse of zvon ringing and ended with what Alexander Morskoi has called "the monotonous, measured throbbing of motors, of machines, a new idol, a new Moloch of the land."[62]

The bells in the zvonnitsa at Rostov-Velikij and a few other important ensembles escaped this fate and are maintained today as monuments of Russia's cultural heritage. One zvon of Russian bells was saved and brought to the United States in the late 1920s. Thomas Whittemore, who had been active in Russian Relief during World War I, persuaded Charles R. Crane of Chicago to purchase eighteen bells from the Soviet government and to present them as a gift to Harvard University.[63] These bells, shipped from Leningrad to New York and then to Boston, were installed in the tower of Harvard's Lowell House in the fall of 1930. Vsevolod Andronov, a former bell ringer in Russia, gave the first demonstration of zvon ringing at Harvard on Easter Sunday of 1931. Until the mid-1930s Andronov made weekly trips from New York to Cambridge to ring the Lowell House zvon in the traditional Russian manner.[64]

During World War II loss of life and destruction of property in the Soviet Union were staggering. With the wanton desecration and demolition of historical monuments in the regions that were overrun and occupied by the Germans, many bells were also lost. One war casualty was the 38-ton bell that Aleksandr Grigor'ev had cast in 1667 for the Savvino-Storozhevskij Monastery near Zvenigorod, famous throughout Russia for its unusually rich and resonant tone as well as for its cryptic inscription (see Chapter 9). In October of 1941, as the enemy was advancing on Zvenigorod, the Russians in great haste tried to lower Grigor'ev's bell from the tower to move it to a safer place. In the process, however, they broke it, and today only its pieces are preserved at the museum in Zvenigorod.[65] The enemy also blew up two of Russia's finest bell towers in Patriarch Nikon's Voskresenskij (New Jerusalem) Monastery on the banks of the Istra and at the Monastery of Joseph of Voloko-

lamsk.[66] The architectural ensemble in both monasteries is presently undergoing restoration, and the bell towers will no doubt be rebuilt. Whether reproductions of their former bells will be cast and installed remains to be seen.

Among the survivors of the war, however, are a few of Russia's most historic bells, including five bells in Novgorod's kremlin. In August 1941, when the three large bells in the zvonnitsa near the St. Sophia Cathedral proved too heavy to be carried from the city with two smaller Novgorod bells, alternative arrangements were quickly improvised as the enemy was approaching the city. The three smaller bells were put on a barge in the Volkhov River, which was sunk during the bombardment; the other two were buried in the ground.[67] According to another source, one large bell "was still on the river bank when the Germans broke into the town. Under shellfire the mayor and his assistants managed to bury the bell, and though the Germans during their 2½ years' occupation asked many people where it was, nobody told them."[68] In 1944, following the liberation of Novgorod, Soviet soldiers raised the three "drowned" bells from the river bed and excavated the other two. But none of the Novgorod bells have been rehung; instead they rest on the ground at the foot of the zvonnitsa inside the kremlin where the three largest once hung.[69]

One of the central forces in Russian history was the rise of Moscow to a position of primacy in the Christian East. By the end of Ivan III's reign Moscow had been designated the Third Rome, heir not only of Constantinople, the new Rome, which the Ottoman Turks had captured in 1453, but also, in the Russian view, of the first Rome.[70] Though this doctrine was never officially embraced or promulgated by the Russian state itself, Ivan III adopted the title *samoderzhets* (the Russian translation of the Byzantine concept of *autokrator*) and eventually incorporated the double-headed eagle of Byzantium in his own seal. The new doctrine also received compelling sanction from the splendid new architecture that began to rise within the Kremlin. Here, in a Muscovite icon of the Imperial Palace in Constantinople, dwelled Ivan III and Sophia Palaeologus, niece of the last Byzantine emperor, Constantine XI.[71]

These architectural affirmations of Moscow's ascendency in the Orthodox East were matched in magnitude by the zvon that resonated above the city like an enormous, invisible dome of booming bronze. In a culture largely dominated by visual and aural images, the Moscow zvon assumed cultic significance as a transcendental expression of "metallic might in a wooden world."[72] For almost four centuries, in wave upon wave of incessant alleluias, "the bronze voice of Orthodoxy" declared the presence of the Third Rome and the piety of its sovereigns.[73] But with the secularization, closing, and even razing of many churches following the October Revolution of 1917, this sound, which in palmier days had made the city tremble, rapidly diminished and will soon fade from living memory.

Part III
Russian Encounters with the West

7

Tower Clocks

THE CURTAIN falls on the final scene of Nikolaj Pogodin's play *The Kremlin Chimes* with Lenin's prophecy as he listens in his study to clock bells in the Kremlin's Spasskij Gate: "Do you hear? They are playing. This is a great thing. When everything has been realized that we are now only dreaming of, arguing over, worrying about, they will be reckoning new time, and that time will be witness to new plans for electrification, new dreams, new daring."[1] Throughout his play Pogodin uses Lenin's repair of the Spasskij clock and its mechanism, damaged in October of 1917, as a symbol of hope for the future. Though Lenin had the chiming cylinder reset to play the *Internationale* instead of the tsarist hymn *Kol' slaven"*, the Kremlin chimes are nevertheless one of the few aural links between the old and new regimes. On December 31 Muscovites stay up to hear the Kremlin chimes ring in the new year.

Chimes made their way into Russia rather slowly, for whereas individual bells seem to have first reached Kievan Russia from the West, further Russian encounters with Western bells and European styles of bell ringing were quite limited.[2] Even when a Western bell was purchased or captured and hung in a church tower with bells cast in Russia, only the most general consideration was paid to its pitch in assigning its function in the tower. The bell virtually lost its Western identity among its untuned companions.

The most extensive dissemination of Western bells in Russia came with the installation of a number of tower or turret clocks, the first of which appeared in Moscow at the beginning of the fifteenth century. Subsequent monumental clocks, with tuned chimes and automatic chiming mechanisms, were installed above several Kremlin gates in the sixteenth century and eventually appeared during the seventeenth and eighteenth centuries in the towers of towns and monasteries throughout Russia. The importation and installation of two successive Dutch carillons in the cathedral tower of the Peter and Paul Fortress in St. Petersburg in the eighteenth century then served to acquaint citizens in the new capital with the bell music of the Low Countries.[3] But change ringing, that uniquely English manner of sounding swinging bells in series of numerical permutations, never reached Russia and remained beyond the Russians' ken. At the end of the nineteenth century, as a result of Aristarkh Izrailev's acoustical experiments and predilection for tuned church bells, attempts were made to promote melodic-harmonic ringing in a few Russian towers. But this was the first time Western ideals for the tuning of individual bells and bell ensembles and European modes of ringing had made any incursion on the native tradition of bell ringing.

The Development of Striking Clocks in Medieval Europe and Their First Appearance in Russia

In addition to announcing church services and sounding alarms, early Western bells eventually acquired another duty—the striking of the hours

41. Miniature from the second Ostermanovskij volume, no. 1324, which shows the tower clock of 1404 in the Moscow Kremlin. From Artsikhovskij, *Drevnerusskie miniatiury*, 85, fig. 26. Permission of Moscow University Press.

from city towers. Before the fourteenth century clocks with escapement mechanisms had not attained sufficient size, versatility, dependability, or accuracy to ring a bell to mark the hour. So medieval towns hired tower wardens—Jantjes, or Town Johnnies, as they were commonly called—to keep track of time with a sundial, hourglass, or small alarm and at the end of each passage of time to strike a bell from a balcony, tower, or rooftop so that its sound could be heard throughout the town.[4] This striking of the hour differed "from all previous means of telling time—water clocks, sand clocks and sundials—which were silent."[5]

The striking tower clock is believed to have appeared in Europe by the beginning of the fourteenth century, and to judge from extant sources, Italian cities may well have been among the first

to have these clocks. As early as 1309 an iron tower clock with a mechanism for releasing a hammer to strike a bell is mentioned at Sant' Eustorgio in Milan.[6] The oldest Italian tower clock for which any general description survives, however, was installed in the campanile of the chapel (now San Gottardo) of the Visconti palace at Milan in 1335. Nine years later a certain Antonio of Padua installed an automatic striking clock designed by Jacopo de' Dondi in the entrance tower of the Carrara Palace in Padua.[7] During the second half of the fourteenth century public clocks—though still without a dial or clock face—began to appear in the towers of civic buildings as well as in the bell towers of churches and are attested to in such northern cities as London, Paris, Rouen, and Metz.

Even if these technological advances reduced the tower duties of the Town Johnnie to winding the clock mechanism twice daily, the builders of medieval tower clocks seemed reluctant to eliminate his presence altogether and very often incorporated into their striking mechanism a pair of bronze or wooden Johnnies on either side of a bell, each with a hammer in one hand. These automated Johnnies (also known as jacquemarts, clock jacks, or quarter jacks) were visible from the ground and were activated at appointed times to strike the clock bell with their hammers just as their human counterparts had done.[8]

It may not have been until the last year of the fourteenth century that visual measurement of time's passage was introduced to tower clocks by attaching dials to the upper walls of the towers, either as a disc with digits rotating below a stationary pointer or as a stationary disc beneath a moving hour hand.[9] Whereas clock dials were useful only during daylight (and even then had to be faced to be read), clock bells continued to communicate the hour day or night to all within the radius of their sound. This aural component still informs those beyond sight of the tower and its dial and remains an integral part of much horological elaboration today.[10]

By the beginning of the fifteenth century public clocks were operating throughout Europe, in cities as distant as Seville and Moscow. The first striking clock in Russia appeared in the Moscow Kremlin during the reign of Grand Duke Vasilij I Dmitrievich (1389-1425).[11] In 1404 a Serbian monk named Lazarus (Lazar'), with the help of his Russian assistants, installed the new clock in a tower beside the Cathedral of the Annunciation. This clock reportedly cost Vasilij 150 rubles, a considerable sum at that time.[12] A passage in the Troitskij Chronicle conveys something of the chronicler's astonishment at the presence of such an instrument in the Kremlin: "This clock (*chasnik*") is called chronographer; for on every hour it strikes a bell with a hammer, measuring and keeping count of the hours night and day; and not by a man striking [a bell], but in a human manner the clock is self-ringing and self-moving. For it has been created, has evolved, and has been elaborated in a marvelous manner by human ingenuity."[13]

A miniature from the second Ostermanovskij volume shows the clockmaker Lazarus standing between Vasilij and two of his retainers on the lower right and the newly built clock in the upper left (figure 41). He appears to be explaining to the duke how the automatic striking mechanism operates. On the front of the bell tower is mounted the clock dial, below which hang three weights—two small and one large—and above which is poised a hammer to strike the outer surface of a bell that is hung (also with a clapper) within the tower and a little above the clock mechanism. Numbers from 1 to 12 are inscribed on the clock dial, expressed as letters or combinations of letters in the Cyrillic alphabet.[14] Since no hand or hands are shown on the clock, the dial must have rotated counterclockwise, probably indicating the correct hour at the top directly below the stem of the hammer.

Two other tower clocks with striking mechanisms were reported in Russia in the fifteenth century. In 1436 Archbishop Evfimij of Novgorod had a striking clock installed above his stone palace.[15] Another was recorded at Pskov in 1477: "Bishop Theofil, when he reached the Cathedral of the Holy Trinity, ordered his own foremen to install a self-striking clock at the Snetogorskij Monastery. That clock the bishop himself had sent earlier through his boyar Avtoman to the Cathedral of the Life-Giving Trinity. . . ."[16]

Chiming Clocks

Toward the end of the fourteenth century tower clocks began to acquire a second bell, of different pitch from the first, on which the "ting-tang" quarters could be struck between the hours. In time a third and fourth bell appeared, each with a new pitch,[17] which permitted the striking of hours on one bell—normally the largest, heaviest, and lowest pitched—and the striking of quarters on some combination of the other three. A clock equipped with five bells gained even greater melodic flexibility.

Actual tunes were probably first rung on clock bells sometime after 1400, and they were refined as the fifteenth century progressed.[18] But it was only during the sixteenth century that chimes came into general use in Europe. As more and more bells were connected to clock mechanisms, clock jacks began to disappear and the *voorslag*, or "forestrike," arose. This brief melodic flourish was originally sounded as a signal before the striking of the hour, then extended to mark the subdivisions of the hour as well. The further elaboration of the *voorslag* eventually gave rise to Flemish and Dutch carillons.[19] Thus the utilitarian striking clock was gradually transformed into a musical instrument of commanding importance in the towns and cities of the Low Countries.

Although no unequivocal line can be drawn between the number of bells that constitute a simple striking clock and the number that qualify an instrument as a chiming clock, one or two bells are generally present in the former, whereas three to twelve or even fifteen bells are present in the latter. During the fifteenth and sixteenth centuries simple tunes were playable on chimes of eight bells whose pitches conformed roughly to a diatonic scale.[20] The addition to an octave of bells of an augmented fourth (e.g., F sharp in the key of C major) and a minor seventh (e.g., B flat in C major) gave greater flexibility and facilitated melodic modula-

42. The clock bell and their hammers that strike the quarters in the tenth tier of the Spasskij Gate, Moscow Kremlin. From Barten'ev, *Moskovskij Kreml'*; 131, fig. 144.

The chiming drum, barrel, or cylinder, as it is variously called, was originally a section of a tree trunk into which spikes were driven.[21] Later it was made of metal and perforated with rows of holes. There were as many rows of holes encircling it as there were bells in the tower to be rung and as many holes in each row as wires from the bells. Pegs were carefully preset in the cylinder's holes to produce the desired tune automatically when the cylinder, mounted on a horizontal axis, was revolved. If the pegs were accurately set, a tune could be played that was melodically and rhythmically precise, even if it could not be inflected dynamically before about 1650.[22]

Clocks and Chimes in the Kremlin's Spasskij Gate

Among the largest of the chimes attached to clock mechanisms in seventeenth-century Russia were those installed in towers over gates to the Moscow Kremlin (figure 43), and the bells in the Spasskij Tower are today the most famous of all clock chimes in the Soviet Union. Set into the east wall of the Kremlin, which borders Red Square, the Spasskij Gate is the most imposing and, in the opinion of many, the most beautiful of the entrances to the Kremlin (figure 44).[23] This gate, whose lower portion was designed and built in 1491 by the Milanese architect Pietro Antonio Solario, provided access to the Kremlin for the tsar, foreign princes, emperors, and ambassadors and their retinues, as well as egress for ceremonial processions associated with services in the Kremlin's churches. Originally known as the Frolovskij, after the Church of Saints Frol and Lavr, which stood nearby, the gate was renamed Spasskij (Saviour) in 1658 in recognition of an icon of Jesus Christ that hung above the entrance that faced on Red Square.[24]

Not even an approximate date for the first clock in the Spasskij Tower can be suggested. That a clock was operating in the tower sometime between 1491 and 1585, and presumably soon after the original gate was finished in 1491, is indirectly documented in a notice of 1585, which reports the salary of a clock technician for the gate.[25] The Godunov plan

tions and transpositions to the dominant and subdominant keys (G major and F major respectively in a C-major chime).

Chimes can be played in three different ways. Though chime bells are traditionally stationary in their mounting, one or more can be fixed to a headstock swung by ropes on a wheel so that they can be rung from the base of a tower. A single player can also ring them by hand from below through a console with levers that are wired to the clappers inside the bells. Alternatively, a revolving cylinder can be placed in the tower to sound the bells automatically at predetermined intervals. Wires control hammers that are poised to strike the bells' exterior surface when the rotating cylinder releases them to fall on the sound-bow (figure 42).

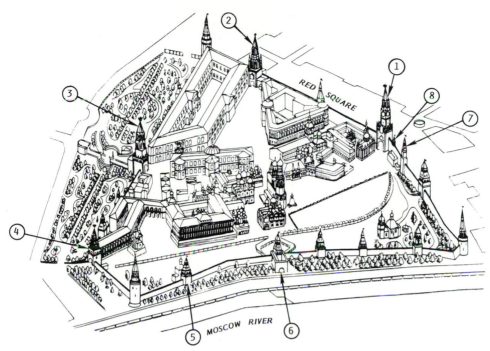

43. Plan of the Moscow Kremlin as it appeared in the nineteenth century. In addition to the Ivan Velikij Bell Tower on Cathedral Square, bells or clocks were installed in the following structures on the Kremlin walls: (1) the Spasskij Gate, (2) the Nikol'skij Gate, (3) the Troitskij Gate, (4) the Borovitskij Gate, (5) the Blagoveshchenskij Tower, (6) the Tajnitskij Gate, (7) the Nabatnyj Tower, and (8) the Tsarskij Tower. From N. Ia. Tikhomirov and V. N. Ivanov, *Moskovskij Kreml'* (Moscow, 1967), 207. Permission of VAAP, Moscow.

of the Kremlin (figure 45) shows no clock dial on the outer façade of the tower. But in 1624 and 1625, Bazhen Ogurtsov, a Russian stonemason, designed and built an ornate upper tower in white stone and brick above Solario's original structure to receive a *new* clock, with its mechanism and bells.[26] Christopher Galloway, a clockmaker from England in the service of the tsar since 1621, supervised the installation of the new clock, its chiming mechanism, and the thirteen bells that Kirill Samojlov had founded.[27] For his work on this clock the tsar conferred on him a large bonus of 100 rubles.

But no sooner had work been completed than a fire in May of 1626 spread into the Spasskij Tower and destroyed Galloway's new clock and all of Samojlov's bells. Restoration and replacement were undertaken a second time, and another clock and a new set of bells were installed and put into operation. Galloway remained in Moscow to serve as technician for the clock for at least a dozen years.[28]

On October 5, 1654, when an epidemic of plague was beginning to abate and while Tsar Aleksei Mikhailovich was away at Smolensk on his Polish campaign, another fire, which had begun before dawn in the wooden interior of the Spasskij Gate, destroyed Galloway's second clock. As the tower's vaulting gave way, Samojlov's clock bells crashed through the structure and shattered.[29] Four months later Patriarch Makarius of Antioch arrived in Moscow with his son and attendant, Archdeacon Paul of Aleppo. Though Paul had not actually witnessed the destruction of the tower, he recorded in his journal what Muscovites had told him about the fire.

44. The Spasskij Gate from Red Square and the Tsarskij Tower on the Kremlin wall (left). From Barten'ev, *Moskovskij Kreml'*, [p. 122], fig. 116.

Above the gate looms an enormous tower, a tall edifice on solid foundations, in which there was located a wonderful city clock made of iron, famous everywhere for its beauty and its mechanism, and for the loud sound of its large bell, which was heard not only throughout the entire city, but even in surrounding villages more than 10 versts away. Last Christmas, because of the devil's viciousness, the wooden beams within the clock caught fire and the entire tower was enveloped in flames together with its clock, bells, and all of their accessory parts which, on falling, by their weight destroyed two vaults of brick and stone. And this rare, marvelous thing—whose restoration to its former state would require an outlay of more than 25,000 dinars [rubles] for workers alone—was ruined. And when from a distance, the tsar laid eyes on this beautiful, gutted tower, whose

decorations and weather vanes were disfigured and [whose] various statues, skillfully carved from stone, were brought down, he shed many tears.[30]

Once more the tower was restored, and a third clock built and installed. Baron von Meyerberg, in Moscow between 1661 and 1662 on an embassy from Emperor Leopold I, has left a description of the new clock "in the Frolovskij Tower above the Spasskij Gate": "It indicates the hour of the day from sunrise to sunset. At the summer solstice, when the days are longest, this clock . . . strikes up to 17 times, and the night then lasts 7 hours. Attached above on the wall is a fixed image of the sun with a pointer, which indicates the hours on a revolving disc, which contains the hours. This clock is the largest in Moscow."[31]

The diameter of the clock dial, according to Meyerberg, was 7.25 arshins (almost 17 feet). In a border around the disc were seventeen gilded copper letters and combinations of letters from the Cyrillic alphabet, and in an inner border were corresponding Arabic numbers from 1 to 17. The disc rotated slowly so that at any given time the correct hour was always at the top directly beneath the lowest ray of the sun's face that was mounted above (figure 46). The restoration of the clock in the Spasskij Gate after the fire of 1654 was followed by another in 1668, when the rusty parts were cleaned by boiling them in an alkaline solution. By the end of the seventeenth century, however, the Spasskij clock had broken down and was in all probability destroyed in the Kremlin fire of 1701.[32]

Soon after his calendar reform of 1700, which brought Russia into the fold of European time, Peter the Great decided to place a Dutch clock in the Spasskij Gate with a twelve-hour dial in the German manner and with bells on which tunes could be played. Peter had heard such chiming clocks during his recent sojourn in Holland, and in 1702 he ordered three Dutch clocks of this kind for Russian towers. By 1704 two of the three had arrived through the northern port of Arkhangel'sk and from there were transported on thirty carts to the residence where General Frants (Franz) Iakovlevich Lefort had lived in the *nemetskaia sloboda*, Moscow's quarter for foreign residents. The clock mechanism for the Spasskij Gate was then carried to the Oruzhejnaia palata in the Kremlin. An expert named J. Garnault supervised the installation of the clock's new twelve-hour dial. His assistants, who even worked on Sundays, had the mechanism in place the following year. And on December 9, 1706, at 9:00 A.M., the new Dutch clock struck for the first time; then at noon its chimes began to play.[33] Another three years were required, however, to complete work on this clock.

All too soon the clock began to show signs of wear. Already in 1732 the clock technician, Gavrila Panikadil'shchikov, noted that it stood in need of immediate repair. But Russian authorities took no action. In a second report he warned that the clock, from lack of attention, had reached the point of dilapidation. He even attached a list of materials needed to carry out the repairs. But his recommendations were still not heeded. Then in 1737 the Spasskij clock was destroyed by the same "Trinity Fire" that ruined the Motorins' Tsar-Kolokol and the clock in the Troitskij Gate as well as devastating much of Moscow.[34] Damage that the Spasskij Gate sustained in the fire was repaired, including restoration of the icon of the Saviour. But its clock was not, and for thirty years no chimes were heard.

In 1763 beneath the Kremlin's Granovitaia palata a large English clock was discovered whose identity has never been clearly established. Five years later Catherine II engaged a Berlin clockmaker name "Fatzi" to install this clock in the Spasskij Tower. His work was supervised by a Russian named Sukin, vice president of the College of Manufacturers in Moscow. When the work was finished in 1770, however, Muscovites were soon surprised: the German clock technicians under Fatzi's direction had pegged the chime cylinder in the Spasskij Tower to play the famous German song *Ach! du lieber Augustin* on Red Square.[35]

By the beginning of the nineteenth century, after almost a hundred years of neglect, the Spasskij Gate itself was rapidly approaching the point of structural collapse. The tower was renovated by order of Alexander I only to be severely damaged ten

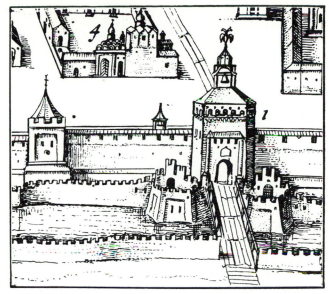

45. Details from the Godunov plan of the Moscow Kremlin (ca. 1605) showing the Spasskij Gate (1) in the Kremlin wall. A bell hangs in the cupola above the gate. In the Tsarskij Tower on the Kremlin wall just to the left of the Frolovskij Gate there is another bell. From Joan Blaeu, *Le Grand atlas ou cosmographie Blaviane* 2 (Amsterdam, 1663).

years later during the French occupation of Moscow. But destruction might have been complete. If someone had not discovered the fuses leading to mines planted under the tower, Solario's original structure of 1491 with its seventeenth-century additions would have been reduced to rubble. In 1815 a group of technicians under the direction of Iakov Lebedev put the clock back in operation. During general renovations of the Kremlin in the following years, the structure itself was further strengthened.

By the middle of the century the Spasskij clock had begun to malfunction once more, and its chimes no longer sounded. This time the Butenop brothers, clockmakers in Moscow, carried out the repairs in 1851 and 1852. They pegged the cylinder to play the hymn, *Kol' slaven" nash" Gospod' v" Sioně* (How glorious is our Lord in Zion), and the *Preobrazhenskij March* at noon, 3:00, 6:00, and 9:00 P.M.[36] At this time the architect Konstantin Ton designed a new metal structure inside the tower with a spiral staircase. Almost a quarter century later a clockmaker named Fremut noted that the

46. Dial of the mid-seventeenth-century clock on the Spasskij Gate, Moscow Kremlin. From Th. Adelung, *Al'bom" Mejerberga: Vidy i bytovyia kartiny Rossii XVII věka*, ed. and enl. A. M. Loviagin (St. Petersburg: 1903), 46, pl. 88. Permission of Sterling Memorial Library, Yale University.

slaven" and the *Preobrazhenskij March*, which had sounded from the Spasskij since the mid-nineteenth century, were pulled out of the chime cylinder, and Mikhail Mikhajlovich Cheremnykh reset the rotating mechanism to ring the beginning of the *Internationale* each noon and a funeral song of the Revolution *Vy zhertvoiu pali* (You fell in sacrifice), at midnight.[39] In October of 1932 on the eve of the fifteenth anniversary of the Revolution, Cheremnykh repaired the chiming mechanism and removed the latter song from the cylinder.[40]

Until 1937 the Spasskij clock had been wound by hand. In that year three electric motors were installed—one to activate the quarters, a second to sound the hours, and another to drive the hands on the clock dial. Today the hour mechanism is electrically wound twice daily. The clock, with its bells, drive mechanism, and machinery for striking the hours and sounding the quarters, occupies the seventh, eight, ninth, and tenth stories of the tower. In the open tier beneath the tent-shaped roof there are nine bells that sound the quarter hours and a large bell of more than 2.33 tons that strikes the hours.[41] The clock bells in the Spasskij Gate are famous throughout the world as the Kremlin chimes (*kremlevskie kuranty*). Their music, now broadcast daily over Radio Moscow throughout the Soviet Union, inspired Lenin's paean to the future at the end of Pogodin's play.[42]

Clocks and Chimes in Other Russian Towers

Though the Spasskij Gate housed the largest and most important clock in the Moscow Kremlin, clock technicians are also mentioned in 1585 for the Troitskij (Trinity) and Tajnitskij (Secret) Gates.[43] By the end of the sixteenth century, then, clocks had presumably been installed in the towers of all three gates on the west, south, and east walls of the Kremlin. In the early seventeenth century a clock technician was also cited for the Nikol'skij Gate (see figure 43),[44] but after 1614 no further mention is made. This clock, if it ever existed, was likely ruined in the same fire of 1626 that destroyed the clock in the Spasskij Gate.[45]

iron parts of the clock had almost rusted through and that the entire mechanism stood in need of basic repairs. Fremut was hired to carry out these repairs and was afterwards appointed clock technician for the Spasskij Gate at a salary of 175 rubles a year.[37] The last restoration during the old regime was undertaken in 1911, when A. V. Ivanov renovated the gate itself and M. V. Volynskij repaired the clock mechanism and its bells.[38]

In October 1917 the Spasskij clock suddenly stopped when artillery shells struck it during the Red Guards' attacks on the Kremlin. Then on Lenin's order, Nikolaj Vasil'evich Berens, a metal craftsman and watchmaker in the Kremlin, made necessary repairs during the summer and early fall of 1918. At that time the two tsarist pieces *Kol'*

In the Godunov plan of the Kremlin a cupola appears above the Tajnitskij Gate in which a single bell is hanging (figure 47). Meyerberg alludes to a striking clock in this gate between 1661 and 1663: "Besides this one [the clock above the Spasskij Gate], there is still another loud striking clock in the Kremlin castle on the other side by the Moscow River; there are no others."[46] Records show that in 1674 the clock in the Tajnitskij Gate was removed.[47] Of four Kremlin clocks apparently functioning at the beginning of the seventeenth century, only two remained in operation after 1674—in the Spasskij and Troitskij Gates.

After the Spasskij clock, the most important Kremlin clock and chimes were those in the tower above the Troitskij (Trinity) Gate (figure 48). Constructed in 1495 on the Kremlin's northwestern wall, the Troitskij Gate was named after the Trinity Monastery, located at one time within the Kremlin near this gate, and provided access to the patriarchal court. By 1585 the Troitskij displayed a clock dial about twenty-eight inches (one arshin) in diameter and contained three bells.[48] In 1613-1614 a clock technician for the Troitskij Gate is mentioned together with those who serviced clocks in the other Kremlin gates. During the mid-seventeenth century the condition of the Troitskij Gate itself steadily deteriorated until much needed repairs were undertaken after 1667.

Tsar Fedor in 1681 ordered a technician named Andreianko Danilov to build a larger clock for the Troitskij Gate. Its dial was to be 1.75 arshins (49 inches) in diameter, and six new bells were to be cast at the Moscow Cannon Yard in weights of 4, 3, 2, 1, 1, and ½ puds (144, 108, 72, 36, 36, and 18 pounds) and added to the three already present. The hour bell was one that Fedor Motorin cast in 1686.[49] In 1685 the Troitskij Gate attained its present height with additions of white stone and brick similar to those already made to the Spasskij Gate. The following year the new clock, with its hour bell and eight smaller bells, was hoisted into the tower.[50]

The new clock and bells of 1686 did not serve long in the Troitskij Gate, for they were replaced by one of the Dutch clocks and chimes that Peter

47. Detail of the Tajnitskij Gate (13) from the Godunov plan of the Moscow Kremlin (ca. 1605). A bell hangs in the cupola above the gate. From Blaeu, *Le Grand atlas ou cosmographie Blaviane.*

the Great had ordered in 1702. By 1705 installation of the new clock was already in progress, but it began to malfunction shortly after Peter's death in 1725. The chimes had already stopped playing in 1731, and at the end of February 1734 the Petersburg carillonneur Johann Förster was assigned to Moscow to repair the clock mechanism. Förster found twenty-six bells in the tower, to which he required the addition of eight lower-pitched bells before he would work on them.[51] He further informed the Senate that the location of the Troitskij Gate was acoustically quite ill-suited for bell music; the ringing would be muffled and poorly heard. But Förster's advice notwithstanding, the Senate ordered bell music restored to the Troitskij Gate, and Förster selected eight compatible bells at the Moscow Cannon Yard to fill out the lower range of the bells already in the tower. Three years later, in the spring of 1737, the Troitskij clock and its bells melted during the Trinity Fire.[52]

Förster returned to Moscow in 1757 to repair the chiming clock in the Troitskij Gate. Whether he actually repaired the clock then is not known.

48. The Troitskij Gate as it appeared before its restoration in 1900. The Kutaf'ia Tower is in the foreground. From Barten'ev, *Moskovskij Kreml'*, [p. 151], fig. 167.

A document from 1775 is preserved that again directs that the clock be put in working order, and nine years later a new clock was built for the gate. Even if the automatic chiming mechanism, which had been connected to the clock, was no longer functioning at this time, its bells were still capable of being played manually, since *Sviatyj Bozhe* (Holy God) had been rung on them at the funeral of Count Chernyshev in 1784 and at the last rites of other prominent Muscovites.[53]

As part of the Kremlin restoration that Alexander I financed soon after his accession to the throne, the Troitskij Gate received the structural attention it needed, but not its clock and chimes. In 1812 the large hour bell again fell (as it had in 1737) and lay useless until 1848 when it was removed and placed with the bells of the Church of St. John the Baptist in the Borovitskij Gate.[54] A fire of 1823 in the Troitskij Tower's fifth tier melted the clock mechanism and twenty-nine bells of various sizes. After this fire the clock was not repaired, and in 1848 its remaining bells were transferred to the clock in the Great Kremlin Palace.[55]

In addition to the striking tower clocks once present in four of the Kremlin's gates, the open watch chamber under the tent roof of the Blagoveshchenskij (Annunciation) Tower (see figure 43) also served briefly as a belfry at the beginning of the eighteenth century. At that time the Blagoveshchenskij received seven bells and functioned as a bell tower for the Church of the Annunciation adjacent to it.[56]

Elsewhere in Moscow chiming clocks were installed in the early eighteenth century at the Vysokopetrovskij Monastery and at the Church of the Archangel Gabriel, also known as the Menshikov Tower. In 1702 a clockmaker named Ivan Zakhar'ev was contracted to build a clock mechanism at the Vysokopetrovskij Monastery. A monastery inventory of 1763 describes the clock as a German one with eight bells; and a later document of 1777 records that the clock underwent repairs.[57] A chiming clock, purchased in London according to Rozanov, was installed in the Menshikov Tower sometime before 1711, when Peter the Great called bell foremen and clockmakers from Holland to service the clocks of Moscow, including the one in the Menshikov Tower. This clock sounded the hour and quarters and at noon played music for half an hour.[58] On June 14, 1723, a bolt of lightning struck the tower and set it on fire. The flames eventually burned through the oak beams on which the bells hung, and a number of persons in the church below the tower were killed when the bells broke loose and plummeted to the ground.[59]

A few of Moscow's tower clocks were built in this century. Shortly after the completion of a building on Novaia Square in 1911 the Moscow firm of A. A. Ėnodin installed a clock in its tower whose six bells were cast at the Finliandskij foundry in Moscow. Its bells, heard for thirty years, were silenced when a bomb that fell in this vicinity during a night air raid in the fall of 1941 damaged the clock's mechanism and knocked its dials from their sockets. Since August 7, 1964, however, the restored clock and its bells have played *Smelo, tovarishchi, v nogu* (Boldly, comrades, in step) on the hour and an abbreviated version of the same on the quarters.[60] The largest clock in the Soviet Union today is near the top of one of the towers of Moscow State University. Installed in 1953 at a height of 249.34 feet, it is also the highest tower clock in the country.[61]

One of the oldest tower clocks in Russia was at the Church of the Archangel Gabriel in the Kirillo-Belozerskij Monastery in northern Russia.[62] Clocks were presumably operating at this monastery in the late fifteenth and sixteenth centuries, and by the end of the sixteenth, "two clocks, one striking and the other for the gates" had been given to the monastery. An inventory of 1601 reports a striking clock in the monastery with two small bells. Exactly when and by whom these clocks for the Kirillo-Belozerskij Monastery were built cannot be determined, but by the end of the nineteenth century, they were no longer extant.[63]

In the mid-seventeenth century on his way from Syria to Moscow, Paul of Aleppo described in some detail the operation of the mechanism for a tower clock at Jassy in Moldavia.[64] He also reported a large iron clock in the tallest of two four-story wooden bell towers at the Kievo-Pecherskaia Lavra, a clock whose bells carried a great distance.[65] Another clock there hung from the exterior of the stone bell tower for the Church of the Trinity. In the evening when the larger clock had finished striking twenty-four hours, it also repeatedly struck a loud warning on an iron beam so those outside the monastery could enter the enclosure before the gates were locked for the night.[66] The present bell tower in the Kievo-Pecherskaia Lavra, built between 1731 and 1745 on a design by J. Schädel, received a chiming clock as soon as it was finished. At the very beginning of the twentieth century Énodin gave this tower a new chiming clock with a mechanism similar to that in the Spasskij Gate of the Moscow Kremlin.[67] Other sixteenth- and sev-

enteenth-century clocks were reported in Russia at the Pafnut'ev-Borovskij Monastery near Kaluga, at the Savvino-Storozhevskij Monastery near Zvenigorod, at the Solovetskij Monastery on an island in the White Sea, at both the Cathedral of the Nativity and the Spaso-Yefim'ev Monastery in Suzdal, and at Kolomenskoe near Moscow.[68] But all of the clocks in Russia, whose bells had marked the passage of time for three centuries since Lazarus' Kremlin clock of 1404, were eclipsed in the early eighteenth century by the carillon that Peter the Great imported from Holland and installed in the cathedral tower in the Peter and Paul Fortress in St. Petersburg.

8

Tuned Bells in Imperial Russia

THE CARILLON developed in the Low Countries in the sixteenth and early seventeenth centuries from the *voorslag*, or "forestrike," on simple tower chimes, but a distinction between chimes and carillons has always been maintained.[1] The bells in both a chime and carillon are fixed to a beam and are therefore stationary, but a carillon has more bells. Whereas eight to twelve bells diatonically tuned—almost always to a major scale—constitute a typical chime, a carillon has twenty-three to seventy or more bells (usually between thirty-five and forty-nine) tuned chromatically. A carillon therefore embraces three to four chromatic octaves.[2] Like a chime, a carillon normally includes a mechanism for automatic playing. But in addition to a keyboard a carillon is also equipped with pedals to provide greater flexibility in performance. And the more precise tuning of the carillon bells permits them to be sounded together consonantly in chords and polyphonic textures.[3] Because chime bells, on the other hand, are normally played melodically, one at a time, their tuning has never been quite so exacting.

The golden age of Dutch carillon building was launched circa 1640 with the arrival in Holland of two bell founders from Lorraine, the brothers Frans and Pieter Hemony. From 1642 until about 1680 the Hemony brothers were responsible, both individually and jointly, for casting about fifty of the world's finest carillons.[4] Automatic striking of the hour and brief ripples of music from a few bells on the subdivisions of the hour had been part of the mechanism in European tower clocks for centuries. But the genius of the Hemony brothers in bell tuning coincided with new technical refinements that Dutch clockmakers introduced in tower clocks. And with these improvements came a tower clock that combined accuracy and dependability with a cylinder for the automatic playing of intricate polyphonic music on the bells of a well-tuned carillon. The nuances of live performances by a carillonneur on a keyboard and pedals could be successfully emulated for the first time in Dutch tower clocks during the latter part of the seventeenth century.[5]

About 150 carillons were built in the seventeenth and eighteenth centuries, and of these, about 120 were installed in towers in the Low Countries. The rest were exported to countries as far away as Portugal and Russia.[6] By the time of the French Revolution, however, with the finest years of Dutch and Flemish carillon manufacture already passed, many carillon bells in France were being melted down for gun metal. Napoleonic France witnessed further dismantling of carillons for recasting as weapons. In fact, according to some estimates, fully two-thirds of all European carillons extant in 1800 had been destroyed by the end of Napoleon's reign.[7] But by that time music from St. Petersburg's second Dutch carillon had been heard from the tower in the Peter and Paul Fortress for almost four decades.

49. The cathedral and its bell tower in the Peter and Paul Fortress, Leningrad. From Igor Grabar, *Russkaia arkhitektura pervoj poloviny XVIII veka* (Moscow, 1954), opp. p. 120. Permission of VAAP, Moscow.

The First Petersburg Carillon

Few eighteenth-century monuments in St. Petersburg reveal the extent of Peter the Great's uncompromising Westernization of Russia more than the Dutch carillon and clock that he had installed in the still unfinished tower of the Cathedral of Saints Peter and Paul in 1720.[8] European bell music, Pe-

ter thus decreed, would crown the new Baltic capital of Russia.

Peter would have heard the bells of several Hemony carillons as well as carillons cast by other Dutch founders during his first visit to Holland in 1697-1698. There were more than half a dozen Hemony carillons in towers at Amsterdam and Leiden at this time, and others in the vicinity of Zaandam. His second exposure to carillon music would have come in 1716-1717 when he visited Bruges, Ostende, Brussels, Namur, and Liège.[9] During this journey, if not earlier, he must have resolved to purchase, perhaps even commissioned, a carillon for the tower of the new cathedral rising inside the fortress in St. Petersburg.

Peter brought his first architect, Domenico Trezzini (ca. 1670-1734), to St. Petersburg from Denmark in 1703 and appointed him to build a new masonry fortress and a large stone cathedral dedicated to Saints Peter and Paul within the fortress.[10] The tower of Trezzini's new cathedral in the northern Protestant style was designed to accommodate the bells and mechanism of a Dutch carillon and clock in addition to a zvon of Russian bells (figure 49). With this structure, Peter broke away from over three centuries of Russian architectural precedents in the Moscow Kremlin.[11] A North German baroque cathedral designed by an Italian-Swiss architect (who had served Frederick IV in Copenhagen) and equipped with a Dutch carillon epitomized the eclectic West European character of the new Russian capital.[12]

Though the cathedral's spire was not completed until the fall of 1723 and work on the sanctuary continued for another decade, the lower stone portion of the tower was finished in 1718, and the first clock and carillon was installed in 1720. St. Petersburg then stood beside Stockholm, Riga, and, a few years later, Danzig, as Baltic ports that owned Dutch carillons.[13] And above the city—with its brooding fortress, busy streets and canals, noisy markets, and bustling docks—the air glistened with the music of the carillon. Peter even favored his new Dutch carillon with architectural primacy in the city. The glint of gold from the cathedral's stiletto flèche, once in place, was the first sign of St.

50. Looking upstream on the Neva toward the Peter and Paul Fortress and Domenico Trezzini's cathedral (before the fire of 1756), St. Petersburg. Engraving after a drawing by M. Makhayev reproduced in Nigel Gosling, *Leningrad: History, Art, Architecture* (London, 1965), 24. Reprinted with permission of Macmillan Publishing Co., from *Leningrad* by Nigel Gosling, as proprietors for Cassel & Co., Ltd. and Studio Vista.

Petersburg to greet the eye of eighteenth-century voyagers as they sailed up the Neva from the Gulf of Finland (figure 50).[14]

Several questions concerning the first Petersburg carillon remain unanswered. Though it was presumably ordered from Holland in 1720, no documents have survived that shed light on the negotiations for the instrument—its commission and contract or the name of the Dutch foundry or founder that cast the bells.[15] The cost of the carillon is a matter of record—45,000 rubles, an enormous sum at that time.[16] We also know that the instrument combined both a carillon with a keyboard (probably including pedals) and a clock mechanism with an automatic chiming cylinder. Each of the thirty-five bells was equipped with two hammers and a clapper.[17] The hammers, which struck the exterior surface of the bells and were controlled by the chiming cylinder, permitted relatively rapid repetitions of strokes. From the clappers inside the bells ran wires connected to levers on the console that the carillonneur could operate. The clock mechanism struck the quarters and the half-hours and played the bells automatically every hour, and at noon each day Johann Christian För-

ster performed selections on the bells.[18] The technician responsible for maintaining the instrument was a man by the curious name of Drunk Miller.

We do not know the pitches of the bells in the first Petersburg carillon, but if the lowest pitched bell was middle C (*c*), as was that of the second carillon (excluding the Quint bell), its thirty-five bells would conceivably have embraced a three-octave range that included the pitches shown in Table 1.[19] This being the case, the first octave, as Percival Price has pointed out, would have lacked the two lowest chromatic notes.[20]

An entry in the diary of Friedrich Wilhelm von Bergholz on August 7, 1721, contains an account of his visit to the tower of the cathedral in the fortress and his impression of the performance by Förster and two of his pupils on the new carillon.

At 12 noon we all . . . climbed the bell tower in the

TABLE 1
Possible Tunings of the Thirty-Five Bells
of the First Petersburg Carillon

Octave	No. of bells	Pitches
First	10	c d e f f$^\sharp$ g g$^\sharp$ a a$^\sharp$ b
Second	12	c^1 c$^{\sharp 1}$ d^1 d$^{\sharp 1}$ e^1 f^1 f$^{\sharp 1}$ g^1 g$^{\sharp 1}$ a^1 a$^{\sharp 1}$ b^1
Third	12	c^2 c$^{\sharp 2}$ d^2 d$^{\sharp 2}$ e^2 f^2 f$^{\sharp 2}$ g^2 g$^{\sharp 2}$ a^2 a$^{\sharp 2}$ b^2
Fourth	1	c^3

NOTE: This table is formulated from Ruban's information on the first Petersburg carillon transmitted in Dimitrij Florinskij, *Istoriko-statis-ticheskoe opisanie sanktpeterburgskago Petropavlovskago kathedral'nago sobora* (St. Petersburg: Tip. Georga Benike, 1857), 3; and from Percival Price's "The Carillons of the Cathedral of Peter and Paul in the Fortress of Leningrad," *The Galpin Society Journal* 17 (February 1964), 67.

fortress to listen to the playing of the chimes scheduled at this time and to survey the panorama of Petersburg. This bell tower is the tallest in the city; there it is extremely interesting to watch the musician's performance, especially for someone who has not seen anything like that. I, however, would not choose his profession for myself because it demands difficult and strenuous movements of the body. He had hardly played one selection when sweat was already pouring from his face. He also made his two Russian pupils play. They had been studying with him not more than a few months but were already playing fairly well. The great clock strikes automatically every quarter-hour and half-hour.[21]

Unfortunately, Bergholz did not record the titles of the selections performed on this occasion.

Almost four hundred feet high from its base to the tip of the cross on its spire, the cathedral tower in the Peter and Paul Fortress did not fail to attract bolts of lightning during electrical storms. In the summers of 1735 and 1748 lightning started two fires in the tower, but both were extinguished before they could cause serious damage. The thunderstorm on the night of April 29-30, 1756, was another matter. When lightning struck the tower about 11:00 P.M., it went unnoticed. Fire gained a foothold, and within two hours the tower's flèche was enveloped in flames. The next morning Trezzini's golden spire had vanished, the tower's wooden

interior was completely gutted, and the Dutch bells of Russia's first carillon had melted in the inferno.[22]

The Second Petersburg Carillon

Not long after the disastrous fire at the Cathedral of Saints Peter and Paul, Empress Elisabeth Petrovna made plans for the reconstruction of the tower and for the purchase of a new clock and carillon. Restoration of the paintings on the vaults in the sanctuary, damaged by the fire in the bell tower, was completed about fourteen months later, on June 23, 1757, when the consecration of the cathedral took place.[23] But the replacement of the carillon was not so quickly or easily resolved.

The empress had enjoined the Chancery for the Construction of Court Buildings and Gardens to replace the clock mechanism and bells in the shortest possible time. Drunk Miller, technician for the first clock and carillon, was the first to submit a proposal, one that called for a dozen foremen, as many skilled assistants, plus up to fifty capable blacksmiths from Sestroretsk near St. Petersburg or the Tula iron foundries.[24] The Senate immediately rejected this hastily drawn plan, since Miller would neither agree in writing to certain specifications nor guarantee the success of the project. Instead, less than two weeks after the fire the chancery chairman authorized Count Aleksandr Gavriilovich Golovkin, the Russian ambassador extraordinary to Holland and privy councilor, to purchase a second Dutch carillon and clock for the cathedral in the Petersburg fortress. Golovkin, instructed to commission the founding of a new carillon if one was not on hand for shipment, accepted a proposal from Barend Oortkras, a clockmaker at The Hague, to cast the bells for the carillon at the foundry of Johannes Nicolaus Derck in Hoorn. Oortkras himself would be in charge of building the clock mechanism and supervising preparations for and the installation of the bells and machinery in the cathedral tower.

Oortkras offered Petersburg the option of purchasing a carillon of thirty-seven bells whose largest bell would weigh 3,200 pounds and be pitched on middle C, or the same carillon plus a Quint bell. The projected weight of the Quint bell was 7,000 pounds, or more than twice that of the largest bell in the basic set. It would be pitched on G, a perfect fourth below middle C. The cost of the second option—with thirty-eight bells, keyboard with pedals, chiming mechanism and cylinder, hammers, and copper wire—was 80,084 guilders 12 stivers, or 32,033 rubles 84 kopecks. The Senate approved the proposal that included the Quint bell and authorized Golovkin to conclude the contract with Oortkras, which both parties signed on July 7, 1757.[25]

Specifications for the second Petersburg carillon were quite detailed (see table 2). Its thirty-seven numbered bells (excluding no. 38, the Quint bell) were designed to cover and slightly exceed a three-octave range from middle C to $d^{\sharp 3}$.

In his study of the two St. Petersburg carillons Percival Price discusses three unusual specifications of the second instrument. He finds the addition at great cost of the G (Quint bell) a fourth below c, the omission of d^3, and the inclusion of $d^{\sharp 3}$ completely indefensible from a purely musical standpoint and concludes that these extensions at either end of the gamut were included so that St. Petersburg's second carillon might be an instrument of slightly greater range than those owned by other eastern Baltic cities.[26] Price notes, however, that instead of a Quint bell on G as specified, a bell pitched on A was actually produced, tuned a minor third rather than a perfect fourth below c.

A second specification called for a keyboard of thirty-seven keys or batons in addition to twenty to twenty-three pedals, unusual on eighteenth-century carillons but theoretically commendable in a very large instrument's design. The more bells whose clappers could be controlled by pedals, the more polyphonic flexibility the instrument would possess. But to specify from twenty to twenty-three pedals on a carillon with a keyboard of only thirty-seven bells was to reduce the number of bells that were not controlled by pedals to between fourteen and seventeen. Apparently Oortkras was to decide in St. Petersburg the exact number of pedals that would be provided.[27] The specification is puzzling.

TABLE 2
Specifications for the Oortkras-Derck Carillon of 1757 for
St. Petersburg

No. of bell	No. of hammers	Pitch of bell	Wt. of bell (lbs.)	Wt. of hammer (lbs.)	Wt. of clapper (lbs.)
38	—	G (Quint)	7,000	—	—
1	2	c	3,200	198	150
2	2	d	2,280	138	91
3	2	e	1,620	99	65
4	2	f	1,430	88	58
5	2	f$^{\sharp}$	1,140	71	45
6	2	g	1,040	64	42
7	2	g$^{\sharp}$	850	53	34
8	2	a	698	44	28
9	2	a$^{\sharp}$	620	38	25
10	2	b	490	28	19
11	3	c^1	450	43	18
12	3	c$^{\sharp 1}$	370	33	15
13	3	d^1	310	30	12
14	3	d$^{\sharp 1}$	270	24	11
15	3	e^1	234	23	9
16	3	f^1	204	20	8
17	3	f$^{\sharp 1}$	171	18	8
18	3	g^1	157	16	7
19	3	g$^{\sharp 1}$	128	13	6
20	3	a^1	108	11	5
21	3	a$^{\sharp 1}$	98	10	4
22	3	b^1	83	9	3.5
23	3	c^2	78	9	3
24	3	c$^{\sharp 2}$	64	8.5	2.5
25	3	d^2	53	8	2
26	3	d$^{\sharp 2}$	46	8	2
27	3	e^2	38	7.75	1.75
28	3	f^2	34	7.5	1.5
29	3	f$^{\sharp 2}$	33	7	1.33
30	3	g^2	30	6.75	1.166
31	3	g$^{\sharp 2}$	26	6	1
32	3	a^2	22	5.5	1
33	3	a$^{\sharp 2}$	19	4	.75
34	3	b^2	17	3.75	.75
35	3	c^3	16	3	.5
36	3	c$^{\sharp 3}$	15	2.75	.5
37	3	d$^{\sharp 3}$	14.5	2.5	.33
Total	101		16,506.5 lbs. (without Quint bell)	1,843 lbs.	[683.576 lbs.]

NOTE : Dimitrij Florinskij, *Istoriko-statisticheskoe opisanie sanktpeterburg-skago Petropavlovskago kathedral'nago sobora* (St. Petersburg: Tip. Georga Benike, 1857), 10-11.

51. Relief and inscription bands on a bell of the Derck carillon of 1757 for the Cathedral of Saints Peter and Paul, Leningrad. The Latin inscription between the two ornamental friezes reads: "HOC OPUS DIREXIT B: F: OORTKRAS HAGAE/IOANNES NICOLAUS DERCK FECIT HORNAE" (B. F. Oortkras of The Hague supervised this work/Johann Nicolaus Derck of Hoorn made [this bell]). From Willy Godenne, *Cloches en URSS* (Malines, 1960), 9. Permission of Franz Peter Schilling, Apolda, E. Ger. and Koninklijke Beiaardschool "Jef Denyn," Mechelen (Malines).

A third unusual feature on the second Petersburg instrument was its projected equalized touch resistance on all the levers that controlled its bells. This, Price explains, would eliminate rapid movement on the smaller bells (required in eighteenth-century carillon music) and by making the touch on the larger bells as light as that for the smaller ones would significantly reduce possibilities for dynamic gradations. Price submits that Derck, the carillon's founder, may have been trying to pass off a poorly tuned instrument under the cover of a technical feature that on paper at least would appear to facilitate performance.[28]

Oortkras began work in Holland immediately, and in November of 1759, he notified Golovkin that the clock mechanism would be ready to ship to St. Petersburg by April of 1760. Oortkras further informed the ambassador that in addition to the one assistant provided in the contract, he would need four other salaried workers. Golovkin granted his request.[29]

By mid-summer of 1760 the carillon destined for St. Petersburg had been successfully cast, had passed inspection, and was transported to the dock to be loaded on the ship that would carry it to Russia (figure 51). On July 22 Oortkras and his five assistants sailed from Holland with the Derck bells, the clock mechanism, parts, and tools for the installation and finishing work. When the Dutchmen reached St. Petersburg toward the end of August, however, they discovered to their surprise and dismay that not only had the bell tower of the Cathedral of Saints Peter and Paul not yet been restored (as they had been given to believe) but that its renovation had not even begun.[30] A small wooden structure had to be built in which to store everything brought from Holland.

Although Oortkras remained in St. Petersburg for the rest of his life in hope of executing the task he had been contracted to perform, he was never to see his carillon installed in the tower of the cathedral or hear the music of its bells. Russian officials placed the accomplished Dutch clockmaker and his five assistants under the direction of Förster and the vindictive Miller, whose proposal the Senate had rejected in favor of the Oortkras plan. The four years of Oortkras' sojourn in the Russian capital were filled with Miller's unpleasant cavilling, which only exacerbated the Dutchman's frustration in his attempts to hasten the refurbishing of the tower so that he might install the carillon and return to Holland. The humiliations Oortkras endured in St. Petersburg may well have contributed to his death there on May 27, 1764.

The carillon remained in storage for more than a decade awaiting installation in the tower, and as Price pointedly notes, the instrument "still has the distinction of never having been paid for."[31] Only one of Oortkras' assistants remained in St. Petersburg for a time after his master died, but he refused the Senate's request to install the carillon, instead returning to Holland, as his four colleagues had.

In 1765 the Senate hired Johann Erdmann Rüdiger, a German clockmaker in St. Petersburg, to evaluate Oortkras' uninstalled clock. Upon examination, Rüdiger declared it to be an instrument of very skilled workmanship and a credit to its maker. But it was not until 1770, after the tower's base was almost finished, that the Russian bells of the cathedral's zvon were hoisted into the lowest tier. Six years later the Chancery for the Construction of Court Buildings and Gardens hired Rüdiger to install the clock and carillon and appointed him carillonneur and clock technician for life. By the end of 1776, after sixteen years of delay, Petersburg finally heard the music of its second Dutch carillon.

On weekdays, with the exception of Saturdays, Rüdiger performed for half an hour between 11:30 A.M. and noon.[32] On Sundays and other holidays, he played between noon and 2:00 P.M. He was also enjoined to change the music in his recitals every four weeks, and the selection of the music was left to his own discretion.[33] Music from the new carillon was thus established in St. Petersburg on a regular basis, but city officials were also notably far-sighted in their attempt to insure its perpetuity. A clause in Rüdiger's contract required him to apprentice five students, two of whom were to receive instruction in playing the carillon, while the other three were to be taught maintenance of the clock, its mechanism, and the bells.

The automatic chiming mechanism sounded the semiquarters, quarters, half-hour, and the hour. A few bells were heard briefly on the semiquarters; on the two quarter-hours several bells gave forth a small chime; and on the half hour the clock activated a number of bells but at only half of their potential volume. Chiming on the hour engaged all the bells at full volume. The half hour was struck on a small bell, and the hour on a large one.[34] In the mid-nineteenth century Florinskij mentions that the striking of the semiquarters had been eliminated. Otherwise, he reports, the chime still operated as it had at the end of the eighteenth century.[35]

When Rüdiger died in 1781, after serving only five years as carillonneur and clock technician, the Senate engaged Johann Georg Strasser to take his place in the cathedral tower. Strasser performed ably for eight years between 1781 and 1789 and through his successful supervision of three students left capable successors to continue his work. In 1817 his son Thoma Ivanov Strasser, Court Clock Master and Technician, was hired to dismantle and overhaul the clock mechanism after several decades of continual service. He also agreed to maintain and repair the clock for a ten-year period and to instruct six apprentices. Upon termination of Strasser's contract in 1827 his students assumed his work.[36]

During the 1830s, however, the carillon in the cathedral tower entered into a period of decline, and by about 1840—through neglect, insufficient funding by Petersburg authorities, or perhaps both—the chiming mechanism had deteriorated beyond use, and live performances on the carillon had ceased as well.[37] In 1858 the chiming mechanism was repaired, and until the October Revolution in 1917 it played *Kol' slaven"* every hour and *Bozhe, Tsaria khrani* (God, save the Tsar) once each day at noon.[38] But for twenty years after the revolution the bells again fell silent. Then on November 6, 1937, after the chiming mechanism had once more been put back in operation and its cylinder reset, Leningrad first heard the melody of the *Internationale* from the cathedral tower.

During the siege of Leningrad in World War II fragments from a bomb that exploded on the grounds of the fortress tore through the cathedral's spire. The impact from the explosion rocked the bell tower itself, forced the clock dials from their sockets, and caused the chime's largest bell to ring several times. Since 1952, following major restoration that began in 1947, flourishes from the clock chime are heard every fifteen minutes, and the melody of the national anthem of the Soviet Union,

Soiuz nerushimyj respublik svobodnykh (Unbreakable union of free republics), plays automatically at 6 A.M., noon, 6 P.M., and midnight.[39] But live performances by a carillonneur have not been heard since before 1840.

Of the five carillons that rang in eastern Baltic cities during the late seventeenth and eighteenth centuries, only the Derck instrument of 1757 for St. Petersburg has survived. The others have been destroyed in fires. A few Russian bells have been mixed with the Petersburg carillon, but the original Dutch instrument remains essentially intact and its performing mechanism could be completely restored at any time.[40]

When Peter the Great first planned his new capital on the Neva, he modeled it after Amsterdam with its canals and even gave it a Dutch name—Sankt Piter Bourkh. The city's design began to change when Jean-Baptiste Alexandre Leblond, who worked in St. Petersburg between 1716 and 1719, laid out the Nevsky Prospect and imposed the beginning of a French radial plan upon the original Dutch design of the city.[41] But for almost a hundred years the periodic flourishes sent forth from the bell tower in the Cathedral of Saints Peter and Paul remained resolutely Dutch, and the polyphony from these tuned bells made the soundscape of the new capital palpably different from that of Moscow, which was dominated by the powerful zvon of untuned Russian bells.

Aristarkh Izrailev's Tuning of Russian Church Bells

Forty years after the second Petersburg carillon had first fallen into disrepair and silence, Aristarkh Aleksandrovich Izrailev (1817-1901), a priest and teacher from Rostov-Velikij, briefly and single-handedly sought to promote Russian interest in harmonic-melodic tuning and Western methods of bell ringing.[42] But Izrailev's attempts to transform the character of Russian bells and bell ringing drew severe criticism, if not actual condemnation, from such campanologists as Rybakov, Privalov, and Olovianishnikov. They feared that his ideas would be far more deleterious to the deeply rooted tra-

dition of Russian zvon ringing than the mere presence of a few chiming clocks and two carillons.[43]

Beginning in 1842 Izrailev had been carrying on acoustical experiments in the physics of sound. He sought in particular to find more exact methods of measuring the number of vibrations generated by a ringing object, and for this purpose he produced an instrument, the sonometer, which could be used to regulate the vibrations of tuning forks.[44] Izrailev's experiments in acoustics continued in work with sets of tuning forks, which he produced himself and exhibited in several cities in Europe and America during the 1870s.[45] This work was officially recognized in 1882 through Izrailev's election to lifetime membership in Moscow University's Imperial Society for Lovers of Natural Science, Anthropology, and Ethnography. But Izrailev was always seeking new applications for his knowledge of the physics of ringing sound.

A casual remark by a Russian peasant is credited with drawing Izrailev's attention to the study of bells and their tuning. A large crowd had gathered around a new bell in Rostov-Velikij to admire the beauty of its reliefs and decorations, when a simple man exclaimed: "How nice! But its voice—what is its voice like? What sort of voice does it have?"[46]

Izrailev soon thereafter undertook to study the noted zvon of thirteen bells at the Uspensky Cathedral in Rostov-Velikij, where he served as priest. Using his sonometer, he measured the number of vibrations generated per second when each of these bells was rung, and he published the results of his investigations in 1884.[47]

In the late 1870s Izrailev produced a set of eighteen small clock bells, which he tuned to a series of definite pitches (figure 52). The pitches embraced a total range of two and a half octaves but formed a gamut that was neither completely diatonic nor chromatic. Izrailev's tuning of these bells was calculated to produce tonic, subdominant, and dominant-seventh chords (I, IV, and V^7) in the key of C major and a tonic and dominant-seventh chord (i and V^7) in F minor—all predicated on Western principles of functional harmony (figure 53). Though Izrailev cites neither the weights of these bells nor the number of vibrations that

52. Pitches of Izrailev's tuning of eighteen small clock bells in the late 1870s. From Olovianishnikov, *Istoriia kolokolov"*, 284.

each generates, the fact that he refers to them as *kolokol'chiki* (small bells) indicates that their fundamental or prime probably lay higher than notated (a bell whose fundamental is on middle C weighs in the vicinity of five thousand pounds).

As a result of his laboratory experiments, Izrailev was convinced that sets of bells with similar compatible tunings could be successfully produced on a much larger scale for use by churches and monasteries. His attention turned to the Cathedral of Christ the Saviour in Moscow, nearing completion and soon to be consecrated.[48] On May 18, 1879, Izrailev wrote Metropolitan Makarij of Moscow of his wish to select and harmonically tune a set of bells for the new cathedral. That fall he submitted his proposal, with specifications for an ensemble of seventeen tuned bells, and he included the number of vibrations per second each bell would generate when struck. Izrailev had worked out these details on a set of seventeen tuning forks (figure 54), and he pointed out that four accurately tuned triads could be sounded, with a number of octave doublings (figure 55). The frequencies that Izrailev gives for his tuning forks (ranging between 222.66 and 1425.02 vibrations per second) indicate that their pitches would lie an octave higher than notated.

At the end of 1880 Izrailev was informed that his proposal had not been approved.[49] But undaunted, he soon after decided to send a communication to the St. Petersburg City Duma, a municipal council, with a proposal for casting a set of tuned bells for the new church to be built on the site of Alexander II's assassination.[50] These bells would produce a minor tonic triad and its dominant. The Duma replied that the proposed bells would receive due consideration when the question of bells for the new church came before its members.

Izrailev proceeded to purchase four bronze bells himself, which he sent to Moscow to be shown at the All-Russian Exhibition of 1882. After the exhibition closed, he presented the bells to the Church of the Resurrection, the new memorial church to Alexander II, under construction beside the Catherine Canal in St. Petersburg. These bells, weighing a total of 251 pounds, were tuned to an A-

53. Chords that could be rung on Izrailev's eighteen small bells. From Olovianishnikov, *Istoriia kolokolov"*, 284.

54. Pitches of Izrailev's seventeen tuning forks. From Olovianishnikov, *Istoriia kolokolov"*, 287.

55. Chords that could be produced on Izrailev's seventeen tuning forks. From Olovianishnikov, *Istoriia kolokolov"*, 288.

TABLE 3
Pitches, Weights, and Frequencies of Four Bronze Bells
Izrailev Tuned in 1882

Bell	Pitch	Weight	Frequencies
1	a^1	2 puds, 15 funts (86 lbs.)	870
2	c^2	2 puds, 20 funts (90 lbs.)	1044
3	e^2	1 pud, 21.5 funts (56 lbs.)	1305
4	a^2	21.5 funts (19 lbs.)	1740

NOTE: A. A. Izrailev, "Muzykal'no-akusticheskiia raboty," *Izvěstiia Obshchestva liubitelej estestvoznaniia, antropologii, i ětnografii* 41, issue 2 (1884), 71.

minor triad whose root was doubled at the octave above (table 3). Accepted before the church had been completed, Izrailev's bells were hung in a temporary chapel on the site.

On February 20, 1884, Izrailev was presented to Alexander III, who had already heard the four bells that Izrailev had tuned. In the tsar's presence he demonstrated an ensemble of smaller bells on which various harmonies could be produced. He rang two hymns for the tsar on these bells: *Bozhe, Tsaria khrani* and *Kol' slaven"*.

Following his audience with the tsar Izrailev received a commission to install tuned bells in the zvonnitsa of the church of the Anichkov Palace in St. Petersburg, an assignment which he successfully completed in 1884 (figure 56).[51] Then he sought to produce compatible melodic and harmonic tunings on a number of bell ensembles and to convince church authorities and civil officials of the superiority of a set of tuned bells over an untuned Russian zvon. By 1892, the year Izrailev celebrated the fiftieth anniversary of his ordination as a priest, he had tuned or proposed tuning for no fewer than a dozen ensembles in Russia and abroad.[52]

ST. PETERSBURG
1. Four bells for a temporary chapel on the site of the Church of the Saviour on the Blood (1882)
2. Church of the Anichkov Palace (1884)
3. Kazan Cathedral

MOSCOW
4. Church built by the Pervushin family at the Donskoj Monastery[53]

ROSTOV-VELIKIJ
5. Plans to modify the zvon in the belfry by elimination of some bells and the substitution of others (1884)

WARSAW
6. House chapel of the First Women's Gymnasium

NIZHNIJ-NOVGOROD
7. Institute of the Nobility of Emperor Alexander II (1885)

KIEV
8. Palace of the Grand Duchess Alexandra Petrovna (1886)

BELEV[54]
9. Widows' Home attached to the memorial church for Empress Elisabeth Alekseevna (1886)

OREANDA
10. Crimean estate of Grand Duke Konstantin Nikolaevich

JERUSALEM
11. Church of St. Mary Magdalene in the Garden of Gethsemane on the Mount of Olives[55]

VAULOVO
12. Church of Aleksandr-Svirskij in the Yaroslavl province (1892)[56]

On the thirteen bells at Vaulovo five triads could be rung: F major, B-flat major, C major, D minor, and A major (figure 57). And five selections could be played: three monophonic chants, *So sviatymi upokoj, Věchnaia pamiat'*, and *Trisviatago pogrebal'nago*; and the two hymns, *Kol' slaven"* and *Bozhe, Tsaria khrani* (figure 58). To judge from the weights Izrailev cites for the Vaulovo bells, which ranged between 352.10 and 13.54 pounds, the fundamental or prime of each would lie an octave higher than notated.

Before Izrailev's work at the end of the nineteenth century no Russian had given serious thought to altering the characteristic clash of untuned colors and superimposed rhythmic strata in zvon ringing. Then Izrailev proposed to introduce tuned bells that would facilitate the performance of chant melodies and polyphonic hymns; and in so doing, declared himself an advocate for Western systems of bell ringing.[57] He believed that the tone of a particular bell was lost when rung with other bells

С. Петербургъ - St.-Pétersbourg   [Аничковъ Дворецъ - Palais Anitchkoff.

56. The Anichkov Palace in St. Petersburg, built between 1741 and 1747. The bells of the palace church hang in the zvonnitsa above the roof line. Courtesy of the National Museum of Finland, Helsinki.

whose tunings were acoustically and musically incompatible. The campaign he launched in the twilight years of imperial Russia, then, was nothing less than a call for completely new criteria in Russian bell manufacture and bell ringing. But Izrailev never succeeded in capturing the imagination or support of authorities who were in a position to implement his ideas on a large scale. His influence

was in fact confined to those dozen sets of bells he had either tuned himself or proposed for tuning during the last two decades of his life. No one stepped forth to continue the cause he had championed, and his tuning of church bells remains only the conclusion to tsarist Russia's contact with Western ideals of campanology.

Although Russian scholars at the turn of the cen-

57. Pitches and chords that could be rung on Izrailev's thirteen tuned bells for the Aleksandr-Svirskij Church in the village of Vaulovo (Yaroslavl province). From Olovianishnikov, *Istoriia kolokolov"*, 297.

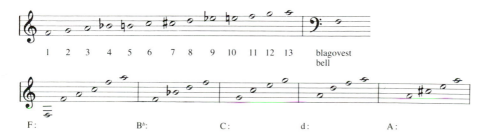

1 2 3 4 5 6 7 8 9 10 11 12 13   blagovest bell

F: B♭:   C: d: A:

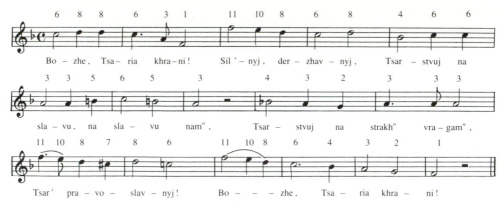

God, save the Tsar! Strong, mighty, Reign for our glory

Reign to instill fright in enemies, O thou Orthodox Tsar!

God, save the Tsar!

58. *Bozhe, Tsaria khrani* as it was rung on Izrailev's thirteen bells for the Aleksandr-Svirskij Church in the village of Vaulovo (Yaroslavl province). From Olovianishnikov, *Istoriia kolokolov"*, 297.

tury viewed Izrailev's work with a certain amount of detached scientific interest and acknowledged the accuracy of his tuning methods, they also regarded tuned bells and melodic-harmonic ringing in Russia as both artificial and unsuitable.[58] Such hothouse cultivation of a foreign performance practice on Russian soil, they pointed out, would only inhibit the free exercise of imagination in the rhythmic improvisations that Russians had come to expect from their bell ringers. Olovianishnikov spoke for the vast majority of Russians on this subject.

Melodic bell ringing may scarcely have any future [in Russia] because it doesn't conform to all traditions of our church's bell ringing and is ill-suited to the very character of [our] bells, which produce a . . . much greater impression if rung rhythmically than if played melodically, as on chimes.[59]

But Olovianishnikov did advocate strengthening the traditional Russian practice of rhythmic zvon ringing, a task that a bell ringer named Aleksandr Vasil'evich Smagin (1843-1896) had in fact already taken upon himself while Izrailev was engaged in his own work.[60]

Today in the Soviet Union the chimes at Novorossijsk, a port on the Black Sea, and those at Khatyn, the site of a Belorussian village near Minsk, are part of Soviet war memorials.[61] And from Red Square in Moscow the music of the Kremlin chimes in the Spasskij Tower is broadcast each day from the Baltic to Kamchatka. For the new regime the chromatic cascades from the Kremlin chimes have become a strangely Western symbol of national unity among the far-flung peoples of the Soviet Union (figure 59).

If our land, as the poet declares, begins from the Kremlin, then with this melody, with the tune of the Kremlin

59. The music of the Kremlin chimes in the Spasskij Gate. From Iu. V. Pukhnachev, *Zagadki zvuchashchego metalla* (Moscow, 1974), 3. Permission of VAAP, Moscow.

chimes, begins each new day in our land. The usual fourfold descent of the bells is always regarded as a signal that separates nights and days, at whatever hour of the day or night it reaches us by radio—whether in Siberia at noon or on Kamchatka in the evening. The morning, which the Kremlin chimes proclaim, is morning on Red Square.[62]

The music of the Kremlin chimes, whose repair Lenin himself had ordered, contains pale echoes from the past—aural ghosts of the great zvon, which once thundered through Red Square and across the entire city of Moscow.

Part IV
The Russian Bell and Bell Founding in Russia

9

The Russian Bell:
Between Europe and Asia

ITS FORM, clapper, and decorative programs are European, the manner in which it is rung was borrowed from Byzantium, but in its sonic ideal, mounting, and the magnitude of some castings it looks toward Asia. The position of the Russian bell between Europe and Asia is partly revealed through the attitude of its founders and of the Russian church toward the nature of bell sound. The tone quality of a bell and the presence or absence of a definite pitch are basically determined by form, substance, and striking agent.[1] Form includes size (height and diameters), weight, proportions, and profile. Profile is understood to be the cross-section of a bell's wall, that is, the contours of its inner and outer surfaces. Substance is the material a bell is made of, normally, but not invariably, some grade of bronze. And the striking agent—its weight, form, substance, and manner of installation—is also important in determining the timbre of a bell. We can expect, then, to see the bells of Europe, Russia, and the Far East sharing certain characteristics of form, substance, or striking agent, while sharply differing in others.[2]

Form

The bells of Asia. The world's first great bells appeared between A.D. 200 and 600 with the spread of Buddhism from India into Korea, China, and Japan. And by approximately the same time that

the earliest church bells were being rung in Latin Europe, large-scale bell casting was developing in the Far East under the aegis of Korean founders.[3] These Asian bells were huge barrel-shaped instruments, struck on their outer surface by an agent of a softer material (figures 60 and 61).[4] They often showed considerable compression in their lower portion, with the diameter at the mouth measuring not more than a ninth larger than the diameter at the shoulder; in fact, the lower diameter of one of these elongated bells was often less than half the bell's height. And unlike the lip of the Western bell, which tapered in from the swell of metal at the sound-bow to form an edge, the bottom rim on an Oriental bell (called a "hoof" on Japanese instruments) was the broadest portion of its almost uniformly thick wall.[5] The largest bells of Burma, China, Korea, and Japan were, together with the great bells of Russia, the most massive musical instruments in the world. Their distinctive features of form, profile, and striking agent gave them a loud, impressive sound of indefinite pitch.[6]

These untuned Asian bells, like the bells in a Russian zvon, were not intended to produce melodic or harmonic patterns in the West European sense. The partials they generated when struck varied considerably from one instrument to another (figure 62). And because the bells were rammed on their outer wall by a wooden beam, their strike note, or fundamental, was recessive to

61 (*above*). A Chinese bell of about 1,000 pounds cast in 1651. This bell without a clapper was suspended by the double dragon on top and was rung by striking with a mallet near its scalloped edge. From Meneely & Co., *Genuine Bell-Metal Bells for Churches, Chapels, Universities, Colleges, Schools, Public Buildings, Factories, Etc. . . .* (Albany, NY, 1904), 38.

60 (*at left*). A large bronze barrel-shaped bell at the Engakuji (Temple) in Kamakura, Japan. The heavy wooden beam (*shumokoku*) is swung to strike the lower portion of the wall. Permission of Shi-hachi Fujimoto.

the point of insignificance.[7] Some Western ears, accustomed to a brighter, more focused and resonant ring, have passed harsh judgment on a number of Oriental bells: "These bells have not the merit of a tolerably fair tone, like those of the Russians, and are of most inferior shape, while their dullness of sound is increased by their being struck with wooden mallets instead of iron clappers. Both the bells of China and its gongs, the latter of which are famous, are made of a peculiar alloy quite remarkable in the hideous tones which it is capable of producing."[8]

The great 155-ton (310,000-pound) Osaka bell of 1902, formerly at the Shi-tennō-ji (temple) was for forty years the largest bell ever rung and was second in weight only to Tsar-Kolokol. Its ring, however, drew responses less enthusiastic than its massive size. According to one who had heard its voice, "the Osaka monster shatters the atmosphere for miles around and sounds something like the crack of doom accompanied by a million angry bees heard through a megaphone!"[9] The Osaka bell, perhaps for this reason, was melted down for its metal during World War II.[10] Yet the voices of some

Chinese and Japanese bells are remarkable for their clarity, depth, and resonance. On a calm night strokes on the great bell of Peking are said to carry for distances up to thirty-one miles.[11]

The bells of Europe. Both European and Asian bells are open forms. But whereas bells in the Far East assumed a more cylindrical "barrel" shape, West European and Russian bells gradually adopted a form that was more conical, with the height and lower diameter more nearly equal.[12] The flared, cup-shaped Western bell, of which the Russian bell is an East European variant, seems to have evolved from the crotal, a small closed bell. Modeled on such natural "bells" as the dried pod with its peas or the gourd with seeds, the crotal contained a pellet or pellets that were sounded by shaking. When the form was opened, its pellet had to be suspended on a string or thong from its interior vertex; thus the open bell with free-swinging, internal clapper that, refined considerably, prevailed in Europe. West European bells, like the pod, gourd, or crotal, were rung by shaking. And when they grew too large to shake, they were mounted in such a way that it was still the bell itself that was set swinging, with the clapper falling against opposite inside points on the sound-bow.[13] This manner of bell ringing is in contrast to both the practice in the Far East of striking the outside of a stationary bell with a wooden beam or cudgel and the tradition in Russia of swinging an internal clapper in rhythmic patterns to meet a stationary bell.

Another major difference between the great bells of Europe and Asia is in the provision made at the top of the bells for suspension. Bells in the Far East were traditionally hung by a single loop from a fixed beam, whereas those in Europe, including Russia, were hung by two, four, six, or in a few instances, eight loops, or cannons, either from a yoke or a fixed beam.[14] Two loops would suffice for a smaller bell, but a large bell (approaching 11,000 pounds) required six loops—two pairs and two singles placed crosswise.[15]

A clapper's contact with the sound-bow of a European bell generates an unusually rich and complex combination of at least a dozen independent

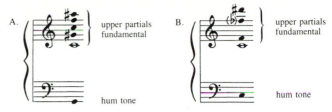

62. Approximate fundamentals and partials on two large, untuned Asian bells of barrel shape. A. From Arthur Lynds Bigelow, *Carillon* (Princeton, 1948), 27. B. From Percival Price, "Bell," *New Grove Dictionary of Music and Musicians* 2:426. Permission of Macmillan Publishers, Ltd. and the author.

partials. A fundamental, or prime, is produced, along with the hum tone, a series of upper partials—tierce (third), quint (fifth), and nominal (octave)—and additional partials above the nominal (figure 63).[16] Each of these partials is generated from a particular segment along the wall of the bell, thus the profile of the bell determines both the frequencies and the intensity of the partials. The thinnest portion of the bell wall, just below the

63. The nomenclature of the European bell showing the points along its wall that generate the most important partials. From Arthur Lynds Bigelow, *The Acoustically Balanced Carillon: Graphics and the Design of Carillons and Carillon Bells* (Princeton University, 1961), [p. 4], fig. 3 (with addition of the cannons). Permission of the Department of Civil Engineering, Princeton University.

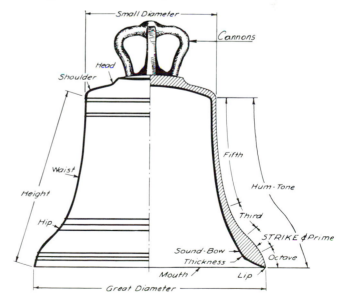

shoulder, generates the quint, and as the wall gradually thickens descending into the sound-bow, the tierce and fundamental (or prime) come into play. The section between the sound-bow and the lip defines the nominal, and the hum tone is drawn from the full length of the bell, shoulder to lip.[17]

On a tuned bell the pitch of the strike-note is identical to that of the fundamental, though its frequency is not measurable, and at least the first five modes of vibration are adjusted so that they are mutually consonant. If the bell is not accurately tuned, a strike-note will only be audible for a brief time. A bell's basic pitch is defined by the fundamental, nominal, and hum tone, but its tone is enriched and colored by the higher partials that emerge above its nominal, some of which are stronger and of longer duration than others.[18] Since the seven upper partials decay quite rapidly, however, their tuning is less critical to the bell's pitch.[19]

Although the lips of European bells are similar, there were nevertheless certain variants established during the thirteenth century that became characteristic of several regions with a history of bell founding. Before World War I at least five different lip profiles could be distinguished among European bells: those indigenous to England, the Low Countries (Holland and Flanders), France, Germany, and Russia (figure 64). English bells show curved contours on both sides of the lip. On French bells both walls are either flat or the outer wall may be slightly rounded, but the larger angle between the lower diameter and the inner wall of the lip reduces somewhat the amount of metal in the sound-bow.[20] (Lips on Italian and Spanish bells are similar to those from France.) The characteristic

bell lip in the Low Countries shows a gently curving exterior wall at the sound-bow and a flat interior with less upward slope than on the French bell. On German bells the inside wall is often rounded, though both walls could also be flat (cf. figure 118 in Appendix C). The flat interior wall and slope on the lip of a Russian bell is similar to these features on Dutch, Flemish, and some German bells, but the outer wall, which initially rises from the lip in a straight line, curves subtly away from this line without producing the characteristic ridge seen on the sound-bows of many German and French bells.

Russian founders also developed a profile for the entire bell, which constitutes a distinctive subdivision among European bells (see figure 121 in Appendix C). They worked out their own method of determining the length of segments that they plotted on a line extending from the bell's lip to its shoulders, used a different system of calculating distances from points along this line to the outer wall of the bell, and formulated their own scale for determining the thickness of the bell's wall as it descended from the thinner portion at the shoulder into the thicker sound-bow.[21]

The formula that Russian founders followed in calculating the lower diameter of bells that would weigh up to 120 puds (4,334 pounds) began with the diameter of a bell half the weight of the one being designed, which they increased by a fourth.[22] For example, the diameter of a bell weighing 8 puds (289 pounds) was computed by taking the diameter of a 4-pud bell, which was 10.75 *vershki* (18.8 inches), and adding to it one-fourth of this measure, or 2.5 vershki.[23] The diameter of the 8-pud bell would therefore be 13.25 vershki (23.18 inches). Similarly, the diameter of a 16-pud bell was 13.25 vershki plus 3.25 vershki, or 16.50 vershki (28.9 inches); and the diameter of a 120-pud bell was 31.75 vershki (55.6 inches). For the diameter of bells weighing more than 120 puds, the percentage of additional length derived from the diameter of the smaller bell was significantly reduced. The upper diameter on Russian bells was equal to no more than two-thirds of the lower diameter.

64. Profiles of traditional bell lips from five regions of Europe: A. England; B. The Low Countries (Holland and Flanders); C. France, Italy, and Spain; D. Germany; E. Russia. After Wendell Westcott, *Bells and Their Music* (New York, 1970), 68. Permission of the author.

A   B   C   D   E

In a Russian bell the relationship of perpendicular height (including cannons) to lower diameter differed somewhat from this ratio in West European bells and departed significantly from that in bells of the Far East.[24] Whereas the height of a Western bell was slightly less than its lower diameter (sometimes only 0.875 of the diameter), and the ratio was almost two to one in Chinese, Japanese, or Korean bells, the height of a Russian bell was generally equal or almost equal to its lower diameter.[25] The thickness of the Russian bell's sound-bow was normally calculated at 0.07 to 0.08 of its lower diameter, while the thickness of the upper portion of the wall was not more than one-third the thickness of the wall at the sound-bow.[26] West European bells had thinner walls than did Russian bells, a feature that gave them a stronger tone with a sharper edge but a somewhat less prolonged ring. The height of the cannons on a Russian bell, according to one source, was one-fifth or one-seventh the height of the bell; according to another, only one-seventh.[27]

Continuous modifications in the profiles of Western bells throughout the Middle Ages and Renaissance were indicative of an uncompromising search among European founders for proportions and contours that would generate the most resonant sound and pleasing timbre. When required, founders would tune the partials of these bells for melodic and harmonic ringing. Figure 65 shows approximate pitches of lower frequencies on an untuned European bell—such as those cast and rung in Russia—whose strike-note is *d* and whose fundamental is middle C. The simultaneous sounding of $C^\sharp$ (hum tone), middle C, *d*, $a^\flat$ (quint), and d^1 (nominal) would produce a strong dissonance, but one that could be tuned on a vertical lathe in a West European foundry. Within limits, a bell's pitch can be lowered by widening the diameter of its mouth through grinding away some metal from the inner surface and raised by filing metal from the outer edge of the mouth to slightly reduce the width of the lower diameter. The tuning of a West European bell thus produces a series of partials that sound a minor triad (fundamental, tierce, and quint) with the doubling of the fundamental at the octave

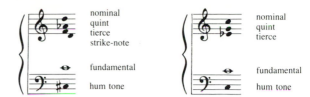

65 (*left*). The approximate fundamental, strike-note, and lower partials on an untuned European bell. From Price, "Bell," 426. Permission of Macmillan Publishers, Ltd. and the author.

66 (*right*). The fundamental and four lowest partials generated by a European bell tuned to middle C. The strike-note is of the same pitch as the fundamental but is not a measurable frequency. From Westcott, *Bells and Their Music*, 42. Permission of the author.

below (hum tone) and at the octave above (nominal) (figure 66).[28] If a bell could not be satisfactorily tuned, it would generally be recast.

Substance

A second factor that determines the tone quality and resonance of a bell is the constituency of the bell metal. Though bronze was always the favored metal for casting bells in southern Europe, iron was used in northern Europe through the ninth century.[29] Iron bells were even reported in Bavaria in the latter half of the fifteenth century, and Ivan IV of Russia is said to have sent a cast-iron bell to the Dosifeev Hermitage in the sixteenth century.[30] Bells of brass, a binary alloy of copper and zinc, were common in China and were also found in Poland, but the timbre of brass bells is significantly inferior to that of bells cast in bronze, and brass lacks the strength of bronze.[31] Steel bells, which Western Europe began to produce widely toward the end of the nineteenth century, notably in Germany and at Sheffield, were only used experimentally in Russia for railroad signals.[32]

No bell cast in an elementary metal has produced a satisfactory much less superior quality of tone. The testimony of poets notwithstanding, gold and silver are both too soft to be used for larger bells and are musically as unsatisfactory as lead.[33] Some small bells have been produced in silver and gold, but still with no aural success.[34] The so-called golden bells that wealthy Russian merchants presented to certain churches in Siberia were actually bronze bells that had been gilded.[35] In the town of Tara, on the left bank of the Irtysh River in the Tobol'sk province, hung six such gilded bells, the largest of which weighed 45 puds (1,625 pounds).[36]

An ideal bell metal insured the proper combination of resilience (the capacity to rebound when struck) and resonance. And the best possible compromise between these two properties existed in bronze, a binary alloy of tin and copper. The tin, which was capable of sustained vibration, produced the finer ring but was quite easily cracked. Copper, less desirable from the standpoint of resonance, was essential for softening the brittle tin. Bronze was also preferred because unlike iron and steel it did not rust. It was therefore well suited for bells that were at least partially exposed to the elements in a tower or belfry.[37] Another feature of bronze was its relatively low melting point, a property that facilitated casting but that, unfortunately, has contributed throughout the centuries to the loss of countless bells in fires.[38]

The composition of bronze has varied somewhat from century to century and from one geographical region to another. By the middle of the first millennium B.C. the Chinese were casting bells in a bronze alloy of approximately four parts copper to one part tin.[39] Japanese bells had a considerably greater proportion of less resonant copper to tin.[40] In the West metal weights have ranged between 70 percent copper and 30 percent tin to 90 percent copper and 10 percent tin, with small amounts of lead, zinc, and even iron.[41] But ever since a Benedictine monk named Theophilus wrote *De diversis artibus* in the first half of the twelfth century, the ratio of copper to tin in European (and Russian) bell metal has remained essentially unchanged:[42] somewhere between 80 to 77 percent copper and 20 to 23 percent tin. These alloys effect the most favorable compromise between resonance and elasticity.

But the proportion of copper and tin was also dependent on the size of a bell. Usually less tin (sometimes as little as 18 percent) was used for very large bells since they had to withstand more powerful blows and hence required a more supple metal.[43] Conversely, more tin (as much as 25 percent) was required for very small bells, because their walls were thicker in relation to their size.[44] Olovianishnikov has shown, at least in the bronze of one old bell, that the percentage of metal content even varied somewhat from one portion of a bell to another (table 4).

The purer the metals used in the bronze, the finer the tone that the bell produced; admixtures and impurities only impair resonance.[45] The best bell metal will also have a fine grain and uniform texture. Another variable that exercises some influence on the relative pitch of a bell is the temperature of the metal at the time it is rung. Warmer air lowers the rate of a bell's vibration by expanding it slightly and thus lowers its pitch. Because all partials that a ringing bell generates are affected equally, however, bells in a chime or carillon remain in tune with themselves and with each other.[46]

Striking Agent

In addition to form and substance, the striking agent affected the tone quality of a bell. The large bronze bells of the Orient, rammed on the lower portion of their outer surface by a horizontally swinging wooden beam (figure 60), block or manually swung wooden cudgel—in any case of a softer material than the bell itself—had a considerably diminished strike-note.[47] In contrast, an internal, free-swinging, iron clapper gave the strike-note its characteristic prominence on European bells. The impact of the clapper on the sound-bow also gave the sound an added surge.[48]

The clapper, or tongue (*iazyk*) for a European bell required a metal that was neither too soft nor too hard. Clappers with wooden padding or cast in too soft a metal (e.g., bronze) would elicit a dull, unfocused tone. They would also wear down in a short time. On the other hand, too hard a clapper would produce a harsh sound because it would give prominence to the upper partials; it would also eventually dent the bell wall at points of repeated impact.[49] More recent experiments with steel clappers have not produced very positive results. Not only are they easily broken but they do not obtain a full-bodied sound from the bell.[50] Neither are clappers that are cast in both soft and hard metals completely satisfactory. Because a fusion of the two metals is difficult to achieve, these clappers also tend to break when they strike the bell wall. Instead, cast iron of a type that was not too hard was found to be the best metal for bell clappers, eliciting the most resonant and satisfactory tone.[51]

To produce the finest ring, a clapper's weight also had to be carefully calculated in relation to the weight of its bell. Generally speaking, the weight of a clapper increased as the size and weight of the bell increased. If a clapper was too light, it would fail to call forth all the partials the bell was capable of producing.[52] Blows from too heavy a clapper, on the other hand, would produce tonal distortion and could eventually crack a bell under repeated strokes.[53] The elasticity of a bell's metal had limits, and like a rubber band, a bell would eventually snap if this capacity were overtaxed.[54]

In the nineteenth century iron clappers for Russian bells were generally produced at a different foundry from the one that produced the bells and then were brought to the bell foundry for installation.[55] Thus a certain variance in the ratio of clapper weight to bell weight is found among bells of this period. In one foundry the weight of the clapper was usually computed at between 0.025 and 0.02 of the weight of the bell.[56] Another foundry cast 1.25 funts (1.13 pounds) of iron in the clapper for each pud (36.113 pounds) of bronze in the bell. And a third foundry cast clappers with from 1.3 to 1.4 funts (1.17 to 1.26 pounds) of metal per pud in the bell.[57] At the Olovianishnikov Foundry in Yaroslavl a clapper for a 1,500-pud bell was cast at about 0.031 the weight of the bell. And if Bogdanov's Great Uspensky Bell of 1817 actually weighs 4,000 puds, then its 125-pud clapper would contain this same proportion of the bell's weight. At this ratio a clapper for the 12,000-pud Tsar-Kolokol, if it had ever been cast, could be projected at about 372 puds (13,434 pounds, or 6.71 tons).

A clapper is comprised of four main sections: (1) a loop (*petlia*) by which it hangs from the crown staple (*vnutrennee ukho*, or "interior ear") on the

Table 4

Variants in the Bronze Composition in Three Portions of an Old Russian Bell

Metal	% in head of bell	% in waist of bell	% in sound-bow of bell
Tin	21.36	20.86	20.62
Copper	75.68	76.69	77.69
Lead	2.96	2.85	2.41

NOTE: N. Olovianishnikov, *Istoriia kolokolov'' i kolokololitejnoe iskusstvo*, 2d ed., enl. (Moscow: Izdanie T-va P. I. Olovianishnikova S-vej, 1912), 382. Olovianishnikov does not explain why the proportions of metal in the middle and lower portions total 100.40 and 100.72 percent, respectively. Analytical errors may be responsible.

inside vertex of the bell, (2) a long shaft or shank whose diameter gradually increases as it approaches (3) the ball, or hammer (*iabloko*, or "apple"), which contains the greatest mass of metal and strikes the sound-bow when the bell is rung, and (4) an abruptly tapering spur of metal below the ball, called the "flight" since its extra weight is required to make the clapper fly properly (figure 67). The clapper for ringing a stationary Russian bell shows a significantly more massive ball than Western clappers intended for swinging bells. Although ideal proportions for clappers remained a Russian foundry owner's secret, they were largely determined by the projected diameter of the ball.[58] The rope or ropes for swinging Russian clappers were tied to the flight below the ball, secured by the ridge at the bottom, so that the rope would not dampen the strike by coming between the ball of the clapper and the sound-bow of the bell.

The method of suspending a clapper inside a Russian bell was determined by the size of the bell. The crown staple was cast in either iron or pure copper since bronze loops were too brittle to support a clapper.[59] In a small bell the clapper was suspended from the crown staple by a leather strap called a baldric, which in Russia was preferably made from walrus hide, since this leather was less elastic than the hide from other animals.[60] Any stretching of the baldric would eventually lower the strike point of the clapper's ball on the sound-

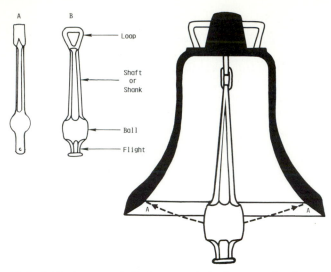

67 (*at left*). Two iron bell clappers. A. Lighter weight clapper for a West European swinging bell. B. heavier clapper for a stationary Russian bell. From Olovianishnikov, *Istoriia kolokolov"*, 401.

68 (*right*). The strike points (A) of the clapper ball on the sound-bow of a Russian bell. From Olovianishnikov, *Istoriia kolokolov"*, 414.

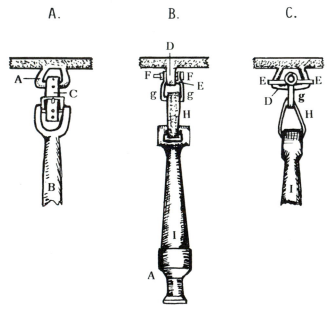

69. Two suspension systems for clappers in Russian bells. A. Lighter clapper hung from the crown staple by a leather strap with buckle. B. and C. Special suspension system for the 125-pud clapper in Bogdanov's Great Uspensky Bell. After Babin (Captain 2d grade), "O russkikh" kolokolakh"," *Gornyj zhurnal"* 4, no. 11 (1861), figs. 16, 17, and 19 in sketch 12.

bow of the bell and would adversely affect the quality of its ring (figure 68). In a bell of moderate size (up to 100 puds, or 3,611 pounds) the clapper was hung by belts or straps wound several times through the crown staple and the loop at the upper end of the clapper (figure 69A).

Views B and C of figure 69 illustrate the more complex system used to suspend the 125-pud (4,514-pound) clapper inside Bogdanov's Great Uspensky Bell in the Kremlin's Ivan Velikij Bell Tower. From the crown staple (D) hangs an iron clevis secured by a pin (F); and the clapper is then hung from this clevis by means of belts and ropes (H). This special suspension system reduces the friction and wear on the belts and ropes that would occur if this unusually massive clapper were suspended in the same manner as the clapper in figure 69A. It also facilitates the swinging of the clapper by eliminating the resistance of belts on the bell's crown staple.[61]

The distance that a clapper hangs from the bell's crown staple also has to be carefully set—and even adjusted from time to time—so that the mid-point on the clapper's ball will strike the bell on the thickest mass of its sound-bow (figure 68). Only here, at this point of maximum elasticity and resonance, is the bell wall capable of withstanding repeated blows and producing an ideal balance of intensity among its various partials. The arc of the clapper's swing has to be further regulated to insure that the ball will be precisely perpendicular to the strike point on the sound-bow.[62] And the ball has to retract immediately upon contact with the sound-bow so that the ring will not be dampened. In ringing a large Russian bell, the clapper is usually swung so that its ball strikes the interior wall of the sound-bow at three points instead of the two points opposite each other customary in ringing Western bells.[63]

Decorative Systems and Inscriptions on Russian Bells

Russian bells belong to the easternmost branch of the European family of bells not only in their form but also in the general style of their decorative programs and in the placement of their inscriptions. Surfaces of both Western and Russian bells are usually articulated with bead lines encircling the upper and lower portions of the bells, which define a horizontal disposition of decorative elements and inscriptions. Because raised areas on the surfaces of small bells could alter the quality of their tone, inscriptions and bas-reliefs were usually cast only on larger bells.[64] Even then, ornamentation was kept as shallow as possible in order to assure the integrity of the instrument's sound.

Decorative schemes on large Oriental bells differ significantly. The walls of many of these bells, as though bound with rope, are partitioned both horizontally and vertically into ranks of panels (see figures 60 and 61). Chinese and Japanese inscriptions, with their characters arranged vertically into columns, are more easily accommodated within such panels. There are some large Chinese bells whose entire surface seems to be organized on a horizontal format more like Western schemes, but in fact they are only covered with engraved inscriptions from sacred scripture that read vertically but are divided by thin horizontal lines into several broad bands encircling the bells. Oriental bells also differ from Western and Russian in having an elaborately "carved" single loop at the top, a slightly raised medallion (usually a stylized lotus) at the point where the laterally swinging wooden beam or block rams the lower wall, and occasionally a scalloped edge: and they characteristically have rows of bosses within the upper panels.

Relief decoration. Before the sixteenth century Russian bells were cast almost without ornamentation. The early bells and bell fragments unearthed in Kiev and elsewhere show only a few bead lines above the shoulder and around the hip (the upper area of the sound-bow). Even as late as 1475 Mikula's bell for the Great Gostinopol'skij Monastery, except for two bands of inscription located just below its shoulder, has only bead lines below its cannons and around its hip (figure 29).

Among the earliest extant Russian bells to be cast with significant decorative systems were those founded at Pskov during the sixteenth century. On

70. Timofej Andreev's bell of 1544 for the Pskovo-Pecherskij Monastery. From I. I. Pleshanova, "O zverinom ornamente pskovskikh kolokolov i keramid," in *Drevnerusskoe iskusstvo: Khudozhestvennaia kul'tura Pskova,* ed. V. N. Lazarev, O. I. Podobedova, and V. V. Kostochkin, (Moscow, 1968), 207. Permission of VAAP, Moscow.

these instruments relief registers alternate with bands of inscription on the portion of the waist just below the shoulder and on the portion near the sound-bow. The extensive surface between these upper and lower zones was generally devoid of ornamentation (figure 70), a feature that distinguishes these bells from those founded during the second half of the seventeenth century and later.

The relief bands on these Pskov bells contain both animal and floral motifs, in a so-called Byzantino-Persian style that, while by no means new in

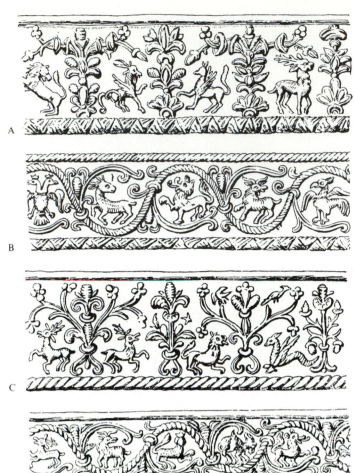

71. Animal and floral motifs on the frieze bands of Pskov bells from the mid-sixteenth century. A. and C. Animals separated by floral motifs. B. and D. Animals framed by an undulating vine. From Pleshanova, "O zverinom ornamente pskovskikh kolokolov i keramid," 209. Permission of VAAP, Moscow.

of inscription disposed above one decorative frieze on the upper portion of the bell and one inscription and one frieze band encircling the sound-bow below the three bead lines around the hip.

After the mid-sixteenth century similar animal and floral motifs began to appear on Novgorod bells, accompanying the transfer of prominence in Russian bell founding from Pskov to Novgorod around 1560.[67] In the hands of Novgorod bell foremen this decorative style continued to flourish throughout the sixteenth and first half of the seventeenth centuries. Even as late as 1683 the decoration of the "Polielejnyj" bell for the Uspensky Cathedral at Rostov-Velikij was relatively simple, still influenced by the older and plainer style (figure 73). Just below the shoulder of this bell an inscription band is separated from two ornamental frieze bands by beading. The rest of the bell's waist is undecorated except for a series of bead lines around its hip. Another inscription and three more bead lines encircled the sound-bow.

Significant changes began to appear around 1650 in the decorative programs on Russian bells. The animal and floral motifs were replaced to a great extent by representations of human figures—relief icons of saints and angels, portraits of contemporary officials (e.g., the patriarch of Moscow and the Russian sovereign)—as well as by coats of arms, baroque cartouches with inscriptions, and medallions with imperial portraits. Individual decorative elements on larger bells were often linked by festoons and garlands.[68] And the previously unornamented waists of bells received more and more attention as inscriptions and decorations began to spread over the entire surface of the bell. The so-called Nikon Bell of 1666 is an early example (figure 74).[69] One decorative frieze covers the shoulder, and two more encircle the sound-bow, while the wall between them contains six bands of inscription. This distribution is unusual on a Russian bell. The end of each line of the inscription is indicated by a rosette, and the following line continues on the band immediately below and to the right.

One of the most unusual types of seventeenth-century Russian bell was the so-called carved bell, a bell designed with apertures in the upper portion

sixteenth-century Russia, was apparently first applied on bells by the founders at Pskov.[65] Heraldic animals, both natural and fantastic, were framed either by undulating vines and tendrils or by flowers and foliage (figure 71).[66] As a rule, both animal and floral motifs occurred in combination, rarely alone. Noteworthy is the absence of any representations of human figures.

The zones of inscription and ornamentation on these Pskov bells were of approximately equal height. Mikhail Andreev's Belozersk bell of 1544 is typical (see detail in figure 72), with three bands

72. Detail of inscription bands and a decorative frieze band on the shoulder and upper waist of a bell that Mikhail Andreev founded in 1544. From Pleshanova, "O zverinom ornamente pskovskikh kolokolov i keramid," 206. Permission of VAAP, Moscow.

of its waist below the shoulder.[70] A 60-pud (2,167-pound) bell that Emel'ian Danilov founded in 1648 (figure 75), is among the finest examples of these bells. It boasts twelve arched "windows" around the upper half of its waist immediately below a decorative frieze and bead lines, and at the base of each aperture a circular medallion pushes up into the space.

More intricately fenestrated—and at 2 puds 4 funts (76 pounds), also considerably smaller—is Dmitrij Motorin's bell of 1687 for the Church of the Intercession of the All-Holy Virgin in the Moscow suburb of Medvedkovo (figure 76). An inscription encircles the bell's waist below the "carved" portion, and bead lines and the founder's inscription relieve the otherwise plain surface of the soundbow. The cannons on this bell are especially unu-

sual. Cannons on Russian bells were generally cast without ornamentation,[71] but here we can see two loops formed by the arched necks of two eagles whose beaks are clamped on either side of a man's head; a third loop (not visible in this photograph) is presumably formed in the same way at the back of the unfortunate man's head. The tradition of carved bells was revived during the second half of the nineteenth century as a specialty at the Ryzhov foundry at Khar'kov, where the foremen believed that fenestration increased the purity of a bell's tone.[72]

73. "Polielejnyj" bell of 1683 in the zvonnitsa of the Uspensky Cathedral at Rostov-Velikij. From *Rostov Velikij* (Moscow, 1971), 42. Permission of Izdatel'stvo "Sovetskaia Rossiia," Moscow.

Inscriptions. Fulgentius Ferrandus' letter to his friend Eugippius *circa* 535 (see Chapter 3) suggests that inscriptions may have been present on Western bells much earlier than is generally acknowledged. But one of the oldest extant instruments with an inscription is the seventh-century bell of Stival on which the letters PIRTURFICISTI are engraved vertically.[73] By the mid-fourteenth century relief inscriptions, built up on the surface of the false bell, were present on many European bells.[74]

The earliest records of Russian inscriptions on bells are found on two previously mentioned bell fragments uncovered in 1946: one from Kiev showing two letters from a Cyrillic relief inscription (ТЬ . . .); and another from the lower church at Old Grodno bearing the Russian word РАБУ ("servant") from a rather roughly executed relief inscription. Though no date can be assigned with certainty to either fragment, the first bell seems to have been cast before the mid-thirteenth century and may have shattered during the Mongol assault on Kiev in 1240. The second bell, if it fell and broke prior to a fire that destroyed the church at Old Grodno in 1183 as some Soviet archeologists believe, may have been one of the first of all European bells to receive a relief inscription.[75] The oldest extant Russian bell with a dated inscription is the bell of 1341 for the Church of St. George (Iurij) at L'vov, which was inscribed by Iakov Skora.[76] From this time on the execution of inscriptions on Russian bells became sharper and more refined.

During the sixteenth and seventeenth centuries inscriptions on Russian bells (especially those from Novgorod, Pskov, and Moscow) were cast largely in *viaz'*, a highly stylized form of the Cyrillic alphabet, which can be compared to the forms of Arabic letters in Kūfic script.[77] Viaz' developed from a mid-eleventh-century Greek style in Byzantine manuscripts, which presented the title or first line of a text in larger and more elongated letters than the rest of the text. In Cyrillic viaz' the principal letters were long and thin and stretched the full height of the text line, while the smaller letters

74. The Bell of Patriarch Nikon (1666). From Iu. M. Zolotov, "Kolokol Patriarkha Nikona," *Sovetskaia arkheologiia* 8, no. 2 (1964), p. 242. Permission of Moscow University Press.

were joined to the larger letters to form ligatures or were placed in the spaces left between them (figure 77).[78]

Viaz' is attested to in South Slavic manuscripts as early as the first half of the thirteenth century, and its spread to Russia coincided with the northward transmission of other South Slavic influences. Several styles of viaz' were transmitted: "natural" viaz' in which letters were ornamented with floral elements; the "geometric" style, which emphasized the harmonious proportion of Cyrillic letters without floral ornamentation; and a mixed style. Only at the end of the fourteenth century does viaz' begin to appear in Russian manuscripts, on Russian frescoes, icons, embroidery, tombstone epitaphs, and cast metal objects such as bells.[79] And the style of viaz' cultivated in Muscovy from the end of the fifteenth century was the simpler geometric viaz', which is the style used in bell inscrip-

75. Emel'ian Danilov's "carved" bell of 1648 at Kolomenskoe. From Rubtsov, *Istoriia litejnogo proizvodstva*, 210, fig. 9. With permission of Izdatel'stvo "Mashinostroenie," Moscow.

tions (figure 78).[80] Viaz' continued to flourish in the seventeenth century but declined in use during the eighteenth; it eventually died out altogether except in certain nineteenth-century publications by the Old Believers.[81]

A typical inscription on a Russian bell may transmit any or all of the following data: the year, and quite often the month and day, of the bell's founding; the name of the church or institution the bell will serve; the name of its founder and/or the name of the foundry; and the bell's weight expressed in puds and funts.[82] Here is a representative example of a fairly complete inscription from an eighteenth-century bell:

On the first day of July in the year 1750, this bell has been cast in Moscow beyond the Prechistenskij Gate for the Church of the Protection of the All-Holy Virgin, which is in Levshino under the care of the priest Ale-

ksej Kirilov and his parishioners; its weight is 80 puds [2,889 pounds]; foreman Konstantin, son of Mikhail, Slizov cast this bell.[83]

Although an inscription may also give the names and titles of the bell's donors as well as brief encomiums to saints, it will generally be more economical and direct than an inscription on a Western bell. A distinction should be made, however, between the typically straightforward inscriptions on most Russian bells and the litanies of names and titles that appear on such imperial commissions as the great bell of 1748 for the Trinity-Sergius Lavra or Bogdanov's Great Uspensky Bell (1817).[84]

Poetic inscriptions, not uncommon on West European bells, are exceptional on Russian instruments. A bell that Afanasij Petrov founded in 1695 for the bell tower of the cathedral in Poltava is one of the few to bear a verse inscription:

In the year one thousand sixteen hundred ninety-five,
In famed Kazikerman captured by the Christians
In the reign of the Russian Tsars Peter, Ioann,
During the hetmanate of Mazepa granted by God,
This bell has been founded for the glory of God,
And for the Church of the Assumption in the town of
        Poltava
From pieces of cannons seized at Kazikerman
With the addition of materials proper for a bell
At the expense of His Grace, the leader of the Poltava
        troops,
Pavel Semenovich, Otrozh of the Ukraine.[85]

Inscriptions on Russian bells, like their Western counterparts, sometimes include passages from Scripture. On the 200-pud (7,223-pound) "Vsesviatskoj" bell of 1664, which formerly hung in the bell tower of the New Jerusalem Monastery, the upper band quoted selected verses from the tenth chapter of Numbers ("And the Lord God ordered Moses to make two trumpets of hammered silver . . ."), and continued with an analogy whose typology was transmitted from antiquity: "And thus the Lord our God has lawfully established for us through divine grace the spiritual trumpets (*dukhovnyia truby*) of a new Israel, resonant cymbals, or to say it with the common designation—bells. . . ."[86] Another large bell cast around 1865 for a church at Votkinsk contained three passages from the Bible.[87]

Of the nine bells Prokopij Grigov'ev cast by himself in the mid-sixteenth century, seven give the date of their founding as September 8, the feast of the Nativity of the Virgin.[88] Study of the inscriptions on thirty-four bells that Pskov foremen cast between about 1520 and 1570 reveals that seventeen of these were poured on feasts associated with the Virgin, five on feasts of the Lord, three on May 9 (The Translation of the Relics of St. Nicholas), and two on July 20 (The Fiery Ascent of Elijah). Smirnova suggests that the wax inscriptions on the false bells for these instruments were prepared well in advance of the projected date of casting and that Pskovian masters sought to time their castings to coincide with the date that had already been committed to the inscription on the bell mold.[89]

A unique inscription appeared on the lower portion of the great bell of 2,125 puds, 30 funts (76,767 pounds), that Aleksandr Grigor'ev founded on September 25, 1667, for the bell tower of the Savvino-Storozhevskij Monastery near Zvenigorod. The upper inscription, disposed in six bands that encircled the bell, though lengthy, was clearly expressed in Russian through the Cyrillic alphabet. After addressing the tsar, tsarina, members of their family, and the patriarchs of Alexandria, Antioch, and Moscow by name and title, this inscription concluded with the bell's date of founding, its weight, and Grigor'ev's name as founder.[90] But the lower inscription, which encircled the bell in three bands, was written in a contemporary Russian diplomatic code (figure 79). Of the numerous letters in this secret alphabet, several were repeated, while others closely resembled each other. One of the puzzling features was that a number of characters in the last three columns had their own special forms and bore no resemblance to the first signs in the inscription.

This lower inscription was first copied from the bell by the noted historian and authority on old texts, Gerard Friedrich Miller (1705-1783), and was published by Johann Vollraht Bacmeister (Ivan Grigor'evich Bakmejster), a librarian at the Academy of Sciences during the second half of the

76. Dmitrij Motorin's "carved" bell of 1687 for the Church of the Intercession of the All-Holy Virgin in the Moscow suburb of Medvedkovo. From Rubtsov, *Istoriia litejnogo proizvodstva*, 236, fig. 30. With permission of Izdatel'stvo "Mashinostroenia," Moscow.

77. Russian viaz' from a Sinodik of 1659 in the State Historical Museum, Moscow. From V. N. Shchepkin, *Russkaia paleografiia* (Moscow, 1967), 53, fig. 15. Permission of VAAP, Moscow.

78. A portion of the inscription in viaz' on the "Sysoj" Bell of 1689 at Rostov-Velikij with the name of its founder, "Foreman Flor Terent'ev." From Iu. V. Pukhnachev, *Zagadki zvuchashchego metalla* (Moscow, 1974), 35. Permission of VAAP, Moscow.

79. The cryptic inscription on Aleksandr Grigor'ev's bell of 1667 for the Savvino-Storozhevskij Monastery near Zevenigorod. From Olovianishnikov. *Istoriia kolokolov''*, 71.

80. The key to the seventeenth-century diplomatic code used for the cryptic inscription on Grigor'ev's bell of 1667. The Cyrillic (Russian) alphabet is in the lefthand column; code signs for each of the six sections of the inscription appear at the top left of each of the six columns. The seventh symbol on the far right, the double-headed eagle, appears at the end of the inscription (not shown in fig. 79). From Pukhnachev, *Zagadki zvuchashchego metalla*, 103. Permission of VAAP, Moscow.

eighteenth century. But the inscription did not attract attention until 1822 when a Russian prince (identified only as P.P.L.), a staff cavalry captain by the name of Skuridin, and Aleksandr Ivanovich Ermolaev (1780-1828) tried to decipher it. Although Skuridin worked out more of the inscription than the prince, only Ermolaev, a numismatist and curator of manuscripts, succeeded in reading it in its entirety.[91] As he deciphered it, the inscription reveals the following:

* By the will of our all good and all generous God * and with the protection of our gracious protector, the Most Holy Sovereign Bogoroditsa [the Virgin], * and because of the prayers of our father and gracious protector, the reverend Savva, the Miracle-Worker, * and by the promise and by the order of Christ's servant, Tsar Aleksei, and by his soulful love and by his heartfelt wish, * this bell is cast for the Church of the Most Holy Bogoroditsa, of her virtuous and glorious Nativity, * and for our great and reverend father Savva, the Miracle Worker, which is in Zvenigorod, called Storozhevskij.[92]

Ermolaev finally cracked the code when he realized that each Cyrillic letter was represented by not one but by at least six different signs. The inscription itself was divided into six sections, each section preceded by a distinctive symbol (indicated in the translation above by asterisks). After each of these signs, a new encoding system took effect (figure 80).[93] For example, in the first section of the code the sign ♭ stood for the Cyrillic letters i or и, but in section four the identical sign represented the Cyrillic T.

This cryptic inscription was in all probability the idea and creation of Tsar Aleksei Mikhailovich himself. Not only had the tsar commissioned the bell (and therefore as donor could be expected to authorize its decorative program and inscriptions), but the reference to him as "the servant of Christ" also suggests that he himself prepared the inscription. He evidently wished to express but also to conceal his piety through this unusual means. Grigor'ev as founder could hardly have taken upon himself the preparation of the second inscription in a secret code without at least the sanction of the sovereign.[94]

As Nicolas Zernov has noted, the Russians differ from other peoples in that "geographically and cul-turally they belong neither to Europe nor to Asia, but form a link between these two continents."[95] Berdyaev takes this further, maintaining that the ambiguity in Russia's cultural identity is not a static condition but one marked by a struggle between dynamic and conflicting forces.[96] Russia's great bells are one expression of the country's unique position on the frontiers of both Europe and Asia. Though the Russians cast their bells in the general form and with the basic profile of European bells, their castings rivaled and eventually surpassed the monumental bells of Asia in magnitude.[97] Though, like Oriental bells, Russian bells were stationary in their mounting, they were rung by means of an internal, free-swinging iron clapper, not rammed with a wooden beam suspended outside the bell or struck with a wooden cudgel on the outside wall. And though Russian bells shared the feature of the clapper with Western bells, in Europe the bell was swung to meet the clapper,[98] whereas in Russia the clapper was swung to meet the bell. In Russian bell ringing, therefore, a performance practice influenced by Byzantium and resembling a percussive principle that was traditional for bell ringing in the Far East was accommodated within the form of an instrument adopted and perfected in the West.

In 1661 Baron von Meyerberg saw the great new bell in the Moscow Kremlin and declared that its magnitude surpassed that of the bell at Erfurt in Saxony or even of the great bell of Peking in the kingdom of China.[99] His intuitive comparisons were remarkable. He had somehow divined the ultimate cultural significance of the monumental Russian bell that Aleksandr Grigor'ev had founded beside the Moscow River, whose waters rise in Europe and finally reach a sea that touches shores in Asia.

113

10

The Russian Bell: From
The Foundry to the Bell Tower

H. B. WALTERS has described the founding of a bell as "nothing more than [running] a layer of metal . . . into a space between two moulds: an inner mould known as the 'core,' and an outer, styled the 'cope' or mantle."[1] Such a synoptical view of bell casting does not take into consideration the several lengthy stages of preparation that must precede the actual pouring of the molten metal, however. Weeks, months, or in some cases, even years of exacting work anticipate the few minutes it takes for the liquid metal to run from the furnace into the cavity between the core and the cope. The founding of a Russian bell was carried out in five successive stages: the designing of the bell, the cutting of the strickle boards, the construction of the molds, the actual pouring of the metal, and the removal of the bell from its mold. Russian founders traditionally omitted a sixth step that was customary in Western Europe, which consisted of tuning the bell by grinding metal from its inside wall.[2] After cleaning and chasing, the newly cast bell was ready to be fitted with its clapper, consecrated, and hoisted into its belfry or tower.

The earliest witness of bell founding on Russian soil appears in a chronicle notice of 1259, which mentions bells cast in the town of Kholm in Galicia.[3] Most of the bells in Kievan Russia and in the early period of Mongol domination are thought to have been cast in the yards or courts of churches and monasteries.[4] By the mid-fourteenth century bell casting was reported in both Moscow and Novgorod, and during the fifteenth century the industry began to develop along highly professional lines. A miniature illustrating the casting of a bell at Tver in 1403 shows the metal from two furnaces being poured into what was probably a clay mold (figure 30).[5] Another miniature from a sixteenth-century Russian manuscript depicts the founding of a bell in Moscow with metal from a single furnace (figure 81). The first detailed information on the technology of bell founding in Russia, however, did not appear until the mid-seventeenth century in Paul of Aleppo's account of the founding of Aleksandr Grigor'ev's great Kremlin bell of 1655 for Aleksei Mikhailovich.[6] Comparison of the techniques employed in the founding of this bell and the Motorins' Tsar-Kolokol of 1735 with those employed in nineteenth-century founding indicates that the basic operations remained essentially the same.[7] Nineteenth-century bell foundries generally contained four work areas: (1) a work shop for pugging clay and preparing the loam and other molding materials; (2) a casting building with a furnace or furnaces and pits where bell molds were formed and the bells cast; (3) a shop with equipment for polishing and sometimes machines for grinding metal from bells when tuning was required; and (4) a warehouse where bells were classified and arranged by weight.[8]

Designing the Bell

A Russian foreman was responsible for determining the size, weight, proportions, and profile of any bell he cast. These he calculated using standard formulas (discussed in Chapter 9), in the case of the profile, an elaborate system based on fractions of the bell's lower diameter (see Appendix C; figure 121). He then prepared a working drawing at full size in order to minimize error in plotting the contours of the bell's inner and outer surfaces. About the same time this was being prepared, specialists were planning their designs for the inscription and decorative scheme. In seventeenth-century Moscow engravers and icon painters at the Pushkarskij prikaz were sometimes assigned to the Moscow Cannon Yard to execute these designs.

At this stage also a foreman estimated the amount of copper and tin that would be required to cast the bell. Though he would have a general idea based on experience and his drawings, he could obtain a more accurate figure by carefully weighing at the outset the amount of wax and clay he would eventually use to build up the false bell: 2.2 pounds of wax was equivalent to about 26.5 to 31 pounds of bronze; and each pound of clay, depending on its degree of purity, equalled 7 to 8 pounds of metal.[9] Biringuccio cautioned founders to provide sufficient metal for overflow and advised them to calculate the weight of the bell's cannons and the melting loss of metal using their own judgment.[10] If too little metal were on hand, a short run would result, that is, the mold (generally the mold for the bell's cannons) would not be entirely filled with metal and the bell would have to be recast. Excessive overestimation would likewise add considerably to the cost of founding.[11]

Making the Strickle Boards

Following his drawing, the foreman prepared two principal strickle boards (*telovye doski* or *shablony dlia formovki*), one cut to the contour of the interior wall of the bell and the other conforming to the profile of the bell's exterior wall.[12] A third, but temporary, strickle board, approximating the shape

81. A sixteenth-century Russian miniature showing the founding of a large bell in Moscow. Another bell is already hanging in a structure behind the furnace. From A. P. Pronshtejn and A. G. Zadera, "Remeslo," in *Ocherki russkoj kul'tury XVI veka*, pt. 1, gen. ed., A. V. Artsikhovskij (Moscow, 1977), 116. Permission of Moscow University Press.

of the interior strickle board, was also prepared. A spindle or stake was attached to each so that the board could be securely set in a socket and rotated 360° to shape both the core mold and the exterior wall of the false bell (figure 82).

Construction of the Molds and the False Bell

Construction of the inner and outer molds and the false bell demanded the most extreme care and accuracy. It also, not incidentally, required the longest time to execute.

First, a sizable casting pit had to be dug, the width and depth of which were determined by the

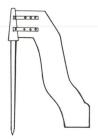

82. A strickle board attached to the spindle on which it rotates to form the outer surface of the false bell. From N. Th. Iartsev, "Kollektsiia po lit'iu kolokolov'," *Izvestiia Obshchestva liubitelej estestvoznaniia, antropologii i ętnografii* 36, no. 2 (1879), p. 50, fig. 2.

height and diameter of the bell to be cast. The pit had to be deep enough so that the top of the bell mold would be slightly lower than the opening in the furnace or furnaces to facilitate the flow of the metal. It had to be wide enough to permit ample passage and working space between its walls and the bell mold (or molds if several bells were to be cast at the same time). Once the pit had been dug, its walls were lined with bricks or stones and reinforced by wooden piles. A circle was drawn on its floor with a diameter that roughly corresponded to the diameter of the bell to be cast. Then the bell mold was built up in a series of stages, from the inside out.

83. The brick foundation on which the core mold of a bell is constructed using a temporary strickle board. From N. N. Rubtsov, "Istoricheskij ocherk razvitiia osnovnykh priemov formovki," *Tekhnologiia litejnoj formy*, ed. N. N. Rubtsov (Moscow, 1954), p. 8, fig. 5. With permission of Izdatel'stvo "Mashinostroenie," Moscow.

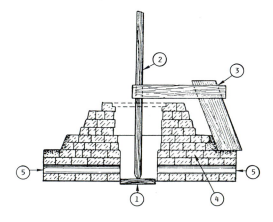

The core (bolvan *or* litso). In the center of the circle drawn to define the circumference of the bell mold ([1] in figure 83) was placed a pointed spindle (2) attached to the temporary strickle board (3); the base of the spindle was enclosed by several layers of brickwork (4). Flues in this foundation (5) would ventilate the fire that would be built inside the core as well as provide avenues by which exhaust gases could escape, insuring that the mold would be uniformly baked. With the rotation of the temporary strickle board the circumference at the base of the core mold could be finalized and a rough brick core built up to about half its total height. The bottom of the cavity inside this core would serve as the ash pit, and the opening at the top as chimney. The temporary strickle board and its spindle were now replaced by the strickle board that would form the final profile of the core (i.e., the contour of the bell's interior wall).

Bricks were first added to the core to refine the form slightly (figure 84), while still remaining well within the strickle board guide.[13] Then the founder applied a mixture of clay, pulverized fireproof brick, and molding sand and gave it the desired shape by sweeping the strickle board around the perimeter of the mold (figure 85). The entire core was then covered with a coating of clay and the strickle board rotated again to remove any excess clay or reveal any depressions. Clay could be added where necessary and the strickle board rotated until the core was uniformly smooth and symmetrical.

Several applications of loam were required at this stage, since shrinkage occurred on drying; each layer was swept clean with the strickle board, wrapped with cord and wire, and allowed to dry thoroughly before a new coat was applied. To hasten this drying process, a wood and charcoal fire was kept burning in the cavity inside the core. Loam applications were repeated until a core was built up whose shape corresponded precisely to the contour defined by the strickle board. The final layer of loam was then covered with a mixture of either powdered brick diluted with kvass (quass) must (a prefermented stage of a Russian beer made from barley, malt, and rye) or ash in soapy water and beer. This coating was essential to prevent the heat of the fire inside the core from cracking the clay.

The false or sham bell (telo *or* rubashka). When the clay of the core had dried completely, its surface was coated with tallow. It was on this greased surface that the founder built up the false bell, a clay model of the bell to be cast in bronze. The second strickle board, cut to the exterior profile of the bell, replaced the first. Then two or three layers of fatty clay were daubed on the core and the strickle board swept around the circumference of the mold. This process was repeated until, as earlier, the contour of the mold was uniformly smooth and symmetrical (figure 86). To prevent the false bell from cracking during drying, linen fibers were added to its layers, and it was wrapped with cord. The outermost layer, made of fine clay, was covered with a mixture of tallow, soap, and wax when finally dry.

At this point inscriptions and ornamentation were modeled on the surface of the false bell with a special mixture prepared in boxes of ten parts wax, twenty parts colophony (a kind of resin from pine trees), five parts red lead, and a half part soot.[14] A fine grade of clay was used to fill any small holes that remained, and with this, construction of the false bell was completed and the building of the cope began.

The cope (kozhukh *or* kolpak). Of the three principal stages in the construction of a bell mold, the formation of the cope required the founder's greatest skill to insure that the bell would be cast with a proper finish. Being careful not to disturb the inscription or relief decorations applied to the false bell, workers first brushed on a liquid substance of finely sifted molding clay mixed with dry and sifted horse manure, cow hair, and chopped flax.[15] This procedure was repeated as many times as necessary to build up a layer 0.19 to 0.27 of an inch thick. Each protective layer took from ten to sixteen hours to dry and harden. When the desired thickness had been reached, a heavier mixture of the same substances was applied in successive layers and allowed to dry. Flax fibers and hair were added after each coating and wrapped with wire in order to prevent the cope from cracking during the baking process. And to strengthen the cope further, workers set vertical iron ribs bound by hori-

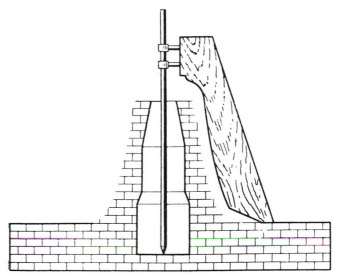

84. The construction of the brick interior of the core mold and shaping of its outer surface with the first strickle board. From B. A. Kolchin, "Remeslo," *Ocherki russkoj kul'tury XIII–XV vekov,* pt. 1: *Material'naia kul'tura* (Moscow, 1968), 208, fig. 1. Permission of Moscow University Press.

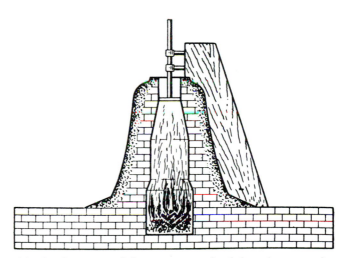

85. The formation of the core over a brick base by using the first strickle board cut to the shape of the bell's interior profile followed by baking from a fire in the cavity of the mold. From Kolchin, "Remeslo," 208, fig. 2. Permission of Moscow University Press.

zontal bands inside the clay. A third application of clay, even thicker than the first two, completed the formation of the cope.[16] To this outer surface were attached iron ribs of even greater thickness than those inside to give the cope an iron frame.

The lower ends of these ribs were bent under

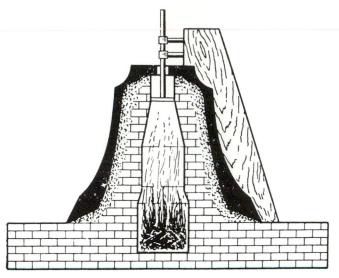

86. Molding the false bell with the second strickle board and its drying through a fire within the cavity of the mold. From Kolchin, "Remeslo," 208, fig. 3. Permission of Moscow University Press.

87. The baking of the cope or upper mold over the false bell. Iron ribs strengthen the outer casing of the bell mold. From Kolchin, "Remeslo," 208, fig. 4. Permission of Moscow University Press.

the lower edge of the cope and the upper ends were bent outward to form hooks by which a derrick could lift the cope from the core. Horizontal bands held these ribs in place around the upper portion of the cope. The bell mold—consisting of core, false bell, and cope—was now ready for baking (figure 87).

Workers again built a fire inside the cavity of the core; and as flames rose, the mold dried and hardened. The layers of grease on either side of the false bell and the wax inscriptions and decorations were also steamed out, which loosened the false bell so that it could simply be sliced with a knife and removed in pieces once the cope was raised. Then the surfaces of both the core and cope were thoroughly cleaned to make sure that they were free from ash[17] and carefully inspected for flaws. If flaws were detected, they were repaired, painted, and dried. At this point an iron loop, or crown staple, for hanging the clapper was inserted in the upper part of the mold. Then workers replaced the cope over the core, locking and sealing the two portions of the mold with clay. The secure and accurate clamping of inner and outer molds was critical, for this is what guaranteed a uniform thickness in the wall of the bell and prevented leakage of molten metal at the bottom. The last step before pouring the bronze was setting the separately constructed mold for the bell cannons in place and fastening them to the top of the bell mold.

The molds for the bell cannons (ushi). Russian founders in the nineteenth century used one of two materials to fashion the models for their bell cannons—plaster of Paris and wax or wood. In using the former, they covered a plaster of Paris core with a thick coat of wax in the desired shape of the cannons, then removed the core when the wax had hardened and very carefully covered the hollow wax shell with damp clay, wrapping it finally with cord. When the clay had dried thoroughly, they baked the form, melting away the wax and leaving a clay mold. In using wood, founders carved each of the cannons' loops individually and covered each with clay. Once the clay had dried, they cut each piece lengthwise, removed the wooden core, and reassembled the two halves of the mold. These individually prepared loop molds were then joined at the top and the assembly strengthened with a covering of clay wrapped in twine and wire. If the mold was for the cannons of a large bell, two handles were attached to its top for ease in moving.

Whether fashioned from wood or plaster of Paris and wax, the mold for the cannons included two or three openings: one, the casting gate, through which the metal was poured; and the other one or two through which air and gases that collected inside the mold during pouring could escape. To prevent any separation from the bell mold during pouring, the mold for the cannons was fitted into a conical pit at the top of the cope and fastened in place by wires attached to the iron bands that encircled the cope. This insured that the bell and its cannons would be cast as a unit. At this point the entire bell mold was locked and stood ready for casting (figure 88).

Final preparations. Before the furnace was tapped, the space between the bell mold and the brick- or rock-lined wall of the pit had to be filled with earth and thoroughly packed. In fact, earth shoveled into the pit was packed every five to seven inches until the entire mold was buried. The weight of the earth between the mold and the wall of the pit braced the cope against the considerable hydrostatic pressure the molten metal would exert as it filled the cavity between the core and the cope and prevented the cope from cracking and releasing liquid metal into the pit.

In Russia the melting of the copper was carried out first in a furnace or furnaces that could generate temperatures of 2,150°F over a period of twelve to fourteen and even up to sixteen hours.[18] After the copper had melted, and five to ten minutes before starting the flow from the furnace, the requisite amount of tin was added.[19] The two metals were thoroughly stirred and skimmed to remove any impurities that may have risen to the surface. Though the amount of waste depended primarily on the purity of the raw metal, a well constructed furnace would only lose from 3 to 4 percent. After the metals had been carefully mixed and the casting gutter cleaned, the molten bronze was ready to be run from the furnace through the pouring gate into the bell mold (figure 89).[20]

Casting the Bell: The Drama of the Pour

Despite careful preparation and precautionary measures, the casting process always entailed certain risks. If the bell mold had not dried sufficiently, if the temperature of the metal was not high enough before being run into the mold, or if trapped gases could not escape from the molten metal, the solidified bronze might be too porous and the bell liable to crack when rung. At other times the bell metal might solidify too rapidly and cause cooling stresses if the outer surface contracted at a faster rate than the inner wall, producing defects in the bell's wall unable to withstand repeated blows of the clapper.[21] If the core should shift during casting, pushed to one side by the weight and pressure from the stream of molten metal, variation in the thickness of the bell wall could easily result. This would produce not only a bell with an unsatisfactory tone but one that would be more likely to crack after repeated ringing. And if the core and cope had not been securely locked, metal could even seep from the mold. Occasionally metal ran into the hollow conical space inside the core mold and made removal of the bell from its mold extremely difficult. The solution when such accidents occurred was generally a recasting of the bell, which meant the beginning of another long process of preparation.

Because no amount of earthly effort assured success in the founding of a bell, prayers, invocations, and benedictions traditionally preceded the mo-

88. A bell mold assembled, locked, and ready for casting. From Rubtsov, "Istoricheskij ocherk razvitiia osnovnykh priemov formovki," 10, fig. 8. With permission of Izdatel'stvo "Mashinostroenie," Moscow.

89. A cross-section of a bell mold in its casting pit with the casting gutter leading from an open hearth furnace to the pouring gate. From Olovianishnikov, *Istoriia kolokolov"*, betw. pp. 396 and 397.

ment when the metal began to flow into the mold. These prayers placed the casting results in the hands of God. In Russian foundries the foundry owner brought an icon into the workshop and set lighted candles before it. Activity ceased and all foundry workers gathered to witness this most solemn moment. The senior foreman removed his hat and crossed himself. Other workers did the same. The foundry owner then read aloud a special prayer for a successful casting, and all foremen and workers, from the youngest and least experienced to the oldest and most accomplished, repeated his prayer. Then the owner ordered all doors to the casting

area closed. The heat and smoke from the furnaces became almost unbearable, the air heavy and difficult to breathe, when finally the owner gave the sign to tap the metal. Several workers pulled a bar, which punctured the plug in the tapping hole to release the molten bronze.[22] And suddenly, like a fiery spring, the liquid bronze rose up from the mouth of the furnace and ran down the casting gutter slowly and evenly into the mold (figure 90). Workers stirred the metal around the pouring gate at the top of the mold constantly to prevent its solidifying and blocking the passage. This entire scene was harshly illuminated by the incandescent bronze and blurred by the smoke and rising heat.[23]

The casting of Bogdanov's Great Uspensky Bell in 1817 was attended by ceremonies even more formal and elaborate than those described above:

90. The drama of the pour, the bell foundry of P. I. Olovia-nishnikov and Sons formerly in Yaroslavl. From Olovianish-nikov, *Istoriia kolokolov"*, betw. pp. 412 and 413.

On the 7th March 1817, the late archbishop Augustin descended into the cavity [the pit] where the bell was to be cast, which measured 32½ feet in depth, and in width 23 feet four inches. He sprinkled this place with holy water, and also the materials for founding the bell. He then gave his benediction to Messrs. Bogdanof and Zibialof [*sic*], who were engaged to re-cast the bell, and ordered all the workmen to come and receive the same with the cross. The melted copper [bronze] was then run off by a gutter into the mould, from the air-holes of which the fiery air burst forth with the splendour of lighted torches. The bell being finished, Augustin gave thanks to God. During the founding of the bell, many of the inhabitants of Moscow were present, and threw among the melted copper, gold and silver, rings &c.[24]

Maurice Baring gives a colorful account of the casting of a bell in a village of the Tambov province sometime during the first years of the twentieth century:

The ceremony was fixed for four o'clock in the afternoon with due solemnity and with religious rites, and I was invited to be present. . . . It was a blazing hot day. The air was dry, the ground was dry, everything was dry, and the great column of smoke mixed with flame issuing from the furnace added to the heat. The furnace had been made exactly opposite to the church. . . . Before the bell was to be cast a Te Deum was to be sung.

It was Wednesday, the day of the bazaar. . . . But this afternoon the bazaar was deserted. The whole population of the village was gathered together on the dry brown grassy square in front of the church to take part in the ceremony. At four o'clock two priests and a deacon, followed by a choir consisting of two men in their Sunday clothes, and by bearers of gilt banners, walked in procession out of the church. They were dressed in stiff robes of green and gold, and as they walked they intoned a plain song. An old card table with its stained green cloth was placed and opened on the ground opposite and not far from the church, and on this two lighted tapers were set together with a bowl of holy water. The peasants gathered round in a semicircle with bare heads and joined in the service, making countless genuflexions and signs of the cross, and joining in the song with their deep bass voices. When I said the peasants I should have said half of them. The other half were gathered in a dense crowd round the furnace, which was built of bricks and open on both sides to the east and to the west, and fed with wooden fuel. The men in charge of the proceeding stood on both sides of it and stirred the molten metal it contained with two enormous poles. On the southern side of the furnace was a channel through which the molten metal when released was to flow into the cast [the mold] of the bell. The crowd which was assembled here was already struggling to have and to hold a good place for the spectacle of the release of the metal when the solemn moment should arrive. Three policemen were endeavouring to cope with the crowd; . . . They were trying with all their might to keep back the crowd, so that when the metal was released a disaster should not happen; but their efforts were in vain, because the crowd was large, and when they pressed back a small portion of it they made a dent in it which caused the remaining part of it to bulge out; and it was the kind of crowd—so intensely typical of Russia—on which no words, whether of command, entreaty, or threat, made the smallest impression. The only way to keep it back was by pressing on it with the body and outstretched arms, and that only kept back a tiny portion of it. In the meantime the Te Deum went on and on; and many things and persons were prayed for besides the bell which was about to be born. At one moment I obtained a place from which I had a commanding view of the furnace, but I was soon oozed out of it by the ever-increasing crowd of men, women, and children. . . . The peasants who were listening and taking part in the Te Deum were like the figures of a sacred picture—women with red and white Eastern headdresses, bearded men, listening as though a miracle were about to be performed, and barefooted children with straw coloured hair and blue eyes running about everywhere. Towards six o'clock the Te Deum at last came to an end, and the whole crowd moved and swayed around the furnace. A Russian crowd is like a large tough sponge. Nothing seems to make any effect on it. It absorbs the newcomers who dive into it, and you can pull it this way and press it that way, but there it remains, indissoluble, passive, and obstinate. . . .

I asked a peasant who was sitting by a railing under the church when the ceremony would begin. "Ask them," he answered, "they will tell you, but they won't tell us." With the help of the policeman I managed to squeeze a way through the mass of struggling humanity to a place in the first row. I was told that the critical moment was approaching, and was asked to throw a piece of silver into the furnace, so that the bell might have a tuneful sound. I threw a silver rouble into the furnace, and then the men who were in charge of the casting said that the critical moment had come. On each side of the small channel they fixed metal screens and placed a large screen facing it. Then the man in charge said in a loud matter-of-fact tone: "Now, let us pray to God." The peasants all uncovered themselves and made a sign of the cross, and a moment was spent in silent prayer. This prayer was especially for the success of the operation which was to take place immediately, namely, the release of the molten metal, since two hours had already been spent in praying for the bell. At this moment the excitement of the crowd reached such a pitch that they pushed themselves right up to the channel, and the efforts of the policemen . . . were pathetic. One man, however, not a policeman, waved a big stick and threatened to beat everybody back if they did not make way. Then at last the culminating moment arrived, the metal was released, and it poured down the narrow channel which had been prepared for it, and over which two logs placed crosswise formed an arch, surmounted by a yachting cap for ornament. It caused a huge yellow sheet of flame to flare up for a moment in front of the iron screen facing the channel. The women in the crowd shrieked. Those who were in front made a desperate effort to get back, and those who were at the back made a desperate effort to get forward, and I was carried right through and beyond the crowd in the struggle. And the bell was born.[25]

Removal of the Bell from the Mold

Once the metal had been poured and the furnace emptied, the founder had to wait for the bronze to solidify before the new bell could be removed from its mold. The time required depended on the size and weight of the bell. A smaller casting of 500 pounds or less cooled overnight; a very large bell might require several days (Grigor'ev's great Kremlin bell of 1655 remained in its pit three days after casting).[26] When the bronze had cooled sufficiently, the packed soil around the mold was removed from the pit, and the cope was broken up to reveal the newly cast bell. The bell was then removed from its mold, its inscriptions and decorations cleaned with metal brushes or chisels to remove oxidized metal and any residue from the mold, and its surface chased and polished. Only then was it ready to be raised up out of its casting pit. Finally came the moment of truth. The new bell was fitted with an iron clapper, and foundry workers waited anxiously to hear the voice of the instrument their weeks of labor had produced. A rich and resonant stroke was greeted with rejoicing.

The Journey to the Bell Tower

To minimize problems of transportation, almost all great Russian bells were cast as close as possible to the bell tower in which they were to be hung. A large casting pit was dug in the churchyard or courtyard of the institution that had ordered the bell. The foreman had to construct melting furnaces close to the pit and bring in all the necessary supplies, including bell metal, tools, and an enormous amount of firewood for stoking the furnace fires. For the Kremlin's Tsar-Kolokol, a special tower was to have been built directly over the pit so that movement of the bell would only have to be vertical. Smaller bells as a rule, and in some instances even bells of considerable weight, were cast in established foundries, however, and had to be transported from the foundry, sometimes over quite a distance, to the church or monastery that had commissioned or purchased them.

Founders had to go to some lengths in Russia to arrange for the transport of large bells. Because roads were generally unable to support the weight of a large bell, especially in the spring and fall, a bell was, when practical, loaded on a flatcar and moved by train. A preferential tariff was available (no. 89 in 1901), calculated at a hundredth of a kopeck per verst (0.663 of a mile) for each pud in the bell's weight. But railroad conveyance was possible only for bells weighing under 1,500 puds (54,170 pounds), because the diameter of heavier bells would not clear bridges and passing trains.[27] If the distance to be covered was not too great and no railroad ran nearby, horses could be harnessed to pull a bell. But eighty horses would be needed to move a bell of 2,000 puds (72,226 pounds) from Valdai to the Trinity Cathedral in St. Petersburg, not only an expensive proposal but one that would have blocked the road between Valdai and Petersburg for a considerable time.[28] Waterways were another means of hauling large bells over a distance.[29] But they were generally used only in the winter when the rivers had frozen over, and some unfortunate instances are recorded of a large bell's breaking through the ice as porters watched helplessly and the instrument sank to the bottom of the river.[30]

On numerous occasions in rural Russia inhabitants of entire villages were recruited to drag large bells on runners or on a sledge (figure 32) from a foundry or train station to a church tower. The two-day portage of Bogdanov's Great Uspensky Bell from his Moscow foundry into the Kremlin was carried out in this manner, and with much ceremony:

On the 23d February 1819 this bell was removed upon a great oak sledge from the foundery [*sic*], Te Deum being previously celebrated. In front of the bell was erected a kind of stage, on which Mr. Bogdanof and others stood. The imperial flag was displayed, and the motions of the machine were regulated by the sound of the small bells suspended over the great bell. Ropes, or cables, were given to the crowd, who disputed the honour, not to say service, of assisting the transportation. At a signal given all was in motion. . . . The Borovitskiya Gates having been previously enlarged, by taking down a small part of the wall, the bell was drawn up hill, and soon lodged at the foot of Ivan Velikii. Te Deum was again celebrated; after which the crowd threw themselves upon Mr. Bogdanof, and kissed his cheeks, his breast, his hands, his clothes, to testify their approbation of his knowledge of his art, and their content at seeing such a fine bell once more within the precincts of the Kremle [*sic*].

Bogdanof then ascended the bell, and bowed three times to each side, amidst the *huzzas* of the multitude.[31]

On reaching its destination, a Russian bell was

often displayed at the base of its tower for people to admire before being hoisted up where it would hang largely out of sight. H. C. Romanoff reports about 1865 that a new bell of 10,950 pounds was displayed for two weeks on the grounds of its church at Votkinsk. During that time strokes on the bell were "sold" to workers and peasants of Votkinsk and its region for three kopecks each. Many offered gifts of more than this amount, and the poor were allowed to hear the bell rung for less or even without paying the three-kopeck fee. Those who paid to hear the bell rung believed that its sound "was beneficial for the soul and conducive to salvation."[32]

Dedication of Bells after Casting

In the medieval West bells, like people, were named, anointed, sprinkled with holy water, and robed; the hope was that the bells would "act as preservatives against thunder and lightning, and hail and wind, and storms of every kind, and that they [would] drive away evil spirits."[33] The origin of the baptism of European bells remains obscure, but the oldest known evidence of this ritual is preserved in the *Liber ordinum*, a book used in Spanish churches before 712.[34] Another reference appears in a capitulary of Charlemagne from 789, where the baptism of bells is prohibited.[35] Centuries later, in 1636-1637, Mersenne quotes the brief benediction pronounced over bells in the Roman Rite: "Lord, may this bell be sanctified and consecrated in the name of the Father, the Son, and the Holy Ghost."[36] Preceding and following these words were other speeches, and the bell was sprinkled inside and out with holy water. The priest then made seven crosses above the bell with oil used in anointing the sick and four crosses within the bell using chrism.

In Russia, too, before a newly cast bell was hung, it was consecrated in a ceremony sanctioned by the Orthodox Church.[37] The *chin" blagosloveniia kampana* (order for the blessing of a bell) found in the enlarged version of the prayer book was performed by a member of the higher clergy (*arkhierej*) or by a priest (*sviashchennik*), who, after leaving the church, approached the bell and sprinkled it with consecrated water.[38] The ceremony of blessing the bell followed.

1. *Blagosloven" Bog" nash"* (Blessed be our God) The clergy then sings *Tsariu nebesnyj* (O heavenly King) in the sixth mode (*glas*).

2. After the opening benediction, the following are read:
Trisviatoe (Thrice Holy)
Otche nash" (Our Father)
Gospodi pomiluj (Lord, have mercy) twelve times
Slava (Glory) ⎫
I nyně (And now) ⎬ Lesser Doxology
Priidite, poklonimsia (Come, let us worship) three times.

3. The Psalms of Praise in which all creation is called upon to praise the Lord with instruments:
Psalm 148: *Khvalite Gospoda s" nebes"* (Praise the Lord from the heavens)
Psalm 149: *Vospojte Gospodevi pěsn' novu* (Sing unto the Lord a new song)
Psalm 150: *Khvalite Boga vo sviatykh" Ego* (Praise God in His holy places).
After the three Psalms follows the Lesser Doxology (*Slava/I nyně*) and then *Alleluia* three times.

4. The deacon then reads the litany *Mirom" Gospodu pomolimsia* (In peace let us pray to the Lord) with special petitions concerning the consecration of the bell for the good of the people.

5. The reading of Psalm 28: *Prinesite Gospodevi, synove Bozhii, . . . prinesite Gospodevi slavu i chest'* (Render unto the Lord, sons of God, . . . render unto the Lord glory and honor).

6. After the reading of Psalm 28, the officiant reads the prayer that begins: *Gospodi Bozhe nash", khotiaj ot" vsekh" vernykh" Tvoikh" vsegda slavim" i pokloniaem" byti* (O Lord our God, who wants always to be glorified and worshipped by all Thy faithful).

7. After this prayer with all heads bowed, the officiant secretly reads the prayer beginning *Vladyko Bozhe Otche Vsederzhiteliu* (O God Father, Ruler Omnipotent) and sprinkles the bell with holy water from above, on all four sides, saying three times: *Blagoslovliaetsia i osviashchaetsia kampan" sej okropleniem" vody seia sviashchennyia, vo imia Ottsa, i Syna, i Sviatago Dukha, amin"* (Blessed and consecrated be this bell by the sprinkling of this holy water, in the name of the Father and of the Son, and of the Holy Spirit, Amen).

8. The bell is also sprinkled inside on four sides and then censed on four sides inside and out. During the

censing the clergy reads Psalm 69: *Bozhe, v″ pomoshch″ moiu vonmi* (O God, harken to my aid).

9. After the reading of Psalm 69, some verses are read from the Book of Numbers (Chapter 10, verses 1-10): "The Lord spoke to Moses saying: 'Make thee two silver trumpets; of hammered work thou shalt make them.'" In this reading from the Book of Numbers is the following passage: "And in the days of your gladness, and on your solemn occasions, and at the beginnings of your months, sound forth with trumpets over [your] burnt offerings," etc.

10. Following the reading from Numbers 10 the following stichera are sung or read: *Zemli i prochim″ stikhiiam″* (For the earth and the other elements) and *Osnovaniia vseia zemli podvizaiaj Bozhe* (O God, who establisheth the foundations of all the earth). During the Lesser Doxology (*Slava/I nyně*) in the fourth mode *Vsiacheskaia edinoiu v″ nachalě soboiu* . . .

(O Lord, who in the beginning hath created everything, by Thine own spontaneous [will] and now acting upon everything indirectly, with the voice of this consecrated bell drive away from the hearts of Thy faithful every oppression and slothful inclination, implant in them Thy awe with reverence, and by Thy power make [them] hasten to prayer, quick to [perform] every good deed, delivering us from all designs of the enemy, and protect the innocent from the pestilence of noxious airs: through the prayers of the Bogoroditsa [Virgin] and of all Thy saints, as Thou alone art merciful).

11. Upon the singing of the stichera, the daily dismissal is pronounced.[39]

Hoisting of Bells into a Tower

After a large Russian bell had been moved to the base of the tower where it was to be hung, a way had to be found to raise it into the tower.[40] This could be accomplished either from within or without the tower (figure 91).

Raising a bell inside a tower was the simplest method and required fewer workers, but it was possible only when construction on the tower was not yet complete and when there were no obstructions to a bell's access into the desired tier. The operation also took several hours. An outside hoist demanded the concerted efforts of a greater number of men but could be accomplished fairly quickly (in only five to ten minutes) and easily. In either

91. Sixteenth-century Russian miniature from the *Tsarstvennaia kniga* (Sinod. bibl. MS. no. 149) showing the outside hoist of a bell into a wooden tower. From N. I. Fal'kovskij, *Moskva v istorii tekhniki* (Moscow, 1950), p. 409, fig. 181. Permission of VAAP, Moscow.

case, Russian engineers used hoisting tackle of hemp ropes and chain blocks for the maneuver, the number and size depending on the weight of the bell.[41] The ropes were controlled by winches, capstans, or in the case of the largest bells, men. Some of the ropes were employed directly in lifting the bell, while others were used to control its lateral swaying and to prevent the bell from striking the tower during its elevation (figure 92).

If the construction and strength of a bell tower would not permit a large bell to be raised by either of the methods above, another procedure was available, although costly and requiring considerably more time and labor. A temporary wooden or iron structure could be built adjacent to the bell tower within which the bell could be raised on chain blocks. The bell would then be moved laterally from the temporary structure to the tier in the bell tower where it was to hang. Since the larger bells occupied the lower tiers in Russian bell towers, the

92. An outside hoist of a 544-pud (19,645-pound) bell into an unidentified Russian bell tower at the end of the nineteenth or beginning of the twentieth century. From Olovianishnikov, *Istoriia kolokolov''*, betw. pp. 402 and 403.

vertical distance of the hoist was minimized. In any case, before a Russian bell was lifted, it was securely wrapped in towels and cloth to protect it from injury. As it was being raised, holy water was sprinkled over it, hymns sung, and prayers said for its safe passage.[42]

H. C. Romanoff has left a vivid description of a hoist he witnessed of a 10,950-pound bell at Votkinsk around 1865.

On the 15th of January, at eleven o'clock, we were warned by a grand clattering of the lesser bells (the old one having been removed to make room for the new one), that if we wished to see the raising of the bell—a religious ceremony—we must make haste. It was a glorious day, "blue and golden," with no wind, consequently the 28° were endurable. We found a considerable crowd outside the church, and feared that it would

be double inside, but were agreeably surprised by the contrary, and I was astonished to find only one lady and two little boys of the nobles among the whole congregation. One of the Priests was reading an acathistus to the Virgin, while the others gradually dropped in, and disappeared behind the altar-screen.

In the body of the church before the royal gates, stood a low naloy, on which were two candlesticks with burning tapers, and a large pewter sort of tureen containing holy water, or rather water that was destined to be blessed. There was a good deal of going backwards and forwards among the Readers and sextons, and evident preparation. At last the High Priest—who, in by no means so handsome canonicals as I had expected on this occasion, issued from the royal gates, followed by three other Priests and the Deacon, and placing himself before the naloy, with his back to the greater part of the congregation, and his face towards the Gates—began a molében, and blessed the water by plunging the cross in it three times, each time holding the same, on taking it out of the water, over another smaller vessel, which the Deacon held, and allowing the drops to fall from the cross into it: with these drops the bell was afterwards sprinkled.

The congregation now approached the naloy, and each, as he kissed the cross, which the High Priest held, was sprinkled by him with water from the first vessel. This is performed by dipping a sort of brush, very like those used for whipping creams, into the water, and by a sharp movement of the wrist dispersing the drops on the heads of the congregation.

A procession was immediately afterwards formed, consisting of the clergy and Readers, churchwardens and sextons, each with something in his hand. Two Readers went before with the church banners; two sextons followed with horrid, dull, waxed dropped lanterns containing tapers, as candles in the usual tall candlesticks would be liable to be blown out. The congregation pressed forward, eager to obtain the nearest possible position to the High Priest; we lingered purposely, and had the best view of all the proceedings from the top of the church steps, which are upwards of twenty in number. At their foot, with a quantity of linen wound round it to prevent its rubbing when it entered the belfry, lay the bell, a mystery of cordage and pulleys twisted about it; and when I looked at the immense mass, I felt nervously doubtful as to whether the means prepared were strong enough to raise it. My companions experienced the same dread, and we moved to the left, lest the 10,950 lbs. should fall on our heads.

The High Priest read a few prayers on reaching the bell, not a word of which was audible, and then proceeded to sprinkle it in the manner I have described, walking round it as he did so. The choir, with the remaining Priests, sang psalms and irmos, but the sound was completely drowned by the hum of voices and the shouts of the workmen to each other as they arranged the cordage; a dozen or so of men were in the belfry, and *five hundred* in the street below, ready to pull at the cords; and when the service, which did not occupy more than five minutes, and which was by no means striking in any respect, was concluded, a great noise ensued, which ended in the signal to begin pulling being given, and in a few seconds the huge mass began to move. The blocks, however, were imperfectly arranged, and they were obliged to lower the bell again while they were being put to rights, and we had to stand an extra ten minutes in the frost. [Here Romanoff quotes a portion of Schiller's "Song of the Bell" in Leveson Gower's translation.]

When it begins to ascend again the shouts ceased, and the crowd made the sign of the cross devoutly, while the melodious singing of the choir, now agreeably audible, accompanied the bell on its rapid progress to its place of final destination.

A great crashing of the lath and plaster about the opening of the belfry rather alarmed the crowd, and an attempt at a rush was made, but no harm was done, and in a few seconds the object of our interest was safely deposited perpendicularly on the temporary floor prepared for it; but it could not be hung for several days, owing to the contrivances required for lifting it in that limited space being out of order, and it was not until the Sunday following that we heard its real tone. I cannot say by what law of acoustics it rang more clearly and sonorously in its gallows [scaffold on the ground] than in the belfry, but such is the fact; everybody was disappointed in its strength and sweetness, but its "voice" is pleasant enough, and of course infinitely preferable to that of its cracked predecessor.[43]

One of the most challenging and controversial of all outside bell hoists in Russia was that undertaken in 1819 to raise Bogdanov's Great Uspensky Bell (at least 4,000 puds, or 144,452 pounds) into the Kremlin's Ivan Velikij Bell Tower. It was engineered through the construction of a temporary tower adjacent to the central (Petrok Malyj) section of the tower where the bell was to hang. But shortly before the day of the hoist Metropolitan Serafim expressed doubts about the capability of Bogdanov's scaffolding tower to support the weight of the new bell during this operation. Only after careful inspection by an architect and his assurances of the structure's sufficiency did the Metropolitan permit Bogdanov to proceed.

On the day set for raising the bell, Metropolitan Serafim together with special church dignitaries arrived at the Cathedral of the Assumption. The square [before the Kremlin cathedrals] was crowded with an immense number of spectators. . . . His Grace . . . consecrated the bell according to the rules of the church and then blessed its elevation. The bell began to rise very quickly and smoothly; it was already halfway, when suddenly cries came from all sides of the square: "The Ivan Velikij is swaying, the hoisting tower is falling!" The crowds of people on the square began to undulate like waves on the ocean; the shrieks of women and children were heard as they were pressed by the crowd. Fortunately Shul'gin, the chief of police, with amazing presence of mind threw himself into the crowd of closely packed people near the seven capstans by which the bell was being raised and with a resolute, reassuring voice declared that this was not true, that this was fabricated by scoundrels! The people calmed down when they saw with their own eyes that neither was the Ivan Velikij Tower shaking nor the hoisting tower falling. During this turmoil, Bogdanov was directing the operations of many capstans by means of a small bell and baton with a handkerchief tied to it. By not moving away from the bell himself, he was able to keep the workers at their positions and by his exemplary efficiency was able to avert a great disaster.[44]

Thus Bogdanov succeeded in placing his bell in the Ivan Velikij Tower that same day. Asked later by Metropolitan Serafim what he would have done if permission had not been granted to hoist the bell as planned, Bogdanov replied without hesitation that he had decided he would raise the bell noiselessly at night with his own workers.[45]

The Suspension of Russian Bells: Problems and Solutions

The systems and structures used for hanging bells were of special concern to founders and bell ringers. Smaller bells generally presented no unusual problems, but the stationary installation of large bells in Russia and Asia often severely taxed, sometimes overtaxed, the ability of bell towers and suspension systems to support their dead weight and to tolerate the vibrations they produced when rung. At the end of the seventeenth century Le Comte saw a 22.25-ton Chinese bell (11 feet 9 inches high with a diameter of 7.5 feet) lying on the ground at Nanking in the ruins of its fallen belfry with three bells of lesser size beside it.[46] In more recent times, too, "It is not uncommon, throughout China, to see enormous bells lying upon the ground, their weight having broken down the towers in which they were suspended.[47]

Unlike the bell towers in Western Europe, most of which were built of stone, the bell towers and zvonnitsy of Russia were generally built of brick and were therefore structurally weaker.[48] In addition, too often they were not adequately reinforced to support the bells they contained.[49] A type of bell tower that seemed especially vulnerable to stress was the one built "over-the-gate" (*kolokol'nia nad" vorotami*). The gateway at the base of this kind of structure had often not been designed to bear the weight of a bell tower and increasing numbers of bells or to withstand the vibrations of the ringing bronze. Cracks developed in the walls of many of these towers. Even in structures that were originally built to contain heavy bells, exigency of design and choice of materials had not always kept pace with the increasing magnitudes of bells acquired.

Problems of structural support and adequate suspension for Russian bells are set forth along with certain solutions in a study by a nineteenth-century Russian engineer, N. Podchinennov.[50] Charged with hoisting and hanging a new bell cast in 1890 that weighed 722 puds (26,074 pounds) and had a 26-pud (939-pound) clapper in an over-the-gate bell tower at the Danilov Monastery in Moscow, Podchinennov observed that the walls and vaulting of this tower showed the effects of excessive stress from a 365-pud (13,181-pound) bell it already contained.[51] The gateway itself he judged to date from the sixteenth century; over this a church had later been added, and above the church, a bell tower.

The entire structure was leaning noticeably toward the southwest.

The 365-pud bell was hung in this tower from two pine beams, placed crosswise one above the other, whose ends were set into the brick masonry, a system that only facilitated the transmission of the bell's vibrations into the tower's walls. Because wooden beams tended to rot and sag, they were often reinforced by being laid across segments of railroad track. And here, as though to insure that the tower would receive full impact from the ringing of the bell, two such supporting rails ran the length of the lower beam with their ends bent back and supported by short segments from other rails. When the bell was rung, the two rails, according to Podchinennov, looked like vibrating strings.[52] In order for the tower to accommodate substantial additional weight and increased stress from ringing the new bell, Podchinennov designed an elaborate framework of iron girders to be constructed inside the bell tower that would direct the bell's weight and its vibrations away from the walls into the lower portions of the structure but would not alter the exterior appearance of the tower.[53]

Problems of support a few miles away in the Kremlin's Ivan Velikij Bell Tower, Russia's largest housing for church bells, were of a different sort. During the second half of the nineteenth century (and contemporaneous with the introduction of cast-iron frames in English towers) some Russian bells were transferred from their wooden beams to iron I-beam support systems,[54] among them the bells in the Bono-Godunov column of the Ivan Velikij Tower. To preserve the tone quality of these bells, the girders were faced on all sides with wooden boards from gun carriages, a casing that significantly reduced, even if it did not completely eliminate, the transmission of vibrations to the iron beam during ringing.[55] The three great bells in the central Petrok Malyj section of the tower—"Polielejnyj," "Reut," and the Great Uspensky Bell—continued to hang from wooden beams until the early part of this century. The considerable bulk of this structure and its massive foundations met the structural requirements for bearing the weight of these bells and for withstanding the effects of their ringing, but the proper suspension of bells of such magnitudes demanded extraordinary measures. Each bell hung from beams made up of multiple timbers stacked one on top of another, whose ends were secured in the walls (figure 93).

The support system for Bogdanov's 4,000-pud Great Uspensky Bell was the most complex of the three. Sixteen stout timbers, placed beside and stacked on top of each other, were secured by iron bands to form an enormous wooden beam 49 inches thick (1 arshin, 12 vershki). This composite beam was in turn supported by another system designed to reinforce the great bell's suspension from above at the midpoint where its load was concentrated. Despite the sturdy construction of this multitimbered beam with its auxiliary bracing, however, by the beginning of the twentieth century it had deteriorated and begun to sag from the weight of the bell. The entire system, together with the suspensions for its two companions on either side, was replaced in 1910 with a riveted iron structure (figure 94).[56] In this new support four wooden blocks were installed to absorb vibrations from the bell's ringing, thereby preventing their transmission to the support system itself.

The suspension systems and special constructions for these three great bells were unusual, even in Russia. The weight of the largest bell at many of the most important foundations in Russia generally fell between 300 and 1,000 puds. Figure 95 shows the manner of suspending a bell in this range, the 450-pud "Lebed'" (Swan) bell in the Ivan Velikij Tower. The bell was oriented with two pairs of cannons (four loops) parallel to the axis of the beam (*a-a*); two single loops ran cross-wise. A short channel-like steel member was placed leg-down over the beam to serve as bearing plate to three double-eye spacer bars (*D*), the outer ones set over the two lengthwise pairs of cannons. Four rods (*C*) hung vertically from the eyes of these two outside spacer bars, fastened on the top by linch pins. At the lower end of each rod was a square eye, located so that each pair of rods straddled the two cannon loops beneath them. An iron key was driven through each pair of eyes and cannon, thus forming a yoke to connect the cannon loops and the beam. The two

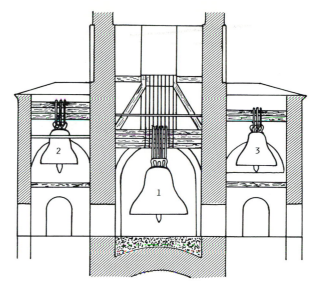

93. The old (pre-1910) suspension systems for three great bells in the central Petrok Malyj structure of the Ivan Velikij Bell Tower in the Moscow Kremlin: (1) Great Uspensky Bell (4,000 puds); (2) "Reut" bell (2,000 puds); and (3) "Polielejnyj" bell (1,500 puds). After Olovianishnikov, *Istoriia kolokolov"*, 404.

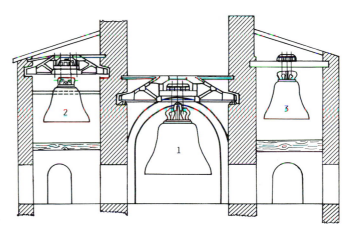

94. The new suspension systems of iron beams installed in 1910 for the same three bells in the Ivan Velikij Bell Tower. After Olovianishnikov, *Istoriia kolokolov"*, 404.

rods (*F*) suspended from the center spacer bar had hooks at their lower ends, each of which engaged one of the two crosswise cannon loops.[57] Thus the cannons of a Russian bell did not touch the beam itself.

Russian bells had to be securely suspended from their beams to withstand shocks from repeated clapper blows. And faulty suspension or a flaw in

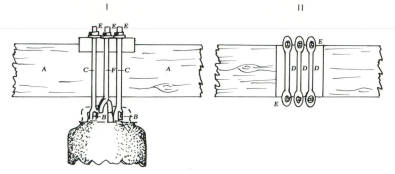

95. Suspension system for the 450-pud (16,251-pound) "Lebed'"
bell in the Ivan Velikij Bell Tower in the Moscow Kremlin: I.
side view; and II. view of beam from above. After Babin, "O
russkikh" kolokolakh"," fig. 12 and 12 bis in sketch 12.

a bell's cannons was occasionally responsible for the bell's breaking loose from its beam and falling, sometimes through the vaults of lower tiers in its tower, to the ground. Of course, suspended in towers as they were, Russian bells were also vulnerable to lightning and the possibility of fire. And they were threatened by the Russian winter when extremely low temperatures made the bronze brittle and more liable to fracture.[58] But a far greater menace was the ringer whose careless handling of the clapper often did irreparable damage.

Broken Bells and Their Repair

Perhaps the most common source of injury to bells in Russia resulted from a breakdown of the microcrystalline structure of the bell metal under repeated blows of the clapper at the same point on the sound-bow. A crack would open at a weakened spot and run upward into the bell's waist.[59] Using excessive force in swinging the clapper against the sound-bow was another common way that Russian bells were broken.[60] In "Kolokol" (The Bell), an early sketch from 1896, Maxim Gorky has dramatized the results of overtaxing the metal of a 600-pud bell. On the eve of Easter Antip Nikitich Prakhov, a wealthy merchant and the bell's donor, ascends the tower where his bell is hanging.

It was three minutes before midnight. Antip Nikitich decided to ring [the bell]. He quickly slipped his watch into the pocket of his waistcoat, crossed himself, and pushed the clapper to the right. He seized it with both hands and . . . pushed it harder and harder. . . . Antip Nikitich, smiling [and] heady from the booming of the bronze, which jangled his nerves, threw the clapper against the edge of the bell with all his might; more and more frequently he struck it. He seemed to want to drown out completely the bell in the city church. . . . Majestically and solemnly the ringing droned on; everything was shaking, and Antip Nikitich blissfully felt himself flying in the air.

Still another blow—and his bell somehow clattered strangely. Prakhov attributed this to the weakness of his stroke and with all his strength flung the clapper to the wall of the bell. At that moment there emerged an odd, abnormal rattling sound. It was so brief and pathetic. It was heard and died out, stifled at once. . . .

A cold blast breathed on Antip Nikitich from somewhere, and he stood rooted to the spot after he released the clapper from his hands. He couldn't believe it. The bronze above his head wheezed somehow. He reached out and silently began to run his fingers over the metal. It was warm, but he could already feel it cooling down beneath his hand.

. . . Prakhov shuddered from head to toe. He had found it. Now he had no doubt—the bell had cracked. A fine fracture had rent its lip, and Antip Nikitich, after firmly grasping the bell with both hands, leaned his forehead against it and froze.[61]

One method of repairing a cracked bell was to open or enlarge the crack and pour molten metal into the space. Although this was intended to at least partially melt the surfaces of the division and fuse the bell wall, the procedure was rarely successful. The bell could not withstand the tension from the contraction of the metal and the impact of the clapper when rung again. Various other methods have been proposed and employed for the repair of fractured bells, including welding, but the ultimate solution was usually a recasting.[62]

A miniature from the sixteenth-century *Tsarstvennaia kniga* shows a Russian bell undergoing repair (figure 96). The accompanying text states that on June 3, 1547, during the ringing of *blagovest* for the evening office, the cannons of this bell broke. The bell fell from its wooden belfry, but it sustained no further damage. In the foreground of the miniature, several workers are forging new iron cannons for the bell, while in the upper portion of the picture, the repaired bell, equipped with a clapper, has already been rehung.[63]

At the end of the eighteenth century Andrew Swinton remarked that "Russians take as much delight in the firing of guns, as they do in the ringing of bells. Artillery, in summer, makes a part of rural entertainments."[64] And indeed, the Russian fascination with the instruments of both church and battle is expressed not only in the proximity in the Moscow Kremlin of Chokhov's Tsar Cannon of 1586 to the Motorins' Tsar Bell of 1735 but also in the frenzy of ringing bells and cannon salvos in the final pages of Tchaikovsky's overture, *The Year 1812*.

Bells were being cast on Russian soil several centuries before cannon, but the same European technology was applied to both, and many Russian masters became equally proficient in the production of both. In times of national emergency bells were particularly vulnerable, however, and were often sacrificed to war efforts.[65] They were also re-

96. Sixteenth-century Russian miniature from the *Tsarstvennaia kniga* (Sinod. bibl. MS no. 149, f. 296) showing the repair of a broken bell. From Nik[olaj] Findejzen, *Ocherki po istorii muzyki v Rossii s drevnejshikh vremen do kontsa XVIII veka*, vol. 1 (Moscow, 1928), 134, fig. 39. Permission of Izdatel'stvo "Muzyka," Moscow.

duced to misshapen hunks of bronze in the frequent conflagrations that swept the wooden churches of Russia. Even so, the bell, not the cannon, ultimately prevailed as the symbol of Russia. And in the great bells of Moscow, cast between 1599 and 1817, the technology of Russian founding reached its apogée.

Part V
The Great Bells of Moscow

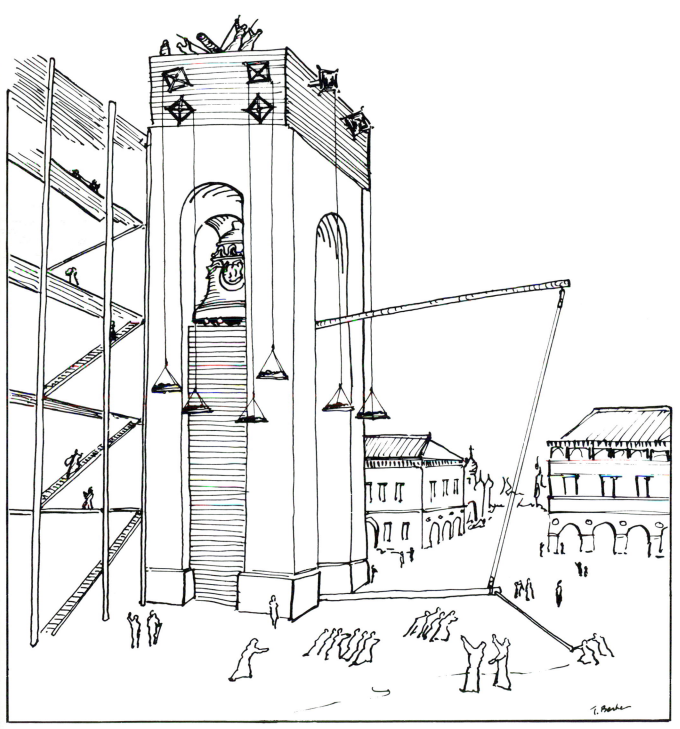

11

The Muscovite Crescendo in Bell Founding

GREEK Archbishop Arsenius of Elasson, who visited Moscow during the reign of Boris Godunov, gazed in amazement at the tsar's great Kremlin bell of 1599 and boldly proclaimed in his travel journal: "Bells of such size and beauty are not to be found in any other kingdom in the entire world."[1] There were, unbeknownst to Arsenius, several older bells of greater magnitude in East Asia. But his words were nonetheless prophetic, for 136 years after the founding of the Godunov Bell the Kremlin did contain the largest and heaviest bell ever cast.

If any single project gave impetus to the casting of the first in a line of truly great bells for the Moscow Kremlin, it was Andrej Chokhov's great cannon "Drobovik" (Fowling Piece) of 1586 for Tsar Fedor Ivanovich (1584-1598) (figure 97).[2] At 2,400 puds (86,671 pounds), Chokhov's mighty weapon, now known as "Tsar-Pushka" (Tsar Cannon), was the heaviest piece of ordnance casting undertaken in Russia to that date and an outstanding example of Muscovite founding, even if it was of no practical military value. The sheer visual impact of this enormous cannon was apparently not lost on Boris Godunov, the tsar's brother-in-law and chief advisor, who twelve years later, having just gained the Russian throne, called Chokhov into his own service.

The great bell so admired by Arsenius, which Chokhov cast for Godunov at the very beginning of his short reign, gave rise to the most celebrated "dynasty" of Russian bells. The bell, also known as the Kremlin Godunov Bell, was twice recast in the mid-seventeenth century during the reign of Aleksei Mikhailovich and recast a third and final time between 1730 and 1735 by Ivan and Mikhail Motorin. The Motorins' bell was the last in this family of great bells and is known as Tsar-Kolokol, so the family has been designated "The Moscow Tsar-Kolokol Line":

1. Godunov Bell (Tsar-Kolokol I)
Cast by Andrej Chokhov in 1599
Weight: *circa* 2,173 puds (78,474 pounds)
Ruined in a Kremlin fire sometime between 1639 and 1651

2. First Aleksei Mikhailovich Bell (Tsar-Kolokol II)
Recasting of the Godunov Bell by Emel'ian Danilov in 1654
Weight: *circa* 8,000 puds (288,904 pounds)
Broken while being rung in 1654

3. Second Aleksei Mikhailovich Bell (Tsar-Kolokol III)
Recasting of the First Aleksei Mikhailovich Bell by Aleksandr Grigor'ev in 1655
Weight: *circa* 10,000 puds? (361,130 pounds)
Ruined in the Kremlin fire of 1701

4. Anna Ivanovna Bell (Tsar-Kolokol IV)
Recasting of the Second Aleksei Mikhailovich Bell by Mikhail Motorin in Ivan Motorin's mold in 1735
Weight: *circa* 12,000 puds (433,356 pounds)

97. Andrej Chokhov's Tsar-Pushka (Tsar Cannon) of 1586, named "Drobovik." From Andreev, *Moskovskij Kreml'*, pl. 152. Permission of VAAP, Moscow.

Ruined in its casting pit during the Trinity Fire of 1737
Raised from its casting pit by Auguste Montferrand and placed on a granite pedestal in the Kremlin in 1836

A second and considerably older family of great Kremlin bells, though of lesser magnitude, began with the casting of Nikolai Nemchin's 1,000-pud Uspensky Bell of 1533 at the beginning of Ivan IV's reign. There is some suggestion that this bell may have been initially recast sometime in the late seventeenth century, but its first fully documented recasting took place in 1760 with Konstantin Slizov's founding of a great bell for Empress Elisabeth Petrovna. Slizov's bell was ruined in the Kremlin explosions that the French detonated in October of 1812 before their departure from Moscow, and Mikhail Bogdanov recast its pieces in 1817. The last bell in this "Moscow Uspensky Line," Bogdanov's

Great Uspensky Bell hangs today in the central structure of the Ivan Velikij Bell Tower and is still capable of being rung.

The third and most recent line of great Russian bells includes two instruments at the Trinity-Sergius Lavra. The first, cast in 1716 by an unknown founder, possibly a foreman from the Moscow Cannon Yard, was broken and useless by 1735, but perhaps as early as 1722. Gavriil Smirnov and Semen Stepanov recast it in 1748 for Elisabeth Petrovna. This bell was removed from its tower at the lavra in early January of 1930 and carried to a foundry where its metal was used in the manufacture of machinery. Because the second of these two bells is also known as "Tsar-Kolokol," this line has been designated "The Tsar-Kolokol Line of the Trinity-Sergius Lavra." Most of the largest bells cast in Russia belong to these three family lines. The history of the Moscow Tsar-Kolokol line is told in the following pages and in Chapter 12.

The Godunov Bell of 1599

Upon his accession to the Russian throne, Boris Godunov (1598-1605) undertook two ambitious and highly visible projects in the Kremlin,[3] eager, if not anxious, to strengthen his oblique claim to the throne and to confirm through both architecture and bell founding what he hoped would become the Godunov dynasty in Russia. In 1599 he commissioned Chokhov to found two large bells.[4] And in 1600 he raised the Bono Tower in the Kremlin to its present height by adding two upper segments crowned by a golden cupola and cross. This architectural stroke cast all Kremlin palaces and churches built during the reigns of his predecessors in the Bono Tower's shadow. An inscription, disposed in three bands around the uppermost cylinder of the tower below its cupola, boldly proclaimed Godunov's establishment of the right of succession for his young son Fedor.[5] The bells that Godunov commissioned were the aural analogue to his extension of the Bono Tower. One was presented to the Holy Trinity Monastery, now the Trinity-Sergius Lavra.[6] The other, cast for the newly established Patriarchate of Moscow, was placed in its own wooden belfry in the midst of Cathedral Square near the Ivan Velikij Bell Tower (figures 98 and 99).[7] Godunov's ostentatious display of this second great bell did not escape Samuel Maskiewicz, a Polish visitor, who saw and heard the bell between 1609 and 1612: "Not far from this church is a bell cast in an enormously large size; it hangs in a wooden tower 2 sazhens [14 feet] high, so that it can better be seen. Twenty-four men can pull the clapper of this bell."[8]

Although Chokhov's Kremlin bell was evidently larger than all others previously cast in Russia, early seventeenth-century sources transmit no data on its dimensions.[9] Several accounts that mention the bell do contain estimates of its weight, however. Two possible figures given in the caption that identifies the bell (no. 25) on the Godunov plan are 2,200 puds and 66,000 *libris* (*livres*). The bell's weight would then convert to either 79,449 pounds, using puds, or 72,732 pounds if this *livre* is equal to 1.102 pounds. Petrus Petrejus and Joan Blaeu record the amount of bronze the bell contained at 336 centners and 336 *quintaux*, respectively; Olearius' figure is 356 centners. The centner in question, measured in multiples of 50 kilograms, or 110.23 pounds, could represent either the basic unit or, as seems more likely, a multiple of two. The *quintal* is measured in multiples of 100 kilograms, or 220.46 pounds. Only if Chokhov's bell were measured in 100-kilogram units would it represent a casting of significantly greater magnitude and weight than Nemchin's 1,000-pud bell of 1533— and, importantly, of comparable weight to Chokhov's own Godunov bell for the Holy Trinity Monastery, which stood at around 1,850 puds. The 50-kilogram unit would give a 336-centner bell, a weight of only 37,037 pounds, or 1,026 puds, just slightly heavier than Nemchin's bell and a little more than half the weight of the lavra bell. At the larger unit of measure, the same bell would weigh 74,075 pounds, or 2,051 puds; and the 356-centner bell in Olearius' estimate would weigh 78,484 pounds (39 tons), or 2,173 puds. Though the figures that sources quote for the weight of this bell

vary somewhat, its weight clearly falls in a range between 74,000 and 80,000 pounds or between about 2,000 and 2,200 puds.[10] No Russian bell founder before Chokhov had cast a bell of such magnitude.

The weight of the clapper alone, according to Maskiewicz's account, was sufficient to require the combined efforts of twenty-four men to swing it to the sound-bow. Two long heavy ropes fastened to the flight of the clapper extended to the ground on either side of the wooden structure that supported the bell. To the ends of each rope were attached smaller ropes, which the ringers—in equal numbers of a dozen on either side—pulled in a kind of tug-of-war exchange to set the clapper in motion. First one group of ringers drew the clapper to its side of the bell; then the other group pulled the clapper to the opposite side. Several men were stationed in the structure itself to guide the strokes of the clapper, controlling the force of its blows and protecting the belfry from excessively strong vibrations.[11]

The Godunov Bell was rung for special occasions of church and state until at least the last third of Mikhail Romanov's reign (1613-1645). It sounded *blagovest* for services in the Uspensky (Assumption) Cathedral on great feasts of the liturgical year. It announced the arrivals, processions, and receptions of foreign dignitaries and ambassadors as well as the tsar's own ceremonial entrances into and departures from Moscow.[12] It may well have rung for the coronations of Vasilij IV Shuiskij (1606) and Mikhail Romanov (1613), and possibly, though not certainly, for the coronation of Aleksei Mikhailovich (1645). Its powerful voice made a deep impression on Western visitors through the first decades of the seventeenth century. Stephan Kakasch, who heard it in 1602 while Boris Godunov was still on the throne, noted that it far exceeded the Erfurt bell in Saxony both in its size and in the volume of its ring.[13] Olearius also saw and heard the bell, which he clearly identifies as the Godunov Bell, during his visits to Moscow in the middle to late 1630s. But Chokhov's great Kremlin bell was ruined in a fire that consumed the wooden

98. Details from the so-called Godunov plan (ca. 1605) of the Moscow Kremlin showing Andrej Chokhov's great bell of 1599 in its wooden tower (no. 25) near the Ivan Velikij Bell Tower (no. 24). To the left is the Cathedral of Archangel Michael and on the right, the Uspensky Cathedral. From Blaeu, *La Grand atlas ou cosmographie Blaviane.*

structure where it hung apparently sometime between the third visit of Olearius in 1639 and the beginning of 1651, when Aleksei Mikhailovich ordered the pieces of the bell recast to form the next great tsar bell.[14]

The First Aleksei Mikhailovich Bell (1654)

With his decree to recast the Godunov Bell for the Kremlin, Aleksei Mikhailovich (1645-1676) also ordered the weight of the new bell increased to 8,000 puds (288,904 pounds).[15] He turned first to Hans Falk of Nuremberg, one of the foreign founders working in Moscow at the time, for plans, budget

estimates, and a schedule for recasting.[16] The proposal Falk submitted required five years to complete and maintained that the metal from the Godunov Bell would not be suitable to use in casting the new bell. Dissatisfied, Aleksei Mikhailovich heard a proposal from a Russian foreman and founders at the Moscow Cannon Yard—Danilo Matveev, his son Emel'ian Danilov, and apprentices Kirill Samojlov, Vasilij Borisov, and Semen Simonov—who assured the tsar that they could successfully recast the Godunov Bell at 8,000 puds with the same inscriptions and decorations that Falk had proposed. Their bell, moreover, would be of the same quality as Falk's, and they could use the metal from Chokhov's bell of 1599.

So eager were the Russians to obtain the tsar's commission for this project that they immediately began to dig a casting pit for the bell. At this point, however, Falk reversed his earlier position and agreed to include the pieces from the Godunov Bell in his own recasting. The Russians were quick to turn Falk's vascillation to their own advantage, but neither Falk nor the Russians would guarantee their work in creating such a large bell. Entrusting a successful outcome to Providence, the Russians reminded the tsar that Falk had only succeeded in casting a 500-pud bell for the Kazan cathedral on his third attempt. The Russians finally persuaded the tsar to grant them the commission with the following petition:

Merciful Sovereign Ts[ar] and G[rand] D[uke] of all Russia, Aleksei Mikhailovich, take pity on us, Majesty, y[our] s[laves]; order us to recast that Sunday *blagovest* bell, for we are accustomed to the bell founding profession. Majesty, do not order him, Ivan [Hans] Falk, to recast that bell. Sovereign Tsar, please have mercy.[17]

On July 5, 1651, Aleksei Mikhailovich assigned the direction of this entire project to Danila Matveev and his son Emel'ian Danilov.[18] Danila Matveev died before he could complete the work. But in early 1654 Emel'ian Danilov successfully cast the great new Kremlin bell on the first attempt.[19] It emerged from its mold at 8,000 puds (288,904 pounds) and was fitted with an iron clapper of 250

99. A. M. Vasnetsov's drawing of 1903, "The Square of Ivan Velikij in the Kremlin," showing the Godunov Bell in its timber structure behind and to the left of the Bono-Godunov Tower. From Bespalova, *Apollinarij Mikhajlovich Vasnetsov 1856-1933*, 86. Permission of VAAP, Moscow.

puds (9,028 pounds).[20] The Russian founders had vindicated the tsar's confidence in their work.

Aleksei Mikhailovich, pleased with a bell of such spectacular size and weight, made the magnanimous offer of five hundred peasant families to Danilov in payment. Danilov, a modest and unassuming man, declined the tsar's gift and requested only a daily allowance, which was granted him for the rest of his life, with the same amount to be paid to his children after his death. The latter provision presumably went into effect almost immediately, for Danilov died during an epidemic of plague that had reached Moscow in the summer of 1654.[21]

Aleksei Mikhailovich had been curious to see how far strokes on Danilov's bell could be heard beyond Moscow. So he sent riders into the countryside around the capital and ordered all the city's bells to be rung simultaneously, whereupon ringers in the Kremlin began to sound the new bell. Its voice, deep and sonorous, rumbled forth across the city beneath the swarming rhythms of all the smaller bells and carried beyond the Kremlin for about 7 versts (4.64 miles).[22] Because they were ringing against the collective zvon, however, those swinging the clapper of Danilov's bell began to increase the force of its blows against the sound-bow. This eventually exceeded the resilience of the bronze, and through a casting defect, perhaps, the new bell "shattered, like glass" without warning. Its booming voice suddenly cracked and disintegrated. The Kremlin's second Tsar-Kolokol, like its founder, came to a sudden and untimely end.[23]

The Second Aleksei Mikhailovich Bell (1655)

Aleksei Mikhailovich decided to have the pieces of Danilov's bell recast at once and ordered them heated and reduced to smaller fragments in preparation.[24] In answer to his call for founders, a confident and enterprising youth stepped forward and convinced the tsar of his ability to successfully complete the project. This young man, Aleksandr Grigor'ev (fl. 1651-1676), was less than twenty years old at the time.[25] He vowed that his bell would be larger, heavier, and better cast than Danilov's, and further, that he would finish the project within a year. The tsar accepted Grigor'ev's bold plan.

Grigor'ev began preliminary work in early February 1655 and before Easter of that year had completed the preparatory stages, including the digging of an enormous pit in the Kremlin and the construction around it of five brick furnaces for melting the metal. When work on the mold was finished, Grigor'ev had masons build a strong wall of several rows of brick around the entire height of the mold. He then packed sand into the space between the mold and this wall to brace the cope against the hydrostatic pressure that the molten metal would exert when poured. Forty or fifty *streltsy* (musketeers) were required to haul the large chunks of metal to the site, plus machinery to put the chunks on the scales and then into the furnaces. According to Paul of Aleppo, Grigor'ev began casting with 2,500 puds (90,283 pounds) of metal in each of his five furnaces—a total weight of 12,500 puds (451,413 pounds).[26] The melting process continued for three days. Though Paul does not indicate the actual date of casting, Murkos, translator of Paul's account, believes that it probably oc-

curred at the beginning of October 1655, when the tsar was away on his Polish campaign.[27] A prelate blessed the work and sprinkled consecrated water over the casting pit. Then the furnaces were tapped to release the liquid metal. Though one of the five gutters cracked, losing some metal, the casting itself was successfully achieved.

The newly cast bell remained cooling in its pit for three days. Then the brick wall and earth around the mold were taken away, the cope removed, and the entire process of cleaning the bell begun. When word reached Moscow of the tsar's imminent return from Smolensk, Nikon, Patriarch of Moscow, accelerated the work of finishing the bell through continuous work night and day so that its voice might greet the tsar's arrival in the capital. The work was completed on December 1.[28] Thus Grigor'ev had kept his promise to the tsar. He had created in only ten months the largest bell cast in Russia until that time.[29]

Paul of Aleppo has described the operation of raising the bell begun on December 1:

Mechanisms and ropes were secured and made ready in our presence, and Muscovites gathered to witness this event. Each of these 16 mechanisms was set in motion by 70 to 80 *streltsy* and above the rope of each mechanism sat a man to coordinate the simultaneous turning of the wheels [capstans?]. . . . Many lines snapped, but they were immediately replaced by others. After a three-day exertion of tremendous force and enormous effort, which defies description, [and] by using the most complicated equipment, they accomplished the raising of the bell and suspended it over its pit at about the height of a man. Above the mouth of the pit they placed stout logs, which covered it completely; on top of these logs they stacked more timbers until this wonder-bell was resting on them. They then proceeded to install the iron clapper, which weighed 250 puds [9,028 pounds] and which was so thick that we had difficulty encircling it with our arms. Its length was more than one and a half times the height of a man. They set about cleaning this marvelous bell inside and out and polishing.[30]

The bell was hung in its own wooden belfry, a temporary structure high enough to suspend the bell but low enough to minimize problems in hoisting.

Then on December 9, 1655, the eve of the tsar's triumphant return to the capital, all Moscow waited to hear the voice of the new bell.[31] Paul of Aleppo reports that it took one hundred *streltsy* pulling on four long ropes tied to the flight of the clapper to swing the clapper to the sound-bow. When the iron pendulum finally struck the sound-bow, what came from the bell left Muscovites transfixed. The ringing, which continued until evening, sent vibrations through the belfry, making its timbers creak and groan. But for a time at least, this structure proved strong enough to withstand the vibrations.

Of the bell's physical properties, its decorative program is documented in a picture of 1661 by Augustin, Baron von Meyerberg (ambassador of Emperor Leopold I of Austria), in Paul of Aleppo's description, and perhaps in a drawing from 1674 by a Swedish visitor to Moscow, Erich Palmquist. One area of the bell's waist contained two apparently rectangular relief portraits; one of Tsar Aleksei Mikhailovich, and next to it, one of his consort, Mariia Miloslavskaia. Above their portraits and centered between them was a third panel with an icon of Jesus Christ (figure 100). The reliefs of the royal couple blessed by the Saviour were on the "front side" of the bell, that is, the side that faced the Kremlin's Uspensky Cathedral.[32] On the opposite side was a relief portrait of Nikon, Patriarch of Moscow, in the full vestments of his office, with a mitre on his head and a crozier in his hand.[33] Just below the shoulders of the bell ran a frieze of six-winged cherubs and seraphs (figure 101). Paul of Aleppo reports two inscriptions, one in large letters above this frieze and another that encircled the lower portion of the sound-bow. According to Meyerberg, the lower inscription recorded that "in the year from the creation of the world 7161 [A.D. 1653], this bell has been cast in Moscow by order of His Gracious Majesty, Tsar and Grand Duke Aleksei Mikhailovich, Autocrat of all Russia, in the eighth year of his holding the scepter."[34]

The differences in the drawings of the great Moscow bell by Meyerberg and Palmquist are difficult to reconcile. Indeed Palmquist's caption (not shown in figure 101) states that the bell he represented was cast in 1637 during the reign of Mikhail

100. Detail of the decorative program on the waist of Grigor'ev's bell founded for Aleksei Mikhailovich in 1655: portraits of Aleksei Mikhailovich (left) and Mariia Miloslavskaia (right) below an icon of Jesus Christ. This surface of the bell faced the Uspensky Cathedral in the Kremlin. From Adelung, *Al'bom Mejerberga*, 27, pl. 64. Permission of Sterling Memorial Library, Yale University.

Fedorovich. The relief decorations visible on this bell's waist—three individual portraits in oval medallions with garlands connecting them—do not conform to the analogous area on the bell Meyerberg has drawn (though for such an important work one would expect a more elaborately ornamented surface than Meyerberg shows). And Paul of Aleppo's description corroborates the arrangement in Meyerberg's drawing. Neither does the Palmquist drawing show an upper and a lower inscription, which Paul of Aleppo describes. Meyerberg for that matter shows only the lower inscription, though he may have intended to copy the upper inscription into what is now an unfilled band around the bell's shoulder (see figure 100).

101. An 11,000-pud Moscow bell reportedly cast in 1637 during the reign of Tsar Mikhail Fedorovich. The clapper lies on the ground below. From Erich Palmquist, *Några widh sidste kongl. ambassaden till tzaren Muskou giorde Observationer öfwer Rysslandh, des wäger, pass meds fastningar och Brantzer* (1674; published in Stockholm, 1898), no pagination. Courtesy of Photoduplication Service, The Library of Congress.

On the other hand, Palmquist calculates the bell's weight at 11,000 puds, which is identical to the information that Kilburger publishes for Grigor'ev's bell of 1655 (see below). And only Palmquist's drawing shows the frieze of cherubs and seraphs that Paul of Aleppo includes in his description; moreover, the two ornamental bands around the upper portion of the sound-bow and below the frieze of cherubs and seraphs are similar, if not identical, to the two analogous relief bands in Meyerberg's drawing. But the two most compelling reasons for regarding the Palmquist drawing as a representation of the 1655 bell by Grigor'ev are that (1) no other source mentions an 11,000-pud bell cast in Moscow in 1637 during the reign of Mikhail Fedorovich and (2) the bell he depicts is the same bell shown in the hoist of 1674 (see figure 103), and that bell was without question Grigor'ev's bell of 1655. Even so, Palmquist's stated year of founding would still be incorrect. Perhaps

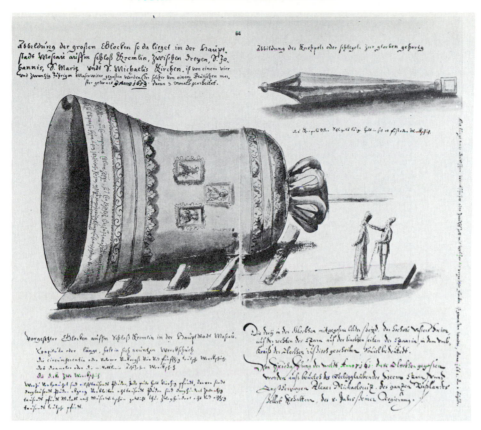

102. Grigor'ev's bell as Meyerberg saw it lying on its sound-bow and shoulder in the Kremlin in 1661. Its clapper also rests on the ground (upper right). From Adelung, *Al'bom" Mejerberga*, 27, pl. 64. Permission of Sterling Memorial Library, Yale University.

this problematical identification of the great Moscow bell in Palmquist's travel diary explains why it has not been previously reproduced in material on Russian bells.

Conflicting data from several witnesses make even an approximate weight for Grigor'ev's bell difficult to determine. Paul of Aleppo, who claims that his information on the bell came from the founder himself, reports the instrument's weight as 12,000 puds (433,356 pounds).[35] Meyerberg later records it at 320,000 funts (8,002 puds, or 288,960 pounds), or somewhat greater than two-thirds of Paul's figure.[36] Between these two extremes are calculations by Kilburger and Palmquist, each of whom transmits 11,000 puds (397,243 pounds).[37] Murkos believes that a fair estimate of the bell's weight would

be around 10,000 puds (361,130 pounds), a figure that also agrees with van Klenk's estimate.[38]

Establishment of the bell's dimensions is also problematical, with figures varying considerably from source to source. According to Meyerberg, the bell was 19 feet high, had a lower circumference of 64 feet, and a lower diameter of 18 feet.[39] Meyerberg's figure for the diameter is not quite compatible with his figure for the circumference, however, for an 18-foot diameter would yield a circumference of only 56.54 feet. Paul of Aleppo records the circumference as 11 *brasse* (63.25 feet), which would make the bell's lower diameter 20.13 feet.[40] But Paul's estimate of the thickness of the metal at the bell's mouth as 1 *brasse*—5 feet 9 inches—seems excessive when compared with a

103. Grigor′ev's bell in the process of being raised in 1674 into the Kremlin structure where it hung until 1701. From Palmquist, *Någre widh sidste kongl. ambassaden till tzaren Muskou*, no pagination. Courtesy of Photoduplication Service, The Library of Congress.

thickness of 2 feet in the sound-bow of the Motorins' Tsar-Kolokol.[41] Meyerberg's measurement of 2 feet of metal at the sound-bow is more credible and is further corroborated in the accounts of Struys and van Klenk.[42] Paul was told that the cost of founding the bell was 50,000 rubles.[43]

The length and weight of the bell's clapper are equally difficult to determine. Paul and van Klenk each give the clapper's weight as 250 puds (9,028 pounds).[44] Kilburger and Palmquist both estimate

440 puds (15,890 pounds).[45] A third figure of 10,000 pounds (277 puds) in Struys is closer to the figure that Paul and van Klenk transmit.[46] The length of the clapper is given variously as more than one and a half times the height of a man, 14 feet, and 22 feet.[47] Van Klenk states that "about fifty bell ringers" were required "to set this bell in motion [*sic*], and therefore it was rung only on feasts and for the reception of ambassadors. And then it booms so frightfully that almost all the ground around shakes and quivers."[48]

Whether it took fifty or a hundred ringers to swing the clapper, history records Grigor′ev's bell as the largest ever rung in Russia. Strokes on this bell were compared to claps of thunder.[49] Whenever the bell was to be sounded at any time other than a great church feast or ceremony of state, the Kremlin sent word throughout the city to warn Muscovites to remove glassware and crockery from their shelves,[50] for the ringing of Grigor′ev's bell, in fact, produced effects that were equivalent to some of those generated by earthquakes in category IV on the XII-point Modified Mercalli Intensity Scale of 1956.[51]

Paul of Aleppo has compared standing beneath this bell to being under an enormous bronze tent.[52] He concludes his account of the bell with an encomium to this instrument and to the tsar who had commissioned it: "There is nothing comparable to this rare object, huge, amazing, and unique in the world; there is not, has never been, and shall never be: it transcends human powers. This fortunate tsar, who produced it during his reign, has surpassed the sovereigns of his time."[53]

Sometime between the end of 1655 and 1661, the bell either fell from its wooden belfry—but without sustaining damage—or was taken down, perhaps because of structural weaknesses that had developed in this housing. For whatever reason, the bell was lying prone on the ground inside the Kremlin when Baron von Meyerberg saw it in 1661. In addition to including a drawing of the bell as he found it (figure 102), Meyerberg also described it:

In the Kremlin we saw a bronze bell of amazing size lying on the ground, and what is more astonishing, it is the work of a Russian master. This bell is taller than the Erfurt [bell] and even the Peking [bell] in the kingdom of China. . . . It is still lying on the ground and awaits a master, who would raise it for arousing a religious feeling in Muscovites by its ringing on feast days, because this people does not wish to be without bell ringing at all, as an absolutely essential condition for worship.[54]

During the first half of 1664 Guy Miege suggests in his report on the embassy of the Earl of Carlisle in Moscow that an unsuccessful attempt of series of attempts had been made to raise the Grigor'ev bell: "When we first came to Mosco, it was upon the ground, in a base Court where it was cast, and during the four monthes and a half we remained there, all they could do was to raise it though but a little from the ground, with the intention to build a Steeple for it in the same place."[55]

The bell must have been hanging once more in some kind of temporary structure by 1669 when Jan Struys visited Moscow, for he heard it rung and wrote that "not far from the Ivan Velikij Tower" was a tower that contained "the greatest bell without doubt in the world, weighing 394,000 lb."[56] Reutenfels recalls from the early 1670s that the bell had been "partly suspended and partly resting on a wooden platform."[57] There had already been many unsuccessful attempts to raise the bell, according to Reutenfels. A number of people had paid with their lives while trying to raise the bell, and as a result, the tsar vowed never again to undertake a similar operation.[58]

But the attention still being given to the problems of hoisting the bell into a permanent structure is evident from three projects that appeared at the end of the 1660s and in the early 1670s. In 1668 a peasant named Nikita Ermolaev built a model of a structure for Grigor'ev's bell, and in January 1671 a *voevoda* (military governor) in Murom sent a certain "Mark Mukhin" to Moscow with a model that demonstrated a means of raising the bell. Nothing further developed from these two proposals. But in 1673 Ivashko Kuz'min, a self-taught mechanic who worked in the Kremlin as a porter, proposed an ingenious method of lifting the bell within a structure supported by two large pylons.

TABLE 5

Grigor'ev's Kremlin Bell between 1655 and 1701, from the Reports of Observers

Locations	Probable dates	Observers
1. Hangs in a wooden structure built over its casting pit	Dec. 1655	Paul of Aleppo
2. Rests on its side on the ground	1661?-1662	Meyerberg
3. Lifted from a prone to an upright position?	betw. Feb. and June 1664	Miege
4. Hangs in a special wooden tower	1668-1670	Struys
5. Partially suspended in a wooden structure	1670-1673	Reutenfels
6. Hangs in a special masonry structure near the Ivan Velikij Bell Tower and the Uspensky Cathedral	1674-1701	Palmquist, Kilburger, van Klenk, Bruyn, Korb

The tsar appointed Kuz'min to put the plan into effect.[59]

An engraving from the travel diary of Erich Palmquist illustrates Kuz'min's method of elevating the bell (figure 103).[60] It shows the bell already in the process of being raised within a specially constructed shaft through use of block and tackle. To assist in the lift, a number of winding drums were placed at the top of this structure from which were suspended counterbalances loaded with rock. There were probably similar drums on the inside of the tower to take up rope as it was payed out by the counterbalance drums. A lever under the lip of the bell raised its mouth so that wooden logs could be inserted to fill the space below. This procedure seems to have been carried out on the three accessible sides of the tower.[61] With each advance in elevation thus supported, a tall wooden substructure began to rise beneath the bell, and in this way the giant instrument was gradually raised into the place where it eventually hung at the top of this structure.

According to Kilburger, an accident occurred during the raising of the bell on December 2, 1673.

104. Two teams of ringers swing the clapper of Grigor'ev's bell at the top of the structure where it hung between 1674 and 1701. The surface of the bell shown here is not an accurate representation of the design on the original bell but is used to transmit the bell's weight and dimensions. From Johann Georg Korb, *Diarium itineris in Moscoviam* (Vienna, [1700]), 190. Courtesy of the Kenneth Spencer Research Library, University of Kansas.

Kuz'min had already raised the bell a certain distance when workers moved it too vigorously, causing it to suddenly break loose and plunge cannons first into the ground. The fall did not damage the bell, but because the ground at the foot of the structure was soft, the bell's upper third—cannons, shoulder, and part of the waist—was buried. The bell was excavated, and the laborious process of lifting began again. By March of 1674, nine months after the initial work had begun, the elevation and installation of Grigor'ev's great Kremlin bell in a structure near the Ivan Velikij Bell Tower and the Uspensky Cathedral was finally accomplished (figure 104).[62]

Kuz'min's successful hoist of possibly 10,000 puds of dead weight to a considerable height was an engineering triumph. Five years later a blacksmith named Anisim Volodimerov built an iron tent-shaped roof and cupola above the structure the bell occupied.[63] Although the exact height of this structure is not known, Cornelis de Bruyn, a Dutch visitor to Moscow in 1702 and 1703, wrote that in order to see the place where the bell had once hung, one had to take 108 steps between the structure for Grigor'ev's bell and the Ivan Velikij Bell Tower.[64]

The history of Grigor'ev's bell between its founding in the fall of 1655 and its destruction in the Kremlin fire on June 19, 1701, may never be established with absolute certainty. But from reports of foreign visitors, summarized in Table 5, we know that the bell remained in the Kremlin for most of forty-six years, twenty-seven of them in Kuz'min's tower. Then the perennial enemy of Russia's bells and her wooden architecture once again attacked the Kremlin. Flames, licking at the beams from which the great bell was suspended, eventually burned through the wood and sent the giant instrument lurching to one side for an instant, then plummeting the length of the shaft. On impact, the ground roared. For three decades the pieces of Grigor'ev's bell formed a large bronze mound at the foot of the Ivan Velikij Bell Tower. Then in 1730, shortly after she was crowned Empress of Russia, Anna Ivanovna decreed that the broken tsar bell would once more be recast. The empress intended the new Kremlin bell to be a worthy monument to the glory of God—and an eternal symbol of her own piety and autocratic power.

12

The Tale of Tsar-Kolokol

LIKE SOME CREATURE of Russian fantasy from the *skazki* (folk tales), the Kremlin's last tsar bell dwelled a hundred years in its subterranean abode before it rose into the light of day. The story of this bell might even be told in the style of the *skazki*, for something of the legendary Russian world of old hovers about its creation by a master bell founder and his son. The epic tale began shortly after Anna Ivanovna was crowned Empress of Russia in 1730. In an *ukaz* (edict) to the Senate dated July 26 of that year the empress declared her intention to recast Grigor'ev's bell of 1655.[1] But she ordered that metal from the older bell, which she recorded at 8,000 puds, be augmented by 2,000 puds for a total weight of 10,000 puds (361,130 pounds).[2] Though no official evidence survives to give credence to the assertion that she solicited foreign founders to recast the bell, Count B. Kh. Minikh states in his memoirs that the empress initially sought a member of the French Academy of Sciences in Paris, a royal goldsmith named Germain, to undertake this work. Astounded at the magnitude of the proposed bell, Germain regarded the project as nothing more than fatuous conceit. He is nevertheless reported to have submitted a proposal with his budget to St. Petersburg. But nothing further was heard of the Frenchman's plan, if indeed it was ever sent.[3]

By 1730 Ivan Fedorovich Motorin (fl. 1687-1735), the most accomplished founder in Moscow, had been engaged in his profession for more than four decades, and a week after the empress had issued her decree, he held the commission for recasting the bell.[4] The commission authorized him to appoint one assistant cannon foreman from the Moscow Arsenal and ten apprentices. For his chief assistant he chose his own son, Mikhail Ivanovich Motorin (fl. 1730-1750).[5] There was no lack of state surveillance, however. Two officers from the Field Artillery Command, Captains Andrej Rukh and Ivan Glebov, were assigned to supervise the project as well as to oversee the purchasing of supplies. In addition, Count Semen Andreevich Saltykov, Governor-General of Moscow, assumed responsibility for directing the entire operation and for reporting on its progress to the empress.

Preliminary Planning

Ivan Motorin's initial steps included supervision of the drafting of full-scale drawings in the artillery office and the casting of a 12-pud (433-pound) model of the final bell.[6] From the very beginning Motorin also gave considerable thought to the formidable engineering feat that loomed at the conclusion of the project—the hoisting of the huge bell from its casting pit into a belfry. He designed two working models of machinery for raising the bell in anticipation of this task and by April 19, 1732, these had been received in St. Petersburg for official approval.[7]

Motorin ordered the excavation of an enormous casting pit, about 33 feet deep and 33 feet in diameter, within the Kremlin between the Chudov Monastery and the east façade of the Ivan Velikij Bell Tower. The bottom of the pit, on which the mold was to be constructed and the bell cast, was reinforced by twelve large oak piles driven into the earth. On these piles an iron grating was laid to support the mold and to provide a stable foundation for casting. Then the walls of the pit, lined with brick, were reinforced by horizontal oak timbers held in place by perpendicular iron beams.[8]

Within the Kremlin a number of temporary wooden structures were built at this time, including a shed over the casting pit and machinery for raising the outer mold from the bell for inspection after casting. A storehouse, a workshop for Motorin and his assistants, a blacksmiths' shop, and a warehouse for supplies were also constructed nearby; Motorin, who insisted on materials and supplies of the highest quality, took measures to protect them from the elements.[9] Finally, an enormous quantity of copper and tin had to be collected to found a bell of the size and weight planned by Motorin. Even if at least 8,000 puds of metal were already available from the pieces of Grigor'ev's bell, several thousand additional puds were needed. For these new materials Motorin requested the highest grade of raw metal—Persian red copper and English tin.[10]

To design the relief decorations on the bell's surface, a special group of artists came to Moscow from St. Petersburg. This team included four foremen of pedestal design whom Peter the Great had sent to Italy for training; Petr Lukovnikov, a foreman skilled in mold making, was another member of this team.[11] From sketches and clay models, three engravers prepared wooden models of the bas-reliefs, friezes, and inscriptions, which when finished, were taken to St. Petersburg for official approval.

Although construction of the four furnaces needed to melt the metal and work on the bell molds had begun in the spring of 1732, progress slackened somewhat in the early summer, and it soon became apparent that preliminary work would not be completed in time to meet the empress' deadline for casting—July 1732. By July, Lukovnikov had only completed his work on the inner core of the mold; the core itself and the cope would not be ready before August 1.[12]

With preparations nearing completion, casting supplies began to accumulate within the Kremlin. Bricks, clay, coal, lime, ropes, logs, boards, and firewood accompanied the arrival of numerous artisans, including masons, stonecutters, and carpenters. The report submitted for the week of January 8-14, 1733, records a total of eighty-three workers engaged in the following tasks: five bricklayers finishing the arched roofs in the furnaces; twenty-six blacksmiths forging articles for the furnaces; some carpenters working on the shed over the casting pit, while others were preparing wooden forms for the cannons of the bell; and forty less skilled workers performing such tasks as pugging clay, mixing lime, and hauling building materials and coal. Five months later one hundred eighty-nine workers were employed on the project.[13]

Despite the demanding labor and the loyalty of the workers assigned to the project, they sometimes received little or no compensation. Mikhail Komarov and Matvej Medvedkov, for example, who began work on the project in October 1730, were paid only in 1742, long after the bell had been cast. On July 13, 1732, when Kirill Kolykhanin, a founding assistant, and the apprentices did not receive their food allowance, they finally submitted a request to the Senate for *per diem* in order to maintain their strength to continue work.[14]

Of all the workers, however, Ivan Motorin himself endured perhaps the greatest deprivation. For almost five years, from the time he accepted the commission in August 1730 until June 1, 1735, he received not a single ruble of the 232 promised him for his work. In order to continue working, Motorin was forced to borrow 300 rubles from a friend. On February 25, 1732, he appealed to the Senate for financial assistance. Although the Senate appropriated 100 rubles, this sum scarcely met his needs. (The financial straits of the father, moreover, were bequeathed to the son when he assumed direction of the project.)

The ultimate insult to Motorin arose in July and August of 1733, when the question was raised whether a bell with bas-relief portraits of Tsar Aleksei Mikhailovich and Empress Anna Ivanovna should bear the name of its founder on the same surface. Diverse opinions on this issue can be traced through a voluminous correspondence. In a report to the empress the Senate finally decided that on the lower edge of the bell, in a place "lower than the lowest grasses," an inscription of nine words might be placed to record Ivan Motorin as founder.[15] The first attempt to cast the bell still lay more than a year away.

Ivan Motorin's Attempt to Cast in 1734

Toward the end of 1733 the initial work had been completed. Ivan Motorin informed the Senate office in January of 1734 of the stage the project had reached and requested that the Senate give immediate authorization to bake the form in which the bell was to be cast, a procedure that would require an entire month.[16] The Senate office was dilatory and, in fact, did not forward Motorin's communication to the Senate for consideration until March 20. When the Senate still did not reply and valuable time was passing, the Moscow authorities decided to assume responsibility for baking the mold. But before Motorin could begin this phase, the Senate office demanded a formal guarantee that the molds would not be damaged during the baking process. Motorin complied. He estimated that this work and all other details preceding the casting itself would occupy the summer and fall of 1734.[17]

Motorin informed Count Saltykov on November 25, 1734, that final preparations could begin and that he expected to cast the bell on November 28. Workers loaded the four furnaces with metal, and at 4:00 A.M. on November 26, 1734, after prayers had been offered in the Kremlin's Uspensky Cathedral for a successful casting, Motorin ordered the furnaces fired and commenced the melting of slightly more than 13,000 puds (469,469 pounds) of metal.[18] Work proceeded smoothly on November 26 and 27 and throughout the day and early eve-

ning of the next day. Then suddenly at 11:00 P.M. on November 28, sixty-seven hours after the furnaces had been fired, the hearthstone at the bottom of two of the four furnaces rose, and molten metal began to seep beneath them. Motorin immediately interrupted the casting process to inspect the furnaces. But on the advice of his son and assistants, he decided to continue, since all the metal needed could be prepared in the two furnaces that were still functioning.[19] Motorin calculated that 6,500 more puds (234,735 pounds) of copper and tin could be added to the metal already in these two furnaces.

Motorin, his assistants, and his workers were completely occupied throughout the early morning hours of November 29 gathering additional metal and hauling it to the casting site in the Kremlin. Six hundred old bells with a total weight of 1,663 puds (60,056 pounds) were hastily brought in from the Moscow Cannon Yard.[20] To these were added 4,137 puds (149,399 pounds) of raw copper and 700 puds (25,279 pounds) of new tin also from the cannon yard. But no sooner had Motorin resumed the melting process than a second accident halted work again. At 7:00 A.M. on November 29 seventy-five hours into the casting schedule, a third furnace cracked and began to release molten metal into the fire.

With these drastic developments, Motorin and his assistants had no alternative but to cancel the entire operation. Metal from the two furnaces was diverted into reserve furnaces built on the site to await a future attempt. But misfortune plagued even this move. During their transfer of the molten bronze, it sputtered and splashed onto the wooden rafters of the casting shed and set the roof on fire. The wooden derrick erected over the pit for raising the cope also caught on fire. This first attempt to cast the empress' bell thus ended in an inferno in the Kremlin on the morning of November 29, 1734. Half of the roof of the shed over the casting pit was burned, and oak beams from the middle of the shed had fallen down on top of the bell mold in the pit.

In assessing causes for the failure of three of his four furnaces, Ivan Motorin decided that the cracks that developed during the melting process were attributable to the excessively high temperature to which the furnaces had been subjected over an extended period of time.[21] His report declared that the damaged furnaces would be dismantled, repaired, and reinforced by the best possible means.[22] But Motorin's first concern was the bell mold. Fearing that the charred timbers that had fallen into the pit might have broken the molds that had taken years to construct, but determined to achieve a successful second casting, he immediately began to excavate the mold and to clean out the pit. He was relieved to find that the forms were undamaged and could be used for the second casting attempt.[23]

In addition to the burden of his failure to cast the great tsar bell, however, a series of personal misfortunes pursued Motorin, climaxed on May 9, 1735, by a fire that destroyed his home and the many mementos he had gathered throughout his long career. On August 19, 1735, a little more than three months later, Ivan Motorin died.[24] He was not to see the successful casting of the monumental bell on which he had labored for five years.

Mikhail Motorin's Casting of His Father's Bell in 1735

Mikhail Motorin petitioned the empress for authorization to direct the second attempt to cast his father's great bell, with Gavriil (Gavrilo) Luk'ianovich Smirnov and Andrej Fedorovich Maliarov as assistants.[25] She granted him the commission, and immediately he resumed the preparatory work. He once again carefully checked the bell mold for damage, and finding it completely whole and serviceable, decided that the casting must be completed by the autumn of 1735 before another winter could possibly crack the furnaces.[26]

This time authorities took exceptional measures to insure successful results. They demanded a written guarantee from the casting foremen; and Prince Ivan Fedorovich Bariatinskij accepted from Count Saltykov's committee the responsibility of maintaining special watch over the work inside the Kremlin.[27] Captains Rukh and Glebov continued their supervision and reported to the Central

Chancery for Artillery and Fortifications. Besides the appointment of assistant cannon foremen Stepan Kop'ev, Kirill Kolykhanin, and apprentice Semen Petrov to assist with casting, eighty-three masons, blacksmiths, metal workers, wood cutters, joiners, carpenters, and other workers served the various needs of Motorin and his assistants. Bricks, water, lime, and coal had to be transported, clay pugged, and bellows pumped. In all, about two hundred people were involved in the work leading to the second attempt to cast. And remembering the disastrous end to the earlier attempt, Moscow authorities took the extraordinary precaution of supplying four hundred men with fire fighting equipment.[28]

Requisite amounts of copper and tin were again assembled. Then on October 20, 1735, the metal was hauled into the Kremlin and put into the four furnaces. The bell mold in the pit was again packed with earth and rubble, so that sole access to the form was now the gating system into which the molten bronze would flow. The preliminary work was completed on November 16.

On November 23 at 1:00 P.M., almost a year to the day after the first attempt to cast, the four furnaces were again fired to begin the melting process.[29] Then just after midnight on November 25, 1735, when the metal had been in the furnaces almost thirty-six hours, Bishop Beniamin of Kolomenskoe, Count Saltykov, Prince Bariatinskij, and Lieutenant General Bark arrived, heading the official delegation to witness the second, and they hoped successful, attempt. At 1:10 A.M. the bishop offered prayers, and gave his blessing for fruitful results. And at 1:13 A.M. Motorin and his assistants watched as the prelate struck a spike that started the flow of metal from the first of the four furnaces. This time there were no accidents. The pouring was completed by 1:49 A.M., only thirty-six minutes after the opening of the first furnace (table 6). Less than a half-hour later Motorin was satisfied that his work had been successful, and he ordered the remaining metal run off into reserve furnaces. Those who had gathered inside the Kremlin in the gelid midnight air had witnessed the founding of the world's largest bell.

TABLE 6
Pouring Schedule for Tsar-Kolokol

Furnace tapped	Time	Duration
First	1:13–1:30 A.M.	17 min.
Second	1:17–1:35 A.M.	18 min.
Third	1:31–1:37 A.M.	6 min.
Fourth	1:36–1:49 A.M.	13 min.
Total time elapsed		36 min.

NOTE: This table is formulated from information in a report dated November 25, 1735 (sheet 118) in N. N. Rubtsov, *History of Foundry Practice in USSR*, trans. from the Russian [2d ed.] (New Delhi: Indian National Scientific Documentation Centre, 1975). 478.

All Moscow was eager to see the bell that would emerge from the mold, as of course were the empress, who had invested a substantial sum in this project, and the founder. When the mold could be excavated and the cope removed several days later, the years of labor—stalked by difficulties, frustrations, delays, and disappointments—were abundantly rewarded. Mikhail Motorin had vindicated his father's faith in the possibility of founding a perfect and beautiful bell of unparalleled size and weight.

Though a successful casting was its own testimony to the founding skills of Motorin and his assistants, their achievement is noteworthy from at least one other standpoint—the speed with which the casting was accomplished. An average of no less than six tons of liquid bronze flowed from the furnaces into the mold each minute during the pouring. Ivan Motorin had purposely designed and built the mold to withstand this unusually rapid rate of casting.[30]

Almost a year after he had cast the bell, Mikhail Motorin's magnum opus was officially recognized and rewarded. On November 1, 1736, he was raised to the rank of Head Foreman of Casting, a promotion that made him the doyen of Muscovite founders.[31]

Plans for the Elevation of Tsar-Kolokol and the Trinity Fire of 1737

Motorin had originally hoped to show the bell within four months of its founding, an interval that he thought would give him enough time to prepare it for inspection.[32] He and his workers had to first remove all residue from the bell by cleaning the bronze with acids. They followed this by "chasing" to eliminate minor imperfections on the bell's inner and outer surfaces. Using a hammer and chisel they cut away any extrusions and with new metal filled in small holes, fissures, or indentations. When the bell had been completely chased, its extensive surface had to be polished. The derrick built over the pit before casting had begun permitted workers to raise the bell slightly from the grating beneath it to clean its lip from below. But the bell was returned to its place on the grating. It was only on July 11, 1736, that official decree authorized the final stages of cleaning, chasing, polishing, and engraving to proceed—in short, everything required to finish the bell.[33] And the process had already taken longer than Motorin had intended.

Ivan Motorin had purposely planned the founding of his great bell inside the Kremlin to minimize problems and hazards of moving such an enormous instrument after lifting it from its casting pit. Indeed a belfry was to be built directly over the pit so that a vertical hoist alone would be required to suspend the bell for ringing. To provide stability and additional buttressing against the powerful vibrations the bell was expected to generate when struck, this zvonnitsa was to be attached to the massive Ivan Velikij Bell Tower by connecting galleries. The galleries would also permit passage between the two structures.[34]

Two proposals for lifting the bell from its pit had appeared before the spring of 1737. A retired soldier named Timofej Khitrov submitted the first of these to Count Saltykov, Governor-General of Moscow, on January 9, 1736, only a month and a half after the bell had been cast. Khitrov estimated that the task would require thirty sailors plus two hundred pine and eighty oak logs, sixty-four ropes, and one hundred twenty-eight blocks. The Moscow Senate office recommended that Khitrov design and submit a working model of his project, and on March 19, 1736, he arrived in Moscow with his model. But there is no further mention of Khitrov or his model. In August of 1736 a peasant named Leontij Shamshurenkov from the town of

105. Tsar-Kolokol in about 1870. The unfinished bas-relief of Empress Anna Ivanovna is on the bell's waist to the left and an inscription cartouche on the right. The Royal Archives, Windsor Castle. Reproduced by Gracious Permission of Her Majesty Queen Elizabeth II.

Yaransk submitted his own plan for raising the bell to the office of the Moscow Senate. The Senate again requested a model of the proposal, and on October 20, 1736, Shamshurenkov presented his model to the artillery office for its inspection. For reasons still unclear, Shamshurenkov's project, like Khitrov's, was never implemented. Mikhail Motorin also worked on this problem and built his own model of a hoisting machine with a specially cast miniature of Tsar-Kolokol, which he sent to St. Petersburg. Whether his plan was ever approved is not known.[35]

Whatever the reasons for the inaction of authorities, disaster continued to stalk the great bell. On May 29, 1737, the Feast of the Holy Trinity, before a structure could be built and the bell raised into it, fire burst into the Kremlin and consumed a large portion of the city as well. The wooden shed above the casting pit in the Kremlin caught fire during this conflagration, sending blazing timbers down into the pit where they began to overheat the bell. Fire fighters in the Kremlin, no doubt aware of the low melting point of bronze, feared that the tsar bell would soon be reduced to a shapeless mass of metal from the intense heat being generated around it, so, with every intention of saving the bell, they poured water into the pit to extinguish the burning wood. But when the cold water hit the red-hot surface of the bell, the injury sustained proved mortal.[36]

In the literature a second explanation of how Tsar-Kolokol was ruined maintains that it was already suspended over the pit and fell when the scaffolding from which it hung began to burn. This version, however, is completely erroneous. Motorin's bell had never hung from a wooden scaffold prior to the fire.[37]

After the Trinity Fire was extinguished, the bell cooled, and the charred debris removed from the pit, Muscovites discovered to their dismay that Tsar-Kolokol, as one writer has expressed it, had "chipped mightily." The "chip" thrown off from the sound-bow weighs about 700 puds (12.63 tons) and is itself heavier than many sizable bells (figure 105).[38] The height of the aperture created in the sound-bow (7 feet 2.5 inches) is broad enough to permit

persons to enter the bell's interior two abreast. In addition to the considerable chunk of metal from the bell's sound-bow, the walls of the bell revealed as many as ten cracks or fissures, some longer and deeper than others. Thus ruined, the bell remained an entire century in the semidarkness of its subterranean tomb.

Description of Tsar-Kolokol

Though the final engraving of the inscriptions and sculpting of the bas-reliefs were never executed, Motorin's Tsar-Kolokol is still a masterpiece. It is the bronze apotheosis of all great bells, one of the most beautifully designed and decorated of all bells; and in magnitude, it remains the supreme achievement in bell founding—in the world as well as in Russia.[39]

Despite persistent rumors of a romantic but unfounded sort that the Russian people in their religious fervor threw a large number of gold and silver objects as well as coins into the molten alloy before the bell was cast, a chemical analysis of the metal in Tsar-Kolokol, which a Colonel Sobolevskij made in 1840 at the laboratory of the Corps of Miners in St. Petersburg, disclosed that the amount of gold and silver in its metal content was negligible:[40]

Copper	84.51%
Tin	13.21
Sulfur	1.25
Zinc, arsenic, and other metals	1.03
Total	100.00%[41]

A previous analysis of the metal composition of Tsar-Kolokol in 1832 revealed that the bell contained only .036 percent gold and .26 percent silver.[42] Traces of substances other than copper and tin (sulfur, zinc, etc.) may have been impurities present in these two principal metals.

Estimates of Tsar-Kolokol's weight have varied considerably. The bell's official weight is given as 12,327 puds 19 funts, a figure obtained by subtracting the amount of metal that remained after casting (2,985 puds 8 funts) from the total weight of the metal (15,312 puds 27 funts) that Mikhail

Motorin placed in the four furnaces at the beginning of the casting process.[43] But as Fal'kovskij has noted, this figure fails to take into account a 3 to 4 percent burning loss that occurs during casting from a good contemporary furnace. Allowing for a 3 percent loss, the actual weight of the bell would stand closer to 12,000 puds (433,356 pounds, or 216.67 tons).[44] Mikhail Motorin had actually cast the bell 2,000 puds heavier than Anna Ivanovna had specified.

The height of the bell alone, according to Fal'kovskij, is 19 feet 3 inches. Its circumference is 60 feet 9 inches, and the diameter at the mouth of the bell would therefore be 19 feet 4 inches. At its sound-bow, the wall of the bell is 2 feet thick.[45] And atop the massive tulip-shaped portion of the bell rise the cannons, four pairs of unornamented consoles that converge at right angles to support a large sphere surmounted by a Greek cross. Although the weight of the cannons are included as part of the bell's total weight, they are not included in the bell's official height.[46] The cost of all materials and labor for casting Tsar-Kolokol, not counting the value of the metal it contains, was 62,008 rubles, a considerable sum at that time, even for the Empress of Russia.[47]

The decorative program on the bell's waist is disposed in four clearly defined areas that are unified and framed, above and below, by two horizontal friezes featuring patterns of vertically articulated foliage that some read as acanthus leaves, others as stylized palm fronds. Two opposite sides of the bell contain inscription cartouches in the French Baroque style, supported by cherubs and ornamental scrollwork (figure 106). The other two areas, on opposite sides between the cartouches, are dominated by full-length relief portraits of Tsar Aleksei Mikhailovich and Empress Anna Ivanovna in their robes of state.[48] Both sovereigns are crowned and hold the orb of Russia in their left hand and the scepter in their right. These bas-reliefs were designed, according to Montferrand, also in the French Baroque style, specifically the schools of Bouchardon and Coysevox.[49] They are unfinished, however, cast only roughly and meant to have been sculpted after casting. Only the heads and upper torsos of the tsar and empress ever took their final form.[50]

Three oval icons are set in the frieze of foliage above the portrait of Aleksei Mikhailovich (figure 107). The larger central medallion is an icon of Jesus Christ, with His right hand raised in blessing

106. Copy of the cartouche on Tsar-Kolokol with the Anna Ivanovna inscription. From Auguste Ricard de Montferrand, *Description de la grande cloche de Moscou* (Paris, 1840), pl. 6. Courtesy of the Fine Arts Library, Indiana University.

107. Copy of the unfinished bas-relief portrait of Tsar Aleksei Mikhailovich on Tsar-Kolokol. From Montferrand, *Description de la grande cloche de Moscou*, pl. 2. Courtesy of the Fine Arts Library, Indiana University.

and His left hand holding an orb like the tsar's. To His right (viewer's left) is an image of the Virgin, and to His left, an icon of John the Baptist. This triptych is further embellished with six cherubs, one each above the representations of the Virgin and John the Baptist, and two above and two beneath the central icon of Christ. Draped garlands extend from the bottom of the two flanking icons across the bell's waist to join the decorative devices on either side of the two large inscription cartouches.

A similar decorative plan is employed on the portion of the bell that features the portrait of Anna Ivanovna. An icon of Jesus Christ occupies the central medallion directly above the empress' head,

assuming the same posture as in the medallion over the tsar's head. On His right (our left) is a smaller icon of St. Peter, and on His left, of St. Anne the Prophetess (figure 108). Cherubs frame the icons as on the opposite side, and draped garlands again link the two outer icons to the decorative devices that surround the two inscription cartouches.

Above and below the multiple bead lines that frame the central decorative zone on the waist of Tsar-Kolokol are additional ornamental friezes. The sound-bow is encircled by a tightly controlled frieze of rosettes within polygonal panels. The frieze immediately below the cannons on the bell's shoulders is also floral, but its treatment is freer than the decoration on the sound-bow (figure 109).

Tsar-Kolokol bears three inscriptions. One of these, set in a decorative cartouche, partially recounts the genealogy of Motorin's bell of 1735 as the successor to Aleksei Mikhailovich's bell of 1655:

By order of the great Sovereign Tsar and Grand Duke, Aleksei Mikhailovich, of blessed and ever-worthy remembrance, Autocrat of all Great and Little and White Russia, the great bell has been cast for the prime Cathedral of the Virtuous and Glorious Assumption of the All-Holy Virgin, containing 8,000 puds of copper [*sic*] in the year from the creation of the world 7162, from the Incarnation of God the Logos 1654; and from this place it began to sound *blagovest* in the year of the creation of the world 7176, of the Nativity of Christ 1668, and it rang until the year of the creation of the world 7208, of the Nativity of the Lord 1701 when, on the 19th day of the month of June, it was damaged because of a great fire in the Kremlin; it remained silent until the year 7239 from the beginning of the world, and from the birth of Christ into the world 1731.[51]

A second inscription, also set in a cartouche, records, though incorrectly, the date Motorin founded his bell for Anna Ivanovna:

By order of the most pious and most autocratic great Sovereign, Empress Anna Ioannovna, Autocrat of all Russia, to the glory of God, glorifying in the Trinity, and in honor of the All-Holy Virgin, for the prime Cathedral of her Glorious Assumption, this bell has been cast from the copper [*sic*] of the former bell of eight thousand puds, damaged in a fire, with the addition of two thousand puds of material, from the creation of the world 7241, from the very Incarnation of God the Logos 1733, and in the fourth year of Her Majesty's successful reign.[52]

The third inscription, shorter and more modest, is located on the bottom edge of the bell facing west and gives the names of the founders: "The Russian foreman, Ivan, son of Fedor, Motorin cast this bell with his own son, Mikhail Motorin."[53]

The voice of Tsar-Kolokol can only be imagined from descriptions of effects produced by the ringing of Grigor'ev's bell during the second half of the seventeenth century. But its probable fundamental can be roughly projected. An extension of Percival Price's formula and table for pitch determination of carillon bells based on weight and lower diameter would place the pitch for Tsar-Kolokol somewhere below C_1, a note two octaves below middle C.[54] This generally agrees with the projection W. W. Starmer made in 1916, though he set the fundamental of the bell on this C_1 (Figure 110),[55] and the hum tone an octave lower on C_2, a note that approaches the lower limits of human pitch perception.[56] These two projections are also in general agreement with another determination of bell pitch from weight cited in the *Harvard Dictionary of Music*.[57] Here a bell of 409,600 pounds would produce a fundamental of C_1. The additional 23,756 pounds of metal in Tsar-Kolokol, plus the fact that in this system the downward extension of pitches by octaves began with a 100-pound bell on c^2 (two octaves above middle C) whose pitch was actually closer to b^1, indicates that the fundamental for Tsar-Kolokol might have been a pitch that leaned heavily toward the flat side of C_1.

A clapper for Tsar-Kolokol has never been found and was probably never cast, but calculating its weight at the traditional 0.031 of the bell's weight, the clapper for Tsar-Kolokol would have weighed about 372 puds (13,434 pounds).[58] The number of ringers that would have been needed to set in motion a clapper of some 6.71 tons can only be imagined from the report of up to one hundred men used to swing the clapper of Grigor'ev's bell. The effects of ringing on those beneath the bell, on the Kremlin's walls and buildings, and in Moscow itself will, alas, never be known.[59]

108. Copy of the Anna Ivanovna surface of Tsar-Kolokol, showing the unfinished bas-relief portrait of the empress and the edges of the two inscription cartouches on the right and the left. Above the empress are relief icons of Jesus Christ (center), St. Anne (right), and St. Peter (left). The plaque on the pedestal is the one that Montferrand placed there in 1836. From Montferrand, *Description de la grande cloche de Moscou*, pl. 7. Courtesy of the Fine Arts Library, Indiana University.

Plans for Recasting, Restoring, and Raising Tsar-Kolokol

Several plans for raising or rehabilitating the broken tsar bell were put forth after the Trinity Fire. Some proposed only raising the bell out of its pit for viewing, others argued in favor of its being recast, while still others imagined that the bell could even be rung if its detached piece might somehow be reintegrated into the mass of its sound-bow. No fewer than seven proposals appeared in the eighteenth century, three of them during the reign of

109. Details of three frieze bands on Tsar-Kolokol. A. Upper frieze around the shoulders of the bell; B. Two lower frieze bands and bead lines on the bell's sound-bow and hip. From Montferrand, *Description de la grande cloche de Moscou*, pl. 1. Courtesy of the Fine Arts Library, Indiana University.

Anna Ivanovna's successor, Elisabeth Petrovna. The first of these was received in January 1747 from Konstantin Slizov, a Moscow founder, who submitted to the Bureau of Artillery and Fortifications a plan for lifting the bell out of the ground and recasting it in a new pit. Slizov's proposal itself was sound and well developed, but his estimated budget of over a hundred thousand rubles led to its indefinite postponement.[60] In 1754 A. K. Nartov (whom Ivan Motorin had consulted on that disastrous night of November 28-29, 1734) examined Slizov's proposal and submitted a budget of only 78,461 rubles for recasting the bell in the same pit Motorin had used. But the Imperial Court did not appropriate

110. W. W. Starmer's projection of (A) the fundamental (C_1) and (B) the hum tone (C_2) of Tsar-Kolokol. From W. W. Starmer, "The Great Bell of Moscow," *The Musical Times* 57 (October 1, 1916): 442.

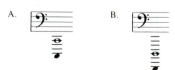

funds.[61] A third proposal for recasting the bell was worked out in December 1759 by three associates of Mikhail Motorin who had assisted in casting the original bell—men named Maliarov, Kop'ev, and Smirnov. But like the two preceding projects, theirs never came to fruition.[62] Mikhail Motorin had died in 1750, and the great bell that he and his father had created remained entombed within the Kremlin.

Only in 1770, during the reign of Catherine II, "the Great" (1762-1796), was interest rekindled in resurrecting the bell. Then the Senate architect, Forstenberg, submitted a plan for restoring rather than recasting the bell; he would raise the bell out of its pit and solder the fragment back into the sound-bow. Forstenberg was convinced that this method of repair would make the bell ringable. The Senate expressed interest in the plan but recommended that Forstenberg first experiment with smaller bells to ascertain whether a satisfactory tone would result. Forstenberg never succeeded in carrying out these experiments, for he succumbed to plague; and his proposal was soon forgotten.[63]

No further proposals were received for the recasting or repair of Tsar-Kolokol until the end of the eighteenth century. The only plans forthcoming recommended raising the bell from its pit. On April 30, 1772, in connection with his projected reconstruction of the Kremlin and building of a great Kremlin palace (1767-1775), V. I. Bazhenov proposed moving both Motorin's Tsar-Kolokol and Slizov's Uspensky Bell of 1760 to other sites in the Kremlin.[64] But Bazhenov's plans to relocate the two great bells were abandoned. He therefore suggested that the pit containing Tsar-Kolokol be covered by wooden planks flush with the ground. Only in 1793, however, under the supervision of I. V. Egotov, a Kremlin architect, was the the pit covered with a wooden "roof" and surrounded by a protective railing.[65] This railing was meant to keep people from walking on the planks covering the large cavity.[66]

The court's attention returned to Tsar-Kolokol in 1797 when Emperor Paul (1796-1801) charged an engineer named J. Guirt with supervising the raising of Motorin's bell.[67] An architect named M. F. Kazakov carried out an inspection of the bell, however, and expressed doubt that it could be successfully raised from its pit.[68] Kazakov recommended that a working model and drawings be made, but he believed there were additional cracks in the bell's wall that could not be seen and that would cause the bell to break apart under its own weight on being lifted from its pit after sixty years.[69]

Conditions had indeed deteriorated in the pit by the time Kazakov inspected the bell at the end of the eighteenth century. Edward Daniel Clarke, who was in Moscow during the reign of Paul, almost lost his life in a near-fatal accident while descending into the pit on rotten ladders.

The bell reaches from the bottom of the pit to the roof. The entrance to the place where it lies, is by a trap door, placed even with the surface of the earth; and beneath the entrance are ladders. We found the steps of the ladders very dangerous; some being wanted, and others broken. In consequence of this the author encountered a very severe fall down the whole extent of the first flight; and narrowly escaped losing his life, in not fracturing his scull [sic] upon the bell. After this accident, a sentinel was stationed at the trap-door, to prevent people from becoming victims to their curiosity. The same person, it is true, might have been as well employed in mending the ladders, as in waiting all day to say that they were broken. The bell is truly a mountain of metal.[70]

At the bottom of the pit Clarke found water, mud, and large pieces of timber. But in spite of the foul air, darkness, and debris, Russians carrying torches descended into the bell's subterranean home on feast days as though entering a sanctuary. They continually crossed themselves on their way down and back and regarded the mound of bronze dimly visible in the flickering light as an object of veneration (figure 111).[71]

Napoleon is said to have considered removing Tsar-Kolokol from its pit for shipment to Paris as a trophy of his Russian campaign, but the bell was theft-proof.[72] Before the French left Moscow, however, the mines they planted in the Kremlin shook all of Moscow and rained debris from the shattered walls of the Ivan Velikij Bell Tower into the pit in which Tsar-Kolokol rested. Only the top of the bell remained visible in the pit above the rubble. After 1819 Alexander I charged General Fabre, a military engineer, with raising Tsar-Kolokol.[73] But Fabre's only accomplishment was cleaning out the pit and removing the debris hurled down by the French explosions. At this time a cover was again placed over the pit, and in 1821 a staircase with a railing constructed by which sightseers could descend through a trap door in the "roof" to view the enormous bell.[74]

At the end of 1834, during the reign of Nicholas I (1825-1855), Vasilij Iakovlevich Lebedev proposed lifting Tsar-Kolokol from its pit and rolling it along an inclined ramp onto a platform (figure 112). The cost would be only 15,612 rubles. Lebedev's plan generated considerable interest among a group of engineers from the Ministry for Means of Communication, and the court assigned Auguste Ricard de Montferrand to study and critique Lebedev's plan.[75] Not unaware of the personal prestige and imperial favor to be garnered through a successful raising and display of Tsar-Kolokol in the Kremlin, Montferrand immediately began to work himself toward the center of this project by pointing out flaws in Lebedev's proposal.[76] The emperor himself approved the Frenchman's plans for the project with the stipulation that the budget for the work must not exceed Lebedev's estimate.[77] In May 1835 authorities in Moscow received Montferrand's approved sketches and plans from St. Petersburg. Preliminary work was quickly begun to raise the bell from its century-long interment.

Since Montferrand was already engaged in the construction of St. Isaac's Cathedral in St. Petersburg, supervision of the first stages of the project fell to Lebedev, who lived in Moscow. But the collaboration of architect and engineer on this project proved to be far from amicable. A new sum of 30,431 rubles, which Lebedev estimated for the work, Montferrand rejected as excessive and submitted his own estimate. Montferrand intentionally underbid Lebedev to force his withdrawal from the project. And his scheme worked, even though the eventual cost of raising Tsar-Kolokol came to 51,648 rubles. By the summer of 1835 Montferrand had established himself in sole charge of the bell's elevation.

The project was to be carried out in two successive stages. The first was the vertical raising of Tsar-

111. Drawing of Tsar-Kolokol in its covered pit about 1809. The representation of a staircase, however, may be premature. According to Clarke, he climbed down into the pit on ladders in 1801; stairs are not reported until 1821. From Edward Daniel Clarke, *Travels in Various Countries of Europe, Asia, and Africa*, pt. 1: Russia, Tartary, and Turkey, 2d ed. (London, 1811), betw. pp. 114 and 115. Courtesy of the University of Cincinnati Libraries.

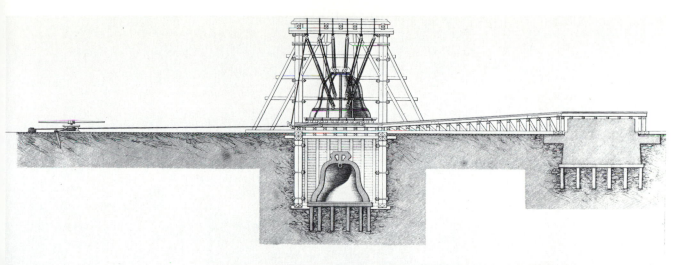

112. Montferrand's cross-section of the pit and derrick for raising Tsar-Kolokol. The ramp for moving it on logs to the granite pedestal extends to the right of the pit. From Montferrand, *Description de la grande cloche de Moscou*, pl. 3. Courtesy of the Fine Arts Library, Indiana University.

Kolokol, followed by movement of the bell along a ramp to a stone platform near the foot of the Bono-Godunov Tower. The bell was then to be lifted from the ramp and lowered onto this pedestal.[78] Preliminary work included building the granite platform and constructing a hoisting derrick over the pit.[79] Montferrand concluded his consultations with F. N. Chelnakov on the masonry for the pedestal on July 12, 1835, and the octagonal stone platform was completed a little more than three months later. Then construction of the hoisting derrick began. This work took approximately 120 carpenters under the direction of foreman Egor Yasin six weeks to finish.

Meanwhile, inside the pit the earth around the base of the bell was removed and water was pumped out so that the ground could dry. Ten navvies then labored to disengage the bell's lip from the hardened earth. During their work they uncovered the remains of the iron grating on which the Motorins had constructed their mold, but after a century in the ground the iron beams had almost become joined to the lip of the bell through corrosion. After the navvies had worked to separate the bell's mouth from the grating, it was ready to be lifted.

On May 1, 1836, Montferrand was waiting impatiently in the Kremlin when word finally came at 10:00 A.M. that the governor-general of Moscow and the Committee on Kremlin Buildings had given orders to begin the raising of Tsar-Kolokol. After clergy had invoked divine blessing for a successful outcome, Montferrand and his workers were so thronged by spectators that they could hardly complete their final preparations. Montferrand at last gave the signal to begin the hoist. His workers leaned into the capstans, the faithful crossed themselves, and ropes groaned as they stretched taut. So strenuous was the initial effort to lift the bell from the floor of the pit that two ropes snapped, and a little later a block broke and was hurled into the scaffolding. But these accidents did not halt the operation. As the bell slowly began to rise, it carried with it four workers on top around its cannons and part of the iron grating below on which it had been cast.

The crowd that only a few minutes ago had pressed excitedly around Montferrand now fell silent and began to retreat. Their festive expectations of success at the beginning had swiftly turned to concern for the outcome of this project. Now only the slow, regular turning of the capstans broke their silence.

113. The wooden derrick Montferrand used to raise Tsar-Ko-lokol on July 23, 1836. From Montferrand, *Description de la grande cloche de Moscou*, pl. 8. Courtesy of the Fine Arts Library, Indiana University.

When the bell had traversed about a third of the distance to ground level, Montferrand noticed that it was listing slightly as a result of the two broken ropes. And the angle it had assumed made its elevation increasingly difficult. When two more ropes gave way, Montferrand signaled to halt the operation. The workers turning the capstans stopped. Three of the four men riding on top of the bell were hastily pulled off. The fourth was sent below into the pit. There in semidarkness beneath the great bronze dome he moved quickly as he carefully set the beams in place onto which the bell would be lowered. Precariously poised in its passage between two worlds, Tsar-Kolokol swayed almost imperceptibly on its remaining ropes. The

crowd, long silent, stopped breathing. Only the creaking from the bell's rigging could be heard. When the worker had finished laying the beams, Montferrand himself descended into the pit and succeeded in bringing the bell to rest without further mishap.[80]

After this unsuccessful operation Montferrand returned to St. Petersburg, where he obtained permission to take some hoisting gear he was using in constructing St. Isaac's Cathedral back to Moscow temporarily. By July 22 Montferrand had marshalled a work force of 480 soldiers under the command of twenty junior officers and an additional 106 carpenters and other workers. At daylight the next day, like some enormous armored creature emerging out of the earth, Tsar-Kolokol was seen to rise slowly from its pit to ground level (figure 113). Montferrand himself has recounted the sequence of events in this operation:

114. Tsar-Kolokol on its platform in the Kremlin shortly after Montferrand had completed his project at the end of July 1836. From Montferrand, *Description de la grande cloche de Moscou*, pl. 9. Courtesy of the Fine Arts Library, Indiana University.

Since all my recent preparations were complete, the operation took place on July 23 in the presence of a large crowd of spectators, including his Eminence the Governor General, important city officials, and members of the Committee on Kremlin Buildings. At 5:00 A.M. after the clergy had finished its prayers for the successful outcome of this operation, I had the soldiers stationed at the capstans. At 6:05 I gave the signal, and the machines began to move. Shortly thereafter the bell, covered with its old dust, was seen to rise slowly from the pit and to fill the space within the wooden frame with its enormous bulk. The operation lasted 42 minutes, 33 seconds and was most successfully accomplished to the great pleasure of the astonished citizens while gazing on this colossus suspended in midair. The pit was covered over immediately with a strong floor of beams which supported the bogie onto which the bell was lowered. . . .[81]

The next day the bell was set on this vehicle, which was then rolled on logs up a gently ascend-ing ramp extending from the pit to a point above the granite pedestal a little over sixty-five feet away. The same derrick employed in hoisting the bell from its pit was then moved and set up above the octagonal platform. Once more the bell was lifted, this time from its vehicle. The vehicle and the end of the ramp and its runway over the platform were removed, and on July 26, the bell was carefully lowered onto this massive granite base (figure 114). The fragment that broke away from the sound-bow in 1737 workers set on the ground propped against the pedestal.

Soon after the bell's removal from the pit and placement on the platform the orb and cross ordered by the tsar were placed on top of the cannons. Montferrand's work was finished.[82] All that remained was to record the accomplishment of his Herculean task on a plaque of bluish-white marble:

This bell has been cast in the year 1733 [*sic*] by order of the Sovereign Empress Anna Ioannovna; it remained in the earth one hundred and three years [*sic*], and by the will of the Most Pious Sovereign Emperor Nicholas I, was placed [here] on the fourth day of August in the year 1836.[83]

Robert Bremner arrived in Moscow four days after Montferrand had placed Tsar-Kolokol on its granite pedestal, a time when all Russia was rejoicing over news of the bell's resurrection.

During our stay, the Kremlin was constantly crowded with people flocking from all parts to see the bell. When we entered it, the fatal gap in its side yawned like the door of an old cathedral. Even a tall man feels himself very small indeed within it. It being the workmen's idle hour, five or six peasants were sleeping within it, among the huge beams and coiled ropes; but these brawny inmates looked small indeed in the monster's womb.[84]

Robert and Clara Schumann reached Moscow in the early spring of 1844, and the Leipzig composer, drawn repeatedly from his hotel to the Kremlin, wrote a poem on the elevation and honored place of the great bell "in the midst of many cathedrals, near the treasury close to the crown jewels of the empire—."[85]

By 1849 if not earlier the interior of Tsar-Kolokol had been consecrated as a chapel, and Russians could enter into the bell's enormous cavity to worship.

Underneath this immense metallic canopy is a chapel, in which is a shrine at which many thousands of the Russians every year offer up their devotions. The entrance to this is through an iron gateway, and the visitor descends several stone steps before he stands upon the paved floor of the chapel. Looking upward and around him, he then for the first time realizes the vast magnitude of this wonderful casting. . . . Imagine a circular room more than twenty feet in diameter, and of proportionate height, and you have some faint idea of the interior of the Tzar-Kolokol.[86]

The Motorins' bell functioned as a chapel until it was secularized with other Kremlin monuments after the October Revolution.[87]

Proposals to Recast or Restore Tsar-Kolokol after Its Elevation

Only a brief epilogue remains in the bell's biography. Toward the end of the nineteenth century several plans were advanced either for recasting the bell or for restoring it. Among the proposals submitted after 1836, three, which appeared at the end of the century, are noteworthy: the plan of a Mr. Roberts from the 1880s; the project of Nikolaj Nikolaevich Benardos in 1890; and the proposal Nikolaj Gavrilovich Slavianov submitted in the early 1890s.[88] One condition attached to the repair of the bell was regarded as inviolable: its decoration and ornamentation must be preserved and its outer surface remain unaltered.[89]

A foreman known only as Mr. Roberts from the Sevastopol steamship workshops believed that all damage to the bell could be satisfactorily repaired by pouring molten metal into the fissures in its walls. A small portion of liquid metal used to fill in the cracks would merge with the surface of the bell.[90] Roberts presumably intended to reintegrate the piece from the bell's sound-bow by this same technique, but because this method, sometimes employed in the repair of cast machine parts, would alter the appearance of the bell's surface, his proposal was not considered.

In 1890 the famous inventor N. N. Benardos offered his own plan for restoring the bell, proposing to weld its broken piece back into the sound-bow by a process of his own invention called *èlektro-gefest*, which involved welding metal with an electric arc.[91] The edges of all cracks and of both the aperture and the piece that fit into it would have to be cut back, however, before repair could be made with the arc. Moreover, oxides would form in places where the welding had been done, resulting in a noticeable difference in the composition and color of the metal. In order to conceal these differences between the old and new metal,

Benardos proposed finishing his work by chasing, polishing, and treatment with acid. He then recommended cladding the bell's surface with gold, silver, or nickel.

In addition to his explanations of the techniques he proposed for repairing the bell, Benardos included plans for moving Tsar-Kolokol and suspending it at a proper height. He even developed a plan for creating an all-Russian monument on Moscow's Sparrow Hills whose focal point would be Tsar-Kolokol.[92] Since Benardos' method of repairing the cracks in the bell's surface would require that they be widened and would significantly alter the appearance of the bell, however, neither his methods nor his proposed monument on Sparrow Hills gained public support or official funding.

In 1892 the attention of a distinguished Russian mining engineer and head of the Perm Cannon Foundry in Motovilikha, N. G. Slavianov, was also directed to the possibility of restoring Tsar-Kolokol.[93] The preceding year he had devised his own technique of welding metal castings with an electric arc. And to test his method, he had carried out a series of experiments during the late winter and early spring of 1893 in which he welded broken pieces back into some relatively small bells and poured metal over the cracks.[94] These experiments were said to be the first in history that successfully repaired broken bells without recasting them.[95]

The proposals of both Benardos and Slavianov were based on the use of an electric arc. They differed, however, in that the electrode in Benardos' arc was carbon, whereas that in Slavianov's arc was metal.[96] Slavianov's method added more metal to the fissure in a bell; Benardos' encouraged more fusion of the base metal (the bell). Of the two proposals, Slavianov's would have been less costly to implement, since wasteful loss of heat would have occurred with the incandescing of carbon in Benardos' *èlektrogefest*.[97] Glubokovskij concludes that Slavianov's experiments leave no doubt that from a technical standpoint his proposed method might have been successful in repairing Tsar-Kolokol.[98]

Furthermore, the tone of several bells that Slavianov had already repaired was described as "excellent." In comparing the plans of Benardos and Slavianov, most contemporaries considered the latter the more feasible and economical of the two.[99] But neither was ever implemented.

Olovianishnikov reports a fourth proposal that appeared around the beginning of the twentieth century from N. V. Podchinennov, who also advocated the use of electrical welding.[100] Recently Tsar-Kolokol has again become the focus of revived interest in determining its condition and the possibilities for its restoration. A scientific study of Tsar-Kolokol was undertaken in 1979 by members of the Military Academy in the name of F. È. Dzerzhinskij, in consultation with representatives from the All-Union Scientific-Research Institute for Restoration. After almost a century and a half of exposure to Moscow winters Montferrand's pedestal itself now stands in need of restoration.[101]

Even if the cast-off piece from Tsar-Kolokol could ever be successfully reintegrated into the bell wall, the crucial question remains—would the tone of the repaired bell be satisfactory? No one seems willing to guarantee even an acceptable tone. In Olovianishnikov's opinion, Podchinennov only revealed his ignorance when he recommended welding the broken piece back into the tsar bell. Olovianishnikov's position on this question was unequivocal. Joining the piece to the bell by any contemporary means was not possible if a normal ring had to be guaranteed.[102]

Tsar-Kolokol stands today in the Kremlin as Montferrand left it on that summer day in 1836. Mute, it remains a purely sculptural monument to the technological genius of Russia's bell founders and to a liturgical destiny that fate had resolved to thwart. But among the Old Believers a legend has persisted that on the Day of The Last Judgment Tsar-Kolokol will rise slowly from its granite pedestal and begin to toll.[103] On that day, at the end of history, the voice of Russia's greatest bell, according to the Old Believers, will proclaim final *blagovest*.

13

The Last of Russia's Great Bells

ABOUT 1570 Heinrich von Staden wrote that in the Moscow Kremlin between the Ivan Velikij Bell Tower and the Uspensky Cathedral hung the largest bell in Muscovy.[1] This great bell of 1,000 puds (36,113 pounds), founded by Nikolai Nemchin in 1533 and originally hung in its own timber structure on the Kremlin's Cathedral Square,[2] was the first bell to bear the name "Tsar-Kolokol." According to sketchy information, Nemchin's bell "was recast at a later time with the addition of bronze";[3] it was christened "Prazdnichnyj" (Feast-day), or "Great Uspensky," in a patriarchal edict of 1689 and moved from its wooden belfry on the square into the Filaret structure of the Ivan Velikij Bell Tower. The first recasting of Nemchin's bell with substantial documentation, however, is the commission that Konstantin Slizov carried out in 1760.

Slizov's Uspensky Bell of 1760 for Elisabeth Petrovna

This commission, granted by Empress Elisabeth Petrovna (1741-1762), launched a second and somewhat lesser line of great Kremlin bells. Slizov's bell, according to its inscription, weighed 3,551 puds 4 funts (128,241 pounds), and its clapper's weight has been placed at 114 puds (4,117 pounds).[4] The bell's circumference was reported as 40 feet 9 inches, and its wall thickness as 16.50 inches.[5] One portion of the bell's surface contained relief icons of Jesus Christ, the Virgin, and John the Baptist; the opposite surface had reliefs of the Assumption of the Virgin, St. Peter the Miracle Worker of Moscow, and Metropolitan Aleksej. Below these icons were grouped portraits of Peter I, "the Great," Catherine I, Elisabeth Petrovna, Grand Duke Petr Fedorovich (the future Peter III), his wife, Grand Duchess Ekaterina Alekseevna (the future Catherine II, "the Great"), and her son, Grand Duke Pavel Petrovich (the future emperor Paul).[6] The inscription read:

In the year from the creation of the world 7268 and from the Incarnation of God the Logos 1760, this bell has been cast in Moscow during the prosperous reign of the Most Pious and Most Autocratic Great Sovereign, Elisaveta Petrovna, Empress of All Russia, in the 19th year of her reign and in the time of their Imperial Highnesses, the gracious Lord, Grand Duke Petr Theodorovich, and his consort, the gracious Lady, Grand Duchess EKATERINA ALEKSEEVNA, and in that of the gracious Lord, Grand Duke PAVEL PETROVICH. Its weight is 3,551 puds 4 funts [128,241 pounds]; the shop foreman, Konstantin, son of Mikhail, Slizov, cast [this bell].[7]

For fifty-two years Slizov's bell served the Kremlin's Uspensky Cathedral. Edward Clarke, one of the last European visitors in Moscow to record his impressions of this bell, reported that in 1800 it hung "near the cathedral" and was "only used upon important occasions: when it sounds, a deep hollow murmur vibrates all over *Moscow*, like the fullest and lowest tones of a vast organ, or the rolling of distant thunder."[8] But as a result of Napoleon's mining of the Ivan Velikij Bell Tower in 1812, Slizov's bell fell to the ground and broke in pieces.

Bogdanov's Great Uspensky Bell of 1817

As part of the reconstruction program undertaken in the Kremlin after Napoleon's retreat, including the restoration of the Ivan Velikij Bell Tower, the large fragments of Slizov's bell were hauled to the Moscow foundry of Mikhail Gavrilov Bogdanov, whom Alexander I (1801-1825) had commissioned to recast the bell. Bogdanov's first step was to reduce the larger pieces of the bell to manageable size. This he accomplished by the very act that had proven fatal to Motorin's Tsar-Kolokol in 1737 during the Trinity Fire. He heated the chunks of Slizov's bell and then caused them to shatter by pouring cold water on the hot metal.[9] Bogdanov recast Slizov's bell on March 7, 1817, and two years later—after many months of chasing, polishing, and finishing its inscriptions and reliefs—the new bell was ready to be transported to its home in the Kremlin (figure 115).

In the summer of 1819, under Bogdanov's personal supervision, the great new Uspensky bell was dragged on a sledge in a festive procession through the streets of Moscow from the foundry into the Kremlin. There it was raised into the central zvonnitsa, the Petrok Malyj portion, of the Ivan Velikij Bell Tower.[10] Tradition maintains that Bogdanov even invested his own resources in the founding of his Great Uspensky Bell and until his death regarded it with paternal affection. On those special days of the year when this bell sounded *blagovest*, he would climb into the Kremlin's bell tower to watch the three ringers beneath the bell who, grasping a rope tied to the flight of the clapper, would begin to swing this massive iron pendant in a circular motion to touch three points on the sound-bow. It was said that Bogdanov's eyes grew moist at the sound of his bell.[11]

The weight and dimensions of Bogdanov's bell are significantly greater than were those of Slizov's. Its height is reported at 21 feet, its diameter from edge to edge, 18 feet, and its reported circumference, 54 feet.[12] Its exact weight is a matter of dispute, but officially it is listed at 4,000 puds (144,452 pounds), which would make it about 449 puds (16,215 pounds) heavier than Slizov's bell.[13] The weight of its iron clapper has been reported at both 120 and 125 puds (4,334 and 4,514 pounds).

One portion of the bell's surface contains a half-length relief of Alexander I, who commissioned the bell; he is crowned and surrounded by implements of war. His cipher (A.) appears on each side of his portrait, and further to his right and left, respectively, are portraits of his consort, Empress Elizaveta Alekseevna, and his mother, Dowager Empress Maria Theodorovna. Above the emperor's head is an icon of Jesus Christ, while to His right is an icon of the Virgin, and to His left, one of John the Baptist. The opposite surface of the bell contains portraits of the three Grand Dukes, younger brothers of Alexander I: Konstantin in the center, flanked by Nikolai (the future Nicholas I) and Mikhail. Because this bell was cast to serve the Uspensky (Assumption) Cathedral in the Kremlin, the medallions above the heads of the Grand Dukes show representations of the Assumption (Dormition) of the Virgin and, on either side, two Russian saints: Aleksej and Ivan (figure 115).[14]

The first part of the inscription on Bogdanov's bell is followed by a bitter indictment of Napoleon and his Grand Armée:

In the year 7325 from the creation of the world, 1817 from the Incarnation of God the Logos on the 22nd day of the month of July, by order of the Most Virtuous Great Sovereign, Emperor, and Autocrat of all Russia, Aleksandr Pavlovich, in the 17th [year] of his reign: in the time of his consort, the Most Virtuous Sovereign Empress Elisaveta Alekseevna: in the time of his mother, the Most Virtuous Sovereign and Empress Mariia Theodorovna: in the time of the Gracious Lord, Tsesarevich and Grand Duke Konstantin Pavlovich, and his consort, the Gracious Lady, Grand Duchess Anna Theodorovna: in the time of the Gracious Lord, Grand Duke Nikolaj Pavlovich, and his consort, the Gracious Lady, Grand Duchess Aleksandra Theodorovna: in the time of the Gracious Lord, Grand Duke Mikhail Pavlovich: in the

time of the Gracious Lady, Grand Duchess Mariia Pavlovna, and her consort: in the time of the Gracious Sovereign Queen of Württemberg, Ekaterina Pavlovna, and her consort: and in the time of the Gracious Lady, Grand Duchess Anna Pavlovna, and her consort.

Upon the happy and triumphal conclusion of terrible and bloody battles and upon the establishment of a lasting peace in all of Europe, this bell was recast from an old one founded in 1760 (and weighing 3,551 puds), [which] was damaged in 1812 by the collapse of the former bell tower, blown up by the furious French, [who] with twenty nations invaded Russia, when they, eventually being punished by a wrathful Lord of Might, Whose name and sanctuaries they dared to desecrate, sought to escape from this capital [and] from God's wrath and fury. Enemies of holiness and mankind, they were pursued and struck down everywhere by the power of God; they covered with their corpses the territory from this capital to the very borders of Russia, and [only] a small portion of them barely managed to survive. Let us sing unto the lord, for Thou hast triumphed gloriously: Thou hast destroyed Pharaoh and his 300's. The weight of this bell is———puds and———funts.[15]

A second inscription records the names of the bell's founders:

This bell has been cast at the Moscow foundry of the merchant of the second guild, Mikhail Gavrilov Bogdanov, by Iakov Zav'ialov, foreman in the same foundry and by Russinov, a cannon foreman of the fourteenth rank at the St. Petersburg Arsenal, by order of His Grace, Archbishop Avgustin.[16]

Muscovites first heard the voice of Bogdanov's bell in the summer of 1819 after its installation in the Ivan Velikij Bell Tower. Some who had heard Slizov's Uspensky bell claimed that the tone of the older bell was superior to that of Bogdanov's recasting. But Priakhin praises Bogdanov's bell as remarkable for the power and majesty of its tone. And Clara Schumann is said to have remarked that the voice of Moscow's Great Uspensky Bell was the most beautiful sound she had ever heard.[17] Priakhin also reports that the pitch of this bell was $A^\flat_2$, notated on the third leger line below the bass staff.[18] This pitch can be taken as the bell's hum tone, with its fundamental, or prime, an octave higher on $A^\flat_1$.

Before the Revolution the Great Uspensky Bell was rung on all the most important feasts of the church year and on certain other solemn occasions. Easter, Christmas, the Assumption of the Virgin, the Feast of the Holy Trinity, and Epiphany were rung in on this bell. And its voice accompanied the procession of the cross (*krestnyj khod*) around the Kremlin each October. The death of a Russian sovereign, a member of the Imperial family, or the Metropolitan of Moscow was announced by three solemn strokes.

Throughout the nineteenth century and until the new regime secularized the Kremlin's cathedrals and churches, the powerful strokes from the Great Uspensky Bell at midnight between Holy Saturday and Easter Sunday signaled other bell ringers in the Ivan Velikij Tower and in bell towers throughout Moscow to begin the festive zvon.[19] When the clapper of this great bell touched its sound-bow, it produced "a tremulous effect over the whole city, similar to what is experienced by any one who stands near a powerful organ when it is played."[20] Bogdanov's bell still hangs today in the Kremlin, silhouetted in the large central arch of the Ivan Velikij Bell Tower (figure 116).

The Elisabeth Petrovna Bell of 1748 for the Trinity-Sergius Lavra

Though the Trinity-Sergius Lavra lies some forty-four miles northeast of Moscow, it has always been closely linked to events in the old capital, and it was often the recipient of expressions of piety from Russian sovereigns. Among the no less than forty bells that once hung in the lavra's mid-eighteenth-century bell tower, three in particular were noted for their unusual size and weight. Of these, one, also known as Tsar-Kolokol, was the monumental bell of 1748 that Elisabeth Petrovna commissioned.[21] The predecessor of this tsar bell was a

115 (*on facing page*). Mikhail Bogdanov's Great Uspensky Bell (1817), which hangs today in the Petrok Malyj structure of the Ivan Velikij Bell Tower in the Moscow Kremlin. From Andreev, *Moskovskij Kreml'*, pl. 81. Permission of VAAP, Moscow.

116. The Ivan Velikij Bell Tower complex in the Moscow Kremlin with two cupolas of the Uspensky Cathedral visible on the right side and the Cathedral of the Archangel Michael on the far left. Tsar-Kolokol rests on its granite pedestal at the foot of the Bono-Godunov tower, and the silhouette of Bogdanov's Great Uspensky Bell can be seen in the large central arch beneath the tall drum and cupola on the Petrok Malyj structure. The Filaret addition, with its large, vacant bell chamber, stands just to the right of the Petrok Malyj structure. From Andreev, *Moskovskij Kreml'*, pl. 84. Permission of VAAP, Moscow.

bell cast in 1716 at 3,500 puds 20 funts (126,414 pounds), which was already recorded as damaged in an inventory of 1735.[22] The empress, during her visit on August 4, 1742, ordered Archimandrite (Abbot) Ambrosij to have the useless bell recast and its weight increased to 4,000 puds (144,452 pounds).

Among those who responded to the call for bell founders was Mikhail Motorin, who estimated that the bell could be recast for 38,369 rubles 27.5 kopecks. But Gavriil Smirnov (who had assisted Motorin in the founding of Tsar-Kolokol) and Semen Stepanov underbid him by 14,821 rubles 42.5 kopecks, and received the commission. They spent two years taking care of the preliminary work and gathered 750 puds of new copper and 250 puds of new tin to add to the metal from the old bell (for a total weight at the beginning of casting of 4,500 puds 20 funts, or 162,527 pounds). But their work suffered a considerable setback on May 17, 1746, when a fire swept through the lavra, destroying not only monastery property but also much of the casting equipment. Undaunted, Stepanov and Smirnov resumed work immediately.[23]

When preparations had been completed on the last day of June 1746, the foremen announced that casting would begin the next day. An All-Night Vigil at the lavra invoked divine blessing on the new bell, and on July 1, at the conclusion of the liturgy in the lavra's Cathedral of the Trinity and in the presence of a large throng, a procession of the cross (*krestnyj khod*) escorted the crowd to the pit where the pour was to be accomplished. All equipment and materials to be used the next day were sprinkled with consecrated water. Workers then fired the furnaces to melt 4,654 puds 14.75 funts of metal.[24] But the attempt to cast the bell was not successful. Because the joint at the base of the mold between the cope and the core was not tightly fastened, metal seeped into the pit during casting and thus left the amount of bronze insufficient to fill the bell's cannons at the top of the mold. By mid-July a report on the mishap had been filed, and on July 29 it was forwarded to St. Petersburg. Elisabeth Petrovna immediately dispatched an artillery general, Prince Vasilij Anikitich Repnin, from Moscow to the lavra to conduct an on-the-spot inspection.

Procedural formalities delayed a second attempt to cast the bell for more than two years. Finally, on September 8, 1748, Archimandrite Arsenij received an *ukaz* from the empress authorizing the final act of pouring the metal. Once again an All-Night Vigil preceded a procession of the cross. Then at 1:20 P.M. on September 10 the furnaces were fired. After two days of melting, the bronze was ready to pour. Services began at the lavra at 9:44 A.M. on September 12, and the casting of the bell was completed eleven minutes after midnight on September 13. This time the work was successful. The task of finishing the bell's surface was assigned to Aleksej Isaev and Petr Fedorov, two workers from the Moscow Arsenal.[25]

Six years after Elisabeth Petrovna had awarded the commission, the largest of the bells to hang in the tower of the Trinity-Sergius Lavra had been founded. The bell's height from its base to its cannons was 4.5 arshins (10.5 feet), its reported circumference was 18 arshins (42 feet), the thickness of its wall at the sound-bow was 10 vershki (17.5 inches), and its reported lower diameter was 6 arshins (14 feet).[26] The bell weighed 4,000 puds (144,452 pounds), and its iron clapper's weight was 90 puds (3,250 pounds).

The bell's decorative program was disposed in four areas. The coat of arms of the Russian Empire occupied one portion, and in the other sections appeared portraits in bas-relief of three members of the imperial family: the reigning Empress Elisabeth Petrovna, Grand Duke Petr Fedorovich, and Grand Duchess Ekaterina Alekseevna. Above the heads of the imperial family were centered representations of the Crucifixion of Christ and the Virgin's appearance to St. Sergius.[27] Above and below the portraits ran a four-line inscription, the first two lines encircling the upper portion of the waist, and the third and fourth, the lower part. The lines, in order from top to bottom, read:

To the glory of the all-holy, consubstantial, lifegiving and indivisible Trinity, the Father and the Son and the Holy Spirit, in honor of the most-blessed Bogoroditsa, ever-Virgin Mary, through the prayers of our reverend and god-bearing fathers, Sergej and Nikon, Igumeny of Radonezh and miracle workers of all Russia.

By the signed and most all-gracious edict of Her Imperial Majesty, our Most Virtuous and Most Autocratic Great Sovereign and Empress Elisaveta Petrovna, Autocrat of all Russia, in the time of Her heir, the grandson of Peter the First.

In the time of the gracious Lord and Grand Duke Petr Theodorovich and his consort, the gracious Lady and Grand Duchess Ekaterina Aleksievna [*sic*], with the blessing of the most-holy ruling Synod of All Russia, during the administration of a member of that most holy Synod, His Grace, Arsenij Mogileanskij, Archibishop of Pereslavl and Dmitrov and Archimandrite of the Holy-Trinity Sergius Lavra, this bell was recast from a former [one] founded in the year 1716 at a weight of 3,319 puds [119,859 pounds]. The weight of this bell is 4,000 puds, which has been cast in this

Trinity Lavra on the twelfth day of September in the year 1748. Foremen Gavrilo, son of Lukiian, Smirnov, and Semen Stepanov founded this bell.[28]

On February 1, 1750, some three thousand people accompanied the bell from its casting site in the lavra to the foot of the new, but still unfinished, tower where Empress Elisabeth Petrovna had ordered it hung.[29] Two days later the bell was hoisted onto a framework of oak posts, where it remained until the bell tower was ready to receive it. Then in December of 1759, more than nine years later, three hundred people assisted in raising the bell into the lowest bell tier of the new tower.[30] The empress' bell sounded *blagovest* from this baroque tower on major feasts of the church year and announced solemn official occasions until the Revolution. At the beginning of January 1930, though, it was removed from the tower and hauled to a foundry where its metal was melted down and reused for industrial purposes.[31] At 4,000 puds, the lavra's Tsar-Kolokol had once ranked with Bogda-nov's Great Uspensky Bell of 1817 as one of the two largest ringing bells in all of Russia.[32]

Through their creation of bells in magnitudes unprecedented in Europe and rivalled only in Asia, Muscovite founders had endowed their church and their sovereigns with iron tongues and voices of resounding bronze. Measured strokes on these great Russian bells became solemn affirmations of Orthodoxy and autocracy, amplifying the person and presence of the Russian monarch throughout and even beyond the limits of Moscow.

14

Bronze Avatars of a Religio-Political Ideology

FOR ALMOST a thousand years bells rang in Russia. The signals that had sounded on Egyptian, Hebrew, and early Christian trumpets were transferred to semantra that the Greeks struck for their calls to services—and finally, by the mid-eleventh century, to bells in Russia. Russian bells both accommodated the metal substance of trumpets and reflected the manual hammer strokes on Byzantine semantra in their manner of ringing. And as they developed on the frontier between Europe and Asia, they combined features of form, installation, and performance practice from both Eastern and Western instruments. In their form and profile they preserved and developed West European ideals. But in their magnitude, stationary mounting, and high visibility they resembled the monumental Oriental bells. In fact, not unlike large temple bells in the Far East, which are suspended only a few feet from the ground, several of the great Kremlin bells were installed temporarily in their own low wooden structures on Cathedral Square where they could be admired, even as Tsar-Kolokol is displayed today on its granite pedestal. Russian bell ringing, too, reflected practices from both East and West. The internal clapper, although characteristic of European bells, was swung in Russia to strike the sound-bow of the stationary bell, in an action more reminiscent of the Eastern practice of striking a bell's outer surface with a cudgel or ramming

it with a suspended wooden beam than of the Western practice of swinging the whole bell to strike the clapper. Direct manual control of the clapper of a stationary bell could reproduce the kind of rhythmic patterns struck on semantra. And like the semantron struck at the Church of the Holy Apostles in Constantinople described by Mesarites, the great bells in the Kremlin's Ivan Velikij Bell Tower rang out like the heartbeat of the people.

Though the achievements of Russian founders remain among the most impressive in Europe from a technological standpoint, a more significant aspect of their prowess in bell casting was the way it expressed and even developed a profoundly Russian religio-political ideology. The Russian *Gigantomanie* in bell casting, as Elmar Arro has called it, was largely associated with the Moscow Cannon Yard and paralleled the dominance of Moscow in the sixteenth and seventeenth centuries. Once the city had assumed the spiritual mantle of Constantinople as the Third Rome, the splendid new Kremlin architecture and the roar of the zvon became visual and aural acclamations of the city's new leadership in the Orthodox East. At the same time, they were symbols of the burgeoning political power and territorial aspirations of the rulers of Muscovy.

That the great Kremlin bells were intended to serve two masters—Orthodoxy and autocracy—was unequivocally expressed in the decorative program on Grigor'ev's great bell of 1655, which featured portraits of the tsar and tsarina on one side—in poses not unlike those of equestrian statues of the king in the *places royales* of French cities—and a relief of the Russian patriarch on the other. Relief icons of Jesus Christ and His saints above the portrait of the royal donor on other bells were meant to express the sovereign's piety. The dual fealty of the Kremlin bells was also evident in their function both as liturgical instruments for announcing services in the Uspensky Cathedral and as instruments of state, accompanying the reception of foreign ambassadors, the Russian sovereign's own ceremonial entrances into and departures from Moscow, and coronations of the tsars and tsarinas.

St. Petersburg, established by Peter the Great in 1712 as the new capital, contributed to the undermining of Moscow's political power and also abandoned the strongly Russian character of the old capital's art and architecture. As "the greatest international achievement of [art during] the age of absolutism," this baroque city drew upon the genius of Italian, French, German, Scottish, and Dutch as well as Russian artists and architects.[1] Its city plan, façades, and bronze sculptures were ideal and highly visible expressions of the baroque predilection for grandiose scale in early eighteenth century Europe. And the music from a Dutch carillon in the tower of the cathedral within the Peter and Paul Fortress only increased St. Petersburg's cultural distance from Moscow.

More indigenous Russian statements of baroque monumentality arose in Moscow through the founding of great bells for the Kremlin in the seventeenth and eighteenth centuries. And this transcendental impulse of the baroque was also expressed in the displays of prodigious team strength required to swing the massive clapper of a great bell. Awesome and earth-shaking utterances from these enormous instruments were calculated to stun the foreign visitor and to convey an aural impression of the presence and power of the august ruler in whose residence they hung.[2]

The baroque artist's enlargement of visual and architectural space is well documented throughout Europe, and the flood plain on which St. Peters-burg and its outlying palaces and parks were built became, in effect, an eighteenth-century laboratory for linear extension on a scale unsurpassed in Western Europe.[3] But Moscow's zvon and its great bells in particular were arbiters of a spatial concept that transcended the confines of architecture. Like the plan of Moscow itself, which radiated outward from the Kremlin in a series of roughly concentric rings, circular space determined by the sound of a great Kremlin bell extended the presence of the Russian capital as far as its strokes were audible.

The establishment of an exterior "acoustical" space is what prompted Aleksei Mikhailovich to order the simultaneous ringing of all the bells of Moscow's churches and monasteries to determine whether Danilov's bell of 1654 could be heard beneath the city's collective zvon and to measure the distance of its carrying power beyond Moscow. With this command the tsar tacitly revealed his interest in the demesne of a nonarchitectural space that was acoustically defined. Exploration of this auditory space[4] beyond the walls of the Kremlin appealed to his imagination, to his concept of what R. Murray Schafer has called the "soundscape."[5] And indeed, on approaching Moscow from Smolensk during the last quarter of the seventeenth century, Western travelers would have been dazzled when the sun ignited the skyline's multitude of gold cupolas like ranks of votive candles. But on the great feasts of Orthodoxy, the soundscape of Moscow would have been no less stirring. With the clamor of thousands of bells from the city's bell towers it was the most impressive aural display in Christendom. On the streets of the capital the incessant concussion of ringing bronze drowned out all conversation, and the powerful strokes on the great Kremlin bells sent tremors through the ground.

Again in the mid-nineteenth century John Murray observed in Russia a blurring of distinction between church and state, an attitude that informed Russia's perspective in politics as well as in monuments. He wrote of Montferrand's Alexander Column, the granite monolith rising almost 155 feet from the square before the Winter Palace: "The idea of this column is, like everything else in Russia, religio-political. It was erected in honour of

117. Mikhail Mikeshin's monument of 1862, *Tysiacheletie Rossii* (Russia of a Thousand Years) inside the Novgorod kremlin. From Thomas Michell, *Russian Pictures* (New York, 1889), 71.

the Emperor Alexander, and is meant to eternalize with his memory that of the re-confirmation of the political constitution and of the security of religion. The attack of the irreligious, unbelieving Napoleon is considered in Russia, not only as an attack on the State, but also as one on the faith."[6] Bogdanov's Great Uspensky Bell of 1817, both in the re-

ligious significance that its inscription ascribed to Russia's repulse of Napoleon and in its dual service to church and state, is a further witness to Murray's observation. Similarly, the Cathedral of Christ the Saviour in Moscow, whose enormous central dome once dominated the city's skyline upstream from the Kremlin, was a monument to the same instincts and was built to commemorate Russia's deliverance from Napoleon in 1812. Tchaikovsky's overture, *The Year 1812*, said to have been motivated by the approaching consecration of this cathedral, was commissioned in 1880 for the All-Russian Exhibition of Arts and Crafts in Moscow.[7] With its motley procession of liturgical music, folk song, national anthems, the zvon of church bells, and salvos from cannon, the overture is a symphonic reflection of the cathedral and celebrates the same Russian alloy of religious and political ideology.

A more subtle and tightly organized example of this same attitude stands today in the Novgorod kremlin, a sculptural embodiment of that religio-political amalgam in Russian history and culture. In 1862 Russia observed her millennium—the thousandth anniversary of the traditional year for the founding of a Russian state. To commemorate this event Mikhail Mikeshin (1835-1896) was commissioned to design and cast a bronze monument for the Novgorod kremlin.[8] Entitled *Tysiacheletie Rossii* (Russia of a Thousand Years), Mikeshin's monument was unveiled with appropriate ceremonies on September 8, 1862, in the presence of Alexander II (figure 117).[9]

Conceived and executed on three principal levels, this monument can be viewed as a synthesis of the three articles of faith that Count Sergej Semenovich Uvarov (1786-1855) proclaimed as a policy for Russian education in 1833—"Orthodoxy, autocracy, and nationality."[10] Around the base of the monument a continuous frieze in high relief contains 109 figures depicting significant events in the nation's historical and cultural development. Represented in this frieze are explorers, states-

men, writers, and artists from the tenth through the mid-nineteenth centuries.[11] On the summit of the monument is an allegorical composition Mikeshin called *Pravoslavie* (Orthodoxy), which shows the guardian angel of the Russian Empire supporting a large cross and protecting the kneeling figure of a woman, who, in native dress and with bowed head, is the personification of Russia.[12] The central portion of the monument contains a series of six tableaux representing six pivotal reigns in Russia's thousand-year history; seventeen figures are distributed around a large bronze sphere, the orb of Imperial Russia and symbol of the autocratic sovereign.[13]

Only from a distance, however, does the symbolic form and larger religio-political significance of Mikeshin's monument emerge, when the entire composition assumes the shape of a great bell.[14] The sculptor's statement is unequivocal. His design proclaims the great bell as the most venerable and enduring symbol of the nation: the historical development and cultural ascendency of Russia during its first thousand years had unfolded beneath the sound of its bells. The measured booming of *blagovest* from a large bell, like blasts from ancient trumpets, called the faithful to services; and under the ringing mantle of smaller bells with their untuned colors and intricately woven rhythms Russians celebrated the feasts of Orthodoxy, rejoiced in victories over their enemies, and announced the anointing and coronation of their sovereigns. The sound of ringing bells seems to envelope the figures on Mikeshin's monument. This chronicle cast in bronze can thus be read as a monument to the bells of Russia and to the reign of their mighty zvon.

Appendices

Appendix A
Bell Founders in Pskov, Novgorod, and Moscow
before the Seventeenth Century

Pskov	Novgorod	Moscow
		Boris (Borisko) (1342-46)
	Mikula (1475)	Fioravanti, Ridolfo (Aristotle) (active in Moscow 1475-85)
		Fedor (Fed'ko) (1488)
		Friazin, Petr (1494-1505)
	Afanas'ev, Ivan (1501)	
Andreev, Mikhail (1520-51)		
Andreev, Anufrij (1520)		
Andreev, Maksim (1520)		
		Friazin, Nikolai (1532)*
		Nemchin, Nikolai (1533)*
Grigor'ev, Prokofij (1534-37)		
Orekhov, Timofej (1534)		
Andreev, Timofej (1534-40)		
Andreev, Ignatij (1542)		
Andreev, Tikhon (1545)	Ilejka (Il'ia) (1545)	
Andreev, Kuz'ma (1551)		
Andreev, Matvej (1[5]51?)		
Semenov, Login (1552-74)		
Vasil'ev, Kuz'ma (1552)		
Oreev, Ignatij (1553)		
	Ivan (1554-66)	
	Mitia (Metia Novgorodets) (1556-67)	
Mikhajlov, Kuz'ma (1557)†	Filipp from Gorodishche (1557)	
Mikhal'ka (1557)		
Grigor'ev, Matvej (1557)	Ul'ianov, Iurij (1557)	
Andrej (1558)	D'iachkov, Ian (1558)	
	Pobereshkov, Vlas (Vlaska) (1558)	
	Pobereshkov, Iurij (1558)	
Mikhajlov, Matvej (1559)†		
Oskarev, Timofej (1559)		
Ivanov, Nestor (1559)		
Bujnosov, Vasilij Ivanovich (1561)	Afonas'ev, Ivan (1561-71)	Luka (1561)
	Erofej Novgorodets (Timofeev) (1563)	
	Timofej Maslenik (1563-97)	
	Kononov, Dmitrij (Dmitriek) (1568)	Chokhov, Andrej (1568)
	Nechajko (1571)	

Pskov	Novgorod	Moscow
		Kuz'min, Pervoj (1581)
		Zvukov, Ivan Gavrilov (1585)
Matveev, Ivan (1587)		Afanas'ev, Ivan (1587-99)
Ivanov, Vasilij (1589-99)	Ievlev, Filipp (1589)	
	Ivanov, Bogdan (1589-99)	
Pankrat'ev, Afanasij (1590-99)		
	Ivanov, Deviatka (1596)‡	
Lavrov, Stepan (1597)		
		Sverchkov, Ivan (1598)‡
		Rodionov, Mikhail (1598-99)‡
Ivanov, Ekim (1599)		
Ivanov, Ivan (1599)		

NOTE: The names of founders in Appendices A and B are taken from three published lists: N. N. Rubtsov, *Istoriia litejnogo proizvodstva v SSSR*, pt. 1, 2d ed., rev. and enl. (Moscow: Gosudarstvennoe nauchno-tekhnicheskoe izd. mashinostroitel'noj literatury, 1962), 197-269; Vladimir Zheleznov, *Ukazatel' masterov" russkikh" i inozemtsev", gornago, metallicheskago i oruzhejnago děla i sviazannykh" s" nimi remesl" i proizvodstv", rabotavshikh" v" Rossii do XVIII věka* (St. Petersburg: Tipo-litografiia S.-Peterburgskoj tiur'my, 1907); and I. E. Zabelin, "O metallicheskom" proizvodstvě v" Rossii do XVII věka," *Zapiski Imperatorskago arkheologicheskago obshchestva* 5 (1855), 110-136. A single date is the year of a founder's earliest known work or the year his name is first documented. Two dates indicate years when a founder is known to have been active.

* Nikolai Friazin and Nikolai Nemchin may be the same man.   † Brothers.   ‡ Active in Moscow?

Appendix B
Seventeenth-Century Bell Founders and Their Students

A. Moscow Founders

Chokhov, Andrej (1568-1629)
  Naumov, Grigorij (1598-1645)
    Tarasov, Fedor (Fed'ka) (1618)
  Karpov, Danilka (1618)
  Bogdanov, Druzhina (1618-1622)
  Grigor'ev, Taras (1622)
  Artem'ev, Semen (Senka) (1622)
  Vasilij Novgorodets (Andreev) (1622)
Vasil'ev, Bogdan (1603-1627)
Ignatij (1607)
Grigor'ev, Filipp (1614-1627)
  Filippov, Foma (1621-1622)
  Kuz'min Eremej (1621-1622)
Nikiforov, Aleksej (1616)
Ekimov (Iakimov), Aleksej (1618-1641)
  Fomin, Foma (Fomka) (1622)
  Kononov (Konon), Kirill (1638)
  Patrikeev, Stepan (1618)
  Alekseev, Petr (1638)
  Pimenov, Andrej (1644)
[Ivanov, Mikhail (1618-1642)]*
  Ivanov, Leontij (Levko, the Blacksmith) (1644-1651)

Samojlov, Kirill (1618-1645) (may be the same founder as Kirill Somov [1634])
  Borisov, Vasilij (Krestechnik) (1622-1645)
  Poluektov, Vasilij (Vas'ka) (1622)
  Matveev, Danila (1622-1651)†
    Denisov, Foma (1638)
    Kirillov, Petr (1638-1643)
    Ivanov, Semen (1638-1675) (also worked under Khariton Ivanov)
    Minin, Larion (Lerka) (1638-1656) (also worked under Aleksandr Grigor'ev)
    Vasil'ev, Anton (1643-1645)
    Vasil'ev, Stepan (1643-1645)
Baranov, Nikifor (Fedorov) (1618-1651)
  Mikhajlov, Semen (1638)
Radushevskij (Radishevskij), Onisim Mikhajlov (1620-1629)
Vasil'ev, Manushka (1620-1630)
Shpilin, Ignatij Maksimov (1621)
  Gavrilov, Il'ia (Ilejka) (1621)
Filippov, Ermolaj (1622)
Falk, Hans (1628-1653)
  Reztsov (Rezets), Ivan Timofeev (1640-1650)

Ivanov, Ivan (1642-1657)
  Aref'ev (Oref'ev), Stepan (Stepanko) (1641-1644)
Vasil'ev, Fedor (1638)
Kir'ianov, Fedor (1638)
Evdokimov, Stepan (1638-1645)
Kirillov, Fedor (1638-1671)
Danilov, Emel'ian (1640-1654)†
Baranov, Filipp (1648-1665)‡
Danilov, Evsevij (1650-1696)
  Kharitonov, Petr (Dubasov) (1677-1702)
  Ivanov, Grigorij (1682-1697)
Borisov, Ivan (1651)
Grigor'ev, Aleksandr (1651-1676)
  Skvortsov, Denis (Skvorets) (1654)
  Ivanov, Petr (Petrushka) (1655)
  Mikhajlov, Pimen (1655)
  Rodionov, Aleksej (1655)
  Dmitriev, Fedor (1655-1671)
    Fedorov, Danila (1666)
  Il'in, Larion (1655-1669)
  Mikhajlov, Stepan (1655-1670)
  Ivanov, Khariton (Popov) (1655-1696)
    Pavlov, Mikhail (1662-1677)
    Romanov, Matvej (1676)
    Ivanov, Iakov (Iakushka) (1677-1700)
    Nikifor[ov], Fedor (1682-1700)
  Skvortsov, Ivan Denisov (Skvorets) (1669-1700)
  Ivanov, Galka Grechnevashnik (1670)
  Kuz'min, Kornilij (Kornilka) (1670)
  Nikiforov, Anikij (1670)
  Vasil'ev, Trofim (1670)
  Andreev, Luka (1670-1696) (also worked under Mart'ian
    Osipov)
  Leont'ev, Vasilij (1677-1683)
Motorin, Fedor Dmitrievich (1651-1687)
  Kniazev, Ivan Ivanov (1684)
Stepanov, Petr (1655-1657)
Ivanov, Gavrila (1655-1671)
[Osipov, Mart'ian (1657-1704)]*
  Ivanov, Ganka (Gavrila) (1700)
Ekimov, Grigorij (1666-1697)
Luk'ian (Luchka) (1676)
Leont'ev, Iakov (1676-1700)
Leont'ev, Fedor (1677-1700)
Mokeev, Semen (1679)
Semenov, Sil'verst (1681)
Andreev, Kiprian (1682)
Ekimov, Isaj (1682-1696)
Nikiforov, Iakov (1682-1696)
Iakovlev, Filat (1682-1696)
Iakovlev, Iurij (1682-1696)
Stepanov, Nikifor (1682-1700)
Maksimov, Iakov (1683)
Il'in, Lavrentij (1683)

Lodygin, Mikhail Matveev (1685-1700)
Andreev, Filipp (1682-1687)
Motorin, Dmitrij Fedorovich (1687-1692)
  Denisov, Vasilij (1689)
Motorin, Ivan Fedorovich (1687-1735)
  Fedorov, Dmitrij (1694)
  Motorin, Mikhail Ivanovich (1735-1750)§
Terent'ev, Flor (1689)
Minachek, Ivan (1690)
Matveev, Mikhail (1690)
Neridin, Vasilij (1693)
Kuz'min, Kuz'ma (1696)
Dekhterev, Abram (1696)||
Dekhterev, Ivan (1696)
Dekhterev, Nikita (1696)
Ageev, Artemij (1700)
Andreev, Zot (1700)
Fedorov, Ivan (1700)
Gavrilov, Efrem (1700)
Spiridonov, Dmitrij (1700)
Kharlamov, Dmitrij (1700)
Mikhajlov, Ivan (1700)
Abramov, Afanasij (1700)
Fedorov, Senka (1701)

B. Bell Founders Outside of Moscow

Pskov
Savva (1614-1619)
Kuz'ma (1614-1619)
Trofim (1619)

Novgorod
Matveev, Dmitrij (1627)
Vasil'ev, Ermolaj (1659)
Turov, Ivan (1674)
Matveev, Ivan (1697-1699)

Ustiug-Velikij
Totskin, Semen (1624-1646)
  Kuznetsov, Nikifor Ivanov (1634-1644)

Trinity-Sergius Lavra
Kipriianov, Terentij (Tren'ka) (1641)
Ignatij (1649)

New Jerusalem Monastery
Paisej, monk (1665)
Sergej, monk (1665-1666)

Vologda
Iosaf "Starets" (elderly monk) (1674)
Ivan (1674)
Kolkol'nik, Nestor (1674)
Porfir'ev, Ivan Sumlianin (1674)

Cheboksary
Nikitin, Savva (1686)
Nikitin, Petr (1686)

B. Bell Founders Outside of Moscow

POLTAVA
Petrov, Afanasij (1695)

AZOV
Ekimov, Grigorij (1696-1697)

Kuz'min, Kuz'ma (1696)
Semenov, Gerasim (1696-1697)

SOLOVETSKIJ MONASTERY
Osipov, Vasilij (1699)

NOTE: Rubtsov, *Istoriia*, 197-269. Indentations indicate foreman-apprentice relationships when known. In some cases it has not been possible to verify whether certain apprentices of bell masters actually cast bells themselves or even whether they continued to work in Moscow after completing their apprenticeship. In a few instances bell founders received their training under cannon foremen. The year or years following each name indicate the date of a founder's earliest extant work or the period in which he was active.
* Although a founder of ordnance, he also supervised at least one apprentice in bell founding.
† Emel'ian Danilov was the son of Danila Matveev.   ‡ Son of Nikifor Baranov.
§ Son of Ivan Fedorovich Motorin.   ‖ Father of Ivan and Nikita Dekhterev.

Appendix C
Profiles of German, French, English, and Russian Bells

On the German bell its lower radius (line AC) is divided into seven equal segments (figure 118). Along line AB are plotted eleven of these segments, each equal to a seventh of the bell's lower radius. An arc is drawn from point A, whose radius (d) is equal to 1.25 segments. This radius determines the point where the sound-bow angle, whose vertex is at p, will fall on the bell's interior wall. The exterior contour of the wall moves sharply away from line AB at n, a point equal to 1.5 segments from A. The outer wall is first plotted by measuring its distance from certain points on line AB. At point 3, the distance perpendicular to line AB is one segment; at point 7, seven-eighths of a segment; and at point 11, again one segment. At 10, the bell wall touches line AB, a point that determines where the shoulder angle will fall. The bell's interior wall is partially constructed from the thickness of the bell itself. The line from 1 to p (the sound-bow) has a wall thickness of one segment; at e, half a segment; at f, a third of a segment; and from g to 0, the wall thickness remains a quarter of the length of a segment. The contours of the inner and outer walls on the lower portion of the bell are realized by drawing four arcs with three different radii. The arcs between p and h, and h and k each have a radius of fourteen segments; for n e, the radius is three segments; and for e f, eleven segments. The profile of the upper portion of German bells (above point 10) founders would sometimes alter or adjust for technical reasons.

In designing the profile for a French bell, the founder first divided radius AC into 7.5 segments (figure 119). Line AB was drawn (with the angle from AC deter-

mined by the length of AB and by the fact that E-d is perpendicular to AC), and twelve segments were plotted on it. Point 12 on AB determined the shoulder. A

118. Profile of a German bell. After Olovianishnikov, *Istoriia kolokolov''*, 389.

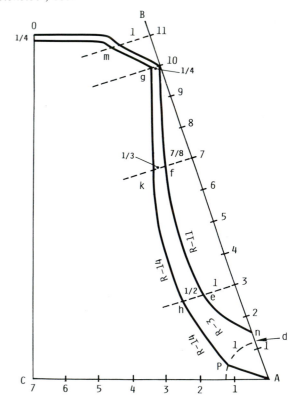

radius (e), whose length was 1.5 segments, extended from point A and determined the apex of the angles on the interior and exterior walls of the sound-bow. The French bell's profile is completed through the drawing of arcs between points 1.5 and h, with a radius of eight segments; between f and k, with a radius of twelve segments; between h and 12, thirty segments; and between k and m, 30.33 segments. To construct the profile of the upper portion of the bell, point p is located on line C n at a distance of eight segments from A. At h the distance of the French bell's outer wall from point 6 on line AB is 1.5 segments. The wall thickness from 1.5 to f, the thickest part of the sound-bow, is equal to one segment, and at k, to a third of a segment. The thickness of the French bell's head or top plate at n is two-thirds of a segment.

The English pattern Grimthorpe used in designing his Westminster bells is constructed on a radius of twelve equal segments (line AE). The thickness of these bells' waist was equal to one thirteenth of its diameter or a third of its sound-bow PQ (figure 120).

119. Profile of a French bell. After Olovianishnikov, *Istoriia kolokolov"*, 389.

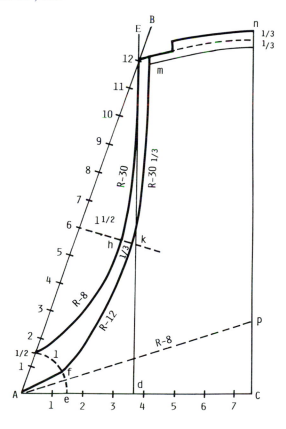

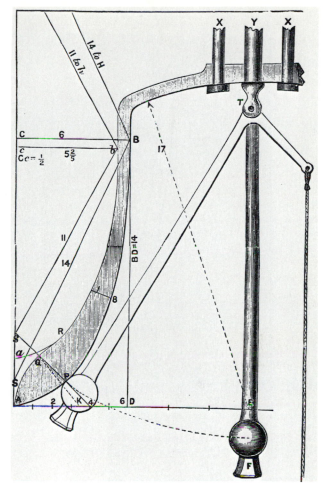

120. Profile of the English Westminster bell. From Edmund Beckett, Lord Grimthorpe, *A Rudimentary Treatise on Clocks, Watches, & Bells for Public Purposes*, 8th ed. (London, 1903), p. 358, fig. 80.

Consider the diameter of the bell mouth divided into 24 equal parts. Then the inside sweep is simply the quadrant of an ellipse, whose semiaxis major AC is 14, and minor BC, 6 'parts'; in which I shall now give all the measures. You see at once the arrangement and lengths of all the vertical and horizontal lines in the figure. To draw this ellipse, mark B at 14 above D, and with radius 14 from centre B mark S, and also H (beyond the size of the page), in the line AC prolonged. S and H are the foci of the ellipse; which is drawn in the well known way, by sticking pins in a table at S and H, through the ends of a thread made just long enough to reach over SBH, and running a pencil along it, keeping it stretched. The pencil will then trace out the elliptic quadrant AP8B, the 8 indicating 8 parts from A, for a purpose I shall mention presently.

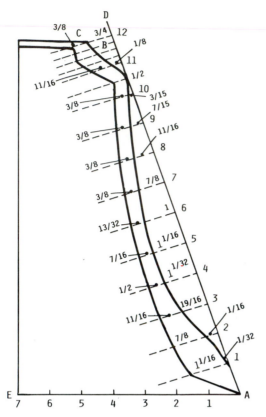

121. Profile of a Russian bell. After Olovianishnikov, *Istoriia kolokolov"*, 389.

The outside can obviously be made of no single curve, but must be compounded of several curves in some empirical way to produce what we find to be the best proportions of thickness throughout. As the thickness of the waist of the bell is to be a third of the sound-bow PQ, which is a 13th of the diameter, *b* must be a 39th, or practically 2 thirds of a 'part,' outside of B. It is necessary to put the minor axis *c b* of this ellipse ½ p. below CB, to make it come right below. From centre *b* with radius 11 mark *s* and *h* for the foci of another ellipse, and then describe the quadrant *aRb*, in the same way as before. The lower part *a* R is useless, and that part of the bell curve is made up thus: —Draw *sQP4* to the point 4 in the base, and mark off PQ = a 13th of the diameter. Then, with a radius of 3½ or 4 (for there is hardly any difference), draw the circular arc AQ, letting the centre K come where it happens. The remaining little bit QR is easily filled up by hand. This makes the thickness = 1 at 8 from A.[1]

The contours on both sides of the sound-bow in this English profile are curved, whereas the two sides of the French bell are both straight. (The Russian bell described below shows a profile that is curved on its outer wall and straight on its inner.) Unlike designs for German, French, and Russian bells, in which a straight edge can be placed that will touch both the lip and the shoulder, this is not possible in the Westminster pattern. A protruding outer wall at the sound-bow throws the straight edge slightly beyond the bell's lip.

In developing a profile for their own bells, Russian founders began with the height of the bell, which they considered the distance from A to point 10.5 on line AD, that is, from the bell's lip to the angle of its shoulder (figure 121). Twelve segments were then plotted along line AD, each of which was equal to one-fourteenth of the bell's lower diameter.[2] Lines are then drawn perpendicular to line AD at each of the twelve points determined by the segments, and the bell's profile was constructed using these lines as guides.

The broken line perpendicular to point 1 determines where the angle will fall on the interior wall of the sound-bow. The distances of the bell's exterior wall from line AD and the varying thickness of the wall itself were measured as segments or fractions of a segment on line AD. Just before point 1 on line AD, the exterior wall of the sound-bow begins to veer gently away from line AD, and the distance here from line AD to the bell's outer wall is a thirty-second of a segment. At point 6, it is one segment, and at point 9, seven-fifteenths of a segment.

The twelve segments along line AD were further divided into quarters. Russian founders called the upper portion of the profile from 10.5 to B the shoulder (*plecho*), a section of the bell that was almost equal to the length of one segment along line AD and, according to Olovianishnikov, was approximately a tenth of the bell's height. The neck (*skejka*), at a half (or two quarters) of a segment, extended from B to C and was approximately equal to one-twentieth of the bell's height. Point C Russian founders called the pointer or arrow (*strelka*) and behind this extended the head or top plate (*skovoroda* or "pan"). The height of the cannons (*ushi* or "ears") for a Russian bell was calculated as one-fifth the height of the bell or slightly more than two segments along line AD.

Appendix D
A Select List of Russian Bells Weighing 36,100 Pounds (1,000 Puds) or More with Comparative Weights of Some of the Largest Bells of Asia, Western Europe, and North America

Russia	Asia	Western Europe and North America	Russia	Asia	Western Europe and North America
1. Moscow Kremlin, "Tsar-Kolokol" (1735) 433,356 lbs.			11. Iur'ev Monastery near Novgorod 75,837 lbs.		
	2. Osaka, Japan (1902)* Shitennō-ji (temple) 310,000 lbs.		12. Tambov, Archbishop's house at the Kazan'skij Monastery 72,226 lbs.		
	3. Mingun (1790)† near Mandalay, Burma 195,000 lbs.		13. Novgorod Province, Kirillo-Belozerskij Monastery 72,226 lbs.		
	4. Kyŏngju, South Korea (771) "Emelie" or "Emilee" 158,731 lbs.		14. Moscow Kremlin, "Reut" (1622) 72,226 lbs.		
	5. Kyoto, Japan (1633) Chion-in Temple 148,000 lbs.		15. Rostov-Velikij, "Sysoj" (1689) 72,226 lbs.		
6. Trinity-Sergius Lavra, Zagorsk, "Tsar-Kolokol" (1748)‡ 144,452 lbs.			16. Leningrad, Great Bell of St. Isaac's Cathedral (mid-19th century) 67,191 lbs.		
7. Moscow Kremlin, "Great Uspensky Bell" (1817) 144,452 lbs.			17. Trinity-Sergius Lavra, Zagorsk, "Godunov" Bell (1600) ca. 66,809 lbs.		
	8. Nara, Japan (732)§ Tōdai-ji (temple) 96,000 lbs.		18. Moscow, Cathedral of Christ the Saviour, "Torzhestvennyj" Bell (hung in S-W tower, 1878)** 59,749 lbs.		
	9. Peking (Beijing), China, Yong Le Bell (ca. 1420) Da Zhong Si (Great Bell Temple) 93,000 lbs.‖		19. Novgorod (1659) 58,286 lbs.		
10. Savvino-Storozhevskij Monastery, Zvenigorod (1667)# 76,767 lbs.			20. Moscow (1878) 57,300 lbs.		

Russia	Asia	Western Europe and North America	Russia	Asia	Western Europe and North America
		21. Cologne Cathedral, "Petersglocke" (1923)†† 56,800 lbs.	32. Village of Miskovo in the Kostroma province and district 37,408 lbs.		
		22. Cologne Cathedral, "Kaiserglocke" (1874)‡‡ 50,000 lbs.	33. Ozery, Moscow province, Kolomenskij district 37,196 lbs.		
	23. Nanking, China (15th century) 50,000 lbs.		34. Belgorod, Kursk province, Holy Trinity Monastery 36,921 lbs.		
24. Trinity-Sergius Lavra, Zagorsk, 46,044 lbs.			35. Moscow, Uspensky Cathedral 36,740 lbs.		
25. Nikolo-Ugreshskij Monastery near Moscow 44,419 lbs.			36. Yekaterinburg, Maksimilianovskij Church 36,655 lbs.		
		26. Vienna, St. Stephen's Cathedral, "Pummerin" II§§ (1951) 44,383 lbs.	37. Tobol'sk (1738)‖‖ 36,530 lbs.		
		27. Paris, Basilica of Sacré-Coeur, "La Savoyarde" (1891) 41,524 lbs.	38. Yaroslavl, Vlasievskij Church 36,402 lbs.		
			39. Khar'kov, Uspensky Cathedral 36,294 lbs.		
28. Iur'ev Monastery near Novgorod 41,169 lbs.			*Bells of 36,113 lbs. hung at:* 40. Kievo-Pecherskaia Lavra		
			41. Moscow, Spaso-Simonov Monastery		
		29. New York, Riverside Church (1930) 40,926 lbs.	42. Moscow province, Bogorodskij district, Nikolo-Berliukovskaia Hermitage		
30. Kursk, Znamenskij Monastery 37,738 lbs.			43. Bronnitsy, Moscow province, Jerusalem Church		
		31. London, St. Paul's Cathedral, "Great Paul" (1881) 37,474 lbs.	44. Pavlovo Posad, Moscow province, Voskresenskij Church		

Russia	Asia	Western Europe and North America	Russia	Asia	Western Europe and North America
45. Dorofeevaia-Iugskaia Hermitage near Rybynsk, Yaroslavl province			48. Ivanovo-Voznesensk, Vladimir province		
46. Rostov-Velikij, Uspensky Cathedral, "Polielejnyj"			49. Village of Kimry, Tver province		
47. Kazan, Blagoveshchenskij Cathedral			50. Odessa, Cathedral		
			51. Pavlovo, Nizhnij-Novgorod province		
			52. Tver, Cathedral		

NOTE: Sources vary considerably in the weights they cite for the world's largest bells. The figures in this appendix should in most cases be regarded as approximate. The Russian bells were presumably extant at the end of the nineteenth century, and weights for a number of them are published in N. Priakhin, "Kolokol'nyj zvon": dostoprimĕchatel'nye kolokola v" Rossii," *Russkij palomnik"*, no. 19 (1886), pp. 171-172. Priakhin, unfortunately, does not include dates of founding with the weights of bells in his list. For some non-Russian bells, see Percival Price, "Bell," *New Grove Dictionary of Music and Musicians* 2, ed. Stanley Sadie (London: Macmillan, 1980), p. 430, table 1: The largest bell in each of twelve countries; and Percival Price, *Bells and Man* (Oxford: Oxford University Press, 1983), 264-273 (App. A: An historical survey of bells around the world).

* This Japanese bell was the largest ever cast in Asia. According to Percival Price it was melted down in 1942 for its metal (*Bells and Man*, 273).

† Today the stationary Mingun Bell is considered the world's largest ringing bell and is second only to Tsar-Kolokol in weight. The weight cited for the Mingun Bell varies considerably. It has been placed as high as 101.4 tons (202,800 pounds) and as low as 87 tons (174,000 pounds). (David A. Boehm, ed. *Guinness 1984 Book of World Records* [New York: Sterling Publishing Co., 1984], 170; and Wilhelm Klein, *Burma*, 2d ed. [Hong Kong: Apa Productions, 1982], 201.)

‡ This is the Russian bell frequently cited in Western sources in or near Moscow under the name "Trotzkoi." It is so named because it hung in the bell tower of the Trinity-Sergius Lavra near Moscow until removed and melted down in 1930.

§ This Nara bell may have been recast in 1239. (H. Batterson Boger, *The Traditional Arts of Japan* [New York: Bonanza Books, 1964], 101.)

‖ Estimates of this Peking bell's weight vary greatly. In publications from the People's Republic of China it is officially cited as 46.5 tons (93,000 pounds). (Liu Junwen, *Beijing: China's Ancient and Modern Capital* [Beijing: Foreign Languages Press, 1982], 143.) Other sources have reported its weight as 106,000 and 120,000 pounds.

This bell was broken in 1941; its fragments are in Zvenigorod.

** This cathedral was demolished in 1931.

†† "Petersglocke" is considered the heaviest swinging bell in the world.

‡‡ "Kaiserglocke" was destroyed during World War I to provide metal for war munitions but was replaced in 1925 by "Petersglocke" (Ernest Morris, *Bells of All Nations* [London: Robert Hale, 1951], 64).

§§ "Pummerin" means "boomer." Pummerin I, a bell of about the same weight cast in 1711, was destroyed during an air raid in 1945.

‖‖ The Tobol'sk bell at 1,011 puds, 22 funts, was the largest in Siberia (N. R., "O kolokolakh" i o kolokol'nom" iskusstvĕ," *Moskovskiia vĕdomosti*, no. 51 [Saturday, April 29, 1850], p. 587n.).

Appendix E
A Linear Scale of the Weights of Thirteen Large Bells Cast in Russia from the Mid-Fourteenth Century to the Early Nineteenth Century

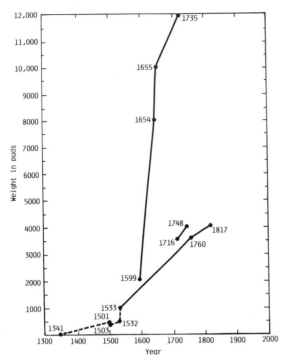

The dotted line that links five Russian bells founded between 1341 and 1533 indicates that these instruments were not related through recastings. Three solid lines connect three family lines of great Russian bells, each of which is the result of a recasting or recastings from an original bell. The oldest of these three Russian bell families is the "Moscow Uspensky Line" with its bells of 1533, 1760, and 1817 (Chapter 13). The apogee of magnitude in Russian bell founding was reached in the "Moscow Tsar-Kolokol Line" with its four great bells of 1599, 1654, 1655, and 1735 (Chapters 11 and 12). The third and youngest family, the "Tsar-Kolokol Line of the Trinity-Sergius Lavra," contains only two bells, those of 1716 and 1748 (Chapter 13). In almost four centuries between 1341 and 1735, the magnitude of bells founded in Russia rose from 25 to 12,000 puds, the equivalent of 903 to 433,356 pounds.

Year of Founding	Founder	Name of Bell	Location or Former Location	Weight in Puds/Pounds
1. 1341	?		Church of St. George (Iurij), L'vov	25/903
2. 1501	Ivan Afanas'ev (Athanas'ev)	Medved'	Moscow Kremlin	450/16,251
3. 1503	Petr Friazin		Moscow	350/12,640*
4. 1532	Nikolai Friazin		Moscow	500/18,057
5. 1533	Nikolai Nemchin		Moscow Kremlin	1,000/36,113
6. 1599	Andrej Chokhov	Godunov Bell	Moscow Kremlin	2,173?/78,474?
7. 1654	Emel'ian Danilov		Moscow Kremlin	8,000/288,904
8. 1655	Aleksandr Grigor'ev		Moscow Kremlin	10,000?/361,130?
9. 1716	?		Trinity-Sergius Lavra, Zagorsk	3,500/126,396
10. 1735	Ivan and Mikhail Motorin	Tsar-Kolokol	Moscow Kremlin	12,000/433,356
11. 1748	Semen Stepanov and Gavriil Smirnov	Tsar-Kolokol	Trinity-Sergius Lavra, Zagorsk	4,000/144,452
12. 1760	Konstantin Slizov	Uspensky Bell	Moscow Kremlin	3,551/128,237
13. 1817	Mikhail Bogdanov	Great Uspensky Bell	Moscow Kremlin	4,000?/144,452?

* The 350 puds in Petr Friazin's bell of 1503 is the weight of its copper only. If a tin content of 20 percent or 87.5 puds is added, this bell's total weight would probably have been about 438 puds (15,817 pounds).

Notes

The following abbreviations are used in the notes:

CSHB   *Corpus scriptorum historiae byzantinae.* Bonn, 1828-1897.
DACL   *Dictionnaire d'archéologie chrétienne et de liturgie.* Paris, 1920-1953.
Izd.   Izdatel'stvo (publishing house)
PG   *Patrologia graeca.* Paris, 1857-1866.
PL   *Patrologia latina.* Paris, 1878-1890.
PSRL   *Polnoe sobranie russkikh lĕtopisej.* 37 vols. St. Petersburg/Leningrad, 1841-1982.
Tip.   Tipografiia (press)
VAAP   Vsesoiuznoe agentstvo po avtorskim pravam (The Copyright Agency of the USSR)

Notes to Author's Explanatory Notes

1. Willi Apel, *Harvard Dictionary of Music,* 2d ed., rev. and enl. (Cambridge, MA: The Belknap Press of Harvard University Press, 1969), 679.

2. Sergei G. Pushkarev, *Dictionary of Russian Historical Terms from the Eleventh Century to 1917,* ed. George Vernadsky and Ralph T. Fisher, Jr. (New Haven: Yale University Press, 1970), 195.

Notes to Chapter 1

1. V. A. Kamenskij, ed., *Pamiatniki arkhitektury Leningrada,* 2d ed., rev. and enl. (Leningrad: Strojizdat, 1960), 425. Viacheslav Ivanov in his poem of 1911, *Sphinxes over the Neva,* reflects on the Russian captivity of these two effigies from Thebes.

2. Now in the Egyptian Antiquities Museum in Cairo the two trumpets measure about 23 and 19.5 inches long, respectively (Hans Hickmann, *Catalogue général des antiquités égyptiennes du Musée du Caire, nos. 69201-69852: Instruments de musique* [Cairo: Imprimerie de l'Institut français d'archéologie orientale, 1949], 143-145). Opinion differs on the metal of the shorter of the two instruments. In Egypt this trumpet was called *šnb*; in ancient Israel it was known as *ḥazozerah*; and in Greece and Rome, as *salpinx* (σάλπιγξ) and *tuba*, respectively.

3. Victor Loret, "Egypte: II. La Trompette," *Encyclopédie de la musique* 1, pt. 1: Histoire de la musique, p. 23. The bronze trumpet in the Louvre is 21.25 inches long and lacks only its mouthpiece.

4. Robert Anderson, "Egypt; I. Ancient Music," *New Grove Dictionary of Music and Musicians* 6, ed. Stanley Sadie (Lon-

don: Macmillan, 1980), 74. The limited number of pitches that can be produced on these three Egyptian trumpets are discussed in Hans Hickmann, *La Trompette dans l'Egypte ancienne,* Supplément aux Annales du service des antiquités de l'Egypte, notebook no. 1 (Cairo: Imprimerie de l'Institut français d'archéologie orientale, 1946; reprint ed., Nashville, TN: The Brass Press, 1976), 30-32, 37.

5. Hickmann, *La Trompette,* 33. Those who heard the two trumpets blown at the Cairo Museum in 1939 described their sound as "shrill and piercing." Arnold C. Brackman, *The Search for the Gold of Tutankhamen* (New York: Mason/Charter, 1976), p. 174. For comments on the timbre and number of pitches available on these Egyptian trumpets by one who has blown them, see Percival R. Kirby, "Ancient Egyptian Trumpets," *Music Book,* vol. 7 of Hinrichsen's Musical Year Book (London: Museum House, 1952), 250-255. According to Kirby, two pitches a major tenth apart could easily be blown on each of the instruments ($B^\flat$ and d^1 on the copper or bronze trumpet and $A^\flat$ and c^1 on the silver); a third pitch two octaves above the lower note of each could also be produced but only with considerable difficulty. Kirby was of the opinion that the third pitch was not used in practice (pp. 250-251).

6. J. Gwyn Griffiths, trans., *Plutarch's De Iside et Osiride* (Swansea: University of Wales Press, 1970), 164. See also Griffiths' commentary on p. 411.

7. Curt Sachs, *The History of Musical Instruments* (New York: W. W. Norton, 1940), 100.

8. Sibyl Marcuse, *A Survey of Musical Instruments* (New York: Harper & Row, 1975), 786.

9. Edouard Naville, *The Temple of Deir el Bahari,* pt. 6 (London: Kegan Paul, Trench, Trübner & Co., 1908), p. 6 (plate CLV).

10. Hickmann, *La Trompette*, 15, fig. 21.

11. Howard Carter, *The Tomb of Tut-ankh-Amen* 2 (London: Cassell and Co., 1927), 31.

12. Hans Hickmann, "Die kultische Verwendung der altägyptischen Trompete," *Die Welt des Orients* 5 (1950): 353.

13. Ibid., 352-353.

14. Eustathius, Archbishop of Thessaloniki, *Commentarii ad Homeri Iliadem* 3 (Leipzig: J.A.G. Weigel, 1829; reprint ed., Hildesheim: Georg Olms Verlagsbuchhandlung, 1960), 65 (ed. Rom., p. 1139, lines 54-57). See B. von Sokolowsky, ed., *Die Musik des griechischen Alterthums und des Orients*, A. W. Ambros' *Geschichte der Musik* I (Leipzig: F.E.C. Leuckart, 1887), 356. Eustathius' term for the Egyptian trumpet was χνούη (*chnouē*), which, as Sachs explains, may have been a Greek transcription from the Egyptian *šnb*, or *šnobē*. Sachs further points out that the modern German verb *schnauben* and Middle High German *snûben* (to blow) may share a common root with the ancient Egyptian *šnb* (*History*, 100; see also Hickmann, *La Trompette*, 21-22).

15. Marcuse believes that the length and the form of the silver Hebrew trumpets indicate their derivation from Egyptian predecessors (*Survey*, 787). See also Alfred Sendrey, *Music in the Social and Religious Life of Antiquity* (Rutherford, NJ: Fairleigh Dickinson University Press, 1974), 189; and Sokolowsky, *Die Musik*, 375. Sachs, who concurs in the external resemblance between Hebrew and Egyptian trumpets, believes that the use of Jewish instruments in pairs was probably not of Egyptian origin (*History*, 113). Whenever a pair of trumpeters is shown in Egyptian art, "they are never represented both playing at the same time" (The Trustees of the British Museum, *The Times* & *The Sunday Times*, *Treasures of Tutankhamun* [Westerham, Kent: Westerham Press, 1972], no. 45: Trumpet).

16. Flavius Josephus, *Antiquities of the Jews*, III, xii, 6, in Benedictus Niese, ed., *Antiquitatum iudaicarum, libri I-V*, vol. 1, *Flavii Iosephi Opera* (Berlin: Weidmannsche Verlagsbuchhandlung, 1955), 216. For an English translation, see William Whiston, trans., *The Works of Flavius Josephus* 1 (New York: United States Book Co., 1890), 224.

17. Marcuse, *Survey*, 787.

18. Numbers 10:3-10. The noun *ḥazozerah* (pl. *ḥazozeroth*) is formed from the verb *ḥazar* (to be present), which signifies that the silver trumpet was a "convoker," or an instrument that signaled a convocation (Sendrey, *Music*, 188).

19. Numbers 10:3-4. Although evidence indicates that the Egyptians did not sound pairs of trumpets together, Kirby has suggested that the code of signals Moses set forth on Sinai was borrowed from Egyptian practice, and that it was, in fact, the pharaohs' code of military signals ("Ancient Egyptian Trumpets," 255).

20. Numbers 10:5-6 mentions only the eastern and southern sides of the camps. Josephus in *Antiquities* (III, xii, 6) reports that there were four alarms blown on the trumpet to give signals to each of the four areas of encampment around the tabernacle (Whiston, trans., *Works*, 225).

21. Yigael Yadin, ed., *The Scroll of the War of the Sons of Light against the Sons of Darkness*, trans. from the Hebrew by Batya and Chaim Rabin (London: Oxford University Press, 1962), 266-270, 292-300, 336, 340-344. Cf. Judges 6:34 and 7:18-22, which explain the military use of trumpets in Gideon's army.

22. In Numbers 10:10 the trumpet is designated an aural reminder of the presence of God among the people (Sendrey, *Music*, 190).

23. See chap. 5, "The Trumpets," in Yadin's Introduction to *Sons of Light against the Sons of Darkness*, 87-113. The purpose of the shofaroth, blown during battle by seven Levites (unlike the religious character of the straight trumpets [ḥazozeroth] blown by six priests), was to terrorize the enemy.

24. II Chronicles 29:26-28; and Ecclesiasticus (The Wisdom of Jesus, Son of Sirach) 50:16-17.

25. II Kings 11:14. Joash, son of Ahaziah, was king of Judah from 835 to 798 B.C.

26. II Chronicles 5:12. Sendrey believes that 120 trumpets may be an exaggeration; a minimum of two trumpets were used at the daily services, but on the high holidays this number could be increased without restriction (*Music*, 191).

27. For the Talmud's description of the liturgical use of trumpets in the Temple, see Joseph Barclay, *The Talmud* (London: John Murray, 1878), 147.

28. James Hastings, ed., *A Dictionary of the Bible* 4 (Edinburgh: T. & T. Clark, 1902), 816. In the Temple, as in battle, the priests blew trumpets of silver, the Levites, instruments of horn (S. M. Lehrman, trans. and ed., *Ḳinnim*, The Babylonian Talmud 6, gen. ed., I. Epstein [London: The Soncino Press, 1948], 24 n. 2. See also J. Benzinger, *Hebräische Archäologie* [Freiburg: Akademische Verlagsbuchhandlung von J.C.B. Mohr, 1894], 277).

29. Maurice Simon, trans. and ed., *Tamid*, The Babylonian Talmud 6, gen. ed., I. Epstein (London: The Soncino Press, 1948), 36-37. See also Ecclesiasticus 50:16-17.

30. Solon Michaelides, *The Music of Ancient Greece: An Encyclopedia* (London: Faber & Faber, 1978), 294.

31. Ibid., 173. The only extant example of a salpinx is an ivory instrument about five feet long from the second half of the fifth century B.C., now preserved in the Boston Museum of Fine Arts (Karl Geiringer, *Instruments in the History of Western Music* [New York: Oxford University Press, 1978], 38).

32. James W. McKinnon, "Tuba (ii)," *New Grove Dictionary of Music and Musicians* 19, ed. Stanley Sadie (London: Macmillan, 1980), 241.

33. J. E. Scott, "Roman Music," *Ancient and Oriental Music*, ed. Egon Wellesz, New Oxford History of Music, vol. 1 (London: Oxford University Press, 1957), 406.

34. McKinnon, "Tuba (ii)," 241.

35. T. K. Cheyne and J. Sutherland Black, ed., *Encyclopaedia Biblica* 3 (New York: Macmillan, 1902), cols. 3231-3232; and Kirby, "Ancient Egyptian Trumpets," 255.

36. With their proclamation in the so-called Edict of Milan in March of 313 Constantine and Licinius guaranteed Christians the same rights and protection that other religions enjoyed in the Roman Empire (A. A. Vasiliev, *History of the Byzantine Empire* 1 [Madison: The University of Wisconsin Press, 1958], 51-52).

37. Pachomius without doubt played a major role in the development of coenobitical monasticism in Egypt, but the distinction that St. Jerome conferred on him as the founder is generally viewed today as overstating it. Pachomius now appears to have been among a number of supervisors of coenobitical houses, though his foundation at Tabennesis became one of the largest in Egypt. (Owen Chadwick, *John Cassian*, 2d ed. [Cambridge: (Cambridge) University Press, 1968], 55; and Derwas J. Chitty, *The Desert City: An Introduction to the Study of Egyptian and Palestinian Monasticism under the Christian Empire* [Oxford: Basil Blackwell, 1946], 20.)

38. Between about 320 and his death in 346 St. Pachomius established nine foundations for men and two for women (M. C. McCarthy, "Pachomius, St.," *New Catholic Encyclopedia* 10:853). By 380 as many as thirteen Pachomian houses may have been functioning in Egypt (Chadwick, *John Cassian*, 6). The Pachomian monasteries resembled small walled towns or Roman military camps and could accommodate a thousand or more monks (David Knowles, *Christian Monasticism* (London: Weidenfeld and Nicolson, 1969), 14; Chitty, *The Desert City*, 22; and Aziz S. Atiya, *History of Eastern Christianity* [Notre Dame, IN: University of Notre Dame Press, 1968], 64).

39. A group of four Pachomian monastic tracts (*Praecepta, Praecepta et Instituta, Praecepta atque Iudicia,* and *Praecepta ac Leges*), which St. Jerome translated from a Greek source in 404, are collectively known as the Rule of St. Pachomius (Amand Boon, ed., *Pachomiana latina*, Bibliothèque de la Revue d'histoire ecclésiastique, no. 7 [Louvain: Bureaux de la Revue, 1932], v). This work, the oldest Christian monastic rule in existence, was actually composed after the death of Pachomius. It belongs to the second half of the fourth century and may therefore reflect coenobitical practices in Egypt that emerged following the lifetime of its alleged author (Armand Veilleux, *La Liturgie dans le cénobitisme pachômien au quatrième siècle*, Studia Anselmiana 57 [Rome: Pontificium Institutum S. Anselmi, 1968], 116; and Rainer Stichel, "Jüdische Tradition in christlicher Liturgie: zur Geschichte des Semantrons," *Cahiers archéologiques* 21 [1971]: 226). A few Coptic remnants of this rule and two recensions of Greek fragments (*Excerpta*) have also survived and provide textual variants for Jerome's Latin translation (Boon, *Pachomiana latina*, xliv-xlviii, 155-162 [Coptic fragments], 163-168 [Latin translation of the Coptic fragments], 169-182 [Greek *Excerpta*]; and L.-Th. Lefort, "La Règle de S. Pachôme [2ᵉ étude d'approche]," *Muséon* 37 [1924]: 2-3).

40. Boon, *Pachomiana latina*, 14 (III), my translation.

41. Ibid., 15 (IX), my translation.

42. Ibid., 171 (no. 3) [IX in St. Jerome's Latin translation]; and Lefort, "La Règle de S. Pachôme," 10.

43. Boon, *Pachomiana latina*, pp. 14 (V), 18 (XXIII), 19 (XXIV, XXVI), 21 (XXXIII), 31 (LVIII), 33 (LXVIII), 39 (XC), and 44 (CXVI).

44. Stichel does not admit the possibility that the trumpet once served early Egyptian monasteries as an instrument of convocation. Though acknowledging Jerome's use of the word *tuba* twice in his translation of Pachomius' rule and the single instance of "salpinx" in the Greek fragments, or *Excerpta*, Stichel insists that because there is a reference to striking or hitting in the following sentence of the Greek excerpt, "trumpet" in both Latin and Greek must be understood to be the semantron. Stichel offers as further evidence Clement of Alexandria's rejection of instruments, including the trumpet, as participants in Christian worship and notes that subsequent sources contain references only to striking as a call to worship or refer to the semantron as a spiritual trumpet or as an earthly manifestation of the angel's horn. ("Jüdische Tradition," 227-228.)

But the very fact that Jerome refers to the *tuba* twice at the beginning of his translation is in itself significant. His first use of *signum* (signal) occurs in section 5 (between the two passages citing the *tuba*), but the other references appear quite a bit later. Jerome may even have intended *signum* to be interpreted in all cases as *tuba*. Furthermore, though Clement of Alexandria (ca. 150-215) excluded instruments in general from Christian worship, the trumpet would have served early foundations only in a convocational capacity and thus cannot be considered a strictly liturgical instrument. Finally, the persistent imagery of trumpeting applied to the semantron and to Russian bells argues persuasively in favor of the trumpet as the archetype of these later instruments of convocation in the Orthodox East.

45. PG 99, col. 1784. In Orthodox monasteries the *kanonarch* is the monk charged with conducting services including the initiating of prescribed singing.

46. *Protoevangelium Jacobi* 8:3. The original Greek text is published in Charles Michel and P. Peeters, *Evangiles apocryphes* (Paris: Librairie Alphonse Picard et Fils, 1911), 18. An English edition is available in Montague Rhodes James' translation, *The Apocryphal New Testament* (Oxford: Clarendon Press, 1975), 42. The *Protoevangelium Jacobi*, formerly known as the Gospel of James, is a Christian apocryphal document of probable Egyptian provenience. The Greek original is generally regarded as the work of a Judaeo-Christian of the Diaspora who pretended to be St. James the Less, son of Alphaeus. It must have been written around 150 since Justin Martyr, Origen, and Clement of Alexandria mention it in their

works. (C. H. Henkey, "Bible III: 5. Apocrypha of the New Testament," *New Catholic Encyclopedia* 2: 405.)

47. Georg Stuhlfauth, "Zur Vorgeschichte der Kirchenglocke," *Zeitschrift für die neutestamentliche Wissenschaft und die Kunde der älteren Kirche* 25 (1926): 263-264.

48. Though practices varied from one monastery to another in the fourth century, Egyptian monks generally assembled for the evening and early morning offices (Chadwick, *John Cassian*, 71).

49. For accounts that describe religious and communal life in the early monasteries of the Thebaid, see Veilleux, *La Liturgie*, 167-197; Chitty, *The Desert City*, 21-26; W. H. Mackean, *Christian Monasticism in Egypt to the Close of the Fourth Century* (New York: Macmillan, 1920), 102, 105; Otto F. A. Meinardus, *Monks and Monasteries of the Egyptian Deserts* (Cairo: The American University at Cairo Press, 1961), 12, 287-288; and Chadwick, *John Cassian*, 68-72. The trumpet also served as a call to prayer in certain Moroccan towns during Ramadan:

At Fez and in other towns the *múdden's* call to the sunset prayer is followed by the monotonous sounds of the *ñfir*, a long and straight trumpet, which is blown by the *nŏffär* for about five or ten minutes. After the call to the evening prayer he again sounds his trumpet from the tower of the mosque, this time for a quarter of an hour; and on the following morning, two hours before daybreak, he ascends the minaret a third time and blows the trumpet for a whole hour. This is repeated on every evening and morning throughout the month, but at sunset time only on the last day of it after the new moon has appeared.

(Edward Westermarck, *Ritual and Belief in Morocco* 2 [London: Macmillan, 1926], 91.) In the mid-nineteenth century, a Lazarist priest noted that in Tibet a lama blows a sea conch toward each of the four cardinal points of the compass as a call to prayer, a sound that was audible within a radius of some three miles (Geo[rge] S. Tyack, *A Book About Bells* [London: William Andrews, 1898; reprint ed., Ann Arbor, MI: Gryphon Books, 1971], 159-160).

Notes to Chapter 2

1. PG 88, col. 937. John Climacus wrote *Scala paradisi* for the monastic community at Raithu (probably El Ṭûr today) on the Gulf of Suez (*John Climacus: The Ladder of Divine Ascent*, trans. Colm Luibheid and Norman Russell [New York: Paulist Press, 1982], xxi, 5). On the divergent opinion about Climacus's dates, see the Introduction to the Luibheid and Russell translation by Kallistos Ware (pp. 2-3).

2. Stichel, "Jüdische Tradition," 227.

3. Francis Halkin, ed., *Sancti Pachomii: vitae graecae*, Subsidia hagiographica 19 (Brussels: Société des Bollandistes, 1932), p. 41: "And when they had struck in the morning for the assembly . . ."; and p. 46: "Therefore whenever they strike during the daytime [to call] the brothers to eat. . . ." The Greek *vita* of Pachomius may have been written as late as 390,

not by those who had known Pachomius themselves but by their immediate successors (Chitty, *The Desert City*, 8); Hans Mertel believes it was probably written between 357 and 368 ("Leben des heiligen Pachomius," appendix to *Des heiligen Athanasius Schriften*, Bibliothek der Kirchenväter 31 [Kempten: Verlag der Jos. Köselschen Buchhandlung, 1917], p. 19). In any case, signaling with an instrument other than a trumpet may have been a feature of Egyptian monastic life unknown to Pachomius but practiced by those who formulated his *vita* during the second half of the fourth century.

4. A.-J. Festugière, ed., "La Première vie grecque de Saint Pachôme," *Les Moines d'Orient*, no. 4, pt. 2 (Paris: Les Editions du Cerf, 1965), pp. 192, 195.

5. Palladius, *Historia Lausiaca*, 43.3, PG 34, col. 1210: "at this time he struck the cells of all with the awakening hammer" (my translation). For a translation of this work, see Robert T. Meyer, *The Lausiac History*, Ancient Christian Writers 34 (London: Longmans, Green and Co., 1965), 120. The information that Palladius transmits in this passage is contained in a section about a certain Adolius, a fourth-century monk, whom he had known in Jerusalem. See also John Cassian, *De coenobiorum institutis*, bk. 4, chap. 12, PL 49, col. 164: "As soon as they hear the sound of blows on the door and also of rapping on cells of the isolated [ones], obviously summoning them to prayer or to some kind of work, each one emulously bursts forth from his quarters . . ." (my translation).

St. Jerome (ca. 340-420) writes toward the beginning of the fifth century that the singing of "Alleluia" at a convent in Bethlehem also provided a signal that summoned the faithful: "After having sung 'Alleluia' (by which signal they were called to assemble), no one was permitted to remain behind" (my translation) Epistola 108: Ad Eustochium Virginem, PL 22, col. 896).

6. Stichel, "Jüdische Tradition," 226. The wooden hammer (*naqoša*) continued to be used during the Middle Ages and was called *Schulklopfer*. It is known in Eastern Europe even in the twentieth century.

7. Ibid., 228. The reason for the semantron's replacement of the trumpet as the principal instrument of convocation in regions where wood was not plentiful is difficult to explain, and sources provide no basis for hypotheses. The trumpet does not seem to have disappeared because of its pagan or military connotations, for the typology of the trumpet and trumpeting was transferred to the semantron.

8. N. Olovianishnikov, who believed that trumpets came into use for Christian services after the reign of Constantine I (d. 337), was also of the opinion that they did not continue long in use (*Istoriia kolokolov" i kolokololitejnoe iskusstvo*, 2d ed., enl. [Moscow: Izdanie T-va P. I. Olovianishnikova S-vej, 1912], 17. Cf. Georg Stuhlfauth, "Glocke und Schallbrett," *Repertorium für Kunstwissenschaft* 41, ed. Karl Koetschau [Berlin: Druck und Verlag von Georg Reimer, 1919], 166).

9. See the *vitae* of the following saints: Euthymios (377-473), Theodosios of Palestine (ca. 423-529), Sabas (439-532),

and Kyriakos of the Souka Laura (449-557) in Eduard Schwartz, *Kyrillos von Skythopolis*, Texte und Untersuchungen zur Geschichte der altchristlichen Literatur, vol. 49, no. 2 (Leipzig: J. C. Hinrichs Verlag, 1939), 133, 159, 160 (Sabas); 227 (Kyriakos); Hermann Usener, *Der heilige Theodosios: Schriften des Theodoros und Kyrillos* (Leipzig: Verlag von B. G. Teubner, 1890), 82, 178-179; Cyril of Scythopolis, "Vie de Saint Sabas," trans. A.-J. Festugière, *Les Moines d'Orient*, no. 3, pt. 2 (Paris: Les Editions du Cerf, 1962), p. 59; and Theodore of Petra, "Vie de S. Théodosios," trans. A.-J. Festugière, *Les Moines d'Orient*, no. 3, pt. 3 (Paris: Les Editions du Cerf, 1963), pp. 43-44; and Cyril of Scythopolis, "Vie de Saint Euthyme," trans. A.-J. Festugière, *Les Moines d'Orient*, no. 3, pt. 1 (Paris: Les Editions du Cerf, 1962), pp. 119-120. See also Karl Krumbacher, "Studien zu den Legenden des hl. Theodosios," *Sitzungsberichte der philosophisch-philologischen und der historischen Classe der k. b. Akademie der Wissenschaften zu München*, Annual 1892 (Munich: Verlag der k. Akademie, 1893), pp. 356-357.

10. Fivos Anoyanakis, *Greek Popular Musical Instruments*, trans. from the Greek by Christopher N. W. Klint (Athens: National Bank of Greece, 1979), 103. Nestorian Christians had carried the semantron to China, as Giovanni de Plano Carpini witnessed in 1246. At the court of the Mongol Khan Guyuk in Karakorum, he reported, "they sing openly and in public and beat the board for services after the Greek fashion like other Christians." (Christopher Dawson, ed., *The Mongol Mission* [London: Sheed and Ward, 1955], 68.) A Latin edition of Giovanni de Plano Carpini's *Istoria Mongalorum* is published in Sinica franciscana 1, ed. Anastasius van den Wyngaert (Quaracchi-Firenze: Apud Collegium S. Bonaventurae, 1929), 3-130. Friar William of Rubruck, who visited Mongol China between 1253 and 1255, also observed that Nestorians "strike a board and chant their offices." He further noted that the Nestorians "also have big bells like ours" and believed that the use of bells among the Nestorians was the reason Eastern Christians did not use them. (William Woodville Rockhill, trans. and ed., *The Journey of William of Rubruck to the Eastern Parts of the World, 1253-55*, The Hakluyt Society, 2d ser., no. 4 [London: The Hakluyt Society, 1900], pp. 116, 144-145.) The *ganti*, a board about six feet by one foot, which Tibetan lamas use to call monks to certain services, is an instrument that may have evolved from the semantra of Nestorian Christians (Rockhill, trans. and ed., *The Journey of William of Rubruck*, 117 n. 2). On the use of wooden beams or boards in other cultures, both Christian and non-Christian, see Marcuse, *Survey*, 17-18. The Buddhist *han* in Japan, a large wooden instrument struck by a mallet, is used, like the semantron, to assemble monks for group meditation (William P. Malm, *Japanese Music and Musical Instruments* [Rutland, VT: Charles E. Tuttle, 1959], 70).

11. John Moschus, *Pratum spirituale*, PG 87³, cols. 2860 (Cap. 11), 2905 (Cap. 50), 2961 (Cap. 104), and 2964 (Cap. 105).

12. Giovanni Mansi, *Sacrorum conciliorum nova et amplissima collectio* 13 (Florence, 1767; reprint ed., Paris: H. Welter, 1902), col. 21 (Nicaea II, A.D. 787). See also Edmund Martène, *De antiquis ecclesiae ritibus* 3, 2d ed. (Antwerp: Typis Joannis Baptistae de la Bry, 1737), col. 15.

13. The Covenant of ʿUmar (caliph from 634 to 644) is a complex document transmitted in several recensions. For studies of the covenant, see A. S. Tritton, *The Caliphs and Their Non-Muslim Subjects* (London: Frank Cass, 1970), 5, 6, 8, 11, and 12; and Antoine Fattal, *Le Statut légal des non-musulmans en pays d'Islam*, Recherches publiées sous la direction de l'Institut de Lettres Orientales de Beyrouth, 10 (Beirut: Imprimerie catholique, 1958), 60-69.

14. Simon Ockley renders the passage from the Covenant of ʿUmar as "they shall not ring, but only toll their bells" (*The History of the Saracens*, 1 [Cambridge: Printed for the sole Benefit of Mrs. Anne Ockley, by Permission of Henry Lintot, Esq., 1757], p. 224). From this error N. I. Privalov states that Caliph ʿUmar's proscription is "the first documented information on the use of bells in Christian churches of the East" ("Kolokol'nyj zvon" na Rusi," *Ezhegodnik" imperatorskikh" teatrov"*, issue 1 [1910], 21, my translation). Another reference to bell ringing also appears in William Muir's discussion of the covenant: "no cross must remain in view outside, nor any church bells rung" (*Annals of the Early Caliphate . . . A.D. 632-680* [London, 1883; reprint ed., Amsterdam: Oriental Press, 1968], p. 213).

15. Edward Gibbon, *The Decline and Fall of the Roman Empire* 2 (A.D. 476-1461) (New York: The Modern Library, 1932), 725 n. 52.

16. Howard Crosby Butler, *Early Churches in Syria, Fourth to Seventh Centuries*, pt. 1: History (Princeton University: Department of Art and Archeology, 1929), 211. The towers on the façades of certain sixth-century churches in northern Syria may have been built to contain the *nāḳūs*. Butler can find no other explanation for the large upper windows in the towers on such churches as those at Ḳalb Lauzeh and Termānîn, and the two arches in the tall tower of the convent at Ḳaṣr il-Benât seem designed for the purpose of suspending the heavy wooden beams of a *nāḳūs*. He suggests that the name of the Syrian town of Bānḳūsa may originally have been Bā-nāḳūs-ā (place of the *nāḳūs*), thus called from the signals struck from its church towers. Ibid. Only in Spain was the term *nāḳūs* used for "bell" (Tritton, *The Caliphs*, pp. 5 n. 1, and 113).

17. Tritton, *The Caliphs*, 7. Cf. Fattal, *Le Statut*, 62.

18. The Covenant of ʿUmar regulated public display of both visual and aural Christian symbols. In addition to limiting the sounding of the *nāḳūs*, bans were also imposed on the building of new churches, on street processions at Easter, and on the display of crosses on churches. (Tritton, *The Caliphs*, 11, 102.) At the beginning of the eighth century the striking of the *nāḳūs* at a Christian monastery while Caliph Al-Walîd stood in the pulpit of a nearby mosque to pronounce the *khotba*

resulted in the monastery's destruction (Ibn Khallikan, *Biographical Dictionary* 3, trans. from the Arabic by Mac Guckin de Slane [Paris: Oriental Translation Fund of Great Britain and Ireland, 1868], 622).

19. Albert of Aachen (Albertus Aquensis or Albert, chanoine d'Aix-la-Chapelle), *Geschichte des ersten Kreuzzugs*, First pt.: Die Eroberung des heiligen Landes (Jena: Verlegt bei Eugen Diederichs, 1923), 315 (bk. 6, chap. 40).

20. PL 67, col. 1109.

21. Justin McCann, ed. and trans., *The Rule of Saint Benedict* (London: Burns Oates, 1952), chap. 22 (p. 70), chap. 43 (p. 102), and chap. 48 (p. 110). In 535 the first mention is made of a bell sent from Carthage to a monastery near Naples (see the beginning of Chapter 3 of this volume), and it suggests that bells were not yet in use on the Italian peninsula. Cf. the use of the Latin word *horologium* to designate any instrument for measuring time—sundial, water-clock (clepsydra), or mechanical weight-driven clock (Hugh Tait, *Clocks and Watches* [Cambridge, MA: Harvard University Press, 1983], 5).

22. PL 105, col. 1201. Metz is located today in northeastern France.

23. P. S. Kazanskij, "O prizyvě k" bogosluzheniiu v" vostochnoj tserkvi," *Trudy* I (1871), Arkheologicheskij svězd" I (Moscow, 1869), 300, 310 n. 1.

24. Abbot Guillaume III of the Abbey of Saint-Germain-des-Près wrote at the end of the fourteenth century that a semantron was used in his time for convocation. And a short Latin inscription on a semantron from the Abbey of Clairmarest near Saint-Omer discloses that hammer blows on this instrument announced the death of monks. (Albert Lenoir, *Architecture monastique*, Collection de documents inédits sur l'histoire de France, 3d ser.: Archéologie [Paris: Imprimerie Nationale, 1852], 154-155.) Both the English *Regularis concordia* (ca. 970) and the eleventh-century *Decreta* (Constitutions) of Lanfranc cite the similar custom of striking a wooden board (*tabula*) to call monks to the bedside of a dying brother (Thomas Symons, trans., *The Monastic Agreement of the Monks and Nuns of the English Nation* [London: Thomas Nelson and Sons, 1953], chap. 12, sect. 65 [p. 65]; and chap. 12, sect. 68 [pp. 67-68]; and David Knowles, trans., *The Monastic Constitutions of Lanfranc* [London: Thomas Nelson and Sons, 1951], 122-123). Even in the late nineteenth century in Rome bells were not rung during Holy Week, but the striking of boards called the faithful to services (N. Korsunskij, *Blagověst"*, 3d ed. [Yaroslavl: Tip. G. Fal'k", 1887], 3).

25. PG 99, cols. 1704ff. Kazanskij points out that the Typikon of the Studion Monastery, founded in 463, was written down only in the mid-eleventh century ("O prizyvě," 312 n. 8).

26. Pavel Savvaitov, ed., *Puteshestvie novgorodskago arkhiepiskopa Antoniia v" Tsar'grad" v" kontsě 12-go stolětiia* (St. Petersburg: Tip. Imperatorskoj akademii nauk", 1872), col. 84. For a French translation of this passage, see Antonij,

Archbishop of Novgorod, *Description des lieux-saints de Constantinople (1200)*, Société pour la publication de textes relatifs à l'histoire & à la géographie de l'orient latin: Série géographique 5 (Paris: Ernest Leroux, 1884?), 97.

27. August Heisenberg, *Grabeskirche und Apostelkirche: zwei Basiliken Konstantins*, Second pt.: Die Apostelkirche in Konstantinopel (Leipzig: J. C. Hinrichs'sche Buchhandlung, 1908), 11-12. The Church of the Holy Apostles, originally a fourth-century foundation of Constantine the Great, Justinian I rebuilt in the sixth century.

28. For a discussion of the con... ...sial Venetian bells allegedly shipped to Constantino... ...ter 3 of this volume.

29. *De sacra precatione*, chap. ... ... col. 557. Other medieval Byzantine sources tha... ...semantra include: Eustathius, *De Thessalonica urbe a Latinis capta* [1185], PG 136, col. 121; "Vita S. Pauli iunioris, in monte Latro [10th century] cum interpretatione latina Iacobi Sirmondi S. I.," *Analecta Bollandiana* 11 (1892): 28; and βίος καὶ πολιτεία τοῦ ἐν ἁγίοις πατρὸς ἡμῶν Ἀθανασίου ἀρχιεπισκόπου Κωνσταντινουπόλεως [end of 13th/beginning of 14th centuries], ed. Hippolyte Delehaye, *Mélanges d'hagiographie grecque et latine* (Brussels: Société des Bollandistes, 1966), 133.

30. N. V. Pokrovskij, *Pamiatniki khristianskoj arkhitektury osobenno russkie* (St. Petersburg: Sinodal'naia tip., 1910), 26.

31. In monastic communities the differences between the sounds of the large and small wooden semantra as well as between wood and metal were used to distinguish among the numerous signals sounded during the day and night (Gabriel Millet, "Recherches au mont-Athos," *Bulletin de correspondance hellénique* 29 [1905]: 140). In addition to wooden and metal instruments, a few examples of the stone semantron (*klepalo kamennoe*) have even been reported. One was once used to announce services at the Solovetskij Monastery in northern Russia (Olovianishnikov, *Istoriia kolokolov"*, 11). Sachs also mentions a "sonorous stone" at a church on the island of Chios (*History of Musical Instruments*, 168-169). And at St. Catherine's Monastery on Sinai a piece of granite is struck by a wooden stick to call monks to Orthros (*utrenia*) (I. Markov, "Bilo," *Pravoslavnaia bogoslovskaia entsiklopediia*, 2: 599).

32. Also called ξυλοσήμαντρο, but more frequently ξύλο (wood), ἱερὸ ξύλο (holy wood), or plural, ἱερὰ ξύλα. In Latin the instrument is known as *lignum sacrum* (holy wood) or *tabula* (board or plank). The derivation of the noun σήμαντρον (correctly accented on the first syllable) is from the Greek verb σημαίνειν (to signal). See also Charles Du Fresne, sieur Du Cange, *Glossarium ad scriptores mediae et infimae graecitatis* 2 (Paris: Apud Anissonios Joan. Posuel, & Claud. Rigaud, 1688; reprint ed., Bratislava: Koebner, 1891), cols. 1359-1360; and see Johann Caspar Suicerus, *Thesaurus ecclesiasticus e patribus graecis ordine alphabetico* (Amsterdam: Heur. Wetstenium, 1682), 947; and "Σήμαντρον" in Θρησκευτικὴ καὶ ἠθικὴ ἐγκυκλοπαιδεία 11 (Athens, 1967), cols. 124-125.

33. Leo Allatius [Leone Allacci], *De templis graecorum re-*

centioribus (Coloniae Agrippinae: Apud Iodocum Kalcovium & Socios, 1645), Epist. I, iii, p. 4; for an English edition, see Leo Allatius, *The Newer Temples of the Greeks*, trans. by Anthony Cutler (University Park, PA: The Pennsylvania State University Press, 1969), 5. See also Hieronymus Magius, *De tintinnabulis* (Amsterdam: Sumptibus Andreae Frisii, 1664), 76-78.

34. Anoyanakis, *Greek . . . Instruments*, 95; and Kazanskij, "O prizyvĕ," 302. Allatius gives the name of one tree from which semantra are made as σφενδάκη, a corruption, he assumes, of σφένδαμνος (maple) (*De templis graec.* [Epist. I, III], 5; *Newer Temples*, 6; see also P. I. Mel′nikov [Andrej Pecherskij], *V″ lĕsakh″*, Polnoe sobranie sochinenij P. I. Mel′nikova, vol. 2, 2d ed. [St. Petersburg: Izdanie T-va A. F. Marks″, 1909], 469n.).

35. Anoyanakis, *Greek . . . Instruments*, 95.

36. Magius, *De tintinnabulis*, 78.

37. Though Seroux d'Agincourt assigns this panel to the eleventh or twelfth century (the date beneath the plate itself reads tenth or eleventh century) (*Histoire de l'art par les monuments* [Paris: Treuttel et Würtz, Libraires, 1823], 3:111; vol. 5, pl. 82), Millet believes that the work is no earlier than the sixteenth century ("Recherches," 135 n. 5).

38. Kazanskij, "O prizyvĕ," 302.

39. The larger wooden instrument is also known today as κόπανος (beater) and τάλαντον (wobbler) (Anoyanakis, *Greek . . . Instruments*, 95). Cf. Constantine Cavarnos who explains the term τάλαντον as "a reminder of Christ's injunction to cultivate one's talents (Matt. 25: 14-30), [and] the sounds produced by the *semantron* when it is struck at the peculiar Athonite rhythm resemble the utterance, 'To talanton, to talanton, to tala—tala—talanton,' thereby reminding the monks of Christ's injunction to cultivate their talents, to strive to grow spiritually by waking up and praying." (*Anchored in God* [Belmont, MA: Institute for Byzantine and Modern Greek Studies, 1975], 157.)

40. Allatius describes the dimensions of the great semantron as "six hands broad, one hand thick, and more than thirty in length" (Allatius, *De templis graec.* [Epist. I, iii], 4; and *Newer Temples*, 5). See also Th. Dombart, "Das Semanterium, die frühchristliche Holzglocke," *Die christliche Kunst* 20 (1924), 55. The largest wooden semantron in Greece is said to be at the Monastery of St. John the Divine (or Evangelist) on Patmos. It is approximately 26.5 feet long, about 6.5 inches wide, and almost 2.5 inches thick. On occasion, two monks strike this semantron with four mallets, one in each hand. (Anoyanakis, *Greek . . . Instruments*, 103.)

41. Anoyanakis, *Greek . . . Instruments*, 95.

42. Ibid., 100, pl. 63.

43. Ibid., 95. On Mt. Athos iron is the only metal reported for semantra. Copper semantra are found on Cyprus, however, an island rich in deposits of this metal. And in Jerusalem at the Church of the Resurrection Kazanskij heard a wooden semantron with steel springs attached to it that vibrated when the wood was struck and produced a pleasing sound (Kazanskij, "O prizyvĕ," 302).

44. A fifth- or sixth-century papyrus from Egypt, which contains an inventory of church furnishings, lists "one rod of iron and a similar small one" (H. Leclercq, "Trois inventaires liturgiques [IVᵉ, VIᵉ, VIIIᵉ siècles] en Afrique et en Egypte," *Didaskaleion* 1 [1912]: 33; and H. Leclercq, "Cloche, clochette," DACL III², col. 1971).

45. Kazanskij, "O prizyvĕ," 304.

46. In addition to figures 14 and 15 in the text, see illustrations on pp. 302-303 in Kazanskij, "O prizyvĕ."

47. Allatius, *De templis graec.* (Epist. I, iii), 4; and *Newer Temples*, 6.

48. Lenoir, *Architecture monastique*, 155.

49. Anoyanakis, *Greek . . . Instruments*, 103.

50. See ibid., 101, pl. 64. In Greek this mallet is called τὸ ῥοπτρὸν, ὁ κόπανος, or τὸ σφυρίον.

51. Ibid., 103.

52. Marie-Joseph Lagrange, *Saint Etienne et son sanctuaire à Jérusalem* (Paris: Alphonse Picard et Fils, Editeurs, 1894), 137. See also Leclercq, "Cloche, clochette," cols. 1974-1975.

53. John Moschus, *Pratum spirituale*, chaps. 11, 50, PG 87, cols. 2860, 2905; and Theodore of Studion, *Iambi de variis argumentis* 10 (Εἰς τὸν κανονάρχην), PG 99, col. 1784. Other references to the *kanonarchos* serving in this capacity are contained in Du Cange, *Glossarium graec.* 1, cols. 583-584.

54. *Iambi de variis argumentis* 16 (Εἰς τοὺς ἀφυπνιστάς), PG 99, col. 1785. This Greek poem by Theodore of the Studion Monastery is addressed to those who struck the semantron to waken sleeping monks. According to Allatius, the semantron was struck by the *laospaktes* (ὁ λᾱοσπάκτης), or summoner of the people, but he also notes that in the Typikon of St. Sabas the *kandelaptes* (ὁ κανδηλάπτης), who lights the lamps or candles, was also responsible for sounding the semantron. Allatius suggests that these duties may have been combined in one person responsible for both sound and light. (*De templis graec.* [Epist. I, iii], 3; and *Newer Temples*, 5; see also Suicerus, *Thesaurus ecclesiasticus*, 947.) Kazanskij cites the *laosynaktes* (ὁ λᾱοσυνάκτης) as the officer at Hagia Sophia charged with striking the semantron and points out that this cleric was known in his time as the *kraktes* (ὁ κράκτης), "the caller," from the Greek verb κράζειν (to call) ("O prizyvĕ," 311 n. 3). In a travel account on Sinai from 1881 Nikodim Pavlovich Kondakov reports that the *kliuchar′*, or keeper of the keys, also struck the semantron at St. Catherine's Monastery to awaken monks and call them to services ("Puteshestvie na Sinaj v″ 1881 godu," *Zapiski Imperatorskago novorossijskago universiteta* [Odessa] 33 [1882]: 43).

55. A. S. Uvarov, "Bilo ili klepalo (Materialy dlia arkheologicheskago slovaria)," *Drevnosti: Trudy Moskovskago arkheologicheskago obshchestva* 1 (1865): 30. *Bilo* is a noun formed from *biti* (to hit or to strike); *klepalo* comes from the verb *klepati* (to strike on metal), used by Russians, Bulgarians, Serbs, and Croats. See also Curt Sachs, *Handbuch der Musikinstru-*

mentenkunde, 2d ed. (Leipzig, 1930; reprint ed., Hildesheim: Georg Olms, 1967), 29. Sometimes the Russian word *drevo* (tree) may also be used to designate the bilo (cf. Greek ξύλο).

56. Korsunskij, *Blagověst"*, 3.

57. Antonij (987-1073), an Athonite monk, returned to Kiev ca. 1050 and lived in one of the caves overlooking the Dnieper River. Soon others began to inhabit nearby caves, and Kiev's Monastery of the Caves (later the Kievo-Pecherskaia Lavra) developed. Theodosij in the 1060's built a dwelling for the hermits above the caves and petitioned authorities in Constantinople for a copy of the Typikon of the Studion Monastery. (Knowles, *Christian Monasticism*, 130, 132.)

58. PSRL I (Lavrentian), p. 80 (1074). In two English versions of this passage "bilo" has been translated "bell" (see Serge A. Zenkovsky, ed. and trans., *Medieval Russia's Epics, Chronicles, and Tales*, rev. and enl. ed. [New York: E. P. Dutton, 1974], 111; and Samuel Hazzard Cross and Olgerd P. Sherbowitz-Wetzor, trans. and eds., *The Russian Primary Chronicle: Laurentian Text* [Cambridge, MA: The Medieval Academy of America, 1953?], 157). The use of a sled to transport a dying person or to carry the deceased to the place of burial was a custom in Kievan Russia (Hazzard and Sherbowitz-Wetzor, *Laurentian Text*, 268 n. 234).

59. PSRL I (Lavrentian), p. 82 (1074). Passages under 1091 and 1182 contain additional references to the bilo at the Monastery of the Caves but do not add to our knowledge of how the instrument was used in early Russia (A. A. Shakhmatov, *Pověst' vremennykh" lět"* 1 [Petrograd: Tip. A. V. Orlova, 1916; reprint ed., The Hague: Mouton, 1969], 266; and PSRL II [Hypatian], p. 126 [1182]). The teachings of St. Theodosij both confirm and amplify the information transmitted in the chronicle: "For when the bilo is struck, it is not proper for us to stay in bed, but to rise for prayer . . ." ("Sochineniia prepodobnago Theodosiia Pecherskago," *Uchenyia zapiski vtorogo otděleniia Imp. akad. nauk"* 2, no. 26 [1856], p. 210) (my translation). Theodosij, father of Russian monasticism, was canonized in 1108 (Nicolas Zernov, *Moscow the Third Rome* [London: Society for Promoting Christian Knowledge, 1938], 23-24).

60. E. Golubinskij, *Istoriia russkoj tserkvi*, vol. 1: Period" pervyj (kievskij ili domongol'skij), 2d ed., rev. and enl. (Moscow: Universitetskaia tip., 1904), 158-159. In about 1606 monks at the newly founded Trinity Monastery on the Lesnoj Voronezh River complained that their foundation was so poorly endowed that it could not purchase bells for the church and that they had to strike a board (bilo) as a call to services ("Doklad" chlena Kommissii P. A. D'iakonova," *Izvěstiia Tambovskoj gubernskoj uchenoj arkhivnoj kommissii* no. 16 [1887], pp. 13-14).

61. PSRL IV (Novg. IV), p. 89 (1382).

62. Ladolf Müller, *Die Legenden des heiligen Sergij von Radonež* (Munich: Wilhelm Fink Verlag, 1967), 117.

63. Kazanskij, "O prizyvě," 306. K. A. Nevolin, *O piatinakh" i pogostakh" novgorodskikh" v" XVI věkě*, Zapiski Imperatorskago russkago geograficheskago obshchestva 8 (St. Petersburg: Tip. Imperatorskoj akademii nauk", 1853), 72, 78-79, 83, 284, 285, 307, and 314.

64. Uvarov, "Bilo ili klepalo," 30.

65. N. Sultanov, *Obraztsy drevnerusskago zodchestva v" miniatiurnykh" izobrazheniiakh" izslědovanie po rukopisi XVI věka: "Zhitie Nikolaia Chudotvortsa,"* Pamiatniki drevnej pis'mennosti i iskusstva 8 (St. Petersburg: Tip. I. Voshchinskago, 1881), 2, 26.

66. Olovianishnikov, *Istoriia kolokolov"*, 17. This bilo, according to Olovianishnikov, is described in N. V. Pokrovskij, *Tserkovno-archeologicheskij muzej S.-Peterburgskoj dukhovnoj akademii* (St. Petersburg, 1909), 42. (Pokrovskij's work was not available to me.)

67. Nik[olaj] Findejzen, *Ocherki po istorii muzyki v Rossii s drevnejshikh vremen do kontsa XVIII veka* 1 (Moscow: Gos. izd. Muzsektor, 1928), IX n. 145.

68. Ibid., IX-X n. 145.

69. In the mid-nineteenth century at the Rykhlovskaia Hermitage in the Chernigov region, the bilo was struck as a call to services after the usual bell ringing. An iron klepalo outside the church was sounded in honor of the Bogoroditsa (Virgin). (Archimandrite Mel'khisedek [Sokol'nikov], *Kratkoe istoricheskoe opisanie Rykhlovskoj-pustyni* [Moscow: Universitetskaia tip., 1844], 54ff.) At the end of the nineteenth century a wooden hand bilo was observed at the Gethsemane Skete (founded in 1844) near the Trinity-Sergius Lavra (S. G. Rybakov, *Tserkovnyj zvon" v" Rossii* [St. Petersburg: Tip. E. Evdokimova, 1896], 21). Not far from the belfry of the Pskovo-Pecherskij Monastery was suspended a long iron bilo, whose tone was judged not unlike that of a bell (Olovianishnikov, *Istoriia kolokolov"*, 16). Elmar Arro reports the striking of bila in Russia at the beginning of the twentieth century and further states that modified examples of the bilo can still be heard in the Soviet Union today ("Die altrussische Glockenmusik: Eine musikslawistische Untersuchung," *Beiträge zur Musikgeschichte Osteuropas* [*Musica slavica*], ed. Elmar Arro [Wiesbaden: Franz Steiner Verlag, 1977], 79). Solzhenitsyn's novel, *One Day in the Life of Ivan Denisovich*, opens with the sound of a hammer striking a rail for reveille.

70. M. I. Pyliaev, "Istoricheskie kolokola," *Staroe zhit'e: ocherki i razskazy o byvshikh" v" otshedshee vremia obriadakh", obychaiakh" i poriadkakh" v" ustrojstvě domashnej i obshchestvennoj zhizni* (St. Petersburg: Tip. A. S. Suvorina, 1892), 287. Because striking a bilo or klepalo normally replaced bell ringing in sketes of the Old Believers, V. G. Korolenko was surprised to learn that a bell in the tower of the Kerzhenskij Monastery, a foundation of the Old Believers, had formerly hung at the Komarovskij Skete (V *pustynykh mestakh*, VI. Po Kerzhentsu; V. Olenevskomu skitu i u "Edinovertsev," sect. 2, *Sobranie sochinenij*, vol. 3: *Rasskazy i ocherki* [Moscow: Gosudarstvennoe izdatel'stvo khudozhestvennoj literatury, 1954], 171-172). A law of 1883 even forbade bells rung at churches of the Old Believers to be visible from out-

side (John Shelton Curtiss, *Church and State in Russia: The Last Years of the Empire, 1900-1917* [New York: Octagon Books, 1965], 135, 230).

Notes to Chapter 3

1. Ferrandus wrote his letter about 535, not in 515 as Eduard Wölfflin reports in "Beiträge zur lateinischen Lexikographie," *Sitzungsberichte der philosophisch-philologischen und der historischen Classe der k. b. Akademie der Wissenschaften zu München*, Annual 1900 (Munich: Verlag der k. Akademie, 1901), 8; and in "Campana, Glocke. Species, Spezerei," *Archiv für lateinische Lexikographie und Grammatik* 11 (1900): 538. See also Herbert Thurston, "The Early History of Church Bells," *The Month* (June 1907), 636 n. 1. Cf. Adolf Jülicher, "Das älteste Zeugnis für kirchlichen Gebrauch von Glocken," *Monatschrift für Gottesdienst und kirchliche Kunst* 7, no. 5 (May 1902), pp. 151-152; and Stuhlfauth, "Glocke und Schallbrett," 164.

2. August Reifferscheid, *Anecdota Casinensia*, Index scholarum in universitate litterarum Vratislaviensi (Winter Semester, 1871-72) (Breslau: Typis Officinae universitatis [W. Friedrich], 1971), 6-7, my translation.

3. Stuhlfauth, "Glocke und Schallbrett," 164. Jülicher believes that church bells were probably being rung in North Africa by at least the year 500 ("Das älteste Zeugnis," 152).

4. Eutychius, Patriarch of Alexandria, *Annales*, PG 111, col. 1069. This is the earliest dated reference to the use of church bells in the Christian East. See also Jean Maspero, *Histoire des patriarches d'Alexandrie depuis la mort de l'empereur Anastase jusqu'à la reconciliation des églises jacobites (518-616)*, Bibliothèque de l'Ecole des hautes études 237 (Paris: Librairie ancienne Edouard Champion, 1923), 162-163; and Edward Rochie Hardy, *Christian Egypt: Church and People* (New York: Oxford University Press, 1952), 137-138. Eutychius was patriarch of Alexandria from 933 to 940.

In the original Arabic of the *Annales* Eutychius uses the word *jaras*, which signifies a metal bell (as distinguished from the wooden nāḵūs) (L. Cheikho, ed., *Eutychii patriarchae Alexandrini annales* 1, Corpus scriptorum christianorum orientalium, vol. 50, reprint of Scriptores arabici, 3d ser., vol. 6 [1906] [Louvain: Imprimerie orientaliste L. Durbecq, 1954], 200). On the subsequent history of church bells in Carthage, Alexandria, and Coptic Egypt, see Percival Price, *Bells and Man* (Oxford: Oxford University Press, 1983), 97.

5. The long-standing tradition of crediting Pontius Meropius Paulinus, Bishop of Nola (ca. 353-431), with the introduction and first use of church bells on the Italian peninsula has proved to be without valid historical foundation. St. Paulinus, who assumed the bishopric of Nola around 409, makes no mention in his own letters of the ringing of bells in his see (PL 61, cols. 153-438). Nor does a detailed description of his basilica at Nola in Campania, which he sent to Severus, give account of bells (Epistola 32, PL 61, cols. 330-343).

6. The oldest known inscription on a church bell is a short vertical inscription engraved on the side of the riveted seventh-century bell of Stival near Pontivy in Brittany (Hersart de la Villemarqué, "Mémoire sur l'inscription de la cloche de Stival près Pontivy, en Bretagne," *Mémoires de l'Académie des inscriptions et belles lettres* 24 [1864], pt. 2, pp. 387-399).

7. Each of these terms seems to have been associated with a particular geographical region. *Campana* or *campanum* is most frequently used in referring to bells in Italy, Africa, and England; *cloca* or *clocca* usually occurs in sources of Irish and German provenience; and *signum* appears in Gallic documents. *Nola* is used in later sources and signifies "bell" in the region of Campania in southern Italy. (Thurston, "Early History," 634-637.) Both *campana* and *signum* eventually came to mean a large tower bell, whereas *nola* was used to refer to a small bell. David S. Landes points out that sometime after the eleventh century the French word for "bell" changed from *sein* or *sain* (from the Latin *signum*) to *cloche*, and the older words have survived in *tocsin* (*Revolution in Time: Clocks and the Making of the Modern World* [Cambridge, MA: The Belknap Press of Harvard University Press, 1983], 68, 407 n. 4).

8. Caesarius of Arles, *Regula ad virgines* (ca. 513), chap. 10, PL 67, col. 1109. See also *The Rule of St. Benedict*, ed. and trans. McCann, chap. 22 (p. 70), chap. 43 (p. 102), and chap. 48 (p. 110).

9. Marcuse, *Survey*, 59.

10. "But wishing to return, he comes at night to that rope by which the bell is set in motion (*de quo signum commovetur*) . . ." (Gregory of Tours, *De Virtutibus Sancti Martini*, bk. 1, chap. 28, in Monumenta germaniae historica: scriptorum rerum Merovingicarum, vol. 1 [Hanover: Impensis bibliopolii Hahniani, 1885], 601-602) (my translation).

11. See Gregory's works in Monumenta germaniae historica: *Historia francorum*, bk. 3, chap. 15 (p. 125); bk. 6, chap. 11 (p. 256); *Incipit de Sancto Gregorio Episcopo* (2.), p. 688; *De Virtutibus Sancti Martini*, bk. 1, chap. 28 (p. 601); bk. 1, chap. 33 (p. 604); bk. 2, chap. 11 (p. 612); bk. 2, chap. 45 (p. 625); bk. 3, chap. 23 (p. 638); bk. 3, chap. 38 (p. 641); *Liber in gloria martyrum*: 9. De puero in igne iactato, p. 495; 75. De sanctis Agaunensibus, p. 538; *Liber vitae patrum* (2.), p. 688; *Liber in gloria confessorum*, 94, p. 809; *Incipit de sancto Nicetio Lugdonensi Episcopo*, p. 701.

12. Just as the nature of the role that Sabinianus' predecessor, Gregory I, "the Great" (590-604), played in the codification of Gregorian chant is still debated, so the attribution to Sabinianus (604-606) of official sanction for the use of bells to announce offices is likewise not clear. Several works that ascribe this legislation to Pope Sabinianus are cited in Lenoir, *Architecture monastique*, 157-158. But the entry for Sabinianus in the *Liber pontificalis* does not mention his alleged institution of bell ringing, which would be a rather significant omission in light of the innovative character of such legislation (see Louis Duchesne, *Le Liber pontificalis* 1, 2d ed. [Paris: E. de Boccard, 1955], 315).

13. St. Columban (ca. 543-615) reportedly rang a bell (*signum*) to summon monks to the side of a dying brother (Jonas of Bobbio, *Vitae sanctorum Columbani, Vedastis, Iohannis*, ed. Bruno Krusch, in Monumenta germaniae historica: Scriptores rerum germanicarum 37 [Hanover: Impensis bibliopolii Hahniani, 1905], 184). Four passages in the *vita* of St. Columba of Iona (ca. 521-597) by Adamnan, Abbot of Hy (d. 704), record the use of bells; two of these use the word *cloca*, and two use *signum* (Alan Orr Anderson and Marjorie Ogilvie Anderson, eds. and trans., *Adomnan's Life of Columba* [London: Thomas Nelson and Sons, 1961], 226, 444, 490, and 528). And The Venerable Bede (673-735) recalls that a bell (*campana*) rang at Whitby (Streanaesheldh) upon the death of the Abbess Hilda in 680, the earliest known reference to the tolling of a passing-bell (The Venerable Bede, *Historia ecclesiastica gentis Anglorum*, ed. Alfred Holder [Freiburg: J.C.B. Mohr, 1895], bk. 4, chap. 23 [p. 207]).

14. Duchesne, *Liber pontificalis* 1:454. Also in the early eighth century, during the lifetime of Ermharius (d. 738), a bell was placed in a small tower to be rung to signal convocation, "as is the custom of churches" (*Gesta abbatum Fontanellensium*, Monumenta germaniae historica: Scriptorum 2, ed. Georg Heinrich Pertz [Hanover: Impensis bibliopolii aulici Hahniani, 1829], chap. 10 [p. 284]). And Turketul, Abbot of Croyland, is reported to have donated a peal of seven bells to his abbey around 970 (*Ingulph's Chronicle of the Abbey of Croyland*, trans. Henry T. Riley [London: Henry G. Bohn, 1854], 107; see also Satis N. Coleman, *Bells: Their History, Legends, Making, and Uses* [Chicago: Rand McNally, 1928], 36-37; and John Robert Nichols, *Bells thro' the Ages: The Founders' Craft and Ringers' Art* [London: Chapman & Hall, 1928], 14-15).

15. Coleman, *Bells*, 37; and Charlemagne, *Capitulare Aquisgranense*, no. 8 (November 801), in *Karoli Magni capitularia*, Monumenta germaniae historica 3, Legum 1, ed. Pertz (Hanover: Impensis bibliopolii aulici Hahniani, 1835), 87.

16. Item 2 in the *Excerptiones*, formerly attributed to Egbert, Archbishop of York (ca. 750), directs all priests to "sound the bells (*signa*) of their churches at appropriate hours of the day and night" (my translation) and then to celebrate the offices sacred to God and instruct the people (PL 89, col. 381). The *Excerptiones* are now thought to be a work of the ninth century (Eric John, "Egbert," *Dictionnaire de spiritualité ascétique et mystique, doctrinaire et historique* 4, pt. 1, col. 340). For a translation of the articles in the *Regularis concordia*, see Symons, trans., *The Monastic Agreement of the Monks and Nuns of the English Nation*, chap. 3, sect. 31 (pp. 28-29); chap. 3, sect. 32 (pp. 29-30); chap. 5, sect. 49 (p. 48); chap. 5, sect. 52 (p. 50); chap. 12, sect. 66 (p. 65); and chap. 12, sect. 68 (p. 67).

17. Bells may have functioned in a civic and secular capacity in Constantinople as early as the sixth century, as H. Leclercq suggests in his article, "Cloche, clochette," col. 1970. In the Museum of St. Irene in Istanbul is a bas-relief from the mon-

ument of Porphyrius carved during the reign of Justin II (565-578) that shows two men striking a bell suspended between two columns (Albert Dumont, "Le Musée Sainte-Irène à Constantinople," *Revue archéologique* [1868], 256). A seventh-century Chinese description of Constantinople discloses that "in the imperial palace there is a human figure of gold which marks the hours by striking bells" (C. P. Fitzgerald, *China: A Short Cultural History*, 3d ed. rev. [London: The Cresset Press, 1961], 328).

18. The three principal sources are: the fourteenth-century chronicle by Andreas Dandolo, published in Cesare Baronio, *Annales ecclesiastici* 15 (864-933) (Barri-Ducis: Ludovicus Guerin, eques Ordinis S. Silvestri, et Socii, 1868), 44, no. 101; the account by Joannes Diaconus (John the Deacon), *Chronicon Venetum*, PL 139, col. 910, and *Chronicon Venetum*, ed. Pertz, Monumenta germaniae historica: Scriptorum 7 (Hanover: Impensis bibliopolii, 1846), 21; and the account of Jacobus Goar, *Euchologion sive rituale graecorum* (Venice: Ex typographia Bartholomaei Javarina, 1730; reprint ed., Graz: Akademische Druck- und Verlagsanstalt, 1960), 450.

19. Though the weights of the Venetian bells are not recorded, a roughly contemporaneous bell that a founder named Tancho (or Tanco) cast specially for Charlemagne (768-814) at St. Gall probably weighed no more than 500 pounds (*Monachi sangallensis de gestis Karoli imperatoris* 1:29, Monumenta germaniae historica: Scriptorum 2, ed. Pertz [Hanover: Impensis bibliopolii aulici Hahniani, 1829], 744. See also Lenoir, *Architecture monastique*, 158-159; and Coleman, *Bells*, 38-39).

20. Emerson Howland Swift, *Hagia Sophia* (New York: Columbia University Press, 1940), 87-88.

21. Symeon Magister, Χρονογραφία (*Annales*), PG 109, col. 753; and George the Monk (Georgius Monachus), Βίοι τῶν νέων βασιλέων (*Vitae recentiorum imperatorum*), PG 109, cols. 904-905. See also A. Petrovskij, "Kolokol"," [*Pravoslavnaia*] *Bogoslovskaia èntsiklopediia* 11 (1910), col. 345. In the second half of the eighteenth century Edward Gibbon seemed to question the authenticity of the ninth-century Venetian bells: "the oldest example [of bells in Constantinople] which he [Ducange] can find in the Byzantine writers is of the year 1040; but the Venetians pretend that they introduced bells at Constantinople in the ninth century" (*Decline and Fall of the Roman Empire* 2:725 n. 52).

22. A translation of Liudprand's *Relatio de legatione Constantinopolitana* by F. A. Wright is contained in *The Works of Liudprand of Cremona* (London: George Routledge & Sons, 1930). Liudprand's only allusion to a bell in the imperial city occurs in an earlier and unfinished work, *Antapodosis* (Retribution) of 955-962, where he points out that Basil's Nea Ekklesia is also called "nine" (*Ennean*) by some people "because the clock that marks the offices always strikes nine" (*Antapodosis*, bk. 3, chap. 34, in Wright, trans., *Works of Liudprand*, 126; and Albert Bauer and Reinhold Rau, *Quellen zur Geschichte der sächsischen Kaiserzeit:* . . . *Liudprands Werke*,

Ausgewählte Quellen zur deutschen Geschichte des Mittelalters 8 [Darmstadt: Wissenschaftliche Buchgesellschaft, 1971], 380, 381 n. 29). This passage suggests that at least one bell was connected to a clock mechanism at the Nea Ekklesia during the time of Liudprand's visit to Constantinople. Price calls this clock a clepsydra or water clock, and its nine strokes "the earliest reference to a clepsydra which rang a bell inside a church. . . ." (*Bells and Man*, 165); on the mechanism of the clepsydra, see Landes, *Revolution in Time*, 9. Whether the striking clock at the Nea Ekklesia incorporated any of the ninth-century Venetian bells, however, cannot be determined.

23. The oldest of the Latin churches in Constantinople was probably the tenth-century Santa Maria de Embula on the Bosphorus, also called Santa Maria of the Amalfitans. For other Latin churches built for European residents in Constantinople during the eleventh century, see Bernard Leib, *Rome, Kiev, et Byzance à la fin du XIᵉ siècle* (Paris: Librairie Auguste Picard, 1924; reprint ed., New York: Burt Franklin, 1968), 82-83; and R. Janin, *La Géographie ecclésiastique de l'empire byzantin*, pt. 1: Le Siège de Constantinople et le patriarcat oecuménique, vol. 3: Les Eglises et les monastères (Paris: Publié avec le concours du Centre National de la Recherche Scientifique, 1953), 582-601. On Mt. Athos, Amalfitan monks founded a Latin monastery, which was already flourishing by the mid-eleventh century (Leib, *Rome, Kiev, et Byzance*, 100-101).

24. Millet, "Recherches," 123. In his account of the Latin conquest of Constantinople, Robert of Clari, who is sensitive to both aural and visual details in his observations, makes no mention of bell ringing by the Greeks in Constantinople before or during the siege (*The Conquest of Constantinople*, trans. Edgar Holmes McNeal [New York: Columbia University Press, 1936]).

25. The Typikon of St. Athanasius of Athos (ca. 958) specifies a bell for calling monks of the Great Laura to the refectory (Philipp Meyer, "[Ὑποτύπωσις καταστάσεως τῆς λαύρας τοῦ ὁσίου Ἀθανασίου]," in *Die Haupturkunden für die Geschichte der Athosklöster* [Leipzig: J. C. Hinrichs'sche Buchhandlung, 1894], 136. See also Millet, "Recherches," 123). According to Michael Psellus (1018-ca. 1078), Emperor Constantine Monomachus (1042-1055) was awakened in the middle of the night by "the sacred bell" (ὁ κώδων ὁ ἱερὸς) (see "Πρὸς τὸν αὐτὸν βασιλέα," Scripta minora I [Orationes et dissertationes], ed. Eduard Kurtz [Milan: Società Editrice "Vita e pensiero," 1936], 27). And in 1174 at St. Nicholas of Casoles in southern Italy "the little semantron or the bell, if there is one," was sounded for the offices of Lichnikon and Orthros (Vespers and Matins) after the great semantron had been struck (Aleksej Dmitrievskij, *Opisanie liturgicheskikh″ rukopisej* 1 [Kiev: Tip. G. T. Korchak″-Novitskago, 1895], 797; and Millet, "Recherches," 123). There is no evidence to suggest that bells were founded in Constantinople at this time, however. Whatever bells were rung there must have been either imported from the West or seized as war trophies.

26. See Oswald Spengler's discussion of the clock and bell as symbols in Western culture, in *The Decline of the West*, vol. 1: Form and Actuality, trans. Charles Francis Atkinson (New York: Alfred A. Knopf, 1957), 134 n. 1. Friar William of Rubruck also noted around 1225 that the Eastern Christians in general did not have bells but that Greeks in Gazaria were exceptional in this respect. (Gazaria, or the land of the Khazars, is a region bordered by the Volga River, Caspian Sea, Caucasus Mountains, and the Black Sea, including the Crimea.) (See *Iterarium Willelmi de Rubruc*, Sinica franciscana 1, ed. Anastasius van den Wyngaert [Quaracchi-Florence: Apud Collegium S. Bonaventura, 1929], 229; for an English translation of this passage, see Rockhill, trans. and ed., *The Journey of William of Rubruck*, 144-145.)

27. Savvaitov, ed., *Puteshestvie novgorodskago arkhiepiskopa Antoniia*, col. 84, my translation.

28. Theodore Balsamon, "Μελέται ἤτοι ἀποκρίσεις," PG 138, col. 1076, my translation.

29. Eustathius, Metropolitan of Thessaloniki, *De Thessalonica urbe a Latinis capta*, PG 136, col. 121, my translation.

30. Olovianishnikov, *Istoriia kolokolov″*, 25. See also Gabriel Millet, *L'Ecole grecque dans l'architecture byzantine* (Paris: Ernest Leroux, 1916), 135; Privalov, "Kolokol′nyj zvon″ na Rusi," 28 n. 1; and Golubinskij, *Istoriia russkoj tserkvi* 1 (2d half): 151-152. Several of these Latin churches remained active after the Greeks had regained control of their city in 1261, though some were transferred across the Golden Horn to Galata (Pera) where the Genoese had concentrated their commercial activities. See R. Janin, *La Géographie ecclésiastique*, pt. 1:3, 582, 588-592.

31. Nicephorus Gregoras, Ῥωμαϊκῆς ἱστορίας (*Byzantina historia*), CSHB 6, pt. 1 (Bonn: Weber, 1829), bk. 6, chap. 7 (p. 192); bk. 7, chap. 5 (p. 236); bk. 8, chap. 11 (p. 356); bk. 9, chap. 3 (p. 406). Significantly, Gregoras uses the verb κρούειν (to strike) in describing the action used in bell ringing, the same verb used to describe the percussive action of the hammer on the semantron. The Russian "Povĕst′ o novgorodskom″ bĕlom″ klobukĕ" (Tale of the White Cowl), written in Novgorod toward the end of the fifteenth century, is set in the second quarter of the fourteenth century when Vasilij was archbishop of Novgorod and mentions Vasilij's ordering bells to be rung (*i povelĕ zvoniti*) in Constantinople (N. Kostomarov, ed., *Pamiatniki starinnoj russkoj literatury* 1 [St. Petersburg: Tip. P. A. Kulisha, 1860], 297). The passage may reveal more about bell ringing in Novgorod at the end of the fifteenth century when it was written, however.

32. Spengler, *Decline of the West*, 134 n. 1. According to Lenoir, an eleventh-century capital from the Church of Saint-Sauveur at Nevers shows a Byzantine church with a bell tower (*Architecture monastique*, 314). The Greeks built three different kinds of structures for their bells: a multistoried, detached tower, tall and massive, similar to the Italian campanile; a low bell tower above a portico or narthex; and a tower that was attached to the main structure of the church (Millet, *L'Ecole*

grecque, 137-138). The third type is particularly characteristic of the churches at Mistra. Almost all Byzantine bell towers were surmounted by a four-sided pyramidal roof.

33. Guillaume Joseph Grelot, *Relation nouvelle d'un voyage de Constantinople* (Paris: Pierre Rocolet, 1680), 124, 128, 132, and pl. between 126 and 127.

34. Swift, *Hagia Sophia*, 86. Grelot describes the belfry as a square structure under 50 *toises* (319.8 feet) high, which was "not able to contain very many bells inside nor [bells] of great size" (*Relation nouvelle*, 132).

35. George Pachymeres, *Historia rerum ab Andronico Palaeologo seniore*, CSHB 25 (Bonn: Weber, 1835), bk. 1, chap. 5 (p. 19).

36. Bell towers at Mistra are found on the following churches: the Metropolis (1310), the Brontochion (before 1311), the Peribleptos (probably built in the first half of the fourteenth century), Hagia Sophia (ca. 1350), and the Pantanassa (between 1428 and 1445) (Gabriel Millet, *Monuments byzantins de Mistra* [Paris: Ernest Leroux, 1910], passim; see also Richard Krautheimer, *Early Christian and Byzantine Architecture*, The Pelican History of Art [Baltimore: Penguin Books, 1965], 356 n. 16; and N. V. Pokrovskij, *Pamiatniki khristianskoj arkhitektury osobenno russkie* [St. Petersburg: Sýnodal'naia tip., 1910], 26-27).

37. Gabriel Millet, J. Pargoire, and L. Petit, *Recueil des inscriptions chrétiennes de l'Athos*, pt. 1 (Paris: Albert Fontemoing, 1904), 35-36 (my translation), and pl. 5.

38. "Lied von der Einnahme Konstantinopel's (1453 nach Chr.)," in Edgar Vincent d'Abernon, *Die heutige griechische Sprache*, trans. from the English by Daniel Sanders (Leipzig: Breitkopf und Härtel, 1890), 220-221; and Demetrios A. Petropoulos, ed., Ἑλληνικὰ δημοτικὰ τραγούδια (Athens: I. N. Zacharopoulos, 1958), 152.

39. Symeon, Archbishop of Thessaloniki, *De sacra precatione*, PG 155, col. 557. A Spanish ambassador who visited Constantinople at the beginning of the fifteenth century offers a similar observation: only at Hagia Sophia did the Greeks use a bell. At other churches they "strike a wooden board to mark the more important moments of the ritual." (Clavijo, *Embassy to Tamerlane, 1403-1406*, trans. Guy Le Strange, The Broadway Travellers, ed. Sir E. Denison Ross and Eileen Power [London: George Routledge & Sons, 1928], 114.)

40. Archimandrite Leonid, ed., *Pověst' o Tsar'gradě (ego osnovanii i vziatii Turkami v" 1453 godu) Nestora-Iskandera XV věka*, Pamiatniki drevnej pis'mennosti i iskusstva 62 (St. Petersburg: Tip. V. Balasheva, 1886), 9-10, my translation. The author of this account, written after the Turkish conquest of Constantinople, was a Russian captured by the Turks.

41. Nicolò Barbaro, *Giornale dell'assedio di Constantinopoli 1453* (Vienna: Libreria Tendler & Co., 1856), 50. See also Steven Runciman, *The Fall of Constantinople 1453* (Cambridge: [Cambridge] University Press, 1965), 130; and Donald M. Nicol, *The Last Centuries of Byzantium, 1261-1453* (London: Rupert Hart-Davis, 1972), 407.

42. Barbaro, *Giornale*, 53-55. "When the watchmen on the towers gave the alarm, the churches near the walls began to ring their bells, and church after church throughout the city took up the warning sound till every belfry was clanging" (Runciman, *Fall of Constantinople*, 133, see also p. 135).

43. Kritovoulos, *History of Mehmed the Conqueror*, trans. Charles T. Riggs (Princeton: Princeton University Press, 1954), 66-67.

44. J. Theodore Bent, "The Fall of Constantinople," *The Antiquary* 7, no. 39 (March 1883), p. 102. The call to worship in Islam is traditionally proclaimed from a minaret by a *muezzin*, the human crier whose voice calls Muslims to prayer five times a day. According to Islamic belief, bell ringing sends forth vibrations that disturb the peace and repose of the invisible spirits of the dead, which are believed to wander in the air. (Coleman, *Bells*, 31. See also F. W. Hasluck, *Christianity and Islam under the Sultans*, ed. Margaret M. Hasluck [Oxford: Clarendon Press, 1929], 189 n. 1.) Contrary to the expressed intentions of Mehmet the Conqueror, Greek churches in Istanbul gradually passed into Turkish hands and became mosques. By the eighteenth century the Greeks held only three of the old churches in the city. (Runciman, *Fall of Constantinople*, 157.)

45. Malcolm Letts, trans. and ed., *The Pilgrimage of Arnold von Harff, Knight*, 2d ser., no. 94 (London: The Hakluyt Society, 1946), 247.

46. Grelot, *Relation nouvelle*, 124.

47. William M. Hennessy, ed., *Annals of Ulster; otherwise Annals of Senat: A Chronicle of Irish Affairs from* A.D. *431 to* A.D. *1540*, 1 (Dublin: Printed for Her Majesty's Stationery Office, by Alexander Thom & Co., 1887), 53, 55; Nichols, *Bells thro' the Ages*, 6. The Bell of St. Patrick's Will is 6 inches high and 5 inches wide at its base. The first known makers of Christian bells (of the riveted type) were "Tasag," "Cuana," and "Mackecht," three smiths that St. Patrick brought to Ireland in the fifth century. (Percival Price, "Bell," *New Grove Dictionary of Music and Musicians* 2, ed. Stanley Sadie [London: Macmillan, 1980], 435.) Members of the Benedictine order in Italy were casting rather than forging handbells at the end of the sixth century (Price, "Bell," 433). The largest pagan Roman bell, from approximately the second century A.D., is slightly over 4 inches high and has a lower diameter of about 6.66 inches (Price, "Bell," 432).

48. Arthur Lynds Bigelow, *Carillon* (Princeton: Princeton University Press, 1948), 31.

49. E. de Coussemaker, "Essai sur les instruments de musique au moyen âge," *Annales archéologiques* 4 (Paris: Au Bureau des Annales archéologiques, 1846): 95 n. 1. The Cologne bell is 16.5 inches high, and it bears the name "Saufang" (pig catch or pig find) because tradition holds that a sow happened to uncover it in a marsh about the year 613.

50. Other examples of seventh-century riveted bells include the so-called Bell of St. Godebert at Noyon, France, and the Bell of St. Gall.

51. Arthur Lynds Bigelow, *The Acoustically Balanced Carillon: Graphics and the Design of Carillons and Carillon Bells* (Princeton University: Department of Graphics, School of Engineering, 1961), 2-3.

52. Alberto Serafini, *Torri campanarie di Roma e del Lazio nel medioevo*, vol. 1: Text (Rome: Pompeo Sansaini, 1927), 9. See also Leclercq, "Cloche, clochette," cols. 1964-1966; and J.-B. de Rossi, "Cloche, avec inscription dédicatoire du VIIIᵉ ou du IXᵉ siècle, trouvée à Canino," *Revue de l'art chrétien* 40 (1890): 3.

53. Other examples of primitive Italian bells are the bell of San Benedetto in Piscinula (second half of the eleventh century), the Pisan bells of 1106, 1154, and 1173, and the Verona bell of 1149 (Coleman, *Bells*, 231; and Sachs, *Handbuch der Musikinstrumentenkunde*, 38).

54. Margarete Schilling, *Glocken und Glockenspiele* (Gütersloh, W. Ger.: Prisma Verlag, 1982), 17, fig. 20. The oldest bell of the so-called Theophilus or Theophile type, according to Sachs, seems to be a German bell of 1098 at Drohndorf in Anhalt (*Handbuch der Musikinstrumentenkunde*, 38).

55. Nils-Arvid Bringéus, *Klockringningsseden i Sverige*, Nordiska Museets Handlingar 50 (Stockholm: Nordiska Museet, 1958), 20.

56. Bigelow, *The Acoustically Balanced Crillon*, 2; and Bigelow, *Carillon*, 35-36. Also Sachs, *Handbuch der Musikinstrumentenkunde*, 38.

57. Bigelow, *Carillon*, 37-38; and Coleman, *Bells*, 231.

58. Karol Badecki, *Dzwony starodawne z przed r. 1600 na obszarze B. Galicji* (Cracow: Wydane z zasiłkami Polskiej Akademji Umiejętności, 1922), 6, 41.

59. Bigelow, *The Acoustically Balanced Carillon*, 2-4.

60. Schilling, *Glocken*, 22.

61. Wendell Westcott, *Bells and Their Music* (New York: G. P. Putnam's Sons, 1970), 27-28; and Bigelow, *The Acoustically Balanced Carillon*, 5, 9.

62. Korsunskij, *Blagovest"*, 8.

63. For a testimony from 1496-1499, see Letts, *The Pilgrimage of Arnold von Harff*, 238. Two sixteenth-century witnesses are cited in Johann Boemus, *Omnium gentium mores, leges, & ritus* (Antwerp: In aedibus Ioan. Steelsii, 1542), 47; and S. O. Dolgov, "Vtoroe khozhdenie Trifona Korobejnikova [1593]," in *Chteniia v" Imperatorskom" obshchestvě istorii i drevnostej rossijskikh" 1887*, bk. 1, p. 16. In the early seventeenth century Captain Jacques Margeret observed that the Greeks under Turkish rule did not have bells (*The Russian Empire and Grand Duchy of Moscow: A 17th-Century French Account*, trans. and ed. Chester S. C. Dunning, Series in Russian and East European Studies, no. 5 [Pittsburgh, PA: University of Pittsburgh Press, 1983], 26; see also *Zapiski Marzhereta i Prezidenta de-Tu: Skazaniia sovremennikov" o Dmitrii Samozvantse*, pt. 3 [St. Petersburg: Tip. Imperatorskoj rossijskoj akademii, 1832], 33). The notable exception to the general suppression of bells and bell ringing among the Greeks was on Mt. Athos, as Paul Ricaut (also Rycaut) noted

in *The Present State of the Greek and Armenian Churches, Anno Christi, 1678* (London: John Starkey, 1679): "In every Monastery they have bells: such as they daily use are small, but those of greatest bigness, are of about 4 or 500 weight [between around 450 and 560 pounds], which they ring at Festivals, when they would make the greatest noise and rejoicing: on these their Clocks strike, which are fixed like those on our Churches in England; which are not to be found, as I remember, in any other place in Turkey, unless at Buda, where I saw one of this sort" (pp. 261-262). See also Kazanskij, "O prizyvě," 305. In a letter of October 7, 1843, Archimandrite Leonid wrote that in Istanbul only a certain Roman Catholic church had bells, but he could not explain why the Turks had made an exception. The Turks apparently did not extend the same privilege to Greek and Russian churches in the city. (*Pis'ma sviatogortsa k" druz'iam" svoim" o Sviatoj Gorě athonskoj*, pt. 1, 2d ed. [St. Petersburg: Tip. E. Fishera, 1850], 10-11.)

Notes to Chapter 4

1. Though 862 is recognized as the year of the "calling of the Varangians," the semilegendary arrival of Riurik in northern Russia, may have occurred about six years earlier. (George Vernadsky, *A History of Russia*, 5th rev. ed. [New Haven: Yale University Press, 1961], 31.)

2. Photius, *Epistolae*, PG 102. cols. 736-737.

3. For studies that interpret various attempts to convert the Russians prior to 988/989, see Francis Dvornik, *The Slavs: Their Early History and Civilization*, Survey of Slavic Civilization 2 (Boston: American Academy of Arts and Sciences, 1956), 199-211; A. V. Kartashev, *Ocherki po istorii russkoj tserkvi* 1 (Paris: YMCA Press, 1959), 70-124; Alexander A. Vasiliev, *The Russian Attack on Constantinople in 860* (Cambridge, MA: The Mediaeval Academy of America, 1946), 229-230; and A. P. Vlasto, *The Entry of the Slavs into Christendom* (Cambridge: [Cambridge] University Press, 1970), 236-295 (chap. 5).

4. Samuel Hazzard Cross and Olgerd P. Sherbowitz-Wetzor, trans. and ed., *The Russian Primary Chronicle: Laurentian Text*, 3d printing, 1973 (Cambridge, MA: The Medieval Academy of America, 1953), 77. Russian Christians are mentioned for the first time in the Laurentian Chronicle in connection with the ratification of a commercial treaty with Byzantium in 945 in the Church of St. Elias (ibid., 238 n. 53). Cross discusses the probable location of this church in Kiev in "The Earliest Medieval Churches of Kiev," *Speculum* 11 (1936), 477-478.

5. Mas'ūdī, an Arab geographer and historian, who traveled extensively in the East, was born in Baghdad toward the end of the ninth century and died in 956 or 957. His earliest writings date from 912. There is nothing, however, to indicate that the information Mas'ūdī transmits on the *Slaviane* and *Rusy* was acquired from direct contact with and observation

of these two peoples. (A. Ia. Garkavi [Harkavy], *Skazaniia mu-sul'manskikh" pisatelej o slavianakh" i russkikh" (s" poloviny VII věka do kontsa X věka po R. Kh.* [St. Petersburg: Tip. Imp. akademii nauk", 1870; reprint ed., The Hague: Mouton, 1969], 120-121).

6. Ibid., 125, my translation. See also Findejzen, *Ocherki po istorii muzyki*, 22.

7. Garkavi, *Skazaniia*, 143.

8. A number of studies on the history of bells in Russia state that they were present in Kiev in 988, but no author cites a specific passage from a primary source to support this statement. See Olovianishnikov, *Istoriia kolokolov"*, 29; and Iurij Vasil'evich Pukhnachev, *Zagadki zvuchashchego metalla* (Moscow: Izd. "Nauka," 1974), 76. In his poem "Bylina o kreshchenii Rusi" (Bylina on the Baptism of Russia) S. Drozhzhin fancies that bell ringing (*kolokol'nyj zvon"*) accompanied Vladimir's official baptism of his subjects at Kiev in 988/989 (P. P. Romanovich, *Russkaia starina v" rodnoj poėzii* [Novgorod: Tipo-litografiia Gub. pravleniia, 1890], 21). And the evidence that Mas'ūdī presents also suggests that bell ringing could have accompanied this important event. But no proof can be cited.

9. Vladimir I granted this church a tithe (*desiatina*) from his property and from the cities of Russia (George Vernadsky, *Kievan Russia*, vol. 2, *A History of Russia* [New Haven: Yale University Press, 1948], 66). On the history of this church in Kiev, see A. I. Nekrasov, *Ocherki po istorii drevnerusskogo zodchestva XI-XVII veka* (Moscow: Izd. Vsesoiuznoj akademii arkhitektury, 1936), 21-22; and Cross, "Earliest Medieval Churches," 481-488.

10. Princess Olga's wooden Cathedral of St. Sophia from the tenth century had burned in 1017.

11. The wooden Cathedral of St. Sophia built at Novgorod in 989 had burned in 1045.

12. PSRL III (Novg. I), p. 2 (1066). Vseslav Briachislavich (d.1101) became prince of Polotsk in 1044.

13. The mention of bells among the booty collected after the capture of medieval Russian towns implies that they were not only uncommon but also of considerable value (N. N. Rubtsov, "Ocherki po razvitiiu litejnogo proizvodstva," *Litejnoe proizvodstvo*, no. 12 [1936], p. 24).

14. "Pamiatniki drevle-russkoj dukhovnoj pis'mennosti: zhitie prepodobnago Antoniia Rimlianina." *Pravoslavnyj sobesědnik"* 1858, pt. 2, 164, my translation. Andrej, Abbot of the Monastery of St. Antonij (1147-1157), allegedly wrote the *vita* of St. Antonij Rimlianin. Antonij's "nationality" has never been clarified; he has been identified as both a Russian and a Roman. (Leib, *Rome, Kiev, et Byzance*, 91.) On the interpretation of "Rimlianin," see also M. N. Tikhomirov, *The Towns of Ancient Rus*, trans. from 2d Russian ed. by Y. Sdobnikov (Moscow: Foreign Languages Publishing House, 1959), p. 188. According to M.-J. Rouët de Journel, Antonij was born in Rome in 1067 and spent twenty years in solitude between 1086 and 1106 after which he left (Italy?) for Novgorod (Mo-

nachisme et monastères russes [Paris: Payot, 1952], 34 n. 1). In the first half of the twelfth century Novgorod was reported to have 230 churches.

15. PSRL II (Hypatian), p. 27 (1146).

16. Ibid., p. 100 (1171).

17. PSRL I (Lavrentian), p. 152 (1169), my translation.

18. *Slovo o polku Igoreve* (Moscow: Gosudarstvennoe izd. khudozhestvennoj literatury, 1954), 4, 6, my translation. This epic poem relates the ill-fated campaign of Prince Igor of Novgorod-Severskij against the Polovtsians in 1185.

19. Ibid., 28, my translation. Vseslav is Prince Vseslav Briachislavich of Polotsk who took bells and chandeliers in 1066 from the St. Sophia Cathedral in Novgorod.

20. Dmitrij Dubenskij, *Russkiia dostopamiatnosti*, pt. 3 (Moscow: Universitetskaia tip., 1844), 199-200 n. 202. Dubenskij suggests three possible interpretations of the second passage.

21. See Privalov, "Kolokol'nyj zvon" na Rusi," 22; and Olovianishnikov, *Istoriia kolokolov"*, 29. Privalov says that bells came to Russia from Byzantium; Olovianishnikov believes they came from the West. Joel Carmichael (*A Cultural History of Russia* [London: Weidenfeld and Nicolson, 1968], 55-56) says the bell was a gift from Byzantium. E. Golubinskij maintains that it had to have come from the Germans and not from the Greeks (*Istoriia russkoj tserkvi*, 1 [2d half], 152). See also A. S., "Kolokola," *Věra i tserkov'*, no. 2 (1905), p. 308. Gleb Rahr also believes that the bell was brought to Russia from the West ("Cloches et carillons en Russie," in *Encyclopédie des musiques sacrées* 2, gen. ed., Jacques Porte [Paris: Editions Labergerie, 1969], 211). But N. Aristov states that in all probability Greek foremen first came to Russia and were then followed by native foremen (*Promyshlennost' drevnej Rusi* [St. Petersburg, 1866], 118). Rubtsov, too, says that "the first Russian bell founders were obviously Greeks" and that Russian masters appeared later. His opinion is apparently based on the report of several bronze sculptures, which Vladimir, after his own baptism, brought to Kiev from the Greeks in Cherson. ("Ocherki po razvitiiu," 24.)

22. Leop[old] Karl Goetz, *Deutsch-russische Handelsgeschichte des Mittelalters*, Hansische Geschichtsquellen 5 (new series) (Lübeck: Druck der Lübecker Verlagsanstalt Otto Waelde Komm.-Ges., 1922), 541. Foreign merchants called "Rugi" are mentioned in the Raffelstätter Customs Statute (Vernadsky, *Kievan Russia*, 338). An important study of trade and foreign relations in Kievan Russia is V. T. Pashuto, *Vneshniaia politika drevnej Rusi* (Moscow: Izd. "Nauka," 1968).

23. Goetz, *Deutsch-russische Handelsgeschichte*, 541; Vernadsky, *Kievan Russia*, 340-341; and B. Grekov, *Kiev Rus*, trans. Y. Sdobnikov (Moscow: Foreign Languages Publ. House, 1959), 651-653.

24. See Samuel H. Cross, "Medieval Russian Contacts with the West," *Speculum* 10 (1935), 139; Leib, *Rome, Kiev et Byzance*, 143-178; and Grekov, *Kiev Rus*, 651-652.

25. Pashuto, *Vneshniaia politika*, 138; Jack Lindsay, *Byzan-

tium into Europe (London: The Bodley Head, 1952), 403; Cross, "Medieval Russian Contacts," 141-142; and Vernadsky, *Kievan Russia*, 338.

26. Grekov, *Kiev Rus*, 652; and Pashuto, *Vneshniaia politika*, 123.

27. Cross, "Medieval Russian Contacts," 142.

28. Ivan Beliaev, *Istoriia goroda Pskova i pskovskoj zemli*, Razskazy iz″ russkoj istorii, bk. 3 (Moscow: Synodal′naia tip., 1867), 4; and Vernadsky, *Kievan Russia*, 270, 339.

29. A. Storozhenko, "O sushchestvovavshikh″ v″ g. Kievě rimsko-katolicheskikh″ khramakh″," in *Eranos: Sbornik″ statej po literaturě i istorii v″ chest′ zasluzhennago professora Imperatorskago Universiteta Sv. Vladimira Nikolaia Pavlovicha Dashkevicha* (Kiev: Tip. Imp. Universiteta Sv. Vladimira, 1906), 244-245.

30. The bell weighs 42.76 pounds, has a total height (with its cannons) of 16.92 inches, and a lower diameter of 13.58 inches. Its clapper was not found. But fragments from two other bells were uncovered at "Maloe gorodische." This site is in the Ukraine on the banks of the Teterev River in the Korotyshevskij district of the Zhitomirskij province. (R. I. Vyezzhev, "Kolokola drevnego Gorodeska," *Kratkie soobshcheniia Instituta arkheologii*, issue 9 [1959] [Kiev: Izd. Akademii nauk Ukrainskoj SSR, 1960], 104-107.)

31. The etymology of the Russian *kolokol* (bell) is of little help in tracing the provenience of this instrument in Kievan Russia. Vasmer believes that a Proto-Slavic **kolkolŭ* is probably related to Lithuanian *kañkalas* (little bell), and the latter he connects with Sanskrit *kalakalas* (confused cries, noise). Although consonants analogous to the "k" and "l" in *kolokol* occur in such West European words for "bell" as *klokke, klocka, Glocke,* and *cloche,* this may be only onomatopoeic coincidence, and the resemblance in any case is more apparent than real. The West European words seem to go back to the Celtic **klokko-* or **klokkā,* which were widely borrowed on the Continent. The Slavic **kolkolo-* may be onomatopoeic and perhaps related to the Slavic **golgolo-* and hence to *glagol* (verb or word). The latter designated the more highly ordered sounds of human speech, the former, the cacophonous "speech" of ringing bronze. For the etymology of *kolokol,* see Max Vasmer, *Etimologicheskij slovar′ russkogo iazyka* 2, trans. from the German and enl. by O. N. Trubachev (Moscow: Izd. "Progress," 1967), 294; Manfred Mayrhofer, *Kurzgefasstes etymologisches Wörterbuch des Altindischen* 1 (Heidelberg: Carl Winter, Universitätsverlag, 1956), 177; and Erich Berneker, *Slavisches etymologisches Wörterbuch* 1, 2d ed. (Heidelberg: Carl Winter's Universitätsbuchhandlung, 1924), 547.

Because copper and iron objects produced by foreign founders were superior in quality to domestic work, the Russians either brought Greek foremen to their southern founding centers and German foremen to their eastern centers, or they imported articles that these artisans had cast (Aristov, *Promyshlennost′ drevnej Rusi,* 118). If bells in certain Russian towns were originally rung by swinging the bells themselves, as some

iconographical material indicates, then the case for a Western source for Russian bells, at least in some parts of Russia, would be significantly strengthened. Percival Price is of the opinion that "the bell founding craft which flourished in Russia in the 17th and 18th centuries was derived from German Baltic sources" ("Bell," 435-436).

32. Nikolaj Zakrevskij, *Opisanie Kieva* (Moscow: Tip. V. Gracheva, 1868), 289; and M. M. Zakharchenko, *Kiev″: teper′ i prezhde* (Kiev: S. V. Kul′zhenko, 1888), 209. The height of the bell that is complete is 15.75 inches, and its cannons are 5.25 inches high. The bell's lower diameter is 17.5 inches and its upper diameter, 12.25 inches; the metal is slightly more than 1 inch thick, and the bell's weight is about 81.25 pounds. (Zakrevskij, *Opisanie Kieva,* 289.) The Desiatinnaia Church suffered extensive damage during a fire in 1017 and was sacked in 1171 and 1203. Though the bells uncovered in the ruins of the church may have fallen on any of several occasions before 1240, their burial in the foundations of the church during the assault of Khan Batu in that year seems likely (Cross, *Medieval Russian Churches,* 6; see also P. I. Korenevskij, "Arkheologicheskiia raskopki v″ Kievě," *Istoricheskij věstnik″* 121 [1910]: 982-984).

33. Findejzen believes that Vladimir brought the two bells from Greece (*Ocherki po istorii muzyki,* IV n. 62).

34. "O khodě otkrytiia drevnostej v″ Kievě do nachala 1836 goda," *Zhurnal″ ministerstva narodnago prosvěshcheniia* 12 (1836), sect. 2, pp. 266, 269; and Ivan Fundukle, *Obozrěnie Kieva v″ otnoshenii k″ drevnostiam″* (Kiev: Tip. I. Val′nera, 1847), 51.

35. For a list of these bells and bell fragments, see M. K. Karger, *Drevnij Kiev* 1 (Leningrad: Izd. Akad. nauk, SSSR, 1958), 378-379; see also p. 570, fig. 43. In chronological order of their discovery, or publication of their discovery, the three whole or almost whole instruments are: a large bronze bell weighing up to 3 puds (108 pounds) recovered in 1901 on the town site of Devich′-gora near the village of Sakhnovka, with loop-shaped cannons similar to those on one of the two Desiatinnaia bells; a well-preserved bell found in 1907 on Khorevaia Street in the lower city (Podol) of Kiev; and an almost complete bell (lacking only its cannons) unearthed in 1937 not far from the site of the Desiatinnaia Church. The height of the bell found in 1907 is 14.87 inches (8.5 vershki); its diameter is 11.81 inches (6.75 vershki) (B. I. and V. I. Khanenko, *Drevnosti pridneprov′ia* 6 [Kiev: S. V. Kul′zhenko, 1907], 42, fig. 42.

36. PSRL I (Lavrentian), p. 173 (1194).

37. Leib believes that bell founding began in Russia about the middle of the twelfth century (*Rome, Kiev, et Byzance,* 92 n. 3).

38. Karger, *Drevnij Kiev,* 378-379.

39. Ibid., 387-388; and M. K. Karger, "Rozkopki na sadibī Kiïvs′kogo īstorichnogo muzeiu," *Arkheologīchnī pam″iatki URSR* 3: Rannī Slov″iani ī Kiïvs′ka Rus′ (Kiev: Vidavnitstvo Akademīï nauk Ukraïns′koï RSR, 1952), 10.

40. N. N. Voronin, *Materialy i issledovaniia po arkheologii drevnerusskikh gorodov*, vol. 3: *Drevnee Grodno po materialam arkheologicheskikh raskopok 1932-1949 gg.*, Materialy i issledovaniia po arkheologii SSSR, no. 41 (Moscow: Izd. Akad. nauk SSSR, 1954), 119-120.

41. On a number of later Russian bell inscriptions, the founder often refers to himself as a servant of God (*rab" Bozhij*).

42. Relief inscriptions on European bells were not common until the thirteenth century.

43. Zernov, *Moscow the Third Rome*, 29; and Sergej Fedorovich Platonov, *Moscow and the West*, trans. and ed. Joseph L. Wieczyński, Russian Series 9 (Hattiesburg, MS: Academic International, 1972), ix.

44. B. A. Rybakov, *Remeslo drevnej Rusi* (Moscow: Izd. Akad. nauk SSSR, 1948), 532. In 1246 during a visit to the court of the Great Khan, Giovanni de Plano Carpini met a number of Russians and Hungarians with whom he conversed in French and Latin. He reported that the Great Khan held a Russian goldsmith named Cosmas (Kosma) in high regard. (*The Mongol Mission*, ed. Christopher Dawson, and trans. by a nun of Stanbrook Abbey [London: Sheed and Ward, 1955], 66.)

45. Excavations have shown that the city of Gorodesk was among the most productive manufacturing and trade centers in the western regions of Kievan Russia during the twelfth and first part of the thirteenth centuries. But it never recovered from the Mongol devastation of 1241 and after 1257 ceased to exist. (R. I. Vyezzhev, "Raskopki 'Malogo Gorodishcha' letopisnogo Gorodeska," *Kratkie soobshcheniia Instituta arkheologii*, issue 10 [Kiev: Izd. Akademii nauk Ukrainskoj SSR, 1960], 134-135; and P. P. Tolochko, *Kiev i kievskaia zemlia v epokhu feodal'noj razdroblennosti, XII-XIII vekov* [Kiev: Naukova dumka, 1980], 157.) For summaries of the effects of the Mongol conquest and occupation on Russian industry in the thirteenth and fourteenth centuries, see Rybakov, *Remeslo drevnej Rusi*, 525-538; George Vernadsky, *The Mongols and Russia*, A History of Russia, vol. 3 (New Haven: Yale University Press, 1953), 338-341; and Joseph T. Fuhrmann, *The Origins of Capitalism in Russia: Industry and Progress in the Sixteenth and Seventeenth Centuries* (Chicago: Quadrangle Books, 1972), 12-16.

46. David MacKenzie and Michael W. Curran, *A History of Russia and the Soviet Union* (Homewood, IL: The Dorsey Press, 1977), 86; Vernadsky, *The Mongols and Russia*, 340; N. N. Rubtsov, *History of Foundry Practice in USSR*, trans. from the Russian [2d ed., rev. and enl.] (New Delhi: Indian National Scientific Documentation Centre, 1978), 21.

Kiev was never to recover its former industrial leadership in Russia. Novgorod and Pskov, though they were not conquered by the Mongols, were still adversely affected and only achieved preeminence in casting during the mid-fourteenth century with the revival of the metallurgical industry. (Vernadsky, *The Mongols and Russia*, 338, 340.) Bell founding in Novgorod, Pskov, and northeastern Russian towns depended upon the importation of considerable quantities of nonferrous metals (A. L. Khoroshkevich, *Torgovlia velikogo Novgoroda s pribaltikoj i zapadnoj Evropoj v XIV-XV vekakh* [Moscow: Izd. Akademii nauk SSSR, 1963], 316).

47. PSRL II (Hypatian), p. 196 (1259), my translation. Kholm, now the Polish town of Chełm, is located near the Polish-Russian border between Lublin (Poland) and Kovel (USSR). This chronicle entry should not be used, as Pukhnachev does, to assert that bells were first cast in this year by *native* Russian founders (*Zagadki*, 77). An inscription on portions of a bronze church chandelier (*panikadilo*) unearthed in 1840 during excavation of a church on the site of Vshchizh discloses that it was cast in 1166 by a foundryman named "Konstantin." Though no Konstantin is known to have cast bells, this name stands first in the long roll of Russian founders. (A. N. Sokolov, *Osnovy litejnogo proizvodstva* [Leningrad: Lenizdat, 1958], 6; and Rybakov, *Remeslo drevnej Rusi*, 253.) Rybakov supplied the missing letters of this inscription to reveal the founder's name. See also Rubtsov, *History*, 395, no. 259.

48. PSRL II (Hypatian), p. 223 (1288), my translation.

49. N. M. Karamzin, *Primĕchaniia k" Istorii gosudarstva rossijskago (Tom" IV, V, i VI)*, ed. Aleksandr Smirdin (St. Petersburg: Tip. Imperatorskoj akademii nauk", 1852), 132 (note 182 to vol. 4). The name "Tiurik" " is derived from a word of Turkish origin meaning "bag" or "sack."

50. PSRL I (Troitsk.), p. 282 (1305); and the Suzdal Chronicle in *Lĕtopis' po lavrentievskomu spisku*, izd. Arkheografičeskoj kommissii (St. Petersburg: Tip. Imp. akad. nauk", 1872), 501 (1305).

51. PSRL III (Novg. I), p. 81 (1342); and PSRL X (Nikon.), p. 217 (1346). The entry of 1346 states that Boris Rimlianin cast the bells.

52. Aristov, *Promyshlennost'*, 118; and Rybakov, *Tserkovnyj zvon"*, 22.

53. A. N. Nasonov, ed., *Pskovskie letopisi*, issue 2 (Moscow: Izd. Akademii nauk SSSR, 1955), 107 (6902 = 1394).

54. A. S. Orlov, *Bibliografiia russkikh nadpisej XI-XV vv.* (Moscow: Izd. Akad. nauk SSSR, 1952), 122, no. 123 (1341), my translation. See also Petr Keppen, *Spisok" ruskim" pamiatnikam", sluzhashchim" k" sostavleniiu istorii khudozhestv" i otechestvennoj paleografii* (Moscow: Tip. S. Selivanovskago, 1822), 105n.

55. A thorough study of the L'vov bell's inscription and its literature is published in Badecki, *Dzwony starodawne*, 88-94. The Cyrillic letters of the four words in the second part of the inscription, which mentions Skora Iakov, run from right to left.

56. P. N. Batiushkov, *Pamiatniki russkoj stariny v" zapadnykh" guberniiakh" imperii*, issue 6 (St. Petersburg: Tip. i khromolitografiia A. Transhelia, 1874), 122 n. 6, my translation.

57. Citations of a fire at Rostov-Velikij in 1408 and the Mongol raid on Vladimir (northeast of Moscow) in 1410 appear in *Lĕtopis' po lavrentievskomu spisku*, Izdanie Arkheo-

graficheskoj kommissii (St. Petersburg: Tip. Imp. akad. nauk", 1872), 510, 511. In 1450 a large bell was brought to Moscow from a small town (PSRL VI [Sof. I], p. 270 [1450]). Some Pskovians, during a raid into foreign territory in 1460, seized some religious objects, including four bells (PSRL III [Pskov. I], p. 219 [1460]).

58. Orlov, *Bibliografiia*, 128, no. 210 (1420). This bell is now preserved in the treasury at the lavra.

59. N. I. Repnikov, "Pamiatniki ikonografii uprazdnen-nogo Gostinopol'skogo monastyria," *Izvestiia Komiteta izucheniia drevne-russkoj zhivopisi*, issue 1 (1921), 14-15, my translation. The lower diameter of Mikula's bell is 2.55 feet. This "Mikula" is the first Novgorod founder who is known by name. (A. I. Semenov, "Novgorodskie litejnye i oruzhejnye masterskie v XV-XVI vv.," *Sbornik issledovanij i materialov Artillerijskogo istoricheskogo muzeia Krasnoj armii* 1 [1940], 240.) See also Rubtsov, *History*, 413, no. 334.

60. Orlov, *Bibliografiia*, 147, no. 244 (1487 [*sic*]). For date, cf. Nikolaj Fetter, "Drevnosti Pafnut'eva monastyria," *Istoricheskij věstnik* 43, no. 2 (February 1891), p. 598.

61. In 1151 Andrej Bogoliubskij left Vyshgorod in the region of Kiev for the newly opened lands around Vladimir and Suzdal. The icon of the Virgin (now called the Virgin of Vladimir), which had probably been carried from Constantinople to Kiev in the early twelfth century, was brought to Vladimir in 1155. In 1157 Andrej Bogoliubskij proclaimed himself prince of Vladimir, Suzdal, and Rostov, and by the end of the thirteenth century Vladimir had become the see of the Russian metropolitan.

Moscow first enters recorded history in 1147 as a possession of Prince Iurij Dolgorukij of Rostov-Suzdal. At that time it was still a small town of relative insignificance in central Russia (PSRL II [Hypatian], p. 29 [1147]; and PSRL IX [Nikon.], p. 172 [1147]).

62. After the Mongol invasion the metropolitan of Kiev had no permanent see in Russia but moved from one city to another, most of which were in ruins. Metropolitan Peter, who frequently visited Moscow, died and was buried there in 1326. According to a legend current at the end of the fourteenth century, the metropolitan had promised Ivan Kalita that if he built and dedicated a church to the Bogoroditsa (Virgin) and would bury him in it, Moscow would one day stand supreme over all other Russian cities. (Robert Lee Wolff, "The Three Romes: The Migration of an Ideology and the Making of an Autocrat," *Daedalus* [Spring 1959], 297.) Theognost, Peter's successor, remained in Moscow and through this decision strengthened Moscow's ecclesiastical primacy among Russian cities (Zernov, *Moscow the Third Rome*, 30-31n). A study of Moscow's rise during the first half of the fourteenth century is J.L.I. Fennell's *The Emergence of Moscow, 1304-1359* (London: Secker & Warburg, 1968).

63. PSRL X (Nikon.), p. 211 (1339). In this same year, a scribe had also compared the Grand Duke of Moscow to three great Byzantine emperors: Constantine I, Justinian I, and Manuel I Comnenus. Wolff, "The Three Romes," p. 297.

64. John Meyendorff, *Byzantium and the Rise of Russia: A Study of Byzantino-Russian Relations in the Fourteenth Century* (Cambridge: Cambridge University Press, 1981), 226.

65. Nikolai Voronin, *Vladimir, Bogolyubovo, Suzdal, Yuryev-Polskoi: Old Russian Towns*, trans. Kathleen Cook (Moscow: Progress Publishers, 1971), 20.

66. PSRL III (Novg. I), p. 81 (1342). See Rubtsov, *History*, 21, 323, no. 56.

67. PSRL X (Nikon.), p. 217 (1346); PSRL VII (Voskr.), p. 210 (1346). Why a foreman named Boris would carry the sobriquet "Rimlianin" (the Roman) is difficult to explain. A native Italian artisan would not be expected to be named Boris unless he had changed his name after arriving in Russia and embracing Russian Orthodoxy. Ivan Zabelin, however, believes that Boris was Italian and regards his presence in Moscow in the 1340s as an early instance of that great influx of Italian artisans to Russia during the last quarter of the fifteenth century (*Istoriia goroda Moskvy*, pt. 1, 2d ed. [Moscow: Tip.-litografiia N. N. Kushnerev, 1905], 152; see also V. A. Bogusevich, "Litejnyj master Mikhail Andreev," *Novgorodskij istoricheskij sbornik*, issue 2 [1937], 91). Rybakov believes that this Boris may have been a foundryman from western Russia, where influences of the Roman Catholic Church were strong, or that he may have learned his founding art in "Roman" (Roman Catholic) regions (*Remeslo drevnej Rusi*, 602 n. 25). Cf. M. N. Tikhomirov who states that this "Borisko" was either Russian or from a south Slavic region, perhaps Bulgaria (*Drevnaia Moskva [XII-XV v.v.]* [Moscow: Izd. MGU, 1947], 122). Only the Nikonovskaia Chronicle transmits the sobriquet "Rimlianin."

68. PSRL V (Pskov. II), p. 23 (1420). Cf. Rubtsov, *History*, 359, no. 109. Pskov had first sought assistance from German artisans.

69. "In Novgorod the Great veche bells ring." (Roman Jakobson and Dean S. Worth, eds., *Sofonija's Tale of the Russian-Tatar Battle on the Kulikovo Field* [The Hague: Mouton & Co., 1963], 30, verse 21). The number of bells founded in Novgorod and the volume of their collective zvon may have indeed been considerable by the beginning of the fifteenth century. Ghillebert de Lannoy reports that when he visited Novgorod in 1413 there were 350 churches in that city ("Voyages et ambassades [1399-1450]," in *Oeuvres de Ghillebert de Lannoy*, ed. Charles Potvin [Louvain: Imprimerie de P. et J. Lefever, 1878], 33).

70. PSRL IV (Novg. IV), p. 89 (1382). The devastation of Moscow in 1382 was Khan Tokhtamysh's revenge for the Mongol defeat at Kulikovo Pole two years before.

71. For information on the introduction of artillery and the founding of heavy weapons in Russia during the last quarter of the fourteenth century, see Rubtsov, *History*, 25-29; A. P. Lebedianskaia, "Ocherki iz istorii pushechnogo proizvodstva

v moskovskoj Rusi," in *Sbornik issledovanij i materialov Artillerijskogo istoricheskogo muzeia Krasnoj armii* 1 (1940): 58-59; and Artsikhovskij, "Oruzhie," 411-412.

72. A. V. Artsikhovskij, "Oruzhie," *Ocherki russkoj kul'tury XIII-XV vekov*, pt. 1: Material'naia kul'tura (Moscow: Izd. Moskovskogo universiteta, 1969), 411-412. James H. Billington discusses the relationship between cannon and bell in *The Icon and the Axe* (New York: Alfred A. Knopf, 1966), 37-43.

73. A violent anti-Mongol uprising put down at Tver in 1327 only strengthened Moscow's position, however (Basil Dmytryshyn, ed., *Medieval Russia: A Source Book, 900-1700*, 2d ed. [Hinsdale, IL: The Dryden Press, 1973], 151).

74. PSRL XV (Tversk.), cols. 470-471 (1403). Pavel Stroev, ed., *Sofijskij vremennik″ ili ruskaia lětopis' s″ 862 po 1534 god″*, pt. 2 (1425–1534) (Moscow: Tip. Semena Selivanovskago, 1821), 201 (1478). "Blagovestnik" is a bell on which *blagovest* is sounded as a call to services.

Earlier the voice of a veche bell that Prince Aleksandr Vasil'evich of Suzdal (1327-1332) had ordered brought back to Vladimir had been described as "pleasing to God" (*boguugoden″*) (Akademiia nauk SSSR, Institut istorii, *Novgorodskaia pervaia lětopis' starshego i mladshego izvodov* [Moscow: Izd. Akad. nauk SSSR, 1950; reprint ed., Slavistic Printings and Reprintings, no. 216, ed. C. H. van Schooneveld, The Hague: Mouton, 1969], 469 [appendix 2]).

75. N. P. Likhachev, ed., *Inoka Thomy Slovo pokhval'noe o blagověrnom″ velikom″ kniazě Borisě Aleksandrovichě*, Pamiatniki drevnej pis'mennosti i iskusstva 168 (St. Petersburg: Tip. M. A. Aleksandrova, 1908), 46. In the fifteenth century Tver also possessed the most advanced artillery among Russian towns (Artsikhovskij, "Oruzhie," 412).

76. Juri Keldysch (Iurij Keldysh), *Geschichte der russischen Musik* 1 (Leipzig: Breitkopf & Härtel Musikverlag, 1956), 76; and Zabelin, *Istoriia goroda Moskvy*, 134. M. Tolstoj, *Sviatyni i drevnosti velikogo Novgoroda*, Russkiia sviatyni i drevnosti, pt. 3 (Moscow: Universitetskaia tip., 1862), 67. The Novgorod veche was first mentioned in 1016. Though a veche convened in towns and cities throughout Kievan Russia, the veche lasted longer at Novgorod (until 1478) and Pskov (until 1510) and was more influential in these two cities. At the sound of the Novgorod veche bell, the assembly convened either within the Yaroslav Court or in the square before the Cathedral of St. Sophia (V. Alekseev, *Narodovlastie v″ drevnej Rusi* [Rostov-on-Don: Izd. "Donskaia Rech'," 1904], 23). The Pskov assembly had its own bell.

77. In 1510 Vasilij III conquered Pskov and abolished its veche. In relocating some two hundred Pskovian families in Moscow, he also took the veche bell from the bell tower of Pskov's Trinity Cathedral. Eight years later he is reported to have sent a large bell to Pskov to replace the veche bell he had taken.

78. Arthur Voyce, *The Art and Architecture of Medieval Russia* (Norman, OK: University of Oklahoma Press, 1967), 105. In 1551 Ivan IV proposed to introduce polyphonic liturgical singing from Novgorod to Moscow (N. Uspenskij, *Obraztsy drevnerusskogo pevcheskogo iskusstva*, 2d ed., enl. [Leningrad: Izd. "Muzyka," 1971], 142).

79. A chronicle entry from 1478 states that this bell was hung on a square in Moscow and rung with the other Kremlin bells (PSRL VIII [Voskres.], p. 199 [1478]). There is speculation that the veche bell was hung in a small structure called the Tsarskij or Storozhevoj (Watch) Tower on top of the Kremlin wall not far from the Spasskij Gate, the main entrance to the Kremlin from Red Square. According to Pyliaev, the veche bell hung here before the same structure was used for the Moscow alarm (*nabatnyj*) bell. (Pyliaev, "Istoricheskie kolokola," 289.)

A legend also grew up around the removal of a Novgorod veche bell to Moscow in 1570 to explain the rise of the manufacture of small bells at Valdaj. According to this legend, Ivan IV was transporting the bell to Moscow when it broke at Valdaj halfway on its journey, whereupon enterprising citizens in the town gathered the fragments and began to cast small bells from them. As we have seen, however, the veche bell of Novgorod had actually been seized and brought to Moscow by Ivan III early in 1478, and the small bell industry at Valdaj did not emerge until the eighteenth century. (K. K. Sluchevskij, *Po severu Rossii: puteshestvie Ikh″ Imperatorskikh″ Vysochestv″ Velikago Kniazia Vladimira Aleksandrovicha i Velikoj Kniagini Marii Pavlovny v″ 1884 i 1885 godakh″*, 1 [St. Petersburg: Tip. Ėduarda Goppe, 1886], 141.) See also Sluchevskij's poem "Novgorodskoe predanie" based on this legend. (*Stikhotvoreniia i poėmy*, Biblioteka poėta, Bol'shaia seriia, 2d ed. [Moscow-Leningrad: Sovetskij pisatel', 1962], 175, note on 426.)

80. R. G. Skrynnikov, *Ivan Groznyj* (Moscow: Izd. "Nauka," 1975), 158.

81. Pavel Iakushkin, *Putevyia pis'ma iz″ novogorodskoj i pskovskoj gubernij*, ed. D. E. Kozhichikov (St. Petersburg: Tip. Torgovago doma S. Strugovshchikova, G. Pokhitonova, N. Vodova i Ko., 1860), 97-98; I. M. Snegirev, "Moskovskij Tsar'-kolokol″," *Russkiia dostopamiatnosti* 3 (1880): 26; and I. I. Vasil'ev, *Arkheologicheskij ukazatel' g. Pskova i ego okrestnostej* (St. Petersburg: Tip. I. N. Skorokhodova, 1898), 41.

82. PSRL XII (Nikon.), p. 157 (1475). See Nicholas V. Riasanovsky, *A History of Russia*, 3d ed. (New York: Oxford University Press, 1977), 141-142. Ivan III dispatched subsequent recruiting missions to Italy in 1488, 1493, and 1499 (Arthur Voyce, *The Moscow Kremlin: Its History, Architecture, and Art Treasures* [Berkeley: University of California Press, 1954], 19).

83. Mention of Ridolfo Fioravanti (or Fieravanti) degli Albertini of Bologna, frequently called Aristotle Fioravanti because of his vast fund of knowledge, first appears in an Italian chronicle under the year 1436. Before coming to Moscow, he had worked in Bologna, Cento, and Venice.

84. Riasanovsky, *A History of Russia*, 141. Using church architecture in the Vladimir region as the model, Fioravanti

built a new Cathedral of the Assumption (Uspenskij sobor) between 1475 and 1479. From 1484 to 1489 architects and builders from Pskov constructed the Cathedral of the Annunciation (Blagoveshchenskij sobor). And Alevisio Novi of Milan designed and built the Cathedral of the Archangel Michael (Arkhangel'skij sobor) between 1505 and 1509. The rulers of Russia were married in the Cathedral of the Annunciation, they were crowned in the Cathedral of the Assumption (even after St. Petersburg had been established as a second capital), and the grand dukes and tsars of Moscow were interred in the Cathedral of the Archangel Michael. (Riasanovsky, *A History of Russia*, 142; also 141.) The Palace of Facets (Granovitaia palata), which Pietro Solario and Marco Ruffo designed, was built between 1487 and 1491.

85. N. I. Fal'kovskij, *Moskva v istorii tekhniki* (Moscow: Moskovskij rabochij, 1950), 254; and E. I. Zaozerskaia, *U istokov krupnogo proizvodstva v russkoj promyshlennosti XVI-XVII vekov* (Moscow: Izd. "Nauka," 1970), 240. The site of the Moscow Cannon Yard would be in the vicinity of Dzerzhinskij Square and Pushkin Street in contemporary Moscow. For a study on its location and plan, see P. Sytin, "Pushechnyj dvor v Moskve v XV-XIX v.v.," *Moskovskij kraeved* 2 (1929): 7-20. Besides bells, cannon, and mortars, the Moscow Cannon Yard also manufactured church chandeliers and gates, bronze doors, candlesticks, and kettles.

86. Although cannon founders (*pushechniki*) are generally distinguished in sources from bell founders (*kolokol'niki*), a distinction in their duties was not always observed in practice. "Cannon men" often produced bells, and "bell men" also cast artillery as well as such smaller articles as crosses and encolpions. An inscription on the bell of 1488 for the Borovskij Pafnut'ev Monastery states that its founder was a cannon foreman named Fed'ko (Orlov, *Bibliografiia*, 147, no. 244 [1487]; cf. Fetter, "Drevnosti Pafnut'eva monastyria," p. 598 for the correct date of the bell's founding). Among the first weapons cast at the Moscow Cannon Shop were a harquebus of 1483 and a cannon of 1485, both the work of a Russian foreman known only as Iakov (Rubtsov, *History*, 457, no. 489).

87. Zabelin, *Istoriia goroda Moskvy*, 153. There are reports that a copper smelting plant built on the Tsil'ma was abandoned once the ore had been exhausted (Rubtsov, *History*, 225).

88. In 1480 the Mongol army under Khan Ahmed withdrew from the banks of the Ugra River southwest of Moscow without engaging the Russians in a conflict. Mongol raids persisted during the sixteenth century, but after this retreat and Ivan III's declaration of independence, the Mongols were powerless to impede the growing authority of the Muscovite state. See J. L. I. Fennell's comments on the events of 1480 in *Ivan the Great* (London: Macmillan, 1961), 86-88.

Notes to Chapter 5

1. Ivan Zakharovich Krylov, *Istoricheskoe opisanie vsekh"*

koronatsij velikikh" kniazej i tsarej rossijskikh" (Moscow: Universitetskaia tip., 1856), 33.

2. Bell founding in sixteenth-century Russia flourished principally in Pskov, Novgorod, and Moscow (Rubtsov, *History*, 34, 36, 38).

3. A. I. Semenov, "Novgorodskie i pskovskie litejshchiki XVI-XVII vekov," *Sbornik Novgorodskogo obshchestva liubitelej drevnostej* 9 (1928): 3; and M. N. Tikhomirov, *Rossiia v XVI stoletii* (Moscow: Izd. Akad. nauk, SSSR, 1962), 338. In Western Europe bell founding had passed from the hands of clerics in the thirteenth century to families of laymen who carefully guarded their professional secrets (Price, "Bell," 435).

4. In 1557 Pskov foremen founded a bell of 170 puds (6,139 pounds) for the Solovetskij Monastery and six years earlier an even larger bell of 400 puds (14,445 pounds) for the Kirillo-Belozerskij Monastery (V. A. Bogusevich, "Pskovskie litejshchiki XVI-XVIII vv.," *Problemy istorii dokapitalisticheskikh obshchestv*, no. 9-10 [1934], p. 158).

5. Semenov, "Novgorodskie i pskovskie litejshchiki," 3; V. A. Bogusevich, "Litejnyj master Mikhail Andreev," *Novgorodskij istoricheskij sbornik*, issue 2 (1937), 87; and Rubtsov, *History*, 309-312. The inscriptions on the two bells that Mikhail, Anufrij, and Maksim Andreev founded for the Spaso-Mirozhskij Monastery in 1520 and 1521 are published in Vasil'ev, *Arkheologicheskij ukazatel'*, 67. In addition to the Andreevs, other prominent families engaged in founding at Pskov included the Mikhajlovs, the Grigor'evs, the Ivanovs, and at the very end of the century, the Matveevs. For a chronological table of bell founders and dates of their work from Pskov, Novgorod, and Moscow reported in Rubtsov, see Appendix A.

6. Bogusevich, "Litejnyj master Mikhail Andreev," 88-89. If Andreev were twenty-five to thirty years old when he began casting in Pskov, he would have been born about 1490, around the time that the Moscow Cannon Yard was established. His last known work is a bell of 1551, a project in which he was assisted by his own sons, Matvej and Kuz'ma (ibid., 90). According to Bogusevich, three bells of Mikhail Andreev were still preserved at Pskov in 1937 (ibid., 85 n. 1).

7. PSRL III (Novg. III), p. 248 (1530); and PSRL III (Novg. II), p. 148 (1530). See epigraph to the preface for my translation of this passage.

8. Bogusevich, "Litejnyj master Mikhail Andreev," 91.

9. Tikhomirov, *Rossiia v XVI stoletii*, 305; and A. I. Semenov, "Novgorodskie litejnye i oruzhejnye masterskie v XV-XVI vv.," *Sbornik issledovanij i materialov Artillerijskogo istoricheskogo muzeia Krasnoj armii* 1 (1940), 240.

10. Rubtsov, *History*, 375, no. 175. For this bell's inscription, see Archimandrite Makarij, *Arkheologicheskoe opisanie tserkovnykh" drevnostej v" Novgorodě i ego okrestnostiakh"*, pt. 2 (Moscow: Tip. V. Got'e, 1860), 280.

11. Makarij, Archbishop of Khar'kov, *Istoriia russkoj tserkvi v" period" razděleniia eia na dvě mitropolii* 8 (St. Petersburg: Tip. Iu. A. Bokrama, 1877), 26. In his list of Novgorod bells Makarij accounts for five sixteenth-century Novgorod bells that

are cited in chronicles, and no fewer than sixteen bells from that century that were still extant at Novgorod in the mid-nineteenth century (*Arkheologicheskoe opisanie*, 278-285).

12. Semenov, "Novgorodskie . . . masterskie," 240; and Semenov, "Novgorodskie i pskovskie litejshchiki," 5, 7. Semen Leont'ev (fl. 1682-1720) was a foreman and gifted cannon founder at the Moscow Cannon Yard; in 1714 he was placed in charge of cannon production at the newly established cannon yard in St. Petersburg (Rubtsov, *History*, 401-403, no. 284).

13. PSRL III (Novg. III), p. 254 (1570).

14. Ibid. From December 1564 to 1572 Ivan IV's residence was in the small town of Aleksandrov, about seventy miles northeast of Moscow.

15. Tikhomirov, *Rossiia v XVI stoletii*, 84. Even at the beginning of the sixteenth century founders working in Moscow had adopted certain technological innovations in their production of cannon that were not being used everywhere in the West, and by mid-century Moscow's artillery was probably among the finest in Europe. (P. P. Epifanov, "Oruzhie i snariazhenie," *Ocherki russkoj kul'tury XVI veka*, pt. 1: Material'naia kul'tura, ed. A. V. Artsikhovskij [Moscow: Izd. Moskovskogo universiteta, 1977], 300; and Rubtsov, *History*, 35.)

16. Rubtsov, *History*, 57. Rubtsov publishes no figures on the number of foremen, foundrymen, apprentices, and assistants in the Moscow Cannon Yard during the reign of Ivan IV.

17. On occasion, Muscovite foremen had assisted founders at Pskov, and in the seventeenth century Nikifor Baranov was sent to Novgorod from Moscow to cast a bell of 1,000 puds (36,113 pounds) (ibid., 34, 57). In 1689 Flor Terent'ev, a Muscovite, was sent to Rostov-Velikij and Pskov to cast bells (N. N. Rubtsov, "Moskovskie litejshchiki XIV-XVII vv.," *Vestnik mashinostroeniia*, no. 11 [1947], p. 69).

18. A. G. Levshin, *Istoricheskoe opisanie pervoprestol'nago v" Rossii khrama* (Moscow: Tip. u Mejera, 1783), 249. Makarij believes that the year 1501 on "Medved' " is probably an error in the inscription from the recasting of 1775. He poses the question whether "Medved' " could be a recasting of the 500-pud Pimen bell that Ivan IV had taken from Novgorod to Aleksandrov in 1570. (*Istoriia russkoj tserkvi*, 27 n. 33.) Rubtsov lists two different bell foremen named Ivan Afanas'ev, a founder from Novgorod who cast "Medved' " in 1501 and a Muscovite founder active between 1587 and 1599 (Rubtsov, *History*, 307, nos. 2 and 3).

19. Zabelin, *Istoriia goroda Moskvy*, 154; I. M. Snegirev, *Pamiatniki moskovskoj drevnosti* (Moscow: Tip. A. Semena, 1842-1845), 110; and N. M. Karamzin, *Istoriia gosudarstva rossijskago* 6, 5th ed. (St. Petersburg: Tip. Éduarda Pratsa, 1842), col. 104 (1503). If the tin content in this bell is calculated at 20 percent, the bell's total weight would be about 438 puds (15,817 pounds). Petr Friazin, a Milanese founder, was active in Moscow from 1494 to 1505 and was among the European foremen who followed Fioravanti in Russia. (Rubtsov, *History*, 440, no. 389.)

20. A. A. Martynov, "Moskovskie kolokola," *Russkij arkhiv"* 34, nos. 1 and 2 (1896), p. 103; and Karamzin, *Istoriia* 7, col. 63 (1532). Cf. Rubtsov, *History*, 426, no. 366.

21. PSRL XIII (Nikon.), p. 72 (1533); PSRL VIII (Voskres.), p. 284 (1533); Zabelin, *Istoriia goroda Moskvy*, 154. The name *Tsar'-kolokol"* (Tsar Bell) was first applied to the 1,000-pud bell that Nemchin cast in 1533 (Petr Ivanov, *Istoricheskiia svěděniia o bol'shom" kolokolě, lezhashchem" v" M. Kremlě, bliz" Ivanovskoj kolokol'ni* [Moscow: Universitetskaia tip., 1835], 11).

22. "Friazin" was a name often given to foreign workers in Muscovite Russia who were natives of southern European (Roman Catholic) regions bordering the Mediterranean, especially Italy, and "Nemchin," a name given to foreign workers from northern and western (Protestant) Europe. In the sixteenth century the latter designation included, but was not limited to, Germans.

23. Martynov, "Moskovskie kolokola," 103. According to Martynov's note, "Lebed' " was subsequently broken and recast in 1775 during the reign of Catherine II. Evidently the inscription from the bell of 1532 was transferred to the bell of 1775 and thereby preserved.

24. Makarij, *Istoriia russkoj tserkvi*, 26.

25. Rubtsov, *History*, 327.

26. A. P. Pronshtejn and A. G. Zadera, "Remeslo," *Ocherki russkoj kul'tury XVI veka*, pt. 1: Material'naia kul'tura, ed. A. V. Artsikhovskij (Moscow: Izd. Moskovskogo universiteta, 1977), 112-113. Kashpir Ganusov cast numerous cannon and harquebuses for the tsar's army in the late 1550s and 1560s; Andrej Chokhov's manufacture of cannon dates from 1568 and dominates the founding of weapons in Moscow from the 1570s until 1629. (Rubtsov, *History*, 387-390, no. 228; 324-339, no. 64.)

27. Raffaello Barberini, "Relatione di Moscovia," in A. Olearius, *Viaggi di Moscovia de gli anni 1633, 1634, 1635, e 1636* (Viterbo, 1658), 196. Some visitors in the nineteenth century reported that the sound of bell ringing in Moscow was "absolutely painful to the ear, and prove[d] an effectual check to conversation on the streets" (Meneely & Kimberly, *Church, Academy, Tower-Clock, Factory, Chime, Court-House, Fire-Alarm, and Other Bells* [Troy, NY: Meneely & Kimberly, 1878], 34). There is no mention of bells or bell ringing, however, in two important earlier reports on Muscovy: by Ambrosio Contarini, who visited Moscow *circa* 1476, and Baron Sigismund von Herberstein, who was there in 1517 and again in 1526. Apparently the zvon in Moscow before about 1530 was not yet remarkable enough to attract their attention.

28. Heinrich von Staden, *The Land and Government of Muscovy: A Sixteenth-Century Account*, trans. and ed. Thomas Esper (Stanford, CA: Stanford University Press, 1967), 47.

29. *The Travels of Sir Jerome Horsey*, Russia at the Close of the Sixteenth Century, ed. Edward A. Bond (London: The Hakluyt Society, 1856), 208; Giles Fletcher, *Of the Russe Commonwealth*, Russia at the Close of the Sixteenth Century,

ed. Edward A. Bond (London: The Hakluyt Society, 1856), 118.

30. Tikhomirov, *Rossiia v XVI stoletii*, 84. For studies on Chokhov and his work, see Rubtsov, "Andrej Chokhov," 18-25; N. N. Rubtsov, "Znamenityj 'litets' Andrej Chokhov," *Litejnoe proizvodstva*, no. 4 (1951), pp. 22-25; and E. L. Nemirovskij's study of his weapons, "Novye materialy ob Andree Chokhove," in *Trudy Instituta istorii estestvoznaniia i tekhniki* 13 (Istoriia mashinostroeniia i transporta) (Moscow: Izd. Akad. nauk SSSR, 1956), 51-66. Nemirovskij places Chokhov's death between January 23 and December 8, 1629 ("Novye materialy," 65).

31. Chokhov apparently served Dmitri I (the first False Dmitri); he named his mortar dated September 27, 1605, "Samozvanets" (the Pretender). He may also have worked for Vasilij IV Shujskij (1606-1610), though no examples or records of his work survives from these years.

32. Kashpir Ganusov, a Belorussian or Livonian founder, was probably among those whom Ivan IV relocated in Moscow during the Livonian War in the 1560s and 1570s (Rubtsov, *History*, 387-388, no. 228).

33. Chokhov's "Drobovik" should not be confused with the large cannon Tsar-Pushka that Paolo Debosis cast a century earlier in 1488. Chokhov's other noteworthy cannons include "Akhiles" (1617) and "Troil" (1590). (Rubtsov, "Znamenityj 'litets,' " 23-24.)

34. "Chokhov (Chekhov) Andrej," *Bol'shaia sovetskaia ėntsiklopediia* 29 (1978), 234. Other outstanding Muscovite founders of the sixteenth century include Ganusov, a foreman named Ignatij, and Ivan Afanas'ev.

35. A. Dmitrievskij, *Arkhiepiskop" elassonskij Arsenij i memuary ego iz" russkoj istorii* (Kiev: Tip. Imp. universiteta sv. Vladimira, 1899), 97. For details on Chokhov's casting of the Godunov Bell, see Chapter 11 in this volume.

36. Rubstov, "Andrej Chokhov," 24. The bell's name "Reut" is thought to come from the Reut River in the Kursk province (Snegirev, *Pamiatniki moskovskoj drevnosti*, 113 n. 15). On the basis of the bell's sound, "Reut" has also been explained as a derivative from *revun* (howler, roarer) (Arthur Voyce, *The Moscow Kremlin: Its History, Architecture, and Art Treasures* [Berkeley: University of California Press, 1954], 134 n. 16).

37. Ivan Zabelin, "Dopolneniia k" dvortsovym" razriadam" po porucheniiu grafa Dmitriia Nikolaevicha Bludova, sobrannyia iz" knig" i stolbtsov" prezhdebyvshikh" dvortsovykh" prikazov" arkhiva oruzhejnoj palaty," *Chteniia v" Imperatorskom" obshchestvě istorii i drevnostej rossijskikh" pri Moskovskom" universitetě*, bk. 3 (July-September 1882), col. 291 (March 1622).

38. Another source gives the bell's weight as 19 puds, 26 funts (710 pounds) (G. P. Dem'ianov, *Illiustrirovannyj putevoditel' po Volgě 1898 g. [ot" Tveri do Astrakhani]*, 4th ed. by M. V. Kliukin [Nizhnij-Novgorod: Tip. Gubernskago pravleniia, 1898], 79). The thickness of the bell's wall (presumably at its sound-bow) is 1.5 vershki (almost 2.66 inches) and its lower circumference is 3 arshins, 12 vershki (8.75 feet) (Vasilij

Serebrianikov, "Ssyl'nyj uglichskij kolokol" v" Tobol'skě," *Moskovskiia vědomosti*, no. 98 [Tuesday, August 17, 1854], p. 414, middle col.).

39. George Vernadsky, "The Death of Tsarevich Dimitry: A Reconsideration of the Case," *Oxford Slavonic Papers* 5, ed. S. Konovalov (Oxford: At the Clarendon Press, 1954), 3. In Uglich the *d'iak* (secretary) Bitiagovskij served the tsar as supervisor of the district financial administration and controller of the Uglich palace estate.

40. Ian Grey, *Boris Godunov, the Tragic Tsar* (London: Hodder and Stoughton, 1973), 115; R. G. Skrynnikov, *Boris Godunov* (Moscow: Izd. "Nauka," 1978), 74. "The Commission made special efforts to establish who had ordered the tocsin [alarm] to be sounded, but obtained no definite answer. Mikhail Nagoy asserted that he heard the tocsin at the palace and rushed to the yard because of it. Vasilisa Volokhova, on the other hand, said that the tocsin started when the Tsaritsa and her brothers were already in the yard. A *stryapchiy* [officer] of the *Kormovoy Dvorets* (Food Department), Subota Protopopov, testified that Mikhail Nagoy ordered him to tell the sexton, Feodot Ogurets, to sound the bell. The sexton said that before he could have reached the Church of the Saviour, the church janitor, Maksim Kuznetsov, had already begun to sound the alarm." (Vernadsky, "Death of the Tsarevich Dimitry," 18 n. 1.) In all probability there were two alarms rung, separated by a short interval. Kuznetsov, who lived at the church, rang the first alarm, which brought the Nagois and Ogurets running into the courtyard. Because Kuznetsov's alarm was not strong enough, Ogurets presumably climbed into the tower and began ringing the bell again. His louder blows on the bell drew the citizens of Uglich, who expected to find a fire (Vladimir Klejn, *Uglichskoe slědstvennoe dělo o smerti tsarevicha Dimitriia, 15-go maia 1591 goda*, pt. 1: Diplomaticheskoe izslědovanie podlinnika, Zapiski Imperatorskago moskovskago arkheologicheskago instituta imeni imperatora Nikolaia II, 25, ed. A. I. Uspenskij [Moscow: Pechatnia A. Snegirevoj, 1913], 90-92).

41. George Vernadsky, *The Tsardom of Moscow, 1547-1682*, pt. 1, A History of Russia, vol. 5 (New Haven: Yale University Press, 1969), 196-197; Skrynnikov, *Boris Godunov*, 84; and Grey, *Boris Godunov*, 118.

The best study of the proceedings of the investigation of Dmitrij's death is Klejn, *Uglichskoe slědstvennoe dělo*. Accounts of the tragedy and its subsequent investigation and testimonies are also published in Thedor Kissel', *Istoriia goroda Uglicha* (Yaroslavl: Gubernskaia tip., 1844), 237-288; and in *Zhitie sviatago Dimitriia Tsarevicha*, Obshchestvo liubitelej drevnej pis'mennosti i iskusstva 36 (St. Petersburg: M. M. Osipova, 1879), 15-16. For more recent interpretations of these events, see S. F. Platonov, *Boris Godunov, Tsar of Russia*, trans. L. Rex Pyles, The Russian Series 10 (Gulf Breeze, FL: Academic International Press, 1973), 125-152; Vernadsky, "Death of the Tsarevich Dimitry," 1-19; Grey, *Boris Godunov*, 112-119; Skrynnikov, *Boris Godunov* 67-84; and Ol'ga

Berggol'ts, "Pokhod za nevskuiu zastavu," in *Dnevnye zvezdy* (Leningrad: Sovetskij pisatel', 1971), 182-187. The investigating commission that Vasilij Shuiskij headed, after weighing the evidence, declared that the death of the tsarevich had been accidental and occurred when Dmitrij, during an epileptic seizure, fell on the knife he was holding. Pushkin's play and Musorgsky's opera, however, are both predicated upon Boris' instigation of the murder of Dmitrij and explore the psychological dimensions of his alleged guilt and remorse.

42. Berggol'ts, "Pokhod," 184. See also Rybakov, *Tserkovnyj zvon"*, 26; and I. A. Kovalev and I. B. Purishev, *Uglich: putevoditel' po gorodu i okrestnostiam*, 2d ed. (Yaroslavl: Verkhne-volzhskoe knizhnoe izd., 1971), 10-11. And see N. R., "O kolokolakh" i o kolokol'nom" iskusstvě," *Moskovskiia vědomosti* 51 (Saturday, April 29, 1850), 587, middle col.

43. Serebrianikov, "Ssyl'nyj uglichskij kolokol"," 414, lefthand col.; and Victor and Jennifer Louis, *The Complete Guide to the Soviet Union* (New York: St. Martin's Press, 1976), 310. In addition to the exiled bell from Uglich, a number of other bells called *plěnnye* (captive) were also condemned to Siberia. Most of these bells were taken from Poland with Polish prisoners who had been sent to towns in Siberia. (N. R., "O kolokolakh"," 587, middle col.)

44. Rybakov, *Tserkovnyj zvon"*, 26; Serebrianikov, "Ssyl'nyj uglichskij kolokol"," 414, middle col.; and I. M. Snegirev, "Moskovskij Tsar'-kolokol"," *Russkiia dostopamiatnosti* 3 (1880), 26 n. 25.

45. Dem'ianov, *Illiustrirovannyj putevoditel'*, 79.

46. George Kennan, *Siberia and the Exile System* 2 (New York: The Century Co., 1891; reprint ed., New York: Russell & Russell, 1970), 420-422.

47. Dem'ianov, *Illiustrirovannyj putevoditel'*, 79-80. In the mid-nineteenth century several Russian publications suggested that the bell in Tobol'sk might not be the original Uglich bell at all but a recasting of it (Serebrianikov, "Ssyl'nyj uglichskij kolokol"," 413, righthand col.). For an account of these deliberations, see "Ssyl'nyj kolokol"," *Istoricheskij věstnik"* 34, no. 10 (October 1888), pp. 255-256. In his guide to Russia, Karl Baedeker, without further explanation or details, wrote that the bell was "an eighteenth-century reproduction" of the original bell, which had melted in a fire at Tobol'sk in 1677 (*Russia with Teheran, Port Arthur, and Peking: Handbook for Travellers* [Leipzig: Karl Baedeker, 1914; reprint ed., New York: Arno Press & The New York Times, 1970], 349). According to Serebrianikov, however, there is no evidence, not even a suggestion, to support this assertion ("Ssyl'nyj uglichskij kolokol"," 414, middle col.).

48. Berggol'ts, *Dnevnye zvezdy*, 184-186.

49. *Warhafftige Relation der reussischen und muscowitischen Reyse und Einzug dess durchleuchtigen hochgebornen Fürsten und Herren, Herren Hertzog Johansen dess Jüngern auss königlichem Stamm Dennemarck . . .* (Magdeburg: Johan Francken, 1604), 9-10. Cf. Baron Korf, "Prints" datskij Ioan" v" Rossii," *Sěvernyj arkhiv"*, no. 8 (April 1822), 89-90.

50. Petrus Petrejus, "Istoriia o velikom" kniazhestvě mo-skovskom"," in *Chteniia v" Imperatorskom" obshchestvě istorii i drevnostej rossijskikh" pri Moskovskom" universitetě*, bk. 4 (1865), 5-6. On p. 646 of the German edition (*Historien und Berichte von dem Gross-fürstenthumb Muschkow* [Leipzig, 1620]) the figures vary somewhat—from a minimum of two or three bells to a maximum of six, seven, ten and twelve bells.

51. "Kakash" i Tektander": Puteshestvie v" Persiiu cherez" Moskoviiu 1602-1603 gg.," trans. from German by A. I. Stankevich, *Chteniia v" Imperatorskom" obshchestvě istorii i drevnostej rossijskikh"*, bk. 2 (1896), 18. In 1917 there were approximately 520 churches in Moscow. With a projected average of eight bells per church the number of bells in the city at that time would have been over 4,000. (*Sredniaia Rossiia s poslesloviem "Prodely vandalisma"* [Frankfurt/Main: Possev-Verlag, 1980], appendix 1.)

52. Petrejus, "Istoriia," 6.

53. Joseph T. Fuhrmann, *The Origins of Capitalism in Russia: Industry and Progress in the Sixteenth and Seventeenth Centuries* (Chicago: Quadrangle Books, 1972), 52. Annual rate of production at the Moscow Cannon Yard during the seventeenth century is difficult to determine. Small alarm bells and church bells were cast quickly; on the other hand the founding of a great bell could require at least a year's work, and producing a large cannon occupied workers up to eighteen months. (V. G. Gejman and N. V. Ustiugov," "Manufaktura," *Ocherki istorii SSSR*, [vol. 4:] Period feodalizma XVII v. [Moscow: Akademiia nauk, 1955], 94.) Though the Time of Troubles (*Smutnoe vremia*) in Russia has been viewed in its broadest extent from the death of Ivan IV in 1584 until about 1618, the period cited here begins with the accession of Boris Godunov in 1598 and concludes with the establishment of the Romanov dynasty in 1613.

54. Rubtsov, *History*, 45-46, 225-226. See also Vernadsky, *The Tsardom of Moscow*, pt. 1, pp. 303-304; pt. 2, pp. 668-669; and Gejman and Ustiugov, "Manufaktura," 87.

55. Rubtsov, *History*, 226-227.

56. I. M. Snegirev, *Pamiatniki drevniago khudozhestva v" Rossii* (Moscow: Tip. Vědomostej Moskovskoj gorodskoj politsii, 1850), 37.

57. Rubtsov, *History*, 57. Cf. S. Bogoiavlenskij, "O Pushkarskom" prikazě," *Sbornik" statej v" chest' Matvěia Kuz'micha Liubavskago* (Petrograd: Tip. B. D. Brukera, 1917), 371, 373.

58. Among the Russian monasteries where bell casting was carried out in the seventeenth century were the Holy Trinity Monastery (Trinity-Sergius Lavra), the New Jerusalem Monastery, and the Solovetskij Monastery. At the New Jerusalem Monastery two monks named Sergej and Paisij became accomplished founders (Rubtsov, *History*, 438, no. 380; 448-449, no. 428). In a letter that Bishop Ivan of Rostov-Velikij sent to a friend, he discloses: "Do you want to know what . . . I do, then listen: I cast bells in my yard, and the people wonder at it" (Rubtsov, *History*, 37 n. 9).

59. As late as the 1670s, however, Moscow foremen still had to travel considerable distances from the capital to cast bells on the spot. In 1674 Khariton Ivanov and four of his students

were sent to Kazan to recast three bells that had melted there in a fire. They returned to Moscow only in the fall of 1676. (Rubtsov, *History*, 380.)

60. Rubtsov has examined and pubished materials pertaining to Russian founding in the seventeenth century from various archives in the Institute of the History of the USSR, Academy of Sciences, Leningrad Branch. His study of founding practices and publication of selected documents are contained in *History*, esp. pp. 36-39, 49-59, 73-82, and 307-462. Information in the text is drawn principally from Rubtsov's pioneering research in these sources.

61. A bell foreman at the Moscow Cannon Yard named Fedor Dmitriev (*sic*), when asked when the mold for recasting a bell for Yaroslavl would be ready, replied that "the bell pattern would be ready by March 1 . . . as it was being prepared at his home" (noted in Rubtsov, *History*, 37).

62. Ibid., 416-417, no. 344.

63. After Chokhov, Aleksej Ekimov (or Iakimov) (fl. 1618-1641) is regarded as the most gifted and experienced bell founder in Russia in the seventeenth century. Others of exceptional ability include Kondratij Mikhajlov (fl. 1590-1629), Grigorij Naumov (fl. 1598-1645), Nikifor Baranov (fl. 1618-1651), Emel'ian Danilov (fl. 1640-1654), and Aleksandr Grigor'ev (fl. 1651-1676).

64. See Part V for the history of the great bells of Moscow founded in the seventeenth and eighteenth centuries.

65. G. Spasskij, "O kolokolakh", dostoprimĕchatel'nykh" po svoej velichinĕ," *Gornyj zhurnal"* 1, no. 1 (January, 1833), p. 136; and L. I. Denisov, *Pravoslavnye monastyri rossijskoj imperii* (Moscow: Izdanie A. D. Stupina, 1908), 478. Some sources erroneously report the weight of Grigor'ev's bell as 2,425 puds 30 funts.

66. Paul of Aleppo, *Puteshestvie antiokhijskago patriarkha Makariia v" Rossiiu v" polovinĕ XVII vĕka*, issue 3, trans. from Arabic by G. Murkos (Moscow: Universitetskaia tip., 1898), 197.

67. The numerous *prikazy* (administrative bureaus or departments) in the structure of the Muscovite state each had a board headed by at least one boyar. One boyar and two secretaries (*d'iaki*) administered the *Pushkarskij prikaz*. Toward the end of the seventeenth century, more than forty *prikazy* oversaw the business of various state interests. (Vernadsky, *History of Russia*, 142-143.) This Cannon Bureau is first mentioned in 1577 as the *Pushechnyj prikaz*. Between 1678 and 1682 the Cannon Bureau was incorporated within the structure of another department, the Cavalry Bureau (*Rejtarskij prikaz*). Then it again became independent for eighteen years. But it was superseded by the Artillery Bureau (*Artillerijskij prikaz*) in 1700. (Bogoiavlenskij, "O Pushkarskom" prikazĕ," 361, 367-369.)

68. Sytin's "Pushechnyj dvor v Moskve v XV-XIX v.v.," 7-20, is a study of the Moscow Cannon Yard, its location and appearance, from the travel reports and city plans of foreign observers.

69. Rubtsov, *History*, 54-55, 59.

70. In 1598-1599 the Moscow Cannon Yard had three foundry foremen (with Andrej Chokhov as senior foreman), two bell foundrymen, and twelve apprentices (Rubtsov, *History*, 73-74). In the 1630s the cannon yard employed more than a hundred workers, and in 1637 personnel numbered one hundred thirty-four: five cannon founders and thirty-seven apprentices, two bell founders and ten apprentices, six foremen for casting church chandeliers and fourteen apprentices, one foreman for melting metal and five apprentices, seven tinsmiths, two sawyers, three workers for moving supplies, fourteen cannon smiths, eight carpenters, and twenty cannon draymen (Bogoiavlenskij, "O Pushkarskom" prikazĕ," 371).

71. Bogoiavlenskij, "O Pushkarskom" prikazĕ," 374-375.

72. As senior foreman, Andrej Chokhov earned an annual salary of 30 rubles (Rubtsov, *History*, 73).

73. Bogoiavlenskij, "O Puskarskom" prikazĕ," 372.

74. Although Russian founders apparently kept no professional secrets from each other, some foreign foremen, such as the German, Hans Falk, would dismiss Russian assistants and apprentices at certain points in the casting process to keep knowledge of his procedures from them. This may partially explain the Russian casters' antipathy toward Falk and the highly competitive attitude that developed in the Moscow Cannon Yard. See B. A. Kolchin, *Metallurgy and Metalworking in Ancient Russia*, trans. from Russian (Jerusalem: Israel Program for Scientific Translations, 1967), 101.

75. Rubtsov, *History*, 74, 80.

76. Kolchin, *Metallurgy*, 102. On apprenticeship in Kievan Russia, see also Tikhomirov, *Towns of Ancient Rus*, 115-116.

77. V. Snegirev, *Moskovskie slobody* (Moscow: Moskovskij rabochij, 1947), 75.

78. In 1684 one apprentice in bell founding received an annual salary of five rubles, but he received this amount only after he had served his stipulated period of apprenticeship. Ibid.

79. N. N. Rubtsov, *Istoriia litejnogo proizvodstva v SSSR*, pt. 1, 2d ed., rev. and enl. (Moscow: Gosudarstvennoe nauchno-tekhnicheskoe izd. mashinostroitel'noj literatury, 1962), 55, my translation.

80. Gejman and Ustiugov, "Manufaktura," 95.

81. Rubtsov, *Istoriia*, 247, my translation.

82. Bogoiavlenskij, "O Pushkarskom" prikazĕ," 372.

83. In 1651 Levka [Leontij] Ivanov was transferred to the state stables to produce horseshoes (Rubtsov, *History*, 382, no. 203).

84. [M. N. Zagoskin,] *The Young Muscovite; or the Poles in Russia*, 2, ed. Captain Frederic Chamier (New York: Harper & Brothers, 1834), 216.

Notes to Chapter 6

1. Rubtsov, *History*, 228; and William L. Blackwell, *The Beginnings of Russian Industrialization, 1800-1860* (Princeton: Princeton University Press, 1968), 17. New plants were established and old ones expanded in the Urals, the Olonets

district, in the White Sea-Onega region, and near Lipetsk and Ustiug. (A. N. Sokolov, *Osnovy litejnogo proizvodstva* [Leningrad: Lenizdat, 1958], 8.)

2. During the battle of Narva, about 8,000 Swedish troops defeated 40,000 Russians (MacKenzie and Curran, *A History of Russia and the Soviet Union*, 187).

3. Rubtsov, *History*, 229-230. Under pressure from the tsar, Motorin cast 113 cannon between 1701 and 1704 (N. N. Rubtsov, "K istorii razvitiia litejnogo proizvodstva v Rossii," *Trudy po istorii tekhniki*, issue 7 [1954], 52).

4. Charles Lord Whitworth, *An Account of Russia as It Was in the Year 1710* (Strawberry-Hill, S. Middlesex, England: Horace Walpole, 1758), 107-108. Apparently not all of the church bells brought to the Moscow Cannon Yard at this time were melted down for recasting as cannon, for in 1734, in order to complete the lower range of the chimes in the Kremlin's Troitskij Gate, Johann Förster selected eight bass bells from among some six hundred that had been gathered in 1701 and were still stored at the state foundry (S. P. Barten'ev, *Moskovskij Kreml': v" starinu i teper'* 1 [Moscow: Sinodal'naia tip., 1912], 164).

5. Rubtsov, *History*, 82.

6. The yearly fluctuation in the manufacture of artillery during the first decade of the eighteenth century is an illustration of how production flow at the Moscow Cannon Yard was never fixed but rose and fell according to orders submitted for certain items (ibid., 64, and 65, table 3).

7. The first bell produced in Russian America (Alaska) is thought to have been cast in 1795 at Kodiak. About fifteen years later a foundry in Sitka began to cast bells for Russian Churches in Alaska (Alfred Mongin, "The Russian Orthodox Churches of Alaska," *Orthodox Alaska* 8, nos. 3 and 4 [December 1979], p. 22).

8. Zernov, *Moscow the Third Rome*, 95.

9. Rubtsov, *History*, 64.

10. M. E. Falkus, *The Industrialisation of Russia, 1700-1914* (London: Macmillan, 1972), 20-21, 23.

11. The St. Petersburg Cannon Yard was built between 1711 and 1713 under the direction of engineer and Lieutenant General Georg Wilhelm de Hennin (1676-1750). Grand Master of Ordnance Jacob Bruce (1670-1735), a Russian of Scottish ancestry, was placed in charge of production at the cannon yard. On its establishment and early production, see E. I. Zaozerskaia, "Manufaktura," in *Ocherki istorii SSSR*, [vol. 5:] *Period feodalizma, Rossiia v pervoj chetverti XVIII v. preobrazovaniia Petra I* (Moscow: Izd. Akademii nauk SSSR, 1954), 96; A. V. Predtechenskij, ed., *Peterburg petrovskogo vremeni* (Leningrad: Leningradskoe gazetno-zhurnal'noe i knizhnoe izd., 1948), 57-59; and Sokolov, *Osnovy litejnogo proizvodstva*, [9].

12. Predtechenskij, *Peterburg*, 58-59.

13. Other Russian founders of distinction who flourished during the reign of Peter I included Iakov Dubinin, Karp Osipov, Iosif Balashevich, Login Zhikharev, and Semen Leont'ev (Olovianishnikov, *Istoriia kolokolov"*, 38).

14. The history of Ivan Motorin's Tsar-Kolokol is presented in Chapter 12 of this volume. Notices on his other works and biographical information appear in N. N. Rubtsov, "Ivan Fedorovich i Mikhail Ivanovich Motoriny," in *Liudi russkoj nauki: tekhnika*, ed. I. V. Kuznetsov (Moscow: Izd. "Nauka," 1965), 26-29; and in Rubtsov, *History*, 417-420, no. 345.

15. In 1687, probably the year Fedor Dmitrievich died, Ksen'ia Motorina gave her stepsons, Ivan and Dmitrij Motorin, a quarter of the family possessions, including the Motorin foundry, located in the parish of St. Sergius the Miracle Worker in Pushkari within that section of Moscow known as the Earthern City (*Zemlianoj gorod*). Fedor Dmitrievich seems to have headed the foundry for only a year. In 1712 the Motorin plant was destroyed in a fire, and several years were required to rebuild it. (Rubtsov, *History*, 416, 420.) Then when Mikhail Motorin died in 1750, the foundry passed from the hands of the Motorins to Konstantin Slizov. Rubtsov has calculated the year of Ivan Motorin's birth around 1660, assuming that he was probably twenty-five to thirty years old when he and his brother Dmitrij established their own foundry ("Ivan Fedorovich," 26). G. A. Boguslavskij puts the year of his birth in the 1670s. (*Tsar'-kolokol* [Moscow: Moskovskij rabochij, 1958], 18.)

16. Dmitrij Fedorovich Motorin apparently flourished during the last two decades of the seventeenth century and was noted for his skill in designing the decoration on the surface of his bells and for the superior tone quality of his castings. Between 1682 and 1696 Dmitrij worked as a foreman in bell founding at the Moscow Cannon Yard and in November of 1687 (1686?) cast a "carved" bell for the Church of the Holy Virgin on the ancestral estate of Prince Galitsyn near Moscow. (Rubtsov, *History*, 416, no. 343.)

17. The first of these commissions came in 1704 when Ivan Motorin cast a 798-pud (28,818-pound) bell for the Ivan Velikij Bell Tower in the Moscow Kremlin. This bell, originally called the "Velikopostnyj" (Lenten) bell, is known today as the "Semisotnyj" (Seven-hundred [-pud?]) bell. About the same time, Motorin founded the "Voskresnyj" (Sunday) bell of 3,400 puds (122,784 pounds). And in 1708 the Trinity-Sergius Lavra engaged him to recast its broken bell of 1427 as a new 161-pud (5,814-pound) bell called "Baran" (Ram). (Rubtsov, "Ivan Fedorovich," 27, 29.)

18. P. V. Sytin, *Istoriia planirovki i zastrojki Moskvy*, vol. 1: 1147-1762, Trudy Muzeia istorii i rekonstruktsii Moskvy, pt. 1, ed. F. N. Salov (Moscow: Moskovskij rabochij, 1950), 189.

19. Karamzin, *Primĕchaniia k" Istorii gosudarstva rossijskago*, 55 (n. 182 to vol. 6). See Chapter 4 of this volume, fig. 32.

20. Barten'ev, *Moskovskij Kreml'*, 221, my translation. In an inventory of 1701 four bells were listed in the Nabatnyj Tower. The small, brick Tsarskij Tower (see fig. 44) was constructed in 1680 for the Spasskij alarm bell and is situated on the Kremlin wall south of the Spasskij Tower. From this spot, beneath an older wooden structure, Ivan IV, according to tradition, watched

events in Red Square. Alarm bells had also formerly hung above the Spasskij, Tajnitskij, and Troitskij Gates in the Kremlin walls. (N. Zakharov, *Kremlevskie kolokola*, 2d rev. ed. [Moscow: Moskovskij rabochij, 1980], 6.) The Nabatnyj Tower, built in 1495 with additions in 1680, overlooks Red Square opposite St. Basil's Cathedral not far from the Spasskij Gate.

21. On the Plague Riot and its aftermath, see John T. Alexander, *Bubonic Plague in Early Modern Russia: Public Health & Urban Disaster* (Baltimore: The Johns Hopkins University Press, 1980), 177-212.

22. L. Krekshina, ed., *Po Kremliu: kratkij putevoditel'*, 5th ed., enl. (Moscow: Moskovskij rabochij, 1975), 26; Uspenskij, "Nabatnyj kolokol''," 614-620; and G. Esipov, "Nabatnyj kolokol''," *Istoricheskij věstnik''* 4 (1881): 418-420.

23. Rubtsov, *History*, 418-419. In 1727 Ivan Motorin also cast a bell to serve as the "Polielejnyj" bell at the Moscow Church of Konstantin and Elena. The inscription on this bell does not record its weight, however. (*Putevoditel' k'' drevnostiam'' i dostopamiatnostiam'' moskovskim''*, pt. 1 [Moscow: Universitetskaia tip., 1792], 207-208.)

24. *Fabriki i zavody vsej Rossii: svěděniia o 31,523 fabrikakh'' i zavodakh''* (Kiev: Knigoizd. T-va L. M. Fish'', 1913), nos. 3715 and 3744. Another source indicates that the Samgin factory in Moscow was established a decade earlier in 1783. At the end of the nineteenth century it was considered the foremost bell foundry in Russia. (*Bibliograficheskij ukazatel' po istorii fabrik i zavodov: knigi i broshiury [na russkom iazyke]* [Moscow: Ogiz, 1932], 26, no. 110.) Konstantin Slizov established the bell foundry of N. D. Finliandskij in Moscow (N. Priakhin, "Kolokol'nyj zvon": dostoприměchatel'nye kolokola v'' Rossii," *Russkij palomnik''*, no. 20 [1886], p. 182n., righthand col.).

25. Bells not exceeding 20 puds (722 pounds) were founded in the smaller pit; the larger pit was used for casting bells weighing up to 130 puds (4,695 pounds). (Johann Gottlieb Georgi, *Bemerkungen einer Reise im russischen Reich in den Jahren 1773 und 1774* 2 [St. Petersburg: Gedruckt bei der Kaiserl. Akademie der Wissenschaften, 1775], 689.)

26. Olovianishnikov, *Istoriia kolokolov''*, 409-410.

27. Ibid., 411-412.

28. E. Ziablovskij, ed., *Statisticheskoe opisanie rossijskoj imperii v'' nyněshnem'' eia sostoianii*, pt. 5 (St. Petersburg: Tip. Provitel'stvuiushchago Senata, 1815), pp. 81-82.

29. *Vospominaniia ochevidtsa o prebyvanii frantsuzov'' v'' Moskvě, v'' 1812-m'' godu* (Moscow: Tip. M. P. Zakharova, 1862), 50-51, my translation.

30. Quoted from p. 386 of Mr. James' *Journal of a Tour in Germany, Sweden, Russia, Poland*, etc., in William Macmichael, *Journey from Moscow to Constantinople in the Years 1817, 1818* (London: John Murray, 1819), p. 4. According to Eugene Tarle, there were five explosions in the Kremlin between October 21 and 23, the last of which occurred at daybreak on the twenty-third (*Napoleon's Invasion of Russia, 1812*, trans. G. M. [New York: Oxford University Press, 1942], 324-325).

31. *Vospominaniia*, 278. Among the other Kremlin towers destroyed in 1812 was one where records and documents from the Cannon Bureau concerning the history of bells were stored. Some of these papers were sold for packing material in Moscow markets; other were brought from the ruined tower into another building, but were damaged when that building collapsed. By the time this archive was studied in 1870, two of the four boxes of materials that had survived the Kremlin explosions had been lost. The other two boxes had been deposited in the Moscow Arsenal. (Rubtsov, *History*, 89.)

32. Falkus, *Industrialisation of Russia*, 31. The rapid growth of Russian industry during the mid-nineteenth century is reflected in the productivity of the bell foundry of the Kapustin brothers in Tver. During the four years between 1846 and 1850 production increased more than threefold. (Kalmykov, "Obozrěnie manufakturnoj promyshlennosti Tverskoj gubernii v'' 1850 godu," *Zhurnal'' manufaktur'' i torgovli* 4 [1851]: 92.)

33. Rubtsov, *History*, 181. A study of the private bell foundries in Russia during the eighteenth, nineteenth, and early twentieth centuries still awaits investigation of their archives in the Soviet Union.

34. Ministerstvo finansov'', Department'' Torgovli i Manufaktur, *Fabrichno-zavodskaia promyshlennost' i torgovlia Rossii*, 2d ed., rev. and enl. (St. Petersburg: Tip. I. A. Efrona, 1896), 75.

35. Mary J. Taber, *Bells: An Anthology* (Boston: Richard G. Badger, 1912), 19.

36. N. R., "O kolokolakh'' i o kolokol'nom'' iskusstvě," *Moskovskiia vědomosti*, no. 50 (Thursday, April 27, 1850), p. 578, righthand col.

37. N. Gorchakov, "O bol'shikh'' kolokolakh''," *Moskovskiia gubernskiia vědomosti*, no. 17 (1844), p. 200; and N. R., "O kolokolakh'' i o kolokol'nom'' iskusstvě," *Moskovskiia vědomosti*, no. 51 (Saturday, April 29, 1850), p. 588, middle col.

38. Howard P. Kennard, ed., *The Russian Year-Book for 1912* (New York: Macmillan, 1912), 402. See also Blackwell, *Beginnings of Russian Industrialization*, 73-74; Robert Sears, *An Illustrated Description of the Russian Empire*, new ed., rev. and enl. (New York: Robert Sears, 1855), 103-105. Preparations for the fair began each year at the end of May or beginning of June and commerce lasted until ice blocked navigation on the Volga and Oka. (Dem'ianov, *Illiustrirovannyj putevoditel' po Volgě 1898 g.*, 166, 168.) The fair was not held from 1917 to 1921 but was revived briefly for nine summers beginning in July of 1921. It was shut down permanently after 1929. (N. P. Eroshkin, "Nizhny-Novgorod Fair," *Great Soviet Encyclopedia* 17 [1978], 581.)

39. Henri Troyat, *Daily Life in Russia Under the Last Tsar*, trans. Malcolm Barnes (New York: Macmillan, 1962), 218. See also Baedeker, *Russia*, 345. In 1844 bells sold at the fair for 10 to 11 rubles per pud, but in 1845, for only 9 rubles 25 kopecks to 10 rubles 50 kopecks per pud (P. Mel'nikov, *Nizhegorodskaia iarmarka v'' 1843, 1844 i 1845 godakh''* [Nizhnij-Novgorod: Gubernskaia tip., 1846], 62). Through the bell market at this great fair, bells were sold and distributed in

towns and villages along the Volga and Oka rivers (Mel'nikov, *Nizhegorodskaia iarmarka*, 61).

40. Ministerstvo finansov″, *Fabrichno-zavodskaia promyshlennost'*, 75. Founding of bronze church bells represented by far the greatest number of items cast with copper at this time (S. M. Prokudin-Gorskij, "O sovremennom″ sostoianii litejnago děla v″ Rossii," *Zapiski Imperatorskago russkago tekhnicheskago obshchestva* 30, no. 4 [April 1896], p. 74).

41. These plants were located in Moscow, Voronezh, Yaroslavl, Valdaj, Kostroma, and Yeniseisk (in Siberia) (I. Éjzen, "Kolokol″: istoricheskij obzor″ po povodu ego 1500-lětiia," *Niva* 9 [1894], col. 119). In addition to the Moscow plant of Iosif Nikitich Purishev, which recast broken bells, advertisements early in 1895 in *Tserkovnyia vědomosti* indicate the activity of provincial bell foundries. (*Tserkovnyia vědomosti* no. 3 [January 21, 1895], pp. 116-117; no. 7 [February 18, 1895], p. 286; no. 8 [February 25, 1895], p. 322.)

42. V. I. Kovalevskij, gen. ed., *Rossiia v″ kontsě XIX věka* (St. Petersburg: Tip. Akts. Obshch. Brokgauz″-Efron″, 1900), 305.

43. Éjzen, "Kolokol″," col. 119. The town of Valdaj, not far from St. Petersburg, was also famous for its bells, "the sweetness and depth of the tone of which are unsurpassed" (H. C. Romanoff, *Sketches of the Rites and Customs of the Greco-Russian Church*, 2d ed. [London: Rivingtons, 1869], 267).

44. V. P. Bezobrazov, ed., *Otchet″ o Vserossijskoj khudozhestvenno-promyshlennoj vystavkě 1882 goda v″ Moskvě*, vol. 3: *Raboty ěkspertnykh″ kommissij* (St. Petersburg: Tip. V. Bezobrazova, 1883), 56-57. Nikolaj Dmitrievich Finliandskij, owner of the foundry that bore his name, was the grandson of Bogdanov, who founded the Great Uspensky Bell in 1817 (Priakhin, "Kolokol'nyj zvon″," 182n.).

45. Bezobrazov, *Otchet″*, 57.

46. Nik[olaj] Findejzen, "So Vserossijskoj vystavki v″ N.-Novgorodě," *Russkaia muzykal'naia gazeta* 3, no. 9 (September 1896), cols. 1018-1020. The largest of seven Russian bells at the Holy Trinity Orthodox Cathedral in San Francisco was cast in 1888 at the Moscow bell foundry of N. D. Finliandskij. The inscription on the sound-bow records that it weighs 144 puds 5 funts (5,205 pounds) and that it was founded "In memory of the miraculous rescue of the Russian Emperor Alexander III, together with the imperial family, October 17 [1888]." On that date the tsar and his family narrowly escaped with their lives in a train accident near the town of Borki in the Ukraine. (The San Francisco bells later narrowly escaped destruction themselves. Several days before the earthquake of April 18-19, 1906, they had been removed from their belfry in the old cathedral on Powell Street, which was scheduled to undergo structural repairs.) (*The Restoration of Holy Trinity Cathedral, San Francisco, California*, booklet published by the cathedral, [p. 4].)

47. Olovianishnikov, *Istoriia kolokolov″*, 412.

48. Olovianishnikov bells were shown in Moscow (1886), Nizhnij-Novgorod (1896), Yaroslavl (1903), New Orleans (1885), Paris (1889), and Chicago (1893) as well as in other cities (ibid., 413).

49. The reigning emperors who visited the Olovianishnikov bell foundry were Alexander I in 1823, Nicholas I in 1834 and 1841, and Alexander II in 1858 (ibid., 412). In 1913 the Olovianishnikov bell foundry was open to visitors daily from 6 to 11 A.M. and from 1 to 6 P.M. (Yaroslavskaia ěkskursionnaia komissiia, *Yaroslavl' v″ ego proshlom″ i nastoiashchem″: istoricheskij ocherk″-putevoditel'* [Yaroslavl: Tip. Gubernskago pravleniia, 1913], 5). See also Olovianishnikov, *Istoriia kolokolov″*, 412-413. Three Olovianishnikov bells from the nineteenth century are now on display in an exhibit of Russian and Dutch bells at the Yaroslavl Museum-Preserve of History and Architecture.

50. In 1913 there were four bell foundries operating in the Nizhegorodskij province and two each in Moscow, Saratov, and Warsaw (then a part of Russia). Other plants that produced bells were located in Buzuluk (Samara province), Voronezh, Rostov-on-the-Don, Valdaj, Perm province, Kozlov (Tambov province), Tiumen (Tobol'sk province), Pesochino (Khar'kov province), and Yaroslavl. (*Fabriki i zavody vsej Rossii*, nos. 2048, 3081, 3438, 3510, 3533, 3536, 3715, 3744, 3767, 3769, 3771, 3772, 3779, 3909, 3910, 3913, 3921, 3971, and 4003.)

51. Walter Duranty, " 'Cemetery of Bells' at Nijni Novgorod," *New York Times* (August 7, 1922), 3.

52. Matthew Spinka, *The Church and the Russian Revolution* (New York: Macmillan, 1927), 102-103, 128ff., 132-133. In 1929 a church bell was rung to summon parishioners to a village church in the Moscow province as authorities arrived to haul away a broken bell for scrap metal (John Shelton Curtiss, *The Russian Church and the Soviet State, 1917-1950* [Boston: Little, Brown and Co., 1953], 234).

53. Spinka, *Church*, 105. Citizens of the new Russia found bell ringing tiresome and complained that it interfered with radio programs and with the sleep of workers on the night shift (Curtiss, *Russian Church*, 238-239).

54. Curtiss, *Russian Church*, 81.

55. "In a Sort of Runic Rhyme," in *Bells and Carillons: A Scrap Book*, compiled by the Music Department, Boston Public Library (Boston, MA, 1942), 25. In the late 1920s and early 1930s a number of fine Russian bells were collected and sold abroad as scrap metal (see Price, *Bells and Man*, xviii, 106, 197, 270, and 272). In early December of 1927 a Russian merchant ship docked at Le Havre with a load of church bells, shattered and bored with holes, to be sold for scrap ("Soviet, Needing Funds, Sells Church Bells for Metal," *New York Times* [December 4, 1927], sect. 3, p. 8).

56. Boleslaw Szczesniak, trans, and ed., *The Russian Revolution and Religion: A Collection of Documents Concerning the Suppression of Religion by the Communists, 1917-1925* (Notre Dame, IN: University of Notre Dame Press, 1959), 171, no. 107 (reported June 12, 1923, in Moscow *Izvestiia*). In the town of Melekess near Ulianovsk (formerly Simbirsk)

the confiscation of bells from four churches yielded twenty-two tons (1,218 puds) of metal (*New York Times* [January 31, 1930], p. 3).

57. Curtiss, *Russian Church*, 238-239.

58. Ibid., 239.

59. Boris Pilnyak (Boris Vogau), "Mahogany," in *Dissonant Voices in Soviet Literature*, ed. Patricia Blake and Max Hayward, (New York: Pantheon Books, 1962), 76. Pilnyak recounts a similar event at Kolomna in his novel of 1930, *The Volga Flows to the Caspian Sea*, trans. from the Russian (London: Peter Davies, 1932), 53.

60. Vasili Peskov, *This is My Native Land*, trans. from Russian by Fainna Glagoleva (Moscow: Progress Publishers, 1976), 85.

61. "Many Ikons Burned by Russian Peasants . . . Moscow Church Bells Silenced," *New York Times* (January 31, 1930), p. 3.

62. Alexander Morskoi (Alexander N. Fishman), *Bells of Russia* (Boston: Bruce Humphries, 1947), 165. William Allen White also observed this transformation: "In modern Russia the machine has taken the place that religion had in old Russia. . . . All over Russia, from the Baltic to the Pacific, great machines are turning raw material into finished products. Machines that make other machines are rising all over the land, and machines that make machines that make machines are building everywhere ("Machine is Called Deity of Russians," *New York Times* [October 2, 1933], 19).

63. Information differs on the original home of the Harvard bells in Russia. Accounts in Boston newspapers report that the seventeen [*sic*] bells shipped to the United States were among some thirty-six bells from a small church near Leningrad, some of which had already been removed and melted down for their metal. Mason Hammond indicates that this zvon had formerly hung in the Danilov Monastery in Moscow. ("The Lowell House Bells," *Bulletin of the Guild of Carillonneurs of North America* 5, no. 1 [December 1950], p. 17.)

64. Though all eighteen bells were originally installed in the tower of Lowell House, the fourth heaviest but oldest was later removed and placed in the Baker Library belfry of the Harvard Business School. The total weight of the zvon was estimated at about 27 tons. The largest bell weighs nearly 14 tons (actually 722 puds), is nine feet high, and was cast in 1890. The oldest bell in the group was founded in 1790, and the most recent, in 1904. (Hammond, "The Lowell House Bells," 17-24.) Hammond's published article incorrectly identifies the donor as Richard T. Crane, though the original manuscript of this article at Lowell House correctly identifies him as Charles R. Crane (*Boston Transcript*, October 11, 1930; *Boston Globe*, April 6, 1931; *Boston Post*, October 11, 1934; and an unidentified Boston paper, October 11, 1934, in *Bells and Carillons: A Scrap Book*, 56, 71).

65. T. V. Nikolaeva, *Drevnij Zvenigorod* (Moscow: "Iskusstvo," 1978), 186. A representation of this famous bell was

included in the coat of arms for Zvenigorod in the eighteenth century.

66. Hubert Faensen and Vladimir Ivanov, *Early Russian Architecture*, trans. Mary Whittal and with photographs by Klaus G. Beyer (London: Paul Elek, 1975), 468, 469. The entire collection of church bells in the Pskov museum was also lost during the occupation (É. S. Smirnova, "Dva pamiatnika pskovskogo khudozhestvennogo lit'ia XVI v.," *Sovetskaia arkheologiia* 6, no. 2 [1962], p. 243).

67. See A. Budiak, ed., *Novgorod* (Leningrad: Lenizdat, 1967), 137. The three largest bells, which formerly hung in the zvonnitsa of the St. Sophia Cathedral, are: a bell of 1,614 puds (58,286 pounds) founded in 1659 by Ermolaj Vasil'ev of Pskov; a bell of 590 puds (21,307 pounds) founded at the Iur'ev Monastery, Novgorod, in 1839; and a bell of 300 puds (10,834 pounds), the work of Vasilij, Iakov, and Fedor Leont'ev in 1677. The other two bells are: a 200-pud (7,223-pound) instrument of 1599 founded by Vasilij and Ioakim Ivanov and Afanasij Pankrat'ev from the Khutynskij Monastery near Novgorod, and an 80-pud (2,889-pound) instrument of 1589 that Boris Godunov donated to the Dukhov Monastery in Novgorod. The last three bells were on the barge that sank in the river. The largest bell was first hung in the zvonnitsa in 1650 but fell and broke in 1659. The present bell of 1659 is a recasting of the earlier one. (Richard Moore and Hilary Sternberg, eds., *Fodor's Soviet Union 1979* [New York: David McKay, 1979], 316.)

68. *Times*, January 31, 1944, quoted in Ernest Morris, *Bells of All Nations* (London: Robert Hale, 1951), 162. This account differs somewhat from the Budiak account.

69. A recent visitor to Novgorod, when she inquired why the bells of the St. Sophia Cathedral had not been rehung in their zvonnitsa, was told that they would be reinstalled as soon as structural repairs could be made on the belfry.

70. One of the first documents to refer to Moscow as "the new Constantinople" was Metropolitan Zosima's *Exposition of the Easter Cycle* (1492); and in *The Legend of the White Cowl*, written in Novgorod toward the end of the fifteenth century, the land of Russia if not Moscow itself was perceived as the third Rome. In the early sixteenth century Filofej of the Eleazarov Monastery at Pskov formulated the definitive statement of the doctrine of the Third Rome: "For two Romes have fallen, but the Third stands, and a Fourth shall never be" (Wolff, "The Three Romes," 291). Moscow's new role in the Orthodox East was officially recognized in 1589 when the patriarch of Constantinople elevated the city to the rank of a fifth patriarchal see (after Constantinople, Antioch, Alexandria, and Jerusalem) with his consecration of Metropolitan Job as patriarch of Moscow. For a succinct exposition of the origins and sources of the so-called doctrine of the Third Rome, see Donald W. Treadgold, *The West in Russia and China: Religious and Secular Thought in Modern Times*, vol. 1: *Russia, 1472-1917* (Cambridge: [Cambridge] University Press, 1973), 19-23; and Wolff, "The Three Romes," 291-311. See also Baron John Meyendorff and Norman H. Baynes, "The Byzantine Inher-

itance in Russia," in *Byzantium: An Introduction to East Roman Civilization*, ed. Norman H. Baynes and H. St. L. B. Moss (Oxford: Clarendon Press, 1949), 369; and George Ostrogorsky, *History of the Byzantine State*, rev. ed., trans. Joan Hussey (New Brunswick, NJ: Rutgers University Press, 1969), 572.

71. Wolff, "The Three Romes," 303; and Riasanovsky, *History*, 141-142.

72. Billington, *The Icon and the Axe*, 2.

73. See Marthe Blinoff's translation of A. I. Herzen's article of 1842, "Moscow and Petersburg," in *Life and Thought in Old Russia* ([University Park, PA]: The Pennsylvania State University Press, 1961), 187.

Notes to Chapter 7

1. Nikolaj Pogodin, *Trilogiia o V. I. Lenine: "Chelovek s ruzh'em," "Kremlevskie kuranty," "Tret'ia pateticheskaia"* (Moscow: Sovetskij pisatel', 1960), 148, my translation from revised version of 1955.

2. One of the earliest references to a foreign bell in Russian territory is in a charter (*gramota*) of 1284, which transmits the lawsuit of Prince Fedor Rostislavich of Smolensk over a German bell (R. I. Avanesov, ed., *Smolenskie gramoty XIII-XIV vekov* [Moscow: Izd. Akademii nauk SSSR, 1963], 62-63; for a translation of this document, see H. W. Dewey and A. M. Kleimola, trans. and eds., *Russian Private Law in the XIV-XVII Centuries: An Anthology of Documents*, Michigan Slavic Materials, no. 9 [Ann Arbor, MI: Department of Slavic Languages and Literatures, University of Michigan, 1973], pp. 50-51). Details on the litigation over this German bell cannot be determined from the information in the charter.

Bells of the fifteenth, sixteenth, and seventeenth centuries from Germany, Denmark, France, and Italy have been reported in Russian bell towers, but the majority of foreign bells in Russia appear to be Dutch (see Snegirev, "Moskovskij Tsar'-kolokol"," 27-28). One of the oldest extant Western bells in Russia is an instrument of 1417 at the Solovetskij Monastery, which bears a macaronic inscription in Latin and Early New High German (M. F. Mur'ianov, "Nadpis' drevnejshego kolokola Solovetskogo monastyria," *Pamiatniki kul'tury*, New discoveries, Annual 1975 [Moscow: "Nauka," 1976], 192-193). A late fifteenth-century instrument is the 1,264-pound German bell of 1493 cast at Hagenow in Mecklenburg and property of the Church of the Ascension at the Pecherskij Voznesenskij Monastery in Nizhnij-Novgorod. Ivan IV allegedly seized this bell at Dorpat during the Livonian War (1558-1583). (Pavel Mel'nikov, "Lifliandskij kolokol" XV stolětiia v" Nizhnem"-Novĕgorodĕ," *Otechestvennyia zapiski*, pt. 33, no. 3 [1844], pp. 42-44; and Baedecker, *Russia*, 343.) At the end of the nineteenth century, three non-Russian bells were hanging in the bell tower of the St. Sophia Cathedral in Vologda. Two were cast in Amsterdam; the third, a 500-pud (18,057-pound) bell of 1686 from Lübeck with a Latin inscription, was brought to Vologda during the reign of Peter the Great, where it served the cathedral as the largest bell in its tower. (Priakhin, "Kolokol'nyj zvon"," 197.)

A 10-pud (361-pound) bell with Oriental inscriptions belonged to the cathedral at Krasnoyarsk in Siberia at the end of the nineteenth century. This Asiatic bell was discovered around 1820 during the excavation of a burial mound on the steppe in the Minusinskij district of the Yenisej province. ("Zamĕchatel'nye kolokola pri sobornoj tserkvi v" Krasnoiarskĕ," *Zhurnal" Ministerstva vnutrennikh" dĕl"*, pt. 17, no. 3 [1847], pp. 479-480 [a drawing of this bell can be found at the end of part 17].)

3. That Russians had earlier been aware of significant differences between their own techniques of bell ringing and the melodic-harmonic style cultivated on European chimes and carillons may have been expressed through the term *malinovyj zvon* (mellow ringing), which occurs in Muscovite sources from the sixteenth and seventeenth centuries. *Malinovyj zvon* has been equated with the style of Russian bell ringing called *trezvon* and described as "very pleasing" and "soft in timbre" (Akad. nauk SSSR, Institut iazykoznaniia, *Slovar' sovremennogo russkogo literaturnogo iazyka*, 6 [L-M] [Moscow-Leningrad: Izd. Akad. nauk SSSR, 1957], col. 532). But the same term has also been interpreted as a way of distinguishing the harmonious and consonant sounds produced on the tuned bells of a Western carillon from the untuned and dissonant colors in Russian zvon ringing. The word *malinovyj* is viewed as a Russian adjectival form of the French name for the Belgian town of Malines (Mechelen in Flemish), and *malinovyj zvon* is thus understood as a Russian expression that designates the special Western style of carillon ringing in Malines and other cities and towns of the Low Countries. (Gleb Rahr, "Cloches et carillons en Russie," *Encyclopédie des musiques sacrées* 2, gen. ed., Jacques Porte [Paris: Editions Labergerie, 1969], 211. See also Iurij Vasil'evich Pukhnachev, *Zagadki zvuchashchego metalla* [Moscow: Izd. "Nauka," 1974], 122; and Billington, *The Icon and the Axe*, 643 n. 89.)

4. Percival Price, *The Carillon* (London: Oxford University Press, 1933), 11; and Percival Price, "Bells and Music," *Bulletin of the Guild of Carillonneurs in North America* 19, no. 1 (April 1968), p. 32. Price notes that in some places the musical art of the Town Johnnie may have developed along more sophisticated lines than striking the hour on a single bell and cites Dubrovnik as a town that had five or six bells the Johnnie could ring. A small alarm gave the Johnnie the signal for striking the large bell or bells in the tower. See Ernest L. Edwardes, *Weight-driven Chamber Clocks of the Middle Ages and Renaissance*, vol. 1: Old Weight-driven Chamber Clocks, 1350-1850 (Altrincham, England: John Sherratt and Son, 1965), 15-19.

Friedrich Christian Weber, during a visit to Russia between 1714 and 1720, observed that in Moscow at the house of each boyar there was a watchman who marked the hours by striking a large board with a wooden hammer (cf. the bilo discussed in Chapter 2) (*The Present State of Russia* 1, trans. from the High Dutch [London: W. Taylor, 1723; reprint ed., London: Frank Cass, 1968], 127). At Nizhnij-Novgorod watchmen in courtyards of the nobility struck a large cast-iron plate at intervals throughout the night as proof that they were awake ([Zagoskin], *The Young Muscovite*, 191). Johann Georg Kohl reported that even in the mid-nineteenth century a watchman in some Russian communities struck the hours on a bell (*Russia* [London: Chapman & Hall, 1844], 228n.). In chap. 34 of Turgenev's novel *Dvorianskoe gnezdo* (A Nest of Gentlefolk), Lavretsky, sitting in the Kalitins' garden at midnight, listens as a watchman strikes a board. The second act of Anton Chekhov's *Uncle Vanya* opens and closes with the tapping of a night watchman in the garden of Serebriakov's house.

5. R. Murray Schafer, *The Tuning of the World* (New York: Alfred A. Knopf, 1977), 55. Clepsydras or water-clocks could strike bells, however (Tait, *Clocks and Watches*, 8).

6. Edwardes, *Weight-driven Chamber Clocks*, vii, 45 n. 1; and J. Drummond Robertson, *The Evolution of Clockwork* (London: Cassell & Co., 1931), 31. For an explanation of the mechanism in fourteenth-century tower clocks, see Samuel Guye and Henri Michel, *Time & Space: Measuring Instruments from the 15th to the 19th Century* (New York: Praeger, 1971), 19. An important study of Western European tower clocks is Alfred Ungerer's *Les Horloges astronomiques et monumentales les plus remarquables de l'antiquité jusqu'à nos jours* (Strasbourg: Chez l'auteur, 1931). See also Schilling, *Glocken*, 125-128. For the history of two fourteenth-century clocks at Perpignan and Nieppe, see Landes, *Revolution in Time*, 192-197.

The oldest tower clock in Paris is the instrument that Henri de Vic (also Henry de Vick, Heinrich von Wych, or Henry Wieck [or Wiek]) of Württemberg had built by 1370 in the tower of the Royal Palace, now the Palais de Justice, though its single bell was not installed until the following year (Robertson, *The Evolution of Clockwork*, 50-51). The earliest extant town clock that strikes the quarters is Jehan de Félains' clock of 1389 at Rouen (Eric Bruton, *The History of Clocks and Watches* [New York: Rizzoli International Publications, 1979], 37, 246-247).

7. Edwardes, *Weight-driven Chamber Clocks*, 46-47, 55-56; and Robertson, *The Evolution of Clockwork*, 32-33.

8. On the etymology of the French name *jacquemart*, see Ungerer, *Les Horloges*, 16-17. Ernest Morris devotes chap. 11 in his *Tintinnabula: Small Bells* (London: Robert Hale, 1959), 128-136, to clock jacks. See also Price, *Bells and Man*, 173-174; and Marcuse, *Survey*, 61. In Orvieto a clock jack has been sounding the hours for some six centuries (Price, "Bells and Music," 32. On English clock jacks, see Nichols, *Bells Thro' the Ages*, 203-206). After the palace clock of 1356 in Perpignan had been malfunctioning for at least eight years, King John I in 1387 decided to hire two men for a penny a day to ring the hours on the clock's bell (Landes, *Revolution in Time*, 195).

9. Because the earliest records of clock dials (*sfere*) in Italy attached to the outside of buildings date only from 1399-1400, Edwardes concludes that "it may be taken for granted that dials were quite unknown for true 'turret' [tower] clocks in the fourteenth century. . . ." (*Weight-driven Chamber Clocks*, 55, 44.) Here Edwardes distinguishes between outside dials on towers and interior dials for "nave clocks" within a cathedral or church. He believes that the clock of Old St. Paul's in London, alluded to in 1286 and to which Walter the Orgoner attached a dial in 1344, was in all probability a "nave clock" inside the church (ibid., 44, 62-63). Robertson also maintains that fourteenth-century clocks "had neither dial and hour circle nor hand" (*The Evolution of Clockwork*, 62).

10. N. Hudson Moore, *The Old Clock Book* (New York: Tudor Publishing Co., 1911), 6-7; and Willis I. Milham, *Time & Timekeepers* (New York: Macmillan, 1945), 56. For insights into the impact of the mechanical clock on Western civilization and its cultural significance in the Western world, see Lewis Mumford, *Technics and Civilization* (New York: Harcourt, Brace and Co., 1934), 12ff.; Schafer, *Tuning of the World*, 55-56; and Carlo M. Cipolla, *Clocks and Culture: 1300-1700* (London: Collins, 1967), 15-75. The English word "clock" originally referred only to the bell on which the hours were struck (cf. French *cloche*, Dutch and Flemish *klokke*, and German *Glocke*). In English, however, the distinction between the bell which sounded the hours and the mechanism that regulated the striking (*horloge*) became blurred.

11. A. M. Plechko, *Moskva: istoricheskij ocherk"* (Moscow: Tip. É. Lissner" i Iu. Roman", 1883), 39. On Russian tower clocks of the fifteenth century, see Boris Georgievich Radchenko, *Moskovskie chasy* (Moscow: Moskovskij rabochij, 1980), 4-9.

12. PSRL VIII (Voskres.), p. 77 (1404).

13. PSRL XVIII (Simeon. and excerpts from Troitsk.), p. 281 (1404), my translation. See also PSRL XI (Nikon.), p. 190 (1404). *Chas"* is Russian for "hour." The chronicler suggests in this passage that he was accustomed to a Town Johnnie (Ivanushka) who rang a bell each hour by striking it with his hammer. (Radchenko, *Moskovskie chasy*, 8.)

14. The Voskresenskij Chronicle reports that the Moscow clock of 1404 was a "very marvelous thing and with a moon" (PSRL VIII [Voskres.], p. 77 [1404]). Although clock dials with phases of the moon were known in the fourteenth and fifteenth centuries, this information does not agree with the analogous passage in the Troitskij Chronicle nor with the clock shown in the sixteenth-century miniature from the second Ostermanovskij volume (A. V. Artsikhovskij, *Drevnerusskie miniatiury kak istoricheskij istochnik* [Moscow: Izd. MGu, 1944], 84-85).

15. PSRL III (Novg. I), p. 112 (1436); and PSRL III (Novg. II), p. 239 (1436).

16. PSRL IV (Pskov. I), p. 254 (1477), my translation. See also A. N. Nasonov, ed., *Pskovskie letopisi*, issue 2 (Moscow: Izd. Akad. nauk SSSR, 1955), p. 207 (1477). The Snetogorskij

Monastery, with its Church of the Nativity of the Virgin, was established in the thirteenth century on the right bank of the Velikaia River about one third of the distance between Pskov and Lake Peipus.

17. The French word *carillon* (derived from Medieval Latin *quadrillionem*) originally meant four stationary bells that were struck to mark the hours and quarters (Westcott, *Bells and Their Music*, glossary, p. 1). Arthur Lynds Bigelow points out that in medieval art one sometimes sees a player, often the seated figure of King David, striking a row of four small bells with a hammer (*Carillon*, 40). Although the French term *carillon* can be applied to an ensemble of more than four stationary bells, the large sixteenth-, seventeenth-, and eighteenth-century tower instrument in the Low Countries, *beiaard* in Flemish and Dutch and "carillon" in English, is called *carillon de Flandre* in French. Price points out that confusion of terminology might have been avoided if both French and English had adopted the word *beiaard* for this large instrument (*The Carillon*, 12-13).

The best known of the four-pitch quarters is the Cambridge Quarters, later called the Westminister Quarters. William Crotch (1775-1847) composed these at King's College, and they were rung for the first time about 1793 at the Church of St. Mary the Great, Cambridge. (Nichols, *Bells Thro' the Ages*, 207; and Price, *Bells and Man*, 180.)

18. A chime is "a [diatonically] tuned series of bells capable of producing melody" (Westcott, *Bells and Their Music*, 34). See also the summary of a course of lectures by W. W. Starmer on "Bells, Carillons, and Chimes," in *The Musical Times* 51 (June 1, 1910), 373. The so-called Kremlin chimes above the Spasskij Gate, however, originally had twenty-five (two octaves of) chromatically tuned bells.

19. Price, *The Carillon*, 13-14. One of the earliest chiming mechanisms is reported at the Sint-Niklaaskerk in Brussels by 1381. This feature appeared on tower clocks more and more frequently during the fifteenth century (p. 129).

20. H. B. Walters, *Church Bells of England* (London: Oxford University Press, 1912), 111. For the most accurate chronology in the development of tower clocks and bells through the sixteenth century, see Guye and Michel, *Time & Space*, 21-26.

21. Starmer, "Bells, Carillons, and Chimes," 373. According to Westcott, the revolving chiming cylinder was an invention of the early fourteenth century (*Bells and Their Music*, 33).

22. About four days' work was required to change the pegs in the chiming cylinder of the carillon at Mechelen (Malines). Up to six different hammers may be available to strike a single bell in carillons at Bruges and elsewhere, and for each hammer a peg had to be set in the chiming cylinder. (Thomas Rees, *Egypt and the Holy Land To-day* [Springfield, IL: State Register Co., 1922], 369.) For an explanation and illustration of how a chiming cylinder is set to sound the beginning of Stephen Foster's *Suwanee River* (*Old Folks at Home*), see Coleman, *Bells*, 183-184. See the definition of "chiming cylinder" in the glossary to this volume.

23. Of the structures in the Kremlin walls discussed in this chapter, only the Blagoveshchenskij (Annunciation), Nabatnyj (Alarm), and Tsarskij are towers in the strictest sense of the word. The Spasskij, Troitskij, Tajnitskij, Borovitskij, and Nikol'skij "towers" were all gates that provided access into the Kremlin (the Tajnitskij's entrance has been sealed since 1930), but because they each have superstructures above their gates, they are called towers. General guides to the history of the Kremlin's walls and towers are A. Goncharova and A. Khamtsov, *Steny bashni Kremlia*, 2d ed., enl. (Moscow: Moskovskij rabochij, 1960); and Krekshina, ed., *Po Kremliu*.

24. The Frolovskij Gate was also earlier known as the Frololavr'skij or the Ierusalimskij (Zabelin, *Istoriia goroda Moskvy*, 184; and Barten'ev, *Moskovskij Kreml'*, 123). Two stone plaques over the exterior and interior portals record the history of the tower's construction. The one on the Red Square side is inscribed in Latin; and the one on the Kremlin side in Russian. Both read: "Ioann Vasil'evich, by the grace of God, Grand Duke of Vladimir, Moscow, Novgorod, Tver, Pskov, Viatka, Iugra, Perm, Bulgar, and other [places] and Sovereign of All Russia, in the thirtieth year of his reign ordered these towers built; in the year 1491 from the Incarnation of the Lord, Pietro Antonio Solario, a Milanese, constructed [them]" (Barten'ev, *Moskovskij Kreml'*, 129, my translation; see also Th. I. Rychin, *Istoricheskoe opisanie moskovskikh″ kremlevskikh″ soborov″, tserkvej i monastyrej i ikh″ sviatyni*, 3d ed., enl. [Moscow: Tip. A. Gattsuka, 1882], 235).

25. Zabelin, *Istoriia goroda Moskvy*, 186; and Barten'ev, *Moskovskij Kreml'*, 139.

26. The old clock, weighing 60 puds (2,167 pounds), was sold in September 1624 to the Spasskij Iaroslavskij Monastery for 48 rubles (Th. Adelung, *Al'bom″ Mejerberga: vidy i bytovyia kartiny Rossii XVII věka*, rev. and enl. by A. M. Loviagin [St. Petersburg: Izd. A. S. Suvorina, 1903], 162; and Zabelin, *Istoriia goroda Moskvy*, 187).

27. Bogoiavlenskij, "O Pushkarskom″ prikazě," 374. Galloway's Russian assistants came from the Ustiug district: Zhdan, a clockmaker, and his son and grandson, Shumilo Zhdanov and Aleksej Shumilov (N. Ia. Tikhomirov and V. N. Ivanov, *Moskovskij Kreml'* [Moscow: Izd. literatury po stroitel'stvu, 1967], 128).

28. Only two clock dials appeared on the Spasskij Gate in the second quarter of the seventeenth century, each showing seventeen hours—one dial of this clock faced out on Red Square, and another was visible within the Kremlin. The dials on this clock apparently counted, and its bells struck, only the hours of daylight (see Meyerberg's description of the clock in the Spasskij Tower installed after the fire of 1654 in Adelung, *Al'bom″ Mejerberga*, 160-161). Friedrich Christian Weber reported that even in the second decade of the eighteenth century "the common Russian people count the hours of the day from sunrise to sunset" (*The Present State of Russia*, 128).

29. Barten'ev, *Moskovskij Kreml'*, 140.

30. Paul of Aleppo, *Puteshestvie*, 3:6, my translation. Patriarch Makarius and his son arrived in Moscow on February 2,

1655, and the tsar returned to the capital in the same month. Paul was either misinformed or was himself in error on the date of the fire.

31. Adelung, *Al'bom" Mejerberga*, 160-161, my translation.

32. Zabelin, *Istoriia goroda Moskvy*, 191.

33. The second clock and its chimes were installed in the so-called Menshikov Tower (Church of the Archangel Gabriel) in Moscow, and the third chiming clock, in the Ingermanland Chancery near the Menshikov Tower (ibid., 191-192).

34. Ibid., 193.

35. Barten'ev, *Moskovskij Kreml'*, 148n. This English clock may possibly have been one that Galloway had built in the second quarter of the seventeenth century. The name of the Berlin clockmaker may have been Watse, possibly Fassy.

36. *Kol' slaven"* (1825), Dmitrij Bortnianskij's setting of a Russian Masonic hymn by the poet M. M. Kheraskov, was the official anthem of the Imperial Russian Army (Iu. V. Keldysh, *Russkaia muzyka XVIII veka* [Moscow: Izd. "Nauka," 1965], 444). The origins of the *Preobrazhenskij March* are uncertain. The composer of the melody of this march may have been Ferdinand Haas (1787-1851). Its melody is found in a collection of marches (no. 94) for the Prussian Army whose rhythm and style A. Th. L'vov (1798-1870) possibly altered and published in his own arrangement for the Preobrazhenskij Regiment, which Peter the Great had established in 1687. (See Tenor, "Kto kompozitor" nashego nyněshniago narodnago gimna?" *Russkaia muzykal'naia gazeta*, no. 52 (December 31, 1903), cols. 1313-1314; and "Kto avtor" narodnago gimna?," *Russkaia muzykal'naia gazeta*, no. 8 (February 22, 1904), cols. 198-205.)

37. Rychin claims that around 1880 the Spasskij Tower contained thirty-six bells and that the chime mechanism played *Kol' slaven"* at 8 o'clock in the evening (*Istoricheskoe opisanie*, 240).

38. According to Alexandra Anzerowa, the bells in the Spasskij clock, before it was damaged during the Revolution, played the melody, *Wir beten an die Macht der Liebe* (a German *contrafactum* of *Kol' slaven"*?), at noon and at midnight (*Aus dem Lande der Stummen* [Breslau: Bergstadtverlag, 1936], 236).

39. At the end of the nineteenth and beginning of the twentieth centuries the *Internationale* became the rallying song of the international socialist labor movement. Its words, written in 1871 by Eugène Pottier (1816-1887), were first published in 1887, and in 1888 Pierre Degeyter (1848-1932), a French woodcarver, set Pottier's poem as a song. A Russian translation of the first, second, and sixth stanzas of the Pottier poem, which A. Ia. Kots had made in 1902, was adopted as the national anthem of the new government after the Bolshevik revolution. Though no longer the national anthem of the USSR, it remains the official hymn of the Communist Party. *Vy zhertvoiu pali* became part of the revolutionary movement in Russia in the mid-1880s. For background on these two songs, see Sim. Drejden, "Internatsional," and E. Kann-Novikova, "Vy zhertvoiu pali v bor'be rokovoj," in *Biografii pesen* (Moscow: Izd. Politicheskoj literatury, 1965), 14-52, and 117-136;

and Paul Nettl, *National Anthems* (New York: Storm Publishers, 1952), 129.

40. Radchenko, *Moskovskie chasy*, 27.

41. Ibid., 29; and Goncharova and Khamtsov, *Steny bashni kremlia*, 50. In 1769 Semen Mozhzhukhin cast the hour bell at 135 puds (4,875 pounds) (Barten'ev, *Moskovskij Kreml'*, 133).

42. Pukhnachev, *Zagadki*, 3. The Spasskij clock and Kremlin chimes were worked on again in 1974 (Radchenko, *Moskovskie chasy*, 32-33). The familiar descending chromatic scale is rung on eleven of the chime bells (Schilling, *Glocken*, 148).

43. Zabelin, *Istoriia goroda Moskvy*, 186. The old Tajnitskij (Secret) Gate was begun in 1485 and razed in 1770. The present gate was built between 1771 and 1773. Formerly there had been a secret well inside the gate, which gave it its name (Krekshina, *Po Kremliu*, 21).

44. Zabelin, *Istoriia goroda Moskvy*, 186. The Nikol'skij Gate was built in 1491, the same year as the Spasskij Gate, and received its name from an icon of St. Nicholas the Miracle Worker placed above its portal. The present Gothic style tower above the gate belongs to the early nineteenth century and was not extant when a clock was apparently in the gate. (Krekshina, *Po Kremliu*, 33; see also Rychin, *Istoricheskoe opisanie*, 240-242.)

45. Barten'ev, *Moskovskij Kreml'*, 172.

46. Adelung, *Al'bom" Mejerberga*, 161, my translation.

47. Barten'ev, *Moskovskij Kreml'*, 195.

48. Ibid., 161.

49. Ibid., 163.

50. Ibid., 162-163.

51. Förster learned that in 1731 Count Semen Andreevich Saltykov had removed the clock bells from the tower of the Church of the Archangel Gabriel (Menshikov Tower) and had transferred them to the Troitskij Gate (ibid., 164).

52. Ibid.

53. Zabelin, *Istoriia goroda Moskvy*, 193. The funeral for Count Z. G. Chernyshev took place in the late summer of 1784.

54. The Borovitskij Gate of 1490, oldest of the entrances to the Kremlin, received its name from the thick pine forest (*bor*) that once covered the rise above the river that the Kremlin now occupies (Krekshina, *Po Kremliu*, 18).

55. Barten'ev, *Moskovskij Kreml'*, 165.

56. Krekshina, *Po Kremliu*, 20. At the end of the seventeenth century the lower portion of the Blagoveshchenskij Tower (built in 1487-1488) was extended upward as a tent-shaped roof with a lookout chamber. The tower is named for an icon of the Annunciation it once contained and for the Church of the Annunciation built next to it at the beginning of the eighteenth century (not to be confused with the Cathedral of the Annunciation on the Kremlin's central square). This church was razed in 1933 during restoration of the Blagoveshchenskij Tower.

57. Archimandrite Grigorij, "Vysokopetrovskij monastyr' v" Moskvě," *Russkiia dostopamiatnosti* 3 (1880): 40-41.

58. N. P. Rozanov, "Tserkov' Arkhangela Gavriila v" Moskvě,

na Chistom″ prudĕ, ili Menshikova bashnia," *Russkiia dosto-pamiatnosti* 2 (1883): 7-8.

59. Ibid., 11.

60. Radchenko, *Moskovskie chasy*, 38-41. L. P. Radin set his poem, "Smelo, tovarishchi v nogu," to a Russian melody in 1897.

61. Ibid., 34-37.

62. As early as 1477 at the Kirillo-Belozerskij Monastery an elder named Dionisij (d. between 1511 and 1514) is cited as a clockmaker; and almost a century later in 1569 three clock-makers, Tikhon, Theognost, and Gerasim, lived at this mon-astery (Nikolaj Nikol′skij, *Kirillo-Bĕlozerskij monastyr′ i ego ustrojstvo do vtoroj chetverti XVII vĕka [1397-1625]* 1 [St. Petersburg: Sẏnodal′naia tip., 1897], 176 n. 1).

63. Ibid., 175-177. Founders in sixteenth-century Pskov often cast bells for cities and monasteries in the north. In 1537 two Pskov founders, Krivoj Nos and Timofej Andreev, founded a 60-pud bell for a tower clock whose location was not specified. (Rubtsov, *History*, 312.)

64. Paul of Aleppo, *Puteshestvie* 1:62-63.

65. This clock struck once on a small bell for the quarters and four times softly to signal the beginning of the hour fol-lowed by the appropriate number of strokes on a large bell. The clock dial was placed outside on the wall of the bell tower and was a disc that indicated the hours of daylight. (Ibid. 2:54.)

66. Ibid.

67. S. Bezsonov, ed., *State Museum of the Kiev-Pechersk Lavra: A Short Guide*, trans. Natasha Johnson (Kiev: Mi-stetstvo Publishers, 1975), 60; and A. V. Kudritskij, ed., *Kiev: ėntsiklopedicheskij spravochnik* (Kiev: Glavnaia redaktsiia Ukrainskoj Sovetskoj Ėntsiklopedii, 1982), 67.

68. The upper tier of the bell tower at the Savvino-Storo-zhevskij Monastery contained a large striking clock of Polish provenience, which Tsar Aleksei Mikhailovich had brought from Smolensk and presented to the monastery. When Paul of Aleppo visited this monastery in 1655, he remarked that the clock bells had not yet been installed (*Puteshestvie* 4:132). The old-est extant mechanism for a Russian tower clock is one that Semen Chasovik of Novgorod made in 1539 for the Solovetskij Monastery. This clock mechanism and others are on display in the Organnaia Palace Museum-Preserve at Kolomenskoe. (Radchenko, *Moskovskie chasy*, 9-17.) In the bell tower of the Solovetskij Monastery, a striking clock and four small German bells were among the possessions listed in an inventory fol-lowing the siege of 1676 (Sergej Al. Belokurov, *Biblioteka i arkhiv″ Solovetskago monastyria poslĕ osady [1676 goda]* [Moscow: Universitetskaia tip., 1887], 5).

Notes to Chapter 8

1. Percival Price, "Carillon," *New Grove Dictionary of Mu-sic and Musicians* 3:781-782; and Price, *The Carillon*, 15. Three early instruments that represent a transitional stage between chimes and carillon are reported at Dunkirk in 1437, Alost (Belgium) in 1487, and Antwerp in 1540 (John Camp, *Bell Ringing: Chimes, Carillons, Hand Bells; The World of the Bell and the Ringer* [Newton Abbot, England: David & Charles, 1974], 110). Price cites three later instruments cast by the Waghevens family that, though still large chimes in their ranges, nevertheless point toward the carillon: "a series of seven bells for Alost in 1539, fourteen for Ghent in 1543, and seventeen for Tournai in 1544" (*Bells and Man*, 179). The chromatic scale of a carillon requires a greater number of bells per octave than the diatonic scale of a chime. For the derivation of the word "carillon," see Chapter 7, n. 17.

2. Westcott, *Bells and Their Music*, 95. The carillon at the University of Kansas, one of the largest in North America, contains fifty-three bells and embraces nearly four and a half chromatic octaves.

3. The natural key of C major was probably the most com-mon key in which most seventeenth-century carillons pro-duced in the Low Countries were pitched, though the precise pitch might even vary from one C instrument to another. As for their tuning, earlier carillons (e.g., those of the Hemony brothers) were untempered, and the performance of poly-phonic music was possible only in certain keys. Some instru-ments, beginning in 1770, began to employ equal tempera-ment, and others sought to effect a compromise between older and newer standards of tuning. Price remarks that "the ma-jority of Continental carillons are so faultily tuned that it is impossible to decide whether their scale is tempered or un-tempered . . ." (*The Carillon*, 97-98).

4. Frans (François) Hemony (ca. 1609-1667) and his brother Pieter (Pierre) (1619-1680) were jointly commissioned in 1642 to cast their first set of bells at Zutphen near Arnhem for a town tower clock. They settled in Zutphen until 1657 when Frans was sent by royal decree to Amsterdam. Pieter man-aged his own foundry in Ghent but joined his brother in Am-sterdam in 1664 where they again worked together until Frans' death. From 1667 to about 1680 Pieter carried on his profes-sion alone. (Hans Klotz, "Hemony," *New Grove Dictionary of Music and Musicians* 8:475; see also Price, "Bell," 436; and Price, *The Carillon*, 23-31.) "The Hemonys were . . . the first to make chromatic carillons and to extend the compass to three or more octaves" (Klotz, "Hemony," 476). Their work in Hol-land set a standard of excellence in carillon building compa-rable to that which Amati, Guarneri, and Stradivari estab-lished for Italian baroque string instruments (Thomas D. Rossing, *The Science of Sound* [Reading, MA: Addison-Wes-ley Publishing Co., 1982], 252-253).

5. Percival Price, "The Carillons of the Cathedral of Peter and Paul in the Fortress of Leningrad," *The Galpin Society Journal* 27 (February, 1964): 64. Carillon bells are struck by internal clappers when played by a carillonneur from a key-board with pedals; they are sounded by external hammers when rung automatically.

6. Price, "Carillon," 782. Cf. Price, "The Carillons of the Cathedral of Peter and Paul," 65.

7. Westcott, *Bells and Their Music*, 90.

8. The principal sources for the two Dutch carillons in the cathedral tower are two works by Dimitrij Florinskij: *Istoriko-statisticheskoe opisanie sanktpeterburgskago Petropavlov-skago kathedral'nago sobora* (St. Petersburg: Tip. Georga Be-nike, 1857), 1-31; and *Sobor" vo imia sviatykh" pervoverkhov-nykh" apostolov" Petra i Pavla v" S.-Peterburgskoj krěposti* (St. Petersburg: Tip. Departamenta udělov", 1882), 1-27, 39. Another important document for the first carillon is I. Th. Ammon's translation, *Dnevnik" kamer"-iunkera F. V. Berkh-gol'tsa, 1721-1725*, pt. 1: 1721, new ed. with supplementary notes (Moscow: Universitetskaia tip., 1902), 78, 96-97. The sources for Florinskij's studies were taken from archives of the cathedral, the offices of the fortress commandant, and the church consistory. In addition, Florinskij consulted Vasilij Ru-ban's historical, geographical, and topographical description of St. Petersburg from 1779 (Andrej Ivanovich Bogdanov, *Isto-richeskoe, geograficheskoe i topograficheskoe opisanie Sankt-peterburga . . . a nyně dopolnennoe i izdannoe . . . Vasil'-em" Rubanom"* [St. Petersburg, 1779]); significant informa-tion on St. Petersburg by P. Svin'in in 1818; and a short his-tory of the Peter and Paul Cathedral found in the remarks of Protopriest Ioakim Kochetov on the consecration of the cathe-dral in 1833. The passage from Bergholz's diary is quoted in Petr Petrovich Pekarskij, *Peterburgskaia starina* (St. Peters-burg, 1860), 331. Materials drawn from Florinskij and Pekar-skij also appear in Olovianishnikov, *Istoriia kolokolov"*, 316-327. An account of the second Petersburg carillon is contained in Willy Godenne's *Cloches en URSS* (Malines: Ecole royale de Carillon "Jef Denyn," 1960), 7-13, 17-19, but the principal modern study of the Petersburg carillons is Percival Price's article, "The Carillons of the Cathedral of Peter and Paul," 64-76. On the history of the cathedral, see E. Timofeeva, "Pervonachal'nyj oblik Petropavlovskogo sobora," *Arkhitek-turnoe nasledstvo* 7 (Leningrad-Moscow: Gosudarstvennoe izd. literatury po stroitel'stvu i arkhitekture, 1955), 93-108; L. I. Bastareva and V. I. Sidorova, *Petropavlovskaia krepost'*, 2d ed., rev. and enl. (Leningrad: Lenizdat, 1972), 80-90; and S. M. Serpokryl, compiler, and A. E. Suknovalov, ed., *Lenin-grad: putevoditel'* (Leningrad: Lenizdat, 1972), 102-106.

9. On Peter the Great's two visits to the West in 1697-1698 and 1716-1717, see Robert K. Massie, *Peter the Great: His Life and World* (New York: Alfred A. Knopf, 1980), 178-233, 624-656.

10. On May 16, 1703, ground was broken on Hare Island in the Neva River for the wooden and earthen fortress of Sankt Piter Bourkh (later called the Peter and Paul Fortress). Do-menico Trezzini began construction on the present brick and stone fortress on May 30, 1706, a project that was not finished until 1740. Work was even resumed during the 1770s and 1780s when the walls overlooking the Neva were faced with granite (Bastareva and Sidorova, *Petropavlovskaia krepost'*, 10, 14-20). Trezzini's new stone cathedral, which replaced his ear-lier wooden church, was begun in early May of 1712 and was

consecrated on June 29, 1733 (Timofeeva, "Pervonachal'nyj oblik," 94-95).

11. An analogous transformation in the portraiture of the tsar along Western lines is discussed by Michael Cherniavsky, *Tsar and People: Studies in Russian Myths* (New Haven: Yale University Press, 1961), 79.

12. See Price, "The Carillons," 66; and Christopher Mars-den, *Palmyra of the North: The First Days of St. Petersburg* (London: Faber and Faber, 1942), 58.

13. The twenty-eight-bell Hemony carillon for the Tyska kyrkan in Stockholm was the oldest of the carillons in the eastern Baltic. Cast in 1663, it was destroyed in a fire of 1878. (Price, *The Carillon*, 213.) A thirty-five-bell Derck carillon of 1737/1738, installed in the St. Katharinenkirche at Danzig, was lost during a fire in 1905, and the twenty-eight bells of the carillon of 1698 at the Church of St. Peter in Riga, the work of Claude Frémy, were destroyed, according to Schil-ling, in a fire of 1721 (*Glocken*, 146, 148, 150). Cf. Price, who states that the bells of the Riga carillon were dispersed throughout Latvia during the eighteenth and nineteenth cen-turies (*The Carillon*, 212).

14. Even in the mid-nineteenth century the tower of the cathedral in the fortress was challenged only by the lesser spire on the Admiralty and by the dome on the new Cathedral of St. Isaac (William Palmer, *Notes of a Visit to the Russian Church in the Years 1840, 1841*, selected and arrg. by Car-dinal Newman [London: Kegan Paul Trench & Co., 1882], 26-27).

15. Florinskij's statement that the carillon was *ordered* in 1720 is probably based upon his interpretation of the passage in Ruban's amplification of Bogdanov's book that mentions the tower clock and its thirty-five bells having been "ordered from Amsterdam at a cost of 45,000 rubles, and *installed* [italics mine] in the bell tower in 1720" (Bogdanov, *Istoricheskoe . . . opisanie*, 254). Whether the instrument was ordered the same year that it was installed is questionable.

Schilling suggests that the bells of the first carillon were the work of Jan Albert de Grave (also Jan Alberts de Graave), a gun and bell founder active in Amsterdam during the first quarter of the eighteenth century (*Glocken*, 148). The names of Claes Noorden and Jan Albert de Grave appear as founders on two bells of 1702 in the Moscow Kremlin's Spasskij Tower (Barten'ev, *Moskovskij Kreml'*, 133). In 1717 de Grave had cast a carillon of thirty-seven bells for the Parochialkirche in Ber-lin, and in 1722 he produced a forty-bell instrument for the Garnisonkirche in Potsdam (Ernest Morris, *Bells of All Na-tions* [London: Robert Hale, 1951], 144). Cf. Price who indi-cates that the bells may have been cast at the Derck foundry in Hoorn, Holland, the same foundry that produced the sec-ond Petersburg carillon. Peter the Great had worked in the shipyards at Zaandam near Hoorn during his first visit to the West in 1697-1698 and may have remembered the Derck foundry for the ship bells it probably produced. (Price, "The Carillons," 67.) Only two carillons have been identified as the work of Johann Melchior Derck and his sons: the Danzig instrument of 1737/1738 and the second Petersburg carillon of 1757 (Price, *The Carillon*, 208, 212). On Johann Melchior Derck of Meiningen, active between 1717 and 1753, see Ulrich Thieme and Fred C. Willis, eds., "Derck, Johann Melchior," *Allgemeines Lexikon der bildenden Künstler von der Antike bis zur Gegenwart* 9 (Leipzig: E. A. Seemann, 1913), 94-95.

16. Bogdanov, *Istoricheskoe . . . opisanie*, 254; and Florinsky, *Opisanie*, 2-3.

17. Bogdanov, *Istoricheskoe . . . opisanie*, 254.

18. Johann Christian Förster from Holstein became a carillonneur and advisor in Russia on bells, their placement, and installation. He was sent to Moscow in 1734 to make a recommendation on the bells in the Kremlin's Troitskij Tower (see Chapter 7 of this volume) and is last mentioned in 1757 in connection with his installation of bells in an older Cathedral of St. Isaac in St. Petersburg. (Price, "The Carillons," 67-68.)

19. The largest bell of the second Petersburg carillon was called the Quint because it was to be pitched on *G*, a fifth above a hypothetical bell on *C*, an octave below bell no. 1 on middle C (Price, "The Carillons," 75 n. 12). Until the eighteenth century it was rare for a carillon's range to descend as low as middle C (Bigelow, *Carillon*, 46).

20. Considerations of expense still take precedence over casting a carillon with a complete chromatic scale in the lowest part of its range. For the price of two large bells on $c^{\sharp}$ and $d^{\sharp}$ an entire additional octave of smaller treble bells could be purchased.

21. Ammon, *Dnevnik" . . . Berkhgol'tsa*, 1:96-97, my translation. On July 24, 1721, Bergholz had noted that the bells were played each day from 11:00 A.M. until noon and were sounded automatically every hour and half-hour (p. 78).

22. Florinskij, *Opisanie*, 4-5. See also Timofeeva, "Pervonachal'nyj oblik," 98; and Bastareva and Sidorova, *Petropavlovskaia krepost'*, 84.

23. Florinskij, *Opisanie*, 6.

24. Tula was an important industrial center south of Moscow, and at Sestroretsk near St. Petersburg there was a small-arms factory, which Peter the Great had established.

25. Florinskij, *Sobor" . . . Petra i Pavla*, 14, 15. The contract was awarded to the lowest bidder. Golovkin also received a second proposal from another foreman with a budget of 86,500 guilders: 55,000 for the clock and 31,500 for the bells, their hammers, and clappers.

26. Price, "The Carillons," 69. By commissioning a second carillon with thirty-eight bells in 1757, St. Petersburg would not only equal but even surpass Danzig, whose thirty-five-bell instrument of 1737/1738 was cast while St. Petersburg's first (thirty-five-bell) carillon was still functioning. The carillons in both Stockholm and Riga contained only twenty-eight bells each.

27. Ibid., 69-70. According to Price, the specifications for clappers imply that the Quint bell was to be rung from both the console and the clock (ibid., 75 n. 15).

28. The Dutch carillonneur who came to Danzig in 1738 to play the Derck carillon in that city declared that the instrument was so out of tune that the inspector who let it out of Holland must have either been drunk or had had his ears plugged with gold (ibid., 70).

29. Florinskij, *Opisanie*, 16-17.

30. The Dutchmen arrived in St. Petersburg on August 28, according to Florinsky in *Opisanie*, 19. In *Sobor" . . . Petra i Pavla*, 18, however, Florinsky gives the date as August 22. The rebuilding of the cathedral's tower and its *flèche* was only begun in 1768 (four years after Oortkras' death) and continued until 1777. The lower stone portion of the tower, however, was finished in 1771 (Timofeeva, "Pervonachal'nyj oblik," 105).

31. Price, "Carillons," 74. Godenne reports the existence of letters in Russian archives from Oortkras' widow, who sought without success to obtain payment for the work her husband had done on the carillon in both Holland and St. Petersburg (*Cloches en URSS*, 12). In 1820 a grandson of Oortkras even appeared in St. Petersburg for the purpose of collecting payment on his grandfather's work. As far as can be determined, neither the widow nor the grandson was successful. (Florinskij, *Sobor" . . . Petra i Pavla*, 22n.)

32. At 11:00 A.M. trumpeters and oboists from the regimental garrison in the fortress played for a half-hour before Rüdiger's performance on the carillon (Bogdanov, *Istoricheskoe . . . opisanie*, 255; see also Florinskij, *Opisanie*, 25n.).

33. Florinskij, *Opisanie*, 25. There is no record of the pieces that Rüdiger performed on his recitals, but as Price has noted, the preparation of five hours of music each week (assuming that he did not repeat selections from day to day) would require considerable time for the arranging and copying of music alone ("The Carillons," 72).

34. Florinskij, *Opisanie*, 25-26. In Belgium some clocks emit brief ripples of music at 7.5, 22.5, 37.5, and 52.5 minutes past the hour. Bell sounds that mark these four semiquarters are designated in Flemish as *wekkering* or *halfkens*. In Act III, scene 2 of Tchaikovsky's opera, *Pikovaia dama* (*The Queen of Spades*), whose action the composer has placed during the reign of Catherine II, the hour bell in Oortkras' clock strikes midnight from the fortress tower.

35. Florinskij, *Opisanie*, 26. The cathedral's bell tower contains three tiers. The lowest level has fourteen Russian bells that served the liturgies and offices in the cathedral; the second tier houses the clock mechanism and the carillon bells; and the third is empty. (Florinskij, *Sobor" . . . Petra i Pavla*, 39; see also Olovianishnikov, *Istoriia kolokolov"*, 117.) The transfer of Russian bells from the Pereslavskij Uspenskij Cathedral at Suzdal to the tower of the Cathedral of Saints Peter and Paul in the fortress at St. Petersburg in 1789 is related in A. A. Potapov, "Perevozka pereslavskikh" kolokolov" v" peterburgskij Petropavlovskij sobor"," *Vladimirskiia eparkhial'nyia vědomosti*, no. 38 (1907), pp. 593-599.

36. Florinskij, *Opisanie*, 27.

37. Ibid., 27n. In his guide to Russia of 1849 John Murray makes no mention of carillon music or chimes in the tower of

the Cathedral of Saints Peter and Paul (*Hand-book for Northern Europe; including Denmark, Norway, Sweden, Finland, and Russia*, new ed., pt. 2: Finland and Russia [London: John Murray, 1849], 478, 479).

38. Shilling, *Glocken*, 149. According to Baedeker in the 1914 edition of his travel guide to Russia, a cannon was fired from the Peter and Paul Fortress every day at noon, and the clock in the tower still played the Russian national anthem, *Bozhe, Tsaria khrani*, at noon and the hymn *Kol' slaven"* every hour (*Russia*, 173; see also Meriel Buchanan, *The Dissolution of an Empire* [London: John Murray, 1932; reprint ed., New York: Arno Press & The New York Times, 1971], 11; and Otto Keller, *St. Petersburg and its Environs* [St. Petersburg: Kügelgen, Glitsch, & Co., (1913)], 79-80). Aleksej Fedorovich L'vov is credited with writing the music for *Bozhe, Tsaria khrani* in 1833 to a poem by V. A. Zhukovsky (Nettl, *National Anthems*, 128; see also Nik[olaj] Bernshtejn, *Istoriia natsional'nykh" gimnov"* [Petrograd: Tip. Glavnago upravleniia udělov", 1914], 3-10.

39. Serpokryl and Suknovalov, *Leningrad: putevoditel'*, 104-106; Bastareva and Sidorova, *Petropavlovskaia krepost'*, 84; and Schilling, *Glocken*, 149-150. The anthem of the Soviet Union appeared at the end of 1943 with words by Sergej Mikhalkov and E. L. Gistan and music by Aleksandr Vasil'evich Aleksandrov (1883-1946) (Nettl, *National Anthems*, 130).

40. Godenne, *Cloches en URSS*, 13.

41. Billington, *The Icon and the Axe*, 181; Germain Bazin, *The Baroque: Principles, Styles, Modes, Themes* (Greenwich, CT: New York Graphic Society, 1968), 119, 314; and Massie, *Peter the Great*, 608-609.

42. Izrailev graduated from the Yaroslavl Seminary in 1840 when he was twenty-three and was consecrated the following year as a deacon in the Peter and Paul Cathedral in Petrovsk. Following his ordination as priest at Rostov-Velikij in 1842, he taught religion and singing. (Rybakov, *Tserkovnyj zvon"*, 42.)

43. The most detailed account of Izrailev's work with tuned bells is his own article, "Muzykal'no-akusticheskiia raboty," *Izvěstiia Obshchestva liubitelej estestvoznaniia, antropologii, i ětnografii* 41, issue 2 (1884), pp. 67-72. For other accounts and evaluations, see Rybakov, *Tserkovnyj zvon"*, 42-47; and Olovianishnikov, *Istoriia kolokolov"*, 282-304. A résumé appears in Privalov, "Kolokol'nyj zvon" na Rusi, 41-43. The material in this chapter is drawn primarily from information on Izrailev and his work published in these sources.

44. For Izrailev's description of his pendular sonometer and its use, see "Muzykal'no-akusticheskiia raboty," 59-61. As Price points out, Izrailev's experiments with tuning forks and bells in Russia were part of a larger European resurgence of interest in bells and their tuning at the end of the nineteenth and beginning of the twentieth centuries ("Bell," 429).

45. Izrailev's tuning forks were shown at the Moscow Polytechnical Exhibition of 1872, the Vienna International Exhibition in 1873, the Philadelphia Exhibition in 1876, the Paris National Academy in 1879, and the All-Russian Exhibition at Moscow in 1882 (Rybakov, *Tserkovnyj zvon"*, 43).

46. Olovianishnikov, *Istoriia kolokolov"*, 283.

47. *Rostovskie kolokola i zvony*, Pamiatniki drevnej pis'mennosti 51 (St. Petersburg: Tip. M. M. Stasiulevicha, 1884).

48. Under construction throughout the mid-nineteenth century, the monumental Cathedral of Christ the Saviour (or Church of the Redeemer, as it was sometimes called) was begun in 1838 but was not consecrated until May 26, 1883, in the presence of Alexander III.

49. Among the reasons cited for rejecting Izrailev's proposal were the following: (1) to tune the bells would require the shaving of metal from their interior surfaces; (2) the commission had received no definite information on the amount of weight the bells would lose through shaving and was therefore not certain whether this loss would adversely affect the strength of the bells; and (3) the proposal contained no estimate of the project's cost, an amount that could possibly prove prohibitive in light of other work that the commission had already approved (Olovianishnikov, *Istoriia kolokolov"*, 288).

50. Built between 1883 and 1907, the Church of the Resurrection (also known as the Church of the Saviour on the Blood) was the work of Al'fred Aleksandrovich Parland, who designed it in the style of the Cathedral of St. Basil on Red Square in Moscow. This Petersburg church stands in the street by the Catherine (now Griboedov) Canal on the very spot where, on March 1, 1881, a group of nihilists bombed and mortally wounded Alexander II. (Baedeker, *Russia*, 118.)

51. Izrailev's nine bells for the Anichkov Palace church were tuned to three chords: a tonic F-sharp-major triad (F$^\sharp$-A$^\sharp$-C$^\sharp$), a sub-dominant B-major triad (B-D$^\sharp$-F$^\sharp$), and a sub-mediant D-sharp-minor triad (D$^\sharp$-F$^\sharp$-A$^\sharp$).

52. List in text is taken from Olovianishnikov, *Istoriia kolokolov"*, 294 n. 1.

53. *Bozhe, Tsaria khrani* and *Kol' slaven"* could be rung on these bells.

54. Belev is located about eighty miles southwest of Tula.

55. These six bells were tuned to a G-minor chord (G-D-G-B$^\flat$-D-G) and were cast in Yaroslavl at the foundry of the Olovianishnikov brothers (Rybakov, *Tserkovnyj zvon"*, 44).

56. This church was one of two located on the country estate of senator and privy councillor Vladimir Pavlovich Mordvinov, who had built near it a fairly low, but elegant, stone bell tower (K. I., "Garmonicheskij zvon" tserkovnykh" kolokolov"," *Litovskiia eparkhial'nyia vědomosti*, no. 34 [1893], 286).

57. Izrailev's work recalls an earlier dichotomy in Russian music during the second half of the nineteenth century between Anton and Nicholas Rubinstein, with a more Western and academic orientation, and Mily Balakirev, mentor for the group called "The Russian Five" (*moguchaia kuchka*), who advocated the mining and use of native materials in Russian music. On the Slavophiles and Westernizers, see D. S. Mirsky, *A History of Russian Literature from its Beginnings to 1900*, ed. Francis J. Whitfield (New York: Vintage Books, 1958), 169-173, 228-230; and MacKenzie and Curran, *History*, 306-309.

58. Izrailev's bell tuning received enthusiastic endorse-

ment, however, from the author of an article (signed only "K. I.") in a church periodical published in Lithuania: "How fine it would be, one thought, if this pure musical ringing of bells were indeed to penetrate into that region [the provinces of western Russia] where even now Russian Orthodox life has to reckon with the hostile power of the militant Roman faith; how fine it would be if these measured melodic sounds could reverberate louder and louder from our Orthodox cathedrals and drown the untuned droning of the bells swinging from Roman churches that loom so proudly" (K. I., "Garmonicheskij zvon″," 286, my translation).

59. Olovianishnikov, *Istoriia kolokolov″*, 270. For other critiques of Izrailev's work in bell tuning, see Rybakov, *Tserkovnyj zvon″*, 46-47; Privalov, "Kolokol'nyj zvon″," 42-43; Pukhnachev, *Zagadki*, 109.

60. Smagin and his work will be discussed in the second volume of this study.

61. The bells of Novorossijsk on the Black Sea are particularly noted for the music that Dmitrij Shostakovich composed for them in 1960. At Khatyn near Minsk, chimneys, each surmounted by a bell, stand on the sites of the former inhabitants' dwellings before World War II. (Victor and Jennifer Louis, *The Complete Guide to the Soviet Union*, 197.) Other chimes in the Soviet Union are located in Sevastopol, Odessa, Kiev, and Kaunas, Lithuania. From the tower of the Seaman's Club in Sevastopol, chimes play the refrain from Vano Muradeli's song *Legendarnyj Sevastopol'*, *nepristupnyj dlia vragov* (Legendary Sevastopol, impregnable to enemies); the Odessa chimes ring a theme from Isaak Dunaevskij's operetta *Belaia akatsiia* (The Locust Tree); above Kalinin Square in Kiev, chimes play the melody of the folk song, *Reve ta stogne Dnipr shirokij* (The broad Dnieper roars and groans); and since 1959 from the tower of the Museum of History and Revolution in Kaunas, Lithuania, has come music from the thirty-five bells of the only carillon in the Soviet Union that can be played by a carillonneur, (Schilling, *Glocken*, 150.)

62. Pukhnachev, *Zagadki*, 3, my translation.

Notes to Chapter 9

1. Rubtsov, *History*, 72. See also Olovianishnikov, *Istoriia kolokolov″*, 400-401. In his treatise published in 1540 Biringuccio set forth four criteria for producing bells with a fine tone: good metal, good form, suitable dimensions, and a clapper proportionate to the bell's weight (*The Pirotechnia of Vannoccio Biringuccio*, trans. from the Italian with an introduction and notes by Cyril Stanley Smith and Martha Teach Gnudi, The Collector's Series in Science, ed. Derek J. Price [New York: Basic Books, 1959], 270 [bk. 6, chap. 12]).

2. Olovianishnikov, *Istoriia kolokolov″*, 253; and N. R., "O kolokolakh″ i o kolokol'nom″ iskusstvě," *Moskovskiia vědomosti*, no. 49 (Tuesday, April 25, 1850), p. 569, righthand col.

3. Price, "Bell," 431, 434. With the advent of Buddhism in China also came a change in the form of Chinese bells from a rectangular or oval horizontal cross-section to a circular cross-

section, a change that significantly extended the sound decay (ibid., 431).

4. Bigelow, *The Acoustically Balanced Carillon*, 1. See also Appendix D to this volume for the weights and dates of founding of some of the largest Asian bells.

5. Price, "Bell," 428.

6. N. R., "O kolokolakh″," 569, righthand col. See also Gatty, *The Bell*, 50. Price points out that the voices of the great bells of the Far East produce "a deep, prolonged and far-carrying note simulating the sacred sound 'Om' " ("Bell," 434).

7. Bigelow, *Carillon*, 27.

8. Meneely & Kimberly, *Bells*, 38. One founder attributes the distinctive tone of Chinese bells to their form, which he describes as "a very prolate hemispheroid." (Edmund Beckett, Lord Grimthorpe, *A Rudimentary Treatise on Clocks, Watches, & Bells for Public Purposes*, 8th ed. [London: Crosby Lockwood and Son, 1903], 356.)

9. T. Philip Terry, *Terry's Japanese Empire Including Korea and Formosa* (London: Constable & Co., 1914), 616. See also Coleman, *Bells*, 316-317.

10. Price, *Bells and Man*, 273.

11. Liu Junwen, *Beijing: China's Ancient and Modern Capital* (Beijing: Foreign Languages Press, 1982), 144.

12. Bigelow, *Carillon*, 26; and Price, "Bell," 428. As Percival Price has noted, however, the more conical, flared form of bell is not exclusive to the West but is also present in Asia (particularly in India and Nepal) and evolved without influence from European examples. (See figures in *Bells and Man*, pp. 23, 30, 56, 27.) The Great Mingun Bell in Burma "although flared [in its lower portion], has the broad flat top of the south-east Asian bronze drum." (Ibid., 33.)

13. Bigelow, *Carillon*, 28; and Bigelow, *The Acoustically Balanced Carillon*, 1, 2; Marcuse, *Survey*, 58-59; Price, "Bell," 424-426; and Camp, *Bell Ringing*, 12. Just as some crotals contain several pellets, open bells with multiple clappers have appeared (Olovianishnikov, *Istoriia kolokolov″*, 253). "Potshaped" or "barrel-shaped" designates a hollow object whose sides are almost perpendicular and whose height exceeds its diameters. The other principal form of vibrating body in the Orient is bowl-shaped, "an object absolutely convex, with a diameter far exceeding its height," that developed into the gong. (Bigelow, *Carillon*, 26.) Despite their obvious difference in form Ernest Morris draws attention to a relationship between large Chinese bells and gongs. Like gongs they are stationary in their mounting and are struck on their outside wall by wood (a substance softer than the bell itself). What Morris regards as a true bell is an instrument with an internal metal clapper set in motion by swinging the bell itself (*Tintinnabula*, 47).

14. Western bells today are usually cast without cannons and with a flat boss on their head or top plate. The top of a European swinging bell is fastened directly to a stock, or in the case of stationary carillon and chime bells, to a beam, by a crown staple bolt through its top plate.

15. Olovianishnikov, *Istoriia kolokolov′*, 393. Cannons with

six loops are normal on large bells. Because of the enormous size and weight of Motorin's Tsar-Kolokol and Bogdanov's Great Uspensky Bell of 1817, however, they were cast with cannons of eight loops (Babin [Captain 2d grade], "O russkikh″ kolokolakh″," *Gornyj zhurnal″* 4, no. 11 [1861], p. 213).

16. Although there is general agreement among campanologists on the names "tierce," "quint," and "nominal" for the three upper frequencies generated by a tuned bell, labels for the two lowest frequencies vary. Since the second lowest frequency is the dominant or principal pitch of a bell, most campanologists call this the "fundamental"; they regard the prolonged lowest frequency an octave below as a sub-harmonic, which they call the "hum tone" (see Price, *The Carillon*, 87; Camp, *Bell Ringing*, 85; Engelbert Wiegman van Heuven, *Acoustical Measurements on Church-Bells and Carillons* [The Hague: De Gebroeders Van Cleef, 1949], 13, 75; and Westcott, *Bells and Their Music*, 42). But because the lowest member of the natural series of harmonics (overtone series) is known as the fundamental, Bigelow has used this term for the lowest frequency generated by a ringing bell (which he also designates hum tone). What Price, Camp, Heuven, and Westcott call the fundamental, Bigelow labels the "prime" (*The Acoustically Balanced Carillon*, [6]). I too prefer to call this the fundamental. The strike note is a fleeting frequency that merges with the fundamental that is an octave below the nominal on a tuned bell. The strike note, however, can also be distinguished briefly in bells whose fundamental does not lie an octave below the nominal. (Price, "Bell," 427.)

17. The thinner waist and shoulder of a bell were sometimes regarded as the necessary means for suspending the heavier mass of metal at the sound-bow without altering its tone when rung (H. B. Walters, *The Church Bells of England* [London: Oxford University Press, 1912], 33). A bell of uniform wall thickness, according to Satis Coleman, would produce a dull nonresonant sound when struck (cf. the tone and timbre of the great Oriental bells) (*Bells*, 71).

18. A bell's size will determine its pitch—the larger the instrument, the lower the pitch of its fundamental (Camp, *Bell Ringing*, 14). In this connection, Percival Price points out that the thinner the wall of a bell, the lower its pitch will be: "when two bells of the same outside form and size have different thicknesses, the thicker bell will sound a higher note. Thus there is a gradual increase in the proportional thickness of the bells in the upper register of most carillons, so as to give them enough mass of metal to be heard along with the much larger bells in the lower register." Price's observation is published in a general information sheet on bells from the American Bell Association.

19. For explanations of the acoustical properties of a ringing bell, see Westcott, *Bells and Their Music*, 49-57; Lord Rayleigh, "On Bells," *The London, Edinburgh, and Dublin Philosophical Magazine and Journal of Science* (5th ser.) 29, no. 176 (January 1890), 1-17; Heuven, *Acoustical Measurements*; and Johannes Biehle, "Die Analyse des Glockenklanges," *Archiv für Musikwissenschaft* 1 (1919): 289-311.

20. Because older French bells lacked the thicker sound-bow of other European bells, they had a thinner, weaker tone (Bigelow, *Carillon*, 38, 39).

21. Olovianishnikov, *Istoriia kolokolov″*, 388.

22. Ibid., 386.

23. Olovianishnikov indicates that fractions of less than one fourth of a vershok in diameter lengths were not taken into consideration in computations, however (ibid.).

24. Tyack, *A Book About Bells*, 29.

25. Tyack points out that Tsar-Kolokol (1735) in Moscow is almost as high as it is wide at its mouth and that another large bell in Moscow—presumably Bogdanov's Great Uspensky Bell—is 21 feet high and 18 feet in diameter (ibid; see also Priakhin, "Kolokol′nyj zvon″," 171).

26. N. Vasil′ev, "Otlivka kolokolov″," *Tekhnicheskij sbornik″* 12, no. 8 (1871), col. 124.

27. Olovianishnikov, *Istoriia kolokolov″*, 388; and N. R., "O kolokolakh″," 569, righthand col.

28. Before the Hemonys, founders had tuned their bells "by chipping off appropriate amounts" of metal from the inside, "an inherently inaccurate process resulting in a lack of symmetry in the shape of the bell and consequently [in] disadvantages for the tone. The Hemonys ground the bell on a lathe, thus achieving both a symmetrical structure and a previously unattainable degree of accuracy [in tuning] to about 1/20 of a semitone." (Klotz, "Hemony," 475.) Since Russian bells, like those of Asia, are traditionally untuned, the processes of tuning will not be discussed here, but see Price, *The Carillon*, 86ff.; Camp, *Bell Ringing*, 84-87; and Coleman, *Bells*, 71-73.

29. Camp, *Bell Ringing*, 13; and Arthur Lynds Bigelow, "Bells," *New Catholic Encyclopedia* 2: 260. Copper and tin, the two metals in bronze, were readily available in southern Europe.

30. Bruce L. Simpson, *History of the Metal-Casting Industry*, 2d ed. (Des Plaines, IL: American Foundrymen's Society, 1969), 101; and E. V. Barsov, *Iz istorii kolonizatsii i kul′tury rostovskago kraia* (Moscow, 1902), quoted in Rubtsov, *History*, 44. Iron was the only ore to be extracted in Kievan Russia; copper and tin had to be imported from the Caucasus and Asia Minor (Vernadsky, *Kievan Russia*, 111-112). From the beginning of the second millennium A.D. some large Japanese and Chinese bells were cast in iron (Price, "Bell," 434).

31. Louis J. Gallagher, trans., *China in the Sixteenth Century: The Journals of Matthew Ricci; 1583-1610* (New York: Random House, 1953), 22; Heuven, *Acoustical Measurements*, 4; and Westcott, *Bells and Their Music*, 46. Other combinations of metals in which bells have been cast include a German alloy of nickel, copper, and aluminum advertised at the beginning of this century (Pukhnachev, *Zagadki*, 60). In the mid-1860s an alloy was developed for the casting of bells, hammers, anvils, and other objects that was reportedly cheaper than bronze. Its components consisted of twenty parts iron filings, eighty parts steel, four parts manganese, and four parts borax. To increase the alloy's toughness, two or three parts of wolframite (iron manganese tungstate) could be added. ("No-

vyj splav″ dlia kolokolov″," *Gornyj zhurnal″*, pt. 1, bk. 3 [1865], p. 689 [from *The Mining Journal*, no. 1519, 1864].) For a listing of alloys other than bronze (e.g., iron/antimony, copper/phosphorus, and copper/aluminum) in which experimental bells were being cast at the beginning of the twentieth century in the United States, see James Larkin, *The Practical Brass and Iron Founder's Guide: A Treatise on Brass Founding, Moulding, the Metals, and their Alloys, etc.*, new ed., rev. and greatly enl. (Philadelphia: Henry Carey Baird, 1907), 111-112.

32. *Fabrichno-zavodskaia promyshlennost'*, 75. Grimthorpe remarked that "if the object of bells is to make the greatest noise for the least money, steel bells are very good ones . . ." (*A Rudimentary Treatise*, 364).

33. "The most inveterate of all popular delusions about bells is the notion that old bells had silver in them, and that all bells would be improved by it" (Grimthorpe, *A Rudimentary Treatise*, 364; see also Larkin, *Practical . . . Guide*, 110).

34. Nichols, *Bells thro' the Ages*, 65; and Rybakov, *Tserkovnyj zvon″*, 17. In 1847 a bell containing a substantial amount of silver was unearthed from a tomb in the village of Belkolodezo in the Tula province ("Drevnij kolokol″, najdennyj v″ Tul'skoj gubernii," *Zhurnal″ Ministerstva vnutrennikh″ děl″*, pt. 18, no. 4 [1847], p. 146). Another bell reputed to be of silver was founded in Khar'kov on June 5, 1890, at the Ryzhov Bell Foundry for the Cathedral of the Assumption in that city (Pyliaev, "Istoricheskie kolokola," 316). Perhaps the most unusual Russian bells, in their substance, were the stone bells reported in 1561 at the Solovetskij Monastery (Gemp, *Skaz o Belomor'e*, 126). One of these, carved during the administration of Igumen Zosima, was still extant in the nineteenth century (*Al'bom″ vidov″ Solovetskago monastyria i snimkov″ drevnostej i dostoprimѣchatel'nostej, khraniashchikhsia v″ ee riznitsě*, photo no. 35).

35. Pukhnachev, *Zagadki*, 58-59.

36. N. R., "O kolokolakh″ i o kolokol'nom″ iskusstvě," *Moskovskiia vědomosti*, no. 51 (Saturday, April 29, 1850), p. 587, middle col.

37. The color of a bronze bell when removed from its mold and after cleaning is a silver-gray. After hanging in a tower for some time, the bronze undergoes a natural aging or seasoning and corrodes to a gray-green patina. (Camp, *Bell Ringing*, 86.)

38. Bell bronze melts around 880°C (1616°F) (Olovianishnikov, *Istoriia kolokolov″*, 382). Cf. copper, which melts at 1083° C (1981.4° F), and tin, whose melting point is 232° C (449.6° F) (Dudley C. Gould, ed., *AFS Metalcasting Dictionary*, 1st ed. [Des Plaines, IL: American Foundrymen's Society, 1968], 48, 172). Harry Jackson points out that one of the interesting and enigmatic anomalies of bronze is its malleability at low temperatures: "When bronze is heated, it tends to become more brittle, and when gradually cooled becomes more malleable, as opposed to iron or steel, which become malleable and elastic at a high temperature and less so at a lower temperature" (*Lost Wax Bronze Casting* [Flagstaff, AZ: Northland Press, 1972], 76, fig. 105).

39. Price, "Bell," 434.

40. Bronze in some Japanese bells contains ten parts copper, four parts tin, one-half part zinc, and one-half part iron (T. I. Tikhonov, "O bronzakh″ voobshche i o kolokol'nykh″ v″ chastnosti," *Izvěstiia Tomskago tekhnologicheskago instituta Imperatora Nikolaia II* 25, no. 1 [1912], p. 10).

41. Westcott, *Bells and Their Music*, 45. The addition of zinc to bell metal is said to make the ring more shrill (Jones & Company, Bell Founders, *Troy Bell Foundry* [Troy, NY: A. W. Scribner & Co., 1870; reprint ed., Ovid, NY: W. E. Morrison, 1984], 34). Older ratios of bell metal (copper: tin) were prescribed at 3:1, 13:4, and 5:1. Cannon bronze contains a significantly higher percentage of copper than bell bronze and varies between 89-91% copper and 11-9% tin. Bronze for casting sculpture contains 86.66% copper, 6.66% tin, 3.33% lead, and 3.33% zinc (Tikhonov, "O bronzakh″," 9, 15).

42. Theophilus, *De diversis artibus* (The Various Arts), trans. C. R. Dodwell (London: Thomas Nelson and Sons, 1961), 154. See also J. Smits van Waesberghe, *Cymbala (Bells in the Middle Ages)*, Studies and Documents 1 (Rome: American Institute of Musicology, 1951), 17; Vyezzhev, "Kolokola drevnego Gorodeska," 107 n. 4; Kalmykov, "Obozrěnie manufakturnoj promyshlennosti," 92-93; and Rubtsov, *History*, 73.

43. The 84.51% copper to 13.21% tin used in the bronze alloy for Tsar-Kolokol (see Chapter 12) can be attributed to the unprecedented size of this bell and to the founders' anticipation of the force of blows they expected from its clapper on the sound-bow.

44. The greater the amount of tin in the bronze, the higher a bell's pitch. In addition to a higher pitch, the hardness of metal produced by the tin also increases the resonating quality of the bell. (Westcott, *Bells and Their Music*, 66-67.) During the first half of the seventeenth century Mersenne wrote that up to a third of the metal in the bells of some clockmakers was tin for greater resonance. He remarks that they added this much tin at the risk of the bells' breaking, just as too little tin will impair their ring. (Marin Mersenne, *Harmonie Universelle (The Books on Instruments)*, trans. Roger E. Chapman [The Hague: Martinus Nijhoff, 1957], 503.)

45. In the mid-sixteenth century Biringuccio advised founders to use a good quality of tin without any lead (*Pirotechnia*, 268 [bk. 6, chap. 12]). Grimthorpe points out that very small quantities of iron, lead, zinc, arsenic, and sulfur in analyses of bell metal are only impurities and should not be considered ingredients of the bell metal. (*A Rudimentary Treatise*, 364.) Walters notes that the copper used in modern bell metal, because of improved smelting procedures, is purer than the copper used before the nineteenth century (*Church Bells of England*, 33).

46. Westcott, *Bells and Their Music*, 75.

47. Twelve men were required to swing the beam to strike the exterior surface of the great bell in Kyoto. This bell is 18 feet high, 9.5 inches thick, 9 feet in diameter, and weighs about 74 tons (148,000 pounds). ("A Wonderful Bell," article

from a Boston paper preserved in the Boston Public Library's copy of Gatty, *The Bell,* attached in front of the book.)

48. Bigelow, *Carillon,* 27; and Price, "Bell," 433.

49. To avoid indentation and possible cracking of a bell by blows from its clapper, English ringers periodically "quarter-turn" their bells so that the clapper's blows will fall on a different place on the sound-bow (Walters, *Church Bells of England,* 30; and Nichols, *Bells thro' the Ages,* 71-72).

50. Olovianishnikov, *Istoriia kolokolov",* 401.

51. Westcott, *Bells and Their Music,* 74.

52. On this point, see Grimthorpe, *A Rudimentary Treatise,* 376.

53. Coleman, *Bells,* 68. The second Big Ben bell in the Parliament tower in London cracked when the bell's wall could no longer sustain blows from its clapper (*London Times,* May 23, 1882).

54. Westcott, *Bells and Their Music,* 75. Cf. Biringuccio's remarks on and his calculations for the weights of clappers in proportion to the weight of their bells (*Pirotechnia,* 272-273 [bk. 6, chap. 13], and 455, app. A).

55. N. Th. Iartsev, "Kollektsiia po lit'iu kolokolov"," *Izvěstiia Obshchestva liubitelej estestvoznaniia, antropologii, i ětnografii* 36, no. 2 (1879), pp. 49, 51.

56. Vasil'ev, "Otlivka kolokolov"," col. 123.

57. Babin, "O russkikh" kolokolakh"," 216. For a table that cites ideal clapper weights for bells up to 1,500 puds (54,170 pounds), see Olovianishnikov, *Istoriia kolokolov",* 417-419. According to Larkin, for bells cast in the United States at the beginning of the twentieth century eight pounds of clapper weight were calculated for every 200 pounds of bell weight; thus a clapper would weigh 4% of the bell's total weight (*Practical . . . Guide,* 113).

58. Babin, "O russkikh" kolokolakh"," 217. Westcott says that at the bell foundry of Petit & Fritsen the diameter of the clapper's ball is calculated to equal the thickness of the sound-bow multiplied by 2.4. The higher pitched, smaller bells, which have proportionately greater wall thickness than larger bells, also have clapper balls that are proportionately thicker. (*Bells and Their Music,* 74.)

59. Babin, "O russkikh" kolokolakh"," 211.

60. Ibid., 217. In the first half of the twelfth century, Theophilus recommended that bell clappers be hung from a thick strap of leather from the neck of a stag (*De diversis artibus,* 158).

61. Babin, "O russkikh" kolokolakh"," 217.

62. Westcott, *Bells and Their Music,* 75. Olovianishnikov's appeal for correct suspension of bell clappers based on his periodic inspections of bells suggests that many were not carefully installed in Russian bells at the beginning of the twentieth century (*Istoriia kolokolov",* 413-415).

63. Meneely & Kimberly, *Bells,* 38.

64. Grimthorpe, describing a bell at St. Peter's in Rome, notes that "it is loaded . . . with ornaments in high relief, which are sure to injure the sound . . . (*A Rudimentary Treatise,* 389).

65. Semenov, "Novgorodskie i pskovskie litejshchiki," 4. Among early examples of this decorative style on Russian bells were three mid-sixteenth-century bells in the cathedral bell tower of the kremlin at Gdov, two of which are dated 1551 and 1561. The decorations on these bells are described and their inscriptions published in P. Pokryshkin, "Tserkvi pskovskogo tipa XV-XVI stol. po vostochnomu poberezh'iu Chudskago ozera i na r. Narově," *Izvěstiia Arkheologicheskoj komissii* 22 (1907): 20.

66. Natural animals include birds, bears, horses, elk, deer, and rabbits; among the mythological or fantastic creatures are sphinxes, griffins, double-headed birds, and unicorns.

67. Semenov, "Novgorodskie i pskovskie litejshchiki," 4.

68. For the decorative programs on Grigor'ev's Kremlin bell of 1655, the Motorins' Tsar-Kolokol of 1735, and Bogdanov's Great Uspensky Bell of 1817, see Chapters 11, 12, and 13, respectively, in this volume.

69. This bell of about 154 pounds is not quite 19 inches high and is the work of two monks of the New Jerusalem Monastery, a founder named Sergij and an engraver named Paisij (Iu. M. Zolotov, "Kolokol Patriarkha Nikona," *Sovetskaia arkheologiia* 8, no. 2 (1964), pp. 242-43).

70. Snegirev, "Moskovskij Tsar'-kolokol"," 19; and Snegirev, *Pamiatniki moskovskoj drevnosti,* 36.

71. On the cannons of some Russian bells, according to Olovianishnikov, the only decorative device is a few interweaving lines (Olovianishnikov, *Istoriia kolokolov",* 393). Oriental bells, by contrast, had more ornate, sometimes sculpturally elaborate, single loops on top. Numerous Chinese bells show two dragons back to back with their bodies arched and joined to form the bell loop (see figure 61). The sphere and cross that Nicholas I ordered placed on the cannons of Tsar-Kolokol is another rare suggestion of ornamentation atop a Russian bell.

72. Bezobrazov, ed., *Otchet" o Vserossijskoj khudozhestvenno-promyshlennoj vystavkě,* 57. See also the large hole at the top of the great bell in Peking "for tonal purposes" (Westcott, *Bells and Their Music,* app. and p. 4 of glossary).

73. Translation of the engraved inscription on the bell of Stival is problematical. Hersart de la Villemarqué believes that the language of this inscription represents the first stage of Celto-Breton and devotes an entire article to a discussion of its translation. He divides the letters of the inscription into *Pir turfic is ti* and translates them as "How sweetly you ring." ("Mémoire sur l'inscription de la cloche de Stival," 399.) Others have suggested that this inscription may be corrupt Latin and should be read: *Pirtur ficisti* (Peter has made [this bell]) (H. Leclercq, "Cloche, clochette," DACL III², cols. 1963-1964).

74. N. I. Fal'kovskij, *Moskva v istorii tekhniki* (Moscow: Moskovskij rabochij, 1950), 243.

75. See Chapter 4, nn. 38 and 40, for citations on both of these bell fragments.

76. See Chapter 4, n. 55. The letters of the last four words of this inscription run from right to left, as did entire inscriptions cast on bells before the fifteenth century.

77. Cf. the more or less general use of Gothic script on bells cast in Western Europe beginning in the fourteenth century (Nichols, *Bells thro' the Ages*, 99).

78. E. F. Karskij, *Slavianskaia kirillovskaia paleografiia* (Leningrad: Izd. Akad. nauk SSSR, 1928; reprint ed., Moscow: Izd. "Nauka," 1979), 241. The oldest dated Cyrillic inscription in viaz' dates from 1230 and appears on the marble victory column of Bulgarian Tsar John Asen II (1218-1241) in the Church of the Forty Martyrs at Trnova. (V. N. Shchepkin, *Russkaia paleografiia* [Moscow: Izd. "Nauka," 1967], 43.)

79. The earliest dated examples of viaz' in Russian are contained in a *stikhirar'* (sticherarion) of 1380, a manuscript copied and preserved at the Trinity-Sergius Lavra (ibid., 44).

80. Ibid., 44-45; and Karskij, *Paleografiia*, 242. See also Robert Auty and Dimitri Obolensky, eds., *An Introduction to Russian Language and Literature*, Companion to Russian Studies 2 (Cambridge: Cambridge University Press, 1977), 45-47; and L. V. Cherepnin, *Russkaia paleografiia* (Moscow: Gos. izd. politicheskoj literatury, 1956), 257ff., 386ff.

81. Shchepkin, *Russkaia paleografiia*, 49.

82. The year on Russian bells cast before the eighteenth century is normally expressed as A.M. (*anno mundi*) or the year from the creation of the world. On the inscriptions of many Russian bells, the name of the founder is often rendered in a more formal manner, e.g. "Konstantin" Mikhajlov" syn" Slizov"" (Konstantin, son of Mikhail, Slizov), instead of "Konstantin" Mikhajlovich" Slizov"." A number of inscriptions from Russian bells are published in Olovianishnikov, *Istoriia kolokolov"*, 65-80, 131-158.

83. Ibid., 141, my translation. Percival Price has published translations of inscriptions from several Russian bells (*Bells and Man*, xviii, 106, 276-279).

84. For inscriptions on these two bells, which were imperial commissions, see Chapter 13.

85. Rubtsov, *Istoriia*, 248, my translation. During Peter the Great's Azov campaign of 1695-1696 an attack on the Turkish fort at Kazikerman at the mouth of the Dnieper River was a major objective of the Russians' western offensive. Two other examples of Russian bell inscriptions in verse are quoted in Olovianishnikov, *Istoriia kolokolov"*, 158.

86. Archimandrite Leonid, "Istoricheskoe opisanie stavropigial'nago Voskresenskago Novyj Ierusalim" imenuemago monastyria," 90-91, my translation. See also the Greek expression ἡ πνευματικὴ σάλπιγξ (the spiritual trumpet) in John Climacus' *Scala paradisi* (see Chapter 2 in this volume).

87. The Scripture quoted was The Song of the Three Children (in the fiery furnace), from an addition to the book of Daniel; Psalm 55: 18; and Matthew 16: 18 (Romanoff, *Sketches*, 259 [in the King James version of the Psalms the verse quoted in Romanoff is 17]).

88. The years for six of the bells are 1533, 1547, 1548, 1549, 1550, and 1551; the year of casting is not recorded on the seventh bell. (Smirnova, "Dva pamiatnika," 244-245.)

89. Ibid., 245-246.

90. Ėjzen, "Kolokol"," col. 124; and Olovianishnikov, *Istoriia kolokolov"*, 67-68. For a translation of the upper inscription, see Price, *Bells and Man*, 278. See also G. Spasskij, "O kolokolakh", dostoprimečatel'nykh" po svoej veličině," *Gornyj zhurnal"* 1, no. 1 (January 1833), pp. 134-136.

91. Olovianishnikov, *Istoriia kolokolov"*, 68.

92. Spasskij, "O kolokolakh"," 136-137, my translation.

93. Pukhnachev, *Zagadki*, 101.

94. N. R., "O kolokolakh"," 588, lefthand and middle cols. For background on Russian cryptography (*tajnopis'*), see Karskij, *Paleografiia*, 249-258.

95. Nicolas Zernov, *The Russians and Their Church*, 3d ed. (London: S.P.C.K., 1964), 2.

96. Nicolas Berdyaev, *The Russian Idea* (Boston: Beacon Press, 1962), 2.

97. The great bell of 1790 at Mingun, Burma, at 97.5 tons and with a lower diameter of 16 feet 3 inches, is considered the largest ringing bell in the world today (Westcott, *Bells and Their Music*, 12). One of the large Nanking bells was 12 feet high, 7.5 feet in diameter, and 23.56 feet in circumference. The weight of the bell was estimated at 50,000 funts (45,150 pounds). ("Bol'shie kolokola," *Biblioteka dlia chteniia* 4, no. 4, sect. 7 [1834], p. 70.) In the mid-nineteenth century there were seven very large bells in Peking that were rung to mark the five watches of the night in the Chinese capital. One of these bells measured 12.5 feet high, 13.5 feet in diameter, had a circumference of 42 feet, 5 inches, and weighed 120,000 pounds. (Gatty, *The Bell*, 49-50.) The weight of the bell now hanging in the Great Bell Temple is officially cited as 46.5 tons (93,000 pounds). See also Appendix D to this volume.

98. A few large Spanish bells in the Giralda Tower in Seville are notable exceptions to this rule in Western Europe. The mounting of these bells is stationary, and they are rung manually in the tower by ropes tied to their clappers. (See Ernest Morris, *Bells of All Nations* [London: Robert Hale, 1951], 145.)

99. Adelung, *Al'bom" Mejerberga*, 98.

Notes to Chapter 10

1. Walters, *Church Bells of England*, 36.

2. Jane Yolen, *Ring Out! A Book of Bells* (New York: The Seabury Press, 1974), 101.

3. PSRL II (Hypatian), p. 196 (1259). Toward the end of the twelfth and during the first half of the thirteenth centuries, as founding technology developed in Kievan Russia, metal objects began to be cast in hard forms made from wax models. Such forms have been unearthed at Kiev, Novgorod, Grodno, and other sites. (N. N. Stoskova, *Drevnerusskoe litejnoe delo [domongol'skij period]* [Moscow: Akademiia nauk SSSR, 1954], 10.)

4. According to Olovianishnikov, Russians themselves first

began casting bells at Kiev in the mid-thirteenth century. After the Mongol yoke descended, disrupting native founding, he believes that bells were again imported from Germany. (*Istoriia kolokolov''*, 32.)

5. One of the final sequences in Andrej Tarkovskij's film *Andrei Rublev* (Mosfilm Studio, 1966) depicts the founding of a Russian bell in 1423. This episode traces a youth's creation of a large bell from his digging of the casting pit and selection of clay for the mold through the various founding processes to his breaking of the mold and the raising and ringing of the new bell.

6. Paul of Aleppo, *Puteshestvie* 3:109ff.; and 4:91ff. Two of the most detailed early sources on the founding of Western bells are Theophilus' *De diversis artibus*, which probably dates from the first half of the twelfth century, and Vannoccio Biringuccio's *Pirotechnia*, which was published posthumously in 1540. Both of these treatises are available in English translations. Biringuccio (1480-1539) has been called the "father of the foundry industry," and in his *Pirotechnia* he transmits virtually all information available on metallurgy and founding during his lifetime. Walter Odington briefly mentions bell founding in pt. 3 (De cymbalis faciendis) of his *Summa de speculatione musicae* (ca. 1300) (ed. Frederick F. Hammond, Corpus Scriptorum de Musica 14 [Rome: American Institute of Musicology, 1970], 85). Marin Mersenne discusses acoustical properties of bells in the Seventh Book of Percussion Instruments in *L'harmonie universelle* (1636-1637) (an English translation has been published by Roger E. Chapman).

Information on casting in Russia occurs in a few eighteenth-century sources but is mainly transmitted in nineteenth- and twentieth-century works. For sources that describe preparatory work for and the casting of Tsar-Kolokol in 1735, see Chapter 12 n. 1. See also Georg Wilhelm de Hennin, *Opisanie ural'skikh i sibirskikh zavodov 1735* (Moscow: Gosudarstvennoe izd. "Istoriia zavodov," 1937), 423-428; Iartsev, "Kollektsiia po lit'iu kolokolov''," 49-51; Babin, "O russkikh'' kolokolakh''," 205-217; N. R., "O kolokolakh'' i o kolokol'nom'' iskusstvě," *Moskovskiia vědomosti*, no. 50 (Thursday, April 27, 1850), pp. 578-580; Vasil'ev, "Otlivka kolokolov''," 121-128; Olovianishnikov, *Istoriia kolokolov''*, 393-399; Rubtsov, *History*, 182-188; N. N. Rubtsov, "Istoricheskij ocherk razvitiia osnovnykh priemov formovki," in *Tekhnologiia litejnoj formy*, ed. N. N. Rubtsov (Moscow: Gosudarstvennoe nauchno-tekhnicheskoe izd. mashinostroitel'noj i sudostroitel'noj literatury, 1954), 8-10; and Rybakov, *Remeslo*, 600-612.

7. Rubtsov, "Ivan Fedorovich," 34. European bells are normally cast mouth down so that the sound-bow, which will receive the clapper's blows, will have the greatest chance for a solid casting by bearing the greatest pressure from the metal during pouring (Grimthorpe, *A Rudimentary Treatise*, 366).

8. N. R., "O kolokolakh''," 578, righthand col. Foundries also needed to be located beside or near a water supply and have access to fine clay for the preparation of bell molds. The mid-nineteenth-century bell foundries of Zinkevich, Samgin,

and Bogdanov in Moscow were all situated on "Balkan," a pond 16 feet deep with steep banks. The bottom of this pond was pure clay, which workers used in their loam molding and which, impervious to water, kept the pond—without springs in its bed and collecting only rain water and melting snow—from drying up during the year.

9. A given size bell varied in weight only slightly from an established norm in Russian foundries. An increase in weight up to 5% was permitted and a decrease of not more than 3%. (Babin, "O russkikh'' kolokolakh''," 208 n. 1.)

10. *Pirotechnia*, 266 (bk. 6, chap. 12). Loss of metal during melting usually amounted to 1 out of every 36 pounds.

11. In 1871 the factory price for a Russian bell stood between 16 and 18 rubles per pud (Vasil'ev, "Otlivka kolokolov''," 128).

12. Before the rotary strickle board came into use in Russia during the fourteenth and fifteenth centuries, the wax models for bells were hand made (Rybakov, *Remeslo*, 248).

13. Theophilus advises that the core of a bell mold be built around a dry piece of oak equal to the length (height) of the bell (*De diversis artibus*, 150 [chap. 85]).

14. Babin, "O russkikh'' kolokolakh''," 209-210.

15. Rubtsov, "Istoricheskij ocherk," 9. Cf. Olovianishnikov, who describes the mixture he used as two parts fatty clay, finely ground and sifted, and one part ordinary clay or pulverized brick (*Istoriia kolokolov''*, 396); and Ivan Dvigubskij, who reported that in the early nineteenth century the clay was mixed with horse manure, hair, and hemp (*Nachal'nyia osnovaniia tekhnologii*, pt. 1 [Moscow: Universitetskaia tip., 1807], 179-180). The organic matter was added so that its consumption during baking would leave the mold finely porous, and gases from the molten metal could thereby escape during casting. If proper means for the escape of these gases had not been provided, they could make the metal itself porous, or worse, cause an explosion. (Jones & Company, Bell Founders, *Troy Bell Foundry*, 35.)

16. The cope for a 100-pud (3,611-pound) bell was slightly over 4.37 inches thick; that for a 1,000-pud (36,113-pound) bell was 10.5 to 12.25 inches thick (N. R., "O kolokolakh''," 279, lefthand col.). Babin reports that the thickness of the cope for a 500-pud bell had to be between 5 and 7 inches. ("O russkikh'' kolokolakh''," 210.)

17. Biringuccio has described the way in which both parts of an Italian bell mold were baked in the first half of the sixteenth century.

Having thus brought everything properly to its end and wishing to cast, you must bake both moulds. First the core is surrounded with dry brick ends like a little furnace, built as high as the core with a distance of four *dita* [3.82 inches] between the core and the wall; this entire space is then filled with charcoal. The cope is placed over the charcoal, resting on the wall of the furnace so that this is also baked with the same fire. Then a flaming fire of dry wood is applied between the cope and the core until the coals begin to ignite the charcoal. Then the fire is gradually ignited down to the very bottom and bakes both the moulds. In case either the core or the cope has formed any cracks or flaking of improperly joined clay, repair them with a plaster of white of egg. (*Pirotechna*, 267 [bk. 6, chap. 12].)

18. Furnaces for melting bell metal in mid-nineteenth-century Russia were essentially the same as those used during the second half of the seventeenth century. The quantity of firewood required to melt the metal for bell casting depended on the weight of the bell: 3 sazhens (21 feet) of pine for 100 puds (3,611 pounds); up to 10 sazhens (70 feet) of wood for 1,000 puds (36,113 pounds); and up to 30 sazhens (210 feet) for 10,000 puds (361,130 pounds). (N. R., "O kolokolakh"," 579, lefthand and middle col.) Grimthorpe had heard that Russian founders used charcoal to melt the copper and tin. The advantage of charcoal over wood, he explains, would be that "wood contains so much moisture that it takes much longer to get the requisite heat up with it, and it is notoriously a bad thing to keep the metal long melted getting up the heat." (*A Rudimentary Treatise*, 366-367.)

19. N. R., "O kolokolakh"," 579, middle col. Larkin advises that when adding the tin, it should be pushed down to the bottom of the previously melted copper to keep a substantial portion of the tin from volatizing and burning before it combines with the copper (*Practical . . . Guide*, 129).

20. Theophilus stresses the need for calm but alert workers during the melting process: "When you see a green flame rise, the copper is beginning to melt. . . . The work at this point does not require indolent workmen but quick, keen ones for fear the mould be broken by carelessness of any kind, or some one gets in the way of, or hurts, another or makes him lose his temper, which is to be guarded against at all costs." (*De diversis artibus*, 154-155.)

21. Westcott, *Bells and Their Music*, 46-47.

22. A hearth furnace usually has a tap hole that is plugged with a friable, brick-like mixture of refractory material (e.g., fireclay and sawdust). This substance is picked out or punctured with a pointed tapping bar to release the flow of metal from the furnace.

23. N. R., "O kolokolakh"," 579, righthand col.; and Pyliaev, "Istoricheskie kolokola," 294-295.

24. Robert Lyall, *The Character of the Russians and a Detailed History of Moscow* (London: R. Cadell, 1823), 209.

25. Maurice Baring, *Russian Essays and Stories* (London: Methuen, 1908), 81-88.

26. Harry Jackson notes that the length of time a bronze sculpture remains in its mold also varies in his work according to the temperature of the air: "If it's in the middle of the winter, we might wait a little longer because the hot bronze exposed to the cold air would crack like splintered crystal" (*Lost Wax Bronze Casting*, 76, pl. 105).

27. Olovianishnikov, *Istoriia kolokolov"*, 402.

28. Th. G. Solntsev, "Moia zhizn' i khudozhestvenno-arkheologicheskie trudy," pt. 3, *Russkaia starina*, no. 3 (1876), p. 644. Coachmen brought seven bells weighing a total of 319 puds 7 funts (11,526 pounds) from Pereslavl to the tower of

the cathedral in the Peter and Paul Fortress at St. Petersburg in 1789 and early 1790 (Potapov, "Perevozka Pereslavskikh" kolokolov"," 593-599).

29. In 1861 the Moscow foundry of A. P. Bogdanov cast two bells, one of 20 puds 10 funts and the other of 10 puds 32 funts (731 and 390 pounds), for the Serbian Monastery of Dečani. The two bells were shipped by frigate from St. Petersburg to Lisbon where they were transferred to another vessel at the end of 1862. Their odyssey through the Mediterranean and Adriatic is chronicled in Marchenko's article, "Prikliucheniia russkikh" kolokolov" otpravlennykh" v" Serbiiu v" 1863 g.," *Russkaia starina* 94 (1898): 149-153.

30. Olovianishnikov, *Istoriia kolokolov"*, 402. The Great Bell of China in Peking was moved in winter on ice: ". . . water was poured along the roadway to form [an] 'ice route' along which the bell was hauled to its destination by oxen. Next, at the base of the bell tower, a mound was constructed and coated with ice, and the bell was pushed up the side of the mound to come to rest on its top." (Liu Junwen, *Beijing: China's Ancient and Modern Capital* [Beijing: Foreign Languages Press, 1982], 144.)

31. Lyall, *The Character of the Russians*, 209-210.

32. Romanoff, *Sketches*, 262-263.

33. Lefévere, *A Short History of Bells*, 6. For information on ceremonies associated with the baptism and dedication of Western bells, see Nichols, *Bells thro' the Ages*, 133-135; Walters, *Church Bells of England*, 256-261; and Coleman, *Bells*, 84-95.

34. Leclercq, "Cloches, clochettes," col. 1968.

35. PL 97, col. 188: "*ut clocas non baptizent.*" Walters draws attention to remarks of Martène, who believes that Charlemagne's capitulary only proscribed baptism of small bells (*clocae*). Baptism was continued and even required for the larger bells (*signa* or *campanae*) (*De ritibus ecclesiae*, bk. ii, chap. 21 [1788 ed., vol. 2, 297] quoted in Walters, *Church Bells of England*, 256).

36. Mersenne, *Harmonie universelle*, 501. A lengthy prayer (actually a ceremony) for the blessing of a church bell is transmitted in the so-called Pontifical of Egbert of York (732-766). This pontifical, however, is not Egbert's work but dates from *circa* 950. (*The Pontifical of Egbert, Archbishop of York, A.D. 732-766*, The Publications of the Surtees Society 27 [Durham: George Andrews, 1853], 117-119.)

37. The earliest record of a Russian bell with a name comes from 1290. Two princes of Rostov-Velikij (Dimitrij and Konstantin Borisovich) sent a bell called "Tiurik"" (bag, sack) to a Bishop Tarasij at Ustiug-Velikij (Karamzin, *Priměchaniia*, 132 [note 182 to vol. 4]; see also Chapter 4 of this volume). Russian bells have been named after saints ("Gavriil"), persons ("Sysoj"), objects ("Krest'" [cross], "Neopalimaia kupina" [the burning bush]), animals ("Baran" [ram], "Medved'" [bear]), or conditions, such as "the one that calls the hungry" ("Golodar'"), a bell rung at Rostov-Velikij for certain services during Lent (Olovianishnikov, *Istoriia kolokolov"*, 56-57).

38. K. T. Nikol'skij, *Posobie k" izucheniiu ustava bogosluzheniia Pravoslavnoj tserkvi*, 5th ed., rev. and enl. (St. Petersburg: Gosudarstvennaia tip., 1894), 781.

39. Ibid., 781-782, my translations.

40. See Chapter 11 of this volume for the procedures Ivashko Kuz'min used in 1674 to raise Aleksandr Grigor'ev's great bell of 1655 into its belfry in the Moscow Kremlin.

41. Father Aleksandr, a bell ringer at the Solovetskij Monastery, reported that bells were raised and lowered from towers with special belts woven from *rovduga* (unteased deer hide) because of their strength (Gemp, *Skaz o Belomor'e*, 129).

42. Edna Dean Proctor, *A Russian Journey* (Boston: James R. Osgood, 1873), 67; and Olovianishnikov, *Istoriia kolokolov"*, 402, 403.

43. Romanoff, *Sketches*, 263-266. The damaged bell, which the new bell replaced in the tower at Votkinsk, was broken up into small pieces and carried to Slobodskoj for recasting. Biringuccio explains that the tone of a new bell improves after being rung for about a year for two reasons: the blows of the clapper on the sound-bow lead to the consolidation of the rim, and if the bell metal emerged with any porosity after casting, "rain water produces a substance similar to rust [corrosion]" which closes the pores in the metal (*Pirotechnia*, 270-271 [bk. 6, chap. 12]).

44. G. Istomin, *Ivanovskaia kolokol'nia v" Moskvě*, 2d ed., rev. and enl. (Moscow: Tip. Obshchestva rasprostran. poleznykh" knig", 1893), 27, my translation. By "hoisting tower" (*kalancha*, literally "watchtower") they meant the scaffold that Bogdanov had built beside the Ivan Velikij Bell Tower through which the bell was to be lifted from the ground and then transferred into the central arch of the Petrok Malyj Zvonnitsa.

45. Ibid. For the description of an outside hoist of a 722-pud bell through scaffolding adjacent to the bell tower at the Danilov Monastery in Moscow, see N. Podchinennov, "Ustrojstvo i ustanovka zheleznoj konstruktsii dlia priv̌sa kolokolov" na drevnej kolokol'ně Moskovskago Danilova Monastyria," *Biulleteni politekhnicheskago obshchestva*, no. 2 (1909), 72-74.

46. Tyack, *A Book About Bells*, 101.

47. Meneely & Kimberly, *Bells*, 38.

48. Podchinennov, "Ustrojstvo," 61.

49. Auguste Ricard de Montferrand in 1845 noted the generally poor suspension systems used for tower bells in Russia and in his design for St. Isaac's Cathedral in St. Petersburg took particular care to provide adequate and architecturally congruent support for the eleven bells to be distributed in the four belfries around the cathedral's great dome (*Eglise cathédrale de Saint-Isaac: description architecturale, pittoresque et historique de ce monument* [St. Petersburg: Chez F. Bellizard et Co., 1845], 52).

50. "Ustrojstvo," 59-75.

51. The bells of the Danilov Monastery were shipped to Harvard University in the late 1920s (see Chapter 6 of this volume). The 722-pud bell cast in 1890 is the largest bell in the tower of Lowell House.

52. Podchinennov, "Ustrojstvo," 66.

53. Ibid., 70.

54. Olovianishnikov, *Istoriia kolokolov"*, 403, 405.

55. Ibid., 405.

56. Zakharov, *Kremlevskie kolokola*, 26. The new iron suspension system for the Great Uspensky Bell weighed 450 puds (16,251 pounds); that for "Reut," 250 puds (9,028 pounds); and that for "Polielejnyj," 150 puds (5,417 pounds) (Olovianishnikov, *Istoriia kolokolov"*, 405).

57. Ibid., 393; Babin, "O russkikh" kolokolakh"," 215-216; see also pp. 213-215, and figs. 8-15 in sketch 12.

58. Olovianishnikov, *Istoriia kolokolov"*, 393.

59. Westcott, *Bells and Their Music*, 46, 47, 54. Note the fracture on the Liberty Bell in Philadelphia.

60. In England, this Russian manner of bell ringing is known as "clappering," a "lazy and pernicious practice," which has cracked more bells than all other means combined (Grimthorpe, *A Rudimentary Treatise*, 379).

61. Maxim Gorky, *Sobranie sochinenij*, 1: Proizvedeniia 1892-1896 (Moscow: Gos. izd. khudozhestvennoj literatury, 1960), 261-262, my translation. Korolenko begins his "Pavlovskie ocherki" (Sketches from the Village of Pavlovo) of 1890 with "Reflections on the Bell at Pavlovo." Awaiting the first stroke of the clapper and expecting to be inundated by waves of sound pouring from this massive bell, Korolenko was disappointed by its pitiful broken wheeze. The impaired tone, he was told, was caused by a fracture that had opened in the bell's wall. Above a large piece of metal missing from the lip of the bell, a wide crack ran upward into its waist. (In *Sobranie sochinenij*, 9: Publitsistika [Moscow: Gos. izd. khudozhestvennoj literatury, 1955], 7-11.)

62. Grimthorpe, *A Rudimentary Treatise*, 367-368. Biringuccio explains a method for welding cracked bells that employs a sleeve extending from the furnace to heat and soften the bell in the area of the crack (*Pirotechnia*, 275-277 [bk. 6, chap. 15]). For a description of the operation followed in filling up a crack in a bell, see Larkin, *Practical . . . Guide*, 132-133. Larkin explains, however, that "bells repaired in this manner never possess their original pure and beautiful tone, and are not very durable."

63. PSRL XIII, pt. 2 (Tsarstv. kn.), pp. 453-454 (1547). See also Findejzen, *Ocherki po istorii muzyki*, 133-134. Olovianishnikov describes how broken cannons on a bell can be replaced by new iron loops without affecting the bell's tone. A new piece or new pieces are forged from iron and bolted to portions of the cannons remaining on the bell. It is also possible, he says, to drill holes in the top of the bell and to rehang it by iron bolts. (*Istoriia kolokolov"*, 402.)

64. Andrew Swinton, *Travels into Norway, Denmark, and Russia in the Years 1788, 1789, 1790, and 1791* (Dublin: W. Corbet for W. Jones & J. Rice, 1792), 292.

65. Billington, *The Icon and the Axe*, 37, 40; and Joel Car-

michael, *A Cultural History of Russia* (London: Weidenfeld and Nicolson, 1968), 55. On at least one occasion, however, a Russian bell was created from gun metal. In the tower of the Cathedral of the Nativity at Kishinev is a bell of almost seven tons (388 puds) that was cast from Turkish weapons captured during the Russo-Turkish War. (Victor and Jennifer Louis, *The Complete Guide to the Soviet Union*, 151.) See also the inscription on Afanasij Petrov's Poltava bell of 1695 in Chapter 9.

Notes to Chapter 11

1. Dmitrievskij, *Arkhiepiskop" elassonskij Arsenij*, 97, my translation. Although the Great Mingun Bell of Burma was not cast until 1790, several monumental Oriental bells antedated those Arsenius saw and heard in Moscow: Nara, Japan (A.D. 732); Kyŏngju, Korea (A.D. 771); and two fifteenth-century bells in Peking and Nanking, China. The famous Kyoto bell of 1633 was a younger contemporary of the Godunov Bell. See Appendix D.

2. For a description of Chokhov's "Drobovik," see Rubtsov, *History*, 329-331. The entire length of the barrel is 17.64 feet; the diameter of the mouth is 35.87 inches and the metal is 7.44 inches thick around its barrel, which was designed to fire stone shells of 52 puds (1,878 pounds). The weapon was founded to satisfy the desire of Tsar Fedor Ivanovich to possess the world's largest cannon. (Voyce, *The Moscow Kremlin*, 43.) An equestrian relief of Tsar Fedor on the barrel of this weapon gives it its popular name, "Tsar-Pushka" (Tsar Cannon).

3. There are no less than seven important sources that mention the Godunov Bell of 1599: (1) an account by Greek Archbishop Arsenius of Elasson (Alessone) in Thessaly, who lived in Moscow between 1589 and 1611 (Dmitrievskij, *Arkhiepiskop" elassonskij Arsenij*, 97); (2) an anonymous report on the journey of Prince John of Denmark to Moscow in 1602 to marry Ksen'ia, the daughter of Boris Godunov; although the Danish prince died suddenly on October 28 of that year before the marriage took place, mention of the Godunov Bell is preserved in *Warhafftige Relation*, 10; (3) observations by Stephan Kakasch, who was sent by Emperor Rudolf of Austria on an embassy to Persia in November 1602 ("Kakash" i Tektander": Puteshestvie v" Persiiu cherez" Moskoviiu 1602-1603 gg.," trans. from German by A. I. Stankevich, in *Chteniia v" Imperatorskom" obshchestvě istorii i drevnostej rossijskikh"* [1896], bk. 2, 18); (4) an account by Samuel Maskiewicz, a Pole who lived in Moscow between 1609 and 1612 during the Time of Troubles and the Polish occupation of the capital (see Alojzy Sajkowski and Władysław Czapliński, *Pamiętniki Samuel i Bogusława Kazimierza Maskiewiczów [Wiek XVII]* [Wroclaw: Zakład narodowy im Ossolińskich, 1961], 148); (5) a record by Petrus Petrejus (Per Persson), a Swede who spent four years (ca. 1604-1608) in the service of Russia during the Time of Troubles and the first years of Vasilij Shuiskij's reign (pt. 1 of "Istoriia," 3); (6) Adam Olearius' information on the

great Kremlin bell from the 1630s (reprint ed. of *Vermehrte newe Beschreibung der muscowitischen und persischen Reyse* [Schleswig, 1656; reprint ed. by Dieter Lohmeier, Tübingen: Max Niemeyer Verlag, 1971], 147-148; Samuel Baron trans. and ed., *The Travels of Olearius in Seventeenth-Century Russia* [Stanford: Stanford University Press, 1967], 114); and (7) Joan Blaeu, *Le Grand atlas ou cosmographie Blaviane (La Géographie Blaviane)* 2 (Amsterdam: Chez Jean Blaeu, 1663), p. 20c, lefthand col. For secondary literature that treats the four generations of bells in the Moscow Tsar-Kolokol Line, see Boguslavskij, *Tsar'-kolokol*, 6ff; and Zakharov, *Kremlevskie kolokola*, 26ff.

4. Dmitrievskij, *Arkhiepiskop" elassonskij Arsenij*, 97.

5. Until the coronation of Boris Godunov, only descendants of Riurik had ruled Moscow (see Chapter 4).

6. The Godunov Bell that Andrej Chokhov cast for the Holy Trinity Monastery is believed to weigh between 1,700 and 2,000 puds (61,392 and 72,226 pounds) (E. Golubinskij, *Prepodobnyj Sergij Radonezhskij i sozdannaia im" Troitskaia lavra* [Moscow: A. I. Snegirevoj, 1892], 199). In 1744 Empress Elisabeth Petrovna ordered Boris' name as donor chiseled from this bell's inscription (Ieromonakh Arsenij, "O Tsar'-kolokolě Sviato-Troitskoj Sergievoj lavry," *Zapiski Otdeleniia russkoj i slavianskoj arkheologii Russkago arkheologicheskago obshchestva* 3 [1882]: 108). Elisabeth's vengeance on this bell is not only a projection of her disdain for Boris as a usurper but also attests to the Romanov dynasty's strong legitimistic sentiments in the eighteenth century. The empress' failure to provide an heir only intensified her attitudes. During his visit to the Holy Trinity Monastery in 1655, Paul of Aleppo saw the Godunov Bell in the old bell tower: "In it there is a bell comparable to the great bell of the capital [Moscow]. They say that one of the tsars made both. Its sound is as thunderous as that of the other bell" (*Puteshestvie* 4:37, my translation). Arsenij mentions that Ivan Zhukov, who saw the Godunov Bell in the mid-eighteenth century, estimated its weight at 1,700 puds (61,392 pounds). Hieromonk Pavel cited the bell's weight at 1,800 puds (65,003 pounds). And Metropolitan Platon in a short history of the Russian church gives the bell's weight as 2,000 puds (72,226 pounds). (Arsenij, "O Tsar'-kolokolě Sviato-Troitskoj Sergievoj lavry," 108-109.) Rybakov estimates the bell's weight at perhaps 1,850 puds (66,809 pounds) (*Tserkovnyj zvon"*, 38; I[van] S[negirev], *Putevyia zapiski o Troitskoj lavrě* [Moscow: Tip., Augusta Semena, 1840], 22; and L. I. Denisov, *Pravoslavnye monastyri rossijskoj imperii* [Moscow: Izdanie A. D. Stupina, 1908], 457).

7. European church bells are traditionally suspended inside a belfry or tower at a considerable distance from the ground and are not easily visible. The Godunov Bell, however, was installed in a wooden structure on the Kremlin's Cathedral Square, not unlike the installation of large bells near Buddhist temples. The latter are normally hung under pavilions only a few feet from the ground to permit worshippers to feel their vibrations when rung. (Price, "Bell," 430.)

8. Sajkowski and Czapliński, *Pamiętniki*, 148. Besides his extension of the Kremlin's Bono Tower and commissioning of Chokhov's two great bells, Boris Godunov also had a tower built for the Lutheran church in Moscow's foreign quarter (*nemetskaia sloboda*). The three bells that the tsar donated to this tower tolled at the funeral of the Danish prince who had come to Moscow to marry Boris' daughter Ksen'ia. (Conrad Bussow, *Moskovskaia khronika, 1584-1613* [Moscow: Izd. Akademii nauk SSSR, 1961], 86, 211.)

9. Without citing a source for its information, one later article quotes the bell's circumference at 84 feet, its diameter at 18 feet, and a wall thickness (presumably at the sound-bow) of 2 feet (Priakhin, "Kolokol'nyj zvon'," 181). The first two figures are suspect, however. A diameter of 18 feet would yield a circumference of 56.54 feet not 84 feet.

10. The figures of "over 33 tons" and "over 35 tons" (66,000 pounds and 70,000 pounds), cited by Arro and Danilevskij, respectively, fall somewhat below the weights quoted in primary sources. Arro, "Die altrussische Glockenmusik," 112; and Danilevskij, *Russkaia tekhnika*, 117.

11. Olearius, *Vermehrte newe Beschreibung*, 147-148; and Baron, *Travels*, 114.

12. Petrejus, "Istoriia," 3; *Warhafftige Relation*, 10; and Olearius, *Vermehrte newe Beschreibung*, 147.

13. "Kakash" i Tektander": Puteshestvie," 18. The "Maria Gloriosa" bell, with which Kakasch compares the Godunov Bell, was cast in 1497 for the Erfurt Cathedral in Saxony by the Dutch founder, Geert van Wou. At an estimated weight of 14 tons (28,000 pounds), this bell was for a long time the largest in Western Europe; its unusually fine and resonant tone can still be heard today. (Westcott, *Bells and Their Music*, p. 4 of glossary.)

14. Adam Olearius was in Moscow as a representative of Duke Frederick III of Holstein in 1634, 1636, 1639, and 1643. A particularly devastating fire destroyed a large portion of the city on June 2, 1648. (Fuhrmann, *Tsar Alexis*, 20-21.)

15. The principal source that transmits information on the great Moscow bells of 1654 and 1655 is the travel journal by Paul of Aleppo, *Puteshestvie* 3:110-113; and 4:91-95. The most valuable source on Russian bell founding from the seventeenth century is also Paul's. An English translation of Paul's description of the second Aleksei Mikhailovich bell is William Palmer, ed., *Testimonies Concerning the Patriarch Nicon, the Tsar, and the Boyars, from the Travels of the Patriarch Macarius of Antioch . . .* , vol. 2: *The Patriarch and the Tsar* (London: Trübner and Co., 1873), 258-260 (pt. 7, bk. 13, chap. iv).

Though no pictures of Danilov's short-lived bell survive, information about it is transmitted in Paul of Aleppo, *Puteshestvie* 3: 110-111; and G. Murkos' commentary, 4: iii. See also Boguslavskij, *Tsar'-kolokol*, 7-8; Zakharov, *Kremlevskie kolokola*, 27-28; Rubtsov, *History*, 166-169; and Olovianishnikov, *Istoriia kolokolov'*, 166. That Aleksei Mikhailovich himself enjoyed the sound of bells is mentioned in Pierre Martin de La

Martinière, "Puteshestvie v" sěvernyia strany (1653 g.)," trans. and with notes by V. N. Semenkovich, in *Zapiski Moskovskago arkheologicheskago instituta* 15 (1912), 137.

16. Hans Falk, a founder from Nuremberg, was active as a cannon foreman in Moscow from 1628 until 1653. In 1632 he founded a bell for the Rozhdestvenskij Monastery in Vladimir and on March 26, 1641, was commissioned to cast a 700-pud bell for the Uspensky (Assumption) Cathedral in the Moscow Kremlin. (Rubtsov, *History*, 358-359, no. 108.)

17. Rubtsov, *Istoriia*, 105, my translation.

18. The struggle between Hans Falk and the Russian foremen to wrest the commission from the tsar reveals the highly competitive spirit between European and native Russian founders in the Moscow Cannon Yard during the seventeenth century.

19. Rubtsov, *History*, 408. Paul of Aleppo describes Emel'ian Danilov as a man of small size, unprepossessing appearance, and little strength, who would never come to mind for accomplishing such a task (*Puteshestvie* 3:111). Although Paul does not report the date when Danilov cast the bell, it was doubtlessly founded in 1654 since Paul, in Moscow during 1655, refers to that event as having taken place "in the previous year." Conflicting information has been transmitted, however. From one of the inscriptions on Tsar-Kolokol of 1735, which states that its predecessor (i.e., Grigor'ev's bell of 1655) was cast in 1654, some sources have pushed the year of Danilov's bell back to 1653. The inscription on Grigor'ev's bell, as Meyerberg reports, contains 1653 as the (anticipated) year of founding, a statement which only adds to the confusion of dating the two great bells (Adelung, *Al'bom" Mejerberga*, 100). But from Paul's statement, there is sufficient reason to believe that Danilov's bell was cast in 1654, since Grigor'ev's was cast in 1655.

20. Paul of Aleppo, *Puteshestvie* 3:110.

21. On the particularly virulent epidemic of plague in 1654 during Muscovy's conflict with Poland and Lithuania, see Alexander, *Bubonic Plague*, 17-19.

22. The distance a bell's voice travels depends on several factors and conditions beyond the composition of the instrument's metal. The sound can carry two or even three times as far over water as on land since the latter tends to absorb sound. Clear, calm weather also increases the carrying power of a bell's voice; rain, snow, fog, and dampness reduce this distance and muffle the sound. The carrying power of a smaller bell with a more penetrating ring is greater than that of larger instruments. "It is a great mistake to suppose that bells may be heard in proportion to their weight . . . that is, that a 2,000 lb. bell will be heard twice as far as a 1,000 lb. bell. The larger bell does not possess anything like the resonant surface, doubled, of the smaller." The voices of swinging bells carry even farther than those of stationary bells because the upturned mouth of the swinging bell projects its voice out of the tower. ("Bell Facts from C. S. Bell Catalogue," in *Bell Basics—A Brief Review*, a leaflet from the American Bell Association, 3.)

According to Eric Sloane, the sound of a large bell will carry at least three miles; with wind and high pressure, it may be heard distances of up to six miles. Under ideal conditions the limit for the carrying distance of a ringing bell is normally nine miles. (*The Sound of Bells* [New York: Doubleday, 1966], 20.) Some of the great Asian bells, however, are reported to carry thirty or forty miles.

23. Paul of Aleppo says that the tsar left Moscow on a campaign after the bell had been broken and that Danilov then succumbed to the plague (*Puteshestvie* 3:111). This probably took place sometime around early July of 1654 when Aleksei Mikhailovich left Moscow to launch a siege of Smolensk that lasted three months. The plague reached Moscow about this time and for this reason the tsar and his family spent the winter of 1654-1655 at Viaz'ma between Moscow and Smolensk. The tsar returned to Moscow only in early February of 1655 about the same time that Patriarch Makarius and Paul of Aleppo reached the city. (Fuhrman, *Tsar Alexis*, 67-68; Alexander, *Bubonic Plague*, 18; and R. Ernest Dupuy and Trevor N. Dupuy, *The Encyclopedia of Military History from 3500 B.C. to the Present*, rev. ed. [New York: Harper & Row, 1977], 578.)

24. Paul of Aleppo's account of the commissioning and casting of Aleksei Mikhailovich's second bell is reported in *Puteshestvie* 3:111-113; 4:91-95; and see Murkos' notes, 4: iii-v. See also Boguslavskij, *Tsar'-kolokol*, 8-17; Zakharov, *Kremlevskie kolokola*, 28-32; Rubtsov, *History*, 169-174; and Olovianishnikov, *Istoriia kolokolov"*, 160-170, 177.

Eleven other works report the second Aleksei Mikhailovich bell: (1) Augustin, Baron von Meyerberg, saw the bell when he was in Moscow in 1661 and 1662. See *Voyage en Moscovie d'un ambassadeur, conseiller de la chambre impériale, envoyé par l'Empereur Leopold au Czar Alexis Mihalowics, Grand Duc de Moscovie* (Leiden: Chez Friderik Harring, 1688), 115-117; or a more recent French ed. *Relation d'un voyage en Moscovie* 1 (Paris: Librairie S. Franck, 1858), 109-110. O. Bodianskij published a Russian translation, "Puteshestvie v" Moskoviiu barona Avgustina Majerberga," in *Chteniia v" Imperatorskom" obshchestvě istorii i drevnostej rossijskikh" pri Moscovie* 1 (Paris: Librairie S. Franck, 1858), 109-110. O. Bodianskij published a Russian translation, "Puteshestvie v" M[iege], *A Relation of the Three Embassies from His Sacred Majestie Charles II to the Great Duke of Muscovie, the King of Sweden, and the King of Denmark . . . 1663 & 1664* (London: Printed for John Starkey, 1669), 138. (3) Johann Philipp Kilburger's report of his trip to Moscow in 1673 and 1674 in B. G. Kurts, *Sochinenie Kil'burgera o russkoj torgovlě v" tsarstvovanie Aleksěia Mikhailovicha* (Kiev: Tip. I. I. Chokolova, 1915), 175-176. (4) Erich Palmquist's unpaginated album of 1674 is valuable for two plates, one that shows the operation of raising the bell into its tower, and another that may be a drawing of the bell of 1655, though 1637 is given as the year of casting. See *Någre widh sidste kongl. ambassaden till tzaren Muskou giorde Observationer öfwer Rysslandh, des wäger, pass meds fastningar och Brantzer* (1674; printed in Stock-

holm: Generalstabens Litografiska Anstalt, 1898). (5) Jan Janszoon Struys lived in Russia from 1668 until 1670 and mentions the bell in *The Perillous and Most Unhappy Voyages of John Struys . . .*, trans. John Morrison (London: Samuel Smith, 1683), 134. (6) Jakob Reutenfels (Yakov Rejtenfel's) was in Moscow between 1670 and 1673. See "Skazaniia," sect. 2, chap. 12, p. 97. (7) The Dutchman Koenraad van Klenk, who was in Moscow in 1675, devotes a few lines to a description of the bell in *Posol'stvo Kunraada fan"-Klenka k" tsariam" Aleksěiu Mikhajlovichu i Theodoru Aleksěevichu* (St. Petersburg: Tip. Glavnago upravleniia udělov", 1900), 522. (8) Bernard Tanner, *Opisanie puteshestviia pol'skago v" Moskvu v" 1678 godu*, trans. from Latin with notes and introduction by I. Ivakin (Moscow: Universitetskaia tip., 1891), 58. (9) Philippe Avril, *Travels into Divers Parts of Europe and Asia*, trans. from French (London: Tim Goodwin, 1693), 78-79. (10) Johann Georg Korb was one of the last European visitors in Moscow to see the bell before its destruction in the fire of 1701. Korb's account of his visit in 1699 is published in *Diarium itineris in Moscoviam* (Vienna: Typis Leopoldi Voigt, Universit. Typog., 1700), 190, pl. (11) By the time Cornelis de Bruyn reached Moscow in 1702, the bell had already been destroyed in a fire the previous year. Bruyn records this fact in his *Voyages*, vol. 3: *Voyages de Corneille le Bruyen par la Moscovie, en Perse, et aux indes orientales* (Paris: Jean-Baptiste-Claude Bauche, 1728), 124.

25. According to a manuscript document, Aleksandr Grigor'ev became a foreman at the Moscow Cannon Yard in November 1651, when he was probably not more than seventeen years old (Rubtsov, *History*, 367). As an apprentice of foremen at the Moscow Cannon Yard, who had trained earlier under Andrej Chokhov, Grigor'ev, by 1654, after some three years on the job, had acquired the reputation of an experienced founder. Paul of Aleppo's description of Grigor'ev is as unflattering as his portrait of Emel'ian Danilov: "a youth of short stature, frail, thin, less than twenty years old, [and] still without any beard at all" (*Puteshestvie* 3:111).

26. *Puteshestvie* 3:113.

27. Ibid., 4:iii. Between August 4 and September 20, 1655, as Grigor'ev's work continued, Paul was in Novgorod with his father (ibid., 4:92 n. 1).

28. Ibid., 4:92-93.

29. Grigor'ev's achievement in casting this bell for the tsar was recognized through his promotion to the rank of Foreman to the Sovereign, a title which appears with his name on the inscription of a 300-pud bell dated October 1, 1666, for the Simonov Monastery in Moscow. Grigor'ev gained further distinction in founding a large bell with a cryptic inscription for the Savvino-Storozhevskij Monastery near Zvenigorod in 1667. Both bells were noted for the exceptional quality of their tone and for their resonance. The last reference to Grigor'ev and his work appears in 1676. (Rubtsov, *History*, 172-173, 367-371.)

30. Paul of Aleppo, *Puteshestvie* 4:93, my translation.

31. Ibid., 4:94; and Fuhrmann, *Tsar Alexis*, 71. Aleksei Mi-

khailovich no doubt first heard the bell from the palace where he spent the night of December 9 about two miles from Moscow.

32. The visual and verbal representations of the sovereign's piety on such great bells were much more than perfunctory recitals of religious virtues and the placement of the ruler's portrait beneath icons of Jesus Christ and His saints. They were viewed in Russia as crucial to the spiritual destiny of the nation and the Russian people.

The myth of the pious ruler drew its strength from the eschatology of Russian political theory. From its beginning around 1500, the Third Rome, Moscow, was the chief fact in the economy of salvation. Upon the orthodoxy and personal piety of the tsar depended the salvation of Russia as a state and thereby the salvation of the whole world. As the saint-prince insured the individual salvation of his people, so the pious tsar guaranteed the salvation of the individual and of the new abstraction of the community—the State which was based on an eschatological *raison d'être*. It was this eschatological foundation for the myth of the ruler which was undercut by Peter the Great.

(Cherniavsky, *Tsar and People*, 71.) On the piety of Aleksei Mikhailovich, see Fuhrmann, *Tsar Alexis*, 89-90, 93-95.

33. The appearance of portraits of the sovereign and his consort on one side of this bell and the head of the Russian Church on the other is not surprising in light of the close relationship that Aleksei Mikhailovich had established with both Patriarch Joseph and Patriarch Nikon in the early 1650s. From November 1651 the tsar and Patriarch Joseph jointly signed state documents. Toward the end of 1654 Aleksei Mikhailovich made Nikon "Grand Sovereign" (*Velikij gosudar'*) and raised him, at least for a time, to the level of co-ruler of Muscovy. In 1619 Mikhail Romanov had likewise conferred on his own father, Patriarch Filaret, the title "Grand Sovereign." (Fuhrmann, *Tsar Alexis*, 44, 67.)

34. Adelung, *Al'bom" Mejerberga*, 100, my translation. The year 7161 (1653) on the inscription of this bell can perhaps be explained as the projected year for casting that appeared in the inscription for Danilov's bell, which may have been reproduced verbatim on Grigor'ev's bell of 1655.

35. *Puteshestvie* 4:94, iii. Grigor'ev's puzzling response to Paul's question was that the bell weighed "up to 12,500 puds less 500 [puds]." He may mean that approximately 12,500 puds of metal were put into the five furnaces—Paul attests to that—but the burning loss during the casting process amounted to 500 puds (which equals an anticipated 4%).

36. Adelung, *Al'bom" Majerberga*, 98; and Bodianskij, "Puteshestvie . . . Mejerberga," 67. According to Meyerberg, Grigor'ev began casting with 440,000 funts (11,002 puds) of metal. Melting loss during the casting process he estimated at 120,000 funts (3,001 puds), an incredible loss of 27.285%, which would reduce the actual weight of the bell to 320,000 funts (8,002 puds). Reutenfels also reports the bell's weight at 320,000 funts (8,002 puds) ("Skazaniia," 97. Cf. Murkos' discussion of the bell's weight in *Puteshestvie* 4:iv n. 2).

37. According to Kilburger, the bell weighed 11,000 puds, a figure he computed as follows:

15,000 puds		metal originally placed in five furnaces
− 2,000 puds		first loss of metal in furnaces [ca. 13.35%]
13,000 puds		
− 3,000 puds		metal lost in casting [ca. 23.1%]
10,000 puds		
+ 1,000 puds		silver and precious objects added by patriarch and prominent Muscovites
11,000 puds		

(Kurts, *Sochinenie Kil'burgera*, 176.) Kilburger's figures for the loss of metal during melting and casting appear far too high. See also Palmquist's identical calculation of the bell's weight at 11,000 puds (*Någre widh sidste kongl. ambassaden till tzaren Muskou*, data cited beneath the picture of the bell that he claims was cast in 1637 during the reign of Mikhail Fedorovich). At 394,000 pounds (10,910 puds), Struys' figure stands close to that of Kilburger and Palmquist (*The Perillous and Most Unhappy Voyages*, 134).

38. *Puteshestvie* 4:iv n. 2. At 400,000 funts (10,002 puds), van Klenk's estimate approximates the figure Murkos believes to be correct (*Posol'stvo Kunraada fan"-Klenka*, 522).

39. Adelung, *Al'bom" Mejerberga*, 98; and Bodianskij, "Puteshestvie . . . Majerberga," 67.

40. *Puteshestvie* 4: 94, iii. At 5.75 feet per *brasse* the bell's circumference would be 63.25 feet, a figure that Murkos rounds off to 64 feet.

41. Murkos believes it quite likely that the copyist of the original manuscript wrote by mistake one *bāʿ* here instead of one *diraa* (*Puteshestvie* 4:iii n. 2). The *bāʿ* is equal to a fathom (6 feet) and the modern Egyptian *diraa* to 22.88 inches, or 1.90 feet.

42. Adelung, *Al'bom" Mejerberga*, 98; Bodianskij, "Puteshestvie . . . Majerberga," 67; Struys, *The Perillous and Most Unhappy Voyages*, 134; and *Posol'stvo Kunraada fan"-Klenka*, 522. Philippe Avril gives the thickness of the metal as a cubit, a unit that can vary between 17 and 21 inches (*Travels*, 79). Kilburger, however, cites the thickness of the wall at its lowest edge as 1.25 arshins (35 inches or almost 3 feet) (Kurts, *Sochinenie Kil'burgera*, 175).

43. *Puteshestvie* 4:94, iii. Murkos equates Syrian dinars with Russian rubles.

44. *Puteshestvie* 4:93; *Posol'stvo Kunraada fan"-Klenka*, 522. According to van Klenk, the clapper weighed "more than 10,000 funts," a figure that converts to 250 puds.

45. Kurts, *Sochinenie Kil'burgera*, 176; Palmquist, *Någre widh sidste kongl. ambassaden till tzaren Muskou*, data cited beneath the picture of the bell.

46. Struys, *The Perillous and Most Unhappy Voyages*, 134.

47. *Puteshestvie* 4:93; Adelung, *Al'bom" Mejerberga*, 98; Bodianskij, "Puteshestvie . . . Majerberga," 67; *Posol'stvo Kunraada fan"-Klenka*, 522; and Kurts, *Sochinenie Kil'burgera*, 176.

48. *Posol'stvo Kunraada fan"-Klenka*, 522. The bell was

also rung for Peter I's marriage to Evdokiia Lopukhina on January 1, 1689 (Avril, *Travels*, 78). Van Klenk must certainly mean that the clapper, not the bell itself, was set in motion.

49. *Puteshestvie* 4:94. Philippe Avril is the only witness who reports that because of the bell's enormous size, the only way of sounding it was to strike it with a hammer (*Travels*, 79). Avril may have observed the use of a hammer, but the plate in Korb's diary and information in several contemporary accounts testify that swinging the clapper was the normal way of ringing the bell (Korb, *Diarium itineris in Moscoviam*, 190, pl.). Avril also makes the curious statement that "at this very time [the bell was] a cubit in thickness, altho' they have been oblig'd to take away 40,000 pound of metal from it, to make it sound."

50. Struys, *The Perillous and Most Unhappy Voyages*, 134.

51. An intensity of IV on the Modified Mercalli Scale (1956 version) is an earthquake of sufficient strength to make "windows, dishes, [and] doors rattle. Glasses clink. Crockery clashes" (Charles F. Richter, *Elementary Seismology* [San Francisco: W. H. Freeman, 1958], 137).

52. *Puteshestvie* 4:93. Guy Miege estimates that "fifty men might very well stand within it" (*A Relation of the Three Embassies*, 138).

53. *Puteshestvie* 4:94, my translation. Paul of Aleppo was correct. Until the manufacture of modern ship propellers, Russian bells were the largest of all single-cast objects (Price, "Bell," 436).

54. Bodianskij, "Puteshestvie . . . Mejerberga," 67, my translation. Cf. Adelung, *Al'bom" Mejerberga*, 97-99; and Augustin, Baron von Meyerberg, *Voyage en Moscovie*, 115, 117. Meyerberg seems to be the only seventeenth-century Western visitor to Moscow also aware of the great fifteenth-century bell at Peking.

55. Miege, *A Relation of the Three Embassies*, 138.

56. Struys, *The Perillous and Most Unhappy Voyages*, 134.

57. Reutenfels, "Skazaniia," 97, my translation.

58. Ibid.

59. Boguslavskij, *Tsar'-kolokol*, 14, 16.

60. Palmquist, *Någre widh sidste kongl. ambassaden*.

61. Fal'kovskij, *Moskva v istorii tekhniki*, 411.

62. Kurts, *Sochinenie Kil'burgera*, 175-176.

63. Snegirev, "Moskovskij Tsar'-kolokol"," 4 n. 2, sect. 3 (document of September 31 [*sic*], 1680, in the archives of the Oruzhejnaia palata).

64. Bruyn, *Voyages*, 124.

Notes to Chapter 12

1. Ivanov, *Istoricheskiia svědeniia*, 15-16. Some of the sources that document the commissioning and casting of Anna Ivanovna's Tsar-Kolokol have been published by Petr Ivanov in *Istoricheskiia svědeniia*. An extract of the history of the founding of Tsar-Kolokol prepared in the Bureau of Artillery and Fortifications is published in Ivan Zabelin, ed., *Materialy dlia istorii, arkheologii, i statistiki goroda Moskvy*, pt. 2 (Moscow: Moskovskaia gorodskaia tip., 1891), cols. 1046-1049; see also documents, cols. 830-832, 840, 871-873, 880. An English translation of materials in the Archives of the Moscow Artillery Historical Museum (Arsenal Fund, Reg. No. 3, File No. 126) from 1730 through 1736 is published in an appendix in Rubtsov, *History*, 463-479. Substantial accounts of the history of Tsar-Kolokol are available in Russian in Boguslavskij, *Tsar'-kolokol*, 17ff.; Zakharov, *Kremlevskie kolokola*, 33-60; and Rubtsov, "Ivan Fedorovich," 29-35. These three works also include material from sources not available in Ivanov, Zabelin, and Rubtsov, *History*.

2. Because the empress and her contemporaries believed that Grigor'ev's bell had been cast in 1654 and contained 8,000 puds, this year and this weight appear in the "Aleksei Mikhailovich inscription" on the Motorins' bell of 1735 (Ivanov, *Istoricheskiia svědeniia*, 15). Murkos explains this error as confusion, after eighty years, of Danilov's bell of 1654 with Grigor'ev's of 1655 (Paul of Aleppo, *Puteshestvie* 4:ii, v).

3. Ivanov, *Istoricheskiia svědeniia*, 5-6. This passage from the memoirs of Count Minikh also appears in an article by Ivanov, "Istoricheskiia svědeniia o bol'shom" kolokolě, lezhavshem" v" zemlě, bliz" Ivanovskoj kolokol'ni," *Moskovskiia vědomosti*, no. 44 (1842), pp. 903-904. See also Snegirev, "Moskovskij Tsar'-kolokol"," 4-5.

4. Rubtsov, *History*, 465 (sheet 4). Motorin's *familiia* or surname has also appeared as Matorin. For discussion of his work as a founder before Tsar-Kolokol, see Chapter 6 of this volume.

5. Little is known of Mikhail Motorin's biography beyond his work in casting the bell of 1735 for Anna Ivanovna. In 1742 he made an unsuccessful bid to recast a monumental bell for Elisabeth Petrovna in the Holy Trinity Monastery, and he died in 1750. Also on Motorin's staff were a founding assistant skilled in cannon and mortar casting (Kirill Kolykhanin), an assistant clerk (Mikhail Komarov), a scribe (Matvej Medvedkov), and apprentices in cannon casting (Semen Petrov, Nikita Nekrasov, Aleksej Ermolaev, Vasilij Kaftannikov, Ivan Kirillov, Kuz'ma Petrov, Mark Mikhajlov, and Nikita Ivanov) (Arkhiv" Mosk. dvor. kont., opis' 6-ia, delo no. 434; published in Snegirev, "Moskovskij Tsar'-kolokol"," 6-8; and Boguslavskij, *Tsar'-kolokol*, 25).

6. Rubtsov, *History*, 175; Rubtsov, "Ivan Fedorovich," 29; and Zakharov, *Kremlevskie kolokola*, 34-35. Anna Ivanovna donated this 12-pud model of the great bell to the Voskresenskij Church (Church of the Resurrection) on Litejnyj Prospekt in St. Petersburg (G. Bogdanov, *Opisanie Sanktpeterburga ot" nachala zavedeniia ego c" 1703 po 1751 god"* [St. Petersburg, 1779], 214).

7. Ivanov, *Istoricheskiia svědeniia*, 18. Motorin's two models of the machinery to be used for lifting the bell included a cast model of the bell itself weighing 12 kilograms (about 26.45 pounds). What action, if any, authorities in St. Petersburg took on these models is not known. In addition to the two

models that Motorin had constructed, in February of 1733, a blacksmith foreman named Bilov presented his own model at the Admiralty in St. Petersburg. (Boguslavskij, *Tsar'-kolokol*, 23.)

8. Auguste Ricard de Montferrand's description of the casting pit appears in his *Description de la grande cloche de Moscou* (Paris: M. M. Thierry frères, 1840), 5-6; see also Boguslavskij, *Tsar'-kolokol*, 23.

9. Boguslavskij, *Tsar'-kolokol*, 21-22.

10. Rubtsov, *History*, 467 (sheets 30, 36). Cf. Boguslavskij who states that Motorin requested Swedish red copper (*Tsar'-kolokol*, 22). Though Motorin asked for 1,000 puds of Persian copper, he received Siberian red copper instead (Rubtsov, *History*, 467 [sheet 58]). For itemized lists of supplies and materials (including metals) and their costs for casting the bell, see Ivanov, *Istoricheskiia svěděniia*, 24-55.

11. The Italian-trained designers were Vasilij Kobelev, Petr Galkin, Petr Kokhtev, and Petr Serebriakov, and the engravers, Ivan Maksimov, Grigorij Ivanov, and Fedor Ivanov (Zakharov, *Kremlevskie kolokola*, 35; Snegirev, "Moskovskij Tsar'-kolokol''," 5; and Boguslavskij, *Tsar'-kolokol*, 23-24).

12. Boguslavskij, *Tsar'-kolokol*, 24.

13. Ibid., 25.

14. Ibid., 26.

15. Ibid., 28, my translation. "Lower than the lowest grasses" meant that the founder's inscription could be placed in the floral frieze at the base of the sound-bow just above the lip of the bell. The Senate approved a nine-word inscription that recorded Ivan Motorin as founder. Mikhail Motorin's name was added to the inscription, however, for a total of fourteen words.

16. Ivanov, *Istoricheskiia svěděniia*, 18-20; and Rubtsov, "Ivan Fedorovich," 30.

17. Boguslavskij, *Tsar'-kolokol*, 29, 30.

18. The events and details of the first attempt to cast the bell are transmitted in documents (sheets 2-3, 70) translated and published in Rubtsov, *History*, 463-464, 470-472. The melting process began with the loading of 5,723 puds 4 funts of metal from the old bell into the furnaces. The following day an additional 5,276 puds 36 funts of metal were added in two stages (1,276 puds 36 funts of bell pieces plus 4,000 puds of red copper) for a total input of 11,000 puds. On the morning of November 28 another 2,000 puds of raw tin and copper were placed in the furnaces bringing the total to 13,000 puds (469,469 pounds) of metal. (Rubtsov, *History*, 470 [sheet 70]; see also Zakharov, *Kremlevskie kolokola*, 44-45; Boguslavskij, *Tsar'-kolokol*, 31-32; and Snegirev, "Moskovskij Tsar'-kolokol''," 9.)

19. Motorin also consulted cannon foremen Andrej Stepanov and Andrej Arnold, assistant foreman Stepan Kop'ev, and A. K. Nartov, an assessor from the office of the Moscow Mint (Rubtsov, *History*, 470-471 [sheet 70]).

20. These old bells at the Moscow Cannon Yard were evidently instruments that remained from Peter the Great's req-

uisition of bells at the beginning of the eighteenth century for the manufacture of cannon during the Great Northern War. See Chapter 6 of this volume.

21. Boguslavskij, *Tsar'-kolokol*, 33. Motorin's reports on his first attempt to cast at the end of November 1734 and his description of the failures of three furnaces are contained on sheets 72, 101, and 102 of the Moscow Artillery Office (Rubtsov, *History*, 473-474, 475-476).

22. Rubtsov, *History*, 473-474 (sheet 72).

23. Boguslavskij, *Tsar'-kolokol*, 33.

24. Ibid.

25. Rubtsov, *History*, 476-477 (sheet 105).

26. Rubtsov, "Ivan Fedorovich," 32; and Boguslavskij, *Tsar'-kolokol*, 33-34.

27. Rubtsov, "Ivan Fedorovich," 32; see also Rubtsov, *History*, 178, 477 (sheet 116).

28. Boguslavskij, *Tsar'-kolokol*, 34; and Zakharov, *Kremlevskie kolokola*, 47-48.

29. A detailed account of the second casting dated November 25, 1735, is published in Rubtsov, *History*, 478 (sheet 118). Mikhail Motorin had 14,814 puds 21 funts (534,997 pounds) remaining from the metal his father had collected, to which he added 498 puds 6 funts (17,990 pounds) of tin for a total of 15,312 puds 27 funts (552,987 pounds) (Fal'kovskij, *Moskva v istorii tekhniki*, 249). For a description of the stages and procedures required in casting a bell, see Chapter 10.

30. Rubtsov, *History*, 178.

31. Boguslavskij, *Tsar'-kolokol*, 35-36.

32. Rubtsov, *History*, 478 (sheet 118).

33. Ibid., 479 (sheet 119). In this decree the empress also ordered drawings made of all reliefs and inscriptions on the bell. These drawings would be used to ascertain whether there were any engravers who would finish the bell's decorations for fees lower than those the engravers in Moscow had requested.

34. Montferrand, *Description*, 6.

35. Boguslavskij, *Tsar'-kolokol*, 36-38.

36. Montferrand, *Description*, 6. See also Rubtsov, *History*, 181.

37. See Lyall, *The Character of the Russians*, 202-203; and Jonas Hanway, *An Historical Account of . . . Travels from London through Russia . . .* , 1 (London: Sold by Mr. Dodsley, 1753), 93. John Murray's explanation is the most far-fetched of all: "It is said that the tower in which it originally hung was burnt in 1737, and its fall buried the enormous mass deep in the earth, and broke a huge fragment from it" (*Hand-book for Northern Europe*, 551; see also Sears, who transmits this version in *An Illustrated Description*, 365).

Though J. Ross Browne reports two explanations of the bell's damage, he assumes that it was once suspended and fantasizes on the way in which Tsar-Kolokol was rung and the effect of its sound (*The Land of Thor* [London: Sampson Low, Son & Marston, 1867], 144-146; cf. Snegirev, who objectively states both the real and false versions of how the bell was ruined, in "Moskovskij Tsar'-Kolokol''," 6). William Spottiswoode, on the other hand, writes: "It is clear to me that the bell was never rung, or even suspended. . . . That it was never raised would seem evident from the fact, that beneath it was found the iron grating on which the core is built previous to forming the mould, and the bell was found in the hole in which it had been originally cast." (*A Tarantasse Journey through Eastern Russia in the Autumn of 1856* [London: Longman, Brown, Green, Longmans & Roberts, 1857], 248-249; see also Robert Bremner, *Excursions in the Interior of Russia* 2 [London: Henry Colburn, 1839], 58; Zakharov, *Kremlevskie kolokola*, 49; and Boguslavskij, *Tsar'-kolokol*, 38-39.)

38. Fal'kovskij says the broken piece of Tsar-Kolokol weighs 12.5 tons (*Moskva v istorii tekhniki*, 250). The 12-pud model of Tsar-Kolokol that Ivan Motorin cast earlier is reported to have split at the Church of the Resurrection in St. Petersburg at the very moment that the great bell was ruined in Moscow (Bogdanov, *Opisanie Sanktpeterburga*, 214).

39. A plan was considered to cast a bell for the Paris Exhibition of 1889 that would be "larger than any other in the world—even than the two-hundred ton 'Tsar Kolokol' in Moscow." This projected clock bell was conceived as an aural symbol of Paris, and was to have been of such size that its strokes on the hours could be heard in the most distant suburbs of the capital. But the Eiffel Tower was built instead. (Price, *Bells and Man*, 176.)

40. W. W. Starmer, "The Great Bell of Moscow," *The Musical Times* 57 (October 1, 1916): 441. Several sources mention the presence of gold and silver in the bronze: Murray, *Handbook for Northern Europe*, 551 ("and every one who had a fraction of the precious metals threw into the melting mass some offering either of silver or gold"); Hanway, *An Historical Account*, 93 ("For every one ambitious to contribute towards it, threw some gold or silver into the furnaces, which were four in number"). See also Edward Daniel Clarke, *Travels in Various Countries of Europe, Asia, and Africa*, pt. 1: Russia, Tahtary, and Turkey, 4th ed., vol. 1 (London: T. Cadell and W. Davies, 1816), 150-151; but cf. Olovianishnikov, *Istoriia kolokolov"*, 182.

41. Montferrand, *Description*, 10.

42. Starmer estimates that gold coins worth £300,000 in 1916 would have to have been present in the bell metal of Tsar–Kolokol to register 1.00% in the analysis of its metal components ("The Great Bell of Moscow," 441).

43. Zabelin, *Materialy dlia istorii*, 2, cols. 1048-1049.

44. Fal'kovskij, *Moskva v istorii tekhniki*, 250. Fal'kovskij's figure of 12,000 puds (433,356 pounds) should be considered the actual weight of Tsar-Kolokol. For a list of weights and dates for a number of the world's other great bells, see Appendix D of this volume.

45. The dimensions of the bell cited here are taken from Fal'kovskij, *Moskva v istorii tekhniki*, 250, who has transmitted the figures from Adelung, *Al'bom" Mejerberga*, 103. There is, however, a surprising lack of consensus among the sources that report the dimensions of Tsar-Kolokol. The height of the

bell is quoted at 20 feet in Hubert Faensen, Vladimir Ivanov, and Klaus G. Beyer, *Early Russian Architecture*, trans. Mary Whittal (London: Paul Elek, 1975), 411; and 20 feet 7 inches in Snegirev, *Pamiatniki drevniago khudozhestva*, 35; and 21 feet 3 inches in Sears, *An Illustrated Description*, 366. Zakharov quotes 6 m, 14 cm (20 feet 1.75 inches) in *Kremlevskie kolokola*, 49.

Varying diameters cited for the bell include 21.5 feet in Faensen, *Early Russian Architecture*, 411; 22 feet 8 inches in Snegirev, *Pamiatniki*, 35; and 6.9 m (22.63 feet) in Danilevskij, *Russkaia tekhnika*, 120. L. Krekshina and Zakharov both estimate 6 m, 60 cm (21.65 feet) in *Po Kremliu*, 116; and *Kremlevskie kolokola*, 49.

The circumference of the bell will vary, of course, according to the diameter. Boguslavskij reports the circumference as 20 m 75 cm (68 feet); Boguslavskij's diameter of 6 m 60 cm (21.65 feet) is compatible with this circumference. (*Tsar'-kolokol*, 48.)

The thickness of the bell wall in its lower portion at the sound-bow is generally reported as 24 inches or 2 feet but has also appeared as 23 inches (Starmer, "The Great Bell of Moscow," 442; and Nichols, *Bells thro' the Ages*, 30. According to J. Ross Browne, the thickness of the bell wall "varies from three feet [*sic*] to three inches" (*The Land of Thor*, 145).

46. Karl Baedeker gives the height of Tsar-Kolokol including its cannons and top ornament (but not the pedestal) as 26 feet (*Russia*, 281).

47. Boguslavskij, *Tsar'-kolokol*, 48. Of this amount, 12,787 rubles were paid to those who worked on the project.

48. No portrait of a Russian patriarch appears on Motorin's Tsar-Kolokol of 1735. After 1700, on the death of Patriarch Adrian, the patriarchal throne of Russia officially remained unfilled, though Stefan Iavorskij, Metropolitan of Riazan, carried out the duties of the patriarch. In 1721 Peter the Great replaced the Patriarchate of Moscow with the Holy Synod.

49. Montferrand, *Description*, 10. Charles Antoine Coysevox (1640-1720), a French sculptor in the service of Louis XIV, provided much of the decoration and statuary for the Palace of Versailles. In the mid-eighteenth century Edme Bouchardon (1698-1762) was regarded as one of the foremost French sculptors who worked in the classical style.

50. Some have criticized the decoration and inscriptions as poorly executed (Sears, *An Illustrated Description*, 366; and Murray, *Hand-book for Northern Europe*, 551).

51. Snegirev, "Moskovskij Tsar'-kolokol"," 2-3, my translation. The absence of any reference to the Godunov Bell of 1599, which preceded Aleksei Mikhailovich's bell of 1654, may be attributable to the ill repute in which Boris Godunov was held.

52. Ibid., 3, my translation. The year 1733 was the anticipated date of casting. Because of delays and an unsuccessful first attempt to cast, the bell was not actually founded until two years later. By using the same bell mold in November 1735 that had been prepared in 1733, Mikhail Motorin could not alter the year originally prepared on the inscription. Like-

wise the weight of Tsar-Kolokol, which appears on the inscription (10,000 puds) is the weight that the empress had initially specified and does not reflect the true weight of the bell (12,000 puds) after casting.

53. Ibid., 3, my translation.

54. "Two bells made of exactly the same material and in exactly the same form (homologous dimensions) will sound an octave apart when one bell has *half the diameter of the other.* The bell sounding the octave higher note will also *weigh one-eighth* of the other bell." (From the first page of "Bell Basics: A Brief Review" published and distributed by the American Bell Association.)

Diameter (in inches)	Weight (in pounds)	Pitch
[240]	[327,680]	[C_1]
120	40,960	C
60	5,120	c (Middle C)
30	640	c^1
15	80	c^2
7.5	10	c^3
3.75	1.25	c^4

55. Starmer, "The Great Bell of Moscow," 442.

56. A hum tone on C_2 would correspond to the third lowest white key on the piano. In the equally tempered scale on the piano C_2 and B_3 generate 32.703 and 30.868 Hz (cycles per second), respectively (see table 3 in Nicholas Bessaroboff, *Ancient European Musical Instruments* [Cambridge, MA: Published for the Museum of Fine Arts, Boston, by Harvard University Press, 1941], 9). The lowest tone that the human ear can generally distinguish as a pitch has a frequency of about 20 Hz. (Llewelyn S. Lloyd, "Pitch notation," *New Grove Dictionary of Music and Musicians* 14, ed. by Stanley Sadie [London: Macmillan, 1980], 788).

57. Willi Apel, "Bell," *Harvard Dictionary of Music*, 2d ed., rev. and enl. (Cambridge MA: The Belknap Press of Harvard University Press, 1969), 89. (In this article a different system of pitch designation is used: c^1 = my c and C = my C_1.)

58. See Olovianishnikov's table with clapper weights for bells up to 1,500 puds in *Istoriia kolokolov"*, 417-419. The 17-foot clapper presently lying on the platform inside the cavity of Tsar-Kolokol belonged to another and unidentified bell and is not the clapper that was intended for Motorin's bell (I. K. Kondrat'ev, *Sědaia starina Moskvy* [Moscow: Izd. knigoprodavtsa I. A. Morozova, 1893], 138 n. 1).

59. Perhaps some idea of the sound Tsar-Kolokol would have generated may be conveyed in Percival Price's description of the voice of the 158,731-pound "Emelie" (A.D. 771) in Kyŏngju, Korea. When struck, this barrel-shaped Asian bell "shudders and gives a great boom. This slowly decreases to a hum, then to a vibration so low in pitch it is more felt than heard. This decreases so slowly that there is no precise moment of its stopping. One can only realize that whatever came out of the bell has gone." (*Bells and Man*, 36.)

60. Boguslavskij, *Tsar'-kolokol*, 39.

61. Ibid.

62. Ibid., 40.

63. Ibid.; and M. Glubokovskij, "Tsar'-kolokol" i proekty ego vozobnovleniia," *Russkoe obozrěnie* 4 (1894): 871.

64. Vasilij Ivanovich Bazhenov (1737 or 1738 to 1799), one of Russia's leading architects during the second half of the eighteenth century, championed the neo-Classical style in Russia. In 1775 Catherine II decided not to implement his radial plan for integrating the Kremlin with the principal arteries of Moscow (I. M. Glozman and O. V. Mamontova, "Bazhenov, Vasilii Ivanovich," *Great Soviet Encyclopedia* 2 [1983], 658).

65. Ivan Vasil'evich Egotov (1756-1814), a Moscow architect at the end of the eighteenth and beginning of the nineteenth centuries, was a student of M. F. Kazakov (see n. 68 below).

66. Boguslavskij, *Tsar'-kolokol*, 40.

67. Montferrand, *Description*, 7.

68. Matvej Fedorovich Kazakov (1738-1812) was the architect of the Moscow Senate building in the Kremlin, a project which occupied him for more than a decade between 1776 and 1787.

69. Boguslavskij, *Tsar'-kolokol*, 41.

70. Clarke, *Travels in Various Countries*, 150.

71. Ibid., 151.

72. Pukhnachev, *Zagadki*, 80; and Schilling, *Glocken*, 28.

73. Montferrand, *Description*, 7.

74. Pukhnachev, *Zagadki*, 80-81.

75. The French architect and engineer, Auguste Ricard de Montferrand (1786-1858), who arrived in St. Petersburg in 1816, had gained distinction in Russia by 1836 through his plans for and construction in progress on St. Isaac's Cathedral in St. Petersburg (begun in 1818 and completed in 1858). Between 1830 and 1834 Montferrand had also raised the Alexander Column in the vast square before the Winter Palace.

76. Montferrand's struggle with Lebedev is chronicled in Boguslavskij, *Tsar'-kolokol*, 41-44.

77. Montferrand indicates that Nicholas I wished to build a bell tower to contain Tsar-Kolokol once it had been raised from its pit. The enormous size of the bell, however, did not make this feasible, and it was placed on a granite platform instead. (*Description*, 7-8.)

78. Rubtsov, *History*, 181.

79. Montferrand's work on this project before July 23, 1836, is described in Olovianishnikov, *Istoriia kolokolov"*, 182-188; Boguslavskij, *Tsar'-kolokol*, 44-45; Zakharov, *Kremlevskie kolokola*, 51-57; and Schilling, *Glocken*, 84-90.

80. Montferrand, *Description*, 8-9. According to Boguslavskij, though not mentioned by Montferrand, there was an attempt to raise the bell on the morning of April 27, 1836. In his account 550 workers managed to lift the bell only a short distance when a block broke on one of the capstans and halted the operation. (*Tsar'-kolokol*, 44.)

81. Montferrand, *Description*, 9-10, my translation. See also the account by K. Sh., "O podniatii tsaria kolokola v" Moskvě,"

Sěvernaia pchela, no. 185 (Friday, August 14, 1836), pp. 737-738. According to this report, six hundred soldiers were stationed at the capstans, and the entire operation was carried out without any noise.

82. According to Montferrand, the monument (including its granite platform) is 34 *pieds* tall from the ground to the top of the cross (Montferrand, *Description*, 10). If the *pied* that Montferrand uses is equal to 1.066 feet, then the monument's total height would be 36.24 feet.

83. Ibid., 11, my translation. Several errors are transmitted in this inscription: (1) the bell, as previously noted, was cast not in 1733, but in 1735. The former date was obviously taken from the Anna Ivanovna inscription on the bell; (2) the bell only lacked four months of being in its pit 101 years—from November 25, 1735 (the date of its casting), to July 23, 1836, when Montferrand raised it; (3) according to Montferrand's statement in *Description*, 10, the bell was placed on its pedestal on July 26, not on August 4, a discrepancy that cannot be explained by a difference between calendars. Montferrand may mean that he attached the plaque with its inscription to the pedestal on August 4 after having set the bell there on July 26.

84. Bremner, *Excursions*, 59.

85. Georg Eismann, "Robert Schumanns Moskauer Gedichte," *Beiträge zur Musikwissenschaft* 1 (1959): 35.

86. Browne, *The Land of Thor*, 145.

87. Sears, *An Illustrated Description*, 367; and Murray, *Hand-book for Northern Europe*, 552. According to Percival Price, the chapel and its altar within Tsar-Kolokol remained until about 1932 (*Bells and Man*, xvii).

88. The nationality of Mr. Roberts is not stated. He may have been an Englishman, or perhaps an American, who served as a casting foreman at the Russian Company for Steam Navigation and Commerce in the Sevastopol workshops. Nikolaj Nikolaevich Benardos (1842-1905) was an important inventor and is considered the father of electric-arc welding. For information on his work, see V. P. Nikitin, "Nikolaj Nikolaevich Benardos," in *Liudi russkoj nauki: tekhnika*, ed. I. V. Kuznetsov (Moscow: Izd. "Nauka," 1965), 290-299. Nikolaj Gavrilovich Slavianov (1854-1897) was another pioneer in electric-arc welding. On Slavianov's contributions, see V. P. Nikitin, "Nikolaj Gavrilovich Slavianov," in *Liudi russkoj nauki: tekhnika*, 419-427. The most comprehensive descriptions and analyses of these three proposals for the restoration of Tsar-Kolokol at the end of the nineteenth century are contained in Glubokovskij, "Tsar'-kolokol″," 872-893. See also "Restavratsiia Tsaria-Kolokola," *Den'*, no. 1703 (March 10, 1893), p. 1; and Andrej Kapitskij, "Demonstratsiia sozvězdij," *Nauka i zhizn'*, no. 50 (December 12, 1892), p. 796.

89. Glubokovskij, "Tsar'-kolokol″," 878; and "Vozmozhnoe priměnenie ėlektricheskoj otlivki N. G. Slavianova," *Ėlektrichestvo*, no. 8 (April 1893), p. 128. Some expressed the opinion of leaving Tsar-Kolokol the way it was without attempting

to repair it (Staryj Moskvich, "Tsar'-kolokol″," *Moskovskaia gazeta*, no. 47 [1893], p. 52, col. 6).

90. Glubokovskij, "Tsar'-kolokol″," 872.

91. The plans of Benardos with a critique of his methods are contained in "Proekt″ N. N. Benardosa dlia ispravleniia Tsar'-kolokola," *Nauka i zhizn'*, no. 8 (1893), pp. 125-126. Benardos proposed *ėlektrogefest* in 1882 as a means of "connecting and disconnecting metals by the direct action of an electric current." This method was predicated on utilizing an electric (or voltaic) arc between a carbon electrode and the work piece. Benardos patented *ėlektrogefest* in 1885 in a number of countries (including the U.S.), and it was immediately employed in metalworking shops both in Russia and abroad. ("Benardos, Nikolai Nikolaevich," *Great Soviet Encyclopedia* 3 [1975], 162.) On arc welding itself, see Emil F. Steinert, "Arc welding," *McGraw-Hill Encyclopedia of Science and Technology* 1, 5th ed. (New York: McGraw-Hill, 1982), 670-673; and J. A. Oates, *Modern Arc Welding Practice* (London: George Newnes, 1961), 2. On the early history of the electric arc in Russia, see M. Glubokovskij, "Ėlektricheskaia otlivka metallov" i eia priměnenie," *Moskovskiia vědomosti*, no. 353 (December 21, 1892), p. 4.

92. Boguslavskij, *Tsar'-kolokol*, 47-48.

93. The details of Slavianov's proposal are explained and his plan compared to Benardos' project in the article "Vozmozhnost' ispravleniia Tsar'-Kolokola po sposobu N. G. Slavianova," *Nauka i zhizn'*, no. 6 (1893), pp. 89-93.

94. For a list of the broken bells and their weights which Slavianov repaired in the Motovilikhinskij Factory at Perm, see "Ėlektricheskoe ispravlenie kolokolov″," *Nauka i zhizn'*, no. 17 (1893), p. 270; and Glubokovskij, "Tsar'-kolokol″," 882-888. The largest bell Slavianov worked with weighed 330 puds (11,917 pounds).

95. Glubokovskij suggests that Slavianov's proposed method could also be used for repairing the cannons ("ears") on the 2,000-pud Kremlin bell "Reut" ("Ėlektricheskaia otlivka metallov″," 5, col. 5 from left).

96. "Vozmozhnost' ispravleniia . . . N. G. Slavianova," 91.

97. "Vozmozhnoe priměnenie . . . N. G. Slavianova," 128.

98. Glubokovskij, "Tsar'-kolokol″," 888; see also "Ėlektricheskoe ispravlenie kolokolov″," 270. The Russian words *prevoskhodnyj* (superb, outstanding), *prekrasnyj* (fine, beautiful), and *otlichnyj* (excellent) describe the tone of these bells. Despite Glubokovskij's confidence in the results of Slavianov's work, it is questionable whether the state-of-art in Russian welding at the end of the nineteenth century would support his claim.

99. "Vozmozhnoe priměnenie . . . N. G. Slavianova," 128; and "Vozmozhnost' ispravleniia . . . N. G. Slavianova," 93. The question of repairing Tsar-Kolokol was debated in the Russian press in 1893; using pertinent quotations Glubokovskij has summarized this controversy in "Tsar'-kolokol″," 888-890.

100. Olovianishnikov, *Istoriia kolokolov''*, 190, 192. Podchinennov also designed a support system for bells in the bell tower over-the-gate at the Danilov Monastery in Moscow (see Chapter 10).

101. Zakharov, *Kremlevskie kolokola*, 59.

102. Olovianishnikov, *Istoriia kolokolov''*, 191.

103. Ibid., 192.

Notes to Chapter 13

1. Heinrich von Staden, *The Land and Government of Muscovy*, 44.

2. Most secondary sources on bells in the Kremlin's Ivan Velikij Bell Tower contain accounts of the Great Uspensky Bell. See Zakharov, *Kremlevskie kolokola*, 18-22; and Istomin, *Ivanovskaia kolokol'nia*, 24-28.

3. Ivanov, *Istoricheskiia svĕdĕniia*, 11. See also Priakhin, "Kolokol'nyj zvon''," 182.

4. Spasskij, "O kolokolakh''," 131.

5. Edward Daniel Clarke, *Travels in Various Countries of Europe, Asia and Africa*, 1, 4th ed. (London: T. Cadell and W. Davies, 1816), 147. If the circumference of Slizov's bell were 40.75 feet, then its lower diameter would have been only a fraction less than 13 feet.

6. Spasskij, "O kolokolakh''," 131-132. The portraits of three eighteenth-century rulers were conspicuously absent from the decorative program on Slizov's bell: Peter II, Ivan VI, and Anna Ivanovna. The first two tsars, a child and an infant, never reigned in their own right. The omission of Anna's portrait can be explained by her rivalry with Elisabeth Petrovna. They each belonged to different lines of the imperial family, and Elisabeth, who regarded her own line as superior, overthrew the regency that Anna had established for Ivan VI.

7. Levshin, *Istoricheskoe opisanie*, 247-248, my translation.

8. Clarke, *Travels*, 147.

9. C. Piazzi Smyth, *Three Cities in Russia* (London: Lovell, Reeve & Co., 1862), 73.

10. For an account of the procession which accompanied the transport of this bell from the foundry to the Kremlin and its elevation into the tower, see Chapter 10 of this volume.

11. Istomin, *Ivanovskaia kolokol'nia*, 24-25.

12. Lyall, *The Character of the Russians*, 211. But cf. Lyall's height for Bogdanov's 4,000-pud bell with the reported height of only 10.5 feet for the 4,000-pud bell of 1748 at the Trinity-Sergius Lavra. With a diameter of exactly 18 feet, the bell's circumference would be 56.54 feet. If the circumference were only 54 feet, however, then the bell's diameter would measure about 17.18 feet.

13. The weight of Bogdanov's bell is not recorded on its inscription as published by Istomin, and the "official" figure of 4,000 puds (144,452 pounds) has been questioned in at least two studies. Istomin reports that Bogdanov himself, in his enthusiasm over this project, increased the bell's weight to 6,000

puds (216,678 pounds) (*Ivanovskaia kolokol'nia*, 24). Arsenij, on the other hand, calculated the bell's weight at considerably less than the 4,000 puds generally cited and believes that it only contains 3,375 puds 18 funts (121,898 pounds) of metal ("O Tsar'-kolokolĕ," 67 n. 1).

14. Lyall, *The Character of the Russians*, 211. According to Istomin, the bell also bore a portrait of Avgustin, Metropolitan of Moscow (*Ivanovskaia kolokol'nia*, 25).

15. Istomin, *Ivanovskaia kolokol'nia*, 25-26, my translation. For some reason Bogdanov omitted the bell's weight from its inscription. Alexander I, who became tsar on March 12, 1801, would have been in the fifth month of the seventeenth year of his reign on July 22, 1817. The title "Tsesarevich" preceding the name of Grand Duke Konstantin Pavlovich on the inscription indicates that at the time of casting he was heir to the throne. In the secret manifesto of August 16, 1823, however, he relinquished his claim to the throne in favor of his younger brother, Nikolaj Pavlovich, who in 1825 became Nicholas I.

16. Ibid., 26.

17. This information is transmitted by Maurice Baring in *A Year in Russia*, 2d ed. (London: Methuen, 1907), 164. Clara Schumann had two opportunities to hear Bogdanov's bell: when she and Robert were in Moscow in the early spring of 1844 and in 1864, eight years after Robert's death, when she made a second concert tour of Russia.

18. "Kolokol'nyj zvon''," *Russkij palomnik''*, no. 20 (1886), p. 182. Cf. the projected pitch for the 12,000-pud Tsar-Kolokol in Chapter 12 of this volume.

19. Ibid.

20. Gatty, *The Bell*, 49.

21. A comprehensive study of Elisabeth Petrovna's bell of 1748 for the Trinity-Sergius Lavra is available in Arsenij's "O Tsar'-kolokolĕ," 65-111.

The two other large bells in the tower of the Trinity-Sergius Lavra are the "Polielejnyj" bell, or Godunov Bell, of 1600 (ca. 1,850 puds, or ca. 66,809 pounds) and the "Kornoukhij" (Crop-eared) Bell founded in 1683 at 1,275 puds (46,044 pounds) by Fedor Dmitrievich Motorin. The Godunov Bell, though smaller than "Kornoukhij," weighs more. (Golubinskij, *Prepodobnyj Sergij Radonezhskij*, 198-199; see also Rybakov, *Tserkovnyj zvon''*, 38.)

22. Arsenij, "O Tsar'-kolokolĕ," 67-69. The inscription on Elisabeth Petrovna's bell of 1748 records a somewhat lesser weight for the 1716 bell (3,319 puds, or 119,859 pounds). See N. Gorchakov, who also lists this earlier bell's weight as 3,319 puds ("O bol'shikh'' kolokolakh''," 198). Bergholz visited the monastery on July 20, 1722, and wrote that the largest bell there was cast in 1709 and weighed "350 p[uds] [12,640 pounds] or 14,000 f[unts] [12,642 pounds]" (Ammon, *Dnevnik''* . . . *Berkhgol'tsa*, 2:180). Bergholz's statement is puzzling since three earlier bells weighing much more than 350 puds were presumably in the old bell tower at the time of his visit and

were being rung: "Kornoukhij" (1683) at 1,275 puds; "Polie-lejnyj" (the Godunov Bell) of 1600 at approximately 1,850 puds; and "Lebed'" (1594) at 625 puds. Nineteenth-century sources mention no bell at the lavra of 350 puds cast in 1709. Though he emphatically confirms his citation of the bell's weight as 350 puds with a parallel equivalent of 14,000 funts, Bergholz possibly omitted one digit from these weights. A bell of 3,500 puds would weigh 140,000 funts, but this error would not reconcile the difference of seven years in the bell's date of founding.

23. Arsenij, "O Tsar'-kolokolě," 68-70.

24. Ibid., 71. If these figures are reliable, they indicate that about 155 more puds of metal were on hand in addition to the 750 puds of new copper and 250 puds of new tin that Stepanov and Smirnov had added to the bell of 1716. Arsenij notes that the metal for the new bell included 161 puds from a broken lavra bell of 1427 named "Baran" (Ram) (p. 71 n. 9).

25. Ibid., 93-97.

26. Ibid., 108. The figures Arsenij cites for the circumference and diameter of the bell, 42 feet and 14 feet, respectively, do not exactly correspond. If the bell's diameter were 14 feet, then its circumference would be almost 44 feet; on the other hand, if the circumference were 42 feet, the bell's diameter would have to be about 13.36 feet. Priakhin transmits the lower diameter as 6 arshins 8 vershki (or 15 feet 2 inches), a diameter that would produce a circumference of almost 47 feet 8 inches ("Kolokol'nyj zvon"," *Russkij palomnik*", no. 21 (1886), p. 195).

27. Arsenij, "O Tsar'-kolokolě," 97.

28. Ibid., 107-108, my translation.

29. Ibid., 68, 98. On December 8, 1742, Elisabeth Petrovna had directed Kirill, the new archimandrite, to install the as-yet-uncast bell in the as-yet-unfinished bell tower. The empress had also cautioned that the bell tower's foundations should be carefully constructed to bear the weight of the new bell.

30. Ibid., 101. The date in December when the bell was raised into the tower is not stated.

31. "Moscow, Jan. 4. . . . the newspapers report today that the heaviest bell in Russia, a seventy-ton monster two feet thick, given by the Empress Elizabeth to the Troitski Monastery near Moscow, now a museum, has been removed to a foundry" (Walter Duranty, "Kalinin Urges Reds to Push Grain Programs," *The New York Times* [January 5, 1930], 8).

32. Arsenij states that though the weight of the lavra bell of 1748 is recorded on its inscription as 4,000 puds (144,452 pounds), according to bell foremen, 4,065 puds (146,799 pounds) of metal were cast ("O Tsar'-kolokolě," 67). The great bell at the lavra thus may have been somewhat heavier than Bogdanov's Great Uspensky Bell in Moscow. Those who had heard the sound of both bells described the ring of the lavra's bell as "pleasant, even, and quite strong, but not very dense." With respect to tone quality, if not weight, then, the lavra bell was surpassed by the bell in the Moscow Kremlin. (Pria-

khin, "Kolokol'nyj zvon"," *Russkij palomnik*", no. 21 [1886], 195).

Notes to Chapter 14

1. Bazin, *The Baroque*, 26.

2. Their intent was therefore partly theatrical, not unlike the "epiphanies" of Byzantine emperor Constantine VII Porphyrogenitus (913-959), who appeared before foreign representatives in the throne room of the Imperial Palace in Constantinople amid the play of elaborate machinery and mechanical animals. (F. A. Wright, trans., *The Works of Liudprand of Cremona*, 207-208 [bk. 6, chap. 5].)

3. Bazin, *The Baroque*, 26. See also Sigfried Giedion, *Space, Time and Architecture: The Growth of a New Tradition*, 5th ed., rev. and enl. (Cambridge, MA: Harvard University Press, 1967), lv-lvi; and William Fleming, *Arts and Ideas*, 3d ed. (New York: Holt, Rinehart and Winston, [1968]), 404.

4. The existence of auditory space was apparently formally recognized in the 1950s by Edmund Carpenter and Marshall McLuhan in "Acoustic Space." *Explorations in Communications: An Anthology*, ed. Edmund Carpenter and Marshall McLuhan (Boston: Beacon Press, 1960), 65-70. Carpenter and McLuhan consider auditory space "a sphere without fixed boundaries, space made by the thing itself, not space containing the thing. It is not pictorial space, boxed in, but dynamic, always in flux, creating its own dimensions moment by moment. It has no fixed boundaries; it is indifferent to background." Ibid., 67.) At the very end of the nineteenth century Maurice Ravel anticipated the notion of acoustic space in his title for a pair of pieces for two-pianos, *Sites auriculaires*. The second of the two compositions is entitled "Entre cloches."

5. R. Murray Schafer, *The Tuning of the World* (New York: Alfred A. Knopf, 1977), 7. As corollaries to his term "soundscape," Schafer introduces such concepts as "sonography" (cf. photography), "earwitness," and "soundmark" (cf. landmark). He further remarks that without "earlids," "the sense of hearing cannot be closed off at will." (Pp. 7-11.)

6. Murray, *Hand-book for Northern Europe*, 512. See a similar observation of C. Hagbert Wright in his essay on Moscow: "the religious history of Russia is so interwoven with the national life of Russia that the one appears almost to include the other" (Winifred Stephens, ed., *The Soul of Russia* [London: Macmillan, 1916], 15). See also Marthe Blinoff, *Life and Thought in Old Russia* (University Park, PA: The Pennsylvania State University Press, 1961), 84; and Joseph Wilbois, *Russia and Reunion*, trans. C. R. Davey Biggs (London: A.R. Mowbray, 1908), 101.

7. Konstantin Ton's Cathedral of Christ the Saviour, under construction for almost half a century, was consecrated in the presence of Alexander III on May 26, 1883, and was demolished in 1931. Tchaikovsky's overture received its premiere in Moscow on August 8, 1882.

8. Mikeshin's other major works include his monuments to

Catherine II, "the Great," in Leningrad; to Bogdan Khmelnitsky in Kiev; to Alexander II in Rostov-on-Don; to Yermak in Novocherkassk; to Mikhail Obrenović in Belgrade; and to the Portuguese constitution in Lisbon.

9. M. Karger, *Novgorod the Great* (Moscow: Progress Publishers, 1973), 104. For a history of the Novgorod monument and its sculptor, see *Pamiatnik "Tysiacheletie Rossii"* (Moscow: Izd. "Sovetskaia Rossiia," 1974); and E. N. Maslova, *Pamiatnik Tysiacheletiiu Rossii* (Leningrad: Lenizdat, 1972). In his work on the Novgorod monument, Mikeshin was assisted by the sculptors, I. N. Shreder, R. K. Zaleman, N. A. Lavretskij, M. A. Chizhov, and A. M. Liubimov (*Pamiatnik* [1974], 19).

10. Uvarov's doctrine was endorsed and promulgated by the tsar himself and became the ideological maxim in the Russia of Nicholas I. See chap. 3 (Official Nationality: The Ideas) in Nicholas V. Riasanovsky, *Nicholas I and Official Nationality in Russia, 1825-1855* (Berkeley: University of California Press, 1969), 73-183. A translation of Uvarov's doctrine from a survey of his first decade in office (1833-1843) appears on pp. 74-75.

11. Among the 109 figures on the relief at the monument's base are Cyril and Methodius, Nestor, Yermak, and Ivan Susanin. The base of the monument is constructed of six 35-ton blocks of Serdobol granite brought from the shores of Lake Ladoga, and its foundations extend 33 feet into the ground. The monument is 51.5 feet high. To cast the figures, the sphere, and reliefs required 65 tons of bronze. (*Pamiatnik* [1974], 19; and Budiak, ed., *Novgorod*, 136.)

12. Maslova, *Pamiatnik*, 55-56.

13. The six tableaux grouped around the bronze orb commemorate the reigns of: (1) Riurik, the semilegendary founder of the Russian state, whose shield bears the date 862; (2) Vladimir "the Great," Prince of Kiev, who officially christianized Russia in 988/989; (3) Dmitrij Donskoj, Grand Duke of Moscow, whose victory over the Mongols at Kulikovo Pole in 1380 was decisive in the eventual liberation of Russia from Oriental domination; (4) Ivan III, "the Great," who was largely instru-

mental in Moscow's unification of Russian lands at the end of the fifteenth and early years of the sixteenth centuries; (5) Mikhail Romanov, the first Romanov tsar, crowned in 1613, flanked by Kuz′ma Minin and Prince Dmitrij Pozharskij, who returned the Kremlin to Russian hands at the end of 1612; and (6) Peter I, "the Great," the founder of a new Russian capital on the Baltic at the beginning of the eighteenth century. Each of these rulers is oriented around the sphere so that he looks out in the general direction of the principal political, military, or cultural event of his reign: Riurik faces south toward Kiev; Vladimir, to the southwest and Byzantium; Dmitrij, to the southeast in the direction from which the Mongols entered Russia; Ivan III, to the east toward Moscow; Mikhail Romanov, to the northwest and to Poland, which ruled Russia before he was established on the throne; and Peter I, to the north toward his new capital on the Neva. (See Maslova, *Pamiatnik*, 15, 58-66.)

14. Ibid., 55. In the winter of 1943-1944, during the occupation of Novgorod, the Nazi General von Herzog had the monument dismantled in preparation for its removal to Germany as a victory trophy. When the Red Army liberated Novgorod on January 20, 1944, the monument lay in pieces scattered in the snow around its base. By November 2, 1944, the Russians had reassembled the monument inside the Novgorod kremlin. (*Pamiatnik* [1974], 71.)

Notes to Appendix C

1. Grimthorpe, *A Rudimentary Treatise*, 357, 359.

2. The lower diameter at the base of the Russian bell was derived from its height, first by subtracting a third of the height and then by multiplying the difference by 2. For example, if a bell's height was 9 vershki (15.75 inches), its lower diameter would be computed: 9 vershki − 3 vershki = 6 vershki × 2 = 12 vershki or 21 inches. On a bell with a lower diameter of 21 inches, each of its fourteen segments would be 1.5 inches long. (Olovianishnikov, *Istoriia kolokolov″*, 388.)

Glossary

Material in this section has been drawn from a number of works including the following: for basic terminology, Wendell Westcott, *Bells and Their Music* (New York: G. P. Putnam's Sons, 1970), and Percival Price, "Bell," *New Grove Dictionary of Music and Musicians* 2, ed. Stanley Sadie (London: Macmillan, 1980), 424-437; for terms associated with the Russian Orthodox Church, Martine Roty, *Dictionnaire russe-français des termes en usage dans l'église russe* (Paris: Institut d'Etudes Slaves, 1980); for terms and concepts encountered in Russian sources before the October Revolution, Sergei G. Pushkarev, *Dictionary of Russian Historical Terms from the Eleventh Century to 1917*, ed. George Vernadsky and Ralph T. Fisher, Jr. (New Haven: Yale University Press, 1970); for casting terminology, *AFS Metalcasting Dictionary*, compiled and ed. by Dudley C. Gould, 1st ed. (Des Plaines, IL: American Foundrymen's Society, 1968), and *Vocabulary of Foundry Practice in Six Languages: English, Czech, German, French, Polish, Russian* (New York: Macmillan, 1963).

ARCHAIC BELL: A "sugarloaf" form of Western bell that appeared in the late twelfth century, cast with an elongated and upward tapering waist (q.v.) and a narrow, rounded shoulder (q.v.). Unlike the primitive bell (q.v.) that preceded it, the archaic bell had a concave rather than convex waist, and its wall was thicker above the hip (q.v.).

ARCHIMANDRITE: The title of the head of a large, important Russian monastery. Generally translated "abbot."

BALDRIC: The leather strap or belt on which a bell clapper hangs from the crown staple (q.v.).

BALL OF THE CLAPPER: The spheroidal portion of a clapper toward its lower end—between the shaft (q.v.) and the flight (q.v.)—that has the greatest mass of metal. Called *iabloko* (apple) in Russian.

BEAD LINES: The thin horizontal ridges that encircle Western European and Russian bells as part of their decorative programs.

BEIAARD: Flemish and Dutch for "carillon" (q.v.).

BELL METAL: A bronze alloy that usually contains a ratio of about four parts copper (80%) to one part tin (20%).

BILO (pl. Bila): Russian for the wooden semantron (q.v.).

BLAGOVEST: The ringing of a single bell to announce services in Russia.

BLAGOVESTNIK: The liturgical name of a bell on which *blagovest* (q.v.) was sounded. Normally the largest bell in a Russian tower.

BOGORODITSA: The Russian name for the Virgin. Literally, "the god bearer," from the Greek Θεοτόκος.

CAMPANILE: Italian for a free-standing or detached bell tower. The term is often used in English-speaking countries for a bell tower that contains a carillon. The Russian equivalent for bell tower is *kolokol'nia*. Cf. zvonnitsa.

CANNONS OF A BELL: Known as *ushi* (ears) in Russian, cannons are the bronze loops that rise from the head (q.v.) or top plate of a bell. They are fixed to a stock (q.v.) for a swinging bell or to a wooden or metal beam for a stationary bell.

CARILLON: The Guild of Carillonneurs in North America has defined a carillon as "a musical instrument consisting of at least two octaves of carillon bells arranged in chromatic series and played from a keyboard permitting control of expression through variation of touch." Further, the partials (q.v.) of carillon bells are "in such harmonious relationship to each other as to permit many such bells to be sounded together, in varied chords, with harmonious and concordant effect." The word "carillon" was originally applied to a chime (q.v.) of four bells (*quadrillionem*).

CARILLONNEUR: The musician who performs on a carillon by depressing large wooden hand keys (or batons) and pedal keys.

"CARVED" BELL: A Russian bell cast with windows or apertures in its wall; the fenestration was thought to improve the tone quality of the bell.

CHANGE RINGING: A traditional English style of bell ringing in which swinging tower bells are rung according to an ordered and predetermined series of numerical permutations.

CHIME: A musical instrument usually of not more than two octaves of stationary bells tuned in a diatonic series. A chime often consists of a diatonic octave of eight bells that can be played either automatically by a rotating chiming cylinder (q.v.) or manually on a chime stand with wooden levers and sometimes pedals.

CHIMING CYLINDER: Also chiming barrel and chiming drum. Westcott explains this mechanism as a "metal cylinder— sometimes wood—whose surface is perforated, often with thousands of holes, for receiving projecting pegs or cogs. Mounted on a horizontal axis, it is made to rotate, in the early days by a suspended weight whose cable unwound from the barrel shaft. The pegs engage levers attached by wire to hammers mounted outside the bells, and as the barrel revolves, the levers are pushed down, thereby pulling the hammers away from the bells. When the levers become disengaged, the hammers fall through a spring to strike the bells. Sometimes there are as many as five hammers per bell in order to permit the rapid repetition of a note."

CLAPPER: The striking agent suspended inside Western European and Russian bells, generally cast in iron. Called *iazyk* (tongue) in Russian.

CLOCK JACKS (Jacquemarts): Automated figures, often cast or carved as men in armor, that are part of mechanisms in tower clocks. These mechanical figures strike the hours on a bell with their hammers or battle-axes.

COPE: The upper part of a bell mold, which fits over the core (q.v.), or inner mold, and which contains on its inner surface the impression that will produce the inscriptions, decorations, as well as the outer contour of the cast bell. In Russian, *kozhukh* (mantle, casing) or *kolpak* (dome, cover).

CORE: The inner bell mold on which the false bell (q.v.) is constructed. The core will determine the contour of the bell's interior cavity. *Bolvan* (blockmold, dummy) or *litso* (face) in Russian.

CROTAL: A relatively small, generally spheroidal instrument of closed form whose holes or slots are narrower than the diameter of the unattached pellet or pellets within (e.g., sleigh bells). Cf. gong.

CROWN: See cannons.

CROWN STAPLE: The loop at the interior vertex of a bell from which the clapper is suspended.

EARS OF A BELL: See cannons.

FALSE BELL: The clay model for a bell constructed on the core (q.v.), or inner mold. The false bell (*telo* [body] or *rubashka* [jacket] in Russian) is removed after the cope has been formed over it and baked, and the cavity left between the core and the cope is filled with molten bronze when the bell is poured.

FLIGHT OF A CLAPPER: The short spur on the clapper below the ball (q.v.) to which a rope or ropes are tied for swinging the clapper in Russian zvon ringing (q.v.). So-called because the ballast it provides makes the clapper fly.

FUNDAMENTAL: The frequency that is the principal pitch of a bell's ring. Also sometimes called the prime. *Zvon* (ring) in Russian.

GATE: The opening at the top of a bell mold through which the molten metal enters the cavity between the core (q.v.) and the cope (q.v.).

GONG: A metal instrument of Asian origin, usually cast and hammered in the form of a circular disc and struck with an agent of a softer material.

GREAT OR LARGE DIAMETER OF A BELL: See lower diameter of a bell.

HAMMER: See chiming cylinder and semantron.

HARMONICS: See partials.

ḤAZOZERAH (pl. Ḥazozeroth): The silver Hebrew trumpet first made and used on Sinai and blown during sacrificial rites in the Temple at Jerusalem.

HEAD OR TOP PLATE OF A BELL: The relatively flat surface at the top of a bell from which its cannons (q.v.) rise. *Golova* (head) in Russian.

HEADSTOCK: See stock.

HEARTH FURNACE: A shallow dishlike basin covered with a refractory brick roof. Flame from fires beside the hearth pass between the hearth and the roof, causing the metal in the hearth to melt.

HEIGHT OF A BELL: The distance that is measured on a bell's exterior from its lip (q.v.) to its shoulder (q.v.).

HIP OF A BELL: On the wall of a bell, that point where the wall thickness at the top of the sound-bow (q.v.) begins to taper into the waist (q.v.).

HOOF OF A BELL: On Japanese bells, the thickest part of the wall at its mouth.

HUM TONE: The lowest partial (q.v.) generated when a bell is rung. On a tuned carillon (q.v.) or chime (q.v.) bell, the hum tone is a sub-harmonic sounding an octave lower than the prime or fundamental (q.v.). *Gul* (hum or drone) in Russian.

IEROMONAKH (Hieromonk): A Russian monk ordained as a priest. Sometimes translated "priest-monk."

IGUMEN or HEGUMEN: The title given to the head of a smaller, less important Russian monastery and sometimes translated as "prior." From the Greek ἡγούμενος.

IVAN VELIKIJ BELL TOWER: The three-part architectural complex in the Moscow Kremlin that contains the bells formerly rung for services in the Uspensky Cathedral. The central Petrok Malyj Zvonnitsa of 1532-1543, built for the largest bells, is flanked by the Bono-Godunov column (1505-1508; 1599-1600) and the Philaret structure (1624).

JACKET: See cope.

JACQUEMARTS: See clock jacks.

KANONARCH (κανόναρχος or κανονάρχης): The monk in an Orthodox foundation charged with conducting services, initiating prescribed singing (especially the kanon in the morning office), and striking the semantron in some monasteries.

KLEPALO (pl. Klepala): Russian for the iron or metal semantron (q.v.).

KOLOKOL: Russian for "bell."

LAVRA: In the early days of monasticism a *laura* (λαύρα) was a group of scattered caves, cells, or huts for anchorites organized around a central place for communal worship and under the supervision of a superior. St. Athanasius of Athos founded the Great Laura on Mt. Athos in the mid-tenth century.

The Russian term *lavra* was derived from the Greek *laura*. It designates a large Russian monastery of the highest importance, independent of the local bishop, and under direct authority of the head of the Russian church. Between 1833 and the October Revolution, there were four *lavry* in Russia: (1) the Kievo-Pecherskaia Lavra (fd. 1051; became a lavra in 1598), (2) the Trinity-Sergius Lavra near Moscow (fd. ca. 1345; became a lavra in 1744), (3) the Alexander-Nevsky

Lavra in St. Petersburg (fd. 1710; became a lavra in 1797), and (4) the Pochaevskaia-Uspenskaia Lavra in Volynia (first mentioned in sixteenth-century sources; became a lavra in 1833).

LIP OF A BELL: The edge around the mouth (q.v.) of a bell formed by the meeting of its inner and outer walls. Also known as the rim or brim of a bell; *kraj* (edge) in Russian.

LOAM: A pasty mixture of clay, silt, and sand, usually with considerable organic matter. It is mixed with water to make a thick compound, which is used to build the inner and upper molds of bells, the core (q.v.) and the cope (q.v.) (as in "loam molding" or "loam mold").

LOWER DIAMETER OF A BELL: The diameter of a bell measured from opposite points on its lip (q.v.).

MALINOVYJ ZVON: A Russian term whose derivation is disputed. This term now refers to a style of bell ringing with a soft and pleasing timbre. Some, however, have seen in this term a reference to the carillon music of the Low Countries in which *malinovyj* is regarded as an adjectival form of Malines, a city in Belgium.

MANTLE: See cope.

MELTING LOSS: The irretrievable loss of metal during the melting process.

METROPOLITAN: The title of the head of the Russian church from the official conversion of Russia at the end of the tenth century until Tsar Fedor Ivanovich established the Patriarchate of Moscow in 1589. Between 1700 and 1917 when there was no Patriarch of Moscow (q.v.), metropolitans were the highest ranking members of the Russian clergy. In the nineteenth century there were metropolitans in Kiev, Moscow, and St. Petersburg.

MOUTH OF A BELL: The large circular opening of a bell formed by its lip (q.v.).

NABATNYJ KOLOKOL: Russian for "alarm bell" or bell that sounds the "tocsin."

NĀKŪS, NĀQŪS: A wooden instrument of convocation used in Christian communities of the Levant. The nākūs consists of two suspended logs or large wooden beams whose ends struck each other when swung.

NOMINAL: The partial a tuned bell generates that is an octave above its fundamental (q.v.), or prime. Though of brief duration, the nominal is important in defining a bell's pitch.

OVERTONES: See partials.

PARTIALS: The independent frequencies generated by a vibrating bell. The series of partials that emerge from a ringing bell affect its timbre (q.v.) as well as determine its pitch. See fundamental, hum tone, strike-note, tierce, quint, and nominal.

PASSING-BELL: In the West, the tolling of a bell for a dying person. Thought to protect the departing soul from evil spirits.

PATRIARCH OF MOSCOW: The head of the Russian church from 1589 until the death of Patriarch Adrian in 1700, and again from 1917 to the present. Peter the Great abolished the Patriarchate of Moscow and in 1721 established the Holy Synod as the highest administrative body in the Russian church. The office of Patriarch of Moscow was not restored until the Church Council of 1917.

PRIKAZ: An administrative bureau or department in the Muscovite government. See Pushkarskij prikaz.

PRIME. See fundamental.

PRIMITIVE BELL: The name used to identify bells cast from the end of the eighth century until the early years of the thirteenth century. The primitive bell had a convex shape with a profile (q.v.) of uniform wall thickness.

PROFILE OF A BELL: The vertical cross-section of a bell showing variations in metal thickness created by the contours of its inner and outer walls.

PUSHKARSKIJ PRIKAZ: Literally Cannon Bureau. The state department in Moscow whose responsibilities included supervision of the operations and organization of the Moscow Cannon Yard, in the late sixteenth and seventeenth centuries.

QUINT: One of the lower partials (q.v.) of a tuned bell pitched at the interval of a fifth above its fundamental (q.v.) or prime.

QUINT BELL: The largest and heaviest bell in the second Dutch carillon for St. Petersburg. It was called the Quint bell because its pitch was to be tuned a fifth above a hypothetical bell on C, an octave below the carillon's first bell on c (middle C). Its pitch, theoretically on G, was a fourth below that of the carillon's first numbered bell.

RIVETED BELL: An early kind of church bell manufactured between the fifth and mid-eleventh centuries from hammered sheets of metal (generally iron) fastened by rivets. Sometimes called a forged bell.

SALPINX (ἡ σάλπιγξ): The straight trumpet of the ancient Greeks, usually of metal, though the sole surviving example is of ivory.

SEMANTRON (pl. Semantra): The Byzantine instrument of convocation still used by Orthodox churches and monasteries. The semantron is a wooden plank, beam, or piece of metal struck with a hammer or mallet.

SHAFT or SHANK OF A CLAPPER: Portion of a clapper between the ball and its upper loop. The diameter or density of the shaft gradually increases from the upper loop to the ball (q.v.).

SHAM BELL: See false bell.

SHANK OF A CLAPPER: See shaft or shank of a clapper.

SHOFAR: The Hebrew instrument made from an animal horn, often that of a ram.

SHOULDER OF A BELL: That portion of a bell at the sharp curve from the upper part of its waist (q.v.) into the head (q.v.). *Plecho* (shoulder) in Russian.

SKETE: In the Eastern Orthodox Church a community of monks belonging to and dependent on an autonomous parent monastery. A skete consists of a dwelling or cluster of dwellings around a church and is often established in a remote area.

SMALL DIAMETER OF A BELL: See upper diameter of a bell.

ŠNB: The straight, metal trumpet of the ancient Egyptians.

SOUND-BOW: The thickest portion of a bell's wall between its lip (q.v.) and its hip (q.v.), and the place where the clapper strikes the bell. *Val* (swell) in Russian.

STOCK: A wooden or metal frame mounting for suspending a Western bell to be rung by swinging.

STRELTSY: Literally "shooters." Musketeers in a military corps that Ivan IV established in the mid-sixteenth century. Between their field assignments *streltsy* were also employed in nonmilitary projects.

STRICKLE BOARD: A template mounted to revolve about a spindle and cut to the contour of either the bell's inner or outer profile and rotated to form the two molds, core (q.v.) and cope (q.v.), in which the bell will be cast. Also known as sweep template, loam board, and forming board; in Russian *telovaia doska* (board for [molding] the false bell) or *shablon dlia formovki* (pattern for molding).

STRIKE-NOTE: a fleeting frequency, produced on a bell at the moment of the clapper's impact, that lies an octave below the nominal (q.v.) on tuned bells. On tuned bells the pitch of the strike-note will coincide with that of the fundamental; on untuned bells, when the fundamental and the nominal are not an octave apart, the difference between the fundamental and the strike-note will be briefly audible.

STRIKE POINT: A point on the interior wall of a bell's soundbow (q.v.) that receives the blows of the clapper (q.v.).

THEOPHILUS BELL: A form of European bell that appeared in the eleventh century with stocky proportions resembling a beehive. It is named for the monk Theophilus Presbyter (fl. early twelth century), whose treatise *De diversis artibus* contains a chapter on bell founding.

TIERCE: The partial (q.v.) on a tuned bell pitched a minor third above its fundamental (q.v.) or prime.

TIMBRE: The quality of sound as distinguished from its pitch. Timbre may be harsh, mellow, or strident. Partials (q.v.) generated by a vibrating object influence timbre.

TONGUE OF A BELL: See clapper.

TOP PLATE OF A BELL: See head or top plate of a bell.

TRINITY FIRE: The great Moscow fire that swept through the Kremlin on Trinity Sunday, May 29, 1737, and resulted in irreparable damage to Tsar-Kolokol.

TRINITY-SERGIUS LAVRA: The Holy Trinity Monastery that St. Sergius of Radonezh founded, probably in 1345, about forty-four miles northeast of Moscow. It became an important center of learning and a focal point of pilgrimage in medieval and modern Russia. Designated a lavra in 1744.

TSAR-KOLOKOL: The world's largest bell, now on a pedestal at the foot of the Ivan Velikij Bell Tower in the Moscow Kremlin. The bell's mold was the work of Ivan Motorin; his son, Mikhail Motorin, successfully cast the bell in his fa-ther's mold on November 25, 1735.

TSAR-PUSHKA: The name by which Andrej Chokhov's great cannon of 1586 is generally known. Chokhov's own name for this cannon was "Drobovik" (Fowling Piece).

TUBA: The straight metal trumpet of the ancient Romans.

UPPER DIAMETER OF A BELL: The interior diameter in the upper portion of a bell, measured from opposite points that correspond to the shoulder (q.v.) on the exterior.

UPPER LOOP OF CLAPPER: The aperture in a clapper at the upper end of the shaft (q.v.) through which the baldric (q.v.) passes to suspend the clapper from the crown staple (q.v.). *Petlia* (loop) in Russian.

VECHE BELL: A bell in medieval Russian cities (especially Novgorod and Pskov) rung to convoke the town assembly, or *veche*.

VELIKIJ KNIAZ': The title held by rulers of several larger principalities in medieval Russia. The ruler of Moscow had been designated *velikij kniaz'* before Ivan IV assumed the title Tsar of All the Russias, in 1547. *Velikij kniaz'* is rendered in English as Grand Duke, Great Prince, or Grand Prince. Later, in imperial Russia, it was the title held by brothers of an emperor.

VIAZ': A decorative and highly stylized Cyrillic script often used for inscriptions on Russian bells from the sixteenth century.

VOEVODA: The military governor of a Russian town that the tsar appointed from the Russian nobility.

VOORSLAG: Dutch for "forestrike" from a chiming tower clock. The brief melodic flourish automatically sounded on the subdivisions of the hour and the signal preceding the striking of the hour.

WAIST OF A BELL: The broad midsection on a bell's wall between its hip (q.v.) and shoulder (q.v.) that generally contains a decorative program. *Pole* (field) or *seredina* (middle) in Russian.

YOKE: See stock.

ZVON: Russian word that can designate either the collective sound generated by the ringing of Russian bells, or a group or set of Russian bells hanging in a tower or zvonnitsa (q.v.). *Zvon* is also the word used for a bell's fundamental (q.v.) or prime.

ZVONNITSA: A Russian belfry that is a masonry structure with apertures in which bells are hung from cross beams.

ZVON RINGING: The traditional Russian style of bell ringing in which a rope or ropes tied to the flight (q.v.) of a clapper (q.v.) are pulled to draw it to the sound-bow (q.v.) of the bell. Rhythmic patterns are struck on each bell whose tempos vary according to the pendular speed of the clapper.

Bibliography

I. Ancient Trumpets, Semantra and Related Instruments, and Bells in Byzantium and the West

Albert of Aachen (Albertus Aquensis or Albert, chanoine d'Aix-la-Chapelle). *Geschichte des ersten Kreuzzugs*. First pt.: Die Eroberung des heiligen Landes. Jena: Verlegt bei Eugen Diederichs, 1923.

Allatius, Leo (Leone Allacci). *De templis graecorum recentioribus*. Coloniae Agrippinae: Apud Iodocum Kalcovium & Socios, 1645.

————. *The Newer Temples of the Greeks*. Trans. Anthony Cutler. University Park, PA: The Pennsylvania State University Press, 1969.

Amalarius of Metz. *De ecclesiasticis officiis*. PL 105.

Anderson, Alan Orr, and Marjorie Ogilvie Anderson, eds. and trans. *Adomnan's Life of Columba*. London: Thomas Nelson and Sons, 1961.

Anderson, Robert. "Egypt; I. Ancient Music." *New Grove Dictionary of Music and Musicians* 6: 70-75. Ed. Stanley Sadie. London: Macmillan, 1980.

Anoyanakis, Fivos. *Greek Popular Musical Instruments*. Trans. from the Greek by Christopher N. W. Klint. Athens: National Bank of Greece, 1979.

Arro, Elmar. "Das Ost-West-Schisma in der Kirchenmusik über die Wesensverschiedenheit der Grundlagen kultischer Musik in Ost und West." *Musik des Ostens*, no. 2, pp. 7-83. Kassel: Bärenreiter, 1963.

Balsamon, Theodore. "Μελέται ἤτοι ἀποκρίσεις." PG 138.

Barbaro, Nicolò. *Giornale dell' assedio di Constantinopoli 1453*. Vienna: Libreria Tendler & Co., 1856.

Baronio, Cesare. *Annales ecclesiastici*. Vol. 15 (864-933), Nicolai Annus 8—Christi 865, no. 101. Barri-Ducis: Ludovicus Guerin, eques ordinis S. Silvestri, et Socii, 1868.

Bauer, Albert and Reinhold Rau. *Quellen zur Geschichte der sächsischen Kaiserzeit: Widukinds Sachsengeschichte, Adalberts Fortsetzung der Chronik Reginos, Liudprands Werke*. Ausgewählte Quellen zur deutschen Geschichte des Mittelalters. Vol. 8. Darmstadt: Wissenschaftliche Buchgesellschaft, 1971.

Bede, The Venerable. *Historia ecclesiastica gentis Anglorum*. Ed. Alfred Holder. Freiburg: J.C.B. Mohr, 1895.

Bent, J. Theodore. "The Fall of Constantinople." *The Antiquary* 7, no. 39 (March, 1883), pp. 100-103.

Benzinger, J. *Hebräische Archäologie*. Freiburg: Akademische Verlagsbuchhandlung von J.C.B. Mohr, 1894.

Bigelow, Arthur Lynds. "Bells." *New Catholic Encyclopedia* 2: 259-263.

————. *Carillon*. Princeton: Princeton University Press, 1948.

————. *The Acoustically Balanced Carillon: Graphics and the Design of Carillons and Carillon Bells*. Princeton University: Department of Graphics, School of Engineering, 1961.

Biringuccio, Vannoccio. *The Pirotechnia of Vannoccio Biringuccio*. Trans. from the Italian with an introduction and notes by Cyril Stanley Smith and Martha Teach Gnudi. The Collector's Series in Science. Ed. Derek J. Price. New York: Basic Books, 1959.

Bona, Ioannes. *Rerum liturgicarum libri duo*. Rome: Typis Nicolai Angeli Tinassij, 1671.

Boon, Amand, ed. *Pachomiana latina: Règle et épitres de S. Pachôme, épitre de S. Théodore et "Liber" de S. Orsiesius*. Latin text by St. Jerome. Appendix: La Règle de S. Pachôme: Fragments coptes et Excerpta grecs, ed. L.-Th. Lefort. Bibliothèque de la Revue d'histoire ecclésiastique, no. 7. Louvain: Bureaux de la Revue, 1932.

Brachman, Arnold C. *The Search for the Gold of Tutankhamen*. New York: Mason/Charter, 1976.

Bruton, Eric. *The History of Clocks and Watches*. New York: Rizzoli International Publications, 1979.

Caesarius of Arles, St. *Regula ad virgines*. PL 67.

Camp, John. *Bell Ringing: Chimes, Carillons, Hand Bells; The World of the Bell and the Ringer*. Newton Abbot, Devon, England: David & Charles, 1974.

Cassian, John. *De coenobiorum institutis*. PL 49.

————. *Institutions cénobitiques*. Trans. Jean-Claude Guy. Sources chrétiennes, no. 109. Paris: Les Editions du Cerf, 1965.

Chadwick, Owen. *John Cassian*. 2d ed. Cambridge: [Cambridge] University Press, 1968.

Cipolla, Carlo M. *Clocks and Culture, 1300-1700*. London: Collins, 1967.

Coleman, Satis N. *Bells: Their History, Legends, Making, and Uses*. Chicago: Rand McNally, 1928.

Coussemaker, E. de. "Essai sur les instruments de musique au moyen âge." *Annales archéologiques* 4. Paris: Au Bureau des Annales archéologiques, 1846.

Cyril of Scythopolis. "Vie de Saint Euthyme." Trans. A.-J. Festugière. *Les Moines d'Orient*, no. 3, pt. 1. Paris: Les Editions du Cerf, 1962.

————. "Vie de Saint Sabas." Trans. A.-J. Festugière. *Les*

Moines d'Orient, no. 3, pt. 2. Paris: Les Editions du Cerf, 1962.

Dawson, Christopher, ed. *The Mongol Mission*. London: Sheed and Ward, 1955.

"De minoribus vesperis." In *Acta sanctorum, Iunii*. Vol. 2. Antwerp: Apud Viduam & Heredes Henrici Thieullier, 1698; reprint ed., Brussels: Editions Culture et Civilisation, 1969.

Dmitrievskij, Aleksej. *Opisanie liturgicheskikh" rukopisej* 1. Kiev: G. T. Korchak"-Novitskij, 1895.

Dombart, Th. "Das Semanterium, die frühchristliche Holzglocke." *Die christliche Kunst* 20 (1924): 51-63, 77-78.

Dressler, Johannes. "Die Glocke: Ihre Geheimnisse, esoterische Symbolik und Magie." *Natur und Kultur* 52 (1960): 23-30.

Du Cange, Charles Du Fresne, sieur. *Glossarium ad scriptores mediae et infimae graecitatis* 2. Paris: Apud Anissonios Joan. Posuel, & Claud. Rigaud, 1688; reprint ed., Bratislava: Koebner, 1891.

Duchesne, Louis. *Le Liber pontificalis*. Vol. 1. 2d ed. Paris: E. de Boccard, 1955.

Edwardes, Ernest L. *Weight-driven Chamber Clocks of the Middle Ages and Renaissance*. Vol. 1. Old Weight-driven Chamber Clocks, 1350-1850. Altrincham, England: John Sherratt and Son, 1965.

Egbert, Archbishop of York[?]. *Excerptiones*. PL 89.

Eustathius, Archbishop of Thessaloniki. *Commentarii ad Homeri Iliadem*. Vol. 3. Leipzig: J.A.G. Weigel, 1829; reprint ed., Hildesheim: Georg Olms Verlagsbuchhandlung, 1960.

————. *De Thessalonica urbe a Latinis capta*. PG 136.

Eutychius, Patriarch of Alexandria. *Annales*. PG 111.

Fattal, Antoine. *Le Statut légal des nonmusulmans en pays d'Islam*. Recherches publiées sous la direction de l'Institut de Lettres Orientales de Beyrouth 10. Beirut: Imprimerie catholique, 1958.

Festugière, A.-J., ed. and trans. "La Première vie grecque de Saint Pachôme." *Les Moines d'Orient*, no. 4, pt. 2. Paris: Les Editions du Cerf, 1965.

Fitzgerald, C. P. *China: A Short Cultural History*. 3d ed. rev. London: The Cresset Press, 1961.

Gatty, Alfred. *The Bell: Its Origin, History, and Uses*. London: George Bell, 1848.

Geiringer, Karl. *Instruments in the History of Western Music*. New York: Oxford University Press, 1978.

Goar, Jacobus. *Euchologion sive rituale graecorum*. Venice: Ex typographia Bartholomaei Javarina, 1730; reprint ed., Graz: Akademische Druck- u. Verlagsanstalt, 1960.

Gould, Dudley C., ed. *AFS Metalcasting Dictionary*. 1st ed. Des Plaines, IL: American Foundrymen's Society, 1968.

Gregoras, Nicephorus. Ῥωμαϊκῆς ἱστορίας (*Byzantina historia*). CSHB 6. Bonn: Weber, 1829.

Gregory of Tours. *Historia francorum* and other works. Monumenta germaniae historica: Scriptorum rerum Merovingicarum, 1. Ed. Georg Heinrich Pertz. Hanover: Impensis bibliopolii Hahniani, 1885.

Grelot, Guillaume Joseph. *Relation nouvelle d'un voyage de Constantinople*. Paris: Pierre Rocolet, 1680.

Griffiths, J. Gwyn, trans. *Plutarch's De Iside et Osiride*. Swansea: University of Wales Press, 1970.

Grimthorpe, Edmund Beckett, Lord. *A Rudimentary Treatise on Clocks, Watches, & Bells for Public Purposes*. 8th ed. London: Crosby Lockwood and Son, 1903.

Guye, Samuel, and Henri Michel. *Time & Space: Measuring Instruments from the 15th to the 19th Century*. New York: Praeger, 1971.

Halkin, Francis, ed. *Sancti Pachomii: vitae graecae*. Subsidia hagiographica 19. Brussels: Société de Bollandistes, 1932.

Heisenberg, August. *Grabeskirche und Apostelkirche: zwei Basiliken Konstantins*. Second pt.: Die Apostelkirche in Konstantinopel. Leipzig: J. C. Hinrichs'sche Buchhandlung, 1908.

Hennessy, William M., ed. *Annals of Ulster; otherwise, Annals of Senat: A Chronicle of Irish Affairs from* A. D. *431, to* A.D. *1540*. Vol. 1: A.D. 431-1056. Dublin: Printed for Her Majesty's Stationary Office, by Alexander Thom & Co., 1887.

Heuven, Engelbert Wiegman van. *Acoustical Measurements on Church-Bells and Carillons*. The Hague: De Gebroeders van Cleef, 1949.

Hickmann, Hans. *Catalogue général des antiquités égyptiennes du Musée du Caire, nos. 69201-69852: Instruments de musique*. Cairo: Imprimerie de l'Institut français d'archéologie orientale, 1949.

————. "Die kultische Verwendung der altägyptischen Trompete." *Die Welt des Orients* 5 (1950): 351-355.

————. *La Trompette dans l'Egypte ancienne*. Supplément aux Annales du service des antiquités de l'Egypte, notebook no. 1. Cairo: Imprimerie de l'Institut français d'archéologie orientale, 1946; reprint ed., Nashville, TN: The Brass Press, 1976.

Ioannides, Costas D. "Quasi-liturgical Hymns." *Kypriakai spoudai* 33 (1969): 53-126.

John Climacus (Scholastikos). *Scala paradisi*. PG 88.

John the Deacon (Joannes Diaconus). *Chronicon Venetum*. Monumenta germaniae historica: Scriptorum 7. Ed. Georg Heinrich Pertz. Hanover: Impensis bibliopolii, 1846.

————. *Chronicon Venetum*. PL 139.

Jonas of Bobbio. *Vitae sanctorum Columbani, Vedastis, Iohannis*. Ed. Bruno Krusch. Monumenta germaniae historica: Scriptores rerum germanicarum, 37. Hanover: Impensis bibliopolii Hahniani, 1905.

Jones & Co., Bell Founders. *Troy Bell Foundry*. Troy, NY: A. W. Scribner & Co., 1870; reprint ed., Ovid, NY: W. E. Morrison, 1984.

Jülicher, Adolf. "Das älteste Zeugnis für kirchlichen Gebrauch von Glocken." *Monatschrift für Gottesdienst und kirchliche Kunst* 7, no. 5 (May 1902), p. 151-152.

Karoli Magni Capitularia. Monumenta germaniae historica 3: Legum 1. Ed. Georg Heinrich Pertz. Hanover: Impensis bibliopolii aulici Hahniani, 1835.

Kazanskij, P. S. "O prizyvě k″ bogosluzheniiu v″ vostochnoj tserkvi." *Trudy* 1 (1871), Arkheologicheskij svězd″ 1 (Moscow, 1869): 300-318.

Loret, Victor. "Egypte: II. La Trompette." *Encyclopédie de la musique* 1, pt. 1: Histoire de la musique, pp. 22-23.

Luibheid, Colm, and Norman Russell, trans. *John Climacus: The Ladder of Divine Ascent*. New York: Paulist Press, 1982.

McCann, Justin, ed. and trans. *The Rule of Saint Benedict*. London: Burns Oates, 1952.

Magius, Hieronymus. *De tintinnabulis*. Amsterdam: Sumptibus Andreae Frisii, 1664.

Marcuse, Sibyl. *A Survey of Musical Instruments*. New York: Harper & Row, 1975.

———. *Musical Instruments: A Comprehensive Dictionary*. Garden City, NY: Doubleday, 1964.

Markov, I. "Bilo." *Pravoslavnaia bogoslovskaia èntsiklopediia* 2, cols. 598-600. Ed. A. P. Lopukhin. St. Petersburg: Prilozhenie k″ dukhovnomu zhurnalu "Strannik″," 1901.

Martène, Edmund. *De antiquis ecclesiae ritibus*. Vol. 3. 2d ed. Antwerp: Typis Joannis Baptistae de la Bry, 1737.

Meneely & Kimberly. *Church, Academy, Tower-clock, Factory, Chime, Court-house, Fire-alarm, and Other Bells*. Troy, NY: Meneely & Kimberly, 1878.

Mersenne, Marin. *Harmonie Universelle (The Books on Instruments)*. Trans. Roger E. Chapman. The Hague: Martinus Nijhoff, 1957.

Meyer, Philipp. "[Ὑποτύπωσις καταστάσεως τῆς λαύρας τοῦ ὁσίου ᾿Αθανασίου]," *Die Haupturkunden für die Geschichte der Athosklöster*. Leipzig: J. C. Hinrichs'sche Buchhandlung, 1894.

Milham, Willis I. *Time & Timekeepers*. New York: Macmillan, 1945.

Millet, Gabriel. *L'Ecole grecque dans l'architecture byzantine*. Paris: Ernest Leroux, 1916.

———. *Monuments byzantins de Mistra*. Paris: Ernest Leroux, 1910.

———. "Recherches au mont-Athos." *Bulletin de correspondance hellénique* 29 (1905): 55-141.

———, J. Pargoire, and L. Petit. *Recueil des inscriptions chrétiennes de l'Athos*. Pt. 1. Paris: Albert Fontemoing, 1904.

Morris, Ernest. *Bells of All Nations*. London: Robert Hale, 1951.

———. *Tintinnabula: Small Bells*. London: Robert Hale, 1959.

Moschus, John. *Pratum spirituale*. PG 87³.

Mumford, Lewis. *Technics and Civilization*. New York: Harcourt, Brace and Co., 1934.

Naville, Edouard. *The Temple of Deir el Bahari*. Pt. 6. London: Kegan Paul, Trench, Trübner & Co., 1908.

Nevolin, K. A. *O piatinakh″ i pogostakh″ novgorodskikh″ v″ XVI věkě*. Zapiski Imperatorskago russkago geograficheskago obshchestva, bk. 8. St. Petersburg: Tip. Imperatorskoj akademii nauk″, 1853.

Nichols, John Robert. *Bells thro' the Ages: The Founders' Craft and Ringers' Art*. London: Chapman E. Hall, 1928.

Niese, Benedictus, ed. *Antiquitatum iudaicarum, libri I-V*. Vol. 1. Flavii Iosephi Opera. Berlin: Weidmannsche Verlagsbuchhandlung, 1955.

Otte, Heinrich. *Glockenkunde*. 2d ed., rev. and enl. Leipzig: T. O. Weigel, 1884.

Pachymeres, George. *Historia rerum ab Andronico Palaeologo seniore*. CSHB 25. Bonn: Weber, 1835.

Palladius. *Historia Lausiaca*. PG 34.

———. *The Lausiac History*. Trans. Robert T. Meyer. Ancient Christian Writers 34. London: Longmans, Green, and Co., 1965.

Patay, Pál. *Alte Glocken in Ungarn*. Gyoma: Druckerei Kner, 1977.

Petropoulos, Demetrios A., ed. Ἑλληνικὰ δημοτικὰ τραγούδια. Athens: I. N. Zacharopoulos, 1958.

Pfundner, Josef. *Katalog der Glockensammlung*. Vienna: Libicky, 1976.

Pokrovskij, N. V. *Pamiatniki khristianskoj arkhitektury osobenno russkie*. St. Petersburg: Synodal'naia tip., 1910.

Price, Percival. "Bell." *New Grove Dictionary of Music and Musicians* 2: 424-437. Ed. Stanley Sadie. London: Macmillan, 1980.

———. *Bells and Man*. Oxford: Oxford University Press, 1983.

———. "Bells and Music." *Bulletin of the Guild of Carillonneurs in North America* 19, no. 1 (April 1968), pp. 26-37.

———. "Carillon." *New Grove Dictionary of Music and Musicians* 3: 781-784. Ed. Stanley Sadie. London: Macmillan, 1980.

———. *The Carillon*. London: Oxford University Press, 1933.

Psellus, Michael. Πρὸς τὸν αὐτὸν βασιλέα. Scripta minora 1 (Orationes et dissertationes). Ed. Eduard Kurtz. Milan: Società Editrice "Vita e pensiero," 1936.

Regulae S. Pachomii translatio latina. PL 23.

Reifferscheid, August. *Anecdota Casinensia*. Index scholarum in universitate litterarum Vratislaviensi (Winter Semester, 1871-72). Breslau: Typis Officinae universitatis (W. Friedrich), 1871.

Riley, Henry T., trans. *Ingulph's Chronicle of the Abbey of Croyland*. London: Henry G. Bohn, 1854.

Robertson, J. Drummond. *The Evolution of Clockwork*. London: Cassell & Co., 1931.

Rockhill, William Woodville, trans. and ed. *The Journey of William of Rubruck to the Eastern Parts of the World, 1253-55*. The Hakluyt Society, 2d ser., no. 4. London: The Hakluyt Society, 1900.

Rossi, J.-B. de. "Cloche, avec inscription dédicatoire du VIIIᵉ ou de IXᵉ siècle, trouvée à Canino." *Revue de l'art chrétien* 40 (1890): 1-5.

Sachs, Curt. *Handbuch der Musikinstrumentenkunde*. 2d ed. Leipzig, 1930; reprint ed., Hildesheim: Georg Olms, 1967

———. *The History of Musical Instruments*. New York: W. W. Norton, 1940.

Savvaitov, Pavel, ed. *Puteshestvie novgorodskago arkhiepi-*

skopa Antoniia v″ Tsar′grad″ v″ kontsě 12-go stolětiia. St. Petersburg: Tip. Imperatorskoj akademii nauk″, 1872.

Schilling, Margarete. *Glocken und Glockenspiele.* Gütersloh, W. Ger.: Prisma Verlag, 1982.

Schwartz, Eduard. *Kyrillos von Skythopolis.* Texte und Untersuchungen zur Geschichte der altchristlichen Literatur. Vol. 49, pt. 2. Leipzig: J. C. Hinrichs Verlag, 1939.

Sendrey, Alfred. *Music in the Social and Religious Life of Antiquity.* Rutherford, NJ: Fairleigh Dickinson University Press, 1974.

Serafini, Alberto. *Torri campanarie di Roma e del Lazio nel medioevo.* Vol. 1. Rome: Pompeo Sansaini, 1927.

Simon, Maurice, trans. and ed. *Tamid.* The Babylonian Talmud 6. Gen. ed., I. Epstein. London: The Soncino Press, 1948.

Simpson, Bruce L. *History of the Metal-Casting Industry.* 2d ed. Des Plaines, IL: American Foundrymen's Society, 1969.

Smits van Waesberghe, J. *Cymbala (Bells in the Middle Ages).* Studies and Documents 1. Rome: American Institute of Musicology, 1951.

Sokolowsky, B. von, ed. *Die Musik des griechischen Alterthums und des Orients.* A. W. Ambros' Geschichte der Musik 1. Leipzig: F.E.C. Leuckart, 1887.

Starmer, W. W. Summary of a course of lectures on "Bells, Carillons, and Chimes." *The Musical Times* 51 (June 1, 1910): 372-373.

Stichel, Rainer. "Jüdische Tradition in christlicher Liturgie: zur Geschichte des Symantrons." *Cahiers archéologiques* 21 (1971): 213-228.

Stöbe, Paul. "Noch einmal die Campana." *Monatschrift für Gottesdienst und kirchliche Kunst* 7, no. 7 (July, 1902), pp. 236-237.

Strabo, Walafrid, Abbot of Reichenau. *De ecclesiasticarum rerum exordiis et incrementis.* PL 114.

Stuhlfauth, Georg. "Glocke und Schallbrett." *Repertorium für Kunstwissenschaft* 41: 162-167. Ed. Karl Koetschau. Berlin: Druck und Verlag von Georg Reimer, 1919.

———. "Zur Vorgeschichte der Kirchenglocke." *Zeitschrift für die neutestamentliche Wissenschaft und die Kunde der älteren Kirche* 25 (1926): 262-266.

Suicerus, Johann Caspar. *Thesaurus ecclesiasticus e patribus graecis ordine alphabetico.* Amsterdam: Heur. Wetstenium, 1682.

Swift, Emerson Howland. *Hagia Sophia.* New York: Columbia University Press, 1940.

Symeon, Archbishop of Thessaloniki. *De sacra precatione.* PG 155.

Symons, Thomas, trans. *The Monastic Agreement of the Monks and Nuns of the English Nation.* London: Thomas Nelson and Sons, 1953.

Tait, Hugh, *Clocks and Watches.* Cambridge, MA: Harvard University Press, 1983.

Theodore of Petra. "Vie de S. Théodosios." Trans. A.-J. Fes-tugière. *Les Moines d'Orient*, no. 3, pt. 3. Paris: Les Editions du Cerf, 1963.

Theodore of the Studion Monastery. *Iambi de variis argumentis.* PG 99.

Theophilus. *De diversis artibus* (The Various Arts). Trans. C. R. Dodwell. London: Thomas Nelson and Sons, 1961.

The Trustees of the British Museum, *The Times & The Sunday Times. Treasures of Tutankhamun.* Westerham, Kent: Westerham Press, 1972.

Thurston, Herbert. "The Early History of Church Bells." *The Month* (June 1907), pp. 634-637.

Tournefort, Pitton de. *Relation d'un voyage du Levant.* Paris: L'Imprimerie royal, 1717.

Tritton, A. S. *The Caliphs and their Non-Muslim Subjects.* London: Frank Cass, 1970.

Tyack, Geo[rge] S. *A Book About Bells.* London: William Andrews, 1898.

Ungerer, Alfred. *Les Horloges astronomiques et monumentales les plus remarquables de l'antiquité jusqu'à nos jours.* Strasbourg: Chez l'auteur, 1931.

Usener, Hermann, ed. *Der heilige Theodosios: Schriften des Theodoros und Kyrillos.* Leipzig: Verlag von B. G. Teubner, 1890.

Uvarov, A. S. "Bilo ili klepalo." (Materialy dlia arkheologicheskago slovaria). *Drevnosti: Trudy Moskovskago arkheologicheskago obshchestva* 1 (1865): 30-31.

Vernet, Marc. *Cloches et musique.* Neuchâtel: A la Baconnière, 1963.

Villemarqué, Hersart de la. "Mémoire sur l'inscription de la cloche de Stival près Pontivy, en Bretagne." *Mémoires de l'Académie des inscriptions* 24 (1864), pt. 2, pp. 387-399.

Vocabulary of Foundry Practice in Six Languages: English, Czech, German, French, Polish, Russian. New York: Macmillan, 1963.

Walters, H. B. *Church Bells of England.* London: Oxford University Press, 1912.

Westcott, Wendell. *Bells and Their Music.* New York: G. P. Putnam's Sons, 1970.

Wölfflin, Eduard von. "Beiträge zur lateinischen Lexikographie." *Sitzungsberichte der philosophisch-philologischen und der historischen Classe der k. b. Akademie der Wissenschaften zu München*, pp. 3-9. Annual 1900. Munich: Verlag der k. Akademie, 1901.

———. "Campana, Glocke. Species, Spezerei." *Archiv für lateinische Lexikographie und Grammatik* 11 (1900): 537-544.

Wright, F. A., trans. *The Works of Liudprand of Cremona: Antapodosis, Liber de Rebus Gestis Ottonis, Relatio de Legatione Constantinopolitana.* London: George Routledge & Sons, 1930.

Yadin, Yigael, ed. *The Scroll of the War of the Sons of Light against the Sons of Darkness.* Trans. from the Hebrew by

Batya and Chaim Rabin. London: Oxford University Press, 1962.

Yolen, Jane. *Ring Out!: A Book of Bells*. New York: The Seabury Press, 1974.

II. Bells and Bell Casting in Russia

Chronicles and Other Primary Sources

A number of documents from the Cannon Bureau (*Pushkarskij prikaz*) are published in N. N. Rubtsov, *Istoriia litejnogo proizvodstva v SSSR*, pt. 1, 2d ed., rev. and enl. (Moscow: Gosudarstvennoe nauchno-tekhnicheskoe izd. mashinostroitel'noj literatury, 1962). This material is also available in the translation of Rubtsov's work, *History of Foundry Practice in USSR* (New Delhi: Indian National Scientific Documentation Centre, 1975).

Akademiia nauk SSSR, Institut istorii. *Novgorodskaia pervaia letopis' starshego i mladshego izvodov*. Moscow: Izd. Akademii nauk SSSR, 1950; reprint ed., Slavistic Printings and Reprintings, no. 216, ed. by C. H. van Schooneveld, The Hague: Mouton & Co., 1969.

Arkheograficheskaia komissiia, ed., *Polnoe sobranie russkikh″ lĕtopisej*. 37 vols. St. Petersburg/Leningrad: 1841-1982.

Avanesov, R. I., ed. *Smolenskie gramoty XIII-XIV vekov*. Moscow: Izd. Akademii nauk SSSR, 1963.

Dewey, H. W., and A. M. Kleimola, trans. and eds. *Russian Private Law in the XIV-XVII Centuries: An Anthology of Documents*. Michigan Slavic Materials, no. 9. Ann Arbor, MI: Department of Slavic Languages and Literatures, University of Michigan, 1973.

Jakobson, Roman, and Dean S. Worth, eds. *Sofonija's Tale of the Russian-Tatar Battle on the Kulikovo Field*. The Hague: Mouton & Co., 1963.

Kostomarov, N., ed. "Povĕst' o novgorodskom″ bĕlom″ klobukĕ." *Pamiatniki starinnoj russkoj literatury* 1. St. Petersburg: Tip. P. A. Kulisha, 1860.

Likhachev, N. P., ed. *Inoka Thomy Slovo pokhval'noe o blagovĕrnom″ velikom″ kniazĕ Borisĕ Aleksandrovichĕ*. Pamiatniki drevnej pis'mennosti i iskusstva 168. St. Petersburg: Obshchestvo liubitelej drevnej pis'mennosti, 1908.

Nasonov, A. N., ed. *Pskovskie letopisi*. Issue 2. Moscow: Izd. Akademii nauk SSSR, 1955.

Orlov, A. S. *Bibliografiia russkikh nadpisej XI-XV vv*. Moscow: Izd. Akademii nauk SSSR, 1952.

"Pamiatniki drevle-russkoj dukhovnoj pis'mennosti: zhitie prepodobnago Antoniia Rimlianina." *Pravoslavnyj sobesĕdnik″* 1858, pt. 2, pp. 157-171, 310-324.

Slovo o polku Igorevĕ. Moscow: Gosudarstvennoe izd. khudozhestvennoj literatury, 1954.

Stroev, Pavel, ed. *Sofijskij vremennik″ ili ruskaia lĕtopis' s″ 862 po 1534 god″*. Pt. 2 (1425-1534). Moscow: Tip. Semena Selivanovskago, 1821.

Zenkovsky, Serge A., ed. and trans. *Medieval Russia's Epics, Chronicles, and Tales*. Rev. and enl. ed. New York: E. P. Dutton, 1974.

Foreign Observers, on Russian Bells, Casting, and Founders

Adelung, Friedrich von. *Kritiko-literaturnoe obozrĕnie puteshestvennikov″ po Rossii do 1700 goda i ikh″ sochinenij*. Pts. 1 and 2. Trans. from German by Aleksandr Klebanov. Moscow: Universitetskaia tip., 1864.

Adelung, Th. *Al'bom″ Mejerberga: vidy i bytovyia kartiny Rossii XVII vĕka*. Rev. and enl. by A. M. Loviagin. St. Petersburg: Izd. A. S. Suvorina, 1903.

Ammon, I. Th., trans. *Dnevnik″ kamer″-iunkera F. V. Berkhgol'tsa, 1721-1725*. Pts. 1 and 2, new ed. with expanded notes. Moscow: Universitetskaia tip., 1902.

Avril, Philippe. *Travels into Divers Parts of Europe and Asia*. Trans. from French. London: Tim Goodwin, 1693.

Barberini, Raffaello. "Relatione di Moscovia." In A. Olearius, *Viaggi di Moscovia de gli anni 1633, 1634, 1635, e 1636*. Viterbo [Italy], 1658.

Baring, Maurice. *Russian Essays and Stories*. London: Methuen, 1908.

Baron, Samuel H., ed. and trans. *The Travels of Olearius in Seventeenth-century Russia*. Stanford, CA: Stanford University Press, 1967.

Blaeu, Joan. *Le Grand atlas ou cosmographie Blaviane*. Vol. 2. Amsterdam: Chez Jean Blaeu, 1663.

Bodianskij, O. "Puteshestvie v″ Moskoviiu barona Avgustina Majerberga." *Chteniia v″ Imperatorskom″ obshchestvĕ istorii i drevnostej rossijskikh″ pri Moskovskom″ universitetĕ*, bk. 3 (July-September 1873).

Bremner, Robert. *Excursions in the Interior of Russia. . . .* Vol. 2. London: Henry Colburn, 1839.

Browne, J. Ross. *The Land of Thor*. London: Sampson Low, Son, & Marston, 1867.

Bruyn, Cornelis de. *Voyages*. Vol. 3: *Voyages de Corneille le Bruyen par la Moscovie, en Perse, et aux Indes orientales*. Paris: Jean-Baptiste-Claude Bauche, 1728.

Bussow, Conrad. *Moskovskaia khronika, 1584-1613*. Moscow: Izd. Akademii nauk SSSR, 1961.

Clarke, Edward Daniel. *Travels in Various Countries of Europe, Asia, and Africa*. Pt. 1: Russia, Tartary, and Turkey. 2d ed. London: T. Cadell and W. Davies, 1811.

―――. *Travels in Various Countries of Europe, Asia, and Africa*. Vol. 1. 4th ed. London: T. Cadell and W. Davies, 1816.

Dmitrievskij, A. *Arkhiepiskop″ elassonskij Arsenij i memuary ego iz″ russkoj istorii*. Kiev: Tip. Imp. universiteta sv. Vladimira, 1899.

Fletcher, Giles. *Of the Russe Common Wealth*. Russia at the Close of the Sixteenth Century. Ed. Edward A. Bond. London: The Hakluyt Society, 1856.

Garkavi (Harkavy), A. Ia., trans. *Skazaniia musul'manskikh″ pisatelej o slavianakh″ i russkikh″ (s″ poloviny VII vĕka do*

kontsa X věka po R. Kh.). St. Petersburg: Tip. Imperatorskoj akademii nauk″, 1870; reprint ed., The Hague: Mouton, 1969.

Georgi, Johann Gottlieb. *Bemerkungen einer Reise im russischen Reich in der Jahren 1773 und 1774.* Vol. 2. St. Petersburg: Gedruckt bei der Kaiserl. Akademie der Wissenschaften, 1775.

Hanway, Jonas. *An Historical Account . . . of Travels from
London through Russia. . . .* Vol. 1. London: Sold by Mr.
Dodsley, 1753.

Hennin, Georg Wilhelm de. *Opisanie ural′skikh i sibirskikh
zavodov 1735.* Moscow: Gosudarstvennoe izd. "Istoriia zavodov," 1937.

Horsey, Jerome. *The Travels of Sir Jerome Horsey.* Russia at
the Close of the Sixteenth Century. Ed. Edward A. Bond.
London: The Hakluyt Society, 1856.

Johnston, Robert. *Travels through Part of the Russian Empire
and the Country of Poland.* London: J. J. Stockdale, 1815.

Kakasch, Stephan. "Kakash″ i Tektander″: Puteshestvie v″
Persiiu cherez″ Moskoviiu 1602-1603 gg." Trans. from German by A. I. Stankevich. *Chteniia v″ Imperatorskom″ obshchestvě istorii i drevnostej rossijskikh″*, bk. 2 (1896).

Kohl, Johann Georg. *Russia.* London: Chapman & Hall, 1844.

Korb, Johann Georg. *Diarium itineris in Moscoviam.* Vienna:
Typis Leopoldi Voigt, Universit. Typog., 1700.

———. *Tagebuch der Reise nach Russland (1698).* Ed. and
trans. Edmund Leingärtner. Reprint ed., Graz, Austria:
Akademische Druck- u. Verlagsanstalt, 1968.

Kurts, B. G. *Sochinenie Kil′burgera o russkoj torgovlě v″
tsarstvovanie Aleksěia Mikhajlovicha.* Kiev: Tip. I. I. Chokolova, 1915.

La Martinière, Pierre Martin de. "Puteshestvie v″ sěvernyia
strany (1653 g.)." Trans. and notes by V. N. Semenkovich.
Zapiski Moskovskago arkheologicheskago instituta 15 (1912).

Lannoy, Ghillebert de. "Voyages et ambassades (1399-1450)."
Oeuvres de Ghillebert de Lannoy. Ed. Charles Potvin. Louvain: Imprimerie de P. et J. Lefever, 1878.

Laveau, Le Cointe de. *Guide du voyageur à Moscou.* Moscow: L'Imprimerie d'Auguste Semen, 1824.

Liubich-Gomanovich, trans. "Puteshestvie v″ Moskoviiu Ra-
faělia Barberini, v″ 1565 gody: stat′ia pervaia." *Syn″ ote-
chestva* 6, sect. 1 (1842), pp. 3-16.

Lyall, Robert. *The Character of the Russians and a Detailed
History of Moscow.* London: R. Cadell, 1823.

Macmichael, William. *Journey from Moscow to Constantinople in the Years 1817, 1818.* London: John Murray, 1819.

Margeret, Jacques. *The Russian Empire and Grand Duchy of
Moscow: A 17th-Century French Account.* Trans. and ed.
Chester S. C. Dunning. Series in Russian and East European Studies, no. 5. Pittsburgh, PA: University of Pittsburgh Press, 1983.

———. *Zapiski Marzhereta i Prezidenta de-Tu: Skazaniia so-
vremennikov″ o Dmitrii Samozvantsě.* Pt. 3. St. Petersburg:
Tip. Imperatorskoj rossijskoj akademii, 1832.

Meakin, Annette M. B. *Russia: Travels and Studies.* Philadelphia: J. B. Lippincott, 1906.

Meyerberg, Augustin Baron von. *Relation d'un voyage en
Moscovie.* Vol. 1. Paris: Librairie A. Franck, 1858.

———. *Voyage en Moscovie d'un ambassadeur, conseiller de
la chambre impériale, envoyé par l'Empereur Leopold au
Czar Alexis Mihalowics, Grand Duc de Moscovie.* Leiden:
Chez Friderik Harring, 1688.

Miege, Guy. *A Relation of the Three Embassies from His Sacred Majestie Charles II to the Great Duke of Muscovie,
the King of Sweden, and the King of Denmark performed
by the Right Ho[noura]ble the Earle of Carlisle in the Years
1663 & 1664.* London: Printed for John Starkey, 1669.

Montferrand, Auguste Ricard de. *Description de la grande
cloche de Moscou.* Paris: M. M. Thierry, frères, 1840.

Moor, Henry. *A Visit to Russia in the Autumn of 1862.* London: Chapman and Hall, 1863.

[Murray, John]. *Hand-book for Northern Europe; including
Denmark, Norway, Sweden, Finland, and Russia.* New ed.
London: John Murray, 1849.

Olearius, Adam. *Vermehrte newe Beschreibung der muscowitischen und persischen Reyse.* Schleswig, 1656; reprint
ed. by Dieter Lohmeier, Tübingen: Max Niemeyer Verlag,
1971.

Palmer, William. *Notes of a Visit to the Russian Church in
the Years 1840, 1841.* Selected and arrg. by Cardinal Newman. London: Kegan Paul Trench & Co., 1882.

Palmquist, Erich. *Några widh sidste Kongl. ambassaden till
tzaren Muskou giorde Observationer öfwer Rysslandh, des
wäger pass meds fastningar och Brantzer.* 1674; printed in
Stockholm: Generalstabens Litografiska Anstalt, 1898.

Paul of Aleppo (Pavel Aleppskij). *Puteshestvie antiokhijskago
patriarkha Makariia v″ Rossiiu v″ polovině XVII věka.* Is-
sues 1, 2, 3, and 4. Trans. from the Arabic by G. Murkos.
Moscow: Universitetskaia tip., 1896-1898.

Petrus Petrejus (Per Persson). *Historien und Bericht von dem
Grossfürstenthumb Muschkow. . . .* Leipzig: Tipis Bavari-
cis, 1620.

———. "Istoriia o velikom″ kniazhestvě moskovskom″. . . ."
*Chteniia v″ Imperatorskom″ obshchestvě istorii i drevnostej
rossijskikh″ pri Moskovskom″ universitetě*, bk. 2 (April-June
1867) and bk. 4 (1865).

Plano Carpini, Giovanni de. "History of the Mongols." In *The
Mongol Mission.* Ed. Christopher Dawson and trans. a nun
of Stanbrook Abbey. London: Sheed and Ward, 1955.

*Posol′stvo Kunraada fan″-Klenka k″ tsariam″ Aleksěiu Mikhaj-
lovichu i Theodoru Aleksěevichu.* St. Petersburg: Tip. Glavnago upravleniia udělov″, 1900.

Proctor, Edna Dean. *A Russian Journey.* Boston: James R.
Osgood, 1873.

Reutenfels, Jakob (Iakov Rejtenfel′s). "Skazaniia světlějshemu
gertsogu toskanskomu Koz′mě Tret′emu o Moskovii (Padua,
1680 g.)." Trans. from Latin by Aleksej Stankevich. *Chte-*

niia v″ Imperatorskom″ obshchestvĕ istorii i drevnostej sijskikh″ pri Moskovskom″ universitetĕ, bk. 3 (1905).

Romanoff, H. C. *Sketches of the Rites and Customs of the Greco-Russian Church*. 2d ed. London: Rivingtons, 1869.

Sajkowski, Alojzy, and Władysław Czapliński. *Pamiętniki Samuel i Bogustawa Kazimierza Maskiewiczów (Wiek XVII)*. Wrocław: Zakład narodowy im Ossolińskich, 1961.

Sears, Robert. *An Illustrated Description of the Russian Empire*. New ed., rev. and enl. New York: Robert Sears, 1855.

Smyth, C. Piazzi. *Three Cities in Russia*. London: Lovell, Reeve & Co., 1862.

Spottiswoode, William. *A Tarantasse Journey through Eastern Russia in the Autumn of 1856*. London: Longman, Brown, Green, Longmans, & Roberts, 1857.

Staden, Heinrich von. *The Land and Government of Muscovy: A Sixteenth-century Account*. Trans. and ed. Thomas Esper. Stanford, CA: Stanford University Press, 1967.

Struys, Jan Janszoon. *The Perillous and Most Unhappy Voyages of John Struys, through Italy, Greece, Lifeland, Moscovia, Tartary, Media, Persia, East India, Japan, and Other Places in Europe, Africa and Asia*. Trans. from Low Dutch by John Morrison. London: Samuel Smith, 1683.

Swinton, Andrew. *Travels into Norway, Denmark, and Russia in the Years 1788, 1789, 1790, and 1791*. Dublin: W. Corbet for W. Jones & J. Rice, 1792.

Tanner, Bernard. *Opisanie puteshestviia pol'skago v″ Moskvu v″ 1678 godu*. Trans. from Latin with notes and introduction by I. Ivakin. Moscow: Universitetskaia tip., 1891.

Warhafftige Relation der reussischen und muscowitischen Reyse und Einzug dess durchleuchtigen hochgebornen Fürsten und Herren, Herren Hertzog Johansen dess Jüngern auss königlichem Stamm Dennemarck. Magdeburg: Johan Francken, 1604.

Weber, Friedrich Christian. *The Present State of Russia*. Vol. 1. Trans. from the High Dutch. London: W. Taylor, 1723; reprint ed., London: Frank Cass & Co., 1968.

Whitworth, Charles Lord. *An Account of Russia as It Was in the Year 1710*. Strawberry-Hill, S. Middlesex, England: Horace Walpole, 1758.

General Works on Russian Bells and Bell Casting

Only a few pages remain from a lost manuscript on Russian bells by Konstantin Konstantinovich Saradzhev (1900-1942), Russian bell ringer and acoustician. There is reason to believe that Saradzhev's study, had it been preserved and published, would have replaced Olovianishnikov's as the principal Russian monograph on bells and bell ringing. Saradzhev's work is discussed in *Razrushennye i oskvernennye khramy: Moskva i Sredniaia Rossiia s poslesloviem "Predely vandalizma"* (Frankfurt/Main: Possev-Verlag, 1980), p. 156.

Arro, Elmar. "Die altrussische Glockenmusik: Eine musikslavistische Untersuchung." *Beiträge zur Musikgeschichte Osteuropas (Musica slavica)*, pp. 77-159. Ed. Elmar Arro.

Akademie der Wissenschaften und der Literatur Mainz und Musikologisches Institut der Universität Warszawa. Wiesbaden: Franz Steiner Verlag, 1977.

Babin (Captain 2d grade). "O russkikh″ kolokolakh″." *Gornyj zhurnal″* 4, no. 11 (1861), pp. 205-217.

Baedeker, Karl. *Russia with Teheran, Port Arthur, and Peking: Handbook for Travellers*. Leipzig: Karl Baedeker, 1914; reprint ed., New York: Arno Press & The New York Times, 1970.

Éjzen, I. "Kolokol″: istoricheskij obzor″ po povodu ego 1500-lĕtiia." *Niva* 9 (1894), cols. 111-128.

"Kolokola." *Ėntsiklopedicheskij slovar'* 15ᴬ. Ed. I. E. Andreevskij. St. Petersburg: I. A. Efron, 1895.

Korsunskij, N. *Blagovĕst″*. 3d ed. Yaroslavl: Tip. G. Fal'k″, 1887.

Olovianishnikov, N. *Istoriia kolokolov″ i kolokololitejnoe iskusstvo*. 2d ed., enl. Moscow: Izdanie T-va P. I. Olovianishnikova S-vej, 1912.

Petrovskij, A. "Kolokol″." *Pravoslavnaia bogoslovskaia ėntsiklopediia* 11: cols. 343-348. Ed. N. N. Glubokovskij. St. Petersburg: Bezplatnoe prilozhenie k″ dukhovnomu zhurnalu "Strannik″," 1910.

Priakhin, N. "Kolokol'nyj zvon″: dostoprimĕchatel'nye kolokola v″ Rossii." *Russkij palomnik″*, no. 19 (1886), pp. 170-172; no. 20 (1886), pp. 181-184; and no. 21 (1886), pp. 195-197.

Privalov, N. I. "Kolokol'nyj zvon″ na Rusi." *Ezhegodnik″ imperatorskikh″ teatrov″*, issue 1 (1910), pp. 21-45.

Pukhnachev, Iurij Vasil'evich. *Zagadki zvuchashchego metalla*. Moscow: Izd. "Nauka," 1974.

Pyliaev, M. I. "Istoricheskie kolokola." *Istoricheskij vĕstnik″* 42 (1890): 169-204.

————. "Istoricheskie kolokola." *Staroe zhit'e: ocherki i razskazy o byvshikh″ v″ otshedshee vremia obriadakh″, obychaiakh″ i poriadkakh″ v″ ustrojstvĕ domashnej i obshchestvennoj zhizni*, pp. 286-319. St. Petersburg: Tip. A. S. Suvorina, 1892.

Rahr, Gleb. "Cloches et carillons en Russie." *Encyclopédie des musiques sacrées*. Vol. 2. Gen. ed. Jacques Porte. Paris: Editions Labergerie, 1969.

Rubtsov, N. N. *History of Foundry Practice in USSR*. Trans. from the Russian [2d ed.]. New Delhi: Indian National Scientific Documentation Centre, 1975.

————. *Istoriia litejnogo proizvodstva v SSSR*. Pt. 1. 2d ed., rev. and enl. Moscow: Gosudarstvennoe nauchnotekhnicheskoe izd. mashinostroitel'noj literatury, 1962.

Rybakov, S. G. *Tserkovnyj zvon″ v″ Rossii*. St. Petersburg: Tip. E. Evdokimova, 1896.

Books

Aristov, N. *Promyshlennost' drevnej Rusi*. St. Petersburg, 1866.

Artsikhovskij, A. V. *Drevnerusskie miniatiury kak istoricheskij istochnik*. Moscow: Izd. MGU, 1944.

Badecki, Karol. *Dzwony starodawne z przed r. 1600 na ob-*

szarze B. Galicji. Cracow: Wydane z zasiłkami Polskiej akademji umiejętności, 1922.

Barten'ev, S. P. *Moskovskij Kreml': v" starinu i teper'*. Vol. 1. Moscow: Sinodal'naia tip., 1912.

Batiushkov, P. N. *Pamiatniki russkoj stariny v" zapadnykh" guberniiakh" imperii*. Issue 6. St. Petersburg: Tip. i khromolitografiia A. Transhelia, 1874.

Bezobrazov, V. P., ed. *Otchet" o Vserossijskoj khudozhestvenno-promyshlennoj vystavkě 1882 goda v" Moskvě*. Vol. 3. St. Petersburg: Tip. V. Bezobrazova, 1883.

Billington, James H. *The Icon and the Axe: An Interpretation of Russian Culture*. New York: Alfred A. Knopf, 1966.

Blackwell, William L. *The Beginnings of Russian Industrialization, 1800-1860*. Princeton: Princeton University Press, 1968.

Bogdanov, Andrej Ivanovich. *Istoricheskoe, geograficheskoe, i topograficheskoe opisanie Sanktpeterburga ot" nachala zavedeniia ego s" 1703 po 1751 god" sochinennoe G. Bogdanovym", . . . a nyně dopolnennoe i izdannoe . . . Vasil'em" Rubanom"*. St. Petersburg, 1779.

Boguslavskij, Gustav Aleksandrovich. *Tsar'-kolokol*. Moscow: Moskovskij rabochij, 1958.

Carpenter, Edmund, and Marshall McLuhan. "Acoustic Space." In *Explorations in Communication: An Anthology*, pp. 65-70. Ed. Edmund Carpenter and Marshall McLuhan. Boston: Beacon Press, 1960.

Cherniavsky, Michael. *Tsar and People: Studies in Russian Myths*. New Haven: Yale University Press, 1961.

Cross, Samuel Hazzard. *Medieval Russian Churches*. Cambridge, MA: The Mediaeval Academy of America, 1949.

Danilevskij, V. V. *Russkaia tekhnika*. Leningrad: Leningradskoe gazetno-zhurnal'noe i knizhnoe izd., 1947.

Denisov, L. I. *Pravoslavnye monastyri rossijskoj imperii*. Moscow: Izd. A. D. Stupina, 1908.

Dvigubskij, Ivan. *Nachal'nyia osnovaniia tekhnologii*. Pt. 1. Moscow: Universitetskaia tip., 1807.

Fabriki i zavody vsej Rossii: svěděniia o 31,523 fabrikakh" i zavodakh". Kiev: Knigoizd. T-va L. M. Fish", 1913.

Fal'kovskij, N. I. *Moskva v istorii tekhniki*. Moscow: Moskovskij rabochij, 1950.

Falkus, M. E. *The Industrialisation of Russia, 1700-1914*. London: Macmillan, 1972.

Findejzen, Nik[olaj]. *Ocherki po istorii muzyki v Rossii s drevnejshikh vremen do kontsa XVIII veka*. Vol. 1. Moscow: Gos. izd. Muzsektor, 1928.

Florinskij, Dimitrij. *Istoriko-statisticheskoe opisanie sanktpeterburgskago Petropavlovskago kathedral'nago sobora*. St. Petersburg: Tip. Georga Benike, 1857.

———. *Sobor" vo imia sviatykh" pervoverkhovnykh" apostolov" Petra i Pavla v" S.-Peterburgskoj krěposti*. St. Petersburg: Tip. Departmenta udělov, 1882.

Fuhrmann, Joseph T. *Tsar Alexis, His Reign and His Russia*. The Russian Series, vol. 34. Gulf Breeze, FL: Academic International Press, 1981.

Funduklej, Ivan, ed. *Obozrěnie Kieva v" otnoshenii k" drevnostiam"*. Kiev: Tip. I. Val'nera, 1847.

Gemp, Kseniia. *Skaz o Belomor'e*. Arkhangel'sk: Severo-zapadnoe knizhnoe izd., 1983.

Giedion, Sigfried. *Space, Time and Architecture: The Growth of a New Tradition*. 5th ed., rev. and enl. Cambridge, MA: Harvard University Press, 1967.

Godenne, Willy. *Cloches en URSS (Klokken in de USSR)*. Malines, Belgium: Ecole royale de Carillon "Jef Denyn," 1960.

Goetz, Leop[old] Karl. *Deutsch-russische Handelsgeschichte des Mittelalters*. Hansische Geschichtsquellen 5 (new series). Lübeck: Druck der Lübecker Verlagsanstalt Otto Waelde Komm.-Ges., 1922.

Golubinskij, E. *Istoriia russkoj tserkvi*. Both bks. of vol. 1: *Period" pervyj (kievskij ili domongol'skij)*. 2d ed., rev. and enl. Moscow: Universitetskaia tip., 1901, 1904.

———. *Prepodobnyj Sergij Radonezhskij i sozdannaia im" Troitskaia lavra*. Moscow: A. I. Snegirevoj, 1892.

Goncharova, A., and N. Gordeev. *Kremlevskie kuranty*. Moscow: Moskovskij rabochij, 1959.

Goncharova, A. A., and A. I. Khamtsov. *Steny bashni Kremlia*. 2d ed. enl. Moscow: Moskovskij rabochij, 1960.

Istomin, G. *Ivanovskaia kolokol'nia v" Moskvě*. 2d ed., rev. and enl. Moscow: Tip. Obshchestva raprostran. poleznykh" knig", 1893.

Ivanov, Petr. *Istoricheskiia svěděniia o bol'shom" kolokolě, lezhashchem" v" M. kremlě, bliz" Ivanovskoj kolokol'ni*. Moscow: Universitetskaia tip., 1835.

Izrailev, Aristarkh. *Rostovskie kolokola i zvony*. Pamiatniki drevnej pis'mennosti 51. St. Petersburg: Tip. M. M. Stasiulevicha, 1884.

Karger, M. K. *Drevnij Kiev*. Vol. 1. Leningrad: Izd. Akademii nauk SSSR, 1958.

Karskij, E. F. *Slavianskaia kirillovskaia paleografiia*. Moscow: Izd. "Nauka," 1979.

Khmyrov, M. D. *Metally, metallicheskiia izděliia i minerally v" drevnej Rossii*. Corrected and enl. by K. A. Skal'kovskij. St. Petersburg: Tip. V. A. Poletiki, 1875.

Kissel', Thedor. *Istoriia goroda Uglicha*. Yaroslavl: Gubernskaia tip., 1844.

Kolchin, B. A. *Metallurgy and Metal Working in Ancient Russia*. Trans. from Russian. Jerusalem: Israel Program for Scientific Translations, 1967.

Kondrat'ev, I. K. *Sědaia starina Moskvy*. Moscow: Izd. Knigoprodavtsa I. A. Morozova, 1893.

Krekshina, L., ed. *Po Kremliu: kratkij putevoditel'*. 5th ed., enl. Moscow: Moskovskij rabochij, 1975.

Krylov, Ivan Zakharovich. *Istoricheskoe opisanie vsekh" koronatsij velikikh" kniazej i tsarej rossijskikh"*. Moscow: Universitetskaia tip., 1856.

Lamanskij, Vladimir, ed., *Sbornik" chertezhej Moskvy, eia okrestnostej i goroda Pskova XVII stolětiia*. St. Petersburg: Tip. Iosafata Ogrizko, 1861.

Leib, Bernard. *Rome, Kiev et Byzance à la fin du XIe siècle.* Paris: Librairie Auguste Picard, 1924.

Levshin, Aleksandr Georgievich. *Istoricheskoe opisanie pervoprestol'nago v" Rossii khrama, moskovskago bol'shago Uspenskago sobora i o vozobnovlenii pervykh" trekh" moskovskikh" soborov" Uspenskago, Blagověshchenskago i Arkhangel'skago.* Moscow: Tip. Mejera, 1783.

Makarij, Archbishop of Khar'kov. *Arkheologicheskoe opisanie tserkovnykh" drevnostej v" Novgorodě i ego okrestnostiakh".* Pt. 2. Moscow: Tip. V. Got'e, 1860.

————. *Istoriia russkoj tserkvi.* Vol. 1. 2d ed., rev. St. Petersburg: Tip. Iu. A. Bokrama, 1868.

————. *Istoriia russkoj tserkvi v" period" razděleniia eia na dvě mitropolii.* Vol. 8. St. Petersburg: Tip. Iu. A. Bokrama, 1877.

Malinin, V. *Starets" Eleazarova monastyria Filothej i ego poslaniia.* Kiev: Tip. Kievo-Pecherskoj Uspenskoj Lavry, 1901.

Marsden, Christopher. *Palmyra of the North: The First Days of St. Petersburg.* London: Faber and Faber, 1942.

Maslova, E. N. *Pamiatnik Tysiacheletiiu Rossii.* Leningrad: Lenizdat, 1972.

Mel'nikov, P. *Nizhnegorodskaia iarmarka v" 1843, 1844 i 1845 godakh".* Nizhnij-Novgorod: Gubernskaia tip., 1846.

Meyendorff, John. *Byzantium and the Rise of Russia: A Study of Byzantino-Russian Relations in the Fourteenth Century.* Cambridge: Cambridge University Press, 1981.

Ministerstvo finansov" Departament" torgovli i manufaktur". *Fabrichno-zavodskaia promyshlennost' i torgovlia Rossii.* 2d ed., rev. and enl. St. Petersburg: Tip. I. A. Efrona, 1896.

Nikol'skij, Konstantin Timofeevich. *Posobie k" izucheniiu ustava bogosluzheniia Pravoslavnoj tserkvi.* 5th ed., rev. and enl. St. Petersburg: Gosudarstvennaia tip., 1894.

Nikol'skij, Nikolaj. *Kirillo-bělozerskij monastyr' i ego ustrojstvo do vtoroj chetverti XVII věka (1397-1625).* Vol. 1. St. Petersburg: Sýnodal'naia tip., 1897.

Pamiatnik "Tysiacheletie Rossii." Moscow: Izd. "Sovetskaia Rossiia," 1974.

Pashuto, V. T. *Vneshniaia politika drevnej Rusi.* Moscow: Izd. "Nauka," 1968.

Podobedova, O. I. *Miniatiury russkikh istoricheskikh rukopisej k istorii russkogo litsevogo letopisaniia.* Moscow: Izd. "Nauka," 1965.

Putevoditel' k" drevnostiam" i dostopamiatnostiam" moskovskim". Pts. 1 and 2. Moscow: Universitetskaia tip., 1792.

Pyliaev, M. I. *Staraia Moskva: razskazy iz" byloj zhizni pervoprestol'noj stolitsy.* St. Petersburg: Izd. A. S. Suvorina, 1891.

Radchenko, Boris Georgievich. *Moskovskie chasy.* Moscow: Izd. Moskovskij rabochij, 1980.

Roty, Martine. *Dictionnaire russe-français des termes en usage dans l'église russe.* Paris: Institut d'Etudes Slaves, 1980.

Rybakov, B. A. *Remeslo drevnej Rusi.* Moscow: Izd. Akademii nauk SSSR, 1948.

Rychin, Th. I. *Istoricheskoe opisanie moskovskikh" kremlevskikh" soborov", tserkvej i monastyrej i ikh" sviatyni.* 3d ed., enl. Moscow: Tip. A. Gattsuka, 1882.

Schafer, R. Murray. *The Tuning of the World.* New York: Alfred A. Knopf, 1977.

Shchepkin, V. N. *Russkaia paleografiia.* Moscow: Izd. "Nauka," 1967.

Smirnov, S. *Istoricheskoe opisanie Savvina Storozhevskago monastyria.* 2d ed., rev. and enl. Moscow: Tip. V. Got'e, 1860.

Snegirev, I. M. *Pamiatniki drevniago khudozhestva v" Rossii.* Moscow: Tip. Vědomostej Moskovskoj gorodskoj politsii, 1850.

————. *Pamiatniki moskovskoj drevnosti.* Moscow: Tip. A. Semena, 1842-1845.

S[negirev], I[van]. *Putevyia zapiski o Troitskoj lavrě.* Moscow: Tip. A. Semena, 1840.

Snegirev, V. *Moskovskie slobody.* Moscow: Moskovskij rabochij, 1947.

[Sokol'nikov], Mel'khisedek, Archimandrite. *Kratkoe istoricheskoe opisanie Rykhlovskoj pustyni ili Pustynno-rykhlovskago nikolaevskago obshchezhitel'nago muzheskago monastyria.* Moscow: Universitetskaia tip., 1844.

Sokolov, A. N. *Osnovy litejnogo proizvodstva.* Leningrad: Lenizdat, 1958.

Sokolov, N. V., ed. *Litejnoe proizvodstvo: bibliograficheskij ukazatel' literatury po 1955 g.* Moscow: Gosudarstvennoe nauchnotekhnicheskoe izd. mashinostroitel'noj literatury, 1959.

Spasskij, A. G. *Osnovy litejnogo proizvodstva.* Moscow: Gosudarstvennoe nauchno-tekhnicheskoe izd. literatury po chernoj i tsvetnoj metallurgii, 1950.

Stoskova, N. N. *Drevnerusskoe litejnoe delo (domongol'skij period).* Moscow: Akademiia nauk SSSR, 1954.

Tikhomirov, M. N. *The Towns of Ancient Rus.* Trans. from 2d Russian ed. by Y. Sdobnikov. Moscow: Foreign Languages Publishing House, 1959.

Vasil'ev, I. I. *Arkheologicheskij ukazatel' g. Pskova i ego okrestnostej.* St. Petersburg: Tip. I. N. Skorokhodova, 1898.

Voronin N. N. *Materialy i issledovaniia po arkheologii drevnerusskikh gorodov.* Vol. 3: *Drevnee Grodno po materialam arkheologicheskikh raskopok 1932-1949 gg.* Materialy i issledovaniia po arkheologii SSSR, no. 41. Moscow: Izd. Akademii nauk SSSR, 1954.

Vospominaniia ochevidtsa o prebyvanii frantsuzov" v" Moskvě v" 1812-m" godu. Moscow: Tip. M. P. Zakharova, 1862.

Voyce, Arthur. *The Art and Architecture of Medieval Russia.* Norman, OK: University of Oklahoma Press, 1967.

————. *The Moscow Kremlin: Its History, Architecture, and Art Treasures.* Berkeley: University of California Press, 1954.

Zabelin, Ivan. *Istoriia goroda Moskvy.* Pt. 1. 2d ed. Moscow: Tip.-litografiia N. N. Kushnerev" i ko., 1905.

————, ed. *Materialy dlia istorii, arkheologii, i statistiki goroda Moskvy.* Pt 2. Moscow: Moskovskaia gorodskaia tip., 1884.

[Zagoskin, M. N.] *The Young Muscovite; or the Poles in Russia.* Vol. 2. Ed. Captain Frederic Chamier. New York: Harper & Bros., 1834.

Zakharchenko, M. M. *Kiev″: teper′ i prezhde.* Kiev: S. V. Kul′zhenko, 1888.

Zakharov, N. *Kremlevskie kolokola.* 2d rev. ed. Moscow: Moskovskij rabochij, 1980.

Zakrevskij, Nikolaj. *Opisanie Kieva.* Vol. 1. Moscow: Tip. V. Gracheva, 1868.

Zaozerskaia, E. I. *U istokov krupnogo proizvodstva v russkoj promyshlennosti XVI-XVII vekov.* Moscow: Izd. "Nauka," 1970.

Zernov, Nicolas. *Moscow the Third Rome.* London: Society for Promoting Christian Knowledge, 1938.

Zheleznov, Vladimir. *Ukazatel′ masterov″ russkikh″ i inozemtsev″, gornago, metallicheskago i oruzhejnago děla i sviazannykh″ s″ nimi remesl″ i proizvodstv″, rabotavshikh″ v″ Rossii do XVII věka.* St. Petersburg: Tipo-litografiia S.-Peterburgskoj tiur′my, 1907.

Zhitie sviatago Dimitriia Tsarevicha. Obshchestvo liubitelej drevnej pis′mennosti i iskusstva 36. St. Petersburg: M. M. Osipov, 1879.

Articles

Arsenij, Ieromonakh. "O Tsar′-kolokolě Sviato-Troitskoj Sergievoj lavry." *Zapiski Otdeleniia russkoj i slavianskoj arkheologii Russkago arkheologicheskago obshchestva* 3 (1882): 65-111.

Artsikhovskij, A. V. "Oruzhie." In *Ocherki russkoj kul′tury XIII-XV vekov.* Pt. 1: Material′naia kul′tura, pp. 389-415. Moscow: Izd. Moskovskogo universiteta, 1969.

Bogoiavlenskij, S. "O Pushkarskom″ prikazě." In *Sbornik″ statej v″ chest′ Matvěia Kuz′micha Liubavskago,* pp. 361-385. Petrograd: Tip. B. D. Brukera, 1917.

Bogusevich, V. A. "Litejnyj master Mikhail Andreev." *Novgorodskij istoricheskij sbornik,* issue 2 (1937), pp. 83-92.

———. "Pskovskie litejshchiki XVI-XVIII vv." *Problemy istorii dokapitalisticheskikh obshchestv* 9-10 (1934): 157-161.

"Bol′shie kolokola." *Biblioteka dlia chteniia* 4, no. 4, sect. 7 (1834), pp. 70-71.

"Bol′shoj kremlevskij kolokol″." *Zhurnal″ dlia chteniia vospitannikam″ voennouchebnykh″ zavedenij* 3, bk. 12 (1836), p. 445.

Cross, Samuel H. "Medieval Russian Contacts with the West." *Speculum* 10 (1935): 137-144.

"Drevnij kolokol″, najdennyj v″ Tul′skoj gubernii." *Zhurnal″ Ministerstva vnutrennikh″ děl″,* pt. 18, no. 4 (1847), p. 146.

"Ělektricheskoe ispravlenie kolokolov″." *Nauka i zhizn′,* no. 17 (1893), p. 270.

Esipov, G. "Nabatnyj kolokol″." *Istoricheskij věstnik″* 4 (1881): 418-420.

Fetter, Nikolaj. "Drevnosti Pafnut′eva monastyria." *Istoricheskij věstnik″* 43, no. 2 (February 1891), pp. 597-598.

Findejzen, Nik[olaj]. "So Vserossijskoj vystavki v″ N.-Novgoroě." *Russkaia muzykal′naia gazeta* 3, no. 9 (September 1896), cols. 1009-1020.

Gejman, V. G., and N. V. Ustiugov. "Manufaktura." In *Ocherki istorii SSSR.* [Vol. 4:] Period feodalizma XVII v., pp. 87-113. Ed. A. A. Novosel′skij and N. V. Ustiugov. Moscow: Izd. Akademii nauk, 1955.

Glubokovskij, M. "Ělektricheskaia otlivka metallov″ i eia priměnenie." *Moskovskiia vědomosti,* no. 353 (December 21, 1892), pp. 4-5.

———. "Tsar′-kolokol″ i proekty ego vozobnovleniia." *Russkoe obozrěnie* 4 (1894): 867-893.

Gorchakov, N. "O bol′shikh″ kolokolakh″." *Moskovskiia gubernskiia vědomosti,* no. 17 (1844), pp. 198-201.

Grigorij, Archimandrite. "Vysokopetrovskij monastyr′ v″ Moskvě." *Russkiia dostopamiatnosti* 3. Ed. A. Martynov. Moscow: Tip. T. Ris″, 1880.

Hammond, Mason. "The Lowell House Bells." *Bulletin of the Guild of Carillonneurs of North America* 5, no. 1 (December 1950), pp. 17-24.

I., K. "Garmonicheskij zvon″ tserkovnykh″ kolokolov″." *Litovskiia eparkhial′nyia vědomosti,* no. 34 (August 22, 1893), pp. 285-286.

Iartsev, N. Th. "Kollektsiia po lit′iu kolokolov″." *Izvěstiia Obshchestva liubitelej estestvoznaniia, antropologii i ětnografii* 36, no. 2 (1879), pp. 49-51.

"Istoriia otlivki Tsar′-kolokola v″ Moskvě." *Tekhnolog″,* no. 8 (1898), pp. 37-38.

Ivanov, P. "Istoricheskiia svěděniia o bol′shom″ kolokolě, lezhavshem″ v″ zemlě, bliz″ Ivanovskoj kolokol′ni." *Moskovskiia vědomosti,* no. 44 (1842), pp. 903-906.

Izrailev, A. A. "Muzykal′no-akusticheskiia raboty." *Izvěstiia Obshchestva liubitelej estestvoznaniia, antropologii, i ětnografii* 41, no. 2 (1884), pp. 58-72.

Kalmykov. "Obozrěnie manufakturnoj promyshlennosti Tverskoj gubernii v″ 1850 godu." *Zhurnal″ manufaktur″ i torgovli,* nos. 4 and 5 (April and May 1851), pp. 22-96.

Karger, M. K. "Rozkopki na sadibī Kiïvs′kogo īstorichnogo muzeiu." *Arkheologīchnī pam″iatki URSR* 3: Rannī Slov″iani ī Kiïvs′ka Rus′ (Materīali pol′ovikh doslīdzhen′ Institutu arkheologīï Akademīï nauk Ukraïns′koï RSR za 1947-1948 rr.), 5-13. Kiev: Vidavnitstvo Akademīï nauk Ukraïns′koï RSR, 1952.

Karitskij, Andrej. "Demonstratsiia sozvězdij." *Nauka i zhizn′,* no. 50 (December 12, 1892), pp. 794-796.

Kolchin, B. A. "Remeslo." In *Ocherki russkoj kul′tury XIII-XV vekov.* Pt. 1: Material′naia kul′tura, pp. 205-210. Moscow: Izd. MGU, 1968.

Korenevskij, P. I. "Arkheologicheskiia raskopki v″ Kievě." *Istoricheskij věstnik″* 121 (1910): 980-984.

Lebedianskaia, A. P. "Ocherki iz istorii pushechnogo proizvodstva v Moskovskoj Rusi." *Sbornik issledovanij i materialov Artillerijskogo istoricheskogo muzeia Krasnoj armii* 1: 57-84. Moscow: Mashgiz, 1940.

Leonid, Archimandrite. "Istoricheskoe opisanie stavropigial'nago Voskresenskago Novyj Ierusalim" imenuemago monastyria." *Chteniia v" Imperatorskom" obshchestvě istorii i drevnostej rossijskikh" pri Moskovskom" universitetě* 90 (July-September 1874): i-iv, 1-124; 91 (October-December 1874): 125-366; and 94 (July-September 1875): 545-767.

———. "Nadpisi Troitse-Sergievoj lavry." *Zapiski Otdeleniia russkoj i slavianskoj arkheologii Russkago arkheologicheskago obshchestva* 3 (1882): 115-194.

Marchenko. "Prikliucheniia russkikh" kolokolov" otpravlennykh" v" Serbiiu v" 1863 g." *Russkaia starina* 94 (1898): 149-153.

Martynov, A. A. "Moskovskie kolokola." *Russkij arkhiv"* 34 (1896), no. 1, pp. 100-108; no. 2, pp. 274-278; no. 3, pp. 393-400; and no. 4, pp. 555-561.

Mel'nikov, Pavel. "Liflandskij kolokol" XV stolětiia v" Nizhnem"-Nověgorodě." *Otechestvennyia zapiski*, pt. 33, no. 3 (1844), pp. 42-44.

Mur'ianov, M. F. "Nadpis' drevnejshego kolokola Soloveckogo monastyria (predvaritel'noe soobshchenie)." *Pamiatniki kul'tury*. New discoveries. Annual, 1975. Moscow: Izd. "Nauka," 1976, 192-193.

Nemirovskij, E. L. "Novye materialy ob Andree Chokhove." *Trudy Instituta istorii estestvoznaniia i tekhniki.* Vol. 13: Istoriia mashinostroeniia i transporta, pp. 51-56. Moscow: Izd. Akademii nauk SSSR, 1956.

"Novyj splav" dlia kolokolov"." *Gornyj zhurnal"*, pt. 1, bk. 3 (1865), p. 689.

"O khodě otkrytiia drevnostej v" Kievě do nachala 1836 goda." *Zhurnal" Ministerstva narodnago prosvěshcheniia* 12 (1836), sect. 2, pp. 261-279.

"O kolokolakh" i o kolokol'nom" zvoně." *Pravoslavnaia zhizn'* 33, no. 9 (393) (September 1982), pp. 1-12.

"O vozmozhnosti ispravleniia mosk[ovskago] Tsar'-kolokola." *Nauka i zhizn'*, no. 6 (1893), pp. 89-93.

"O vozmozhnosti restavratsii Tsar'-kolokola." *Russkij listok"*, no. 122 (1893).

Pleshanova, I. I. "O zverinom ornamente pskovskikh kolokolov i keramid." In *Drevnerusskoe iskusstvo: khudozhestvennaia kul'tura Pskova*, pp. 204-219. Ed. V. N. Lazarev, O. I. Podobedova, and V. V. Kostochkin. Moscow: Izd. "Nauka," 1968.

Podchinennov, N. "Ustrojstvo i ustanovka zhelěznoj konstruktsii dlia privěsa kolokolov" na drevnej kolokol'ně Moskovskago Danilova Monastyria. (K" voprosu o priměnenii zhelěza pri remontě drevnikh" pamiatnikov" zodchestva)." *Biulleteni politekhnicheskago obshchestva*, no. 2 (1909), pp. 59-75.

Pokryshkin, P. "Tserkvi pskovskogo tipa XV-XVI stol. po vostochnomu poberezh'iu Chudskago ozera i na r. Narově." *Izvěstiia Arkheologicheskoj komissii* 22 (1907): 1-37.

Potapov, A. A. "Perevozka pereslavskikh" kolokolov" v" peterburgskij Petropavlovskij sobor"," *Vladimirskiia eparkhial'nyia vědomosti*, no. 38 (1907), pp. 593-599.

Price, Percival. "The Carillons of the Cathedral of Peter and Paul in the Fortress of Leningrad." *The Galpin Society Journal* 17 (February 1964): 64-76.

"Proekt" N. N. Benardosa dlia ispravleniia Tsar'-Kolokola." *Nauka i zhizn'*, no. 8 (1893), pp. 125-126.

Prokudin-Gorskij, S. M. "O sovremennom" sostoianii litejnago děla v" Rossii." *Zapiski Imperatorskago russkago tekhnicheskago obshchestva*, 30, no. 4 (April 1896), pp. 59-76.

Pronshtejn, A. P., and A. G. Zadera. "Remeslo." In *Ocherki russkoj kul'tury XVI veka*, pt. 1, pp. 99-136. Moscow: Izd. Moskovskogo universiteta, 1977.

R., N. "O kolokolakh" i o kolokol'nom" iskusstvě." *Moskovskiia vědomosti*, no. 49 (Tuesday, April 25, 1850), pp. 568-569; no. 50 (Thursday, April 27, 1850), pp. 578-580; and no. 51 (Saturday, April 29, 1850), pp. 586-588.

Repnikov, N. I. "Pamiatnikiikonografii uprazdnennogo Gostinopol'skogo monastyria." *Izvestiia Komiteta izucheniia drevne-russkoj zhivopisi.* Issue 1. St. Petersburg: Gosudarstvennoe izd., 1921.

"Restavratsiia 'Tsaria-kolokola.'" *Den'*, no. 1703 (March 10, 1893), p. 1.

Rubtsov, N. N. "Andrej Chokhov." In *Liudi russkoj nauki: tekhnika*, pp. 18-25. Ed. I. V. Kuznetsov. Moscow: Izd. "Nauka," 1965.

———. "Istoricheskij ocherk razvitiia osnovnykh priemov formovki." In *Tekhnologiia litejnoj formy*, pp. 5-19. Ed. N. N. Rubtsov. Moscow: Gosudarstvennoe nauchno-tekhnicheskoe izd. mashinostroitel'noj i sudostroitel'noj literatury, 1954.

———. "Ivan Fedorovich i Mikhail Ivanovich Motoriny." In *Liudi russkoj nauki: tekhnika*, pp. 26-36. Ed. I. V. Kuznetsov. Moscow: Izd. "Nauka," 1965.

———. "K istorii razvitiia litejnogo proizvodstva v Rossii." *Trudy po istorii tekhniki*, issue 7 (1954), pp. 50-66.

———. "Kratkij istoricheskij ocherk razvitiia litejnogo proizvodstva." In *Tekhnologiia litejnogo proizvodstva* 1: 5-23. Ed. L. M. Marienbakh. Moscow: Gosudarstvennoe nauchno-tekhnicheskoe izd. mashinostroitel'noj literatury, 1946.

———. "Moskovskie litejshchiki XIV-XVII vv." *Vestnik mashinostroeniia*, no. 11 (1947), pp. 69-72.

———. "Ocherki po razvitiiu litejnogo proizvodstva." *Litejnoe proizvodstvo* 12 (1936): 22-30.

———. "Ot Andreia Chokhova do Ivana Motorina." In *Tekhnologiia litejnogo proizvodstva: Sbornik statej*, pp. 5-24. Ed. V. I. Krylov. Moscow: Gosudarstvennoe nauchno-tekhnicheskoe izd. mashinostroitel'noj literatury, 1955.

———. "Znamenityj 'litets' Andrej Chokhov." *Litejnoe proizvodstvo* (Ministerstvo avtomobil'noj i traktornoj promyshlennosti SSSR), no. 4 (1951), pp. 22-25.

S., A. "Kolokola." *Věra i tserkov'*, no. 2 (1905), pp. 305-310.

Saradzhev, K. S. "Spisok individual'nostej bol'shikh kolokolov vsekh kolokolen g. Moskvy." *Pamiatniki kul'tury.* New discoveries. Annual, 1977, pp. 35-52. Moscow: Izd. "Nauka," 1977.

Semenov, A. I. "Novgorodskie i pskovskie litejshchiki XVI-

XVII vekov." *Sbornik Novgorodskogo obshchestva liubitelej drevnostej* 9 (1928): 3-8.

———. "Novgorodskie litejnye i oruzhejnye masterskie v XV-XVI vv." *Sbornik issledovanij i materialov Artillerijskogo istoricheskogo muzeia Krasnoj armii* 1 (1940): 239-241. Moscow: Mashgiz, 1940.

———. "O nekotorykh Sofijskikh kolokolakh." *Novgorodskoe veche*, no. 4 (1922), pp. 10-12.

Serebrianikov, Vasilij. "Ssyl'nyj uglichskij kolokol″ v″ Tobol'skě." *Moskovskiia vědomosti*, no. 98 (Tuesday, August 17, 1854), pp. 413-414.

Sh., K. "O podniatii tsaria kolokola v″ Moskvě." *Sěvernaia pchela*, no. 185 (Friday, August 14, 1836), pp. 737-738.

Shajtan, M. É. "Germaniia i Kiev v XI v." *Letopis' zaniatij postoiannoj istoriko-arkheograficheskoj komissii* 34, issue 1 (1926), pp. 3-26.

Slavianov, N. G. "Vozmozhnost' ispravleniia Tsar'-Kolokola po sposobu N. G. Slavianova." *Nauka i zhizn'*, no. 6 (1893), pp. 89-93.

Smirnova, É. S. "Dva pamiatnika pskovskogo khudozhestvennogo lit'ia XVI v." *Sovetskaia arkheologiia* 6, no. 2 (1962), pp. 243-247.

Smolenskij, St. "O kolokol'nom″ zvoně v″ Rossii." *Russkaia muzykal'naia gazeta*, no. 9-10 (March 4-11, 1907), cols. 265-281.

Snegirev, I. M. "Moskovskij Tsar'-kolokol″." *Russkiia dosto-pamiatnosti* 3 (1880): 1-28.

Spasskij, G. "O kolokolakh″, dostopriměchatel'nykh″ po svoej velichině." *Gornyj zhurnal″*, pt. 1, bk. 1 (January 1833), pp. 123-143.

Sreznevskij, I. I. "Kolokol″." *Materialy dlia slovaria drevnerusskago iazyka po pis'mennym″ pamiatnikam″*, vol. 3. St. Petersburg: Tip. Imperatorskoj akademii nauk″, 1893.

"Ssyl'nyj kolokol″." *Istoricheskij věstnik″* 34, no. 10 (October 1888), pp. 255-256.

Starmer, W. W. "The Great Bell of Moscow." *The Musical Times* 57 (October 1, 1916): 441-442.

Staryj Moskvich. "Tsar'-kolokol″ (po povodu proekta ego restavratsii)." *Moskovskaia gazeta*, no. 47 (1893), p. 52, cols. 5 and 6.

Strémooukhoff, Dimitri. "Moscow the Third Rome: Sources of the Doctrine." *Speculum* 28, no. 1 (January 1953), pp. 84-101.

Sytin, P. "Pushechnyj dvor v Moskve v XV-XIX v.v." *Moskovskij kraeved* 2 (1929): 7-20.

Tikhonov, T. I. "O bronzakh″ voobshche i o kolokol'nykh″ v″ chastnosti." *Izvěstiia Tomskago tekhnologicheskago instituta Imperatora Nikolaia II* 25, no. 1 (1912), pp. 1-15.

Uspenskij, D. "Nabatnyj kolokol″." *Russkaia starina* 129 (1907): 614-620.

Vasil'ev, N. "Otlivka kolokolov″." *Tekhnicheskij sbornik″* 12, no. 8 (1871), cols. 121-128.

Vorob'ev, A. V. "K datirovke chasozvoni novgorodskogo kremlia." *Kul'tura srednevekovoj Rusi*, pp. 119-122. Posviashchaetsia 70-letiiu M. K. Kargera. Leningrad: Izd. "Nauka," 1974.

"Vozmozhnoe priměnenie ėlektricheskoj otlivki N. G. Slavianova." *Ėlektrichestvo*, no. 8 (April 1893), p. 128.

"Vozmozhnost' ispravleniia Tsar'-Kolokola po sposobu N. G. Slavianova." *Nauka i zhizn'*, no. 6 (1893), pp. 89-93.

Vyezzhev, R. I. "Kolokola drevnego Gorodeska." *Kratkie soobshcheniia Instituta arkheologii*, issue 9 (1959), pp. 104-107. Kiev: Izd. Akademii nauk Ukrainskoj SSR, 1960.

———. "Raskopki 'Malogo Gorodishcha' letopisnogo Gorodeska," *Kratkie soobshcheniia Instituta arkheologii*, issue 10 (1960), pp. 124-135. Kiev: Izd. Akademii nauk Ukrainskoj SSR, 1960.

Westcott, Wendell. "Historical Role of Bells in Religious Practice." *Music* (American Guild of Organists) 5, no. 10 (October 1971), pp. 28-32.

Wolff, Robert Lee. "The Three Romes: The Migration of an Ideology and the Making of an Autocrat." *Daedalus* (Spring 1959), 291-311.

Zabelin, Ivan. "O metallicheskom″ proizvodstvě v″ Rossii do XVII věka." *Zapiski Imperatorskago arkheologicheskago obshchestva* 5 (1855): 1-136.

"Zaměchatel'nye kolokola pri sobornoj tserkvi v″ Krasnoiarskě." *Zhurnal″ Ministerstva vnutrennikh″ děl″*, pt. 17; no. 3 (1847), pp. 479-480.

Zolotov, Iu. M. "Kolokol patriarkha Nikona." *Sovetskaia arkheologiia* 8, no. 2 (1964), pp. 242-243.

Index

Library of Congress Cataloging in Publication Data

Williams, Edward V., 1935-
The bells of Russia.

Bibliography: p.
Includes index.
1. Bells—Soviet Union—History. 2. Bell founding—Soviet Union—History. I. Title.

CC250.S65W55 1985   789'.52'0947   85-3453
ISBN 0-691-09131-5